IRELAND'S IMMORTALS

IRELAND'S IMMORTALS

A HISTORY OF THE
GODS OF IRISH MYTH

MARK
WILLIAMS

PRINCETON UNIVERSITY PRESS
Princeton and Oxford

Published by Princeton University Press
41 William Street, Princeton, New Jersey 08540

In the United Kingdom: Princeton University Press
6 Oxford Street, Woodstock, Oxfordshire OX20 1TW

press.princeton.edu

Paper ISBN 978-0-691-18304-6

Library of Congress Cataloging-in-Publication Data

Names: Williams, M. A. (Mark Andrew), 1980– , author.
Title: Ireland's immortals : a history of the gods of Irish myth / Mark Williams.
Description: Princeton, NJ : Princeton University Press, 2016. | Includes
bibliographical references and index.
Identifiers: LCCN 2015045004 | ISBN 9780691157313 (hardcover : alk. paper)
Subjects: | LCSH: Mythology, Celtic—Ireland. | Ireland—Religion—History.
Classification: LCC BL980.I7 W54 2016 | DDC 299/.16113–dc23 LC record available at
https://lccn.loc.gov/2015045004

British Library Cataloging-in-Publication Data is available

This book has been composed in Linux Libertine
and Albertus MT Std

1 3 5 7 9 10 8 6 4 2

FOR JUSTINE
siur 7 anmcharae

CONTENTS

ILLUSTRATIONS

FIGURES

TABLE

ABBREVIATIONS

A&CM   J. Waddell, *Archaeology and Celtic Myth: An Exploration* (Dublin, 2014).

BBCS   *The Bulletin of the Board of Celtic Studies*

CCHE   J. T. Koch (ed.), *Celtic Culture: A Historical Encyclopedia* (5 vols., Oxford and Santa Barbara, 2006).

CHA   J. T. Koch & J. Carey (ed. & trans.), *The Celtic Heroic Age: Literary Sources for Ancient Celtic Europe & Early Ireland & Wales* (4th edn., Aberystwyth, 2003).

CHIL   M. Kelleher & P. O'Leary (eds.), *The Cambridge History of Irish Literature* (2 vols., Cambridge, 2006).

CMCS   *Cambridge Medieval Celtic Studies* (nos. 1–25), continued as *Cambrian Medieval Celtic Studies* (nos. 26–).

CMT   *Cath Maige Tuired*, ed. & trans. E. A. Gray [ITS 52] (Dublin, 1983).

CSANA   The Celtic Studies Association of North America

CWA&A   J. F. Nagy, *Conversing with Angels and Ancients: Literary Myths of Medieval Ireland* (Ithaca, NY, 1999).

DDDH   R. O'Connor, *The Destruction of Da Derga's Hostel: Kingship and Narrative Artistry in a Mediaeval Irish Saga* (Oxford, 2013).

DIB   *Dictionary of Irish Biography*, ed. J. McGuire & J. Quinn (Cambridge, 2009).

DIL   *Contributions to a Dictionary of the Irish Language*, ed. E. G. Quin, et al. (Dublin, 1973–6).

ÉC   *Études celtiques*

ECI   T. M. Charles-Edwards, *Early Christian Ireland* (Cambridge, 2000).

EIH&M   T. F. O'Rahilly, *Early Irish History and Mythology* (Dublin, 1946).

EIM&S   J. Gantz, *Early Irish Myths and Sagas* (London, 1981).

FATV   H. O'Donoghue, *From Asgard to Valhalla: The Remarkable History of the Norse Myths* (London, 2007).

FFCC   W. Y. Evans-Wentz, *The Fairy-Faith in Celtic Countries* (Oxford, 1911).

I&G   J. Carey, *Ireland and the Grail* (Aberystwyth, 2007).

IIMWL   P. Sims-Williams, *Irish Influence on Medieval Welsh Literature* (Oxford, 2011).

ITS   Irish Texts Society

JRSAI   *The Journal of the Royal Society of Antiquaries of Ireland*

K&LT   E. Bhreathnach (ed.), *The Kingship and Landscape of Tara* (Dublin, 2005).

L&IEMI   E. Johnston, *Literacy and Identity in Early Medieval Ireland* (Woodbridge, 2013).

LGE   *Lebor Gabála Érenn*, ed. & trans. R. A. S. Macalister [ITS 34, 35, 39, 41, 44] (5 vols., London, 1938–56, repr. London, 1993).

NHI   F. J. Byrne, W. E. Vaughan, A. Cosgrove, J. R. Hill, & D. Ó Cróinín (eds.), *A New History of Ireland* (9 vols., Oxford, 1982–2011).

OCT   *Oidhe Chloinne Tuireann: The Fate of the Children of Tuireann*, ed. & trans. R. J. O'Duffy (Dublin, 1901).

PB   R. Hutton, *Pagan Britain* (London & New Haven, 2013).

PHCC   *Proceedings of the Harvard Celtic Colloquium* (Cambridge, MA, 1980-).

PPCP   K. McCone, *Pagan Past and Christian Present in Early Irish Literature* (Maynooth, 1990).

PRIA   *Proceedings of the Royal Irish Academy* (Dublin, 1836-).

RC   *Revue celtique*

SC   *Studia Celtica*

TAM   R. Foster, *W. B. Yeats, A Life: I. The Apprentice Mage, 1865–1914* (Oxford, 1998).

TAP   R. Foster, *W. B. Yeats, A Life: II. The Arch-Poet, 1915–1939* (Oxford, 2003).

TE   *Tochmarc Étaíne*, ed. & trans. O. Bergin & R. I Best, *Ériu* 12 (1934–8), 137–96.

TEI   *Tales of the Elders of Ireland*, trans. A. Dooley and H. Roe (Oxford, 1999) [= *Acallam na Senórach*].

W&TB   T. M. Charles-Edwards, *Wales and the Britons, 350–1064* (Oxford, 2013).

WIFL&M   W. B. Yeats, *Writings on Irish Folklore, Legend, and Myth*, ed. R. Welch (London, 1993).

WOTW   J. Cousins, *The Wisdom of the West: An Introduction to the Interpretative Study of Irish Mythology* (London, 1912).

YA   *Yeats Annual* (London, 1982–).

ZCP   *Zeitschrift für celtische Philologie*

PREFACE

THIS BOOK IS the story of a nation's fantasy, and of the crossing-places where imagination meets belief. Its purpose is to trace the evolution of the divinities of Irish mythology—most frequently known as the *Túatha Dé Danann* or 'Peoples of the goddess Danu'—from the early Middle Ages through to the present.

But who are the Irish gods? Often people who love Greek or Norse myth have never heard of the indigenous divinities of Ireland. Such elusiveness is their calling card: they dissolve into the landscape, here one minute, gone the next. At times they resemble the Olympian divinities as a family of immortals ruled by a father-god, but at others we find them branching into a teeming race of supernatural nobility, an augmented humanity freed from ageing and artistic limit. Paradox is key, for these gods are also fairies; they are immortal, but—like the Norse gods—they can be killed. They are simultaneously a pantheon and a people.

Where to look for them? They lie hidden, literally latent. In some medieval stories they live in Ireland and rule, not from faraway Olympus or Asgard, but from the island's symbolic seat of kingship at Tara. In many other tales they live under the surface of Ireland's landscape, inside hills and prehistoric mounds. But they are not phantasms rising from the earth like a damp vapour: their dwellings open out into a mirror-universe of uncanny splendour. Though their origins lie in Iron Age veneration of earth and water, the gods' affinities are not with nature but with culture. Never depicted in early art and long cut off from pagan ritual, they float—worldly and refined—through the imaginative spaces of Irish literature.

A noteworthy difference between Irish and other mythologies is that sharply outlined personalities among the Irish gods are few, though we might point to the heroic Lug, a radiant and royal man between youth and maturity, or to the Morrígan, a gruesome war-goddess, shapeshifting between woman and crow, eel and wolf, or to Manannán the sea-god, speeding his chariot over an ocean churned to the colour of blood.

Opaque in motivation and unstable of outline, these beings do not lend themselves to a conventional history, especially as my own training is as a literary critic rather than a historian. Nonetheless, this book's focus is overwhelmingly on stories, and concerns the development of a group of characters caught up in the flow of historical change. It follows the Irish gods through many interconnected sources, alighting on key works and summarizing plotlines. Texts in the Irish language are read together with Irish literature in English. It is not intended to be a complete history of the supernatural beings of Irish tradition: there are no leprachauns or pookas here. Nor is it intended as a contribution to comparative mythology or the history of religions, at least not directly; only very rarely do I suggest the shape which pre-Christian Irish belief might have taken. Further, among the peculiarities of the pantheon is the fact that new deities continued to appear centuries after pagan religion had come to an end in Ireland, just as a willow branch will continue to put forth green shoots long after being sawn from the body of the tree. Under such circumstances it would scarcely be possible for me to judge whether a particular deity is 'authentic': I follow the principle of the anthropologist Claude Lévi-Strauss in regarding all iterations as valid and necessary for the meaning of a myth, or of a god, to be fully grasped.

'Myth' is a difficult term to define, but one used often in this book. Greek *muthos*, from which our word derives, originally simply meant 'something said'. The most common interpretation of the word in English, however, is that of a falsehood or an ingrained untruth, and scholars of mythology have long struggled to uproot this meaning from their readers' minds. They tend instead to emphasize the range of ways in which mythic narratives are able to embody responses to the human condition. The Sanskritist Wendy Doniger has mischievously played on this, summing up myth as 'a story that a group of people believe for a long time, despite massive evidence that it is not actually true.'[1] Her definition resonates with the early material examined in this book, for the Túatha Dé Danann were believed by generations of Ireland's medieval and early modern intellectuals to have been historical people, their deeds memorialized in a complex web of legendary history. According to this view, the gods were merely the second-to-last of a sequence of invaders who wrested control over the island in ancient times. For writers in Irish down to the eighteenth century, the myth of Ireland's successive

---

1 W. Doniger, *The Hindus: An Alternative History* (Oxford, 2010), 23.

invasions and associated stories about the Túatha Dé Danann retained great imaginative hold.

A second useful definition of myth is that adopted by Heather O'Donoghue: it consists simply of 'stories about the gods'.[2] But in Ireland it is the word *gods* that causes trouble. When the peoples of Europe became Christian, they had to decide how to think about the gods of their pagan forebears, often concluding that they had been demons who should be forgotten or only contemplated with a shudder. Not so the Irish, who continued to make a conspicuous imaginative investment in their island's native gods; one of the enigmas this book addresses is why this habit of mind should have obtained in Ireland but not in (say) Anglo-Saxon England. A consequence of this continuing interest in the gods was that the divine characters of medieval Irish literature bear only a very uncertain relationship to the deities of Irish paganism. Likewise, a distinctively Irish habit was the assigning of exotic orders of being to former gods in an effort to shoehorn them into a Christian worldview. Some medieval writers asserted that these former gods had been either 'half-fallen' angels or a mysteriously sinless branch of the human race, although neither were fully orthodox positions. It is a fundamental oddity of Irish mythology that while its divine personnel may be strangely 'other'—gifted with supernatural powers, great beauty, or immortal life—before the nineteenth century those beings were only occasionally acknowledged to be, or to have once been, pre-Christian gods. It is also worth noting at this point that any discussion of a monolithic group of Irish gods may in itself be misleading, and that some of the things that puzzle us about their representation may result from our own imperfect knowledge of medieval tradition. Though the literature we have is rich, references to lost manuscripts and tales make it clear that we only have a limited sample of what once existed and what we do have may not be representative. In particular, it is very likely that there were regional variations in traditions about the gods which are now hard to trace due to the limitiations of the surviving evidence.

With this caveat in mind, we come to the structure of the book. *Ireland's Immortals* falls into two halves, with discrete styles and ways of approaching the material. Part One addresses the trajectory of the Irish divinities from the conversion period through to the end of the Middle Ages. It asks three interconnected questions. The first is who or what are the Irish gods; the second asks why they are so unusual, compared to the

2 H. O'Donoghue, *English Poetry and Old Norse Myth: A History* (Oxford, 2014), 1.

gods of other European paganisms; and the third considers the reasons why interest in them persisted in medieval Ireland. In looking squarely at medieval texts as repositories of the values of the people who actually wrote them, rather than trying to look through them in an attempt to glimpse a pre-Christian world, we can answer all three questions by examining the work which the native gods performed within Irish culture during the Middle Ages.

Each chapter addresses a different set of themes and focuses on a small number of key texts. Chapter 1 looks at the Iron Age religious background and what became of the gods as Ireland became Christian during the fifth and sixth centuries, in so far as that process can be traced at all. Chapter 2 compares the earliest saga narratives featuring native supernaturals, 'The Adventure of Connlae' and 'The Voyage of Bran', both of which are short; they date from around the turn of the eighth century. Chapter 3 analyses the society of the gods and weighs their importance as symbols of culture; it does so by looking at two magnificent ninth- or tenth-century sagas, 'The Wooing of Étaín' and 'The Second Battle of Moytura'. Chapter 4 then goes on to examine 'The Book of Invasions', the great edifice of pseudohistory into which the Túatha Dé Danann were slotted during the eleventh and twelfth centuries.

Chapter 5 considers the role of the divinities in relation to the hero Finn mac Cumaill—anglicized as Finn Mac Cool—who became the centre of gravity for a luxuriant body of story from the turn of the thirteenth century. The principal text examined here is 'The Colloquy of the Elders', written c.1220, though the chapter ends by comparing the depiction of the gods in a luminously beautiful saga called 'The Fosterage of the House of Two Vessels', perhaps composed in the fourteenth century. Chapter 6 ends Part One with a brief look at how the gods were imagined, and found wanting, towards the end of the Middle Ages. It examines 'The Tragic Deaths of the Children of Lir'—famously the weepiest of all Irish mythological tales—and compares it with 'The Tragic Deaths of the Children of Tuireann', likewise a late tale, but one focused on bloodletting and vengeance. To close, I turn to 'The Battle of Ventry', a fifteenth-century tale in which the gods help to fight off invaders from Ireland's shores. So rich is the medieval literature that a painful selectivity has been necessary: many sagas and a number of important divinities have been mentioned only in passing.

Part Two represents a fresh starting point, turning from Irish to English and from the largely anonymous writings of the Middle Ages to a range of literary personalities. Some of the men and women who appear in this section—W. B. Yeats, for example—are among the most hallowed of Irish writers. Others, such as the mystic, poet, and painter George Russell, were of the second rank in virtuosity, but of the greatest importance in the story of the Irish gods. After all, almost certainly more people have now heard of divinities such as Lug, the Morrígan, and Manannán than at any previous point in history, and the second half of the book sets out to determine how the multitudinous medieval Túatha Dé Danann slimmed down and came into focus as the pantheon of one of the world's great mythologies. My concern is with the recasting in English of the divinities in the eighteenth, nineteenth, and twentieth centuries, focusing in particular on their importance in the Irish cultural and political *risorgimento*. This body of material, though large, is such that most significant figures can be discussed, though some important areas—such as book illustration and modern writing in Irish—have had to be passed over.

Chapter 7 takes a wide view of the early history of the gods in writing in English, and shows how the concept of a native pantheon only slowly became intellectually available during the eighteenth and nineteenth centuries. Chapter 8 focuses on Yeats and Russell and the role of the Túatha Dé Danann in *fin de siècle* occult nationalism, when for the first time a passionate impetus was felt to recover a lost Irish paganism. It includes the first of two case studies in the book of a single deity, the love-god Óengus, the Mac Óc ('Angus Og'). Chapter 9 focuses on Scotland, where from the 1890s a Celtic Revival parallel to that of Ireland took root. This redefined the pantheon not just as the gods of Ireland, but as the gods of the Gaels on both sides of the sea. The work of that movement's most celebrated literary figure, 'Fiona Macleod', is read alongside that of its most successful visual artist, John Duncan. Chapter 10 considers three early twentieth-century attempts to systematize Ireland's intractably complex mythology under the influence of eastern philosophy, with various degrees of coherence and literary success. Chapter 11 takes us to the present, concluding with a second case study of Óengus and an overview of the Irish gods in classical music, children's literature, and contemporary culture. The book then ends with Chapter 12, which presents some final observations and thoughts about what the future may hold.

A work such as this has some obvious potential pitfalls. In particular it became clear as soon as I started that most Irish divinities could benefit from full-length studies combining the medieval and the modern.

This has already been done by Charles MacQuarrie for the sea-god Manannán, but Lug, Óengus, the Morrígan, and especially the fire-goddess Brigit would richly repay such examination as well. I hope other scholars will undertake this work in future and so add to and correct my findings here. Also, in covering so many texts over such a long time span it is inevitable that I shall have neglected items which some experts will feel should have been discussed. The first draft of the book was a third as long again as the published version and many things I would have liked to have included have been cut. In order to write it I had to familiarize myself with aspects of modern Irish literature of which I had only vague knowledge, and will certainly have failed to notice some relevant material. Worse, writing a long work of systematizing scholarship places the author in the alarming role of arch-ventriloquist, aiming to modulate sympathetically the voices of many writers—poets, annalists, antiquarians, monastics, and mystics—over fifteen hundred years. But it is precisely this long process of development and reclamation which makes the Irish gods so fascinating, and which is one reason for the book.

I have written with two audiences in mind. The first consists of colleagues whose expertise is concentrated in one of the two poles which it addresses: that is, medievalists who want to know more about the reception of Irish myth and scholars of modern Ireland with an interest in the Revival's medieval roots. But I hope still more that the book will be accessible and entertaining to the general public, and this tempts me to add a personal note. As I completed the text I had a vivid dream in which I found myself following the war-goddess, the Morrígan, into a *síd* or 'fairy hill'. The interior—dismally—was completely empty except for wall-to-wall beige carpeting. This book may seem similarly empty to that sector of my readership who feel a deep personal connection to the Irish gods: it will be said that an academic approach suffers from institutional unimaginativeness (that beige carpet). I can only rejoin that no one is more aware of this than I, and that there is a humble value in criticism which explores and explains. Such criticism in no way detracts from the worth of responses rooted in rapture and rich emotion; nor could it, for that is where literature begins.

A NOTE ON TRANSLATIONS AND REFERENCING

Given the audiences at which this book is aimed it has been my policy (against my own inclination) to keep quotations in Irish to a minimum in the body of the text. For the same reason I have felt obliged to use English names for Irish and Latin texts, unless the effect was misleading or barbarous. The Irish original is given when a text is first mentioned. Often translations from Irish are my own, though if there is a recent scholarly rendering of a text I have sometimes used that, duly credited.

In the footnotes, full bibliographic data is given when an article or book is cited for the first time; subsequent references are abbreviated. An exception is the relatively small number of texts, journals, and critical studies cited very frequently: these are given using the acronyms listed under Abbreviations above. Where possible I have tried to cater to the needs of both the specialist and the general reader, directing the one to the original text and the other to a reliable translation.

GUIDE TO
PRONUNCIATION

THERE ARE CONVENTIONAL English spellings and pronunciations for the names of the gods of Greece and Rome (we say *Jupiter* for *Iuppiter*), and for some members of the Norse pantheon; not so for the Irish divinities. This is a problem in as much as Irish and its sister language Scottish Gaelic can seem unpronounceable to those unfamiliar with the Gaelic spelling system, such as the hapless visitor to the Highlands or west of Ireland encountering *Sgùrr a' Ghreadaidh* or *Aonach Urmhumhan* for the first time.

The coverage of this book means that many names might potentially be met with in their Old Irish, Middle Irish, Modern Irish, or (occasionally) Scottish Gaelic guises. All of these would be equally correct, but important shifts in pronunciation took place as Old Irish (roughly AD 600–900) morphed into Middle Irish (*c*.900–1200), which in turn developed into the Early Modern and Modern versions of the language. Scottish Gaelic also has idiosyncrasies of its own. Orthography too is a problem: for experts the difference between, say, Old Irish *Bodb Derg*—a fairy king of Connaught—and Early Modern Irish *Bodhbh Dearg* is superficial, but it may confuse other readers who do not expect names to develop supplementary vowels and *h*'s. To make matters worse, nineteenth- and twentieth-century writers in English often spelled medieval Irish names idiosyncratically: in the penultimate chapter of this book the sea-god *Manannán* (correctly so spelled) appears as *Mananaan*, *Mannanan*, and *Manaunaun*.

My own policy has been to choose a point in time—*c*.AD 875—and to keep names in the form which they had at that stage in the history of the language: later Old Irish. Some suggested pronunciations may therefore look odd to speakers of Modern Irish: in particular the pronunciation of *d* and *g* inside words has changed greatly with time, and Old Irish did not have the extra 'epenthetic' vowels heard in the modern pronunciation of words such as *dearg* (red), or *gorm* (blue). If no Old Irish form of a name is available, then the earliest attested form is given. This system has the advantage that a single Old Irish-based key to pronunciation can be provided, at least for most of the personal names. In a way, I would prefer to provide a fully accurate guide to all these names using the symbols of the International Phonetic Alphabet, but doing so would undermine the goal here, which is to provide a crib useable by the general reader. This key is not aimed at Celtic specialists, but rather at non-specialist readers, who should be able to at least approximate the names in a manner that has some historical justification.[1] In a few cases (the names of some texts and manuscripts, for example), scholars use the modern rather than the medieval pronunciation, and I have followed this convention.

There are two difficult cases. The first is the youthful god *Óengus*, who is discussed extensively in this book. As he was a popular figure his name occurs in at least seven different forms in texts from which I quote: Middle Irish *Aengus*, Scottish Gaelic *Aonghas*, and anglicized *Angus*, *Œngus*, and *Aongus*—among others. The second is the term for the hollow mounds in which the gods were supposed to live: *síd* (plural *síde*) in Old Irish, along with later Irish forms such as *sídhe/sidhe*, Scottish Gaelic *sìth*, and anglicizations such as *Shee* or *Shí*. For clarity, I have sometimes used the tautology '*síd*-mounds'. In both cases the coverage of the book makes variation unavoidable, and I hope this will not cause marked discomfort; I have tried to signal it wherever possible.

As a final note for the general reader, I draw attention here to the convention that when an asterisk is placed before a word, it indicates that that word is a modern philological reconstruction of a lost form or root which is not actually attested in any surviving writing.

STRESS

In the following list, capital letters indicate where the stress falls in words of more than one syllable: almost always this is the first syllable. Monosyllablic names are always strongly stressed.

---

1 My policy is similar to that of Ann Dooley and Harry Roe in their translation *Tales of the Elders of Ireland* (Oxford, 1999), xxxiv–vii; their guide is easy to use and much more accurate for the medieval pronunciation than e.g. that in Marie Heaney's (beautiful) *Over Nine Waves: A Book of Irish Legends* (London, 1994), 243–9, which is based, albeit inconsistently, on Modern Irish. The suggested pronunciations found in popular works on Celtic myth are usually wildly wrong. For Old Irish pronunciation rules using the IPA see T. Charles-Edwards, *ECI*, xvi-viii, plus Appendix 4 of Fergus Kelly's *A Guide to Early Irish Law* (Dublin, 1988).

SOUNDS

During the Old Irish period there was a gradual change in how vowels were pronounced in unstressed, i.e. non-initial, syllables. Early on they all sounded distinctly different, but later they all (with the exception of 'u') became a nondescript 'uh' sound, like the 'a' at the end of English *sofa*, technically called a *schwa* and written as ə in phonetic notation. This was particularly obvious at the *ends* of words: by about 875 the names *Lóegaire* and *Banba*—note the different final vowels—ended when spoken with identical 'uh' sounds of this sort.

The key uses the following five symbols:

i.   ə   the 'uh' sound at the end of *sofa*

ii.   ɣ   a throaty *gh* sound, similar to the *-ch* in Scots *loch* but further back and down in the gullet. Not to be confused with the letter 'y'

iii.   kh   the *ch* in Scots *loch*, spelled with a *k-* to avoid confusion with the *ch* in English *child*, a sound which did not occur in Old Irish

iv.   ð   the *th-* sound at the start of *those*, *that*, and *than*, which is different from the *th-* sound at the beginning of *thick*, *thin*, or *think*

v.   ʸ   indicates that the preceding consonant is 'palatal', that is, accompanied by a y-glide like the *m* in *mew* or the *c* in *cute* (contrast *moo* and *coot*). This often occurs at the end of a word: in a form like the place-name *Crúachain*, given in the key as *KROO-əkh-ənʸ*, the ʸ is there simply to indicate that the final consonant is pronounced like the first -n- in 'onion': it does not add a syllable.

Acallam na Senórach	*AG-əll-əv nə SHEN-or-əkh*
Áeb	*aiv* (to rhyme with English 'hive')
Áed	*aið* (to rhyme with English 'lithe')
Aengus	*AIN-ɣəss* (a Middle Irish form: 'AIN' probably to rhyme with 'fine', but in Anglo-Irish writings this name tends to be pronounced *ENG-guss. See also* Óengus
áes dána	*ice DAHN-ə* (*ice* as in English)
áes síde	*ice SHEATHE-ə* (*ice* and *SHEATHE* as in English)

áes trebtha	*ice TREV-thə* (*ice* as in English)
Aí	approximately the same as English 'eye'
Áine	*AHN-yə* (later *AWN-yə*)
Aillenn	*AL-yən*
Aillén	*AL-yane* (*yane* to rhyme with 'mane')
Airmed	*AR-vəð*
Aisling(e)	*ASH-ling, ASH-ling-ə*
Aldui, Allae	*AL-wee, AL-ə*
Alloid	*AL-əð*
Amairgen	*AV-ar-yən*ʸ
Ana, Anu	*ANə, ANoo*
Aobh	see Áeb
Aoife	*EE-f*ʸ*ə* (or modern *EE-fə*)
Auraicept na n-Éces	*OW-rə-kept nə NAY-gəss*
Badb	*BAð-v*
Balor	*BAL-ər*
Banba	*BAN-vəh* (in later Irish, *BAN-ə-vəh*)
Beira	*BAY-rə* (an anglicization)
Bé Binn	*BAY VIN*
Bé Dreccain	*BAY ðRECK-ən*ʸ (not unlike English 'bathe reckon', said quickly)
Bé Néit	*BAY N*ʸ*ADE* (rhymes with 'made')
Bóadag	*BOW-əð-əɣ* (*BOW* rhyming with English 'crow')
Bóand	*BOW-ən* (*BOW* rhyming with English 'crow')
Bodb Derg	*BOðv D*ʸ*ERg*
Bran mac Febail	*BRAN mack FEV-əl*ʸ
Bregon	*BRE-yən*
Bres	*BRESS* (to rhyme with 'press')
Brian	*BREE-ən* (not like the English pronunciation of the name)
Bride	*BREE-jə* (Scottish Gaelic; <u>not</u> like English 'bride')
Bríg	*BREEɣ*
Brigit	*BRI-ɣid* (anglicized *Bridget* is often substituted, especially when referring to the saint)
Bruig na Bóinne	*BROO(ɣ) nə BOW-n*ʸ*ə* (*BOW* rhyming with English 'crow')
Bua	*BOO-ə*

Buí	*BWEE*
Cáel	*Kail* (like the modern name 'Kyle'); in later Irish this came to be pronounced a bit like the English word 'quail'
Cáer Iborméith	*KAYR IV-ər-vayth* (*KAYR* rhymes with English 'fire'; *vayth* rhymes with 'faith')
Cailleach Bheur	*KAL-yəkh VUR* (*VUR* to rhyme with 'fur')
Caillech Bérri	*KAL-yəkh VAY-rə* (*VAY* to rhyme with 'day')
Caílte	*KYLE-tʸə* (*KYLE* like the modern name 'Kyle') or, later, *KWEEL-tʸə*
Caíntigern	*KAIN-tʸiɣ-ern* (*KAIN* to rhyme with 'pine')
Cairbre	*see* Coirpre
Cas Corach	*KASS KOR-əkh*
Cath Maige Tuired	*KATH MAɣə TOO-rəð*
Cé	*KʸAY* (to rhyme with 'day')
Cermait Milbél	*KʸER-məd MʸIL-vʸayl* (*vʸayl* to rhyme with 'pale')
Cessair	*KʸESS-ər*
Cessán (Ceasan)	*KʸESS-ahn*
Cían	*KEE-ən*
Coirpre	*KOR-brə*
Conchobor mac Nessa	*KON-khəv-ər mack NESS-ə*
Conn	*KON*
Connlae	*KON-leh*
Cormac	*KOR-mək*
Créde	*KRAYð-ə* (*KRAYð* to rhyme with English 'lathe')
Credne	*KREð-nʸə*
Crom Crúach	*KROM KROO-əkh*
Crom Dub	*KROM DUV* (*DUV* like English 'dove', the bird)
Crúachain, Crúachu	*KROO-əkh-ənʸ, KROO-əkh-oo*
Cú Chulainn	*KOO KHULL-ənn* (*KHULL* rhymes with 'skull')
Curcóg	*KURK-ogue* (rhymes with 'vogue')
Cú Roí	*KOO ro-EE* (later *KOO RWEE*)
Dagda	*DAɣ-ðə*
Dáire Donn	*DAH-rʸə DON*
Dairenn	*DARʸən*
Dál Cais	*DAHL GASH*

Dalua	*də-LOO-ə*
Danann	*see* Túatha Dé Danann
Delbaeth	*D^yEL-əv-ayth* (*ay* in the last syllable is like English 'eye')
Dían Cécht	*D^yEE-ən KAYkht*
Díarmait (*later* Diarmaid)	*D^yEE-ər-məd^y*
dindshenchas	*DIN-HEN-khəss*
Donand	*DON-ən*
Donn	*DON*
Éber	*AY-vər*
Echtrae Chonnlai	*EKH-trə KHONN-lee*
Esrus	*ESS-rəss*
Etan	*ED-ən*
Étar	*AID-ər* (quite close to English 'aider', provided the final 'r' is sounded)
Elatha	*EL-ath-ə*
Elcmar	*ELK-vər* (going by Modern Irish *Ealcmhar*)
Eochaid Airem	*YOKH-əð AR-əv*
Eochaid Ollathair	*YOKH-əð oll-ATH-ər*
Eochaidh	*YOKH-ee*
Étaín	The Old Irish pronunciation was probably *AY-dine*, to rhyme with English 'fine', but the name is conventionally pronounced by most scholars in the Modern Irish way, as *AY-deen* (modern *Éadaoin*)
Ethliu	*ETH-l^yoo*
Eithne (Ethne)	*ETH-n^yə*
Éremón	*AY-rə-vone* (*AY* rhymes with 'day'; -*vone* rhymes with 'phone')
Ériu	*AYR-yoo*
Falias	*FAL-ee-əss*
Fand	*FANN*
Ferdoman	*F^yER-DOVən*
Fer Maisse	*F^yER MASH-ə*
Fíachna	*FEE-əkh-nə*
fían, fíana	*FEE-ən, FEE-ən-ə*
fíanaigecht	*FEE-ən-a-yekht*
Fidbadach	*FIð-vəð-əkh*
Fidchell	*FIð-khel*
Fid Rúscach	*FIð ROOS-gəkh*

fili, pl. *filid*	*FIL-ee* (later *FIL-ə*), pl. *FIL-ið*
Findias	*FINN-ee-əss*
Finnbarr	*FIN-var*
Finn mac Cumaill	*FIN mack KU-vəl* (*KU-vəl* rhymes with 'shovel'; later it became *KOO-wəl*, close to English 'cool')
Fintan mac Bóchra	*FIN-tən mack BOW-khrə* (*BOW* rhymes with 'crow')
Fionnghuala	*FᵞONN-yoo-ələ* (= Fionnuala, Finnula)
Fir Bolg	*FEER VOLg* (*FEER* like English 'fear'); later *FEER VOL-əg*
Fir Dé	like English 'fear they'
Flann mac Lonáin	*FLAN mack LON-ahnᵞ*
Flann Mainistrech	*FLAN MANᵞish-trəkh*
Fomoiri	*FOV-o-rə* (roughly rhymes with English 'hoverer')
Fódla	*FOWð-lə* (*FOW* like English 'foe'); later *FOH-lə*, to rhyme with 'Coca *Cola*'
Fúamnach	*FOO-əv-nəkh*
Gilla Coemáin	*GᵞILLə KOI-vahn*
Goibnenn	*GOV-nᵞənn*
Goibniu	*GOV-nᵞoo*
Goirias	*GOR-ee-əss*
Ilbrecc	*IL-vrek*
Immacallam in dá Thuarad	*IM-əg-əll-əv ən DAH THOO-ər-əð*
Immram Brain	*IM-rəv Branᵞ*
Indech	*INN-yekh*
Íth	*EEth* (rhymes with 'teeth')
Iuchar	*YUKH-ər*
Iucharba	*YUKH-ər-və*
Kail	uncertain, because invented by William Sharp: probably rhymes with 'fail'
Keithoir	*KᵞETH-or* (a Middle Irish name, Ceth(e)or, adapted in modernity by William Sharp: this is a guess at how Sharp might have pronounced it)
Lebor Gabála	*LᵞEVər GAVAL-ə*; alternatively *LᵞOWER* (to rhyme with 'flower') *gəWAUL-ə* (*WAUL* like British English 'wall')
Lebor na hUidhre	*LᵞOWER* (to rhyme with 'flower') *nə HIR-ə*

	(the Modern Irish pronunciation is usually used for this manuscript)
Lí Ban	*LEE VAN* (sometimes given as Lí Bán, in which case *LEE VAHN*)
Lochlann	*LOKH-lən*
Lóegaire	*LOI-ɣər-ə*
Luchta	*LUKH-tə*
Lug Lámfhota	*LUɣ LAH-vodə* (the vowel in *Lug* is similar to that in English 'look'; later this name came to be pronounced *LOO*)
Lugaid Fer Trí	*LUɣ-əð FʸER TREE*
Lugaid Mac Con	*LUɣ-əð MACK KON*
Lugaid Riab nDerg	*LUɣ-əð REE-əv NʸErg*
Luigni	*LUɣ -nʸə*
Mac Cécht	*mack KAYkht*
Macha	*MAKH-ə*
Máeltne	*MAILT-nʸə* (*MAILT* like English 'mild' but with the final -d replaced by a t)
Manannán mac Lir	*MAN-ənn-ahn mack LIR*
Mongán mac Fiachna	*MONG-ahn mack FʸAKH-nə*
Medb	*MEð-v*
Míach	*MEE-əkh*
Midir	*MIð-ər*
Míl Espáine	*MEEL ESS-PAH-nʸə*
Mochaomhóg	*mə-KHWEEVE-ogue* (*-ogue* rhymes with 'vogue')
Módhán	*MOW-ðahn* (*MOW* like English 'mow')
Mórfhesa	*MOHR-essə*
Morrígan, Morrígu	*MOR-ree-ɣən, MOR-ree-ɣoo* (thus in Old Irish; in later Irish, the first syllable was often taken to be the word *mór*, 'big', and given an accent—in which case the name should be pronounced *MOH-ree-ɣən* with a long 'o')
Muirias	*MWEER-ee-əss*
Mumain	*MUV-ənʸ* (almost rhymes with English 'oven')
Nemain	*NʸEV-ənʸ*
Nemed	*NʸEV-əð*
Nemglan	*NʸEV-ɣlən*
Néit	*NʸADE* (rhymes with 'made')

Núadu Argatlám	*NOO-əð-oo AR-gad-LAHV*
Óengus	*OIN-ɣəss*
Ollam	*Oll-əv*
Ógarmach	*OWG-ar-vəkh* (*OWG* to rhyme with 'vogue')
Ogma	*Oɣ-mə*
Orchil	*OR-khil* (a goddess invented in the nineteenth century, so pronunciation uncertain)
Partholón	*PARTH-əll-own* (last two syllables sound much like English 'alone')
Rúadán	*ROO-ə-ðahn*
Sadb	*SAðv* (later *sive*, to rhyme with English 'five')
samildánach	*SAV-il-ðahn-əkh*
Scothníam	*SGOTH-nʸee-əv*
Senchán Torpéist	*SHEN-khahn TOR-paysht*
Senchus Már	*SHEN-khəs MAHR*
Seithoir	*SHETH-or* (a Middle Irish name, Seth(e)or, adapted in modernity by William Sharp: this is a guess at how Sharp might have pronounced it)
Semias	*SHEV-ee-əss* (or, if the name is actually *Sémias*, perhaps *SHAVE-ee-əss*: *SHAVE* like English 'shave')
síabair, pl. *síabraí*	*SHEE-əv-ər, SHEE-əv-ree*
Síd	*SHEEð* (much like English *sheathe*); later *Sídhe, Sí*, both pronounced 'shee'
Sinand	*SHIN-ənn*
Slat	*SLAD*
Táin Bó Cúailnge	*TOINʸ* (or *TAWNʸ*) *BOW* (as in 'bow and arrow') *KOOL-ngʸə*
Tait son of Taburn	*TADʸ* son of *TAV-ərn*
Tanaide	*TAN-əð-ə*
Teithoir	*TʸETH-or* (a Middle Irish name, Teth(e)or, adapted in modernity by William Sharp: this is a guess at how Sharp might have pronounced it)
Tírechán	*TʸEER-əkh-ahn*
Tír Tairngire	*TʸEER TARN-gʸir-ə*
Tochmarc Étaíne	*TOKH-vərk AY-deen-yə*
Trén	*TRAYnʸ* (quite close to English 'train')

trénfher	quite close to English 'trainer' provided the final -r is sounded clearly
Tuán mac Cairill	*TOO-ahn mack CAril* (*CA-* as in 'cat', not as in 'car')
Túath Dé	*TOO-əth DAY* ('DAY' as English)
Túatha Dé Danann	*TOO-əth-ə DAY DA-nənn*
Tuire(a)nn	*TOORʸən*
Tuirill	*TOORʸəll*
Tuis	*TUSH* (rhymes with 'hush')
Uchtdelb	*UKHT-dʸelv*
Uí Néill	*EE NʸALE* (*NʸALE* rhymes with 'nail')
Uiscias	*USH-gee-əss* (*USH* rhymes with 'hush')

PART ONE

HIDDEN BEGINNINGS

FROM CULT TO CONVERSION

Every layer they strip
Seems camped on before.
The bogholes might be Atlantic seepage.
The wet centre is bottomless.

—SEAMUS HEANEY, 'BOGLAND'

IN MANY MYTHOLOGIES the gods issue forth from primordial night; in Ireland, the divinities emerge not from the dark abyss of creation myth, but from an enigmatic and patchy archaeological record.

The earliest *written* evidence for native gods comes from early Christian Ireland, not from the pagan period; this is a pivotal fact which must be emphasized. Christianity did not entirely consign the pagan gods to the scrapheap, but the consequences of its arrival were dramatic and affected Irish society on every level. Pagan cult and ritual were discontinued, and a process was set in motion that eventually saw a small number of former deities reincarnated as literary characters. Christianity—intrinsically a religion of the book—enabled the widespread writing of texts in the Roman alphabet. Some of these have been transmitted to the present, with the paradoxical upshot that we owe our ability to say anything at all about the 'personalities' of Ireland's pre-Christian gods to the island's conversion.[1]

---

1 On the complex origins of literacy, see E. Johnson, *L&IEMI*, 9–16, and important analyses by A. Harvey, 'Early Literacy in Ireland', *CMCS* 14 (Winter, 1987), 1–15, and J. Stevenson, 'The Beginnings of Literacy in Ireland', *PRIA* (C) 89 (1989), 137–65. The complexity is partly down to the existence of *ogam*, a system of notches used originally for inscriptions along the edge of a stone; these are almost always of the form '[the memorial] of X, son/descendant of Y...' and appear to be grave and/or boundary markers. Research has shown that ogam was developed in the immediately pre- or partially Chris-

This chapter focuses on the period from the fifth century down to the late seventh, but tighter historical brackets can be put around the conversion process itself. The Christian religion was present in Ireland from at least the early 400s, certainly among British slaves and their descendants, though there may well also have been communities of Irish converts in the areas of the island that had been most exposed to influence from Roman Britain.[2] It is notoriously difficult to pinpoint when a population group can be decisively said to have exchanged one religion for another, but during the 500s the church hierarchy was legally established as a privileged order, and monasticism, Latin education, and ecclesiastical learning thrived. By the year 600, therefore, we can speak of Irish society as already converted on the level of hierarchy and institution.[3] The public worship of pagan gods by high-status individuals had probably come to an end in the mid to late 500s, but occasional, increasingly marginalized manifestations of non-Christian religion seem to have continued until the turn of the eighth century.[4] It is not until that point that druids—the magico-religious specialists of Irish paganism—finally cease to appear in legal texts as a going concern and can be taken to have disappeared from Irish society.[5] It is also worth remembering that all such markers are public and collective: the realm of personal conviction—how people behaved in their homes and felt in their hearts—is irrecoverably lost to us.

Around the year 700—roughly three hundred years after the conversion process began—pagan divinities began to appear in a vibrant litera-

---

tian period, at least as far back as the fourth century, by someone familiar not only with the Roman habit of monumental inscriptions on stone but also (possibly) with Latin grammatical tradition: the alphabet is not, in other words, an inheritance from the immemorial Celtic past. Probably it was also used on wood or bark, but the script's cumbersomeness makes the one-time existence of extended texts in ogam unlikely. Nevertheless, it is clear that at least some members of pre-Christian Irish society were able to write Irish and Latin from an early date.

2 See below, 13.

3 *ECI*, 182; T. M. Charles-Edwards, 'The Social Background to Irish *Perigrinatio*', *Celtica* 11 (1976), 43–59.

4 *ECI*, 244; Charles-Edwards points out that St Columba, born around 520 into a dynasty in the far north-west, is represented as converting the Picts to Christianity, but never his fellow Irishmen—presumably because they were by then largely converted. Johnston (*L&IEMI*, 14) dates the take-up by aristocratic elites of the 'opportunities presented by the new religion' to the second half of the sixth century.

5 See Elva Johnston's comment (*L&IEMI*, 114) that the Irish church had already won the 'long struggle over organised and semi-organised paganism' by the early 700s.

ture written in Old Irish.[6] Two questions immediately present themselves. Why should a Christian people be interested in pagan gods at all? And what was the relationship between the gods whom the pagan Irish had once venerated and the literary divinities who thronged the writings of their Christian descendants?[7]

ARCHAEOLOGY AND ANALOGY

It is traditional in handbooks of mythology to begin with a family portrait of the divinities, detailing their relationships, powers, and attributes.[8] This cannot be done for the gods of Ireland. It could be argued—albeit rather austerely—that we should not speak of Irish pre-Christian deities at all, because everything we know about them comes down to us in writings composed after the island's conversion and may therefore have been filtered through a Christian lens. *All* surviving mythological material from Ireland is the product of a pious and intellectually sophisticated Christian culture, and it is important to hold in mind that from their earliest appearances in the textual record the Irish gods are divorced from cult.

Can we retrieve any information from non-textual sources about the nature of the divinities worshipped by the pagan Irish?[9] The attempt is possible only with caution and if we confine ourselves to general principles. Two tools come to hand: the first is archaeology, and the second is inference drawn from the related societies of Celtic Gaul and Britain.

---

6 Charles-Edwards (*ECI*, 201) makes an illuminating contrast with the Old English poem *Beowulf*, written, much like early Irish literature, in a Christian and monastic context and similarly set in a pre-Christian past. But where Irish saga teems with former pagan deities, the likes of Thunor and Woden are conspicuously absent in the Anglo-Saxon poem; famously the 'paganism' of its characters is a kind of natural monotheism.

7 A recent approach to the change of religions from the perspective of ritual praxis is chapter three of E. Bhreathnach's *Ireland and the Medieval World, AD 400–1000* (Dublin, 2014).

8 See for instance B. Graziosi's recent *The Gods of Olympus: A History* (London, 2013), 1–10.

9 A condensed list of standard works would include M.-L. Sjoestedt, *Gods and Heroes of the Celts* (London, 1949); P. Mac Cana, *Celtic Mythology* (London, 1970); M. (Aldhouse-) Green, *The Gods of the Celts* (Gloucester, 1986); A. Ross, *The Pagan Celts* (London, 1986 [revised edn.]); and B. Raftery, *Pagan Celtic Ireland: The Enigma of the Irish Iron Age* (London, 1994). Points of detail in all these are worth checking against individual entries in *CCHE* for the current consensus.

By its nature, archaeological evidence is of limited value in reconstructing belief systems or mythological narratives, but it does seem that at least some Irish population groups set up anthropomorphic wooden or stone images that may be of gods. One found in the bog of Ralaghan, Co. Cavan, is roughly a metre long and made from a single round trunk of yew: it has a gouged hole in the genital area, which may once have held a carved phallus (Fig. 1.1). Though its sunken eye hollows anticipate the uncanny stare associated with the (characteristically Iron Age) La Tène decorative style, it actually dates to the late Bronze Age, at the beginning of the first millennium BC.[10] Many scholars would place this before the arrival of any form of Celtic speech in Ireland, so there is no guarantee of cultural continuity with the religious practices of over a millennium later.[11] That said, similar sculptures have turned up sporadically in Britain in a more explicitly Iron Age context, suggesting that they may once have been widespread: we cannot tell.[12]

10 M. Stanley, 'Anthropomorphic wooden figures: recent Irish discoveries', in J. Barber, *et al.* (eds.), *Archaeology from the Wetlands: Recent Perspectives* [Proceedings of the eleventh WARP conference] (Edinburgh, 2007), 17–30; A. O'Sullivan, 'Exploring past people's interactions with wetland environments in Ireland', *PRIA* (C) 107 (2007), 147–203.

11 The whole question of the arrival of some form of Celtic speech in Ireland is extremely difficult: we do not know when it happened, who brought it—except that the immigrating population must have been substantial—nor with what degree of violence or lack thereof it spread. More than one variety of Celtic may have been spoken, perhaps for centuries, before the ancestral form of Irish came to dominate. Concise referenced discussion in T. M. Charles-Edwards, 'Introduction: Prehistoric and Early Ireland', *NHI* i., lxvi–lxix.

12 See *PB*, 221–2 for these figures and their possible date-ranges; also A. Burl, *Rites of the Gods* (London, 1981), 213, 226–7. Other Irish wooden figures have been found at Lagore Crannog in Co. Meath (late Neolithic/early Bronze Age) and

FIG. 1.1. Late Bronze Age yew-wood figure, *c.*1000 BC, discovered in Ralaghan, Co. Cavan. Photo: Reproduced with the kind permission of the National Museum of Ireland.

Similar problems of interpretation attend the stone sculpture known as the 'Tandragee Idol', also dated to *c*.1000 BC. Helmeted and grasping his left arm—in pain or in salute?—the figure could represent a human warrior or a native deity (Fig. 1.2). In an instance of the seductive temptation to read archaeological objects in the light of much later literature—and thus to find a politically soothing continuity in the Irish past—it has been suggested that the Tandragee sculpture depicts Núadu Argatlám ('of the Silver Hand/Forearm'), a literary character who loses his arm in battle and has it temporarily replaced by one made of metal.[13] Ellen Ettlinger, who suggested the identification in 1961, felt convinced that the sculptor had depicted the left arm as 'clearly artificial'—but distinctions of this kind surely lie in the eye of the beholder.[14] Additionally, as the story of Núadu's silver prosthesis is first attested in a saga composed nearly two millennia after the Tandragee sculpture was created, any link must be considered at best only a possibility; the figure remains inscrutable.

There are also hints that rivers, bogs, and pools were important in the religious beliefs of the pagan Irish, though Iron Age deposits of artifacts are strikingly rarer in Ireland than in parts of Britain, for unknown reasons: an instance of the enigmatic quality of Irish Iron Age archaeology in general.[15] Ireland can nonetheless boast one of the most spectacular of these, the Broighter Hoard, which was discovered in 1896 buried in heavy agricultural land near to Lough Foyle in County Derry. The original deposition was made close to the water's eastern edge, but the shore of the lake has shifted over the millennia. It includes not only the most splendid torc ever uncovered in Ireland, but also a miniature golden

---

Corlea, Co. Longford (unambiguously Iron Age in date); see F. Menotti, *Wetland Archaeology and Beyond: Theory and Practice* (Oxford, 2012), 193.

13 Elizabeth Gray has provided a useful clutch of references for most Irish deities in her *CMT*; see 130–1 for Núadu; also F. Le Roux, 'Le dieu-roi NODONS/NUADA', *Celticum* 6 (1963), 425–54, which is old but useful.

14 E. Ettlinger, 'Contributions to an interpretation of several stone images in the British Isles', *Ogam* 13 (1961), 286–304. See speculations on the emergence of the motif of Núadu/Nodons' silver limb, which would ascribe it to the first centuries AD, by S. Zimmer, 'The making of myth: Old Irish *Airgatlám*, Welsh *Llaw ereint*, Caledonian Ἀργεντο-κόξος', in M. Richter & J.-M. Picard (eds.), *OGMA: Essays in Celtic Studies in honour of Próinséas Ní Chatháin* (Dublin, 2002), 295–7.

15 See *A&CM*, 79–73 for Irish finds; useful survey of Iron Age water hoards in Britain as well as Ireland in R. Hutton, *Pagan Religions of the Ancient British Isles* (Oxford, 1991), 184–90.

FIG. 1.2. The Tandragee Idol, carved stone image, *c.*1000 BC.
Photo: Reproduced by permission of the Dean and Chapter of
St Patrick's Cathedral (Church of Ireland), Armagh.

boat, complete with tiny oars.[16] The items seem to have been fashioned, and perhaps deposited as well, in the first century BC. Depositions such as this suggest a belief at the time they were made in supernatural beings associated with water, and it should be emphasized that this is all that can be extracted with confidence. In another instance of looking to later literature to explain archaeology, scholars have long speculated that the hoard was a ritual offering to the sea-god Manannán, because Old Irish texts associate Lough Foyle with stories of an inundation and an encounter between the god and a band of human mariners.[17] All this is not to say that connections drawn between medieval written texts and pre-Christian archaeology are of necessity misguided, simply that they must be considered tentative and that it is dismayingly easy to build castles in the air.

Because the archaeological evidence emerges as open to several interpretations we can use it to outline only the most important aspects of how the pre-Christian Irish regarded their divinities. Briefly, there were probably a great number of these, related to specific places, peoples, and to the natural world.[18] They were considered worthy of reverence, and perhaps (as seen) of artistic depiction; some of them seem to have had associations with water—though whether they were supposed to dwell in, under, or through it is unclear. They could be propitiated, and must have been imagined as having uses for the gifts, including animal sacrifice, which human beings offered up to them. Some of this picture can be rounded out by comparison with Gaul and Britain, but one final caveat about the archaeological record should be considered before we move on: it points to the centuries immediately before the conversion began as a period of economic contraction, agricultural decline, and (very likely)

16 Main description in P. F. Wallace & R. Ó Floinn (eds.), *Treasures of the National Museum of Ireland: Irish Antiquities* (Dublin, 2002), 138–9; see Carey, *I&G*, 555–8 for further bibliography.

17 The main personage to meet Manannán is named Bran son of Febal; *Febal* is the source of anglicized *Foyle*. For this story, see below, 56–68. For the Broighter Hoard and the later literature, see Carey, *I&G*, 355–8, and S. Mac Mathúna, *CCHE*, v., 1750–52.

18 Note the suggestive Irish words *bile* 'sacred tree' and (even more strikingly) *defhid*, apparently 'god-tree' (*día* + *fid*) and sometimes used to mean a tree held in special veneration by the inhabitants of a particular area. The latter however could be used as a synonym for the term *fidnemed*, which seems to have meant a tree growing on church land, so the 'paganness' of the concept is unclear. See discussion in *Bechbretha: an Old Irish Law-Tract on Bee-Keeping*, ed. & trans. T. Charles-Edwards & F. Kelly (Dublin, 1983), 108–9.

some degree of political upheaval.[19] Therefore it is possible that late–Iron Age religious values and beliefs reflected such turbulence, so that far from descending changelessly from an immemorial Celtic past, they may have been in considerable flux.

With the turn from Irish archaeology to Celtic Gaul and Britain, written data enters the picture, largely in the form of inscriptions, though there are also important Roman descriptions of Gaulish religious customs. Once again, useful parallels between the religious cultures of these societies and that of Ireland can only be drawn if we stick to broad outlines. Three features emerge as likely to have been shared. The first is that watercourses seem regularly to have been venerated as divinities—usually goddesses, though there are a few river-gods.[20] The second is a welter of local variety, with an enormously large number of named deities attested, though most of these clearly fell into a limited number of overlapping functional types: warrior, trader, hunter, and healer, for instance.[21] Thirdly, neither Gaul nor Britain provide us with evidence for a native pantheon in the Graeco-Roman sense, and this is clearly related to the localism just mentioned. This last presents a puzzle, for it has to be acknowledged that Old Irish literature—as we shall see—*does* in fact provide a loose family of supernatural beings looking something like a pantheon. A deity named the Dagda, literally meaning the 'Good God', forms the centre of gravity within this structure, like the Roman Jupiter; like Jupiter, he has several children and is conspicuously highly sexed.[22]

---

19 Note that Edel Bhreathnach argues the opposite, suggesting 'relative stability on the island', in *Ireland and Medieval Europe*, 41. The eve of conversion seems to have seen economic expansion, bolstered by raiding on and trading with Roman Britain; see *ECI*, 149–63. See also T. Charles-Edwards, 'Nations and kingdoms', in *After Rome* (Oxford, 2003), 25, for evidence that some kind of powerful but partial authority had emerged among elements of the Irish in the mid-fourth century.

20 On Celtic female river-deities, see M. Green, *Celtic Goddesses* (London, 1995), 89–102; river-gods are few and are attested only in overtly Romanized contexts. Mars Condatis ('of the Confluence'), for example, was associated with confluences into the River Wear (and elsewhere), and was also found in Gaul; the deity of the River Tyne was depicted as a mature, masculine figure. But as Graeco-Roman culture tended to visualize rivers as male, examples such as these may represent the overwriting of native convention, though why this should take place in some cases and not others is hard to say; see Hutton, *PB*, 242.

21 See Hutton, *Pagan Religions*, 155–6; raw data in P.-M. Duval, *Les dieux de la Gaule* (Paris, 1993), and N. Jufer & T. Luginbühl, *Les dieux gaulois: répertoire des noms de divinités celtiques connus par l'épigraphie, les textes antiques et la toponymie* (Paris, 2001).

22 The archaeologist Catherine Swift says that '... there is no real reason to suggest

There are a number of ways to resolve this discrepancy. On the one hand, pre-Christian Ireland might have independently developed a pantheon while the Gauls and the Britons did not, though this seems unlikely. Ireland was, and remained after its conversion, a decentralized, rural, and politically fragmented society with a thinly spread population of limited mobility—a situation unlikely to foster the development of a national family of gods.

More persuasive is the second possibility that those members of society who *could* move about thought in terms of a core pantheon. This would mean those who maintained themselves via a professional skill (known as *áes dána*, the 'people of art/talent'), and perhaps especially druids as the island's religious elite. It may be that this is what we find reflected at some removes in the later literature, which does have a striking emphasis on figures associated with skill. People tied to the land would probably have focused more on local divinities of fertility.[23] It is possible that a similar situation obtained in Gaul, and this would explain the sharp contrast between Julius Caesar's famous description of a micro-pantheon of five Gaulish gods—for whom he uses the Roman names Mercury, Mars, Jupiter, Apollo, and Minerva—and the clear epigraphic evidence that Gaulish deities numbered in the hundreds.[24] We know that Caesar spoke with a druid, and that he had a pressing need to understand the attitudes of the powerful in Gaulish society: his account of the gods of the Gauls may reflect solely the beliefs of the learned, mobile elite.[25]

---

a hierarchy along the lines of a classical pantheon among the Irish gods', but this merely underscores the problem of how and when the literary pantheon originated; see her 'The Gods of Newgrange in Irish Literature and Romano-Celtic Tradition', in G. Burenhult & S. Westergaard (eds.), *Stones and Bones* (Oxford, 2003), 53–63, at 55. Note that Eric Hamp has queried the translation 'Good God', arguing that *Dagda* may have meant 'god of the good (i.e. noble) people'; see 'The Dag(h)d(h)ae and his relatives', in L. Sawicki & D. Shalev (eds.), *Donum grammaticum: Studies in Latin and Celtic Linguistics in Honour of Hannah Rosén* (Leuven, 2002), 163–169.

23 The possibility of such a scenario is suggested by the maintenance by the elite—a few centuries later, but in a no less decentralized society—of a complex, high-register language, Old Irish, with almost no evidence of dialect. The language of people lower on the social spectrum would have exhibited regional variations, which were perhaps considerable. On this aspect of Old Irish, see P. Russell, ' "What was best of every language": the early history of the Irish language', *NHI* i., 405–50, at 442–3.

24 *Bell. Gall.* 6. 17. 1–2.

25 Compare M. Aldhouse-Green's maximalist account, *Caesar's Druids: An Ancient Priesthood* (London & New Haven, 2010), with the comments of R. Hutton, *Blood and*

A third possibility is that the whole concept of a family of gods under a father-god might have been adopted by the Irish as a result of contact with Roman culture, though this might have happened at two possible stages: pre-conversion and post-conversion. Pre-Christian Ireland was exposed to significant influence from Roman Britain, and the idea of a pantheon might have been adopted in imitation of the culture of the neighbouring island, as was the custom of commemorating the dead with inscriptions on stone.[26] Alternatively the concept of a pantheon might never have been part of Irish paganism at any stage. Rather, it could have been imported after the island became Christian, as the learned classes of Irish society developed familiarity with Latin litera-ture—not least the poet Virgil's baroquely mythological epic, the *Aeneid*. All these options are possible, but at the present state of our knowledge it is hard to gauge which is most likely.[27]

'UNCLEAN THINGS'

We know of one individual who encountered pagan Ireland first-hand: St Patrick. Exasperatingly, Patrick tells us next to nothing in his surviving writings about the non-Christian religious beliefs and practices to which he must have been exposed.[28]

Much about Patrick's life and mission has been clarified by two gen-erations of brilliant historians, though many obscurities remain.[29] What he was famously *not*, however, was an Irishman. He tells us that he was

---

Mistletoe: The History of the Druids in Britain (London & New Haven, 2009), 2–6; also S. B. Dunham, 'Caesar's perception of Gallic social structures', in B. Arnold & D. Blair Gibson (eds.), *Celtic Chiefdom, Celtic State* (Cambridge, 1995), 110–5.

26 On pre-Christian Ireland as 'both part of a Roman milieu and other than Roman', with contacts via 'trading and raiding, colonisation and slaving' see Johnston, *L&IEMI*, 10–12; her fn.53 gives references to the most recent material evidence for trade networks between Britain and Ireland (and beyond). Survey of Roman influence in the conversion period in L. Laing, 'The romanization of Ireland in the fifth century', *Peritia* 4 (1985), 261–78.

27 See the arguments of V. Di Martino, *Roman Ireland* (Cork, 2003), 135–60, which are interesting but often unsupported or wildly overstated.

28 Useful basic survey in R. Fletcher, *The Conversion of Europe: From Paganism to Christianity, 371–1386 AD* (London, 1997), 80–92; great detail in *ECI*, 182–233. My account owes much to Hutton, *Pagan Religions*, 155–6, to which I merely add detail here.

29 See *ECI*, 214–32, for a scrupulous weighing of the evidence. For Patrick's likely dates, see E. A. Thompson, *Who Was Saint Patrick?* (Woodbridge, 1985); influential collec-

a Briton, born into priestly family which belonged to the local nobility of a Romano-British *civitas*.[30] Abducted as a teenager and enslaved in the far west of Ireland, he managed after six years to escape. Later, having been ordained and then consecrated as a bishop, he felt impelled by a vision to return to evangelize the island where he had been in bondage and to succour its beleaguered Christians, though we know he was neither the island's first missionary, nor even its first bishop. The scholarly consensus is that Patrick's mission should be dated to the fifth century, and probably to its second half, though there is a range of opinions on almost every detail of where, when, how, and why.

Patrick is an indispensable source for the 'changing times' of the conversion period, which began with a pagan cult in full swing. British slaves, right at the bottom of society, probably made up the majority of Christians in Ireland—Patrick himself began as one such—though there may already have been settled communities of Irish converts in the 'Greater Leinster', the eastern and south-eastern region of Ireland, the area which had been most exposed to the culture of Roman Britain.[31] Of Patrick's two surviving writings, the more important for our purposes is the *Confession*, which amounts to a powerful—and powerfully difficult—spiritual autobiography, written in Latin.[32] Ireland's social topography, it reveals, consisted of a patchwork of different kingdoms of variably dense

---

tion of essays in D. N. Dumville & L. Abrams (eds.), *Saint Patrick, A.D. 493–1993* (Woodbridge, 1999).

30 For suggestions about the status of Patrick's family and the implications for his mission, see R. Flechner, 'Patrick's Reasons for Leaving Britain', in P. Russell & F. L. Edmonds (eds.), *Tome: Studies in Medieval History and Law* (Woodbridge, 2011), 125–34. For archaeological evidence bolstering the impression that contact with Britain was crucial in the formation of a Christian milieu in Ireland, see E. O'Brien, 'Pagan and Christian burial in Ireland in the first millennium', in N. Edwards (ed.), *The Early Church in Wales and the West* (Oxford, 1992), 130–7. Charles-Edwards (*ECI*, 186) makes the intriguing suggestion that British missionaries' work was made easier because the Irish gods were 'often identical' to those whom the Britons had formerly worshipped.

31 See *ECI*, 182 and *W&TB*, 182–3. Slaves in early Ireland, as elsewhere, would have performed hard labour while under the constant threat of violence and sexual exploitation. Patrick's writings, incidentally, are remarkable as the only first-hand account of the experience of slavery to have come down to us from antiquity. For awareness in Rome of Ireland's Christians and the concerns behind the decision to send them a bishop, see Bhreathnach, *Ireland in the Medieval World*, 158.

32 Amongst other things, this extraordinary text is also a justification of Patrick's behaviour as a missionary in the context of disputes which are opaque to us but were clearly familiar to his intended audience among the Britons; see *ECI*, 214–33, especially 218–19.

population. There were around a hundred of these *túatha* (singular *túath*).[33] Patrick notes the presence among the Irish of *idola et inmunda*, 'idols and unclean things'.[34] Jacqueline Borsje has noted that while the basic meaning of *idolum* in Latin is 'image', extended definitions include 'apparition' and the like; because a category of supernatural entity appears in the later literature under the native label *scál* ('phantom', 'spectre'), she has suggested that Patrick's word *idola* refers to this class of being.[35] Ingenious as this is, his meaning may have been more prosaic. *Inmunda* in particular suggests *objects*, and it is tempting to imagine Patrick's 'idols and unclean things' as carved figures of the Ralaghan type, together with the ritual trappings of their cult.[36]

After Patrick, nothing in the textual record names or alludes to native deities until the end of the seventh century.[37] To bridge this gap in the evidence about the fate of the gods whom the Irish worshipped during the change of religions, we must again look at parallels with similar societies.[38] These parallels suggest that the customs of animal sacrifice and the makings of offerings to deities—universal among pre-Christian European peoples—were progressively given up or banned. The loss of these

33 On the character of the conversion-period *túath*, see *ECI*, 12–15, and *After Rome*, ed. T. Charles-Edwards, 12–18; for population, see Bhreathnach, *Ireland in the Medieval World*, 38–9.

34 *Confessio*, §41, in *The Book of Letters of Saint Patrick the Bishop*, ed. & trans. D. Howlett (Blackrock, 1994), 80, 81.

35 J. Borsje, 'Monotheistic to a Certain Extent. The "Good Neighbours" of God in Ireland', in A.-M. Korte & M. de Haardt (eds.), *The Boundaries of Monotheism: Interdisciplinary Explorations into the Foundations of Western Monotheism* (Leiden & Boston, 2009), 56.

36 It is conceivable that by *inmunda* Patrick was referring to sacrificial offerings. The question of whether Christians should eat meat from animals sacrificed to idols was of serious concern to the very early Church (see Acts 15:29, where it is forbidden). St Paul believed eating such meat was allowable in itself, but not if it caused a weaker fellow Christian to be troubled in his conscience (1 Corinthians 8:4–13). Surrounded by recent converts, Patrick may have felt that Paul's concern applied.

37 This is not to imply there is a textual gap in the record between the late fifth and late seventh centuries: a highly complex and significant body of texts survives which sheds light on the growth of monasticism and the codification of ecclesiastical and secular law, much of it notoriously difficult for the non-specialist. Native gods, however, do not feature. A good way in is C. Etchingham, *Church organisation in Ireland, A.D. 650 to 1000* (Maynooth, 1999), along with D. Ó Cróinín's indispensible *Early Medieval Ireland, 400–1200* (London & New York, 1995).

38 New light will undoubtedly be shed by R. Flechner & M. Ní Mhaonaigh (eds.), *Converting the Isles* (Turnhout, 2015), one outcome of a major three-year research project, which had—alas—not yet been published as this book went to press.

rituals would inevitably lead to once-important divinities being forgotten—perhaps more rapidly than we would expect, given the dismal life expectancies of the period.[39] Ritual sites would have been closed and abandoned. Edel Bhreathnach suggests that wells and springs formerly associated with pagan gods were widely used by missionaries as sites of baptism by affusion, in which water was poured over the convert's head, thus consecrating the sites via the rites of the new religion.[40] On the social level the vigour of churches and monastic centres would have been reflected in the increased standing of churchmen, even as authority drained from pagan religious functionaries. In Ireland this probably meant the druidic class, and there is good evidence from the law-tracts and penitentials for this process of social demotion, including seventh-century stipulations that druids were no longer to be accorded the privileges owed to members of high-status professions.[41]

If Anglo-Saxon England is anything to go by, after the rulers of a population group converted, the public worship of pagan gods probably took forty to fifty years to disappear, following a brief period in which Christianity and paganism coexisted.[42] In Ireland, this scenario was probably repeated many times in different social groups. As Elva Johnston points out, the island's political diversity meant that conversion must have been an untidy affair, and 'not simply the process of convincing one important dynasty or ruler'.[43] She thus aptly describes Ireland's conversion as 'both fast and slow'—fast because once a people began to change their religion the process could take place relatively speedily, but slow because there were so many peoples to convert.

The Venerable Bede provides a (not unproblematic) narrative of the process of Christianization for Anglo-Saxon England, but there is no

---

39 Observations for a slightly later period, the seventh century, in C. Doherty, 'Kingship in Early Ireland', *K&LT*, 7–10, who points to a continuing concern among churchmen with the Christianization of the landscape, implying that the symbolic conversion of the landscape—'a redefinition of the physical world'—flowed from and followed the conversion of society and the dismantling of pagan cult.

40 See Bhreathnach, *Ireland and the Medieval World*, 134–5.

41 F. Kelly, *A Guide to Early Irish Law* (Dublin, 1988), 60–1, and *The Irish Penitentials*, ed. L. Bieler (Dublin, 1963), 160. A re-assessment of all references to druids in medieval Irish literature—too easily blended with the contradictory accounts of classical writers, and produced in very different cultural circumstances—is strongly to be desired; see comments of Hutton, *PB*, 173.

42 B. Yorke, *The Conversion of Britain: Religion, Politics and Society in Britain, 600–800* (Harlow, 2006), 128.

43 *L&IEMI*, 13.

equivalent for Ireland. Indeed, Patrick's writings make plain that he was not at all interested in giving a sequential account of the conversion process. We do not know, for example, which *túatha* were converted first, which lagged behind, nor how this process was bound up with the expansion of alphabetic literacy. If there was any backsliding, it is not mentioned. Nevertheless, the earliest Irish saints' lives, which date from the seventh century, make plain that—as elsewhere in Europe—pagan deities were sometimes rebranded as evil spirits.[44] Surviving Anglo-Saxon baptismal formulae involve the rejection of pagan deities as demons, and as Irish missionaries played an important role in the conversion of some Anglo-Saxon kingdoms, it is tempting to believe that similar formulae also played a part in the conversion process in Ireland.

TWO DEITIES

With this background in mind, it is worth considering the trajectories in the conversion period of two specific deities, a god and a goddess.

The god Lug is a pivotal figure in a number of medieval sagas, and is one of the most charismatic of medieval Ireland's literary supernaturals—a youthful warrior and ruler 'equally gifted in all the arts', as his sobriquet, *samildánach*, indicates. He was repackaged in the nineteenth century as the Irish god of the sun—a process examined later in this study—and though not a shred of evidence exists for this identification it is still recycled in popular works.[45] Lug's prominence in the literature has led generations of scholars to see him as an after-image of an important pre-Christian deity intimately connected with kingship.[46] Old Irish Lug can only derive from earlier Lugus, and a divinity of that name is attested among a number of Celtic-speaking peoples on the continent, as

---

44 See J. Borsje 'Druids, deer, and "words of power": coming to terms with evil in medieval Ireland', in K. Ritari, *et al.* (eds.), *Approaches to Religion and Mythology in Celtic Studies* (Newcastle, 2008), 128–9, for druids invoking demons (i.e. their gods) in Muirchú's late seventh-century 'Life of Patrick'.

45 See below, 265, 337.

46 For Lug's continued prominence into the Christian period, see T. Ó Cathasaigh, 'The Eponym of Cnogba', originally in *Éigse* 23 (1989), 27–38, and reprt. in M. Boyd (ed.), *Coire Sois: The Cauldron of Knowledge* (Notre Dame, IN, 2014), 155–64. Foundational observations by O'Rahilly, *EIH&M*, 310–4, to be used with caution; overview of medieval references in *CMT*, 126–7.

well as more indirectly in Britain.[47] It has long been thought that Lugus was one of the few Celtic gods with an extensive cult, though Bernhard Maier has recently cast doubt upon his pan-Celtic spread.[48]

In Ireland, it seems accepted that a pre-Christian deity provided the foundation for the medieval Lug. But how do we determine the ways in which this divinity was affected by change of religions—about how, on a more than merely linguistic level, Lugus morphed into Lug? If as before we refer only to what cautious comparison can tell us (supplemented by such securely pre-Christian evidence as there is), then all that can be blandly affirmed is that Lugus was important to at least some groups among the pagan Irish. This much is clear from tribal and personal names, as at least two populations named themselves after him. One was the Luigni, the 'People of Lugus', whose territory in historical times was located in Connaught; the other was the Luigni Temro ('of Tara'), who were associated with Tara in Co. Meath, the symbolic centre of Irish over-kingship.[49] The two peoples may have been branches of a single kindred. Their name appears a number of times in an earlier form, LU-GUNI, upon stones incised in ogam, the cumbersome alphabet of notches which was developed to write Irish in the fourth and fifth centuries.[50] This form crops up on ogam stones in a scattered fashion, suggesting that members of the Luigni were either widely dispersed or that the name was relatively common.[51]

47 The British evidence consists of a few personal and placenames apparently containing the theonym: Welsh *Llywarch* < **Lugumarkos*, 'Stallion of Lugus', for example, and Carlisle < *Castra Luguvalium*, 'the settlement of *Luguwalos*, "he-who-is-strong-in/ like-Lugus"', though these could admit of other interpretations. Less assailable is the name of the literary figure Lleu Llaw Gyffes in the Fourth Branch of the *Mabinogi*, as *Lleu* can only derive independently from earlier *Lugus* and cannot represent a borrowing from Irish *Lug*. Note Charles-Edwards' comments on the punning on the name Lleu and the place name Lothian (= *Lleuddinion*, 'Lleu's Fortress') in one of the *awdlau* of the Old Welsh poem *Y Gododdin* (*W&TB*, 375).

48 See his 'Is Lug to be identified with Mercury (*Bell. Gall.* vi 17, 1)? New Suggestions on an Old Problem', *Ériu* 47 (1996), 127–135.

49 I use *Connaught* to refer to the province, to distinguish it from the *Connachta*, its medieval inhabitants.

50 See D. McManus, *A Guide to Ogam* (Maynooth, 1991), 108, and J. Carey, 'Tara and the Supernatural', *K&LT*, 42–3, fn. 50. It is conventional to transcribe ogam with uppercase letters.

51 Bhreathnach, *Ireland in the Medieval World*, 43–4, notes the Dál Luigne—*dál* is another term for a kin-group—who are listed as a subject people in the eighth-century 'Expulsion of the Déssi'.

By their nature, ogam stones commemorate high-status individuals. A significant number of stones point to a widespread fondness among Irish elites for personal names containing an allusion to the god. One example is LUGUDEC(C)AS—corresponding to Old Irish *Lugdech*, genitive case of the common male name *Lugaid*—which perhaps means 'he who venerates Lugus'.[52] Even more suggestive is LUGUQRIT- (Old Irish *Luccreth*), 'he whose form is like that of Lugus'.[53] That these names continued to be popular in the Christian period in no way implies that the worship of Lugus was maintained, in the same way that those named Apollonius or Dionysius in late antiquity did not continue to worship the gods Apollo or Dionysus. Rather, these were simply names hallowed by tradition, inheritance, and elite usage.

While the above is relatively secure, it is not much to go on. However, as soon as we turn to early medieval depictions of the literary Lug for hints about the pagan Lugus, we are immediately confronted with a mass of aggravating ambiguities. It must be emphasized that although very little can be known for sure about pre-Christian Irish religion, it

---

52 There are several others. LUGUVEC(C)- is twice attested (= Old Irish *Lugech*, *Lugach*), perhaps meaning 'Lugus-like' or 'fighter of Lugus', while another stone apparently commemorates a poet named *Luguttis*, perhaps 'devoted to Lugus'; for these see McManus, *A Guide to Ogam*, 88, 96, 103–4, 108, 125. Note that the group-name *moccu Lugd(a)i*, attested in Old Irish, points to an older *Luguadii*, also probably meaning 'Lugus-like'. On the etymologies, see references in J. T. Koch, 'A Swallowed Onomastic Tale in *Cath Maige Mucrama?*', in J. Carey, et al. (eds.), *Ildánach, Ildírech: A Festschrift for Proinsias Mac Cana* (Llandysul, 1999), 69–71.

53 These names are vulnerable to one of the criticisms made by Maier of continental and British evidence for a cult of Lugus, which is that a homonym, **lugus*, meant 'lynx', figuratively 'warrior' or 'hero' in Celtic, and so words containing the *lugu-* element do not have to refer to the god: the Luigni might have been the 'Heroic Ones', and LUGUQRIT- might have meant 'having the look of a warrior'. On the other hand, no one doubts there *was* a pre-Christian Lugus in Ireland, and confusion between the theonym and the noun for 'warrior' must have been widespread and conducive to deliberate double meanings—especially as heroism is the god's most obvious quality. Scholars have never agreed on the meaning of the theonym; a link to a root meaning 'light' is often suggested but is philologically difficult. (See E. Ellis Evans, *Gaulish Personal Names* (Oxford, 1967), 218–21). On the other hand, John Carey has recently shed doubt on the very existence of the 'lynx' word, and I do not see why the meaning 'warrior, hero' might not have been a dead metaphor derived from the theonym; *DIL* is not clear that the later forms of these words, *lug* and *Lug*, are separate words at all. For these semantic complexities, see S. Ziegler, *Die Sprache der altirischen Ogam-Inschriften* (Göttingen, 1994), 197–200, and J. Carey, 'Celtic **lugus* 'lynx': A phantom Big Cat?', in F. Josephson (ed.), *Celtic Language, Law and Letters: Proceedings of the Tenth Symposium of Societas Celtologica Nordica* (Gothenburg, 2008), 151–68.

does not follow that *all* conjecture on the subject is retrograde and irresponsible. One may reasonably speculate, but it is important not to use the resulting suggestions to anchor larger arguments.[54]

One plausible scenario is that there were multiple Luguses, or versions of him. Surviving texts make clear that the medieval Lug was strongly bound up with ideas and ideals of rulership, and in an island of many *túatha* his divine precursor might well have had any number of local manifestations—hardly an uncommon phenomenon in the pagan religions of ancient Europe.[55] As such, he might have been regarded as an ancestor-deity connected with the legitimization of political authority in many different population groups: the Luigni may have been far from unique.

If different groups in pre-Christian Ireland did indeed have distinctively local takes on Lugus, this may explain a puzzling feature of the written record: that numerous literary figures—often heroes or legendary ancestors, and definitely intended to be mortal—look like alter egos of the god. Scholars have suggested quite a number of these, their names usually containing the *Lug-* root. Luigne Fer Trí, legendary ancestor of the Luigni of Connaught and fosterer of the wise king Cormac mac Airt, is a likely candidate. So is Lugaid Mac Con, a pseudohistorical king of Tara associated with the Érainn people of Munster, whom Cormac, according to legend, displaced as king.[56] Though Mac Con (as he is also known) has a rather villainous role in the later saga literature, early accounts treat him sympathetically, suggesting that he was once a more heroic figure.[57] He in turn may have a doublet in Lugaid Loígde, an important ancestor-

---

54 On the question of how legitimate it is to comb medieval Irish texts for evidence of pagan belief, it cannot yet be said that a consensus has emerged. While discussion looks set to continue, one (influential) view sees the whole exercise as a hiding to nothing; see for instance Elizabeth Boyle's uncompromising review of Bhreathnach's *Ireland in the Medieval World*, in which she condemns 'the ongoing production of speculative prose in the face of the inescapable truth that we have no reliable historical evidence which can attest to the nature of the pre-Christian religion of Ireland' (*Early Medieval Europe* [forthcoming, 2016/7]).

55 See for example R. Parker, *On Greek Religion* (Ithaca & London, 2011), 70–3; it is striking that multiple Luguses (if this is what the 'Lugoves' mentioned in dedications across a wide span of western Europe actually were), are attested outside Ireland, for which see A. Tovar, 'The God Lugus in Spain', *BBCS* 29.4 (1982), 591–9.

56 *ECI*, 144.

57 See comments of Ralph O'Connor, *DDDH*, 315; also *Duanaire Fhinn: The Book of the Lays of Fionn*, ed. E. MacNeill & G. Murphy (London, 1953) [ITS 43], iii., 205–6.

figure for the Érainn.[58] A fourth is Lugaid Riab nDerg ('the red-striped'), who like Mac Con was remembered as a legendary king of Tara.[59]

But Lug's most famous possible avatar is an ally of Mac Con (and in some traditions, his cousin), Finn mac Cumaill. The legendary Finn was the leader of a *fían*—a band of young, aristocratic warrior-hunters—and he became the focus of a lush body of later medieval and modern Gaelic tradition. Scholars have long pointed out structural similarities between the stories associated with Lug and those connected to Finn. The latter's name goes back to *Vindos, the 'Fair One', which may have been a local form of Lugus, perhaps even the form of the god whom members of a *fían* took as their patron deity, since *fían*-bands were a genuine social institution in early Ireland.[60] This list of reflexes could be extended: it has even been argued, less convincingly, that the saints Lachtin and Mo Lua might also be humanized versions of Lugus in origin.[61]

One further special case may be significant, albeit problematic: the crucial bond between Lug and the Ulstermen's greatest hero, Cú Chulainn.[62] According to the great epic *Táin Bó Cúailnge* ('The Cattle Raid of Cooley'), Cú Chulainn is Lug's son. But according to the much shorter tale *Compert Con Culainn* ('Cú Chulainn's Conception'), he is also in some sense his mortal incarnation. There is no way to gauge the age

58 A. Mac Shamhráin & P. Byrne, 'Prosopography I: Kings named in *Baile Chuinn Chétchathaig* and *The Airgíalla Charter Poem', K&LT*, 164–5.

59 Carey, 'Tara and the Supernatural', *K&LT*, 41–4, esp. fn.49; see classic statements from T. F. O'Rahilly on euhemerized reflexes of Lug in *EIH&M*, 202, 284.

60 On Lug and the 'divine' Finn, see J. Carey, 'Nodons, Lugus, Windos', in C.-M. Ternes, *et al.* (eds.), *Dieux des Celtes/Goetter der Kelten/Gods of the Celts* (Luxembourg, 2002), 99–126, plus T. Ó Cathasaigh, '*Cath Maige Tuired* as Exemplary Myth', in Boyd (ed.), *Coire Sois*, 135–54, at 152–3 (originally published in P. de Brún, *et al.* (eds.), *Folia Gadelica: Essays presented by former students to R. A. Breatnach* (Cork, 1983), 1–19). Also P. Mac Cana, 'Fianaigecht in the pre-Norman period', in B. Almqvist, *et al.* (eds.), *The Heroic Process: Essays on the Fenian Tradition of Ireland and Scotland* (Dublin, 1987), 75–99, and see lengthier discussion below, 197–8.

61 See P. Ó Riain, 'Traces of Lug in early Irish hagiographical tradition', *ZCP* 36 (1977), 138–156; cf. D. Blair Gibson on a connection between the obscure Airgialla saint Luchthigern mac Lugdach and the hilltop ritual site of Mooghaun, Co. Clare (*From Chiefdom to State in Early Ireland* (Cambridge, 2012), 43). Suggestive, but too speculative to be persuasive, is B. Lacey, *Lug's forgotten Donegal kingdom: the archaeology, history, and folklore of the Síl Lugdach of Cloghaneely* (Dublin, 2012), which argues for traces of an ongoing connection to the god Lug(us) in the hagiography and historical record of a small and remote early medieval kingdom in Donegal.

62 A theme explored by E. A. Gray, 'Lug and Cú Chulainn: King and Warrior, God and Man', *SC* 24/5 (1989/90), 38–52.

of this tradition; both the texts which attest to it are sophisticated works from a Christian and monastic milieu, and quite basic aspects of Lug's role in them are unclear. In the *Táin* Lug appears to his son Cú Chulainn, who lies gravely injured. Not only does the god heal him—leaving him in a recuperative coma for three days—but he also takes on his son's appearance and fights in his stead on the battlefield.[63] This interlude might be an old theme, but the *Táin*'s Christian shapers went to great lengths to imbue the text with a plausibly 'pagan' atmosphere. Lug's healing of Cú Chulainn resembles episodes from classical epic so closely that medieval literary imitation is a distinct possibility.[64]

In the story of Cú Chulainn's conception, things get still murkier, and it is possible that that the saga's author is sending up pagan gods.[65] Lug—supposedly *samildánach*, 'multitalented'—requires no fewer than three attempts to father a son, a son who is also (apparently) himself.[66] The first child dies in childhood, while the second—fathered sexlessly—is promptly aborted by his mother, who is embarrassed to be a visibly pregnant bride. The third is Cú Chulainn, who is conceived via an act of ordinary sexual intercourse between human beings and is thus Lug's son only in a rather rarified sense. Historically, Irish scholars have been prepared to see this as a 'triple birth', an archaic mythic theme marking the hero out as someone special. It may instead be that persistent echoes of the Gospel infancy narratives are being enlisted here to underscore that the pagan Lug can barely manage what the Christian God had done with

63 *Táin Bó Cúailnge: Recension I*, ed. & trans. C. O'Rahilly (Dublin, 1976), ll.2073–2184. Note that Lug *says* that he will fight in Cú Chulainn's stead, at least: but in Recensions I and II of the *Táin*, when the hero wakes up, Lug tells him the boys of Emain Macha have actually done the job.

64 Ann Dooley has gone so far as to suggest the whole episode may have been inspired by an uncanny incident in Patrick's *Confession*; see her *Playing the Hero: Reading the Irish Saga 'Táin Bó Cúailnge'* (Toronto, 2006), 128–35 (where the Recension I version of the episode is quoted and translated), also 145–55.

65 The saga might well be early; it depends when one thinks a crucial lost manuscript, the *Cín Dromma Snechtai* ('The Book of Drumsnat'), was written. There is longrunning debate on the matter, but a date of *c.*700 is not impossible; see T. Ó Concheanainn, 'The Textual Tradition of *Compert Con Culainn*', *Celtica* 21 (1990), 441–55. Text itself in *Compert Con Culainn and other stories*, ed. A. G. Van Hamel (Dublin, 1933 [reprinted 1978]), 1–8, and translation in *EIM&S*, 131–3. On tone see *PPCP*, 198–9.

66 On the possible influence of the Gospel infancy narratives here, and how we should read the implied parallel between Christ and Cú Chulainn, see *DDDH*, 245, and T. Ó Cathasaigh, 'Mythology in *Táin Bó Cúailnge*' in H. L. Tristram (ed.), *Studien zur Táin Bó Cúailnge* (Tübingen, 1993), 114–32, at 126–8, reprt. in Boyd (ed.), *Coire Sois*, 201–18, at 213–4.

ease—that is, become incarnate and be born of a virgin as a child both divine and human.[67] Neatly, the life of Cú Chulainn was thought by the medieval Irish to have overlapped with that of Christ and, like his, to have lasted thirty-three years.[68]

And yet the possibility remains that behind Lug's relationship to Cú Chulainn there lies a genuinely old tradition of Lugus the divine ancestor, who might embody himself in heroes and rulers. To name a noble boy-child *Luccreth* was to hope for him to be 'like-Lugus-in-form' in the future. Here we may further speculate: if Christianization removed the mobile religious elite—the druids—who had bound the religious traditions of different population groups together, it may have prompted the divine Lugus to disintegrate. The way then opened for local versions of the god to go their separate ways and to develop into a range of different and mortal ancestor figures with distinct regional and genealogical significances.

If our speculation is correct, this splintering into legendary personages was only one of the trajectories of Lugus. The conversion period also brought with it his reincarnation as Lug the literary character, who retained the clearly supernatural status which the likes of Luigne Fer Trí and Lugaid Mac Con had lost. The dynamo driving the crystallization of the literary Lug was probably the rise of the Uí Néill, the multi-branched royal kindred who achieved predominance as a distinct lineage in the northern half of Ireland in the first half of the sixth century, at much the same time that Christianity was becoming firmly established among the island's elites. They were to dominate the high-kingship of Tara for half a millennium.[69] The supernatural Lug of the medieval literature is in many ways *their* Lug; as such he was no cultural fossil, but a figure filtered through a veil of political propaganda in order to underwrite the Uí Néill's claim to the kingship of Tara.[70]

---

67 Note Tomás Ó Cathasaigh's elegant observation (in Boyd (ed.), *Coire Sois*, 8) that in the first conception 'the parents are both divine; in the third they are both human. In the second conception the father is divine and the mother human. We see in this sequence how the hero mediates the opposition between god and man.'

68 'The Conception of Cú Chulainn' would repay greater examination than can be given here; note that Marion Deane's recent retro-mythological reading does not mention its possible satirical subtext ('From sacred marriage to clientship: a mythical account of the establishment of kingship as an institution', in R. Schot, *et al.* (eds.), *Landscapes of Cult and Kingship* (Dublin, 2011), 1–21).

69 *DDDH*, 314.

70 Lugaid Riab nDerg whom we met above was thought of as a key ancestor of the

But why should this require the retrofitting of an ex-god? It is difficult to overestimate the importance of the institution of kingship in early Irish culture: the king was represented as the axis around which secular society revolved, and the high-kingship of Tara was the supreme example, in ideology if not always in political fact.[71] Bart Jaski writes that kings were 'the protagonists in the early Irish annals, the main characters in narrative literature, the focus of praise-poems, the *raison d'être* of the genealogists, the target of praise or curse in hagiography, and the centre of secular power in the legal tracts.'[72] In literature at least, the king was often represented as a 'sacral' figure, whose rule was licensed by a contract with the supernatural realm and who mediated between society and nature.[73] A core of originally pagan concepts continued to attach to the institution, not least the idea of the 'prince's truth' (*fír flathemon*), a just equilibrium in which the ruler's righteousness is reflected in the success of his reign. This success in turn depended on the ruler avoiding a personal checklist of 'prohibited acts' (*gessi*)—another originally pre-Christian idea. But the church also had trenchant views of its own about the nature of monarchy, with the result that in the documentary period the early Irish ideology of kingship encompassed both indigenous and ecclesiastical elements.[74]

Philip O'Leary comments that Irish saga teaches that 'perfect kingship is beyond human scope.'[75] The purpose of the literary Lug may have been to personify the potent native dimension of ideal kingship, just as the Old Testament King David personified the Christian aspect. Lug may have remained imaginatively available during the conversion period because of a strong association with the great annual *óenach* or 'fair', which was held at Tailtiu, now Teltown in Co. Meath. (This was the most famous of such assemblies; there were a number of others.) In the his-

---

Dál Cuinn, the progenitors of the Uí Néill dynasty; see *DDDH*, 314. Tomás Ó Cathasaigh points out that Lug 'is presented as the legitimator of the Dál Cuinn (and hence also the Uí Néill) kings of Tara' ('The Eponym of Cnogba', *Éigse* 23 (1989), 31 [= Boyd (ed.), *Coire Sois*, 158]).

71 Essential one-volume discussion is B. Jaski, *Early Irish Kingship and Succession* (Dublin, 2000), especially 25–88. See also N. B. Aitchison, 'Kingship, society and sacrality: rank, power, and ideology in early medieval Ireland', *Traditio* 49 (1994), 45–75.

72 Jaski, *Kingship and Succession*, 25.

73 Jaski, *Kingship and Succession*, 57–88.

74 Seminal discussion by McCone, *PPCP*, 155–8; see also *DDDH*, 278.

75 P. O'Leary, 'A Foreseeing Driver of an Old Chariot: Regal Moderation in Early Irish Literature', *CMCS* 11 (Summer, 1986), 16, quoted *DDDH*, 308.

torical period, the *óenach* itself involved not only serious political, ecclesiastical, and judicial business, but also horse and chariot racing, and other games and forms of entertainment, along with trade.[76] Tailtiu had become a politically crucial royal site and the Uí Néill's pre-eminent place of assembly by *c.*700, but it seems clear that its roots—especially the link to Lug—went back to the pagan period. Later tradition made Tailtiu the name of Lug's foster-mother, and also asserted that Lug had instituted the games there as part of her funeral rites.[77] The antiquity of that particular idea is debatable, but the *óenach* at Tailtiu was certainly held each year at *Lugnasad* (probably meaning 'the Festival of Lug') at the beginning of August.[78] The very name underscores its relationship to Lug, though the original meaning of the *nasad* element is no longer clear.[79] The custom of holding tribal assemblies at Lugnasad is very likely to be old: it is amongst other things the most obvious and convenient time in the cycle of the seasons for travel.

It must be emphasized that in the historical period the Lugnasad assembly at Tailtiu was not—in any sense at all—a 'pagan' festival; indeed, Tailtiu had a church and was at one point the site of an ecclesiastical synod, probably held at the time of the *óenach* itself.[80] But it is striking that Lug continued to be openly associated with the festival after it ceased to involve his worship as a god. It suggests the Irish had the capacity during the sixth and seventh centuries for a very precise kind of

---

76 *L&IEMI*, 77.

77 See for example the poem by Cúán ua Lothcháin (who died in 1024) on Tailtiu which makes the etymology clear by calling the festival 'Lug's Lugnasad' (*Loga Lugnasad*); *Metrical Dindshenchas*, ed. & trans. E. J. Gwynn (5 vols., Dublin, 1903–35), iv. 150.46.

78 See M. MacNeill, *The Festival of Lughnasa: A Study of the Survival of the Celtic Feast of the Beginning of Harvest* (London, 1962), 311–38.

79 See *DIL* s.v. In 'Cormac's Glossary' (*c.*900) it is understood as *násad*, a word apparently interpreted to mean 'a commemorative gathering', though that might simply represent the glossator's guess based on the word *Lugnasad* itself; see F. Kelly, *Early Irish Farming* (Dublin, 2000), 459. That the festival originated in Tailtiu's funeral-games might itself have been inspired by a homonym (*nás* in *DIL*) meaning 'death, putting to death', the story being concocted when the festival originally in the god's honour was rebranded and historicized. It is tempting to see, with *DIL*, a connection to the verb *nascid*, 'to bind', as in an oath or legal contract; the original Lugnasad might have involved the brokering of political and social contracts under the auspices of Lugus, whose own name—scholars have suggested—may derive from **lugiom*, 'oath', making him not only a god of kingship but also of ties and sureties. But here again the siren song of mere speculation is heard. On Lugus and oaths, see J. T. Koch, 'Further to *tongu do dia toinges mo thuath* etc.', *ÉC* 29 (1992), 249–61.

80 *ECI*, 278–9.

imaginative discrimination, and also that there can have been remarkably little fear of backsliding into paganism.

Memory of Lug may have been preserved thanks to a strategy already visible in the writings of learned Irishmen in the middle of the seventh century. This was to re-imagine the island's pre-Christian past as a local version of the Old Testament, full of scenarios and personages mirroring those of scripture. The point was to emphasize that the Irish had been uniquely ready to receive the truth of Christianity, being already long prepared for it. Part and parcel of this was to reconfigure former deities as people who had lived long ago, and Lug may have been re-constituted as the culture hero of the *óenach*: the invention of ball games, horse-racing and the assembly itself were all ascribed to him.[81] Equally important, he could function as an idealized self-projection of those competing for, and visibly asserting, royal power—most importantly the Uí Néill over-king, who was there to see and be publicly seen, surrounded by his vassals.[82] Catherine Swift tellingly points out that successfully holding the festival of Tailtiu was in itself a display of power, one 'that could bolster a new king or one weakened by defeats elsewhere', because an over-king had to have the political clout to demand the attendance of his more powerful subordinates.[83] Accomplished and aristocratic masculinity, mature but ideally still charged with the potency of youth, continued to be a crucial dimension of social identity among those aspiring to power; thus Lug as 'divine' hero could retain a function in the culture in direct proportion to the extent that he functioned as a role model without flaws.[84]

---

81 J. Carey, 'Tara and the Supernatural', *K&LT*, 43–4; a gloss on the tenth-century 'Colloquy of the Two Sages' reads *is e Lug ar-ránic oenach ocus liathróit ocus echlaim*, 'it was Lug who invented the assembly and the ball and the horse-rod', in which the last two presumably stand metonymically for the sports played during the first. See *Immacallam in Dá Thuarad*, ed. W. Stokes, *RC* 26 (1905), §120. These may well have been old traditions—one is reminded of Caesar's statement (*Bell. Gall.* 6.17), that the Gaulish 'Mercury' (which may have meant Lugus) was considered 'the inventor of all the arts'—but the point is they were just as relevant under the new dispensation.

82 The classic historical account is D. A. Binchy, 'The Fair of Tailtiu and the Feast of Tara', *Ériu* 18 (1958), 113–38.

83 C. Swift, '*Óenach Tailten*, the Blackwater valley, and the Uí Néill kings of Tara', in A. P. Smith, (ed.), *Seanchas: Studies in Early and Medieval Irish Archaeology, History, and Literature in Honour of Francis J. Byrne* (Dublin, 2000), 109–20, at 119.

84 *Óenach Tailten* may have been a very masculine affair, its events reserved for men; a high medieval poem on another Lugnasad *óenach*, the triennial fair at Carmun, considers it worth mentioning (and by implication finds it unexpected) that women as well as men attended, though they did not mix. See Kelly, *Early Irish Farming*, 459.

Earlier I mentioned King David; if Lug functioned as a native parallel for any scriptural figure, it was this most charismatic of Old Testament kings. Kim McCone noted two decades ago that aspects of the medieval Lug echo the life story of David: both are represented as handsome youths, acclaimed warriors, righteous kings, poets, and harpists. Lug's most famous deed in Irish saga—killing the giant Balor with a sling-shot—exactly parallels David's killing of the Philistine giant Goliath.[85] McCone's observation had the effect of making it alarmingly clear just how likely it is that Irish mythology as transmitted to us has been re-modelled along biblical lines. The suggestion here is that King David might be even more important than has been realized; the process of typological remodelling might be pushed back into the 600s, if not ear-lier. By doing so, the literary Lug could be seen as the reanimation of a pagan figure—remembered because of the *óenach* and an association with the pivotal institution of kingship—with an infusion of Davidic tropes that were important because the New Testament emphasized that the line of David ultimately produced Christ himself. Lug's emergence as a 'national' figure may therefore owe at least as much to the Old Testa-ment David as to the Lugus of Irish paganism. A pagan god has been reconfigured as—in part—a native analogue to the most famous of Christ's ancestors. Uí Néill propagandists may well have constructed (or appropriated) a figure savouring of the ancient past but whose face was turned to a new era and who foreshadowed the coming of the new reli-gion. This would be an absolutely typical early-Irish mixture of conser-vatism and creativity.[86] Even in a Christian Ireland, the ideology of king-ship was clearly felt to benefit from the energizing touch of the apparently archaic.

The Uí Néill Lug makes his classic appearance in the tale *Baile in Scáil* ('The Phantom's Frenzy'), written in the ninth century but revised in the eleventh. Lug lures King Conn of the Hundred Battles into a splendid otherworldly feasting hall and, in the form of a tall, handsome, en-throned man, he enumerates to Conn the names and regnal periods of the future kings of Tara.[87] It is strongly implied that all Irish over-kings

85 *PPCP*, 158–9; K. McCone, 'A Tale of Two Ditties', in L. Breatnach, K. McCone, & D. Ó Corráin (eds.), *Sages, saints and storytellers: Celtic studies in honour of Professor James Carney* (Maynooth, 1989), 137–9.

86 *DDDH*, 280.

87 *Baile in Scáil: The Phantom's Frenzy*, ed. & trans. K. Murray (Dublin, 2004) [ITS 58], 16–7 for a summary of Lug's significance in the tale. The English title has become con-

are stand-ins for Lug himself. The tale draws attention to the constructed nature of its Lug by thematizing his contradictory and blurred order of being: looking palpably and impressively divine, he not only denies that he is a supernatural being but asserts that he is of the race of Adam—and dead, to boot. It is also telling that after the earliest period, hints of Lug's association with the claims to kingship of groups other than the Uí Néill are muted. A very early praise-poem (c.600) identifies a dynastic ancestor of the Leinstermen directly with the god as a 'protective Lug' (*Lug scéith*, literally 'a Lug of a shield').[88] The Leinstermen were the principal enemies of the Uí Néill, and after this they do not seem to have claimed Lug for themselves again.

This account, if at all correct, emphasizes just how tricky the category of the 'native' is when talking about the supernatural beings of Irish myth, and is as much about conjecture regarding the nature and traces of pre-Christian Irish religion as I indulge in this book. I have speculated at length on Lug's trajectory during the change of religions to demonstrate precisely why such efforts are self-limiting, and have done so in a way that also showcases the themes of this chapter. In summary, very little survives to shed light on the gods of the Irish Iron Age. Conversion to Christianity represented an extreme cultural transformation, and while attempts to reconstruct pre-Christian ideology are fascinating, the results are relentlessly indeterminate. Tales often only survive in manuscripts copied centuries after a given text was actually composed, and such texts are indefinitely subject to problematic variations of tonal weight and weave. All of these are major stumbling blocks to our understanding.

Above I said that a male and a female deity would be compared. While Lug is one of the best-known figures in Celtic mythology, not so the goddess, whose very identity can only be retrieved via historical linguistics. Her name is embedded in that of an early medieval people from south-west Munster called the Corcu Loígde, meaning the 'Seed of the Calf-Goddess'.[89] Old Irish Loígde (in the genitive) points back to an ear-

---

ventional: 'the ecstatic prophecy of the supernatural being' might be a more accurate rendering of the Irish.

88 For this poem and its context, see J. Carey, 'From David to Labraid: sacral kingship and the emergence of monotheism in Israel and Ireland', in K. Ritari, *et al.* (eds.), *Approaches to Religion and Mythology in Celtic Studies* (Newcastle, 2008), 2–27. It may have influenced *Baile in Scáil*; see *Baile in Scáil*, ed. & trans. Murray, 16–7.

89 *ECI*, 186; precisely what kind of kin-group is implied by the word *corcu* is a matter of dispute. In Hiberno-Latin it is usually translated by *gens*, 'people' (see discussion in

lier deity called, in Primitive Irish, *Loigodēvā, who would be utterly lost to history were it not for the preservation of the old theonym in the name of the kindred.[90] The etymology makes it reasonably certain that the goddess did exist: *Loígde* was the name given in Irish to the river Bandon which flows through the same territory and was probably seen as the embodiment of the goddess.[91] Indeed, the bovine element in the name is echoed by other divine 'cow-rivers' in Celtic-speaking areas, not least the Boyne, the 'cow-white' one, who appears in the literature as the divine woman Bóand.[92] But no supernatural female named 'Loígde' (or *Loígdae) appears in the surviving literature, even though the name itself was preserved both in the name of the people and the river. This may be due to the fact that the political clout of the Corcu Loígde came to an end during the 600s, though they had once been dominant; had they increased in power instead, such a figure might well have emerged in subsequent centuries in texts written within their sphere of influence.[93] The goddess was so forgotten that a Middle Irish treatise on the meaning of names traces that of the Corcu Loígde back to an eponymous ancestor, Lugaid Loígde, who had hunted a fawn (*loíg allaid*)—evidently a new story.[94]

ECI, 96–100), but the concept seems to have become increasingly obsolete by the 700s. There is in fact a link back to Lug here, as the legendary king of Tara Lugaid Mac Con— potentially one of those humanized versions of Lug—was in early texts identified as Mac Con *moccu Loígde*, from this dynasty; see *K&LT*, 164–5.

90 Preserved in an intermediary Primitive Irish form, LOGIDDEAS, on an ogam stone at Thomastown, Co. Kilkenny, for which see *L&IEMI*, 81; on this name see comments of T. Charles-Edwards, *Early Irish and Welsh Kinship* (Oxford, 1993), 155.

91 *EIH&M*, 3; McManus, *Guide to Ogam*, 75.

92 Bóand derives regularly from *bou-vindā ('Cow-white', 'White-like-a-cow'), which name is attested in the form *Bououinda* by the Greek geographer Ptolemy, reflecting the situation *c*.150. Another example, this time from Britain, is the river Wharfe, from (Latinized) British *Verbeia*—if the latter is cognate, as seems likely, with Old Irish *ferb*, a relatively unusual word meaning 'cow'; see *EIH&M*, 3, and G. Isaac, *Place-names in Ptolemy's Geography: an electronic data base with etymological analysis of the Celtic name-elements* [CD-ROM] (Aberystwyth, 2004). For the later association between the mound of Knowth, a few hundred yards from the Boyne, and a supernatural female, Buí, whose name may have meant 'cowlike' (from *bouvjā), see *A&CM*, 24, and H. Wagner, 'Origins of pagan Irish religion', *ZCP* 38 (1981), 6.

93 For the early prominence and then decline of the Corcu Loígde, see D. Ó Cróinín in *NHI* i., 227.

94 *Cóir Anmann: A Late Middle Irish Treatise on Personal Names*, i., ed. & trans. S. Arbuthnot [ITS 59] (Dublin, 2005), 102–3, trans. 140; I have turned Middle Irish form *laeg* back into Old Irish *loíg* to make the etymological connection clear.

A comparison of the fates of Lugus and Loigodēvā makes clear that there was a vast difference between the continuation of idolatrous worship and the retention of significance. When this material has been presented to various audiences, modern Pagans have sometimes suggested to me that the reason particular deities were remembered into medieval times is because they had been particularly beloved. I suspect instead that an Irish deity had to be charged with some ingrained political, ideological, or geographical importance—preferably in combination—in order to survive, in some form, after their cult had been discontinued. By its very nature, conversion siphoned specifically religious significance from the pagan gods, but it is clear that the converting Irish could in some cases sift the cultural cachet of a deity—an association with the ideology of kingship, or with native systems of knowledge, for example—from pagan worship, thus retaining after-images of the god for the secular sphere. These different kinds of association might make former gods gyre off in different directions, explaining something of the sheer complexity of Ireland's literary supernaturals. Tellingly, several divinities—such as the goddess Macha—have evidently related but incompatible forms: a single deity could clearly splinter into several medieval characters.[95]

All this adds up to a melancholy conclusion. Given the likelihood of extreme localization we encountered earlier, it is probable that the vast majority of deities once worshipped by the pagan Irish failed—like Loigodēvā—to be re-embodied as medieval literary characters, and so never crossed over into history.[96] Very local deities and those associated with peoples whose importance dwindled during the conversion period would have been especially vulnerable; they differed from Loigodēvā only in that their names passed into oblivion along with their divinity.

95 There are four (or five) female figures all called *Macha*, three of whom are explicitly associated with the Iron Age site of Emain Macha (Navan Fort, Co. Armagh); see J. Carey, 'Notes on the Irish war-goddess', *Éigse* 19 (1983), 263–75.

96 Note discussion by Charles-Edwards of Eoin Mac Neill's suggestion that in 'gentilic' names with the form *moccu* 'X', the X sometimes referred to a given people's ancestor-deity; another example beyond the *Corcu* (*moccu*) *Loígde* might be the Corcu Duibne, the people of the modern Barony of Corcaguiney, as ogam stones with the phrase MUCCOI DOVVINIAS suggest (but do not prove) the existence of a lost goddess *Doviniā*, Old Irish Duiben/Duibne (*Early Irish and Welsh Kinship*, 150, 155). See Blair Gibson, *From Chiefdom to State*, 28, 56, which somewhat overstates Charles-Edwards' position.

2

EARTHLY GODS

PAGAN DEITIES, CHRISTIAN MEANINGS

He who obeys the Lord and follows the
prophecy given through him... becomes a
god while still moving about in the flesh.

—CLEMENT OF ALEXANDRIA

SOME EARLY SAGAS were mentioned in Chapter 1. But before we turn in greater detail to the written record—focusing on the late seventh and early eighth centuries—we must first tackle a significant problem, one that is crucial for the entire history of the Irish gods: the concept of the *síde*, or 'hollow hills', often anglicized as *shee*.

These supernatural residences are a distinctive oddity of the Irish pantheon, which has no Asgard or Mount Olympus, no place for the gods to gather. 'A *síd*', Jacqueline Borsje tells us, 'is a hill, a megalithic tumulus or pre-Celtic grave-hill. Its inhabitants look like human beings but they are different. In general, they are superior to humanity: they live longer or are even immortal; they are more beautiful and possess supernatural powers.'[1] *Síd*-mounds are usually synonymous with the 'otherworld' (in fact, rather various otherworlds), an intermittently accessible parallel dimension.[2] The space within a *síd*-mound is not isomorphic with its exterior: they are bigger on the inside.[3]

---

1 Borsje, 'Monotheistic to a Certain Extent', 58. See also P. Sims-Williams, '*Kaer Sidi* and Other Celtic Otherworld Terms', in *IIMWL*, 53–78.

2 See *A&CM*, 56, and especially J. Carey, 'The Location of the Otherworld in Irish Tradition', *Éigse* 19 (1982), 36–43.

3 Sims-Williams (*IIMWL*, 63) points out that the Irish 'otherworld' is not a unity: it does not seem to be a single parallel dimension with many entrances, but several different and apparently unconnected parallel worlds. Note that a natural hill can also be a *síd*; cf. *I&G*, 16 fn.3.

Borsje's formula begs a raft of questions, but chiefly the issue of whether a belief that mounds concealed supernatural inhabitants formed part of pre-Christian Irish religion. We have already seen how problematic such questions are. Oddly, though scholars have become increasingly reluctant to credit pagan survivals in the medieval literature it has never been questioned that ancient mounds were genuinely associated with native gods in pre-Christian Irish belief. This is probably because there is no obvious biblical or classical model from which the idea might have been borrowed.[4]

The word *síd* itself comes from Celtic **sīdos*, 'abode', derived from a root related to English 'seat' and 'settle'. Patrick Sims-Williams argues that the core sense 'settlement, abode'—compare the aristocrat's 'country seat'—narrowed over time to mean 'abode of divinities', and eventually 'tumulus', their distinctive abode in Ireland.[5] Evidence for the use of the Celtic word in this sense outside Ireland is extremely sketchy, suggesting that the narrowed meaning was indeed a purely Irish innovation.[6]

Nor does Continental Celtic evidence help. There are some indications that the Gauls did have the concept of some kind of other realm into which the dead were believed to pass, but no reference to mound-dwelling supernaturals appears in any Gaulish (or indeed Romano-British) source that has survived.[7] That said, offerings deposited into water or into the earth suggest a belief in spirits dwelling below the surface of the world, and an attested word in the Gaulish language seems

---

4 See H. Wagner, 'Studies in the Origins of Early Celtic Traditions', *Ériu* 26 (1975), 1–26, at 7. In a now classic essay, T. Ó Cathasaigh says that 'the Otherworld of Irish tradition must... have its roots in ancient ideas' ('The Semantics of *síd*', in Boyd (ed.), *Coire Sois*, 19–34, at 28 [article originally published in *Éigse* 17 (1977–9), 137–55]).

5 *IIMWL*, 56–7, clearly sets out the etymology and semantics, with references to extensive past discussions, amongst which Ó Cathasaigh, 'The Semantics of *síd*', in Boyd (ed.), *Coire Sois*, 19–34, is crucial. Recent exploration by R. Matasović, *Etymological Dictionary of Proto-Celtic* (Leiden & Boston, 2009), 326, who accepts that the words are the same, and says 'the strange combination of meanings "tumulus" and "peace" must have its roots in Celtic mythology.'

6 P. Sims-Williams, *Ancient Celtic Placenames in Europe and Asia Minor* (Oxford, 2006), 111, see also 106–7. Ancient Celtic placenames show forms in *sed-* and *sīd-*; the list of the latter are intriguing but intractable. Sims-Williams significantly finds them too heterogeneous to be worth mapping, and makes negative comments on (e.g.) *Sidon* (291).

7 The Roman poet Lucan referred to a druidic belief that souls survived death to live on in an 'other world' (*orbe alio*), but note Sims-Williams's demonstration that it is probably a mistake to take this phrase to mean 'otherworld' in the sense in which that term is now used, *IIMWL*, 54.

to denote a class of deity who dwelled 'beneath', presumably within the earth.[8] Nonetheless, it is important not to lose sight of the fact that these powers may have been imagined very differently from the subterranean *síd*-beings of medieval Irish literature; there is no way to tell.

Yet from Roman Britain comes limited but suggestive archaeological evidence for the re-use of ancient mounds in ways that may point to religious ritual. Roman-era coins, pottery, tiles, beads, and metalwork have been recovered from most of the major Cotswold-Severn group of Neolithic long barrows, for example, while in Derbyshire, Neolithic tomb-shrines and Bronze Age barrows both show signs of having been sites of ritual deposition. In the latter case, Ronald Hutton notes that 'coins predominated, followed by pottery and then brooches and pins', making them similar to deposits in ritual contexts elsewhere in Roman Britain.[9] But why this re-use? It seems unlikely that such ritual actions represented a direct continuation of native Celtic practices, for they seem only to have gathered pace in the later Roman period: the coins allow for precise datings. It looks instead as though prosperous late Romano-Britons began to look for a spiritual connection to the remote past, and Hutton suggests that this pattern of re-using these ancient monuments reflected an attempt by the Britons to assuage a sense of shock and disconnection from their land, even as the countryside of the province became fully Romanized for the first time.[10] Romano-Britons inhabited a landscape filled with impressive monuments from an earlier period, just as the Irish did, and Hutton suggests that some may have felt the need for a kind of 'retro-paganism', by which these ancestral sites became incorporated into religious practice. The way the ancient mounds dominated the surrounding landscape seems to have been important in their being selected for this kind of re-use. But frustratingly the focus of

8 A first-century AD Gaulish tablet from Chamarlières contains the term *andedion*, perhaps meaning 'gods below'; for discussion, see P.-Y. Lambert, *La Langue Gauloise* (Paris, 1994), 150–9, supplemented by *CHA*, 2–3 and *CCHE* i., 398–9. There is also debate over an extant Gaulish dedicatory dative plural, ανδοουνναβο (*andoounnabo*) which may contain a forerunner of the standard Welsh term for the otherworld, *Annwfn*, perhaps meaning the 'un-world'; see P. de Bernardo Stempel, 'A Welsh Cognate for Gaul. ανδοουνναβο?', *BBCS* 36 (1989), 102–5, disputed by P.-Y. Lambert, 'Gaulois ΑΝΔΟΟΥΝ-ΝΑΒΟ', *ÉC* 27 (1990), 197–99; see too F. O. Lindeman, 'Varia III.2: Gaulish ανδοουνναβο', *Ériu* 42 (1991), 146.

9 See *PB*, 270 for discussion, and 439, fn.106 and 107 for references to the excavation data.

10 *PB*, 270–3; see also C. Swift, *Ogam Stones and the Earliest Irish Christians* (Maynooth, 1997), 19–20.

FIG. 2.1. Cairn T, Neolithic passage-grave at Carbane East hilltop, Loughcrew, Co. Meath, 3500–3300 BC. Photo: Frank Prendergast.

Romano-Britons' interest is not recoverable: it might have been a cult of local deities, or of the dead, or of something else entirely. The first is in fact only one possibility, though Catherine Swift writes of 'a tradition of Roman worship at Neolithic mounds in southern England', and mentions the discovery of Romano-British altars near examples of such monuments.[11]

Were any Irish tumuli reused in a similar way in the immediate pre-conversion era? At Loughcrew, a complex of passage tombs spreads across three hilltops in Co. Meath (Fig. 2.1). One tomb was found to contain over five thousand fragmentary bone slips, some inscribed with designs, along with thirteen bone combs, some amber and glass beads, and some rings of amber and iron, probably all from the first century AD. The archaeologist John Waddell has suggested that the flakes were tools

11 Apparently dedicated to Mars, Minerva, and to a native god pictured with a ram-headed serpent; see C. Swift, 'The Gods of Newgrange in Irish Literature and Romano-Celtic Tradition', in G. Burenhult & S. Westergaard (eds.), *Stones and Bones* (Oxford, 2003), 59.

for divination, deposited at a sacred place; they might just as well be a bronzesmith's trial pieces.[12]

The religious culture of this region does however seem to have had contacts with Britain. A powerful, even unsettling, three-faced sculpture known as the 'Corleck head' was found twelve miles from Loughcrew; it dates to the first or second century AD (Fig. 2.2). Corleck Hill, where it was uncovered, was the site of a passage tomb surrounded by a stone circle, both sadly destroyed in modern times. Was the head a representation of the supernatural being associated with the tumulus? Its closest stylistic affinities are with Romano-British sculpture from Yorkshire, which include two similarly three-faced idols. The custom of carving stone heads may itself have been borrowed from Roman Britain: none has been found west of the Shannon, and there is a particular concentration around south-east Ulster, in an area where early Roman influence was strong.[13]

Still more intriguing is the great complex of Neolithic monuments found in a bend of the river Boyne, thirty miles to the southeast of Loughcrew.[14] The greatest of these is Newgrange, a huge developed passage grave which was constructed c.3300–3200 BC (Fig.2.3). This is normally taken to be 'the síd-mound of the Bruig' (Síd in Broga), which forms the backdrop to many of the medieval literature's most important mythological scenes.[15] There were other significant mounds, including those of Dowth and Knowth, and of the three largest only one lacks an early name, which firmly suggests their continued importance in the early medieval period.[16]

Evidence for Iron Age re-use of Newgrange is limited. Horse bones from the first or second centuries AD might point to equine ritual—or might have been left behind after an old or injured animal had been

12 A&CM, 27; B. Raftery, 'Iron-age Ireland', NHI i., 158–9; wider description of the Loughcrew site in G. Cooney, Landscapes of Neolithic Ireland (Abingdon, 2000), 158–163.

13 E. Rynne, 'Celtic Stone Idols in Ireland', in C. Thomas (ed.), The Iron Age in the Irish Sea Province [Council for British Archaeology Research Report 9] (London, 1972), 79–98.

14 See J. Carey 'Time, Memory, and the Boyne Necropolis', PHCC 10 (1990), 24–36; survey in Cooney, Landscapes of Neolithic Ireland, ch. 5, and A&CM, 15–8. See also C. O'Kelly, Illustrated Guide to Newgrange and the other Boyne monuments (3rd edn., Ardnalee, 1978), and magisterial study by the site's great excavator, M. J. O'Kelly, Newgrange: Archaeology, Art and Legend (London, 1982).

15 G. Stout, Newgrange and the Bend of the Boyne (2002), esp. 48ff, 62ff.

16 Archaeology in M. J. O'Kelly, F. M. Lynch, & C. O'Kelly, 'Three passage-graves at Newgrange, Co. Meath' PRIA 78 (C) (1978), 249–352. See also Swift, 'The Gods of Newgrange', 58.

FIG. 2.2. Three-faced stone head found at Corleck Hill, Co. Cavan,
first or second century AD. Photo: Reproduced with the kind
permission of the National Museum of Ireland.

killed and the flesh eaten by humans or dogs. What is intriguing, however, is the evidence the site provides for Hiberno-Roman contacts. We
know there were Roman traders in Ireland, accessing parts of the island
through the specialized trading centres known as *emporia*.[17] The most
impressive examples of Roman influence—not least the ogam stones—

17 *ECI*, 156.

35

FIG. 2.3. Bruig na Bóinne (Modern Irish Brú na Bóinne), or Newgrange. Almost certainly the medieval *síd in broga*, it was constructed *c.*3300–3200 BC and in the literature is the most important of the *síd*-mounds of Ireland. The white quartz cladding is a controversial modern reconstruction. Photo: © National Monuments Service Photographic Unit, Department of Arts, Heritage and the Gaeltacht.

date from the fourth and fifth centuries AD, and both the Irish Sea and Irish rivers could act as highways. Did Romano-Britons find their way to the Boyne complex—perhaps even as pilgrims? The whole site must have been, and still is, deeply impressive. It is within ten miles of the Boyne estuary, where there was probably a gateway community where trade between Ireland and her neighbours was conducted, so it is not difficult to imagine a context in which Romano-British travellers might have visited the complex.[18] The evidence is not explicit, though the deposits of coins and artefacts at Newgrange look very much like the votive deposits left at Neolithic mounds in Roman Britain, albeit on a smaller scale. Edel Bhreathnach points out that among the deposits clustered around the entrance to Newgrange are two *donativa* from the 320s or 330s—medallions based on coins which were given by the Emperor as presentation-gifts to high-ranking officials. She suggests that these point to Irishmen attaining high-ranking positions in the imperial army, or to 'diplomatic

18 If modern Colp near Drogheda is the medieval *Inber Colptha*, as Charles-Edwards suggests (*ECI*, 156).

gifts exchanged between an Irish king and a visiting emissary.'[19] A torc
with an unintelligible but clearly Roman inscription has been uncovered, while close to the mound of Knowth, one of the 'big three' in the
necropolis, a Roman burial has been revealed.[20]

Overall, it looks highly plausible, though at present unprovable, that
there was a late–Iron Age cult focused on supernatural beings—whether
gods, deified ancestors, or the spirits of the dead—associated with the
mounds of the Boyne necropolis, and perhaps others as well. In the case
of the former, it seems likely that at least a few Romano-British visitors
paid their respects to the local spirits of an imposing site in their usual
way, perhaps bringing to Ireland a 'retro-pagan' fondness for making
offerings at ancient monuments.[21] But if the Boyne complex had been so
important, it remains difficult to explain why there are relatively few
signs of earlier ritual use in a purely Irish context.[22]

Overall, there is no way to ascertain how close the literary gods are
to whatever beings were associated with mounds in the Iron Age, but
archaeologists in particular have found the temptation to connect the
two irresistible. Newgrange itself is the classic example: it is always the
pre-eminent *síd*-mound in the literature, and one with distinctive personnel, being associated with the Dagda, the top god of the literary pantheon, and his son, Óengus. The archaeologist and great excavator of the
site, M. J. O'Kelly, wanted to trace these two all the way back to the gods
worshipped in the Neolithic by the Boyne complex's builders, but this is an
extreme view. More likely is Catharine Swift's suggestion that the cult of
the Dagda and Óengus as gods of Newgrange took shape in the late Iron
Age and under Roman influence.[23] Earlier, I set out the possibility that
the very existence of a pantheon of sorts in medieval Irish literature
might be due to influence from the neighbouring island, and if Swift is
correct, then the core and kernel of Irish mythology begins to look rather
less indigenous than has traditionally been thought. There is no problem
proposing that elements of pre-Christian religious culture might have

19 Bhreathnach, *Ireland in the Medieval World*, 152–3; the medallions are reproduced
in plate 8.

20 References collected in *A&CM*, 17–18; important discussion in C. Swift, 'Pagan
monuments and Christian legal centres in early Meath', *Ríocht na Midhe* 9.2 (1996), 1–26.

21 This was M. J. O'Kelly's view in *Newgrange*, 47–8.

22 Though not none; see Swift, 'Pagan Monuments', 2.

23 Swift is prepared to suggest that a late prehistoric invasion of the Boyne valley
from Britain took place; see 'The Gods of Newgrange', in Burenhult (ed.), *Stones and
Bones*, 55.

spread from Britain to Ireland, as Christianity (signally) was later to do. Rather, I merely point out the possibility that some gods long regarded as distinctively Irish might have coalesced rather late and under Romano-British influence. It is entirely possible, for example, that a mythological figure as important as Núadu of the Silver Arm may have been conveyed into Ireland from Roman Britain. As has long been recognized, Núadu can only go back to an earlier form *Nodons*, and there is clear evidence for a deity of that name in Britain. Rather than the Irish Núadu representing one branch of a shared, ancient 'Celtic' inheritance, his cult could have been imported into Ireland in the third or fourth century AD.[24]

MEN OF THE MOUNDS

Two things are striking about the literary people of the *síd*-mounds: they are human-like, and there are a lot of them. They are not separated from humanity by a chasm of difference, but are closer and 'lower' than the classical deities.

Were such human-like powers a genuine idiosyncrasy of Irish paganism? There are suggestive points of connection between the Irish figures and both Roman and Germanic supernatural beings. It is possible that entities associated with mounds might have been imagined by Roman visitors to occupy a role similar to that played by *numina* in Roman religion: that is, vaguely personified divine presences immanent in the landscape and tied to a particular place.[25] On the other hand, Irish *síd*-beings resemble the 'elves' of Old Norse and (to a much lesser extent) Old English literature to such a degree that it has been suggested they are evidence

24 See J. Carey, 'Nodons in Britain and Ireland', *ZCP* 40 (1984), 1–22. One possibility—and it is only that—comes as a corollary of a bold recent theory of the Dutch Celticist Peter Schrijver. In an unpublished talk in May 2007 (*How Roman Britain made Ireland Celtic*, O'Donnell Lecture, University of Oxford) he has suggested that Celtic speech itself came to Ireland in the first century AD—much later than usually thought—and from Roman Britain. The consequences would be momentous, and Schrijver's theory has not been widely accepted. That said, he notes in particular that a British and Irish tribal group share the name *Brigantes* ('the people of the goddess *Brigantī*') and suggests that the Irish group originated as an emigrating offshoot from the British one: this possibility is detachable from the rest of the theory, and raises the possibility that the important Irish goddess Brigit (from *Brigantī*) could have been another importation from Britain.

25 Note the querying of the concept of *numina* in M. Beard, J. North, & S. Price, *The Religions of Rome: A History* (2 vols., Cambridge, 1999), i., 30–1.

for a widespread north-western European belief in a parallel supernatural race, something common to both Celtic and Germanic cultures.[26] This theory is more often put forward by specialists in Germanic literature than by Celtic scholars, and one significant objection is that in Norse and Anglo-Saxon culture tumuli were not imagined as the dwelling places of ever-living supernaturals, but as more or less the exact opposite—the graves of the restless dead who might emerge to menace the living.[27]

It is possible that, after the end of paganism, one category of supernatural being, the human-like mound dwellers, ballooned in the Irish imagination and absorbed beings who had originally belonged to other orders.[28] Lug, who has impeccable credentials as a former god, is described in the *Táin* as Cú Chulainn's 'father from the hollow hills'.[29] By the eighth century a *síd*-mound had apparently become the *sine qua non* of a literary god. It may be that the concept of the *síd*-mounds grew in importance because Christian intellectuals found it a discrete way to signal the divinity of originally non-Christian figures without directly describing them as gods. However, there are only two surviving statements directly connecting mound-dwelling beings to pre-Christian gods: neither is straightforward to interpret.

The first occurs in an account of the activities of Patrick, written in Latin by an Irish bishop named Tírechán around 690, and made famous by its narrative appeal.[30] On his circuit around the northern half of Ire-

26 See A. Hall, *Elves in Anglo-Saxon England: Matters of Belief, Health, Gender, and Identity* (Woodbridge, 2007). After conversion, the Anglo-Saxons seem to have shifted to viewing elves as demonic relatively slowly; they retain positive associations in many texts, not least in personal names, though note the ambiguities identified by C. Saunders, *Magic and the Supernatural in Medieval English Romance* (Cambridge, 2010), 95.

27 S. Semple, 'A Fear of the Past: the Place of the Prehistoric Burial Mound in the Ideology of Middle and Later Anglo-Saxon England', *World Archaeology* 30 (1998), 109–26.

28 I feel unable to share the confidence of Séamus Mac Mathúna, who says that the people of the *síd* 'were originally supernatural beings of vegetation and fertility, and probably also functioned sometimes as guardians of fire and sacral kingship' ('The Relationship of the Chthonic World in Early Ireland to Chaos and Cosmos', in J. Borsje, *et al.* (eds.), *Celtic Cosmology: Perspectives from Ireland and Scotland* (Toronto, 2014), 53–76, at 74). On page 75 he compares them directly to Norse elves.

29 '*athair a ssídaib*'; *Táin Bó Cúailnge, Recension I*, ed. & and trans. C. O'Rahilly (Dublin, 1976), l.2109, 65, 183.

30 Tírechán was writing with limited knowledge of the historical Patrick of two hundred years earlier, though he did have texts of the saint's own writings. To information gleaned from these he added a series of local stories and traditions, framed as a circular journey undertaken by the saint through the northern half of Ireland. His pur-

land, Patrick and his retinue have come at dawn to the hill of Crúachain, part of the complex of ring forts and other features in what is now Co. Roscommon.[31] Sitting beside a spring on the eastern side of the hill, Patrick meets the two daughters of Lóegaire mac Néill, the king of Tara, who have come for their morning wash. The two princesses are disconcerted by the strangers and imagine them to be supernatural beings: 'they supposed that they were men of the *síd*-mounds or of the earthly gods or an apparition.'[32] The saint quickly disabuses them and answers their charmingly naïve questions about the nature of his God. The pair immediately become Christians and are baptized; upon receiving the Eucharist for the first time, they expire.

This case of mistaken identity inaugurates the native supernaturals as a literary theme in Ireland, in a saint's life, and more than a century after the consolidation of the Irish church. Its importance lies in the fact that it contains in embryonic form a series of crucial cultural strategies in relation to the gods and the people of the *síd*-mounds—and that those strategies, revealingly, already seem to be presupposed, even at this early date.

Because Tírechán's statement about the girls' misconception has attracted an astonishing quantity of critical attention, we must look at it in the original Latin:

> Sed illos uiros side aut deorum terrenorum aut fantassiam estimauerunt.[33]

The grammar is oddly difficult. A recent interpretation by Jacqueline Borsje looks correct, and following her we might translate thus, expanding for clarity:

> But the two girls supposed that Patrick and his followers were men of the *síde*—that is, men of the earthly gods—or an apparition.[34]

---

pose in writing was to strengthen the authority of the bishops of Armagh, the heirs to the community of Patrick, and to emphasize their connection with the most important dynasty of the Irish midlands; see *ECI*, 9–10.

31 Discussion in Bhreathnach, *Ireland in Medieval Europe*, 145–6; discussion and references to the site of Crúachain in *A&CM*, 9–10, 56, 58–61, 109–10.

32 *The Patrician Texts in the Book of Armagh*, ed. L. Bieler with F. Kelly (Dublin, 1979), §26, 142, 143; alternative translation of the whole episode in *CHA*, 210–11.

33 *Patrician Texts*, ed. Bieler, 142.

34 My expansion consists of making the subject (the two girls) and object (Patrick

The problem is that the Latin appears to give us three possibilities (men of the *síde*, the mysterious 'earthly gods', or an apparition), where arguably only two, or perhaps even one, are in fact meant. 'Earthly gods' seems to be an explanatory gloss on the only phrase containing a non-Latin word in the sentence, *viros side* (i.e. *síde*), 'men of the *síd*-mounds'. (This therefore corresponds exactly to the attested Old Irish phrase *fir shíde*.) We may assume that 'earthly gods' is what Tírechán thought *síd*-beings actually *were*, which has major implications regarding both the concept of the people of the *síd*-mounds and their relationship to the literary divinities, and how this concept was developed.[35]

The third term, *fantas(s)ia*, is difficult. Its etymology is suggestively parallel to *taidbsiu*, a common Old Irish term for 'phantom, supernatural being', and one regularly used for entities identified elsewhere as gods or the inhabitants of the *síd*-mounds. It may thus represent an attempt to find a Latin equivalent for the Irish word. Both *fantas(s)ia* and *taidbsiu* are nouns formed from verbs meaning 'show' or 'appear', and both thus basically mean 'something which manifests', 'an apparition'.[36] So these three supposedly different categories here may in fact all refer to only one kind of being—those which Tírechán thought his pagan forebears had worshipped.

As we saw earlier, the term *síd* literally refers to a hill in which the native supernaturals were supposed to live. The trouble is that the relationship of these 'earthly gods' to the idea of megalithic tumuli is not clear here. Does *deorum terrenorum* mean 'of gods who live in the earth'—that is, literally 'within' hollow hills? Scholars have usually assumed so, especially as Crúachain supposedly had entrances to the otherworld. It has also been suggested that we are supposed to take it that the two girls

---

and his retinue) absolutely explicit, and indicating that I think *deorum terrenorum* should be taken as a gloss on *side*, hence the insertion of dashes and the phrase 'that is'.

35 The basic difficulty in interpretation arises from some oddities in the Latinity of the sentence. Latin has two words for 'or', *aut* and *uel*; *aut* separates mutually exclusive words ('are you having a boy or a girl?'), while *uel* separates two terms which refer synonymously to identical or similar things ('take one aubergine, or eggplant'). The fact that *deorum terrenorum* is in the same grammatical case as the Irish word *side*, the genitive plural, strongly suggests that the former is intended as a gloss on the latter, telling the reader without Old Irish what the native term means; but we might have expected *uel* to be used instead of *aut*, so an awkwardness remains either way. Nevertheless Tírechán's meaning seems clear, even if he might have phrased it more conventionally as *uiros side .i. deorum terrenorum*.

36 *Taidbsiu* is the verbal noun of *do·adbat*, 'show, appear'; *fantas(s)ia* is ultimately a Greek word borrowed into Latin and deriving from φαίνεσθαι, 'appear'.

believe the men before them have come up from another dimension—one hidden within the earth.[37] Yet this would be an odd use of the expression: the normal sense of *terrenus* in ecclesiastical Latin was not 'under the earth', but 'of the earthly world', as opposed to heaven.[38]

Fortunately, some solution to the puzzle appears when Tírechán then has the two girls reveal to Patrick exactly what they think a god is. After the saint explains that he is only a servant of the true God, one of them asks:

> Who is 'God' and where is God and whose god is he and where is his dwelling-place? Does your god have sons and daughters, gold and silver? Does he live forever, is he beautiful, is his son fostered by many, are his daughters beloved and beautiful to the people of the world? Is he in the sky or in the earth, or in the water, in the rivers, in the mountains, in the valleys?[39]

Tírechán's purpose here is to present a picture, plausible to his late seventh-century readers, of how a young Irish noblewoman, reared in paganism but about to be sanctified, might think about her ancestral gods.[40] Crucially, there is no mention of hollow hills: a native divinity can reside, according to the girls, in the sky! This suggests that Tírechán's

---

37 Thus Mac Mathúna, who thinks we are supposed to infer that the well itself is the 'point of access', something in which I have less confidence; see his 'The Relationship of the Chthonic World', 55–6.

38 Tírechán might have surely written something like *deorum tumulos incolentium* or *deorum subterrenorum*. There is the possibility that this sequence was influenced by the 'gods coming up from the earth' of 1 Samuel 28:13; in the mid-seventh century an exegete known as the Irish pseudo-Augustine commented on this passage in the biblical text in a discussion of the ability of spirits to form spectral illusions out of the air, for which see J. Carey, *King of Mysteries: Early Irish Religious Writing* (Dublin, 1998), 71. On the other hand Tírechán was a great deal closer to Irish paganism than we are, and some asides he makes on the topic have the ring of truth, e.g. on the 'divine' well of Slán and the druidic doctrine of the destruction of the world by fire. On these see J. Carey, 'Saint Patrick, the Druids, and the End of the World', *History of Religions* 36:1 (1996), 42–53.

39 *Patrician Texts*, ed. Bieler, 142; translation (after the first line) from *CHA*, 210.

40 On this, see C. Doherty, 'Kingship in early Ireland', *K&LT*, 8. Versions of this passage appeared in subsequent Patrician hagiography, not least the ninth-century *Tripartite Life*. One wonders if they influenced a depiction of pagan prayer in the eleventh-century Irish adaptation of Virgil's *Aeneid*, which begins 'Gods of heaven and earth, of the waters, the streams, and the rivers'; as Erich Poppe notes, this is a native addition, as in Virgil's poem Aeneas calls only on the nymphs and the river Tiber. See his '*Imtheachta Aeniasa*: Virgil's *Aeneid* in Medieval Ireland', *Classics Ireland* 11 (2004), 74–94.

use of *terrenus* simply meant 'of the earth' in the 'non-transcendent' sense. Strikingly the girls ask the authentically archaic question '*whose god is he?*', presumably harking back to a past in which gods were associated with particular population groups, as we saw with the lost goddess Loígodēvā's association with the Corcu Loígde.

Thus Tírechán depicts an outmoded paganism that centres around a belief in nature-dwelling gods who are reminiscent of Roman *numina*, but more strongly anthropomorphized. The point is not that this is what Iron Age paganism in Ireland was actually like, but rather that this is how a learned bishop, a hundred and fifty or so years after its end, could imagine it to have been in its heyday: a divine curiosity, and an innocent belief in nature gods. He may also have been influenced by St Paul's statement that even gentiles could infer the existence of God from the visible creation around them.[41] Particularly striking is the note of primal innocence. For the two girls, a god is simply a more powerful and permanent version of their father; they themselves exhibit a kind of radiant narcissism as they imagine the daughters of such a god to be beings very much like themselves writ large. It is important to note that these are good pagans who, by implication, worship the people of the *síd*-mounds—the latter being a concept not seen again until the revivals of the nineteenth century.[42] I suspect that particular generic conventions are being presupposed here, meaning that they were already established by 690; in particular, the reader needs to know that the hill of Crúachain was itself considered a major *síd*.[43] The basic pattern in play here, richly attested in later Irish sagas, is that in which a royal youth meets a *síd*-maiden or a divine woman, who may be going to wash and who has some connection to the idea of 'sovereignty'. They subsequently marry or couple, by vir-

41 See Kim McCone's comments, *PPCP*, 141, and those of Ralph O'Connor, *DDDH*, 279.

42 There is a possible exception in the perhaps eighth-century 'Hymn of Fíacc', which says that the Irish 'used to worship the *síde*; they did not believe in the godhead of the true Trinity' (*Thesaurus Paleohibernicus*, ed. & trans. W. Stokes & J. Strachan (Cambridge, 1903-5, reprt. Dublin, 1975), ii., 317). But this may be an illusion: despite the ubiquity of the anglicization 'shee' to mean 'pagan Irish gods, fairy-folk' in nineteenth-century writing, in Irish it seems to have been rare for the original word (*síde*) to be used in this sense, and *DIL* gives no incontrovertible examples. Thus the original author of the 'Hymn' might have meant that the pagan Irish 'used to venerate the mounds', which (as seen) may have been simply true. This last is a point made by Sims-Williams, *IIMWL*, 67, fn.119.

43 The *síd* of Crúachain seems to have had a particularly sinister reputation, often being associated with monsters, acts of war, and deities of destruction; see *A&CM*, 56–81.

tue of which the royal youth attains the kingship or (sometimes) is confirmed in it. In Tírechán, those elements have been systematically flipped along the axis of gender.[44] Instead, we have a pair of royal maidens who have gone to wash, who meet (they think) a man of the *síd* and then end up 'marrying' the King of Heaven—the theme is made explicit. They thus attain a kingdom, although in quite another sense. Tírechán's studied inversion—indeed, near parody—of inherited motifs is paralleled in texts in Irish which are closely contemporary and to which we will shortly turn.

The crucial point about this episode is that it begins in a world recognizable from secular tradition, in which aristocratic and beautiful people are unfazed to encounter the people of the *síd*; and then as each generic convention is inverted or dismantled, we shift into sacred, Christian space. This dismantling of secular motifs mirrors the conversion of the two girls. The touching quality of the episode lies in the fact that this hagiographical space has a kind of ethnographic dimension—Tírechán spends some time imagining the two girls' pre-Christian sense of divinity, which dimly anticipates Christian truths. It is noteworthy, for example, that divine fatherhood is part of the girls' internal sense of what a god is, as it highlights their useful theological instincts: as Patrick tells them, God is indeed a Father, but he has only one Son.

This inaugural articulation of the concept of the *síd* registers the ambiguity and complexity of the subject. Tírechán's interlude provides limited support for the idea that *síd*-beings did exist in pre-Christian Irish religion as something like *numina*. Being chronologically much closer to those who practised Irish paganism than we are, he found it logical to describe the people of the *síd*-mounds as 'earthly gods', by which he may have meant 'divinities resident within the multifarious dimensions of the natural world'. However, it is puzzling that the word's primary semantic association with tumuli is not particularly strong here. Furthermore, in terms of literary gambits, it is striking that we find parodic strategies and the inversion of apparent conventions from the moment the native gods make their appearance. In one sense, by creating an imagined version of the pagan past Tírechán was doing exactly what

---

44 The gendered dimensions of this episode are noted by J. F. Nagy in a review of C. Harrington, *Women in a Celtic Church: Ireland 450–1150* (Oxford, 2002), *Speculum* 79.4 (2004), 1085–88, and in his 'Myth and *Legendum* in Medieval and Modern Ireland', in G. Schrempp & W. Hansen (eds.), *Myth: A New Symposium* (Bloomington, IN, 2002), 124–38, at 126–7.

later saga-writers did. Over the next centuries saga-authors were to go to great lengths to depict a heroic world in which noble humans and quasi-divine *síd*-beings had once rubbed shoulders. However, here—at the start of the tradition—Tírechán also invokes such a world, only to rescind it immediately.

VERNACULAR WRITING

If Tírechán's anecdote presents difficulties, still more enigmatic are the two stories which have a good claim to being the earliest surviving narratives in Irish: *Echtrae Chonnlai* ('The Otherworld Adventure of Connlae') and *Immram Brain* ('The Voyage of Bran'). 'The Adventure of Connlae' features a *síd*-woman with some relation to the so-called 'woman of sovereignty' or 'sovereignty goddess'. In 'The Voyage of Bran', a phantasmagoric scene brings before us the first literary incarnation of a named native divinity—Mannanán mac Lir, the 'son of the sea'. The perplexities attending any attempt at interpreting these texts are formidable: an appropriate comparison might be Jorge Luis Borges's short stories, which have a similar self-conscious artificiality and elusiveness.

What kind of people were responsible for the composition of these stories—and for the large number of later sagas also set in the pagan past and featuring native supernatural beings? Where did their priorities and affiliations lie?[45] Answering these questions means encountering heated disputes over how native Irish tradition was interblended with Christianity and Latin learning, and at this point the two audiences of this book may have different needs. The scholarly consensus is that the sagas' authors were not mere passive transmitters of pagan myth and ancient tradition. Rather, they were creative authors who hybridized their native inheritance with a vast body of classical and Christian learning, thereby engaging with the issues and demands of their own times. Specialists will openly yawn at the prospect of gesturing yet again towards a set of old debates: as Jonathan Wooding briskly says, 'We all know the basic story'.[46] But as this 'story' may be new to non-specialists, especially if

45 'Saga', while a Norse term, is useful shorthand for Irish vernacular prose narratives as well.

46 J. M. Wooding, 'Reapproaching the Pagan Celtic Past—Anti-Nativism, Asterisk Reality and the Late-Antiquity Paradigm', *Studia Celtica Fennica* 6 (2009), 51–74, at 51.

they know Irish mythology through popular works on Celtic spirituality, it is important to enter once again into the fray.[47]

First, it is abundantly clear that a secular literary tradition in Irish could only have emerged in a Christian context, and that the Bible remained at all times the wellspring and core of Irish literacy.[48] This is because *all* literary composition, vernacular and Latin, depended on alphabetic writing and book production. This was only available via the technology of ecclesiastical education, which was embodied by and enabled in the communal, intellectual, and literate environment of monasticism. It is also clear that the literature we have was produced within elite communities of learning, and that these were based in monasteries, though their personnel were not necessarily all ecclesiastics. Such communities appear over the horizon of history in the late 500s.

Secondly, those responsible for vernacular composition are normally identified as the honoured class of secular, learned professionals known in Irish as *filid* (singular *fili*). Habitually rendered 'poets' in English, the *filid* were in fact a great deal more than that: not only did they play an important educational role, but they were also genealogists and confidants for secular dynasts, acting—in Elva Johnston's words—as the 'custodians of communal aristocratic memories'.[49]

The question of how one should imagine the *filid* allows me to set out the scholarly debates under consideration here.[50] One view, often called 'nativist', dominated the study of early Irish literature until at least the late 1970s, and held that the native learned orders and the ecclesiastical *literati* had formed distinct, even rival, groups. Often the *filid* were regarded as having been continuingly quasi-pagan (in some nebulous manner) and thus invested in the preservation of pre-Christian material.[51] The nativist view accordingly allowed for an archaic origin for the themes and imagery of the vernacular narratives, and at the extreme

---

47 The only attempt to explain the transformation in medieval Irish studies to the general reader has come (tellingly) not from a Celticist but a historian; see Hutton, *Pagan Religions of the Ancient British Isles*, 148–9, which is very clear but now twenty-five years old. At 142–3 in the same volume Hutton provides an amiable critique of the handling of medieval sources by adherents of contemporary Celtic spirituality.

48 See *DDDH*, 244.

49 *L&IEMI*, 20.

50 Useful discussion by T. Ó Cathasaigh, 'Early Irish Narrative Literature', in K. Mc-Cone & K. Simms (eds.), *Progress in Medieval Irish Studies* (Maynooth, 1996), 55–64.

51 Addressed by J. Carey, 'The Three Things Required of a Poet', *Ériu* 48 (1997), 41–58.

end it was suggested that the *filid* could be imagined as the continuation not only of pre-Christian Ireland's intelligentsia, but of its religious elite—Christianized druids, in fact, in touch with a supposedly enduring oral tradition.[52] Jonathan Wooding has astutely pointed out how the nativist view laid stress upon Ireland as the 'keeper of a very ancient culture', and so reflected the cultural politics in the earlier part of the twentieth century, furnishing the country's literature with primal, independent, and oral origins.[53] Both views depended upon a concept of Irish identity as something living in the mouths of the people, thereby retaining its integrity despite cultural onslaught. The nativist view allowed that plenty of pre-Christian belief—conveniently vaguely defined—could be extracted from the medieval literature. The literary after-images of Ireland's gods were therefore taken to be reasonably good likenesses of the deities actually worshipped by the Iron Age Irish. This can be a reassuring thought for lovers of mythology, because (as seen in Chapter 1) if the literature is put to one side, our picture of the gods is dispiritingly threadbare.[54] The nativist position in any simple form is long out of date in the academy, though many readers will recognize that a version of it continues to be recycled by popular writers on Celtic religion.

The opposing view, sometimes called 'anti-nativist', directly challenged these assumptions. Anti-nativists argued that there had been a fusion of the learned orders early in the conversion process, suggesting the *filid* and the Latin *literati* had soon formed a single monastic 'mandarin class', steeped in commentary upon scripture.[55] Far from being a rival community of learning, the *filid* were now seen as submerged within and identifying with the ecclesiastical, Latin-literate establishment. The argument was backed up with powerful evidence for Irish

---

52 On the other hand it is perfectly sensible to suggest that there were high status and learned 'men of art' in pre-Christian Ireland, who may have had a degree of literacy: that some kind of literate class existed in pre- and partially Christian Ireland is shown by the earliest ogam inscriptions. It is not sensible, however, to propose that these individuals became bound up with the elite communities of learning of early Christian Ireland with their identity and curriculum *unaltered* from pagan times.

53 Wooding, 'Reapproaching the Pagan Celtic Past', 69.

54 Enduringly valuable examples of this nativist position are P. Mac Cana, *Celtic Mythology*, and his 'Mythology and the Oral Tradition: Ireland', in M. J. Green (ed.), *The Celtic World* (London, 1995), 779–84.

55 The classic statement of this view is D. Ó Corráin, 'Irish Origin Legends and Genealogy: Recurrent Aetiologies', T. Nyberg, *et al.* (eds.), *History and Heroic Tale: A Symposium* (Odense, 1985), 51–96, especially 51–2.

learning's deep and early engagement with classical and biblical tradition; a number of vernacular texts long thought to be archaic, even 'pagan', were shown to depend upon ecclesiastical material. It was argued that the themes of early Irish literature were mediated and even created by an undergirding Christian vision. Anti-nativists have tended to regard attempts to retrieve pristine mythology as a blind alley. They emphasize that the native gods themselves show signs of having been thoroughly interfused with ecclesiastical and biblical concepts.

Aspects of anti-nativism have long since become a basic part of the intellectual toolkit for scholars of medieval Ireland. One benefit has been a sharpened focus on the detail of early Irish literature as we have it: lapses in the sagas' logic or flaws in their composition can no longer be ascribed to the garbling of oral tales by unsympathetic churchmen. That said, though nativism and anti-nativism are apparently clear-cut and opposed positions in theory, in practice each has allowed for shades of grey. As Thomas Charles-Edwards has written, early Ireland exhibited both a strong sense of its own identity *and* a willingness to embrace the wider world: the two orientations were not mutually exclusive.[56] Wooding—looking back at the decades of sometimes acrimonious debate—points out that nativist scholars were hardly monolithic in their views and in fact accepted as self-evident a lot of what anti-nativists insisted they rejected; anti-nativists in turn have not always been intellectually consistent.[57] As one who came of age after anti-nativism had attained the status of an orthodoxy, I can empathize with Wooding's description of excavating an Iron Age grave as a 'liberating feeling'—precisely because such a monument was indisputably constructed 'by people who believed in a primal Celtic religion and whose cosmology was unaffected by Christian notions'.[58] The thought that pre-Christian Irish beliefs are irretrievable is so ingrained that it is surprisingly bracing to be reminded that those beliefs, and the people who held them, actually did exist.

However, the most crucial thing to emerge from the debate is the sheer complexity of the backdrop to vernacular literary culture. A degree of clarity is gained if we only use the label 'pagan' to mean 'involv-

---

56 *NHI* i., lxxviii.

57 A good example of how a basically nativist position can also be highly nuanced is offered by T. Ó Cathasaigh, 'Pagan Survivals: the Evidence of Early Irish Narrative', in P. Ní Chatháin & M. Richter (eds.), *Ireland and Europe: The Early Church/Irland und Europa : die Kirche im Frühmittelalter* (Stuttgart, 1984), 291–307, reprt. in Boyd (ed.), *Coire Sois*, 35–50.

58 Wooding, 'Reapproaching the Pagan Celtic Past', 65.

ing the worship of non-Christian gods'. The word is deeply misleading if applied to most of the dimensions of native culture which retained significance after conversion, especially that of vernacular learning: no one suggests that the *filid* carried on worshipping pagan deities. Elva Johnston proposes that we think in terms of interlocking intellectual elites, imagining neither a nativist gulf between indigenous and ecclesiastical men of learning, nor an anti-nativist fusion between the two; in her brilliant encapsulation, the *filid* were neither 'druids in disguise or monks in mufti'.[59] We can sensibly picture the *filid* as bridging the ecclesiastical and secular worlds, sharing their fundamental intellectual and religious assumptions with their clerical colleagues. '*Filid*', Johnston writes, 'take their place firmly within the Irish intellectual milieu, even in its monastic context, and can be seen as joining secular and ecclesiastical interests, largely because, although they could be clerics, they formed a basically secular learned class strongly connected with the royal courts.'[60] She makes a telling analogy between the *filid* and the *rhetors* of late Roman antiquity—both were learned professionals, and both were trained in poetry and the forms of persuasive speech appropriate to the secular sphere.

THE PEOPLE OF PEACE

Moving on from a general overview of what we know about the people responsible for the creation of early Irish vernacular literature, we can now return to 'The Adventure of Connlae' and 'The Voyage of Bran'.[61] These tales, both in the characteristic medieval Irish mixture of prose and verse, have been assigned to a date range between the late seventh and the mid-eighth centuries, and scholars agree that 'The Adventure' is the earlier of the two, though perhaps not by very much.[62] Indeed,

---

59 *L&IEMI*, 20.

60 *L&IEMI*, 20.

61 The standard edition is *Echtrae Chonnlai*, ed. & trans. K. McCone, in *Echtrae Chonnlai and the Beginnings of Vernacular Narrative Writing in Ireland* (Maynooth, 2000). See also J. Carey, 'The Rhetoric of *Echtrae Chonlai*', *CMCS* 30 (1995), 41–65, and now K. Hollo, 'Allegoresis and Literary Creativity in Eighth-Century Ireland: The Case of *Echtrae Chonnlai*', in J. Eska (ed.), *Narrative in Celtic Tradition: Essays in Honor of Edgar M. Slotkin* [CSANA Yearbook 8–9] (Hamilton, NY, 2011), 117–28.

62 The linguistic technicalities of dating the texts are complex. See *Echtrae Chonnlai and the Beginnings of Vernacular Narrative Writing in Ireland*, ed. & trans. K. McCone

echoes and inversions of theme and language between the two tales are so striking as to suggest that they were intended to form a pair. They might even be the work of a single individual, though it is more likely that the tales' authors were a pair of associates from the same literary school, based in an unknown Ulster monastery.[63] It is likely that whoever composed them were either contemporaries of Tírechán, or belonged to the following generation.

'The Adventure of Connlae' is set after the birth of Christ but before the coming of St Patrick, and begins with Connlae standing upon the hill of Uisnech—the traditional centre of Ireland. He is next to his father, the legendary king Conn of the Hundred Battles, and standing with them is Conn's druid Corann. Connlae sees a strangely dressed woman approaching, who announces that she is from 'the land of the living ones' and who summons him to the 'Plain of Delight' where there is no sickness or death. Only Connlae can see the woman, though Conn and the druid can hear her. The druid silences her with his magic, and she vanishes; but before she does so she throws Connlae an apple, and although he consumes only the apple for a month, it remains miraculously uneaten. Meanwhile he is filled with longing for the woman. After a month, she reappears when Connlae is seated with his father and calls again for Connlae to come away with her; though his heart is torn, ultimately he leaves his people and goes with her to her supernatural realm, where he becomes immortal.

In 1969 one of the greatest scholars of medieval Ireland, James Carney, described the tale as 'gem-like', revealing different colours as its facets are turned in the light.[64] A persuasive view (if not quite a consensus) has emerged that the whole composition is an intricate Christian

---

(Maynooth, 2000), 29–41, for the date of composition of 'The Adventure'; in the same volume (44, 47–8) McCone also assigns 'an eighth-century date, more likely than not before c.750 AD' to 'The Voyage of Bran'. J. Carey ('On the interrelationships of some Cín Dromma Snechtai texts', *Ériu* 46 (1995) 71–92) argues for an early date for *Echtrae Chonnlai*, perhaps as early as 688. A. Nutt & K. Meyer (*The Voyage of Bran son of Febal to the Land of the Living* (London, 1895–7), 148–9) suggested, then pulled back from, the idea that the two texts are compositions by the same author. McCone (*Echtrae Chonnlai*, 47) argues that *Echtrae Chonnlai* was composed just before *Immram Brain*; J. Carey ('On the Interrelationships', 85) agrees that the former impacted upon the latter.

63 *Echtrae Chonnlai*, ed. McCone, 119.

64 'The Deeper Level of Early Irish Literature', *Capuchin Annual '69* (1969), 160–71, at 162–4—an article which kickstarted all subsequent discussion of the story's meaning and effect.

allegory couched in the language of homily and biblical exegesis, and this has direct bearing on the nature of the supernatural woman who lures Connlae away.[65]

Kim McCone—a trenchant anti-nativist—has set out the case for an allegorical reading.[66] The mysterious woman cannot be an otherworld goddess: rather she is that medieval commonplace, *Ecclesia*, the Church personified.[67] Her language is that of Christian eschatology, in which *life* and *death* have their common New Testament connotations of salvation and damnation respectively (as in Romans 6:23, for example, where 'The wages of sin is death, but the gift of God is eternal life through Jesus Christ our Lord'). As the woman says:

'Grandly does Connlae sit amidst the short-lived dead awaiting terrible death. The everliving living invite you.'[68]

The woman then gives Irish paganism a drubbing, first instructing Connlae's father not to love druidry, and then prophesying the coming of Patrick to Ireland:

'It is in a little while that the Great High King's righteous and decent one will reach your judgments with many wondrous followers. His law will soon come to you. He will destroy the druids of base teaching in front of the black, bewitching Devil.'[69]

---

65 As we have it, the story itself cannot be not of great antiquity, as there is clear evidence that Connlae's disappearance into the otherworld was deliberately engineered to replace an older tradition in which he came to a more conventional end; see *Echtrae Chonnlai*, ed. McCone, 49.

66 Arguments for an allegorical reading can only be baldly summarized here, but see *Echtrae Chonnlai*, ed. McCone, 100–3, and also—more polemically—his *PPCP*, 157–8, on which see P. Sims-Williams's contructively critical review in *Éigse* 29 (1996), 181–96. Note that Hollo ('Allegoresis and Literary Creativity', 123–7) sets out reasons for believing that a nonbiblical text could be written to invite the kind of allegorical reading which was normally applied to scripture.

67 McCone (*Echtrae Chonnlai*, 105) points out that the woman also typologically corresponds to Patrick himself and that Muirchú's mid seventh-century life of the saint may have been an important influence on the text. Hollo ('Allegoresis and Literary Creativity', 122–3) suggests a sapiential dimension to the woman, identifying her with the biblical figure of God's (feminine) Wisdom.

68 *Echtrae Chonnlai*, ed. McCone, 166–70. All quoted translations from this text are McCone's.

69 *Echtrae Chonnlai*, ed. McCone, 174–181.

There is more. The paradisial and sinless overseas realm to which the woman calls Connlae is ruled by an explicitly 'everlasting' king called Bóadag, a peculiar name which seems to imply 'Victorious One'—by implication God himself, victorious over sin and death. It was common as far back as the New Testament to speak of heaven as paradise restored (cf. Luke 23:43, where Jesus promises the repentant thief 'today you will be with me in paradise'), and the woman's home is clearly Edenic. The apple she gives to Connlae brings eternal life, and by implication salvation; it is the mirror image of that given by Eve to Adam in the garden. James Carney brilliantly suggested that the author imagined the apple as coming from the *other* tree in Eden—the Tree of Life, rather than the Tree of Knowledge. Augustine of Hippo thought that if Adam had eaten from this tree he would have become immortal, which is precisely what happens to Connlae.[70] The tale ends with Connlae leaping into the woman's 'crystal boat' and the two of them vanishing, and although the woman says her realm is far and the sun is setting, she adds, 'we shall reach it before night'. We are surely right to see this near instantaneous translation into a state of blessedness in the light not only of Christ's words in Luke quoted above, but also the eschatological mystery of 1 Corinthians 15:52: '... in a moment, in the twinkling of an eye, at the last trump: for the trumpet shall sound, and the dead shall be raised incorruptible, and we shall be changed.'

That a charged Christian coherence is present in the tale is undeniable, and the allegorical view seems persuasive. Nonetheless 'The Adventure of Connlae' has provided fodder for longstanding arguments over the supposed pre-Christian inheritance of Old Irish literature.[71] To clarify this we must first unpack those elements in the text which have a good chance of being traditional, that is, pre-Christian. First among these is the 'woman of sovereignty' theme, which we have already met. Its core is a paradigm almost certainly inherited from the pre-Christian era, and which seems likely to have formed a crucial aspect of the way in which the pagan Irish had imagined the acquisition and successful maintenance of kingship: a noble youth is sought out by a quasi-divine woman, sex with whom confers rulership upon the youth. It is unclear to what degree this was ever a strictly *religious* belief, even in pagan

---

70 *Echtrae Chonnlai*, ed. McCone, 82; Augustine, *De Civitate Dei*, xiii.20 and xiv.26, in *The City of God against the Pagans*, trans. G. E. McCracken and W. Green (7 vols., London, 1957–72), iv., 214, 394.

71 Vehement discussion in *Echtrae Chonnlai*, ed. McCone, 77–95.

times. However, the startling longevity of the sovereignty motif and its importance in the inauguration ceremonies of kings long after Ireland's conversion to Christianity suggests its powerful ideological importance in the ancestral culture. This is a concept to which we shall return, and the 'woman of sovereignty' is a good illustration of the principle that pre-Christian themes and figures connected with the ideological underpinnings of secular power were more likely than others to be re-used in early Christian Ireland.

Tírechán's story of the conversion of the King of Tara's daughters hinted at this structural pattern, though only briefly. Tírechán inverted the inherited theme along the axis of gender, whereas in 'The Adventure of Connlae' the basic form of the sovereignty motif is retained—the royal youth is still sought out by a supernatural woman. However, the motif here is subjected to a similarly meticulous inversion on the level of meaning and signification. Everything except the *structure* of the inherited theme is turned on its head. As McCone says, '… the crucial point is surely that the woman in *Echtrae Chonnlai* proves to be the exact opposite of this stereotype in that she finally persuades Connlae to give up his regal future among mortals for eternal life in a distant sinless paradise. What she bestows is not kingship in this world but immortality in another.'[72]

A second dimension of the text probably also has ancient roots, as the theme of the child or young person enticed away by the quasi-divine people of the *síd* is a very long-lived motif in Irish literature and folklore. It plays as important a role in the text's intricate manoeuverings as the sovereignty mythos. The bold step taken by the author of 'The Adventure of Connlae' is to turn this theme—a royal youth led by a *síd*-woman into the blissful abode of gods—into a metaphor for spiritual conversion to Christianity, and perhaps more specifically to the monastic life. Its trajectory now ends in heavenly, rather than supernatural, joy.

So much is announced in a pivotal and much-discussed pun near the beginning of the tale, and here again the original wording needs to be borne in mind. The *síd*-woman describes to Connlae the life of bliss enjoyed by her people, saying *i síd már at·aam,* 'it is in a great *síd* that we are…'[73] On the one hand this means 'we are in a big hollow hill (*síd*)', but

---

72 *Echtrae Chonnlai*, ed. McCone, 55.

73 *Echtrae Chonnlai*, ed. McCone, 134–6; see Ó Cathasaigh, 'The Semantics of *síd*', reprnt. in Boyd (ed.), *Coire Sois*, 19–34, at 21, who makes important points about whether part of this is a gloss that has crept into the text.

it is also transparently playing on a homonym, *síd*, 'peace'. (The two words may in origin simply be the same; at the very least, they are connected.) Thus another, equally valid, translation of her statement could be 'we dwell within a vast peace', implying her people live within the Christian 'peace of God, which passeth all understanding', of Philippians 4:7.[74] The metaphor of 'place' has been converted into a state of being; the woman's people live in Christ.

This ambiguity is clearly deliberate. What is less clear—and has had critics locked in combat—is why the monastic author of a Christian allegory would have turned to materials rooted in Irish paganism, least of all the people of the *síd*, the very beings whom Tírechán (another learned churchman) had glossed as 'earthly gods'. Yes, they have been transfused with Christian meanings, but here we must ask what might have motivated a pious monastic author to have made use of them at all.

I suggest that pagan gods in a Christian allegory are only a problem if the reader insists on interpreting the text mythologically, rather than theologically. The emphasis here needs to be on the doctrine of divinization, nowadays a rather underemphasized aspect of Christian teaching. It is one, however, that has a strong claim to be the lynchpin of the faith, for it represents the answer to the question 'what actually *is* salvation in Christ?' To be saved means to come to partake in Christ's divine nature through the atonement—to become, in other words, a god. In the words of Athanasius of Alexandria, 'God became man in order that man might become God'.[75]

To encapsulate the doctrine of divinization by saying that human beings might become *gods* rather than *God* became unusual, but the phrasing was respectably biblical and was deployed by the earliest Church Fathers. In Psalm 81:6–7, God says: 'I have said, you are gods, and all of you are children of the Most High. But you shall die like Adam, and fall like one of the princes.' 'The Adventure of Connlae'—turning as it does on the *síd*-woman's desire to rescue Connlae, a king's son, from death—

---

74 So much has been pointed out by many commentators; see Hollo, 'Allegoresis and Literary Creativity', 118, who makes the brilliant point that St Paul states that 'Christ himself is peace' (Ephesians 2:14) who breaks down the barrier between Jew and Gentile: the author of the text may have been making an analogy between that reconciliation and the one between pagan past and Christian present embodied in his story.

75 Irenaeus, Justin Martyr, Augustine, and Maximus the Confessor (amongst many others) all discussed the theme, for which see the patrological overview in A. N. Williams, *The Ground of Union: Deification in Aquinas and Palamas* (Oxford, 1999); also M. J. Christensen & J. Wittung (eds.), *Partakers of the Divine Nature: the History of Development of Deification in the Christian Traditions* (Madison, 2007).

amounts to an extended commentary on these verses.[76] In the Gaelic world the Psalter was the most intensively copied and commented-upon part of the Bible; it was used to inculcate 'beginner's Latin' in monastic pupils, and was fundamental to liturgical life.[77] As Ralph O'Connor explains, 'The various branches of literary training (reading, writing, grammar, rhetoric) reached their highest goal in the correct understanding and dissemination of biblical texts, especially the Psalms, Gospels, and Pauline epistles.'[78] Early Irish exegetes may have found this passage especially profound, as it contains one of the passages of Hebrew scripture quoted by Jesus, in John 10:34: 'Is it not written in your Law, "I have said, you are gods"?'[79] As the Psalmist makes clear, this is precisely Connlae's dilemma: even princes must grapple with the offer of eternal life versus the inevitability of death. 'Gods', as John's Jesus glosses, are those 'to whom the word of God has been spoken'—a group with whom learned Irish churchmen might readily have identified themselves. This passage was expanded upon by the Church Fathers, not least by Clement of Alexandria: 'He who obeys the Lord and follows the prophecy given through him... becomes a god while still moving about in the flesh'—an apt description of the plot of our story, in fact.[80]

That 'The Adventure of Connlae' is about salvation is clear; its difficulties become fewer if we surmise that its author was thinking in terms

---

76 So undergirded by a matrix of scripture is our text that it seems to transform not one but several such biblical passages into narrative; McCone (*Echtrae Chonnlai*, 105) points out how well Matthew 19:29 applies to Connlae: 'And every one that hath forsaken houses, or brethren, or sisters, or father, or mother, or wife, or children, or lands, for my name's sake, shall receive an hundredfold and shall inherit everlasting life.'

77 *ECI*, 180; see fn.128 for the Springmount Bog tablets, containing an early text (c.600) of three psalms, probably used by a monastic teacher to instruct his pupils in reading and writing.

78 *DDDH*, 244. See M. McNamara, *The Psalms in the Early Irish Church* (Sheffield, 2000); also J. F. Kelly, 'Hiberno-Latin Theology' in H. Löwe (ed.), *Die Iren und Europa im früheren Mittelalter* (2 vols., Stuttgart, 1982), ii. 549–67. O'Connor (*DDDH*, 263–4) notes Irish exegetes' attachment to the literal sense of the Psalms and interest in the historical circumstances of their composition. My suggestion that 'gods' of 81:6 were identified with native divinities suggests exegetical minds hovering significantly between the allegorical and the literal. See M. McNamara, 'Tradition and Creativity in Irish Psalter Study', in P. Ní Chatháin, et al. (eds.), *Irland und Europa: Die Kirche im Frühmittelalter* (Stuttgart, 1984), 328–89.

79 Elsewhere in the New Testament, in 2 Peter 1:4, we find God's promise to make human beings 'partakers in the divine nature' (*divinae consortes naturae*).

80 Clement of Alexandria, *Stromata* 7.16, ed. J.-P. Migne, *Patrologia Graeca* (161 vols., Paris, 1857–86), ix., col. 540.

of the theology of divinization. His creative innovation was to identify the 'gods' of the Psalmist with his own island's indigenous divinities, appropriating them as metaphors for redeemed souls. In this way he connected biblical exegesis with figures like Conn and his son Connlae, characters drawn from a body of native genealogical tradition already in existence.[81] If we read it in this way, which is wholly compatible with the views of McCone (and Carney before him), then we catch a glimpse of how the author's circle must have read: the text privileges the implicit, and rewards the reader's ability to see new significance in old motifs. The state of mind revealed is one made acute by the practice of biblical exegesis, comfortable with drawing analogies between spiritual and corporeal things, and with rumination upon the interplay between surface and signification.

'THE VOYAGE OF BRAN'

To McCone, the *síd*-woman 'invites Connlae to peer beneath the superficial attractions of everyday life and perceive things as they really are *sub specie aeternitatis*'.[82] Modes of knowing are emphasized still more insistently in 'The Voyage of Bran', another monastic composition, also pervaded by thoughts of sin and redemption.[83] As previously noted, so thoroughly does it echo and invert 'The Adventure of Connlae' that the two stories may have been conceived as companion pieces; both are believed to have been composed around the same time.[84] There is no space here to set out the similarities, but 'The Voyage' features an ill-fated and less-reflective hero, and is a darker and more cautionary tale than 'The Adventure'.[85] The crucial point about 'The Voyage' for this study is that it contains the first appearance in Irish literature of a named pagan deity, the sea-god Manannán mac Lir.[86]

---

81 On the creative use of the biblical text in early Irish learning, especially in a legal context, see *DDDH*, 246.

82 *Echtrae Chonnlai*, ed. McCone, 110.

83 The standard edition is *Immram Brain: Bran's Journey to the Land of the Women*, ed. & trans. S. Mac Mathúna (Tübingen, 1985).

84 See above, 49–50, for dating references.

85 Discussion in *Echtrae Chonnlai*, ed. McCone, 74 ('one half of a narrative diptych'), 106–17.

86 For this figure see J. Vendryes, 'Manannan mac Lir', *ÉC* 7 (1952–4), 239–54; also C. W. MacQuarrie, *The Biography of the Irish god of the Sea from Immram Brain (c. 700) to Finnegans Wake (1939): the Waves of Manannán* (Lewiston, NY, 2004).

The story tells how one day Bran, son of Febal, hears beautiful music that lulls him to sleep. Upon awakening, he sees beside him a silver branch hung with white blossoms, which he then carries to his royal house. Afterwards, a woman 'in strange garments' appears, and serenades him with an exquisite poem of twenty-eight stanzas about the island paradise where the branch has grown. Sickness and death are unknown there (just as in the land of Bóadag in 'The Adventure of Connlae'). The woman prophesies the Incarnation of Christ, foretelling the birth of 'the son of a woman whose mate is not known', the creator of heaven and earth. Before she departs, she tells Bran to travel across the sea to 'the Land of the Women'. As she disappears, the branch springs from Bran's hand—which, significantly, lacks the strength to keep hold of it—into hers. The next day he gathers a company of twenty-six men and sets off. (In contrast, Connlae had set out *with* the woman who appeared to him but *without* companions, and only after a month of anguished reflection.)

After two days and nights upon the sea, as predicted by the woman in her song, Bran sees a man speeding towards him in a chariot. The man identifies himself as Manannán mac Lir and he recites one of the most famous poems in all Irish literature:

Bran thinks it a wondrous beauty
in his coracle over the clear sea;
as for me, in my chariot from afar,
it is a flowery plain around which he drives.

What is clear sea
for the prowed ship in which Bran is,
is a pleasant plain with an abundance of flowers
for me in a two-wheeled chariot.

Bran sees
many waves breaking over the clear sea;
I myself see in Mag Mon ['the plain of sports']
red-topped flowers without flaw.

Sea-horses [i.e. waves] glisten in summer
as far as Bran has stretched the glances of his eye;
flowers pour forth a stream of honey
in the land of Manannán son of Lir.

The colour of the ocean on which you are,
the bright colour of the sea on which you row:
it has spread out gold and blue-green;
it is solid land.

Speckled salmon leap out of it, from the womb,
from the white sea on which you look;
they are calves, they are lovely-coloured lambs
at peace, without mutual slaying.[87]

Manannán then goes on to discuss the Fall, and then to prophesy the Incarnation for the second time in the story. The passage quoted above is more than merely beautiful: commentators have universally felt that this speech, and 'The Voyage of Bran' as a whole, is in some way *intricately thought*.[88] This sequence can be read as contrasting two different ways of knowing: Bran perceives one version of the world—superficial and tied to time—where Manannán perceives quite another, and with a degree of insight deeper, truer, and keyed to eternity. For John Carey and Máirín Ní Dhonnchadha this is fairly apparent, and they have admirably unpacked this layer of the text and thus its author's 'theory of knowledge'.[89] In a study of revelation in Irish literature, Ní Dhonnchadha writes: 'Texts which turn on issues of human perception inscribe notions of its limitations—humans' inability to see their future in eternity, in tension with their desire to imagine it. In terms of divine time, this future already exists, and consequently, texts which are concerned largely with the past, or with encounters with "ancients" who witness to that past, are open to being read as allegories for the accommodation of all human time within eternity.'[90]

---

87 *Immram Brain*, ed. Mac Mathúna, 39 (text), 52 (trans), with minor alterations. Note that the nominative of *lir*, 'ocean', is *ler*, so *mac Lir* should technically be translated as 'son of Ler' in English; Mac Mathúna's 'Manannán *mac Ler*' is not fully grammatical. I have silently updated suffixless and archaic forms of the name Manannán (*Monand*, *Monindán*) in the translation.

88 See especially P. Mac Cana, 'The Sinless Otherworld of *Immram Brain*', *Ériu* 27 (1976), 95–115; *Echtrae Chonnlai*, ed. McCone, 59–76.

89 J. Carey, 'Time, Space, and the Otherworld', *PHCC* 7 (1987), 1–27.

90 See M. Ní Dhonnchadha, 'Seeing things: revelation in Gaelic literature', *CMCS* 53–4 [= *Croesi ffiniau: Trafodion y 12fed Gyngres Astudiaethau Celtaidd Ryngwladol 24–30 Awst 2003, Prifysgol Cymru, Aberystwyth / Crossing boundaries: Proceedings of the 12th International Congress of Celtic Studies, 24–30 August 2003*, University of Wales, Aberystwyth] (2007), 103–12, at 104.

On a basic level, the sea-god's higher knowledge can be read as a kind of wish fulfillment on the part of clerical men of learning. For the early Irish scholar, the gathering of knowledge—the process of cognition itself—involved the scrupulous exploration of scriptural meaning, the assimilation of commentary, and the unpicking of allegory and typology. It also required the acquisition of facility in Latin—an entirely foreign language—as well as the vernacular. Fascination with and frustration by obscurity thus went hand in hand. It is, therefore, unsurprising to find that reflection on modes of knowing and on different kinds of knowledge is a recurrent preoccupation in early Irish texts.[91] The author seems to think of Manannán and those like him as unstained by original sin, for he has him announce:

Since creation's beginning we exist
without age, without decay of freshness [or of earth],
we do not expect lack of strength through decay,
the Fall has not touched us.[92]

Like the archangels in Milton's *Paradise Lost*, Manannán's mode of knowing is that of an unfallen being. Both effortless and instantaneous, it is capaciously illuminating without need of deductive reasoning. What the clerical scholar struggles to approach, Manannán can do by nature. The sea-god's knowledge is *intellectus* as *apocalypsis*, understanding as the unveiling of hidden realities.[93] Bran, however, seems wholly unmoved by (or unaware of) Manannán's omniscience, his discourse on original sin, or the prospect of the 'noble deliverance' of redemption. Tellingly, he finds nothing to say. Connlae's exclusive focus on his apple, in contrast, provides an image of spiritual nourishment derived from a profound shift in attention.[94]

---

91 A charming and famous example is the ninth-century poem 'Pangur Bán', in which a scholar compares his intellectual work with the mousing skills of his cat, in *Early Irish Lyrics: eighth to twelfth century*, ed. & trans. G. Murphy (Oxford, 1956 [new edn. Dublin, 1998]), 2, 3; for this poem's figurative description of cerebral activity, see G. Toner, '*Messe ocus Pangur Bán*: structure and cosmology', *CMCS* 57 (2009), 1–22.

92 *Immram Brain*, ed. Mac Mathúna, §44, 40 (text), 53 (trans); *immarbus* (= *imarmus*) means 'transgression, sin' but often specifically '*original sin, the Fall*', as it clearly does here; see *Echtrae Chonnlai*, ed. McCone, 131–2; important discussion of this passage in context in its intellectual context in J. Carey, *A Single Ray of the Sun: Religious Speculation in Early Ireland* (Andover, MA, & Aberystwyth, 1999), 29–30.

93 Ní Dhonnchadh, 'Seeing things', 106.

94 *Immram Brain*, ed. Mac Mathúna, §45–8, 41, 54.

Here we must readdress the question of what it means to be saved, in terms of human ontology. Does Christ's redemption provide only the restoration of the cognitive (and other) capacities which were inherent in humans before the Fall? Or does redemption entail transfiguration into an unprecedented state far greater and more glorious? While the latter has always been the standard answer of theologians, medieval exegetes habitually thought typologically—figuring Paradise as the new Eden, Christ as the new Adam, and so on—which introduced an ambiguity. So much is explicit in Connlae's departure, for example, which stands for conversion to the Christian and monastic life (on earth) and for eternal salvation (after death); oddly, his actual redemption takes place off stage. With this in mind, if Carney's suggestion that the apple comes from the Tree of Life is correct, then the woman's home is Eden—and also paradise.

It is doubtful that this kind of subtle fudge troubled either the authors or audience of these stories, but the question of epistemology is acutely problematic. It is difficult, after all, to imagine what an unfallen mode of knowing might look like, except in the terms that the New Testament represented as proper to the redeemed. In 1 Corinthians 13:12, the Apostle Paul provides the classic statement on the latter: 'For now we see through a glass darkly; but then face to face: now I know in part; but then shall I know fully, even as I have been fully known.' Manannán seems to possess this kind of total knowing, and it is part and parcel of divinization, whereby salvation is obtained through partaking in the divine nature. There is a vast patristic literature on this deep, eschatological knowing, or *noesis*, which must be approached through the language of paradox, because, as fallen beings, we cannot access it directly. Its metaphors and images elude the mind's representational capacity, and so 'self-destruct'. This is one way to read Manannán's lyrical double vision: how can the sea be land? How can one thing be two, or two things be one?

In Ireland (and elsewhere) conspicuously holy persons were depicted as receiving anticipatory flashes of this redeemed mode of knowing. About a century or so before the composition of 'The Voyage', Adomnán of Iona ascribed precisely this capacity to Columba in his account of the saint's life. Columba says:

'There are some people—few indeed—to whom the grace of God has given the power to see brightly and most clearly, with a mental grasp miraculously enlarged, at one and the same time as if lit by single sunbeam, even the entire orbit of the whole earth and the sea and sky around it.'[95]

However, what makes Ireland unusual in this respect is that, apparently without undue concern, something essentially indistinguishable from this mode of knowing was ascribed in literary texts to the learned poets of pre-Christian times. Thomas Charles-Edwards shows that Columba's prophetic insight closely resembles the instantaneous, inspired, and irradiating knowledge that belonged to the literary *filid* (etymologically 'seers'). In Irish, it was known as *imbas for·osna*—the 'encircling knowledge which illuminates'.[96]

Such knowledge might be all very well for Columba and his ilk, and even for the imagined poets of the past who could be envisaged as illuminated by a degree of natural grace. But what are we to make of such 'deep' cognition in the mouth of a pagan divinity, and why Manannán specifically?[97] We cannot be wholly certain that Manannán had been a pre-Christian god, though it is highly probable: a famous Irish glossary of *c*.900 describes him as 'god of the sea', and also states that both the Irish and the Britons had once regarded him as such.[98] Furthermore, the name goes back to **Manaw(i)onagnos*, 'one born in or having the nature of the Isle of Man', which seems plausible enough for a deity known on both sides of the Irish sea.[99]

95 See *ECI*, 193, to which I am indebted here; Charles-Edwards notes that the language of this passage borrows directly from Gregory the Great's *Life of St Benedict*.

96 *ECI*, 193–4.

97 Significantly, the same verb-form as *for·osna* is used in the woman's description of Manannán as 'a fair man *who illuminates* level lands', *fer find for-osndi réde,* referring to the god's capacity to demonstrate that the sea is not as Bran perceives it, but has a deeper dimension as a flowery plain (*Immram Brain*, ed. Mac Mathúna, §16, 36).

98 *Sanas Cormaic: an Old Irish glossary compiled by Cormac úa Cuilennáin king-bishop of Cashel in the tenth century*, ed. K. Meyer, in O. Bergin, et al. (eds.), *Anecdota from Irish Manuscripts* (5 vols., Dublin & Halle 1913), iv., 78 [useful single-volume reprnt. Llanerch, 1994]. It may be significant that this particular assertion is made in Latin, indicating scepticism or distaste on the part of the glossator vis à vis Manannán's divinity, for which see below, 81, 162–3.

99 The medieval Welsh literary character *Manawydan* looks like a later borrowing of Irish *Manannán*, as the names only partially correspond etymologically; for this and the Isle of Man etymology see *IIMWL*, 11–13. MacQuarrie (*Biography of the Irish God of the Sea*, 17–58) raises the possibility that Mannanán was made up for the purposes of 'The Voyage of Bran': in the absence of epigraphic evidence attesting to a cult of the god this cannot be disproved, even if the balance of probability weighs against it.

Two observations can be made here. Firstly, as Carney suggests, not only would the allegorical dimension of 'The Adventure of Connlae' have been poignantly relevant to students entering the monastic life, but it and 'The Voyage of Bran' also demonstrated how to write fine Old Irish, just as extracts from the Roman poet Virgil were used to inculcate polished Latinity.[100] One part of reading or teaching a text like the *Aeneid* would have been the glossing of references to classical myth, and it is possible that this dimension of the pedagogical process may have inspired the idea of bringing native divinities (like Manannán) to representational life within a text likewise intended as a teaching tool. With this in mind, it is striking that the first appearance of a named pagan god in Irish literature—a divinity of the sea riding over the ocean in his chariot—bears points of similarity to an episode very near the beginning of Virgil's poem, when the Roman sea-god appears and calms a storm that menaces the hero and his fleet:

> ... thus all the ocean's uproar subsided, as soon as father Neptune,
> gazing over the water, carried through the clear sky, wheeled
> his horses and gave them their head, flying behind in his chariot.[101]

Direct allusions to classical verse are rare and Irish men of learning often did not know a source in its entirety. They instead regularly used mythographies, commentaries, and compilations of extracts.[102] Nonetheless, this was a particularly significant passage within the most important poem by classical antiquity's most celebrated poet. Virgil's scene

---

100 Carney on this point quoted in *Echtrae Chonnlai*, ed. McCone, 48, and later 117: 'the young monastic student, reading this tale, is faced with a problem very similar to Conle's, insofar as he too is "asked to give up all that is familiar for the sake of eternal life." '

101 *Aen.* 1.154–6.

102 See *DDDH*, 230; note essential articles by M. W. Herren, 'Classical and Secular Learning among the Irish before the Carolingian Renaissance', *Florilegium* 3 (1981), 118–57; B. Ó Cuív, 'Medieval Irish Scholars and Classical Latin Literature', *PRIA* 81 (C) (1981), 239–48; R. Hofman, 'Some New Facts Concerning the Knowledge of Vergil in Early Medieval Ireland', *ÉC* 25 (1988), 189–212; D. Dumville, *The Early Medieval Insular Churches and Preservation of Roman Literature* (2nd edn., Department of Anglo-Saxon, Norse, and Celtic, University of Cambridge, 2004), most recently, the essays in R. O'Connor (ed.), *Classical Literature and Learning in Mediaeval Irish Narrative* (Cambridge, 2014). This would be by far the earliest *vernacular* allusion to the poet in Irish tradition: see Hofman, 'Some New Facts', 197.

may have resonated in the mind of a clerical man of learning because it contains the first 'epic simile' in the poem, in which the god is likened to a venerable public official calming a dangerous crowd; the unusual urban, Roman background to the image would have been utterly foreign to students from an entirely rural society with a wholly dissimilar political system.[103] Was the introduction into 'The Voyage of Bran' of a chariot-driving sea-god—echoing the *first* extended simile of Virgil's poem—intended as a consciously inaugural gesture, announcing an initial attempt at the writing of vernacular stories about secular dignitaries such as Bran?[104] We can but wonder.

Secondly, it is worth noting that in the text Manannán is never called a god: he is referred to as a 'man' (*fer*), never a divinity (*día*, or *dé*).[105] Nonetheless, there is evidence that the author may have intended the pagan sea-deity to be read as an allegory of Christ, or of the Christian God.

This suggestion is less bizarre than it might at first appear. In late antiquity and the early Middle Ages, classical deities were frequently appropriated as allegorical symbols for Christian moral notions, especially in pedagogical texts. (Much later in the Middle Ages, Christ himself was sometimes represented allegorically in the form of Cupid, the Roman god of desire, complete with blindfold and darts of love.)[106] It is bold to suggest that our Irish author might have used a similar strategy with a non-classical, native deity, especially at the beginning, rather than the close, of the Middle Ages. However, this would correspond to the idiosyncratic (but nevertheless orthodox) theological figurations to which early medieval Irish churchmen seem to have been prone. The woman who summons Bran predicts his encounter with Manannán and uses terms that already hint at Christianity:

103 If so this reflects a degree of careful attentiveness to Virgil's tropes which was not present when, three or four centuries later, the whole *Aeneid* was adapted into Irish; such similes are typically replaced with passages of more objective description. See Poppe, '*Imtheacta Aeniasa*', 74–94. The simile would have seemed startling even to a Roman reader: see B. Otis, *Virgil: A Study in Civilized Poetry* (Oxford, 1966), 230.

104 *Echtrae Chonnlai*, ed. McCone, 119.

105 On the development of a word with the specific sense 'pagan god', see J. Carey, '*Dee* "Pagan Deity"', *Ériu* 62 (2012) 33–42.

106 The reuse of pagan gods as 'fertilizer' in medieval European allegory and rhetoric is vast topic; the sixth-century *Mythologiae* of Fulgentius, which systematically gave didactic moral interpretations to pagan tales, is one classic example. Basic overview under 'Paganism', in A. Grafton, *et al.* (eds.), *The Classical Tradition* (Cambridge, MA & London, 2010), 675–6.

At sunrise there comes
a fair man who illuminates level lands;
he rides upon the bright plain against which the sea beats,
he stirs the ocean until it is blood.[107]

The coming of dawn evokes the rising 'sun of righteousness' of Malachi 4:2, which exegetes interpreted as an Old Testament prophecy of the Incarnation; in such a context the last line of the stanza can scarcely fail to evoke Christ's saving blood.

A further piece of evidence lies in a Latin letter written by St Columbanus to Pope Boniface IV in 613—roughly a century before the likely composition of 'The Voyage'. Originally a Leinsterman, Columbanus became a monk in the Ulster monastery of Bangor after studying with the great teacher Sinell. He later emigrated to the continent as a pilgrim-exile, where as a monastic founder he enjoyed the most spectacular career of all such early Irish *peregrini*.[108] In the letter he uses a vivid rhetorical image for Ireland's conversion, that of Christ coming over the sea in a chariot: 'The Most Highest pilot of that carriage, who is Christ, the true Father, the Charioteer of Israel, over the channels' surge, over the dolphins' backs, over the swelling flood, reached even unto us.'[109] Equipped with strong Latinity, Columbanus may have had Virgil's Neptune simile in mind as he describes the incarnate Christ rescuing humanity from sin as the sea-god rescues Aeneas and his followers from the storm.[110] 'The Voyage of Bran' may not have been written at Columbanus' monastery of Bangor—though it could have been—but it is undoubtedly a composition made in a northern monastery. This image so closely resembles the representation of Manannán in our text that McCone suggests its author was making a deliberate allusion, rewriting a powerful passage of rhetoric in the work of a revered monastic forefather.[111] Here, Manannán's revelatory 'deep knowing' transforms into something Christological.

---

107 *Immram Brain*, ed. Mac Mathúna, §16, 36, 49.

108 *ECI*, 344.

109 A link first noticed by H. P. A. Oskamp, *The Voyage of Máel Dúin: A Study in Early Irish Voyage Literature* (Groningen, 1970), 80–1; quoted in *Echtrae Chonnlai*, ed. McCone, 111–2.

110 Charles-Edwards notes that for all Columbanus' evident rhetorical training, Virgil is the only Roman poet he can be shown to have read; *ECI*, 177.

111 *Echtrae Chonnlai*, ed. McCone, 112.

Manannán may indeed hark back to Columbanus' marine Christ, but he also seems intended—directly and boldly—to trope God himself. So much is apparent in the text's most baffling feature: the clearly deliberate juxtaposition of two supernatural fatherings—that of Christ by God the Father, and that of the hero Mongán mac Fíachnai by Manannán. Manannán prophesies:

A noble deliverance will come
from the King who has created the heavens,
the Lord will set in motion a just law,
he will be both God and man.

The shape on which you are looking
will come to your parts,
a journey is in store for me to her house,
to the woman in Mag Line.

The shape of the man [speaking] from
the chariot is Manannán son of Lir,
there will be of his progeny in a short while
a fair man in a chalk-white body.

Manann, the descendent of Lir, will lie
a vigorous lying with Caíntigern [= the wife of Fíachna],
his son shall be called into the fair world,
Fíachna will acknowledge him as his son.[112]

Presumably the author wanted to suggest a correlation between the two situations—or enough of one to prompt deep consideration of their differences. This has caused much head scratching, because Mongán mac Fíachnai, who died in 625, was a perfectly historical king of an Ulster people.[113] Charles-Edwards notes that depicting a pagan god as Mongán's father was presumably a literary conceit, remarking that 'what is striking is that it was a possible literary conceit.'[114] Manannán foretells that

---

112 *Immram Brain*, ed. Mac Mathúna, §§48–51, 41–2 (text), 54–5 (trans).

113 Though see discussion of Mongán's historicity, *Compert Mongáin and Three Other Early Mongán Tales*, ed. & trans. N. White (Maynooth, 2006), 58–66; the historical evidence for his father Fíachna is much stronger than that for Mongán himself.

114 *ECI*, 202.

he will not only be the boy's father, but his tutor too, and all this must have been intended as a compliment to the historical Mongán—or rather his descendants—to whom our text ascribes remarkable, almost godlike knowledge and powers. Carney sensibly suggested that the whole thing was 'poetic hyperbole indicating Mongán's prowess at sea', though he is not in fact praised for this skill within the text, which focuses instead on his martial success and wisdom. Nonetheless, Carney may have been thinking along the right lines: there are hints from elsewhere that wisdom was a quality associated with Manannán, which would correspond to his 'deep knowing' in our text.[115] Rhetorically, to be termed Manannán's son would mean to be wise, a quality repeatedly associated with Mongán in later tales.[116]

But the analogy between Mongán and Christ only works if Manannán is given his full value—at least momentarily—as a divinity, and not as an unfallen human or other variety of ontological compromise. Mongán's Christian salvation is clearly signalled when we are told 'the white host will take him under a wheel of clouds, to the assembly which is not sorrowful'—meaning that angels will conduct his soul to heaven. Thus there are clearly things in the text we are intended to take literally cheek by jowl with things which we are not, and this is the source of the discomfort some critics have felt when reading the Mongán section. (Carney acidly described it as 'tasteless'.) Within this deeply Christian text, something presumably figurative, and therefore false, has been placed on the same plane of representation as a similar event which happens to be a central Christian mystery, and therefore true.

What is going on here? It looks like a typological experiment using native mythological figures.[117] Typology is that crucial mode of medieval scriptural interpretation which took events and persons in the Old Testament as allegories, foreshadowings, or sometimes topsy-turvy inversions of those in the New, just as the conception of Mongán echoes that of Christ. As a result, typology became an approach to history, rather than just a way of reading the Bible. For example, Jonah, who spent three

115 James Carney opined that 'the wise man in Irish tradition tends to be begotten by the God of the Sea', *Studies in Irish Literature and History* (Dublin, 1955), 290–1. The examples he gives are Mongán, Morand, and the prophetic infant Noíndiu Noíbrethach ('of the nine judgments'), who was begotten 'by a phantom from the sea' and (like Morand) spoke immediately after his birth.

116 J. Carney, 'Language and Literature to 1169', *NHI* i., 507.

117 See J. Carney, *Studies in Irish Literature and History*, 290, and P. Mac Cana, 'Mongán mac Fiachna and *Immram Brain*', *Ériu* 23 (1972), 102.

days and nights in the belly of the whale before being vomited up onto dry land, was taken as a foreshadowing of Christ's death and descent into Hades before his resurrection upon the third day.[118] However, typology was not normally applied to pagan myths, which were either subjected to moral interpretations or, when they seemed to evoke biblical narratives, were explained as pagan corruptions of events accurately relayed in scripture. (For example, the attempt by the giants to attack the Olympian gods by piling one mountain on top of another was seen as a garbled version of the story of the Tower of Babel.)[119]

Parallels with the life of Christ are a normal feature of medieval saints' lives; in Ireland such echoes allowed authors to make events in the island's past symbolically correspond to those of sacred history.[120] In Muirchú's seventh-century 'Life of Patrick', for example, the saint appears in Tara 'after the doors had been closed'. Here Muirchú makes the parallel with the resurrected Christ in John's Gospel appearing in a locked room quite clear; Patrick thus becomes a 'type' of Christ.[121] Additionally, in the *Vita Prima* of Brigit—Ireland's greatest female saint— the circumstances of her birth clearly echo the Gospel infancy narratives.[122] Both of these saints' lives re-imagined the native past of Ireland as, effectively, a local version of the great narrative relayed in the scriptures, and this became an ingrained habit of thought in early Irish monastic culture; even druids could on occasion be represented as illuminated by divine grace, thanks to the biblical tradition of the gentile prophet.[123] Absolutely characteristic of early Irish intellectual and literary culture is this mixture of exegetical ingenuity, reverence for the legitimizing power of the native past, and (not least) a sense of being really rather special.

---

118 Not least because Jesus makes the analogy between Jonah and himself (Matthew 12:40) and was thus taken to have licensed typological readings of scripture.

119 But see Hollo, 'Allegoresis and Literary Creativity', 125–7.

120 Such modes of figuration are known as *imitatio Christi*, and have a long and complex history; see e.g. J. W. Earl, 'Typology and Iconographic Style in Early Medieval Hagiography', *Studies in the Literary Imagination* 8 (1975), 15–46.

121 See *Echtrae Chonnlai*, ed. McCone, 72.

122 See my own *Fiery Shapes: Celestial Portents and Astrology in Ireland and Wales, 700–1700* (Oxford, 2010), 38–9.

123 See discussion by McCone in *PPCP*, 90–2. For druids one thinks particularly of those of Conchobor, King of the Ulstermen, who are depicted in an eighth-century tale as clairvoyantly able to perceive the Crucifixion 'in real time'; see Williams, *Fiery Shapes*, 17–20.

In hagiography, the purpose of depicting a saint as a parallel of Christ was to demonstrate their extreme sanctity. But this can hardly be the case with the secular Mongán, who, for all his connections with the church, was a king, not a saint; still less can it be true of Manannán. For all the frisson of genuine mystery that attends his doubled vision and account of a sinless paradise, the sea-god can hardly succeed as a 'type' of God himself.[124] It could be argued that the correlation, through its sheer incongruity, focuses the mind on the uniqueness of the Incarnation. Despite the exquisite and eerie imagery of the first half of Manannán's poem, which can be taken in a natural enough way to have some bearing on the world of the spirit, the god confronts us with the cheerful—almost Ovidian—physicality of Mongán's conception. No being conceived of the Holy Spirit here: for this god, 'energetic sex' (lúthlige) with another man's wife is the order of the day.[125]

In all, this part of the tale leaves us with a sense of uncomfortable ethical strangeness, because the parallel between the divine fatherings of Mongán and Christ is clearly deliberate, and, I suggest, unique in medieval European literature. The typological use of Christlike attributes in depictions of the 'good' or 'noble heathen' is reasonably common in Irish sagas, where it underscores the idea that anticipatory glimmers of the true faith might occur in a country not yet Christian. But the situation in our tale is so striking, even extreme, that it is clear that its meaning to the author and his first audience is not yet fully understood; it may never be.[126]

PARODY AND PRECEDENT

We have covered a great deal of ground and so it is worth summing up what this early material says about the divine beings of Irish tradition. The texts do not represent a naive phase of 'primal myth': the first nar-

---

124 Note the comments of Wooding ('Reapproaching the Pagan Celtic Past', 70) on typological parallels between Manannán and Moses in 'The Voyage'.

125 In another early tale, 'The Conception of Mongán' (Compert Mongáin), we find a backstory to these events: Manannán has made a deal with Fíachna to help him out in a sticky spot in battle, in exchange for which he will sire a son upon Fíachna's wife while disguised as her husband. Whether this idea predates the praise of Mongán in 'The Voyage of Bran' or was inspired by it is unclear; see Compert Mongáin, ed. White; also trans. in CHA, 217–8.

126 I am grateful to one of the Press's anonymous readers for pointing this out to me.

rative appearances of the native supernaturals were shaped by a small class of monastic intellectuals, steeped in Christian Latin learning, who were working on the borderlands between the midlands and the north.[127] The embryonic and inaugural turns out to be sophisticated and complex, a long way from the clumsy interference with pre-Christian material that was once assumed. Nor do these early texts present us with a pantheon of distinct deities, whether 'earthly' or otherwise. The 'god-people' (*Túath Dé*) of the later sagas are simply not there, still less the sprawling 'People of the goddess Danu' (*Túatha Dé Danann*)—the best-known name for the Irish gods. This concept appears to have developed as late as the tenth century and is discussed in a later chapter.

We saw that the immortal woman of 'The Adventure of Connlae' was a version of the so-called 'sovereignty goddess' ruthlessly re-purposed as a figuration of the Church, because traditionally alluring to young noblemen. Her fellow *síd*-beings—whom Tírechán had identified as 'earthly gods'—came to stand for the divinized souls of those saved in Christ. The idea that the people of the *síd* inhabited hollow mounds is present (because punned on) in this text, but it is bracketed. Nonetheless, it is the core semantic meaning of the word, and it seems to reflect a genuinely pre-Christian association between supernatural beings and tumuli, one that is also detectable in late Roman Britain. Although the precise content of the belief is unknown, it is probable that at least some of these monuments were thought to be the abodes of divinities in the pagan period; but the idea that a *síd*-mound is the essential accoutrement of an Irish god is probably a later and literary generalization.

It was the very similarity of *síd*-beings to humans that allowed them to serve as Christian images of human perfection, whether unfallen or redeemed. Manannán mac Lir in 'The Voyage of Bran' also seems to have a symbolic dimension: a phantasmagoric sea-traveller who seems to embody a particular kind of 'deep' knowing—visionary, gratuitous, divinely inspired—to which both secular and ecclesiastical *literati* might have aspired, albeit in different but allied ways, at the turn of the eighth century. Indeed, both of these enigmatic monastic compositions are about the nature of knowing. 'The Adventure of Connlae' uncompromisingly demands the ability to unpack allusion and read for submerged meaning. In 'The Voyage of Bran', knowing is instead a visionary un-

---

127 *Echtrae Chonnlai*, ed. McCone, 119, where the compelling suggestion is made that the monasteries of Druim Snechtai (Drumsnat) and Túaim Drecain (Tomregan, Co. Cavan) would be logical places in which to envisage the composition of these stories.

veiling. It portrays the kind of 'face-to-face' seeing that unfallen (and redeemed) beings enjoy permanently, but which ordinary persons— even those who are holy—experience only as rare flashes of unearned grace.

These texts therefore present us with a residue of pre-Christian material transfused with ecclesiastical modes of thought. The pagan gods have not so much been reclaimed as turned inside out: the processes of re-purposing deities and discarding them were clearly intertwined. It was essential that former divinities were, to some extent, cut off from their roots before they were suitable for inclusion in the products of the monastic scriptorium. The reconfiguring of native supernaturals as ideological personifications compatible with Christian learned culture amounts to a kind of conscious forgetting, the creation of an alternative literary universe.

It is worth asking, however, how literal—how carefully circumscribed—this alternative universe was. Did it reflect anything beyond the bounds of the monastery? James Carney saw in these texts an effort to find a place for 'the virtually ineradicable Irish belief in "fairies" or "Otherworld Beings"'—implying that these beings were widely credited with a certain amount of genuine existence.[128] Carney may have been right: the association between native supernaturals and tumuli was genuinely pre-Christian. Yet it is impossible to extract from texts such as these the forms in which that belief may have persisted amongst the laity, so clearly are these tales—and others like them—the products of exegetically trained minds experimenting with fiction.[129]

It is important to remember that the monastic author(s) of these stories wrote in the aftermath of a momentous cultural change that had not only transformed the learned classes of Irish society but also involved the voracious assimilation of a vast amount of data. (This is why the encyclopedist Isidore of Seville was so highly esteemed: his works gave the Irish access to a distillation of the learning of classical antiquity.)[130]

---

128 Quoted in *Echtrae Chonnlai*, ed. McCone, 50.

129 By 'fiction' I mean writing with a distinct and self-conscious creative or imaginative dimension, which nonetheless uses traditional characters (such as Bran, Connlae, and Conn) whom medieval Irish men of learning generally took to have been historical persons. The term should not therefore be taken to imply a rigid contrast with 'history' in this context.

130 See P. Russell, 'The Sounds of a Silence: The Growth of *Cormac's Glossary*', *CMCS* 15 (Summer, 1988), 1–30, 16–27.

This also hints at the source of the detectable anxieties about vernacular composition in the period. McCone notes that these texts may insist so vigorously upon their Christian credentials precisely because writing secular sagas containing pre-Christian figures was a new and daring enterprise, one that was 'likely enough to have been viewed with some suspicion and disapproval in certain monastic circles'.[131] 'The Adventure of Connlae' and 'The Voyage of Bran' inaugurate the tradition, but in doing so they invert themes relating to the mythical sovereignty goddess, the sea-god Manannán, and the people of the *síd* almost to the point of parody. Tírechán does the same. We see tradition and innovation, past and future, fusing in a precarious but often brilliant tension of opposites.

In all, it seems probable that at least some ecclesiastical intellectuals around the turn of the eighth century found pagan divinities a useful way to open up a space for fictive play in the vernacular. Early Irish culture had a proclivity towards harping on the sources of empowering precedent in the ancient past, but it did not permit ideas to be taken over from paganism without considerable change. In later centuries, when anxieties about secularly focused vernacular composition had relaxed, some of the strategies identified above would flower into a rich literature in which native divinities held a prominent place. But for all that, the strange reverberative quality of these early texts—the way they combine literary sophistication with a sense of pristine force—could not have been foretold. It was precisely this originality which greatly enlarged the possibilities for those who came after.

131 *Echtrae Chonnlai*, ed. McCone, 119.

3

DIVINE CULTURE

EXEMPLARY GODS AND THE
MYTHOLOGICAL CYCLE

By piety and hard concentration a man may induce
gods to exercise that useful attribute of divinity, the
ability to break off fragments of their essence.

—MICHAEL AYRTON, *THE MAZE MAKER*

STEREOTYPES OFTEN ATTACH to national mythologies, which are held
to embody the characteristics ascribed to the peoples who shaped them
in an especially concentrated form. If—as the classicist Peter Green insists—Germanic mythology is 'lumpish, violent, and primitive', then
Irish myth has also been stereotyped all too often as fey and involuted,
veering between whimsy and soggy mournfulness.[1]

Mercifully, the Irish sagas of the eighth, ninth, and tenth centuries
rarely exhibit these qualities, although many feature mythological beings and are set in a grandly imagined version of the island's pre-
Christian past.[2] Even for Ireland—whose contribution to world literature
is famously out of all proportion to its size—the proliferation of vernacular story between the eighth and the eleventh centuries must count as an
outstanding contribution to the literary inheritance of humanity. Many
of the most important sagas were composed during a period of historical
transition; the advent of the Vikings in 795 ushered in a period of eco-

1 P. Green, *Classical Bearings: Interpreting Ancient History and Culture* (London, 1989),
16; these stereotypes are addressed by a number of the essays in M. Gibson, S. Trower, *et
al.* (eds.), *Mysticism, Myth and Celtic Identity* (New York & Abingdon, 2013).

2 It seems to have been conventional to keep overt Christianity out of saga-writing
until *c.*1000, after which there was a shift in style and emphasis which included (*inter
alia*) the adaptation into Irish of classical works and an importation of hagiographical
material into the world of the sagas.

nomic and political turbulence and brought to an end the relatively settled culture of early Christian Ireland.[3] Changing times were reflected in
a new kind of literary ambition, with a shift from the production of tiny,
concentrated stories like 'The Adventure of Connlae' to the assembly of
elaborate, integrated prose works—from gem cutting to cathedral building, so to speak.[4]

What role do the native gods play in this rich and various body of
tales? In chapter 2 I suggested that monastic writers composing literature in Irish for the first time had found the gods 'good to think with':
they pressed mythic personages into service in order to emblematize
Ireland's triumphant progression from the pagan past into a glorious
Christian present. It remained the case that a pre-Christian setting could
be used to showcase Christian themes, and in the sagas examined in this
chapter this undergirding vision is less blatant but no less present.[5] Two
in particular, which number among the very finest, are 'The Wooing of
Étaín' (*Tochmarc Étaíne*), a millennium-spanning tale of reincarnation,
and 'The Second Battle of Moytura' (*Cath Maige Tuired*), which describes
the downtrodden gods' rebellion against a race of oppressive enemies.
'The Wooing', in the form in which we have it, probably dates from the
ninth or tenth century, while 'The Second Battle'—apart from an eleventh-
century preamble—is likely to be a creation of the late ninth.[6]

AUTHORSHIP, AUDIENCE, AESTHETICS

First we must look at the broader background. The question of how to
classify Irish sagas has recently become increasingly difficult.[7] The tales

---

3 Literary and historical overviews by M. Ní Mhaonaigh, 'The literature of medieval
Ireland, 800–1200: from the Vikings to the Normans', *CHIL*, i., 32–73; J. Carney, 'Lan-
guage and Literature to 1169', *NHI*, i., 451–510, and (in the same volume), F. J. Byrne, 'The
Viking Age', 609–34. Note the influential if now rather dated account by P. Mac Cana,
'The Influence of the Vikings on Celtic Literature', in B. Ó Cuív (ed.), *Proceedings of the
International Congress of Celtic Studies held in Dublin 6–10 July, 1959* (Dublin, 1962), 78–118.

4 It should be noted that the timespan in play here was also marked towards its end
by gradual linguistic transition, as the classical form of Old Irish (*c*.650–900) gave way to
Middle Irish (*c*.900–1200).

5 See Ralph O'Connor's comments, *DDDH*, 65.

6 See below, 83–4, fn.42, and 78, fn.23, for bibliography on these texts.

7 The old-fashioned scheme, going back to the early twentieth century, began by
shunting hagiographical, apocryphal, and biblical material off to one side to focus only
on secular stories, which were then divided up by content into the Ulster, Fenian, King,

featuring the gods represent only a selection of what survives, and this selection in turn is likely to be only a fraction of what once existed.[8] Many of these are traditionally lumped together under the heading of the 'Mythological Cycle'—or as Tomás Ó Cathasaigh has suggested, the 'Cycle of the Gods and Goddesses'—because a high proportion of the characters within them have generally been taken to be former divinities.[9]

As indicated by the disputes outlined in chapter 2 between 'nativists' and 'anti-nativists', it is hard to gauge the degree to which any of these sagas reflect lost pre-Christian myths. At one extreme, it cannot be argued that *no* archaic undertow can be detected, but on the other hand it is overwhelmingly clear that the mythic patterns and motifs present have been transmuted and transfused with meanings tailored to medieval, Christian Ireland—the period in which the sagas were written. The archaic and the innovative are intertwined, and the contrast between the Mythological Cycle and the body of tales attached to the heroes of Ulster—the 'Ulster Cycle'—is instructive here.[10] Early pieces of evidence

---

and Mythological Cycles. Magisterially represented by R. Thurneysen, *Die irische Helden- und Königsage bis zum 17. Jahrhundert* (Halle/Saale, 1912 [repnt. Hildersheim, 1980]), 4–5, this tradition was continued (with changes of emphasis) in M. Dillon, *Early Irish Literature* (Chicago, 1948). More recently this time-honoured but by now creaky classification was repeated by the late Muireann Ní Bhrolcháin, *An Introduction to Early Irish Literature* (Dublin, 2009). These are not native classifications, but they are convenient; see the comments of E. Poppe, *Of Cycles and Other Critical Matters: Some Issues in Medieval Irish Literature and Criticism* (Department of Anglo-Saxon, Norse, and Celtic, University of Cambridge, 2008). Medieval Irish men of learning themselves did not employ cyclical demarcations of this sort, and preferred to divide stories up thematically—'wooings', 'cattle raids', 'violent deaths', 'elopements', and so on. This too is a system which also has serious problems, even if it is native, because it suppresses the interlinking of sagas which trace the story of the same character or group of characters over the course of time—a concept with which the Irish were perfectly familiar, as the common term *rem- scél*, 'prequel', implies.

8 Depression can be easily induced by the surviving Middle Irish tale-lists, which record storytellers' repertoires. A substantial proportion of the narratives listed are completely lost and we can only make educated guesses concerning their subject matter, though how many of these only ever existed in oral/aural versions and were never put into writing is unknowable; see P. Mac Cana, *The Learned Tales of Medieval Ireland* (Dublin, 1980), 41; on the relationship between written texts and performance in the 'secondary-oral' context of the period, see *L&IEMI*, 1–2, 154–5, and J. F. Nagy, 'Oral Tradition and Performance in Medieval Ireland', in K. Reichl (ed.), *Medieval Oral Literature* (Boston & Berlin, 2011), 279–93.

9 In Boyd (ed.), *Coire Sois*, 3–7, 128–9.

10 See the comments of O'Connor, *DDDH*, 3, and Johnston, *L&IEMI*, 175–6.

suggest that the basics of the Ulster Cycle were in place in the seventh century, perhaps earlier, so that with careful analysis we can make educated guesses about older, oral forms of the stories.[11] However, there is no such evidence for the Mythological Cycle, and as a result, it is not clear whether *any* aspect of a given saga—from large-scale narrative structure down to the finest detail—represents transcription from oral tradition, a radical monastic overhaul of an inherited myth, or medieval invention.

The nature of authorship and audience in the period must also be considered. Storytelling in Irish was one of the responsibilities of the *filid*, the professional poets, and thus the medieval sagas were stories composed by highly ranked, influential men of letters for elite audiences.[12] Their images of the native gods were meant to underpin ideas of social cohesion or the assertion of particular political claims, probable priorities of the ambitious dynasts who were their patrons.[13] And while the *filid*'s body of knowledge was basically secular, their attitudes and aspects of their education overlapped with their ecclesiastical counterparts in the monasteries: they belonged to the space between secular society and the church.[14] This reflects the church's longstanding domination of literate activity in early medieval Ireland, and its largely staunch (and, for medieval Europe, highly unusual) support of secular learning. This intimate interlocking on the intellectual level mirrors the alliance of the secular and religious spheres on a political level, though some basic questions remain about how it all worked in practice.[15]

11 A very early poem, *c*.600, refers to events recognizable as belonging to the Ulster Cycle as *sen eolas*, 'ancient knowledge'; see J. Carney, 'Early Irish Literature: The State of Research', in G. Mac Eoin, *et al.* (eds.), *Proceedings of the Sixth International Congress of Celtic Studies* (Dublin, 1983), 113–30, esp. 119–26, and (more recently) Charles-Edwards's comments on the implications of the name Conchobor Machae mac Maíle Dúin, king of the Airthir around Armagh (d. 698), *NHI*, i., lxxxii.

12 See *L&IEMI*, 151, for a Middle Irish tract describing the audiences of the *filid* as 'kings and rulers and nobles'; Johnston comments that this displays impressive continuity with the earlier, Old Irish period. See too J. F. Nagy, 'Orality in Medieval Irish Narrative: An Overview', *Oral Tradition* 1/2 (1986), 272–301, at 272–3.

13 *DDDH*, 5–6.

14 See *L&IEMI*, 145, for a 'strong monastic component' in the education of *filid*; Elva Johnston reminds us that Irish monasteries were centres of non-clerical as well as clerical populations.

15 Deftly summarized by M. Ní Mhaonaigh, 'The literature of medieval Ireland, 800–1200', *CHIL* i., 36–7; see too *DDDH*, 20–1, and E. M. Slotkin, 'Medieval Irish Scribes and Fixed Texts', *Éigse* 17 (1977–9), 437–50.

My specialist colleagues may be troubled by my use of *literature* and *literary* in relation to vernacular sagas. The learned classes of medieval Ireland were profoundly suspicious of the value of untrue stories: the modern idea of 'imaginative literature' did not exist as a concept in their culture. They thought of themselves as custodians of an ancient past, not as imaginative innovators.[16] Because of this very different sense of truth and its value, Celtic scholars are wary of treating early Irish sagas unreflectively as 'literature'; they are aware that medieval Irish writers crafted pictures of the past in order to yoke them to their patrons' political and religious agendas. According to one influential view, the sagas form a body of narratives in which we can see the claims and ambitions of the present being justified and advanced by reference to the complex body of legendary tradition and genealogy known as *senchas*, 'historical lore': the 'literary' dimension is a by-product of dynastic rhetoric.[17]

Treating literature as the handmaiden of secular and ecclesiastical politics has greatly increased our understanding of how these texts function.[18] But so austere an emphasis on their political context may have forestalled analysis of their aesthetics, so much so that Ralph O'Connor, for example, has found it necessary to argue for the importance of taking this dimension of the sagas seriously. He points out that the creators of the vernacular narratives were not just spin doctors of *senchas*, but were also artists who shaped the structures of their stories, chose their words carefully, and expected their audiences to pay attention to subtle shifts, inversions, and echoes. The 'message' of a saga is

16 The best way into this major theoretical issue is through the implications of the two famous colophons—one Irish, one Latin—attached to the end of Recension II of *Táin Bó Cúailnge* in the twelfth-century Book of Leinster, upon which there is a substantial literature. See especially B. Miles, *Heroic Saga and Classical Epic in Medieval Ireland* (Cambridge, 2011), 1–14, and E. Poppe, '*Grammatica, grammatic*, Augustine, and the *Táin*', in J. T Koch, J. Carey, & P.-Y. Lambert (eds.), *Ildánach, Ildírech: A Festschrift for Proinsias Mac Cana* (Andover, 1999), 203–10.

17 I refer here in particular to Donnchadh Ó Corráin, who has advanced this view in a series of influential publications; see his 'Historical Need and Literary Narrative', in D. Ellis Evans, *et al.* (eds.), *Proceedings of the Seventh International Congress of Celtic Studies* (Oxford, 1986), 141–58, also 'Legend as Critic', in T. Dunne & C. Doherty (eds.), *The Writer as Witness: Literature as Historical Evidence* (Cork, 1987), 23–38, and 'Creating the Past: The Early Irish Genealogical Tradition', *Peritia* 12 (1998), 177–208.

18 See *DDDH*, 6, fn.19 for examples, also 287–96 for important notes of scepticism; the approach is extended to a whole manuscript in D. Schlüter, *History or Fable: The Book of Leinster as a document of cultural memory in twelfth-century Ireland* (Münster, 2010).

neither necessarily singular nor straightforwardly didactic.[19] In other words there is a significant element of conscious artistic excellence in play, so that any proper assessment of a saga must take into consideration the sphere of art as well as that of political promulgation. In relation to the native gods, allowing for the sagas' aesthetic dimension is entirely compatible with the awareness that inherited mythological material was continually being made relevant to contemporary contexts.

There is a further level of complexity here. None of the tales discussed in this chapter survive in manuscripts of the period in which they were originally composed.[20] The sagas of the eighth, ninth, and tenth centuries are only available to us via large compilations made in the twelfth century and later, when Ireland was facing quite different challenges. We will look at this period in detail in the following chapters, but the crucial point here is that our understanding of the saga-writing of the earlier period is determined by what the compilers of several centuries later thought was worth copying and preserving. As a result it remains frustratingly difficult to say when several major narratives were composed; often we can only suggest upper and lower limits, which may be decades, even centuries apart. 'The Wooing of Étaín', one of the two great sagas analysed below, offers an example of the difficulties involved. It is named in a medieval tale-list, which means we can be reasonably sure a version of the narrative existed in the tenth century.[21] But our first surviving *text* consists of a partial copy from the beginning of the twelfth century; there is also a complete copy from the fourteenth century. How then to date the composition of the saga?

One approach involves looking in forensic detail at the language. Is it convincingly Old Irish (*c.*600–900), or, if there are Middle Irish (*c.*900–1200) linguistic features, might these be explained as mechanical updatings by a later scribe copying out an Old Irish original? This is a difficult and technical undertaking, rendered increasingly problematic by the fact that medieval writers felt perfectly at liberty to work parts of older texts into new compositions. The second approach, clearly related to the previously discussed historicist way of reading Irish sagas, is to look for ways in which a text might correspond to the political scenarios of the period in which it might reasonably be thought to have been composed.

---

19 *DDDH*, 7–16, and *passim*.
20 *DDDH*, 20; Ní Mhaonaigh, 'The literature of medieval Ireland', *CHIL*, i., 32–7.
21 Mac Cana, *The Learned Tales*, 42, 68–9.

Neither approach is without problems, although circular reasoning is a particular risk when hunting for political applicabilities.

'The Second Battle of Moytura' provides the classic warning here, as O'Connor has pointed out.[22] It survives in a single sixteenth-century manuscript, but was originally composed in the ninth century and added to in the eleventh. Two separate scholars have argued—in compelling detail—that the tale can be shown to allegorize precise sets of political circumstances. The circumstances they suggest are not only different, but also more than a century apart. While John Carey believes the story to be a parable of Irish-Viking relations in the 800s, Michael Chesnutt instead sees it as an allusion to the battle of Clontarf in 1016.[23] Both suggestions are persuasive and yet they cannot both be correct (at least not in the same way). The gulf between these equally scholarly interpretations has worrying implications for our ability to date texts using this approach. More importantly, it also calls into question our basic ability to understand their contexts and so guess at what their original audiences might have made of them.

NATURE AND IDENTITY

A bewildering variety of largely incompatible opinions about what the gods were is characteristic of early medieval Ireland. John Carey and Jacqueline Borsje, key voices in the debate, have made it plain that the saga-writers were undecided on how to fit the gods into a Christian universe: there were a variety of opinions about their ontology—the nature of their nature.[24] This is usually attributed to cultural anxiety: Irish men of learning are supposed to have recognized that the gods were an important part of the traditional lore of Ireland, but to have worried (as pious Christians) about how such beings should be conceptualized.

---

22 I draw here on *DDDH*, 288.

23 J. Carey, 'Myth and Mythography in *Cath Maige Tuired*', *Studia Celtica* 24–5 (1989–90), 33–69; M. Chesnutt, '*Cath Maige Tuired*—A parable of the Battle of Clontarf', in S. Ó Catháin (ed.), *Northern Lights: Following Folklore in North-Western Europe* (Dublin, 2001), 22–33.

24 See Carey's essay, 'The Baptism of the Gods', in his *A Single Ray of the Sun: Religious Speculation in Early Ireland* (Andover, MA, & Aberystwyth, 1999), 1–38, and useful entry 'Tuath Dé', *CCHE*, v., 1693–6, on which I draw gratefully here; also Borsje's 'Monotheistic to a Certain Extent' in Korte & de Haardt (eds.), *The Boundaries of Monotheism*, 53–82.

One serious conclusion about the ancient gods was that they had been merciful angels sent before the coming of Christianity in order to guide the Irish according to 'the truth of nature'. While only stated once (albeit unequivocally) in the literature, this suggestion was jaw-droppingly daring for early medieval Europe.[25] As previously discussed, a second strategy identified the gods as unfallen human beings who, unstained by sin, were both invisible and immortal.[26] Yet another method was to identify them as a group of 'half-fallen' angels who had failed to take sides in Lucifer's rebellion against God; lastly, they could be condemned outright as demons. These options presented a sliding scale of moral respectability. Off to the side, because involving no attempt at accommodation with Christian teaching, are rare presentations of the native gods as gods proper, or as illustrious humans who had been falsely deified by posterity, in the manner suggested by the ancient fabulist Euhemerus. The last of these was not strongly emphasized in the period covered in this chapter, but went on to become crucial in the central Middle Ages.

How to weigh these possibilities up? Strictly speaking, the only orthodox idea was that the gods had been demons, which was a common strategy for dealing with indigenous divinities in medieval Europe.[27] While never a major theme, in Ireland it is detectable in the earliest Patrician hagiography; it is uncompromisingly expressed in part of a saga probably written in the eleventh century, slightly after the period covered in this chapter:

> For the diabolical power was great before the Faith, so that demons could wage bodily war against men, and could show them beautiful and secret things, as if they were permanent. And so they were believed in. So that it is those apparitions which the ignorant call *síde*, and people of the *síde*.[28]

The author's conviction is clear, but this seems never to have been a widespread view; it also implicitly explodes the value of literature set in

25 Carey, *A Single Ray of the Sun*, 37–8.

26 Useful discussion of the Irish idea of unfallen races in J. Carey, 'The Irish Vision of the Chinese', *Ériu* 38 (1987), 73–80; *A Single Ray of the Sun*, 30–1.

27 *ECI*, 195–6.

28 Trans. by J. Carey, 'The Uses of Tradition in *Serglige Con Chulainn*', in J. P. Mallory & G. Stockman (eds.), *Ulidia: Proceedings of the First International Conference on the Ulster Cycle of Tales* (Belfast, 1994), 85–90, 78; text in *Serglige Con Chulainn*, ed. M. Dillon (Dublin, 1953), ll.844–9. Carey (79) notes this passage's debt to Isidore of Seville.

a pagan past—a literature which was already very rich by the time this passage was written.

In contrast, configuring the ancient gods as unfallen human beings or as neutral angels were important strategies in Ireland. They were, however, *outré* propositions from the point of view of Christian orthodoxy. The first had no scriptural warrant whatsoever, whereas the second ran into difficulties over the question of angelic nature: the standard Christian view affirmed that for angels *all* sins—including that of sitting on the fence—are mortal sins, leading to eternal damnation.[29] Nonetheless, the idea of neutral angels was retained into modernity as one of the main explanations in Irish folklore for the native supernaturals, although whether the idea travelled from folk belief into the early literature or the other way round is unclear.[30] The fact that it occurs first in a famous, densely allegorical Latin text, *Navigatio sancti Brendani abbatis* ('The Voyage of St Brendan the Abbot'), suggests a learned origin. Likely composed in the ninth or tenth centuries, the tale features half-fallen angels who linger on earth in the form of birds.[31] In this guise, they sing the canonical hours and hope that one day God will forgive them and let them back into heaven. In no way are they identified with Ireland's pagan divinities, though otherworldly bird-men do appear in at least one vernacular saga; an audience might well have inferred that these were the pre-Christian gods.[32]

For the Irish, direct acknowledgement of the pagan deities once worshipped by their ancestors was easier in some spheres of learning than in others. One hugely important text, *Sanas Cormaic* ('Cormac's Glos-

29 This may only have been a problem *in potentia*: the mortal nature of angelic sin was not formulated until Aquinas in the thirteenth century (*Summa theologiae*, I-II, Q. 89, Art. 4., 'Whether a good or evil angel can sin venially?').

30 Another major theory identified the fairies with the human dead; this is not apparent in the medieval literature but is greatly emphasized in the fairylore collected in the modern era.

31 *Navigatio sancti Brendani abbatis from Early Latin Manuscripts*, ed. & trans. C. Selmer, (Notre Dame, IN, 1959), 24, and note new edn., *Navigatio sancti Brendani: alla scoperta dei segreti meravigliosi del mondo*, ed. G. Orlandi & R. Guglielmetti (Florence, 2014). For the dating, see D. Dumville, 'Two Approaches to the Dating of *Navigatio Sancti Brendani*', *Studi Medievale* 29 ser. 3.1 (1988), 87–102.

32 The saga to which I refer is the tenth- or eleventh-century 'Destruction of Da Derga's Hostel' (*Togail Bruidne Da Derga*), the author of which seems to have wanted to depict the powers of the otherworld in as enigmatic a manner as possible, taking pains not to identify the bird-men as the native gods explicitly but leaving the audience to take the hint; see *DDDH*, 61, 63.

sary'), notes several Irish divinities in an ostensibly matter-of-fact way. A figure named Néit—who never appears as a character in any surviving saga—is described as 'a war-god among the pagan Irish', while the divine physician Dían Cécht is labelled 'the god of health' (*deus salutis*), exactly as though he were (say) Aesculapius.[33]

Entries like these seem to offer some of the clearest information about the Irish gods that has come down to us, but even here serious complexities still exist, and the information set out cannot necessarily be taken at face value. 'Cormac's Glossary' was first compiled *c.*900, but it was continually added to and revised over subsequent centuries. As a result, many entries referring to native gods became increasingly elaborate and thus more and more likely to reflect the understanding of medieval clerics instead of ancient mythology.[34] At one point, for example, a blatantly non-native god is transplanted to Ireland, when Beltane, the festival at the beginning of May, is explained as 'the fire (*teine*) of Ba'al'—a Canaanite deity well known to the Irish from scripture and the writings of Isidore of Seville.[35] As a result, a completely spurious ancient Irish god named 'Bel' still lingers in popular accounts of Celtic mythology. Furthermore, entries in the Glossary often mix Irish and Latin, and a switch to Latin often seems to indicate a desire to create distance from the content on the part of the glossator. Describing Dían Cécht as *deus salutis*, for example, may indicate not dispassion, but distaste.

Outside glossaries, it is also necessary to ask what kind of vernacular terminology was used for the gods. The most important term, *áes síde*, 'people of the hollow hills', has been previously discussed, but we will revisit it below due to its complex implications. Until the tenth century, a very common strategy in the sagas was to use a euphemism. Instead of

33 This phrase only appears in the Leabhar Breac version of 'Cormac's Glossary' (*Three Irish Glossaries*, ed. W. Stokes (London, 1862, repnt. Felinfach, 2000), 16).

34 See P. Russell, 'The Sounds of a Silence: The Growth of *Cormac's Glossary*', *CMCS* 15 (Summer, 1988), 1–30.

35 *Bil. o Bial .i. dia ídal, unde beltine .i. tene Bil no Beil* = 'Bil, from Bial (= Ba'al), i.e. an idolatrous god. Whence *Beltane*, i.e. the fires of Bil or Bel' (*Sanas Cormaic*, ed. Meyer, 15). Cú Chulainn gives the same explanation—clearly dependent on glossary tradition—in the saga 'The Wooing of Emer' (*Tochmarc Emire*), for which see M. Clarke 'Linguistic Education and Literary Creativity in Medieval Ireland', in P. Ronan (ed.), *Cahiers de l' Institut de Linguistique et des Sciences des Langues* (Lausanne, 2013), 39–71, at 62. *Ba'al* was variously spelled in medieval Latin, including as *Bel*, *Beel*, and *Belus*. Note that the similarity to a widely-attested continental Celtic deity named *Belenus* is a coincidence: the latter name has proved very hard to etymologize securely, as discussed by P. Schrijver, 'On Henbane and Early European Narcotics', *ZCP* 51 (1999), 17–45.

plain 'gods', the collective phrases 'god-men' (*fir dé*), 'god-kindreds' (*cenéla dé*), and especially 'god-people' or 'god-peoples' (*túath dé* or *túatha dé*) were used.[36] This will perhaps fail to strike the modern read as a significant distinction, but medieval Irish writers stuck to this phrasing carefully, and so presumably felt it made the difference between acceptability and unacceptability.[37]

There were two other reasonably common labels for native supernatural beings. The term *scál* seems to denote an uncanny being, sometimes a god, who appears to pass on supernatural information.[38] Its etymology ties it to words for 'shadow'—compare Latin *umbra*, 'shade, dead soul'—but at its root it refers to a 'phantasm'.[39] The word *síabair* (plural *síabrai*) also denotes a spectral or apparitional being: it is related to the verb *síabraid*, 'distort, transform', and so may imply the shapeshifter's ability to adopt illusory outer appearances.[40]

---

36 The idea of a divine race was perhaps less likely to stick in the craw than individual divinities: John Carey notes that this kind of designation—unlike *áes síde*—is used in sagas detailing the gods' activities in the deep past, and so points to the development of a euhemerist strategy towards the gods, imagining them as the exalted but human personages of long ago. See Carey, 'Tuath Dé', 1694.

37 Whether there was any difference of emphasis between *fir, cenéla* and *túath(a) dé* is not now recoverable, because the evidence is so elliptical: it is possible that *túath* in particular implied common descent from a single male ancestor, for which see *L&IEMI*, 73.

38 The *sirite* seems to have been especially associated with the battlefield. The word *airdrech* sometimes also refers to a kind of battlefield spirit, but originally meant 'something looked at, something that appears to the eye' from an Indo-European root **derk-*, 'look, perceive'; an early Irish glossator used it to translate Latin *prodigium*, 'omen, prophetic sign', hinting that *airdrech* may have implied a kind of phantasm. See W. Sayers, 'Airdrech, sirite, and other early Irish battlefield spirits', *Éigse* 25 (1991), 45–55.

39 A major peculiarity of the semantic range of this noun is that it underwent an apparently old extension from '(uncanny) being' to plain 'being, person': for example the compounds *banscál* and *ferscál*—literally a 'woman-' and 'man-*scál*'—just mean 'a female' or 'a male', with no supernatural overtones. We might compare the English 'soul' in the sense 'person' ('a merry old soul'); see M. Ní Dhonnchadha, 'The semantics of *banscál*', *Éigse* 31 (1999), 31–35.

40 J. F. Nagy, *CWA&A*, 156. It is interesting that *síabrai* is the term preferred by the Middle Irish saga 'The Destruction of Da Derga's Hostel' for its ambivalent otherworld beings. The legendary boy-king Conaire the Great is raised up and then doomed to death by their machinations: he is the king, the tale disquietingly tells us, 'whom the *síabrai* exiled from the world'. The point is not that the author wants to discretely avoid mentioning pagan gods, but that he wants to heighten the sense of doom by making them inscrutably collective. That said, the associations of the word cannot always have been sinister, because it occurs in personal names, rather in the manner of Old English *ælf*,

Again, this welter of terminological and ontological variety may stem from the authors' anxiety about the role former divinities might legitimately play within a Christian literary culture, the basic issue being how to explain their supernatural gifts within a cosmos ruled by the Christian God. But it is important to credit the saga-authors' creativity and capacity for irony. The breadth of explanations for the gods meant that it was possible for a saga-writer to choose the one most conducive to the literary effect they were aiming at in a given work.[41] The fictional vampire offers a modern parallel: presumably few writers would assert a belief in their literal existence, but they feel free to reshape the mythology (significant word) of vampirism for the purposes of their fiction, with results variously poignant, comic, politically or socially metaphorical, phantasmagoric, erotic, or horrific. The composers of the Old Irish sagas should be credited with having allowed themselves similar room for manoeuvre with regard to the native gods; only when this is borne in mind can we take the measure of their artistic achievement.

'THE WOOING OF ÉTAÍN'

It is time to see this manoeuvring in practice, and 'The Wooing of Étaín' —a major saga from the mythological cycle—provides an excellent example of the conscious exploitation of the gods' indeterminacy of nature. Composed perhaps in the ninth or tenth century, it is one of the most beautiful and most complex of Irish sagas, and here a plot summary is necessary.[42]

'elf'. The most famous of these is *Findabair*, 'fair-haired *síabair*', daughter of Aillil and Medb of Connaught, whose name is linguistically equivalent to Welsh *Gwenhwyfar* (Guinevere), Arthur's queen.

41 Note O'Connor's parallel comment (*DDDH*, 60) that the otherworld in medieval Irish saga was 'constructed anew in every individual text, and therefore cannot be understood without reference to each text's particular formal strategies'.

42 Two crucial discussions are T. Charles-Edwards, '*Tochmarc Étaíne*: A Literal Interpretation', in J.-M. Picard & M. Richter (eds.), *Ogma: Essays in Celtic Studies in Honour of Próinséas Ní Chatháin* (Dublin, 2002), 165–181, and T. Ó Cathasaigh, '*Tochmarc Étaíne* II: A Tale of Three Wooings', in P. O'Neill (ed.), *Land Beneath the Sea: Essays in Honour of Anders Alqvist's Contribution to Celtic Studies in Australia* (Sydney, 2013), 129–142. Note too W. Sayers, 'Fusion and Fission in the Love and Lexis of Early Ireland', in A. Classen (ed.), *Words of Love and Love of Words in the Middle Ages and Renaissance* (Tempe, AZ, 2008), 95–109; lunar symbolism is found—eccentrically, in my view—by R. Hicks, in 'Cosmog-

The saga falls into three sub-tales. The first opens with a set of sordid events, when the Dagda—the 'Supreme Father' (*Ollathair*) among the gods—uses his powers to get away with adultery. He secretly fathers a son, Óengus, upon Bóand, the eponymous goddess of the River Boyne and wife of the blameless Elcmar. We are told explicitly that the Dagda's descent is from the 'god-peoples' (*tuatha dé*), who thus seem like very shady beings, guilty of the kind of wrongdoings for which Augustine of Hippo had condemned the classical deities.[43] Midir, a significant grandee among the god-peoples, fosters Óengus, who as an adult finagles Bruig na Bóinne (Newgrange) out of Elcmar by means of a ruse.[44]

Visiting Óengus in his new home, Midir is blinded in one eye in an accident. Although he is healed completely by Dían Cécht, the divine physician, Midir demands compensation from his foster son, including that he deliver to Midir the most beautiful woman in Ireland to be his wife. Handily, he has already identified her as Étaín, daughter of Ailill, king of the Ulstermen, a group who seem to belong to a different race to that of the god-peoples. To win her for Midir, Óengus must perform various tasks for Ailill, including clearing plains and diverting rivers, in addition to paying her weight in gold and silver. In this he succeeds—with help from his father the Dagda—and Étaín becomes Midir's wife.

Only at this point do we discover that Midir is already married. While polygamy was a normal aspect of secular Irish life in the earlier Middle Ages, it is no surprise that Midir's first wife is bitterly jealous of her husband's attractive new bride. A powerful sorceress, Fúamnach (perhaps 'noisy one') turns Étaín into a pool of water, out of which emerges a beautiful purple bluebottle the size of a man's head, which buzzes musically and sheds healing dew from its wings.[45] (As an aside,

---

raphy in *Tochmarc Étaíne*', *The Journal of Indo-European Studies* 37:1–2 (Spring/Summer, 2009), 115–29.

43 But note that it is perfectly possible for criticism of the sexual laxity of the gods in traditional myths to be conducted from within a pagan culture; in Greece this began as early as the sixth century BC, when Xenophanes of Colophon objected that Homer had 'attributed to the gods everything that is a shame and reproach among men, stealing and committing adultery and deceiving each other' (quoted in Green, *Classical Bearings*, 132).

44 It is not certain (but plausible) that Midir is a former god: the name looks like it should be connected with the verb for 'judging' (*midithir*). But it may be a borrowing from British and have originally meant 'Mead-King', for which see the comments of J. Uhlich, 'Einige britannische Lehnnamen im Irischen: *Brénainn (Brenden), Cathaír/Catháer* und *Midir*', ZCP 49/50 (1997), 893–5.

45 Note the comments of T. Ó Cathasaigh on the elemental symbolism of this passage, 'The Wooing of Étaín', in Boyd (ed.), *Coire Sois*, 173–186, at 181–2.

this moment illustrates how early Irish saga is distinguished by moments of ferocious weirdness, and so contrasts sharply with the sober
moralizing characteristic of most genres of Old English literature.) A
millennium later, Anglo-Irish romantics prettified this episode by having Étaín take the form of a butterfly; nonetheless, the word used—*cuil*—
definitely means 'fly'.[46]

Midir knows that the fly is Étaín, who accompanies him wherever he
goes. (He does not appear to be able to change her back himself.) But
again Fúamnach magically interferes, conjuring up a storm that blows
the fly away, and she drifts for seven years before landing on Óengus.
Óengus tends her until she returns to health.[47] Fúamnach creates yet
another storm to blow the fly away from Óengus, and after another
seven years she drops, exhausted, into the wine cup held by the wife of
the warrior Étar; the time is now that of the legendary Ulster king Conchobor mac Nessa. Étar's wife drinks from the cup, swallows the fly, and
becomes pregnant. One thousand and two years after her first birth,
Étaín is reborn into a changed Ireland.

In the second part of the saga, Eochaid Airem, the human king of
Ireland, seeks a wife, because the provincial kings will not submit to an
over-king without a queen. He sends messengers to identify the most
beautiful woman in Ireland; they find Étaín, who is now the daughter of
Étar, and who is also completely unaware of her previous existence, including her marriage to Midir. Eochaid marries her, but his brother Ailill also falls for her, and wastes away with unrequited love. Eochaid
leaves Tara on a tour of Ireland, leaving Étaín with the dying Ailill. He
tells her the cause of his sickness, which he says would be cured if she
gave the word. She tells him she wants him to be well, and he begins to
rally. However, he says, the cure will only be complete if she agrees to
meet him for sex on the hill above the house; meeting there means they
will not shame the king in his own house. She agrees to do so three times,

---

46 It was used for the plague of flies that afflicts the Egyptians in Exodus 8:20–32; see
DIL, s.v.

47 Scale and denotation in this passage go strangely awry: the author wants us to
keep Étaín's double nature in mind, so things appropriate to a fly are mixed up, as though
in surreal double exposure, with things appropriate to a young girl. Thus Óengus 'puts
purple clothing' on Étaín (how?!) and though he settles her into a *grianán* or 'sun-room'
(the normal word for the light-filled room in a noble house where women did their sew-
ing) and fills it with health-giving houseplants, he simultaneously seems to be able to
carry the whole thing about with him, like a lantern. I hope to write about this dimension of the text at length elsewhere.

but each time she goes to meet him, she in fact encounters Midir, who has put Ailill to sleep and taken his appearance. On the third occasion Midir reveals his identity and tells Étaín who she really is, but she does not know him. Finally she agrees to go with him, but only if Eochaid agrees to sell her.

In the third part of the story, after Ailill has fully recovered and Eochaid has returned home, Midir comes to Tara and challenges Eochaid to play *fidchell*, 'wood-wisdom', the medieval Irish equivalent of chess. They play for ever-increasing stakes. Eochaid keeps winning, and Midir has to pay up. One loss compels Midir to build a causeway overnight across the bog of the Lámraige, which he does by mobilizing an army of workers from among his people. Finally, Midir suggests to Eochaid that they play for a kiss and an embrace from Étaín; this time Midir wins, having previously played badly on purpose in order to lull Eochaid into a false sense of security. Eochaid tells Midir to come back in a year to collect his winnings, and gathers his best warriors at Tara to prepare for Midir's return. Despite the heavy guard, Midir mysteriously materializes inside the house. Eochaid agrees that Midir may embrace Étaín, but when he does so, the pair fly away up through the skylight, transforming into swans as they do so.

The tale ends with a disastrous coda. Eochaid instructs his men to dig up every *síd*-mound in Ireland until his wife is returned to him. Finally, when they set to digging at Midir's *síd* at Brí Léith, Midir himself appears and promises to give Étaín back. But at the appointed time, Midir brings fifty women who all look alike, and tells Eochaid to pick which one is Étaín. Eochaid chooses the woman he thinks is his wife, takes her home, and sleeps with her; she becomes pregnant and bears him a daughter. Later, Midir appears a final time and tells him that Étaín had been pregnant when he took her; the woman Eochaid has chosen is his own daughter, who had been born in Midir's *síd*. Eochaid is both father and grandfather to his new child.

So runs 'The Wooing of Étaín', though no synopsis can do justice to its haunting quality—oddly reminiscent of Shakespeare's late plays—which turns on loss and restoration and grounds human drama in mythic patterns.

My first observation is that there is a clear shift in the political and ontological status of the former divinities between the scenario in the first sub-tale and that in the third. We begin among the gods, and as the tale opens the Dagda is described in the most explicitly godlike terms found in any Irish saga:

There was a famous king of Ireland from the race of the god-peoples, named Eochaid Great-Father. He was also called the Dagda [the 'Good God'], for it was he who used to work wonders for them and control the weather and the crops. As a result of which men said he was called the Dagda.[48]

All this sounds strikingly like the Roman Jupiter, the 'Father of Gods and Men' who was responsible for weather and rainfall, and whose title was 'Best and Greatest'. He was also notoriously highly sexed, with a penchant for other men's wives: Hercules is conceived when Jupiter deceives Amphitryon, husband of Alcmene, just as the Dagda tricks Bóand's husband Elcmar, which results in Óengus. Normally this similarity is explained by identifying the Dagda and Jupiter as reflexes of a reconstructed Indo-European deity, the 'Sky-Father', and this may well simply be correct.[49] But Jupiter's characteristics were also clearly laid out in Isidore's *Etymologies*—a text greatly revered by the Irish—as well as by Carolingian mythographers. With this in mind, this portrait of the suprahuman Dagda could have been inflected by Irish men of learning's knowledge of the most important of Roman deities.[50] If so, the saga-writer's intention may have been to discreetly underscore the Dagda's divinity, thereby emphasizing that his tale opens in a morally dubious world in which the gods are in charge.

But by the end of the third of the saga's three sub-tales, the ontology of these figures has shifted significantly. As John Carey points out, Midir—definitely a god in the first sub-tale—suddenly implies that he and his kin are unfallen human beings, as though we had returned to the Christian allegories of 'The Voyage of Bran' or 'The Adventure of Connlae':

---

48 Irish text in *Tochmarc Étaíne*, ed. & trans. O. Bergin & R.I. Best, *Ériu* 12 (1938), 137–96; useful translation by J. Carey in *CHA*, 146–165, superseding that of Gantz, *EIM&S*.

49 Calvert Watkins (*How to Kill a Dragon: Aspects of Indo-European Poetics* (Oxford, 1995), 8) pointed out that the second elements of each term in the phrase *Dagda Ollathair*, 'Good-God Supreme-Father', are etymologically cognate with Roman *Iuppiter* and Greek *Zeu pater* ('Father Zeus', in the vocative), and thus are likely to be very old. But compare also Norse *Alföðr* ('father of all', 'all-father'), an epithet for the god Odin which appears occasionally in (probably relatively late) eddic poetry, but more prominently in the narrative framework of Snorri Sturluson's *Edda* which has a clear learned-Christian agenda.

50 Isidore of Seville, *Etymologiae* 8.34–6; see comments on the supposed goddess Ana/Anu below, 187–91.

Stately folk without blemish,
conception without sin, without lust.

We see everyone on every side,
and no one sees us.
It is the shadow-veil of Adam's sin
that has prevented us from being counted.[51]

'Conception ... without lust' hardly describes the Dagda's shenanigans in the saga's first part. It is likely that the author of 'The Wooing of Étaín' was both drawing on and compiling several older traditions here which are lost to us and which may have contradicted each other; nevertheless, his art is sufficiently careful that this wavering can be regarded as a source of calculated literary effect. The important thing is that Midir is addressing a woman, Étaín, whose own nature is unclear; although she does not come from the god-peoples herself, she becomes Midir's second wife in the first sub-tale. Then, transformed by magic, she lives out over a millennium as an insect, before finally being reborn as a human woman. Midir now calls her back, underscoring the idea that all these Étaíns are really one and the same.

But this presents the author of the saga with a problem that becomes the major theme of the second sub-tale. Étaín is persistently half-identified with the sovereignty-goddess, and this foregrounds the fact that she circulates sexually between several men, just as the 'woman of sovereignty' marries a sequence of men in turn.[52] The god-peoples too, as we know from the tale's opening, have no qualms about adultery, and yet our author seems to want to shape the story into a poignant romance of married love between Étaín and Midir. It is here that the deliberate and startling shift into the tropes of Edenic sinlessness does crucial work. Midir's lyrical description of the gods' elysian mode of being causes us to read the story as a tale of remembrance and reunification across more-than-human time—even though different interpretations, perhaps less generous to the divine characters, might be equally justified. Because her marriage to Eochaid is suddenly represented as an interlude of unwilled forgetfulness in an unfallen and eternal life, Étaín can be figured as sexually pure and faithful to her original husband. Midir thus jailbreaks his

51 *Tochmarc Étaíne*, ed. Bergin & Best, 180; see Carey, *A Single Ray of the Sun*, 30–2, for seminal discussion on this point.
52 See Charles-Edwards, '*Tochmarc Étaíne*', 166, 173–6, 178–9.

wife from a world of doomed and fallen beings, just as the immortal woman does for Connlae. The moment of apotheosis too—while exquisite—is blatantly manipulative of audience sympathies. As they heard how Midir and Étaín rose up through the skylight and flew off in the form of birds, a medieval Irish audience must have known, as we do, that wild swans really do mate for life.

LAND AND TERRITORY

It is clear thus far how debate about the nature of the gods could be exploited to powerful literary effect. In the sagas there is a second aspect to this phenomenon in that ideas about the gods' natures were inseparably yoked to the places where they were supposed to live—specifically, their relationship to the geography of Ireland itself. The poem excerpted above is a prime example, as it begins with Midir calling Étain to go with him 'to a land where there is music':

Hair is there like the primrose flower;
on the smooth body there is the colour of snow.

There is no 'mine' or 'yours';
white the tooth, black the brow.
The multitude of our host delights the eye:
the colour of the foxglove is in every cheek.[53]

And yet as seen, the same poem climaxes with Midir asserting that the people of the *síd* are present invisibly 'on every side', implying that their realm is somehow superimposed upon our own like a sheet of tracing paper: the sinless people of the *síd* pass through us, impalpable and unimpeded. Nonetheless, the tale is quite consistent on the point that Midir's *síd*-mound is the perfectly physical Ardagh Hill in Co. Longford.[54]

So there is a mystery here, and it is plain that the *síd*—the fantasy of a contiguous world—is an elliptical and ambiguous concept. Some orienting observations can nonetheless be made in the face of this suggestive blurring of place and state, and (as usual) it is important to put the

---

53 *Tochmarc Étaíne*, ed. Bergin & Best, 180; trans. Carey, *CHA*, 159.

54 A mile and half south of Ardagh, and also known as Slieve Golry/Slievegolry. Old Irish *Brí Léith* means 'Hill of a Grey One'—perhaps meaning Midir himself.

question of the putatively pre-Christian origins of the *síd* to one side and focus on what the medieval texts actually say.

One of the defining propositions of Irish mythology is that at some point in the past the god-peoples removed themselves into subterranean otherworldly dwellings, from which they could subsequently sally forth to help or hinder mortals. Although this removal is generally accepted as a given, the actual textual picture is more complex and contradictory. In the first sub-tale of 'The Wooing of Étaín', which is trying to present a primordial scenario, we find ourselves in a world in which the *síd*-mounds are emphatically *not* (at this stage) openings into supernatural space. We are dealing instead with earthly territory and geography, so much so that the overall political framework in the first sub-tale of 'The Wooing of Étaín' would have had obvious contemporary resonance for the saga's original audiences. The Dagda is settled at the Hill of Uisnech in the midlands, 'for it is there that [his] house was, Ireland stretching equally far from on every side, south and north, to east and west'.[55] He has the ability, which underscores his status as a powerful over-king, to deal out territory in Brega, at some distance from his own seat of power. He also arranges for Elcmar, the man he has cuckolded, to be permanently ejected from Newgrange and given Cleitech instead, on the south side of the Boyne. This situation maps fairly closely onto the political geography of the southern Uí Néill, which was, between the seventh and ninth centuries, the most dominant and powerful Irish dynasty. Although the saga-author was writing about the struggles and set-tos of the gods, earthly Irish territory and its political significance was in the forefront of his mind.[56]

It is appropriate, therefore, that in the first sub-tale of 'The Wooing of Étaín' each individual *síd*-mound seems to function very much like a circular ringfort or *ráth*, the dispersed and usually lightly-defended settlements inhabited by well-off and self-sufficient members of Irish society in the early Middle Ages. Perhaps never stated explicitly, it may be that the Irish envisioned the *síd*-mounds as supernatural ringforts which had been mysteriously hollowed out or roofed over with turf. Neolithic tumuli had a single entrance and many were surrounded with one or more enclosing earth banks, just like a *ráth*, while Newgrange, the most spectacular, was enclosed by a ring of standing stones.[57]

---

55 Now next to the village of Loughnavally, Co. Westmeath.
56 Charles-Edwards, '*Tochmarc Étaíne*', 167.
57 See *L&IEMI*, 75; the more rings a *ráth* had, the higher the status of the person who

Ringforts were usually built in areas of fertile farmland, and in 'The Wooing of Étaín' the *síd*-mounds are imagined as epicentres of social power and land-management.[58] Bóand's cuckolded husband Elcmar is fobbed off with the *síd* of Cleitech, which comes 'with the three lands (*cusna tri tirib*) that are round about it'.[59] A memorable scene finds Óengus and Elcmar—unsurprisingly on poor terms—standing on top of their respective *síd*-mounds, umpiring their 'boy-troops' as they battle it out in the level land in between: their *síd*-mounds come with playing-fields attached. Interestingly the boys are described as playing 'in the Bruig' (*isin Bruig*), which must mean 'in the territory ruled from the Bruig and under the jurisdiction of Óengus', not that lying literally within the tumulus.[60]

A strong strand in early tradition ascribes to the Dagda the responsibility for assigning a *síd*-mound to each individual divinity. In 'The Wooing of Étaín' this process has been completed long before the story opens, which is why Óengus—the Dagda's initially unacknowledged son—has to manipulate his way into possession of the Bruig. There was, however, variation on this point: a separate Old Irish anecdote gives us a glimpse of the Dagda's primordial distribution of the *síd*-mounds, but asserts it was he, not Elcmar, who originally possessed the Bruig, and that Óengus tricked his own father.[61] Despite the differences between the two accounts, both versions feature an Óengus who craves land to administer and to call his own; the whole Bruig imbroglio stems directly from the desire of a king's son for territory in the earthly Ireland.

Early Irish political reality is also reflected in the fact that this primordial Ireland is not socially or ethnically homogenous. 'The Wooing

---

lived there. See also N. Edwards, 'The Archaeology of early medieval Ireland, *c.*400–1169', *NHI* i., 238–9, and D. Ó Corráin's comments at 550–2 in the same volume.

58 The Dagda—admittedly a very biased judge—rules that Elcmar has lost his right to Newgrange precisely because he failed to defend his territory, telling him 'your life was dearer to you than your land (*tír*).'

59 *Tochmarc Étaíne*, ed. Bergin & Best, 146.

60 *Tochmarc Étaíne*, ed. Bergin & Best, 146.

61 'Great too was his [the Dagda's] power when he was king in the beginning; and it was he who divided the *síd*-mounds among the god-men (*Fir Dé*): Lug son of Eithliu in Síd Rodrubán, Ogma in Síd Aircheltrai, the Dagda himself however has Sid Lethet Lachtmaige..., Cnoc Báine, Brú Ruair. They say that, however, Síd in Broga [Newgrange] belonged to him at first'; trans. by J. Carey, *CHA*, 145; text in '*De Gabáil in t-Sída*', ed. & trans. V. Hull, *ZCP* 19 (1933), 53–58, at 56, 57. The ellipsis in the translation is for the phrase *oí asíd* which comes between *Lachtmaige* and *Cnocc Báine* in the text and which appears to be corrupt.

of Étaín' features peoples whose line of descent differs from that of the Dagda and his kin; the Fir Bolg. While the Fir Bolg possess a modicum of social standing, they are explicitly socially subjugated to the Túatha Dé. If 'The Wooing' maps onto the political geography of the eighth century, then the territory and sway of the legendary 'god-peoples' corresponds to that of the southern Uí Néill; the Fir Bolg are therefore equivalent to the Uí Néill's unfree vassal-peoples (*aithechthúatha*), who stood in a tributary relationship to their powerful rulers.[62]

This projection of the politics of early Christian Ireland back onto the mythological past is governed by a single crucial metaphor that carries a significant amount of the tale's ideological message: divinity is aristocracy. There seems to be no essential difference of nature between the god-peoples and the Fir Bolg, which suggests that divinity belongs to the realm of metaphor. As in the highly stratified society of early Christian Ireland, for the god-peoples too nobility and power go hand in hand. This may explain the relentless emphasis on the potency of the Dagda in particular. In 'The Wooing of Étaín' he is a worker of wonders, able to control the weather, manipulate others' perception of the flow of time, and cause plains to be cleared and rivers to spring up in a single night.[63] Power seems to be innate and a matter of descent, in that only members of the god-peoples seem to be able to wield magic. Fúamnach, Midir's first wife, is a particularly frightening example—fostered by a druid, she is able to transform, and then continue to persecute, the unfortunate Étaín.

Étaín's own ancestry is left uncertain, but she is clearly not one of the god-peoples: she seems to possess no magical powers whatsoever and is helpless against Fúamnach's ghastly fury. The reader may rejoin at this point that she still turns from a wet patch on the floor into a fly, and ask who could have transformed her except herself. In fact, this sequence provides the curiously cinematic experience—most unusual in a medieval work—of observing something happening silently in an empty room:

> As Étaín sat down in the chair in the middle of the house, Fúamnach struck her with a rod of purple rowan so that she turned her into a pool of water on the floor of the house. Then Fúamnach went

---

62 Charles-Edwards, '*Tochmarc Étaíne*', 168–9; *L&IEMI*, 75.

63 Three rivers (the 'three sisters', Suir, Nore, and Barrow) spring up before him in 'Fingén's Night Watch', *Airne Fingéin*, ed. J. Vendryes (Dublin, 1953), 17.

to her foster-father Bresal, and Midir left the house to the water into which Étaín had been transformed. After that Midir had no wife. The heat of the fire and the air and the energy of the earth worked together with the water until they made a larva out of the water that was on the floor of the house, and after that made out of that larva a purple fly, which was the size of a man's head and the most beautiful in the land.[64]

The elemental forces of air, fire, and earth act in concert upon the water, but on the face of it it remains unclear exactly who is responsible for this hushed and alchemical gestation.

One answer might be none other than the Christian God. Christian thinkers debated whether creation had been a unique event or whether God had enabled some ongoing mechanism for the replenishment of life. Augustine of Hippo concluded that spontaneous generation was indeed part of the divine plan, pointing to Genesis 1:20: 'Let the waters bring forth abundantly the moving creature that hath life.' The context was an influential commentary upon the biblical book, known to Irish men of learning.[65] Perhaps, as the larva stirs into being amidst the waters which once were Étaín, the showy magic of the god-peoples has been trumped by a greater power, interceding silently and out of sight to preserve Étaín's life. With a subtlety typical of the saga-author, this pivotal episode hints that supremacy over Ireland will not lie in the hands of the pagan god-peoples forever, and that a new dispensation, willed by a greater God, will soon arrive.

BEING AND TIME

The themes we have been considering—power, place, and ontology—work quite differently in 'The Second Battle of Moytura', the second mythological saga this chapter examines. Most likely also a composition of the late ninth century, this tale has substantially rearranged some of its inherited mythic structures, although scholars agree that its basic

---

64 *Tochmarc Étaíne*, ed. Bergin & Best, 152.

65 He also asserts that earth and water are more 'pliant' than other substances and therefore symbolize 'the unformed matter of things', which inflects the larva's mysterious appearance. For knowledge of this commentary in Ireland, see M. Smyth, *Understanding the Universe in Seventh-Century Ireland* (Woodbridge, 1996), 23.

mise-en-scène preserves an old stratum of myth better than 'The Wooing of Étaín'.[66] The god-peoples in this saga seem to have inhabited Ireland immemorially, and although they control its earthly territory—as they do in the first sub-tale of 'The Wooing'—they do not seem to live in *síd*-mounds. The seat of royal power seems to be Tara, just as mortal over-kingship was normally conceived: here, the gods are represented as the earthly 'men of Ireland', and are scaled-up versions of human beings.

In 'The Second Battle', the Túatha Dé battle the Fomorians or *Fomoiri*, a supernatural race clearly associated in late tradition with the sea: the etymology of the name is disputed, but might well mean the 'under (*fo*) sea (*muir*) [beings]'.[67] Later they became the monsters *par excellence* of Irish tradition—variously deformed, fishlike, or fanged—but in several early sagas, including 'The Second Battle', they look much the same as the god-peoples and can be just as beautiful.

'The Second Battle' starts with an account of the loss of Núadu's arm, and his replacement as king by Bres. It then tells how Bres was conceived from a union on the seashore between Ériu of the Túatha Dé and a Fomorian warrior named Elatha. Bres grows up unnaturally fast and oppresses the Túatha Dé. He makes the noblest of them perform the grimiest kind of work, imposes heavy tribute, and fails to show the level of hospitality required in a king. He is deposed, and Núadu—who has had his arm restored with a fully functional silver version by the physician-god Dían Cécht—is restored to the kingship. Bres then appeals to his Fomorian kin for assistance in taking Ireland back, and while his father Elatha makes a principled refusal, another Fomorian leader, Balor of the Evil Eye, agrees to help him and musters an invasion fleet. Meanwhile, the heroic Lug arrives at Núadú's court at Tara. Like Bres, he is a product of miscegenation between the Túatha Dé and the Fomorians, but Lug's father is of the Túatha Dé while his mother is of Fomorian stock. After gaining admittance and impressing the king with his many talents, Lug is given the kingship of the Tuatha Dé. Núadu is then killed by Balor in the battle, but Lug, Balor's grandson, kills the Fomorian

---

66 Reading the saga like this involves detaching its preamble, demonstrably added on when the tale was redacted in the late eleventh century; see J. Carey, 'Myth and Mythography in *Cath Maige Tuired*', 54.

67 Another possibility is 'under-phantoms/spirits', with the *mor-* element cognate with English night*mare*, which may also be the first element in the name of the goddess Morrígan, ('Phantom-Queen'); yet another is 'those who go about upon the sea'. For all these see S. Rodway, 'Mermaids, Leprechauns, and Fomorians: A Middle Irish Account of the Descendents of Cain', *CMCS* 59 (2010), 16–7.

leader with his sling, smashing his deadly eye out through the back of his head where it decimates the Fomorians. Bres is found alive in the aftermath of the battle, and is spared by Lug on the condition that he teaches the Tuatha Dé how to plough, sow, and reap.

The saga has long intrigued scholars of mythology because of its similarity to the demonstrably ancient Indo-European theme of the primordial conflict between the gods and the antigods.[68] In Greece, the Olympian gods fought the Giants and Titans; in India, the Devas battled the (morally indistinguishable) Asuras; in Scandinavia, the gods, the Æsir, clashed with giants and with second-division divinities known as the Vanir.[69] We therefore have an after-image or echo of a mythological war on the grandest of scales; and indeed in 'The Second Battle', the main players on both sides differ markedly from their counterparts in 'The Wooing' (and most other texts) by virtue of being colossally big. It was a common belief among medieval scholars that ancient people had been bigger than themselves, and the Bible testified to the existence of giants before Noah's Flood; these concepts may or may not have influenced the presentation of the gods in the saga, who are—at a rough guess—over two hundred feet tall.[70]

68 E.g. T. Ó Cathasaigh. '*Cath Maige Tuired* as Exemplary Myth', in P. de Brún, et al. (eds.), *Folia Gadelica: Essays presented by former students to R. A. Breatnach* (Cork, 1983), 1–19, at 1, 8 (reprnt. in Boyd (ed.), *Coire Sois*, 135–54).

69 See J. Puhvel, *Comparative Mythology* (Baltimore, 1987), 176–8; the major study of the theme is J. Oosten, *The War of the Gods: the Social Code in Indo-European Mythology* (London, 1985), but the handling of the Celtic material is unsophisticated. Follow-up references for Greece in M. Morford, R. J. Lenardon, & M. Sham, (eds.), *Classical Mythology* (Oxford, 2013 [tenth edn]), 66–7; for India, see Doniger, *The Hindus: An Alternative History*, 88, 108–9; for Norse myth, *FATV*, 11–49. In some cases (e.g. for Greece) the gods' conflict with their enemies is a one-off; in others (e.g. for Scandinavia) it is a continual problem which flares up periodically. Which category the 'original' Irish myth fell into is unclear, but see the comments of Carey, 'Myth and Mythography', 54–5.

70 I am being deliberately, even thuddingly literal here as I think this is a dimension of the story often simply ignored. Medieval writers regularly described ancient heroes and supernaturals as of giant stature and then equally regularly forgot—often within a few sentences—that they had done so; this seems to me to hint at important dimensions to the way they visualized (or failed to visualize) the stories they were telling. In 'The Second Battle of Moytura' we are told that the bowl of the Dagda's ladle is big enough to contain an embracing couple: if that means it is about six feet long, then he must be between two and three hundred feet tall in the story. Later the Morrígan stands astride the River Unshin, implying that she is of similarly gigantic stature. E. A. Gray notes that the tale explicitly ascribes gigantism only to these two, but I doubt that this means, as she

Because these ancient beings are built on a gargantuan scale they can alter the landscape directly by exerting vast physical force. In 'The Wooing of Étaín' the Dagda and Midir both transformed the land, but they did so by dint of magic and (in Midir's case) by acting as foreman of works to hordes of toiling subordinates. In contrast, 'The Second Battle' makes a theme out of land and soil, and things take a more hands-on form: the poor Dagda is reduced at one point to the basest kind of navvying, building ramparts for a tyrant. Indeed the Dagda affords a simple measure of how *big* the gods are in the story, to judge by the trolley he uses to trundle his magical club around the landscape:

> He trailed behind him a wheeled fork which was the work of eight men to move, and its track was enough for the boundary ditch of a province. It is called 'The Track of the Dagda's Club' for that reason. And he was naked, with a long penis.[71]

This episode occurs immediately before one of the most eye-popping sex scenes in all medieval literature, and when the 'track' of the Dagda's 'club' is so closely juxtaposed with his hypervirile penis, the reader may be forgiven for wondering if this might not be a delicate rewriting of a lost older tradition in which the ditch was raised, not by the god's club, but by his manhood dragging on the ground.[72]

In closing this phase of the argument, let us return to the idea of a timeline in the life of the god-peoples—that there came a point in the past in which they vacated the surface of Ireland and went to dwell permanently within the *síd*-mounds. The standard version of this doctrine in medieval Irish writing held that this was the result of regime change, there being a time when the god-peoples had fallen from political supremacy and the Gaels had become the rulers of Ireland in their stead. It is significant that in 'The Wooing of Étaín', with its transmillennial nar-

---

argues, that all the other characters are imagined as human-sized ('*Cath Maige Tuired*: Myth and Structure', *Éigse* 19 (1982–3), 240).

71 *Cath Maige Tuired: The Second Battle of Mag Tuired*, ed. & trans. E. A. Gray (London, 1982), 46, 47. The word *denucht* (*denocht*) = 'stark naked, completely bare'; corrections to Gray's trans. from E. C. Quin's review of her edn., *CMCS* 9 (1985), 101.

72 Though this detail may also be intended to degrade the Dagda; compare the treatment of the befuddled, elderly warrior Iliach in the *Táin*, who fights naked and who is roundly mocked by the assembled hosts because his exposed penis dangles down through his chariot frame. See *Táin Bó Cúailnge: Recension I*, ed. & trans. C. O'Rahilly (Dublin, 1976), 215.

rative arc, this crucial moment happens (so to speak) off stage. While poor Étaín is being buffeted from pillar to post, the entire political landscape changes. 'The Wooing of Étaín' is one of a small number of sagas which cycle down to the present—the human period—so that within the elaborate artificial chronology cultivated by Irish men of learning, the tale ends a few generations before the birth of Christ.[73] And when this happens, we find that Midir's power has shrunk to the confines of his *síd*, Brí Léith. Humans, and specifically the ethnic Irish, rule the land, a transformation underscored by the similarity of names between the kings of Ireland at the beginning and end of the saga. As the saga opens, we are pedantically told that the Dagda's main name is Eochaid *Ollathair*, 'Eochaid Supreme-Father'; the unfortunate husband of the reincarnated Étaín at the end is Eochaid *Airem*, 'Eochaid Ploughman'.[74]

In the third sub-tale of 'The Wooing' there is an uncanny moment that draws attention to this revolutionary change with great subtlety. Midir has come as a complete unknown to the court of Eochaid Airem at Tara, guilefully manoeuvring the return of his wife. Eochaid is unnerved, 'for he was unaware of his [Midir's] being in Tara the night before, and the courts had not [yet] been opened at that time'.[75] We saw that the motif of a supernatural person who mysteriously appears within a locked court had been applied in 'The Adventure of Connlae' to the nameless woman personifying the Church; it had itself been borrowed from the risen Christ of John's Gospel.[76] No longer a token of Christian sanctity, here we find it fully naturalized as a token of otherworldly power. Midir is splendidly dressed and radiantly handsome, but delays—against social protocol—to reveal his name:

> Thereupon he came up to Eochaid. Then Eochaid said, 'Welcome to the warrior whom we do not know.' 'It is for that we have come', said the warrior. 'We do not know you', said Eochaid. 'But I know *you*', replied the warrior. 'What is your name?' said Eochaid. 'Not well known', he replied, 'Midir of Brí Léith'.[77]

---

73 Eochaid Airem is in some accounts the grandfather (and great-grandfather) of Conaire Mór, whose life overlaps with those of the champions of the Ulster Cycle, the central events of which were supposed by some medieval Irish authorities to have occurred around the time of the birth of Christ.

74 As noted by Charles-Edwards, '*Tochmarc Étaíne*', 173.

75 *Tochmarc Étaíne*, ed. Bergin & Best, 174.

76 Perhaps via Muirchú's 'Life of Patrick'; see above, 67.

77 *Tochmarc Étaíne*, ed. Bergin & Best, 174.

'An out-of-the-way place', Midir implies slyly; 'you won't have heard of it'. I suggest that this is not an example of *litotes*, the rhetorical trope of understatement, according to which 'not well known' would be a way of saying 'very famous', for after Midir names himself Eochaid seems none the wiser. And yet the obscurity of Midir's home and identity is belied by his gorgeous attire and by his inscrutable reluctance to give his name and origins. To be the first to state one's identity was to acknowledge that one stood before a social superior, and later in the tale we discover that Midir's current status is very grand indeed. He has become 'king of the *síd*-mounds of Ireland' and thus overlord of the god-peoples, a doctrine not otherwise attested before the early thirteenth century.[78] Midir leaves his status disconcertingly unclear for as long as possible, forcing Eochaid to ask three times, even as his visitor insouciantly declines to take the hint. The Irish of Eochaid's day seem to have forgotten the island's ancient rulers altogether. Thus part of the *frisson* of the saga's denouement is observing the king's dawning realization that his world has suddenly slipped from its normal intelligibility, and that he is dealing with a vastly powerful supernatural being of whom he should be very afraid indeed.

The chronology of 'The Wooing of Étaín' puts Eochaid Airem firmly in the pre-Christian era, but it should be noted that here, as elsewhere in Irish saga, writers never depict the ancient gods as the objects of their ancestors' religious reverence. Gods and mortals encounter each other only as actors in a shared drama: they are united by the setting, not by the medium of cult. (We might contrast classical epic, in which the gods function simultaneously both as characters and as the recipients of human prayer.) There seems to have been a strong taboo in Ireland against the literary depiction of pagan worship in narrative. For example, when pre-Christian heroes in Irish saga swear, they do so 'by the god my people swear by': a deliberately non-specific formula.[79] In contrast, medieval Icelandic sagas do not dwell on pagan practice, but some-

---

78 *Tochmarc Étaíne*, ed. Bergin & Best, 184; *ECI*, 4; see below, 232.

79 R. Ó hUiginn ('*Tongu Do Dia Toinges Mo Thuath* and Related Expressions', in Ó Corráin, *et al.* (eds.), *Sages, Saints and Storytellers*, 332–41) suggests that this formula is a creation of the Christian era and cannot be all that old, but controversy remains: J. T. Koch ('Further to *tongu do día toinges mo thúath*, etc.' *ÉC* 29 (1992), 249–61) argues the exact opposite to Ó hUiginn, saying that the formula has a Common Celtic origin involving trying to avoid saying the name of the god Lugus. See important later discussions by T. Charles-Edwards, '*Mi a dynghaf dynghed* and related problems' in J. F. Eska, *et al.* (eds.), *Hispano-Gallo-Brittonica: Essays in honour of Professor D. Ellis Evans on the occasion of his*

times allusions to pagan worship provide 'period detail' and when necessary to the plot of a saga, they are treated openly. In *Hrafnkels saga* a
horse is dedicated to the god Freyr by the protagonist, who serves as the
god's priest, while the hero of *Víga-Glúms saga* seems to move from the
worship of Freyr to that of Odin. Similar straightforwardness would be
unthinkable in a medieval Irish tale, given the characteristic Irish
vagueness about the gods, their powers, and their places.

This is manifest on the minutest textual level in the third sub-tale of
'The Wooing of Étaín'. At the moment of maximum tension, just before
Midir reclaims his wife, he speaks to her directly, telling her that if he
wins her it will not be by virtue of his *doéas*. As it stands this is a mean-
ingless non-word, but it can be plausibly emended in two contradictory
ways, either as *dóenacht*, 'humanity', or *déacht*, 'divinity'.[80] If the latter, it
is telling that Midir openly confesses his godhood to Étaín as he pre-
pares to elevate her to the same level of being: it is no longer necessary
to cloak his power. The wavering between humanity and divinity cannot be intentional here—the scribe must have meant one or the other—
but the indeterminacy of meaning, being, and motive which it introduces perfectly embodies the artful charge Irish saga-writers could
derive from the native gods.

EXEMPLARS AND EXCESSES

What was the relationship between the society of the gods in the literature and the society of which the saga-writers themselves formed a
part? We saw earlier that the vernacular sagas are compositions for a
political elite by an intellectual one: the society of the god-peoples certainly reflects that of medieval Ireland, but from a thoroughly privileged
standpoint.

One of the oddest romantic fantasies about the so-called 'Celts'—in
itself a dubious concept—is the idea that their cultures were somehow
more egalitarian than the ancient and medieval norm. Early Irish soci-

---

sitxty-fifth birthday (Cardiff, 1995), 1–15, and S. Schumacher, 'Old Irish *Tucaid, Tocad* and
Middle Welsh *Tynghaf, Tynghet* Re-Examined', *Ériu* 46 (1995) 49–57.

80 For *dóenacht*, see *Tochmarc Étaíne*, Bergin & Best, 185, fn.2, while Carey, *CHA*, 161,
suggests *déacht*. The emendation depends on whether one takes the -*s* of *doéas* as a common manuscript abbreviation, originally used for the Latin word *sed*, 'but', but which in
Ireland came to be deployed for the native equivalent, *acht*, and for that sequence of letters when found in another word, especially (as here) the abstract noun suffix -*acht*.

ety provides the classic evidence to the contrary, for it was intensely, almost obsessively, hierarchical. Reality almost certainly differed from the archaic situation enshrined in the early (eighth century) law-tracts, but these do indicate how highly the prescriptive ideal of stratification by rank—which determined legal rights and entitlements—was valued. The most basic division in lay society was between free and unfree. The former category included the more or less noble and well-off persons who were legally independent, while the latter encompassed slaves, 'semi-free' peasants, and indentured serfs, who were permanently under a free person's authority.[81] The striking term used for all free persons—in some law-texts at least—was *nemed*, 'privileged', which etymologically means 'sacral'. In pre-Christian times this may have implied that such persons were ritually acceptable to the druidic class and so were entitled to attend religious assemblies that excluded those lower down the social spectrum.[82] The free were subdivided (in some law-tracts) into the aristocratic *sóernemed* ('free privileged/sacral ones') and the *dóernemed* ('base privileged/sacral ones'), or vassals; by the ninth and tenth centuries this division implied real distinctions of wealth and consumption.[83]

A second social division cut across this distinction between free *nemed* and base *nemed*. Most people were directly dependent on farming, because wealth meant livestock; these were known collectively as the *áes trebtha*, the settled 'farming people'. Quite different was that category of persons who maintained themselves by the exercise of their skill and knowledge. These were known as the *áes dána*, 'people of art/talent', and they were more mobile. By far the most exalted group among the *áes dána* were the *filid*, the professional experts in the memorialization of tradition, aristocratic genealogy, legal precedent, and vernacular composition. The *filid* were the only members of the *áes dána* to be counted as 'free *nemed*', and were on a level with kings, clerics, and lords.[84] All

---

81 B. Jaski in *Early Irish Kingship and Succession* (Dublin, 2000), 39–40, 45.

82 The suggestion is Eoin MacNeill's, adjudged 'a leap in the dark' but also 'exceedingly plausible' by Charles-Edwards (*ECI*, 190, 'Early Irish Law', *NHI*, i., 353–4).

83 *L&IEMI*, 70–1; references to the texts can be found in Jaski, *Early Irish Kingship and Succession*, 38–40.

84 See P. Sims-Williams & E. Poppe, 'Medieval Irish literary theory and criticism', in A. Minnis & I. Johnson, (eds.) *The Cambridge History of Literary Criticism, Volume II: the Middle Ages* (Cambridge, 2005), 292–3, and discussion of the terms in *Bechbretha: an Old Irish Law-Tract on Bee-Keeping*, ed. & trans. T. Charles-Edwards & F. Kelly (Dublin, 1993), 107–9; see also 134, fn.10, below.

the rest, from physicians and judges to smiths, harpists, and carpenters, were 'base *nemed*'.

The broadest view of the society of the god-peoples is provided in 'The Second Battle of Moytura', on which the rest of this chapter focuses. The key point is that almost everyone on the Túatha Dé side who plays a role in the story belongs to the 'people of talent': the *dramatis personae* are poets, men of learning, lawyers, druids, magicians of various stripes, physicians, blacksmiths, bronzeworkers, and craftsmen.[85] In a celebrated incident, when the young champion Lug comes to the court of the king of the god-peoples, he is told that 'no one without a talent (*dán*) enters Tara', and this proclamation is emblematic of the saga's concept of divinity. The nearest to an odd man out is Ogma, whose skill is as a 'champion' (*trénfher*). This was not historically an *áes dána* line of work, but elsewhere Ogma is famed as the inventor of the ogam alphabet; through this he is included as one of the gods associated with the literary arts *par excellence*.[86]

The peculiarity of this scenario is hammered home when Lug compiles a pre-battle roster listing the skills of the Túatha Dé nobles:

> Then in this way Lug addressed each of them in turn concerning their arts, strengthening them and addressing in such a way that every man had the courage of a king or a great lord.[87]

In terms of early Irish social norms, the text does not offer a realistic account—for a start, some of these men are actually women. More importantly, it is especially striking that the *áes dána* have swelled to become co-extensive with the lay nobility, which the reader sees happening on the interior level in the above quotation.[88] The saga-author's ideal of kingship—embodied in the handsome, brave Lug—involves omnicompe-

---

85 The major discussion is Ó Cathasaigh, '*Cath Maige Tuired* as Exemplary Myth', in Boyd (ed.), *Coire Sois*, 135–154, at 147 (originally published in P. de Brún, *et al.* (eds.), *Folia Gadelica: Essays presented by former students to R. A. Breatnach* (Cork, 1983), 1–19).

86 On this see Carey, 'Myth and Mythography', 64, fn.44.

87 *CMT*, 54, 55.

88 Historical evidence for female membership of *áes dána* professions is limited: women *filid* were not wholly unknown but seem to have been very rare (*L&IEMI*, 140, and T. O. Clancy, 'Women poets in early medieval Ireland: stating the case' in C. Meek & K. Simms (eds.), *The Fragility of her Sex? Medieval Irishwomen in their European Context* (Dublin, 1996), 43–72). I would place a small bet that the same was true of women druids in the

tence: Lug's meta-talent is that he encompasses in one person the talents of an entire society, and thus accedes to the kingship of the Túatha Dé.

Núadu, the previous king, is an oddly touching figure. Thanks to his maimed and then restored arm his kingship has already been cast in doubt once. More tellingly he is the only major Túatha Dé figure who is simply a warrior; he has no apparent *dán*, or skill, of his own. When faced with the hypertalented Lug, 'a sage in every art', he does the decent thing and steps down for the common good:

> Then Núadu, when he had seen the warrior's many powers, considered whether he could release them from the bondage they suffered at the hands of the Fomorians. So they held a council concerning the warrior, and the decision which Núadu reached was to exchange seats with the warrior. So *Samildánach* [i.e. Lug, 'the one equally-endowed-with-all-talents'] went into the king's seat, and the king stood up before him until thirteen days had passed.[89]

This is an unusual view of kingly values: while Núadu's actions are congruent with the ideals of justice, prudence, and modesty necessary in Irish rulers, it is never stated that a king should be professionally skilled in the arts of the *áes dána* as well.[90] Despite this, the saga-author clearly feels passionately that Lug's dazzling repertoire of skills makes him more qualified for lordship than his predecessor. (It is worth noting that the Dagda—another king of the Túatha Dé—also explicitly subsumes the talents of others in his own person, although he cuts a very different figure to Lug, and his multi-talentedness lies in the arena of magic.)[91] We begin to sense that in 'The Second Battle', the gods' society—whatever its ancient roots—can be seen as a projection, almost a wish-fulfilment fantasy, of the *filid* as the most socially elevated of the 'people of talent'. The *filid* advised kings, and their careers revolved around the royal courts; like many intellectuals who find themselves close to the workings of

---

pre-Christian period. Women physicians seem to have been particularly responsible for childbirth.

89 *CMT*, 42, 43.

90 *DDDH*, 279, on *Audacht Morainn*; see also C. Sterckx, 'Quand Lugh devient-il roi?', *Ollodagos* 18/2 (2004), 301–5, who makes the case that Lug's replacement of Núadu is merely temporary and for the duration of the battle itself.

91 *CMT*, 44, 45: ' "The power which you boast, I will wield it all myself." "You are the Good God [*Dagda*]!", said everyone, and the name "Dagda" stuck to him from then on.'

political power, the *filid* may have been struck by the thought that they could do a better job of wielding it.

A large number of the gods in 'The Second Battle' function as paradigmatic figures for the *áes dána* professions. We are reminded that 'gods' is an inadequate term for these beings: they are exemplars whom the Irish took to have been, in some sense, historical.[92] Their role was to provide precedent, acting as and acting out prototypical examples of particular professions and institutions. Tomás Ó Cathasaigh points out that the Mythological Cycle is especially rich in such prototypes because it intrinsically deals with events which lie deeper in the past than the other Cycles.[93]

The perception of the gods as exemplary figures possessed of authoritative knowledge was sustained by an ingrained and elite way of thinking, which asserted that 'older is better' and memorialized the past in order to validate the power structures of the present. The *filid* in particular had a great deal invested in the minimization of novelty and in myths of continuity.[94] Among them written knowledge never eclipsed the oral, even though their curriculum interfaced closely with ecclesiastical learning. (So complex is the role played by the native gods in the *filid*'s conception of their own profession that it is discussed separately in the following chapter.)

Nonetheless, the professions represented among the mythological 'people of talent' in 'The Second Battle of Moytura' do not map exactly onto those of real-life early medieval Ireland. There are two glaring differences. First, there are a plethora of people whose gift is to work magic. Actual spellcasters—and druids too, in the early period—were the objects of strong condemnation by law-tracts and penitentials.[95] Druids seem to have disappeared from Irish culture during the early eighth century: a law-tract of that era on church-community relations lumps them, with distaste, among 'satirists and inferior poets and farters and clowns and bandits and pagans and whores and other bad people'.[96] But in common with other saga writers, the author of 'The Second Battle' thoughtfully

---

92 *DDDH*, 289.

93 Ó Cathasaigh (in Boyd (ed.), *Coire Sois*, 140, 147) notes that this is a story full of firsts, including the first satire and the first keening.

94 *L&IEMI*, 71.

95 F. Kelly, *A Guide to Early Irish Law* (Dublin, 1988), 279; L. Breatnach, *A Companion to the Corpus iuris hibernici* (Dublin, 2005), 286–7.

96 *Córus Béscnai*, in *Corpus Iuris Hibernici*, ed. D. A. Binchy [6 vols.] (Dublin, 1978), ii., 526, ll.15–9.

attempts to re-imagine a lost social order in which druids had occupied an exalted place. Where other professions are exemplified by individuals—Dían Cécht in medicine, Credne in bronzesmithing, the obscure Én mac Ethamain in poetry and historical tradition—those who work magic seem to appear as a group. 'Our druids and people of power are numerous', the obstinate doorkeeper of Tara tells Lug.

There seem to be distinctions between specialties, however.[97] The sorcerer (*corrguinech*) causes earthquakes; the druid conjures rains of fire and supercharges the Túatha Dé with courage, while spooking the Fomorians and leaving them unable to urinate; the cupbearer—not, one might have thought, a conspicuously magical role—turns out to be able to prevent Ireland's rivers and lakes from yielding up their waters to the thirsty enemy.[98] We hear too of the god-peoples' two witches (*bantúathaid*), who transform trees, stones, and clods of earth into warriors. Finally, just before the great battle, it is revealed that in a pinch *all* of the *áes dána* seem to possess magical power, for together they 'chanted spells against the Fomorian hosts'.[99]

In all this the saga-author may be reflecting on ways to signal the differences between his time and that of the Túatha Dé. It is usual in medieval Irish literature for the druid to be a magician rather than a pagan priest, but the suspicion dawns that the striking overplus of magic workers in the society of the gods represents a—perhaps unconscious—reflection of the ecclesiastical orders in Irish society. The idea that druids had been unholy mirror images of Christian clerics goes back as far as Muirchú's seventh-century 'Life of Patrick', and while those in 'The Second Battle' are not exactly unholy, their powers are certainly uncanny and massively destructive.

If the presence of powerful sorcerers in tales represents a self-consciously fantastical deviation from the norms of ninth-century Ireland, there is a second difference, less striking but no less revealing; the legal profession. While secular jurists (*brithemain*) were an essential part of the flesh-and-blood *áes dána*, there is no native god, in this saga or any other medieval Irish text, who acts as the prototypical source of legal knowledge. Though there *are* references in the saga to the presence of jurists among the god-peoples, their real-life importance among the *áes dána* has been radically downgraded.

97 *CMT*, 40, 41.
98 *CMT*, 42–5, 96. For parallel instances of this topos, see *DDDH*, 213–4.
99 Witches in *CMT*, 52–55; *áes dána* chanting spells, 46, 47.

Reasons are not far to seek. Firstly, the practice and enforcement of law in early Christian Ireland was diffused among different personnel: jurists, *filid*, canon lawyers, and kings all played a role.[100] More importantly, the law and druidism were the two skilled professions most transformed by Ireland's conversion. Druids, deprived of their status and privilege, disappeared from society altogether, while the legal profession seems to have been brought under the thorough ideological domination of the church at an early date.[101] How compatible was native, pre-Christian legal tradition with canon law and with the Mosaic law of the Old Testament? How was the church to be organized within Irish society, and what form of legal relationship should exist between the church and the *túath*, the wider community? These had been urgent questions in the sixth and seventh centuries.[102]

The law fundamentally differed from (say) medicine or metalworking in that it was impossible for its practitioners to maintain that it had been passed down unchanged from pre-Christian times: the inescapable importance of the church in Irish society meant that evidence to the contrary was everywhere they looked.[103] Though men of learning believed that their legal system was of native origin, they simultaneously maintained that its continuity with the specifically pagan past was limited. This paradoxical attitude to the legal framework was encapsulated in a famous origin legend, found in the prologue to the second recension of

---

100 *L&IEMI*, 136, and see T. Charles-Edwards, *The early mediaeval Gaelic lawyer* [Quiggin Pamphlets on the Sources of Mediaeval Gaelic History 4] (Department of Anglo-Saxon, Norse, and Celtic, University of Cambridge, 1999); but see too R. C. Stacey, *Dark Speech: The Performance of Law in Early Ireland* (Philadelphia, 2007), 151, for the jurist Caratnia as a figure whose professional knowledge has supernatural roots in the otherworld.

101 I do not mention the *filid* as a 'transformed' profession here because it is entirely possible that they came into being as a learned order within the matrix of Ireland's conversion, however insistently they harped upon their ancient roots. On this see Johnston's astute comments, *L&IEMI*, 16–8.

102 Useful survey by Charles-Edwards, 'Early Irish Law', *NHI*, i., 331–70; see also D. Ó Corráin, L. Breatnach, & A. Breen, 'The Laws of the Irish', *Peritia* 3 (1984), 382–438.

103 Ronald Hutton has pointed out to me [pers. comm.] that the idea of a divinity who gives a lawcode to humanity is distinctively Middle Eastern and not characteristic of Indo-European mythologies; Indo-European deities were often, however, patrons of justice. If I had to guess under the auspices of which deity pre-Christian men of law felt themselves to work, I would go for Lugus: his name *may* be related to the word for 'oath' (OIr *lugae*); possibly he was once the god who oversaw contracts and the giving of sureties.

an important early collection of native law, the *Senchas Már* ('Great Tradition'). This story argued that the Holy Spirit had revealed to Ireland's pagan poets and judges the 'law of nature'—meaning the inbuilt human sense of right and wrong. In the same way, Old Testament law had been divinely revealed to the biblical patriarchs and prophets. Both had now been superseded by the law of Christian scripture, and the prologue explains how St Patrick had purged Irish law of elements incompatible with the new religion, forging native and Christian law into a harmonious unity.[104] The elegance of the pseudohistorical prologue lies in the way that it simultaneously asserts continuance and reformation of repertoire, but it also makes clear why the law, as a body of knowledge, could not be fathered on a native deity—a functional role significantly occupied in the *Senchas Már* story by the Holy Spirit.

MIRRORINGS AND REVERSALS

Observations such as these on the gods as emblems of antiquity lead us to a further, crucial, aspect of 'The Second Battle of Moytura': it is a story of traumatic upheaval in the gods' status. Gregory Nagy has observed that Greek mythology was about disequilibrium—how forces at work in the world get or got out of balance—while Greek ritual aimed to restore equilibrium.[105] The literary gods of Ireland have no ritual or cult attached, but in their case too the theme of supernatural forces getting out of balance may be a sign of a genuinely old stratum of material. In the saga the social status of the gods gets radically wrenched out of joint before it is righted; the remainder of this chapter is devoted to examining the system of ideas and ideals which underpins this scenario.

Critics have made plain that 'The Second Battle' can be looked at as a pattern of contrasts and binaries, in which image is answered by mirror image.[106] My own view is that the plot is more like shards of mirror

---

104 This passage has been much discussed; for the text see 'An Edition of the Pseudo-Historical prologue to the *Senchas Már*', ed. & trans. J. Carey, *Ériu* 45 (1994), 1–32; select seminal discussions are McCone, *PPCP*, 92–102; J. Carey, 'The Two Laws in Dubthach's Judgment', *CMCS* 19 (1990), 1–18; and Nagy, *CW&A*, 200–8. See *DDDH*, 247 fn.81 for further references.

105 G. Nagy, *The Ancient Greek Hero in 24 Hours* (Cambridge, MA, 2013), 561, 587.

106 Elizabeth Gray's eloquent structuralist approach has been the main voice here; note her indispensable reading of the entire saga, '*Cath Maige Tuired*: Myth and Structure', *Éigse* 18 (1980–1), 183–209, and *Éigse* 19 (1982–3), 1–35, 230–62. Her work complements the

stuck into the ground at angles to one another: there are multiple lines of reflection, so that every incident finds echoes and inversions in several others. On the most basic level we have the opposition between the god-peoples, who are a just society, and the dastardly Fomorians, who are not. The saga clearly presents the ideal society as an organic whole in which everyone has a role and where people's talents are put to good use. The two races were later polarized in terms of beauty and deformity—the Fomorians were sometimes said to have one leg, one arm, and one eye. However, the author of 'The Second Battle' either does not know this tradition or has chosen to avoid it: for him the god-peoples and the Fomorians possess the same (huge) physical size and shape.

The broad opposition between the races is epitomized by Bres and Lug, unjust and just kings respectively. They are halfbreeds who mirror one another: Bres has a Túatha Dé mother and a Fomorian father, while Lug has the reverse. (The saga's fearsomely patriarchal message is that only paternal blood affects one's character.)[107] Lug gives each professional the honour due for his or her skills, but Bres insists on reducing their noble status to servility, imposing demeaning tasks on the Dagda and Ogma, the most senior pair of brothers among the god-peoples. The Dagda is forced to build ramparts for Bres's fort, while Ogma has to hulk firewood about. Tradition numbered the Dagda among the kings of the Túatha Dé, and under Irish law a king who took up manual labour was deprived of his honour price.[108] Furthermore, the greater the number of banks and ditches around one's ringfort, the higher one's standing, so the Dagda's degrading loss of status is made all the worse by serving to enhance that of Bres; a figure who should live in a kingly house is forced to help build one. The task's brute physicality also serves to undercut the Dagda's magic. In 'The Wooing of Étaín' we saw him use his powers to make massive changes to the landscape, work that came with no shame attached because it was performed without effort. But here the half-starved Dagda is stuck in a ditch, shovelling away, so that Bres's monstrous imposition debases the god's nobility and cripples his power.

---

more historicist and equally seminal investigations of John Carey, 'Myth and mythography in *Cath Maige Tuired*', *SC* 24/25 (1989/90), 53–6, and Kim McCone, 'A Tale of Two Ditties: Poet and Satirist in *Cath Maige Tuired*', in Ó Corráin, *et al.* (eds.), *Sages, Saints and Storytellers*, 122–143.

107 I draw here on N. MacLeod, 'Irish Law and the Wars of the Túatha Dé Danann', in L. Breatnach *et al.* (eds.), *Proceedings of the XIV International Congress of Celtic Studies, held in Maynooth University, 1–5 August 2011* (Dublin, 2015), 75–94.

108 F. Kelly, *A Guide to Irish Law* (Dublin, 1988), 18–9.

Ogma's assigned task is also both apt and abject. That the Túatha Dé's champion or *trénfher*, 'strong man', must haul wood around is bad enough, but the significance goes deeper. Though the saga-author leaves this unmentioned, Ogma was said to be the inventor of the ogam alphabet. In Irish the word for a letter of that alphabet was *fid*, 'wood', so that it may be that the wood he is forced to carry was intended to be a parody of the letters he created. That such tasks should be given to these gods indicates a world thrown into monstrous disorder, and the reversal of social norms would no doubt have induced a shudder of horror in the saga's noble audience.

It emerges, therefore, that a core theme of the saga is the sense of proportion characteristic of the god-peoples versus the lack of proportion endemic among the Fomorians; Fomorian social organization has only two settings, *too much* and *not enough*. The classic instance is the peculiar but pivotal moment at the end of the tale, in which Bres tries to ensure his life is spared by Lug.[109] Lug has a minor figure with him, an otherwise-unknown jurist named Máeltne:

> 'Is there anything else which will save you, Bres?', said Lug.
>
> 'There is indeed. Tell your jurist that they [the god-peoples] will reap a harvest every quarter in return for sparing me.' Lug said to Máeltne, 'Shall Bres be spared for giving the men of Ireland a harvest of grain every quarter?' 'This has suited us', said Máeltne. 'Spring for ploughing and sowing, and the beginning of summer for maturing the strength of the grain, and the beginning of autumn for the full brightness of the grain, and for reaping it. Winter for consuming it.'
>
> 'That does not save you', said Lug to Bres.
>
> 'Máeltne has given bitter alarms!', said he.
>
> 'Less rescues you', said Lug.
>
> 'What?', asked Bres.
>
> 'How shall the men of Ireland plough? How shall they sow? How shall they reap? If you make known these things you will be saved.'
>
> 'Say to them, on Tuesday their ploughing; on Tuesday their sowing seed in the field; on Tuesday their reaping.'[110]

---

109 Discussed by W. Sayers, 'Bargaining for the Life of Bres in *Cath Maige Tuired*', *BBCS* 34 (1987), 26–40.

110 *CMT*, 68, 69.

This episode is frequently identified as the apogee of the tale's Indo-European archaism, the acquisition by the gods—who are already excellent warriors and craftspeople—of the secrets of cultivation, forced out of a race of more primitive beings who are connected with the earth's fertility.[111] Tomás Ó Cathasaigh says that Lug had 'no competence in agriculture until he wrested it from Bres'.[112] The great mythographer Georges Dumézil saw this episode as the incorporation of the 'third function'—agricultural productivity—by the priestly and warrior sectors of society, the 'first' and 'second' functions in his formulation of ancient Indo-European ideology.

I must admit to a certain scepticism that the right thing is being fastened onto here: the episode seems oddly vestigial in the context of the tale as a whole.[113] The most recent scholar to have examined this incident in detail, William Sayers, argues that it is simply not the case that the Túatha Dé in the saga know nothing of farming before Bres is strong-armed by Lug; to me this seems quite correct. The Túatha Dé certainly know about livestock, for we hear how their cattle were commandeered by the Fomorians, and as Máeltne's words to Bres show, the Túatha Dé are also perfectly *au fait* with the seasonal cycle of ploughing the land and sowing and reaping cereal crops.[114] Why then does Lug need Bres's help? The Túatha Dé seem simultaneously to know and not to know.

One solution is to accept that Ó Cathasaigh and Dumézil are correct in thinking that the 'secrets-of-agriculture' theme is archaic, but to suggest in addition that the saga author has tried, not entirely successfully, to adapt that inherited theme to support his basic cultural ideal: that the wisdom and justice of Túatha Dé society is underpinned by balance and proportion, qualities which the Fomorians signally lack. We remember

---

111 See especially G. Dumézil, *Jupiter, Mars, Quirinus* (Paris, 1941), 171–2, and *Mythe et épopée* (Paris, 1961), i., 289–90; a scepticism anticipated by P. Mac Cana, *Celtic Mythology* (London, 1970), 60–4, and S. O'Brien, 'Indo-European Eschatology: A Model', *Journal of Indo-European Studies* 4 (1976), 295–320.

112 Ó Cathasaigh, in Boyd (ed.), *Coire Sois*, 145.

113 With exceptions such as Tomás Ó Cathasaigh and the late Proinsias Mac Cana, use of Dumézil's ideas by Celtic scholars has been low-key. Dumézil's 'trifunctional hypothesis' has attained a high degree of acceptance among Indo-Europeanists, but controversies remain: note the strong criticism in W. W. Belier, *Decayed Gods: Origin and Development of Georges Dumézil's Idéologie Tripartite* (Leiden, 1991).

114 *CMT*, 71, and Sayers, 'Bargaining for the Life of Bres', 27. Sayers makes an ingenious case that Bres's words in this passage amount to a trick, each phrase he uses being sufficiently semantically ambiguous to amount to a curse in the guise of a boon.

that Bres tries to bargain for his life by offering the Túatha Dé four harvests a year and the prospect of cows which are never out of milk. Máeltne and Lug rightly refuse this grotesque (and exhausting) distortion of the natural rhythm of the seasons.[115]

MEDICINE AND MURDER

The effect of this opposition between Túatha Dé proportion (balance) and Fomorian disproportion (imbalance) is not monolithic in the saga. The overall impression given by the god-peoples of a justly articulated society is enhanced by a single lurid counter-example: the physician Dían Cécht's murder of his son.

The episode begins after Núadu has lost an arm in combat:

Now Núadu was being treated, and Dían Cécht put a silver arm on him which had the movement of any other arm. But his son Míach did not like that. He went to the arm and said 'joint to its joint and sinew to sinew'; and it healed in nine days and nights. The first three days he carried it against his side, and it became covered with skin. The second three days he carried it against his chest. The third three days he would throw white wisps of black bulrushes after they had been blackened in a fire.[116]

Dían Cécht did not like that cure. He hurled a sword at the crown of his son's head and cut his skin to the flesh. The young

---

115 A point well made by E. A. Gray, 'Cath Maige Tuired: Myth and Structure', Éigse 19 (1982–3), 251–2: 'Bres's suggestion would disrupt the natural order of the agricultural cycle... four harvests would mean four ploughings, four sowings, and four reapings: four times the labour, with no period of time set aside for rest and enjoyment of the yield.'

116 Gray comments that the 'third element of Míach's medical practice, casting wisps or tufts of blackened rush, remains obscure' (CMT, 85). Edward Pettit ('Míach's Healing of Núadu in Cath Maige Tuired', Celtica 27 (2013), 167–71) ingeniously suggests that Núadu is imagined as having to extract starchy white fibres from charred bulrush roots, the fiddly task demonstrating his restored dexterity. He may well be right, and I certainly agree on the latter point; but could the phrase—I diffidently suggest—be a reference to a throwing game, like our darts? If one took the tufty end of a bulrush, sharpened the stem to a point and blackened the tip in a fire to harden it, it would then make a very serviceable dart. The point is that Núadu's healing is progressive, so that this third stage must represent the restoration of full functioning: if he can throw rush-darts, all his joints are working and he has regained fine motor control in his fingers.

man healed it by means of his skill. He struck him again and cut his flesh until he reached the bone. The young man healed it by the same means. He struck the third blow and reached the membrane of his brain. The young man healed this too by the same means. Then he struck the fourth blow and cut out the brain, so that Míach died; and Dían Cécht said that no physician could heal him of that blow.

After that, Míach was buried by Dían Cécht, and three hundred and sixty-five herbs grew through the grave, corresponding to the number of his joints and sinews. Then Airmed [Míach's sister] spread her cloak and uprooted those herbs according to their properties. Dían Cécht came to her and mixed up the herbs, so that no one knows their proper healing qualities unless the Holy Spirit taught them afterwards. And Dían Cécht said 'Though Míach no longer lives, Airmed shall remain.'[117]

This famous episode is remarkably difficult to interpret. As Edward Pettit has recently pointed out, there is strong evidence that it is a late creation and not part of any putative substrate of myth.[118] I suggest that the story of Míach's murder at his father's hands was the invention of the author of the saga, and like Pettit I am deeply sceptical of any interpretations of the sequence that detect archaic Indo-European patterns of ideas.

It is certainly clear that the saga-author felt able to make radical changes to traditions about the Túatha Dé in order to fit them into his opposing in-tales and patterns of moral inversion. For example, there is good evidence that in order to make Bres a foil for Lug, the author deliberately turned him into the villain of the tale. Elsewhere he is a card-carrying member of the Túatha Dé: the Dagda sends Elcmar off to visit him in 'The Wooing of Étaín', and in texts written a century or so after 'The Second Battle', but probably representing older tradition, Bres's father Elatha is no Fomorian king, but a major ancestor among the god-

---

117 *CMT*, 32, 33. I have changed Gray's 'hand' to 'arm' (*lám* meant both).

118 See again Pettit, 'Míach's Healing of Núadu', 158–71. I am unconvinced by Gray's analysis of this episode—in which she finds pervasive Dumézilian second and third-function symbolism ('*Cath Maige Tuired*: Myth and Structure', *Éigse* 19 (1982–3), 9–12). She writes that 'there is no suggestion that Dían Cécht's response is excessive': I cannot believe that a ninth-century audience—in a society in which kinslaying was regarded with especial horror—would think this, or that they would find Míach's cure 'negative, "excessive"' or 'intrusive', rather than miraculous and impressive. Dían Cécht does not emerge from the incident 'supreme', as Gray says, but as deeply and obviously flawed.

peoples. The Dagda and Ogma number among his sons.[119] We have re-turned to the idea that saga-authors could make bold artistic choices and shifts of emphasis when handling the native gods. The line between myth making and myth breaking is blurred, as a direct result of the fact that these gods were objects of representation in a culture in which they were no longer worshipped. Again, the Greeks offer an analogy. Tragedians could not radically change the attributes of gods who were the focus of contemporary cult (though they could select from variant myths), but they *could* innovate to some degree with non-divinities. The first audience of Euripides' *Medea*, for example, was probably shocked by the play's climax: the heroine was not traditionally responsible for the murder of her children, and the play represents a single playwright's twisting of an inherited story into a new shape.[120]

By staging a brutal contrast, the episode of Dían Cécht's murder of his own child highlights what the author feels the Túatha Dé should be. Meritocracy was only one part of the law of status as it related to the *áes dána*—for the *filid*, at least, paternal ancestry was also crucial. But the episode's representation of intergenerational conflict seems basically meritocratic in that a father reacts with an access of rage and jealousy to his son's professional superiority.[121] (One wonders how often such feel-ings actually arose in professional families in medieval Ireland when natural talent differed.) Humility and unselfishness are key virtues in this tale, but Dían Cécht is filled with pride and spite. We remember that in the face of Lug's excellence Núadu stood down as king of the god-peoples, an act clearly seen as innately correct. But Dían Cécht's rival is his own son, whose medical talent can restore the missing limb which he

119 Thus Carey, 'Myth and Mythography', 56–8. The title of the saga in the (unique) sixteenth-century MS—'This tale below is the Battle of Moytura and the Birth of Bres son of Elatha and his reign'—seems to underscore the impression that the text's account of Bres is a noteworthy innovation. If 'bad Bres' were a part of the age-old tradition of the second battle, why was it necessary to insert the title of his 'conception tale' at the very beginning of the saga? See *CMT*, 7–8.

120 That this astonishing play only came third in the City Dionysia festival has long been taken as evidence that Euripides' innovation did not find favour; nonetheless it soon became a canonical part of the myth. On this see M. Ewans, *Opera from the Greek: Studies in the Poetics of Appropriation* (Aldershot, 2007), 55.

121 Ó Cathasaigh (in Boyd (ed.) *Coire Sois*, 46–50) discusses this incident in terms of intergenerational conflict. See T. Charles-Edwards, 'The Context and Uses of Literacy in Early Christian Ireland', in H. Pryce (ed.), *Literacy in Medieval Celtic Societies* (Cambridge, 1998), at 70–2, and Johnston, *L&IEMI*, 136 on the legal background to the *filid* having hon-our prices dependent on both skills and ancestry.

himself can only artificially imitate in silver. Like Bres's offer of four harvests a year, Núadu's cybernetic prosthesis identifies the conspicuously
unnatural—the inorganic, the unseasonal—as a chief marker of 'Fomorian'
unrighteousness. Here artificial enhancement is the prelude to murder,
and in this episode Dían Cécht makes himself Fomorian in his values.[122]

There are good reasons to think that this episode in the saga is an innovation and not something inherited from older mythology. Firstly,
there are a number of other medieval accounts of the healing of Núadu,
but not one of them mentions the killing of Míach by Dían Cécht.[123] Furthermore, a version of the story in the twelfth-century Book of Leinster
not only omits Míach's murder, it omits Míach completely. Instead, Dían
Cécht and the metalworker Credne—appropriately enough—are assigned
the task of restoring Núadu's arm; this version probably represents the
oldest tradition. The episode as a whole is also oddly inconsequential:
there is no attempt to bring Dían Cécht to justice for his crime, despite
the fact that the narrative has already featured—immediately before—a
murder investigation plus autopsy, conducted upon the satirist Cridenbél.[124] More tellingly, later in the saga, Míach is alive again, without explanation, and is assisting his father in the operation of a magical healing well.[125] These discrepancies are strongly suggestive that this new
episode was not fully worked into the texture of the tradition—or even
into the texture of the saga itself.

Secondly the murder makes nonsense of Dían Cécht's role as the exemplar of the profession of medicine. This is striking because he is so
well-attested in this capacity in sources outside 'The Second Battle'; his
name, for example, is attached to a medico-legal tract, *Bretha Déin Chécht*
('The Judgments of Dían Cécht'), which addresses the compensations
due for personal injury.[126] It is worth noting that bodies of legal judge-

122 Dían Cécht is not by any means an unmoderated villain; it is striking that the
only member of the Túatha Dé who is obviously rotten to the core—the greedy satirist
Cridenbél—also has to do with precious metal, via which he meets his end, being unable
to digest gold (*CMT*, 30–1). See comments below, 118, 122–3.

123 See the comments of Gray, *CMT*, 85; the same point is made—with full references—by Pettit, 'Míach's Healing of Núadu', 160–1.

124 *CMT*, 30–1.

125 *CMT*, 54, 55; Pettit, 'Míach's Healing of Núadu', 161.

126 For the text, see 'Bretha Déin Chécht', ed. O. Bergin, *Ériu* 20 (1966), 1–66. There is
some difficulty about the meaning of the god's name. As length-marks were often not
written in by Irish scribes, the first element (often spelled *Dian*) is likely to be *dían*, a
common adjective meaning 'swift'. The second element may mean 'power', but we only
know this from 'Cormac's Glossary' (*Sanas Cormaic*, ed. Meyer, 36–7) which glosses the

ments were also fathered on the gods Goibnenn, Credne, and Luchtaine.[127] As Neil MacLeod has noted, our 'mythological' story mirrors the tract's concerns with the compensations for injury, the grading of wounds according to an ascending scale of seriousness, and the payments due to physicians.[128] It appears the legal text has influenced the supposedly 'mythological' story, not the other way around, for the overall effect is a massive, undermining irony, especially as the legal context of Míach's murder is made explicit. The god's legal character as the originator of judgments is inverted in the saga: he causes injury rather than cures it, and breaks the law rather than prescribes it.

Thirdly, the whole thing has a learned, inkhorn air. Dían Cécht's children have schematic names, for both are measures of the kind an apothecary might use. Míach means 'bushel (of grain)' and Airmed a 'dry measure'; MacLeod has pointed out that the size of cuts and other injuries were measured in grains, again suggesting that the inspiration for these figures lay in the law.[129] The names *might* be old—in Greek myth the children of the healer-god Asklepios are even more schematic—but they also look suspiciously artificial, especially as *airmed* in particular is a learned glossary word. Finally, the detail that three hundred and sixty-five herbs grew from Míach's grave clearly draws on the early grammatical handbook *Auraicept na n-Éces* ('The Scholar's Primer'), which asserts that three hundred and sixty-five is the number of bones and sinews in

---

word (in this very name) as *cumachta*, '(magic) power', but this may originally have been simply a guess; there was also a word *cécht*, 'ploughshare', presumably not relevant. Wikipedia—of all places—has the unreferenced suggestion that the second element could be a noun from earlier *k^wok^w-o-, cognate with English 'cook' and 'concoction': the healer-god's name would thus originally have meant something like 'Speedy Potion' or even 'He-who-is-Swift-with-Healing-Remedies.' The major problem is that this root is only attested in the Brittonic branch of Celtic, which makes this otherwise attractive suggestion unlikely. See J. Vendryes, *Lexique etymologique de l'Irlandais ancien* (Dublin & Paris, 1959), C-52, R. Matasović, *Etymological Dictionary of Proto-Celtic* (Leiden & Brill, 2009), 180, and (with caution) *EIH&M*, 472–3.

127 One of the things that disqualified someone from acting as a judge (*brithem*) was being unversed 'in the judgments of Dían Cécht and Goibniu and Credne and Luchtaine': see R. Thurneysen, 'Aus Dem Irischen Recht V.', *ZCP* 18 (1930), 363, and *Irische Texte* iii., 26. Goibniu aside, these were included in the so-called pseudohistorical prologue to the *Senchus Már* in a list of old authorities whose works were in existence and were accepted in as much as they were compatible with Christian law.

128 N. MacLeod, 'The Not-So-Exotic Law of Dian Cécht', in G. Evans, *et al.* (eds.), *Origins and Revivals: Proceedings of the First Australian Conference of Celtic Studies* (Sydney, 2000), 381–400.

129 MacLeod, 'The Not-So-Exotic Law', 386.

the human body. The parts of the body are used extensively in the *Auraicept* to image the subdivisions of native grammatical learning. We are clearly in that world, and a further sign of Dían Cécht's metaphorical 'Fomorian-ness' is his sudden desire to destroy knowledge. Although Airmed has gathered all the separate herbs and sorted them out on her cloak, her father scatters them, 'and from that time no one has known the virtue of herbs unless taught by the Holy Spirit'. Perhaps this scene contains an element of social commentary: it teaches that native systems of learning are vulnerable not just to attrition by time, but also, more insidiously, to wrong values among those who profess expertise. The author asserts in a rare moment of overt piety that true knowledge is inspired by God, echoing the doctrine of the pseudohistorical prologue to the *Senchas Már*, in which the Holy Spirit was said to have inspired the framing of good laws among the pagan Irish. Even if this episode is not the invention of the author of 'The Second Battle'—which is perfectly possible given his *áes dána* orientation—it is clearly rooted in the lore of the *filid*, not in that of physicians. It is difficult to imagine that Irish physicians could have told this sordid story about their own professional exemplar, because in a sense it is an origin legend for pharmacological ignorance.

My final reason for thinking this episode to be an innovation is more tentative. It closely resembles another (probably genuinely mythological) anecdote found only in sources later than 'The Second Battle' itself. This is a constant problem when dealing with Irish myth, because the fact that a tradition about a divinity appears in an early text does not mean that tradition is genuinely pre-Christian, nor must every apparently mythological detail in a later text necessarily be a medieval invention. The story upon which the killing of Míach may be modelled is found in one version of the *dindshenchas* ('Placename Lore') associated with the river Barrow (*Berba*).[130] Such lore of significant places was a crucial part of the curriculum of the *filid*.[131] As is typical for *dindshen-*

---

130 Verse in *The Metrical Dindshenchas*, ed. E. Gwynn (5 vols., Dublin, 1903–35), ii., 62, 63; prose in 'The Prose Tales in the Rennes *Dindshenchas*', ed. & trans. W. Stokes, *RC* 15 (1894) 272–336 and 418–84, at 304–5. Unusually for *dindshenchas* the actual etymology is not fanciful: *Berba(e)* really does mean the 'seething' river (< *b^her-w-yā*) in a way that was transparent to Irish speakers thanks to the verb *berbaid* 'boils, cooks'. See D. N. Parsons & P. Sims-Williams (eds.), *Ptolemy: Towards a linguistic atlas of the earliest Celtic place-names of Europe* (Aberystwyth, 2000), 104.

131 See *Dá ernail déc na filidheachta*, ed. R. Thurneysen, *Irische Texte* iii., 1, §2; T. Ó Concheanainn, 'The three forms of *Dinnshenchas Érenn*', *Journal of Celtic Studies* 3 (1981) 88–131; P. Mac Cana, 'Place-names and mythology in Irish tradition', in G. W. MacLennan

chas we have the story in two forms, an allusive poem and a piece of explanatory prose.

These two works differ in minor details, but it is the basic plot that is important. The Morrígan has a son named Méiche, whose heart contains three serpents. If these grow they will lay waste to Ireland—presumably after bursting through Méiche's chest wall.[132] Dían Cécht extracts Méiche's heart—fatally—and incinerates it and the snakes. The ashes are so toxic that when he throws them into the river Barrow (*Berba*) the water churns—hence its name, 'Seething One'. All the fish in the river are boiled alive.

In this tale, Dían Cécht again kills someone's son, though this time not his own, and again the intervention takes destructively surgical form, with the extraction of the heart; we recall that Dían Cécht ended his son's life by cutting out his brain.[133] The Méiche episode is an early version of that cliché of contemporary medical drama: should an infected individual be sacrificed to prevent an inevitable threat? Lastly the names are similar: the genitive of *Míach* is in fact *Méich*. Could a pair of wholly unrelated stories have existed in which the healer-god kills a youth by extracting, in each case, a vital organ? Given the similarity of the characters' names, it is surely unlikely.

There are several convincing reasons to think that the *dindshenchas* story is the prototype. Firstly, although Méiche's death at the hands of Dían Cécht is horrifying, the divine physician's intervention is nonetheless diagnostic. The murder of Míach in contrast turns that role on its head. (As an aside, one *can* imagine Irish physicians transmitting the story of the Morrígan's son, for it is an encapsulation of the kind of ethical dilemma which they must have faced, not least in the case of complications in childbirth: when is it right for a doctor to kill in order to save?) Secondly, the contextual detail of the Míach episode in 'The Second Battle' is overtly legal, learned, and Christian, while the 'feel' of the Méiche story is more mythological, for the adders in Méiche's heart seem to embody and concentrate the destructive energies of his mother, the goddess of war.

(ed.), *Proceedings of the first North-American Congress of Celtic Studies* (Ottawa, 1988), 319–341; P. S. Hellmuth, 'The *Dindshenchas* and Irish literary tradition', in J. Carey *et al.* (eds.), *Cín Chille Chúile, Texts, Saints and Places: Essays in Honour of Pádraig Ó Riain* (Aberystwyth, 2004), 116–26.

132 The verse refers to only one serpent, with three coils.

133 Note MacLeod's comments on *Bretha Déin Chécht* and brain injuries, 'The Not-So-Exotic Law', 386.

While there are various manuscript versions of the Méiche story, only the oldest versions (in the early twelfth-century Book of Leinster) actually name Dían Cécht as the executioner.[134] Elsewhere an entirely separate warrior named *Mac* Cécht is consistently said to have done the deed.[135] Certain determination is not possible, but the fact that both the verse *and* the prose accounts of this story in the Book of Leinster—which are separate in the manuscript—name Dían Cécht as Méiche's killer suggests that this is the older tradition. If the story of Míach's killing was inspired by that of Méiche, as I suggest, then it may well have been the creation of the original author of 'The Second Battle'. It slots into the ideological patterns of his tale a little too neatly, while at the same time feeling oddly out of place on the level of plot. (If the episode were removed from the text of 'The Second Battle' we would never guess that something was missing.)[136] The shift in the *dindshenchas* story from Dían Cécht to Mac Cécht might have come about when the 'new' story of Míach's slaying entered circulation in the late ninth century: there would be a need to differentiate the new tradition from the older story, the elements of which had been recast.[137]

In terms of the values of Túatha Dé society, Dían Cécht's arrogant murder of Míach identifies him as one of very few exceptions that prove the rule: envy and excess are characteristically 'Fomorian', even when found among the Túatha Dé. While the god-peoples labour under the Fomorian yoke, Bres is a wretched host by the standards of an early Irish noble: we are told that no matter how many times the god-peoples came

134 *The Book of Leinster, formerly Lebar na Núachongbála*, ed. O. Bergin & R. I. Best, *et al.* (5 vols., Dublin, 1954–83), iv., 858 (verse) and iii., 702 (prose).

135 T. F. O'Rahilly's arguments (*EIH&M*, 66, 125, 472–3) that Dían Cécht and Mac Cécht are in origin both doublets of an ancient sun-god are misguided and so of little help here. (Dían Cécht himself has no connection to the sun: O'Rahilly was led to think he did via an etymology of the name which is probably incorrect). There are also *two* Mac Céchts in Irish tradition, one a more or less human warrior in the service of the legendary king Conaire the Great, and one a member of the god-peoples; see *DDDH*, 131, 142–4.

136 Gray ('*Cath Maige Tuired*: Myth and Structure', *Éigse* 19, 1–13) makes the apt point that this part of the saga makes up a sequence focusing on contrasting paternal-filial relations: it is certainly the case that Dían Cécht's rivalry with Míach inverts the supportive relationship between Óengus and the Dagda in the immediately preceding episode, though in both cases the son's knowledge and insight is superior to that of the father.

137 If so this must have happened by the writing of the Book of Leinster: an embedded stanza of verse in the Book of Leinster prose *dindshenchas* about Berba names Mac Cécht as the killer, even though preceding prose names Dían Cécht.

to visit him, as they left 'their breaths never smelled of ale'.[138] But when open war between the two peoples is about to begin, they go to the opposite extreme, for when the Dagda is sent on an embassy, the Fomorians grotesquely overfeed him on pain of death, leaving him stuffed to the gills. It is to this episode—and its even less savoury aftermath—that we now turn.

GOOD CLEAN DIRT

The in-tale of the Dagda's visit to the Fomorian camp and his return journey is a subversive meditation on what makes a god 'exemplary': that is, the extent to which he or she embodies the values which the author thinks should triumph. It is also perhaps the most disconcerting episode in the entire medieval Irish corpus, for it encompasses force-feeding, female-on-male fisticuffs, defecation, and the outdoor copulation of titanic beings (twice); as such it genuinely merits the over-used term 'Rabelaisian'.[139]

The story begins on the eve of the long-delayed showdown between the god-peoples and the Fomorians. The Fomorian forces are about to make landfall and camp at Mag Cétne, about twelve miles north of what is now Sligo Town.[140] Our passage is a sexual and scatological interlude in preparation for battle, and it forms a thematically distinct subsection, as one of two parallel passages in the saga in which the Dagda is the protagonist. (The first is the Dagda's confrontation with—and justified killing of—the parasitic Cridenbél, who demands the best bits of the god's dinner while he is being forced to dig ramparts for Bres's fort.)[141]

The action falls into three episodes of increasing length. In the first, the Dagda has a sexual encounter with the war-goddess, the Morrígan, whom he finds straddling the river Unshin and washing a few days before Samain. After their love-making, the Morrígan, gifted with pro-

---

138 *CMT*, 32, 33.

139 Whitely Stokes left these passages out of his earlier edition ('The Second Battle of Moytura', *RC* 12 (1891), 52–130, 306–8); astonishingly for a very major saga and the keystone of the mythological cycle, an unbowdlerized English translation was not available until Gray's 1983 edition. There is an Early Modern Irish version of the tale, in which this episode is not included (*Cath Muighe Tuireadh: The Second Battle of Magh Tuireadh*, ed. B. Ó Cuív (Dublin, 1945)).

140 Misspelt as Mag *Scétne* in the text; see *CMT*, 140.

141 *CMT*, 28, 29; 30, 31.

phetic insight, pinpoints the location of the Fomorians' future landfall and promises her supernatural help in weakening and destroying their king, Indech mac Dé Domnann. She asks that the *áes dána* among the god-peoples come to meet her: they do so and, presumably at her instruction, chant spells against the Fomorians—the supernatural equivalent of laying mines in the sand dunes.

In the second episode, on the eve of Samain itself, Lug sends the Dagda on a mission deep into enemy territory. He is to gather intelligence and delay the Fomorians while the god-peoples gather for battle. Approaching the Fomorian camp as an ambassador, the Dagda asks for and receives a temporary truce. He is monstrously ill-treated by his hosts, who feed him a gargantuan helping of porridge on pain of death. Bloated but successful, the Dagda falls asleep.

The third and longest episode, set shortly afterwards, finds the Dagda wambling westwards towards Tráig Eba, a beach in Carbury on the coast of Sligo. He is distended and lethargic but also more-or-less naked from the waist down—standard non-aristocratic Irish dress.[142] He meets the beautiful daughter of Indech the Fomorian king, and she mocks him for his temporary impotence. Demanding a piggyback to her father's house, this formidable young woman beats the Dagda up twice, thrusting him waist deep in the earth the first time and causing him to lose control of his bowels on the second. (In the Cridenbél sequence which this in-tale mirrors, we found the Dagda stuck in a hole in the ground after being systematically underfed; here again he is in a hole in the ground after being systematically *over*fed.) The action then shifts to a war of words between the two of them centred on the Dagda's multiple names. During this sparring match the balance of power mysteriously shifts and an unspoken accommodation is reached. After further relieving his bowels at some length—on purpose this time—the Dagda carries the girl on his back for a spell before they have intercourse. A second sequence of verbal parrying takes place, at the end of which the girl changes sides. She then promises her new lover's people powerful supernatural help against her own kinfolk.[143]

---

142 The 'indecent' trouserlessness of the Irish was much remarked upon by their neighbours; see *IIMWL*, 24–8.

143 The only previous discussion is P. K. Ford, 'The *which* on the wall; obscenity exposed in early Ireland', in J. M. Ziolkowski, *Obscenity: Social Control and Artistic Creation in the European Middle Ages* (Leiden, 1998), 176–90, which argues that the Dagda is thoroughly emasculated in the sequence.

Our passage turns on satire, and this depends—familiarly—on the contrast between the god-peoples's measuredness and Fomorian immoderation. The Fomorians have been satirized for not being generous, so when the Dagda falls into their hands they go to the opposite extreme, turning the virtue of generosity into a cynical vice:

> The Fomorians made porridge for him to mock him, because his love of porridge was great. They filled for him the king's cauldron, which was five fists deep, and poured in four score gallons of new milk and the same quantity of meal and fat into it, and boiled them all together with the porridge. Then they poured it into a hole in the ground, and Indech said to him that he would be killed unless he consumed it all; he should eat his fill so that he should not satirize the Fomorians.[144]

As he is forced to eat, the Dagda makes two quips—both, in their way, proverbial. 'Then the Dagda said, "this is good food if its broth is equal to its taste". But when he put the full ladle into his mouth he said, "its poor bits do not spoil it", as the wise man said.'[145] He thus turns the tables on the Fomorians, satirizing them in turn: such breezy equipoise highlights how, despite dire circumstances, he insists on posing as an enthusiastic guest, robustly cleaning his plate and complimenting the chef.[146]

The difference between the god-peoples and the Fomorian invaders is expressed—in this passage especially, but also throughout the saga—through opposed representations of the body. When the Dagda couples with the daughter of the Fomorian king, the aesthetics of a previous seduction scene are inverted. Earlier in the saga, Ériu, a woman of the god-peoples whose name significantly means 'Ireland', has been lured into a sexual encounter with Elatha, a Fomorian king of faintly sinister beauty:

> Then she saw that it was a man of fairest appearance. He had golden yellow hair down to his shoulders, and a cloak with bands

---

144 *CMT*, 46, 47.

145 *CMT*, 46, 47.

146 The proverbs are close to falling into the category of ironic antiproverbs known as 'wellerisms' to sociolinguists, which typically consist of a proverb plus an attribution to speaker (e.g. '"Much noise and little wool", said the Devil as he sheared a pig'.) The effect is to underscore the Dagda's stoical wit.

of gold thread around it. His shirt had embroidery of gold thread. On his breast was a brooch of gold with the lustre of a precious stone in it. Two shining silver spears and in them two smooth riveted shafts of bronze; five circlets of gold around his neck. A gold-hilted sword with inlayings of silver and studs of gold.[147]

It has been cogently suggested that this part of the saga is an allegory for the disastrous consequences of Irish-Viking miscegenation; it is likely to be the saga-author's own invention.[148] But oddly, Elatha appears to lack a face. In early saga texts, the description of beautiful people tends to follow a fairly clear formula: the description starts with the hair—its colour and sometimes its length and texture—then the eyes and eyebrows, cheeks and lips, followed by the fabrics and garments in which the body is clad; for male characters an account of their weaponry is included. Especially with men, the trunk and the body as a whole below the head tend to be elided by the clothing, and the central description of the face tends to be in primary, often clashing, colours.[149] But in the case of Elatha we do not get a description of the face at all. Coupled with the metallic imagery, the account amounts to a suppression of the flesh—a subliminally disquieting inorganicism and blankness. Bres 'the beautiful' is the result of this union, under whose rule the god-peoples suffer a disastrous eclipse.

This first sex scene—inaugurating disaster for the god-peoples—is flipped on its head by the Dagda's tryst with the Fomorian princess, the daughter of Indech. No glamorous clothes or kingly accoutrements here:

> Then the Dagda got out of the hole, after letting go of the contents of his belly, and the girl had waited for that a long time. He got up then, and took the girl on his back; and he put three stones in his belt. Each stone fell from it in turn—and it has been said that they were his bollocks which fell from it. The girl jumped on him and whacked him across the arse, and her curly bush was revealed. At that point the Dagda gained a mistress, and they had sex. The mark remains at Beltraw Strand where they coupled.[150]

147 *CMT*, 26, 27.
148 The major conclusion of Carey, 'Myth and Mythography'.
149 See *DDDH*, 57–8.
150 *CMT*, 48, 49 (translation made somewhat less genteel).

In a reverse of the Ériu-Elatha coupling, here a Fomorian noblewoman is persuaded to have sex by a sorry, even ludicrous figure, to the eventual great advantage of the god-peoples. It needs to be remembered that the Dagda is not only sexually successful but carries out his mission successfully to boot: one ninth of the Fomorian forces are destroyed by his actions.[151] It is a kind of dirt-magic: though soiled and beshitten, his performance is a form of *aristeia*, the glorious self-display of the Homeric warrior. It is his sexual capacity and his titanic ability to ingest and excrete which allow him to win through, decisively shifting the balance of power in favour of the god-peoples.[152]

Gorging and defecation in this episode are aspects of a vital theme in 'The Second Battle' as a whole, and that is the contrast between the organic and the inorganic.[153] It returns us to the idea of the proper relation of parts to wholes, for one of the major dimensions of this saga is the knitting together of people and their land. We have seen that Bres offered Lug a harvest every season, as well as cows that give unceasing milk: far from being spirits of fertility, the Fomorians in the saga are characterized by a monstrously exploitative and unnatural relationship to the organic world, in a strange anticipation of contemporary agribusiness. (In the late twentieth century a number of writers reimagined them as personifications of technology run amok and degrading the environment—a view for which 'The Second Battle' provides a certain justification.)[154]

The theme of the organic—of the earth and agriculture, feeding and dunging—plays out in the sequence in a series of variations. The Dagda eats from a pit in the earth, and ends up defecating in a hole in the ground, manuring the soil.[155] The play on edibility and inedibility in the saga has a part in this complex of ideas too. Where the Dagda eats gravel with his Fomorian porridge with no ill effects, Cridenbél, the misshapen satirist who had been extorting the god's food, is given porridge with gold coins in it: he chokes on them and dies. John Carey has commented

---

151 *CMT*, 50–1.

152 In another instance of the mirror-images characteristic of this saga, the Dagda's digestive capacity inverts the death of the parasitic Cridenbél, who was unable to pass the gold the Dagda had concealed in his food.

153 On this theme in the literature as a whole, see D. Edel, ' "Bodily Matters" in Early Irish Narrative Literature', *ZCP* 55 (2006), 69–107.

154 See below, 476.

155 On the great value of (cattle) manure, see F. Kelly, *Early Irish Farming* (Dublin, 2000), 229–30.

on the strange phrase—'an unnatural plant'—used to describe the coins. Money grows without earth: it is, he says, 'an inorganic commodity assigned spurious life by the conventions of the marketplace', and spuriousness, greed, and inorganicism are prime Fomorian markers.[156]

That the outwardly unprepossessing may contain great power appears to be the message of the most mysterious part of the episode, namely the series of names which the Dadga gives himself in the first of his two verbal battles with Indech's daughter:

> ... and she forced him to carry her upon his back three times. He said that it was a *geis* for him to carry anyone who would not call him by his name. 'What is your name?' she asked. 'Fer Benn ['Man of Mountains'],' he said. 'That name is too much!' she said. 'Get up, carry me on your back, Fer Benn.' 'That is indeed not my name,' he said. 'What is?' she asked. 'Fer Benn Brúach,' he answered. 'Get up, carry me on your back, Fer Benn Brúach,' she said. 'That is not my name,' he said. 'What is?' she asked. Then he told her the whole thing. She replied immediately and said, 'Get up, carry me on your back, Fer Benn Brúach Brogaill Broumide Cerbad Caic Rolaig Builc Labair Cerrce Di Brig Oldathair Boith Athgen mBethai Brightere Tri Carboid Roth Rimaire Riog Scotbe Obthe Olaithbe...'[157]

There are other lists of names in our text as a whole, but this particular instance is a conventional device familiar from other Irish sagas: a supernatural personage is asked to identify themselves and utters a list of alliterating nicknames, some of which seem resonant and archaic, others spontaneous and tailored to the situation. This device seems designed for situations in which a supernatural figure wants to hint at some future fate without setting it out plainly: its purpose is for building tension and narrative foreshadowing. The speaker simultaneously gives too much information and yet not enough, and normally the effect is sinister: it is used, for example, in 'The Destruction of Da Derga's Hostel' when the goddess of death appears to the doomed king Conaire.[158] But here the effect is absurd rather than unsettling. I suggest that we are not supposed to believe for a moment that the Dagda is telling the truth

---

156 Carey, 'Myth & Mythography', 61.

157 *CMT*, 48, 49; minor correction of translation in first clause from Quin, review of Gray, *Cath Maige Tuired*, 101.

158 See *DDDH*, 147–50.

about this supposed *geis*, a kind of personalized 'prohibited act'.[159] Rather I think we are meant to read this as a ruse on his part, designed first to play for time and second to make the girl aware of his divine power and so hint that the two of them might come to a mutually beneficial arrangement. By deploying a mixed bag of his names and titles, the author seems be determined to have the Dagda display strategic thinking in a tight spot.

The names the Dagda gives are themselves unusual, and not all of them are certainly interpretable. Essentially they involve the intercutting of the dignified with the sordid, recapitulating in miniature the Dagda's appearances in the saga as a whole. They begin with *Fer Benn* 'Man of Mountains', which might also mean 'man of prongs', perhaps—given his aggressive flirtation—with a sexual subtext. The phrase *Di Brig* might mean 'God of Power', which he certainly is, possibly with a pun on the name of his daughter, Bríg.[160] More certain is *Roláech builc*, 'great warrior of the belly'.[161] Others are crude and refer to his present condition: he is *Brúach*, 'the Paunched', and even *Cacc*, 'Shit'. But some of the nicknames he gives himself are mysterious: they include 'Being' (*Buith*) and the resonant *Aithgein mBethai*, 'Rebirth of the World'.[162] With this in mind, it is entirely possible that elements from this scene may have been part of the 'original' mythology of the Dagda. One of the names we have seen elsewhere, and it could plausibly be interpreted as a cult title: this is *Oldathair* (more commonly spelled *ollathair*), 'Supreme Father'. Other names in the list might belong to the same category.

How all this might have been interpreted by the saga's original late ninth-century noble audience is unclear. The author is interested first and foremost in the idea of the success of the gods as prototypical 'people of talent', but he is also conscious of the social context—good kingship—in which those talents are most productively to be exercised. The saga presents the views of the professional men of learning and the no-

---

159 For these see T. Charles-Edwards, '*Geis*, Prophecy, Omen, and Oath', *Celtica* 23 (1999), 38–99.

160 *CMT* is notoriously orthographically odd. Because the names here are obscure, a copyist could easily misunderstand a phrase *da bríg*, 'god of power'—here I follow *EIH&M*, 128–9 on *da* as a pretonic form of *día*, 'god', used in names—as 'two powers'; as *bríg* is feminine he might then have corrected the form to *dí/di*, the feminine form of the numeral 'two'.

161 Or 'Great Warrior, Belly' as two separate names. Note I have put all the names into the nominative case; in the text they are vocatives.

162 For further suggestions on the list of names, see *CMT*, 100.

bility; it is this combination of perspectives that makes reading 'The Second Battle' a particularly vivid experience. The Dagda emerges from this episode as an 'earthly god'—to reuse Tírechán's phrase—in a very literal way. He has learned from his period of servile ditch digging. His behaviour exhibits humility, in the sense of connection to the *humus*, the soil, for he eats from a hole in the ground and fills another trench with dung. Despite and through all this he maintains an improbable virility. Rightful occupation of the land means submitting to the organic. The obscenity fits into the saga-author's vision of a whole society, one connected to itself and to the land.

This vision subversively cuts across other aspects of early medieval Irish ideology, most particularly the idea that physical beauty in a man is a sign of suitability for kingship.[163] Bres's father is beautiful but oddly alien, while Bres's own beauty is in direct proportion to his unsuitability for kingship. (The point is laboured: the saga-author tells us the word *bres* is used as a word applicable to anything beautiful, like our 'nonpareil'.)[164] This is a text which is suspicious of vacuous good looks. The systematic griminess of the Dagda has its place, and perhaps its own nobility too, in that he conspicuously declines to stand on his own dignity for the sake of his people. What we have in this crucial passage is not ugliness contrasted with beauty, but filth versus flash. Wry, brave, earthy, full of appetite, endearingly long-suffering, the Dagda has a kind of Falstaffian vitalism. He is notably untouchable by satire, unlike the Fomorians: he lacks a form of vulnerability to which they are helplessly prone. This is a suggestive and subversive idea of nobility, very different to that of Lug but no less vital to the god-peoples' success.

The influence of the *filid* is clear in this ideological arrangement, for the idea that the initially unprepossessing may conceal deep worth and beauty is a celebrated theme in the lore of the professional poets. In more than one anecdote an unattractive, filthy, or uncouth figure transforms himself into a personage of luminous talent, and this is clearly a metaphor for the practice of poetry itself: rebarbative to begin with, but ending in beauty.[165] In the *filid*'s terms, the one becomes the other; in 'The Second Battle' the same essential idea is present, but the two poles are personified as the Dagda and Lug. They are separate individuals who

163 *DDDH*, 195–7, 200–4, 224–6.

164 *CMT*, 28, 29, 81.

165 Discussed in detail below, 175–9, but note P. K. Ford, 'The blind, the dumb, and the ugly: aspects of poets and their craft in early Ireland and Wales', *CMCS* 19 (1990), 27–40.

work together towards the single aim of the flourishing of the Túatha Dé. The underlying ideal is the same: when skilfulness is needed, the ugly (the difficult, inconvenient, recalcitrant, rebarbative, disgusting, etc.) can be a paradoxically potent source of strength—a lesson quite lost on the Fomorians.

CONCLUSION

The word 'culture' in the title of this chapter was used in order to highlight two themes which have emerged from the discussion. The first is the relationship between the literary gods and the real-life social hierarchies of Viking-age Ireland, and the role they played in mirroring that culture back to itself. The second is the emphasis laid on the relationship of the gods to Ireland's landscape and cultivated earth. We thus have culture and cultivation, but no cult; this situation had three consequences.

First, because the gods lacked a religious dimension in medieval Ireland, they were open to being creatively re-purposed. Though traditions and tales about them were handed down among men of learning, these were clearly malleable. Variation was possible, according to the saga-author's literary needs and aims—including the possibility of radical changes, as in the character of Bres. The effect is of a tradition with one foot on the brake and one on the accelerator. Very old patterns (such as the conflict between the gods and the Fomorians) were preserved even as new figures like Míach were worked into the pantheon long after the demise of Irish paganism. Strands of lore were being constantly added long after the gods had ceased to be objects of veneration; this is not unexpected when characters are still filled with vivid cultural life.

Secondly, giving the saga-authors credit for individual creativity goes some way to explaining the weirdly *granular* texture of Irish mythology. By this I mean that our sense of the 'personality' of a given deity has to be assembled from widely varied sources, and the resulting collage sometimes fails to cohere. It is hard to get a sense of each god as an individual personality, unlike the Greek gods. Apollo may have many aspects, but he is recognizable as Apollo across many different texts; Midir—to choose a contrasting figure—can only be captured at a lower resolution. Part of this is simply due to the conventions of Irish literature, in which it was not normal to tell stories in verse: prose was the medium for narrative. This means that references to the gods in verse often allude to stories about them without setting them out plainly, and often such poetic allusions are our *only* evidence for a particular story. The fate of the Morrígan's son Méiche is a prime example: who was his father? How did the Morrígan react to the killing of her son? *Why* did Méiche have three serpents in his heart? We simply do not know.

Finally, even though the medieval Irish sagas cannot be counted as pagan mythology in any simple or straightforward way, it is remarkable that the Irish gods nonetheless do most of the jobs performed by divinities within pre-Christian European cultures. The gods' conflicts and triumphs anatomized the archetypal and ever-recurring tensions within human life; they stood as sources of empowering precedent. Most of all, they embodied and encoded the deep past of the island, and it is to the ways in which that deep past was imagined that we now turn.

4

NEW MYTHOLOGIES

PSEUDOHISTORY AND THE LORE OF POETS

A sound magician is a demi-god.

—CHRISTOPHER MARLOWE, *DOCTOR FAUSTUS*

SO FAR WE have looked at some four centuries of developing tradition. As seen, a certain orchestrated haziness is characteristic of the way in which saga-authors handled the native gods, and this could be exploited for literary effect. As with Manannán's epiphany to Bran or that of Midir to the unhappy Eochaid Airem, the gods intrude and then are lost to sight, leaving the question of their nature and potency open. (If you do not know what a being *is*, you cannot guess what it intends to do to you.) Slipperiness combines unsettlingly with the capacity to overpower.

This haziness underlies the recurrence of phases of strenuous mythological revival in Irish literary history, in which attempts are made to tie the gods down within some new and less-ambiguous intellectual frame. The best known of these phases—the nineteenth-century Irish Revival— is examined later in this book, but some of its foundations were laid a millennium earlier, when the intellectual energies of Irish scholars were first galvanized by the prospect of clarifying the ancient past and the place of the gods within it.

HOW THE GAEL BECAME

This chapter investigates the tenth, eleventh, and twelfth centuries in relation to Irish literary history, crossing the millennial divide. Irish military success in the later tenth century brought the Viking wars to an end and stabilized the political scene, enabling a many-faceted scholarly revival and reorganization of monastic learning.[1] Works typical of the time clearly aimed to bolster Ireland's cultural memory, so that we find attempts to rescue, reassess, and revive the writings of several centuries before. Irish largely replaced Latin as the language of scholarship, older sagas were redacted, and several large, famous manuscripts—effectively one-volume libraries of vernacular texts—were produced. In these are found the earliest extant copies of most of the treasures of the early medieval literature, so that what descends to us from that literature undoubtedly owes something to the tastes of the clerical compilers of the central Middle Ages.[2]

A crucial dimension of this cultural stocktake was the creation of a chronological narrative for the island's past, which would integrate all the sources—biblical, native, and classical—known to Irish scholars.[3] This seductive fabrication, often called the 'synthetic history', possessed two core strands, both of which revolved around the question of who had held power over the island. The first strand investigated the story of the Gaels and how they had come to Ireland, while the second tackled the story of the island's pre-Gaelic inhabitants, imagined as a sequence of settlers or invaders. The gods were represented as the last pre-Gaelic, 'prehistoric' people to have wrested control over Ireland. This was a development of an idea which had been around since the eighth century at least: that there had once been a time, long ago, when the god-peoples had been in charge. Thomas Charles-Edwards points out that this looks like a procedure for denying pagan divinities any existence in the present—where Christian orthodoxy would have demanded that they be regarded as demons—by relegating them to an 'innocuous past'.[4] Thus distanced, they could be regarded safely, even with admiration, as figures of cultural significance.

---

1 This is a vast topic; the best introduction to the intellectual background is M. Herbert, 'Crossing Historical and Literary Boundaries: Irish Written Culture Around the Year 1000', in P. Sims-Williams and G. A. Williams (eds.), *Crossing Boundaries/Croesi Ffiniau* (Aberystwyth, 2007) [= *CMCS* 53/4 (2007)], 87–101; see also *L&IEMI*, 130.

2 A substantial recent study is Schlüter, *History or Fable?*

3 On the increasing importance of chronology in Irish learning during the tenth century, see M. Ní Mhaonaigh, 'The literature of medieval Ireland, 800–1200', *CHIL*, i., 46, and P. J. Smith, 'Early Irish Historical Verse, the Evolution of a Genre', in P. Ní Chatháin & M. Richter (eds.), *Ireland and Europe in the Early Middle Ages: Texts and Transmission/ Irland und Europa im früheren Mittelalter: Texte und Überlieferung* (Dublin, 2002), 326–41, 335.

4 *ECI*, 200–1.

I often use the term 'pseudohistory' here and in the title to this chapter, but not in a derogatory manner. Our contemporary sense of what history is ('what really happened') differs from that of medieval writers, who regularly shaped stories about the past involving blatantly artifical narratives and genealogies. The purpose of these stories was to explain and exemplify how the past related to the present, often by giving accounts of how peoples, places, and political institutions had come into being. For our purposes, the crucial innovation of the Irish pseudo- or synthetic history lay in its explicit insistence that the Túatha Dé had been a race of men and women—not gods, phantoms, unfallen human beings, half-fallen angels, nor any other form of theological exotica. The importance of this development can hardly be overstated, as a basic faith in the fundamental historicity of this narrative prevailed for centuries, so that it effectively became Ireland's official framework for its native gods. They were to float within it, as though pickled in brine, until the middle of the nineteenth century.

After several centuries of development, the culmination of the synthetic history came in the final quarter of the eleventh century with *Lebor Gabála Érenn* ('The Book of Invasions'). A highly influential Middle Irish prose-and-verse treatise, it was written in order to bridge the chasm between Christian world-chronology and the prehistory of Ireland.[5] To the learned classes of medieval Ireland, as elsewhere, the primary source for ancient history was the Bible; its narrative had been explicated and expanded by early Christian writers who had established precise chronologies for biblical events. As part of this process figures from classical mythology such as Jason or Theseus—who were considered fully histori-

---

5 Literally 'the book of the taking/settling/conquest of Ireland'. 'The Book of Invasions' is conventional in English, but *Lebor Gabála* is also common and I use both here. Best introductions both by John Carey: *The Irish National Origin-Legend: Synthetic Pseudohistory* [Quiggin Pamphlets on the Sources of Mediaeval Gaelic History 1, 1994], and 'Lebor Gabála and the legendary history of Ireland', in H. Fulton (ed.), *Medieval Celtic Literature and Society* (Dublin, 2005), 32–48. The (very problematic) edn. is *Lebor Gabála Érenn*, ed. & trans. R. A. S. Macalister (5 vols., London, 1938–56, repr. London, 1993), henceforth *LGE*. John Carey (*A new introduction to Lebor Gabála Érenn, the Book of the Taking of Ireland, edited and translated by R. A. Stewart Macalister* (Dublin, 1993)) assesses Macalister's edn., while R. M. Scowcroft ('Leabhar Gabhála, Part I: The Growth of the Text', *Ériu* 38 (1987), 81–142) offers a helpful skeleton key to using it (139–42). Carey has himself produced an indispensable critical edition and translation of Recension I ('*Lebar Gabála*, Recension I' [unpublished PhD dissertation, Harvard University, 1983]); the general reader will find it easier to get hold of his revised translation of the same recension in *CHA*, 226–71.

cal—were sometimes slotted into the timeline of the kings and high priests of Israel. A further important dimension to this medieval infilling of the Bible was the attempt to trace the descent of the various peoples of the world, past and present, all the way back to notional ancestors in the Book of Genesis. But here Ireland's men of learning came to a dead end: they possessed a conspicuously lush body of traditions about the origins of the peoples of their own island, but could find no reference to the Irish either in scripture or the works of Christian world history. So who, they asked themselves, were they? And where had they come from?

All versions of *Lebor Gabála* provided the same basic answer (Fig. 4.1 and Fig. 4.2).[6] There are two strands to the story, and the first begins with Noah. Thanks to the Flood he becomes the last common ancestor of humanity. His (non-biblical) granddaughter Cessair and her entourage of a hundred and fifty women and three men are the first human beings to arrive in Ireland. Desperately searching for shelter from the coming deluge, all of them drown—except for one Fintan mac Bóchra, who escapes in the form of a salmon and magically lives on in various forms for

---

6 The diagrams downplay the differences between versions, especially over the various time-spans. *Lebor Gabála* is probably the single most complex work to survive from medieval Ireland: it continually attracted new material, so that within a century of its composition it had already been recast into three different recensions, plus a welter of subrecensions, each of which added, subtracted, and rearranged material, sometimes cross-pollinating with each other. This is evidence of the treatise's immediate impact and popularity, but as a result it has proved impossible for scholars to edit a single 'original' text of *Lebor Gabála*, and Macalister's five-volume edition is simultaneously indispensible and unusable. Further, the tract's mutations are so technical as to be impossible to summarize for the general reader. Extremely briefly, each recension of *Lebor Gabála* grew from the conflation of older ones, and the text(s) grew idiosyncratically from copy to copy. The recensions relate as follows. The earliest, *c.*1075, seems to have been a truncated version known as the *Míniugud*. Then, apparently at much the same time, Recension I emerged, which added a selection of material to the *Míniugud* and was closely related to it. Recension II is a revision of Recension I, completed very soon after Recension I itself; not only did Recension II borrow passages from a version of *Míniugud*, it also attached the whole *Míniugud* text as an appendix. Recensions I and II (in various sub-versions) were then repeatedly expanded by borrowings from each other and from external sources, until they were eventually fused together as Recension III, perhaps at the end of the twelfth century. An early modern version by Mícheál Ó Cléirigh comprises Recension IV, which is not relevant here. The details of how these four recensions are embodied in the surviving manuscript witnesses are complex and cumbersome. See Carey, 'Lebar Gabála, Recension I', 19–20, and R. M. Scowcroft, 'Mediaeval Recensions of the *Lebor Gabála*', in J. Carey (ed.), *Lebor Gabála Érenn: textual History and Pseudohistory* (London, 2009), 1–20.

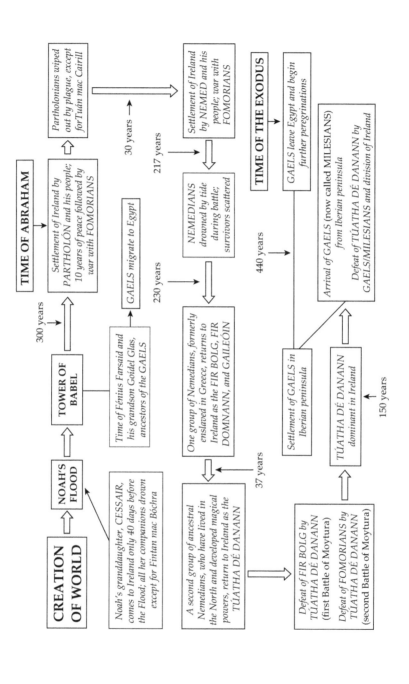

FIG. 4.1. The timeline of Irish prehistory in 'The Book of Invasions'.

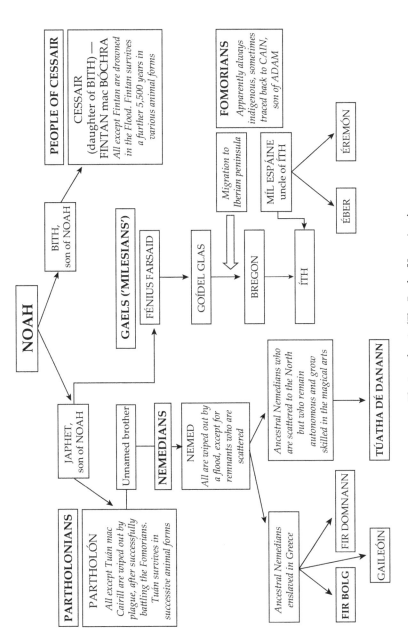

FIG. 4.2. The invaders in 'The Book of Invasions'.

NOAH

BITH, son of NOAH

PEOPLE OF CESSAIR

CESSAIR (daughter of BITH) — FINTAN mac BÓCHRA
All except Fintan are drowned in the Flood. Fintan survives a further 5,500 years in various animal forms

JAPHET, son of NOAH

PARTHOLONIANS

PARTHOLÓN
All except Tuán mac Cairill are wiped out by plague, after successfully battling the Fomorians. Tuán survives in successive animal forms

Unnamed brother

NEMEDIANS

NEMED
All are wiped out by a flood, except for remnants who are scattered

Ancestral Nemedians enslaved in Greece

FIR BOLG

FIR DOMNANN

GAILEÓIN

Ancestral Nemedians who are scattered to the North but who remain autonomous and grow skilled in the magical arts

TÚATHA DÉ DANANN

GAELS ('MILESIANS')

FÉNIUS FARSAID

GOÍDEL GLAS

BREGON

ÍTH

Migration to Iberian peninsula

MÍL ESPÁINE uncle of ÍTH

ÉBER

ÉREMÓN

FOMORIANS
Apparently always indigenous, sometimes traced back to CAIN, son of ADAM

133

three and a half millennia. He thus becomes one of the most authoritative 'ancient witnesses' to the tradition.[7]

Cessair's line thus comes to a dead end. After Cessair, the next settlers are the people of Partholón son of Sera, a distant descendant of Cessair's uncle, Japhet, a son of Noah.[8] The Partholonians are wiped out by plague, but in some versions, as with Fintan mac Bóchra, a single survivor escapes the catastrophe: this is Tuán mac Cairill, who also survives through the ages in successive animal guises.[9]

The next wave of settlers, the people of Nemed, descend from one of Partholón's brothers. *Nemed*—originally meaning 'sacral'—is the native word Irish law-tracts used for free persons of rank, but the semantic range of the term is exceedingly complex. When applied to a person (as here, presumably) it meant 'dignitary', but it could also refer to the legal inviolability or privilege attaching to such a person, and to the concept of sanctuary, and to a sacred place which offered such sanctuary; it should be noted that in the latter sense it was regularly used to mean 'church'.[10] Its use here underscores the belief among the Irish that their society's roots went deep into the past. They imagined that Nemed's descendants had introduced some of the island's most enduring political and geographical institutions, including kingship itself, the siting of royal power at Tara, and the division of the country into provinces.

With the exception of a very few, Nemed's kin are obliterated by the incoming tide during a seashore battle against the Fomorians—whose own origins, incidentally, were never fully agreed upon.[11] Some of these bedraggled survivors make for Britain, where they become the ancestors

7 See E. Nic Cárthaigh, 'Surviving the Flood: Revenants and Antediluvian Lore in Medieval Irish Texts', in K. Cawsey & J. Harris, *Transmission and Transformation in the Middle Ages: Texts and Contexts* (Dublin, 2007), 40–64.

8 Medieval learned tradition made Japhet the ancestor of the peoples of Europe—later antiquarian scholars sometimes termed the languages of Europe the 'Japhetic' tongues after him—and the Irish considered themselves no exception: all subsequent inhabitants of the island were said to be of Japhet's line.

9 Tuán is mentioned in Recension I but this may be a later addition; otherwise he is not known in *Lebor Gabála* outside the composite Recension III. See J. Carey, 'Scél Tuáin meic Chairill', *Ériu* 35 (1984), 93–111, fn. 28.

10 See K. McCone, 'Notes on the Text and Authorship of the Early Irish Bee-Laws', *CMCS* 8 (Winter, 1984), 45–50, at 48–9, reviewing *Bechbretha*, ed. & trans. Charles-Edwards & Kelly, in which the term *nemed* is discussed on 107–9.

11 See S. Rodway, 'Mermaids, Leprechauns, and Fomorians: a Middle Irish Account of the Descendants of Cain', *CMCS* 59 (Summer, 2010), 1–17, and M. Clarke, 'The lore of the monstrous races in the developing text of the Irish *Sex aetates mundi*', *CMCS* 63 (Summer,

of the Britons. Others find their way to Greece, where the Greeks enslave them and force them to hulk soil up mountains to create agricultural land. There they acquire a new name from the leather sacks they use for this task: *Fir Bolg*, 'Bag Men'. After many generations these Bag Men throw off the Greek yoke and return, now subdivided into three groups, to resettle Ireland.

Meanwhile other remnants of Nemed's scattered people head north. There they grow skilled in the magical arts and develop augmented, more-than-human capabilities; the later recensions add the detail that they pursued this intriguing curriculum in four mysterious cities. This race is the pseudohistory's take on the god-peoples. In time, they too return to their ancestral Ireland, now under the rule of their relations, the Fir Bolg; distant kinship notwithstanding, the god-peoples defeat and dispossess them, taking the island for themselves.

So much for the first of *Lebor Gabála*'s two strands. The second strand follows the adventures of another people descended from Japhet, son of Noah, who are destined to become the Gaels. At the disaster of the Tower of Babel, a Scythian nobleman named Fénius Farsaid ('Irishman the Pharisee') extracted all the best bits of humanity's jumbled languages and from them pieced together the world's first artificial, 'perfect' language: Irish.[12] (A typical piece of medieval Irish *amour propre*, that; Michael Clarke calls it 'staggeringly self-assertive'.)[13] It is Fénius Farsaid's grandson, Goídel Glas, who gives his name to the people and their language, *Goídelc*, modern *Gaeilge*. After a series of peregrinations clearly modelled on those of the Israelites in the Book of Exodus, the descendants of Goídel Glas and his grandfather Fénius settle in what is now Spain and Portugal. From the top of a tower in Braganza, their king Bregon glimpses Ireland over the sea one winter's evening—an oddly haunting detail. Later Bregon's grandson Míl Espáine ('Spanish Soldier') invades the island and

---

2012), 15–50. John Carey ('*Lebar Gabála*, Recension I', 57) notes that the Fir Bolg seem to somehow summon the Fomorians when they begin to alter the Irish landscape.

12 This itself was an idea of some antiquity, as old as the seventh century; it is found in the central core of that fountainhead of quasi-scientific vernacular *grammatica* in Ireland, 'The Scholar's Primer' (*Auraicept na n-Éces*). For the text of the episode, see A. Ahlqvist, *The Early Irish Linguist: An Edition of the Canonical Part of the Auraicept na nÉces* (Helsinki, 1983), 47, lines 2–10; see also J. Carey, 'The Ancestry of Fénius Farsaid', *Celtica* 21 (1990), 104–12.

13 M. Clarke, 'Linguistic Education and Literary Creativity in Medieval Ireland', in P. Ronan (ed.), *Cahiers de l' Institut de Linguistique et des Sciences des Langues* 38 (Lausanne, 2013), 37–70, 50.

defeats the Túatha Dé. The Gaels, also known after Míl Espáine as the 'sons of Míl' (often 'Milesians' in later works), now rule Ireland, and the god-peoples in turn find themselves dispossessed.

This bare account fails to convey what it is actually like to read 'The Book of Invasions', suppressing the differences between recensions and giving little sense of the pseudohistorians' complex chronologies or their Tolkienesque enthusiasm for the family trees of imaginary persons. (It must be admitted that *Lebor Gabála*—important though it is among medieval Irish writings—is not the place to seek for wrenching emotional force.) What it does highlight however is the manner, reminiscent of Romanesque architecture, in which simple, repeating structures are decorated with teeming surface detail. These governing structures are basically biblical—Exodus and Flood—and insistent leitmotifs include plagues, migrations, dispossessions, the colonizations of deserted lands, and the reduction of once-sovereign peoples to servile status under oppressive rulers.[14]

Versions of this pseudohistorical scheme seem to have emerged into the mainstream of Irish learning during the later 900s, when the lore of the professional poets began to influence monastic authors deeply and significantly.[15] We do not know who gave it its lasting form as 'The Book of Invasions', but their task was complete by around 1075; the various recensions and subrecensions which rapidly followed were the work of many hands extending over the next two or three generations.

These scholars—busily rearranging, cross-referencing, and interpolating—looked for much of their immediate source material to didactic accounts of Irish history put into verse by a small number of poets during the late tenth and eleventh centuries.[16] When compared with contemporary ideas of writing history, these early ideas and methods differed greatly; for us it is obvious to put faith in close scrutiny, the comparison of sources, and the evidence of eyewitnesses, but the redactors of *Lebor Gabála* preferred to conflate and layer variant traditions in a sedimentary, accretive mass. The prose-and-verse form of the treatise perfectly suited this approach, because the verse was basically primary

---

14 This dimension of the text's deep structure has been admirably examined by Scowcroft, who notes that these themes were also commonplaces of medieval Irish political reality; see 'Leabhar Gabhála, Part II: The Growth of the Tradition', *Ériu* 39 (1988), 1–66, at 21.

15 *L&IEMI*, 145.

16 See Carey, '*Lebar Gabála*, Recension I', 17–20.

and fixed, while the prose might not only allude to variant versions of a given incident, but also attempt to bring them into harmony.

The compilers of *Lebor Gabála* seem to have drawn from the work of four poets in particular. The earliest was the Armagh cleric Eochaid ua Flainn (d.1004), described in the Annals of Ulster as a 'sage of poetry and historical tradition', marking him out as a top scholar.[17] His poetry seems to have been designed to accompany a pseudohistorical tract which was one of the major nuclei around which the original *Lebor Gabála* condensed. This tract must therefore have been in existence by 1004, when Eochaid died, and its contents can be distilled from *Lebor Gabála* as we have it.[18] The second poet is a shadowy Connaught figure named Tanaide, who may have died *c.*1075.[19] A major poem on the reigns of the various kings of the god-peoples is ascribed to him in the first and third recensions of *Lebor Gábala*, and his allusion to the familiar story of the loss and restoration of Núadu's arm gives the flavour of the kind of didactic verse produced by the pseudohistorical school:

Noble slender Núadu ruled for seven years
over the fair-haired wolf-pack;
[that was] the eager fair-headed man's reign
before coming into Ireland.

It is in grievous Mag Tuired, without predestined death,
the yoke of battle fell;
his kingly arm was severed
from the bright champion of the world.

---

17 This dating for Eochaid ua Flainn depends on taking him to be the same man as the similarly-named Eochaid ua *Flannucáin*, a long-standing view which, while not proven, seems to be gaining ground; see Carey, '*Lebar Gabála*, Recension I', 50–1, and (more recently) M. Ó Mainnín, 'Eochaid Ua Flainn agus Eochaid Ua Flannucáin: Súil Úr ar an bhFianaise', *Léann* 2 (2009) 75–105.

18 Scholars term this lost—or submerged—tract 'α', and is one of the primary two branches descended from a single canon, known as ω: proto-α must therefore be before 1004, Eochaid's obit. This α formed the core of both *Míniugud* and Recension I, though not of Recension II, which accessed ω via a different intermediary.

19 All identifying details about Tanaide are late and problematic. He may have belonged to a branch of the Uí Maelchonaire and to have held the *ardollamnacht*, the 'top-poethood', of Connaught; see Carey, '*Lebar Gabála*, Recension I', 52–4. The date of Tanaide's *floruit* is difficult to determine beyond it belonging somewhere in the first three quarters of the eleventh century; note Scowcroft's scepticism, '*Leabhar Gabhála*, Part II', 4 fn.6.

Bres ruled seven years, no bright interval;
on account of his beauty, the lord of poems
held the kingship of the plain of tender nuts,
until the arm of Núadu was healed.[20]

And so on in this vein for another six quatrains; the kennings, stereo-typed phrases, and asides on display here are all characteristic of the genre. To be fair to the poets, they were labouring under exacting and untranslatable metrical demands and the poems of *Lebor Gabála* are su-perb examples of the kind of learned versifications of historical memory in which they specialized. Nonetheless, it is easy to see why it was found desirable to attach a prose apparatus setting out the actual data under curation.[21]

The work of the third of the four poets, Gilla Cóemáin mac Gilla Samthainne (*fl.*1072), would not be especially relevant to the representa-tion of the gods were it not that we know that he had something to do with an important prose tract, the *Lebor Bretnach*. This text provides cru-cial evidence for how the gods were imagined by the learned personnel of the period: Gilla Cóemáin may himself have been responsible for it.[22] We will come to this tract in due course. The last of our four poets was not used, it seems, by the original compiler of *Lebor Gabála*. The distin-guished scholar Flann Mainistrech, 'of the Monastery' (d.1056), was head of the monastic school at Monasterboice, in what is now Co. Louth.[23] Poems of his were nonetheless rapidly incorporated into *Lebor Gabála* as it underwent recasting and interpolation, and some of them are of great importance. One, examined below, gleefully details how each god met his or her death.

These poets were the fountainhead for the national narrative which 'The Book of Invasions' made canonical. But what sources had these

20 The translation is John Carey's (*CHA*, 275); earlier trans. and original text in his 'Lebar Gabála, Recension I', 294–5, 138.

21 The poets wrote in a mode known as *dán dírech*, 'strict-metre syllabic poetry', and often in variations on a fiendish seven-syllable metre called *deibhidhe*, which required complex internal and final rhyme and alliterative ornament.

22 On Gilla Coemáin (or Cóemáin) mac Gilla Samthainne note P. J. Smith, *Three Historical Poems ascribed to Gilla-Cóemáin: a Critical Edition of the Work of an Eleventh Century Irish Scholar* [Studien und Texte zur Keltologie 8] (Münster, 2007).

23 See Carey, 'Lebar Gabála, Recension I', 54, and M. Ní Mhaonaigh, 'Flann Mainis-trech', in S. Duffy (ed.), *Medieval Ireland: an encyclopedia* (Abingdon & New York, 2005), 180–1. Nineteen of Flann's poems survive, amongst other works, for which see *L&IEMI*, 139, fn.51.

poets drawn upon in turn? The answer lies in the pre–*Lebor Gabála* development of the synthetic history. A core of ideas about the geographical origins and peregrinations of the Gaels—clearly involving at least some written and scholarly material, but still developing and shifting outline—seems to have been in existence before the tenth century. The Bible provided the major model for this kind of history, augmented by Christian authorities and biblical commentators; the pseudohistorians' curious connection between the Gaels on the one hand and Spain, Greece, and Scythia on the other was derived from these latter sources. To a significant degree this connection was based on the kind of false etymologies loved by medieval scholars. The idea of a link between Ireland and Spain—whence Íth son of Bregon had first seen the Gaels' future homeland—goes back to the encyclopedist Isidore of Seville, who thought of Spain as the 'mother of races' and had (wrongly) connected *Hibernia* and *(H)iberia*.[24] Isidore also derived the Greeks from Noah's son Japhet and ascribed Greek connections to the Gauls (*Galli* in Latin); because of the similarity of the names, Gaeldom's men of learning soon took the latter to be a reference to themselves.[25]

Another example of this kind of 'etymological history' was the standard assertion (very odd to modern eyes) that the ancestors of the Irish had ultimately come from Scythia, an area notoriously vaguely imagined in the Middle Ages, but roughly to be identified with modern Ukraine and Kazakhstan. Scythia features in several early Irish sources as well as all versions of *Lebor Gabála*, and the connection was based merely on the resemblance between two Latin words, *Scythae*, 'Scythians', and *Scotti*, the normal term for the Irish.[26] Even Míl Espáine, the ancestor of the invading Gaels and thus putative forefather of all the ethnic Irish, was an etymological figment. Transparently not originally a name, it is rather a translation of the Latin phrase for 'a soldier of Spain' (*miles Hispaniae*)—a form which actually occurs in the earliest pre–*Lebor Gabála* account of the wanderings of the Gaels to survive.[27] It is a tribute to the ingenuity of Ireland's learned classes that the huge edifice of 'The Book of Invasions' could be built upon such slight foundations.[28]

24 Carey, *The Irish National Origin-Legend*, 23.

25 B. Jaski, ' "We are of the Greeks in our origin": new perspectives on the Irish origin legend', *CMCS* 46 (2003), 1–53.

26 See J. Carey, 'The Ancestry of Fénius Farsaid', *Celtica* 21 (1990), 108.

27 This is the *Historia Brittonum* ('History of the Britons'), discussed below, 142–3. For Míl (sometimes *Míled*), see Scowcroft, 'Leabhar Gabhála, Part II', 19.

28 It is sometimes excitably claimed that genetic analysis—which shows a link be-

STRUCTURE AND SEQUENCE

Irish pseudohistorical tradition is plainly a mare's nest, but nonetheless the stages of its growth can be reconstructed.[29] The point may not need labouring, but the story of successive invasions is demonstrably not pre-Christian; it developed gradually in early Christian Ireland.[30] The very concept of a universal history of this kind belongs to medieval learning, not native tradition. But no race of people lacks a story about where they come from, and the original nucleus of the pseudohistory was the narrative of the coming of the Gaels.[31] We know that material about the legendary ancestors of the Irish existed as early as the seventh century, because early poetry associated with Leinster mentions Ír, Éber and Éremón—figures who later appear among the grandsons of Míl Espáine in the story of the Gaelic takeover.[32] Míl himself, however, could not have entered the tradition before the late seventh century—when, thanks to the writings of Isidore, the Irish first conceived of the Spanish-Irish connection—and so a good amount of soldering new material onto old was clearly going on.[33]

---

tween the inhabitants of Ireland and those of the present day Basque country—points to the historical truth of *Lebor Gabála*. As the *idea* of the Ireland-Spain connection can be conclusively shown to be a learned development of the seventh century, this is a coincidence—particularly as the same genetic markers are also very common in Britain. For a witty recent account by a scholar *au fait* with the archaeology, genetic analysis, and medieval literature, see J. P. Mallory, *The Origins of the Irish* (London & New York, 2013), especially chapter seven.

29 The most detailed statement about the development of the various recensions and the relation of their manuscript witnesses is Scowcroft, 'Leabhar Gabhála', Part I'.

30 Though note J. Carey, 'Native elements in Irish pseudohistory', in D. Edel, *Cultural Identity and Cultural Integration: Ireland and Europe in the Early Middle Ages* (Dublin, 1995), 45–60.

31 See *ECI*, 580, for evidence that the Irish in the earliest period did not think of themselves as one people with a single common ancestor, underscoring the fact that the pseudohistory is a medieval development.

32 See Carey, *Irish National Origin*-Legend, 9–10; see *CHA*, 56–7 for these early poems.

33 Elva Johnston points out that the fiction of descent from Míl as a common ancestor became more and more central in the ninth and tenth centuries AD, and can be seen as a response to the presence of the Vikings in Ireland. For the first time the Irish were having to live at close quarters with groups who were culturally and ethnically different from themselves, and among Ireland's elites this constellated a sense of collective identity in the form of shared ancestry; see *L&IEMI*, 86–7.

A rudimentary written account of the Gaels' wanderings already existed by the ninth century, at least two centuries before the composition of *Lebor Gabála*. This can be verified because of an important didactic poem, known from its first line as *Can a mbunadas na nGaedel* ('Whence Did the Irish Originate?'), which cannot have been composed later than 887, when its author, Máel Mura Othna, died.[34] While we know the compiler of *Lebor Gabála* did not use this poem, minute details embedded in *Lebor Gabála* about the wanderings of the Gaels chime so closely with it that a single source must ultimately have fed into both; this source must therefore have been in existence, in written form, before 887.[35]

Crucially, 'Whence Did the Irish Originate?' does mention the god-peoples. It tells us that the Gaels, having travelled from Scythia via Spain, reached Ireland and found the Túatha Dé *already there*: there is no suggestion of older inhabitants. It also contains suggestions that the god-peoples began by being less than friendly, and though the phrasing is obscure we are clearly told that the Túatha Dé gave the men of the Gaels wives in exchange for their being allowed to keep half of the island. The poem does not actually make explicit, as documented elsewhere, that this means the half which lies beneath the earth's surface, but this seems likely.[36]

This is striking on two levels. First, it is broadly compatible with the representation of the god-peoples in the Old Irish sagas, although it contains details of a primordial encounter between men and gods, which the sagas do not. One strand of saga-tradition had depicted the god-peoples as the island's antediluvian aboriginals, still in residence because free from original sin and therefore invisible and immortal; this is precisely the situation in the third part of 'The Wooing of Étaín', for example. Secondly, there is no suggestion in Máel Mura's poem that the god-peoples have shipped in from anywhere else: they are in their native

---

34 Máel Mura, learned poet and historian, is an excellent and early example of pre-occupations emerging in monastic circles. He was a member of the community of Othain (hence *Othna*), now Fahan, Co. Donegal; for his life, see J. Carey, 'In search of Mael Muru Othna', in E. Purcell & P. MacCotter, *et al.* (eds.) *Clerics, Kings and Vikings: Essays on Medieval Ireland in Honour of Donnchadh Ó Corráin* (Dublin, 2015), 429–39, and for the poem see *L&IEMI*, 129 fn. 203, and Scowcroft, '*Leabhar Gabhála*, Part II', 8–9; no modern translation and commentary upon this crucial work exists, though a diplomatic Irish text can be found in R. I. Best, *et al.* (eds.), *The Book of Leinster, formerly Lebar na Núachongbála* [6 vols.] (Dublin, 1954–83), iii., 516–23.

35 Scowcroft, '*Leabhar Gabhála*, Part II', 8–9.

36 Scowcroft, '*Leabhar Gabhála*, Part II', 9, fn.19.

place. This corresponds to the major 'mythological' sagas like 'The Second Battle of Moytura', and certainly before *c.*900 there seems to be no assertion anywhere that the Túatha Dé had been invaders.[37] This—and the very mythological-looking idea of intermarriage between gods and Gaels—was emphatically excluded from the tradition by the compiler(s) of *Lebor Gabála*.

While the body of tradition about the migrations of the Gaels was clearly primary, by the mid-tenth century it had been gradually augmented by accounts of the preceding settlements or invasions. Traditions about the pre-Gaelic settlements spread like suckers from the root-story of the Gaels. Partholón seems to have been worked in first.[38] His name is the Irish version of 'Bartholomew' and learned Irishmen could read in Isidore that this was a Syriac name meaning 'he who holds up the waters'.[39] Accordingly, Partholón became *mac Sera*, 'son of the Syrian', and the first man to settle Ireland after the waters of the Flood subsided.[40] Nemed seems to have been added next as another doublet of Míl, which results in three different invasions: Partholón, Nemed, and the Gaels under Míl.

This scenario is precisely what appears in the earliest account of the Irish invasion histories to have survived. It is not an Irish text, but a Welsh one, the *Historia Brittonum* ('History of the Britons'), composed in Latin by an unknown cleric somewhere in Gwynedd *c.*829/30.[41] Its author devotes some time to the origins of the inhabitants of his neighbouring island, and says that he has taken his information from 'the most learned of the Irish.'[42] His account is recognizably a kind of proto-

---

37 This includes 'The Second Battle of Moytura' if, as John Carey notes, we remove the pseudohistorical preamble about the origins of the Túatha Dé, which we know to be a later addition tacked onto the saga because its is clearly borrowed from *Lebor Gabála*; see G. Murphy, 'Notes on *Cath Maige Tuired*', *Éigse* 7 (1953–5), 195, and J. Carey, 'Myth and Mythography in *Cath Maige Tuired*', *SC* 24 (1989), 53–69, at 54. The first mention of them as invaders seems to be *Scél Tuáin*, *c.*900; see below, 147–8.

38 Tellingly, material about Íth—normally thought of as Míl's father—is also found attached to Partholón, supposed to have lived thousands of years earlier. This strongly suggests that the story of Partholón had budded off from that of Míl.

39 Scowcroft, '*Leabhar Gabhála*, Part II', 58.

40 Carey, Irish National Origin-Legend, 8.

41 See Charles-Edwards' comments, *W&TB*, 437–8; see also *L&IEMI*, 85.

42 *peritissimi Scottorum*: see *Historia Brittonum*, ed. Th. Mommsen, *Chronica Minora Saec. IV. V. VI. VII.* [*Monumenta Germaniae Historica AA* 13] (Berlin, 1898), iii., 156. Useful text and translation in *Nennius, British History, and the Welsh Annals*, ed. & trans. J. Morris (London, 1980).

Lebor Gabála and it is a crucial witness to the early development of the synthetic history. For the author of the *Historia Brittonum*, there were only three sets of Ireland's invaders: 'Partholomus', 'Nemedius', and the *miles Hispaniae*—Míl Espáine.[43]

The standard first settlement—the company of Cessair—is absent from the *Historia Brittonum*. As mentioned, Cessair's settlement is a kind of stillbirth, and it seems to have been a very late addition to the tradition and continued to be of doubtful canonicity for some time.[44] It is interesting, therefore, that she may nonetheless be of some antiquity. John Carey has plausibly suggested that she was originally a Leinster figure, perhaps a goddess associated with the confluence of the rivers Nore, Barrow and Suir near Waterford, one of the most impressive features of Ireland's hydrology.[45] If this is so, we can observe antique material still being incorporated into the synthetic history long after it had already assumed its basic shape. Also conspicuous by its absence in the *Historia Brittonum* is the invasion of the Túatha Dé. It is this absence that brings us at last to a consideration of the position of the god-peoples within the pseudo-history, and within *Lebor Gabála* in particular.

It has long been clear to scholars that the gods were the last major group to be incorporated into the synthetic history, which is hardly surprising. Nemed and Partholón had no currency outside pseudohistorical tradition, but there existed a substantial body of independent material about the god-peoples that varied conspicuously in detail and tone, which made them awkward to assimilate.

There is both direct and indirect evidence for the process of integration. Direct evidence includes the absence of the gods in the list of invasions in *Historia Brittonum*, c.830, as just noted; significantly, they are also omitted in a ninth-century set of synchronisms preserved in the Book of Ballymote. (A 'synchronism' matches up the lives or reigns of different persons, establishing who was contemporary with whom.)[46] Further evidence is visible within *Lebor Gabála* itself, which carefully makes Ireland's various invasions keep time with 'world empires'—the Assyrians, Persians, and so on. The Túatha Dé are the only race whose

---

43 Later he does mention one *Builc*, having clearly misunderstood the 'bags' of the Fir *Bolg* as a personal name.

44 The learned Gilla Cóemáin can be observed changing his mind about Cessair, for example.

45 J. Carey, 'The Origin and Development of the Cessair Legend', *Éigse* 22 (1987), 37–48.

46 Scowcroft, 'Leabhar Gabhála, Part II', 29–30.

reign does *not* synchronize with such an empire, and this points to their having been belatedly spliced into the scheme.

Indirect evidence for the late integration of the gods is provided by one of the notorious perversities of Irish mythology: confusingly, its gods fight not one, but *two* 'Battles of Moytura'.[47] In chapter 3, we examined the second of these, which features the conflict between the god-peoples and the Fomorians and has deep roots in Indo-European mythology. The *first* battle, on the other hand, is the conflict in which the incoming god-peoples defeated their predecessors, the Fir Bolg. The scholarly consensus has long been that the second battle, because of its obviously archaic roots, is the original, while the first is merely an uninspired doublet. It seems likely that the idea of a battle between the Túatha Dé and the Fir Bolg was a rationalizing invention of the pseudo-historical school, intended to supplant the tradition of a mythological conflict between the gods and the Fomorians. This may have been part and parcel of stripping the god-peoples of their supernatural status, but it had been made necessary by the fact that the Túatha Dé had been shoehorned into the narrative of successive invasions. Instead of the Gaels defeating the Fir Bolg, the Túatha Dé—now wedged between the two—had to play both roles, vanquishing the Fir Bolg on the one hand before themselves being vanquished by the incoming Gaels on the other. We will investigate the sheer *oddness* of this scenario in mythological terms later, for it has the ethnic Irish inflicting military defeat upon their own gods. But in retaining the ancient tradition of a Túatha Dé victory at Moytura, while redefining the vanquished as the human Fir Bolg rather than the supernatural Fomorians, the pseudohistorians no doubt felt that they had arrived at a tidy solution. Unfortunately for them (but fortunately for students of mythology) the Fomorians' defeat by the god-peoples was clearly tenacious in tradition and impossible to uproot.[48] This explains the doubling of the Moytura battles in *Lebor Gabála* as we have it.

It seems that the initial integration of the gods into the scheme of invasions probably took place late in the ninth century, and indeed 'The

---

47 See G. Murphy, 'Notes on *Cath Maige Tuired*', *Éigse* 7 (1953–5), 191–8.

48 'Cormac's Glossary', *c*.900, gives an anecdote about the craft-gods Goibniu, Credne, and Luchta forging weapons for the battle, and assigns it to the *senchus*, 'historical lore' of Ireland: this may well be around the same time as the original composition of 'The Second Battle'; *Sanas Cormaic*, ed. K. Meyer, *Anecdota from Irish Manuscripts*, ed. O. Bergin, R. I. Best, K. Meyer, & J. G. O'Keefe (Halle, 1912), iv, 83–4.

Second Battle of Moytura' may originally have been composed as a grand restatement of the traditional doctrine in the face of an ersatz version intended to supplant it.[49] The second battle was in turn absorbed into the structure of the pseudohistory during the eleventh century: the poems of Eochaid ua Flann and Tanaide only mention the first battle, but Flann Mainistrech knew of both, significantly terming them the 'first' and the 'great' battles of Moytura, respectively.[50] Carey points out that saga tradition added lustre to stretches of *Lebor Gabála* here; in Recension I, for example, the narrative of the second, or 'great', battle is significantly less dry than that of the first. There is some evidence that the idea of the 'first' battle against the Fir Bolg never really took off in Irish tradition outside the pseudohistorical school: a lacklustre Middle Irish saga on the subject appears to be an attempt to promote the story in literary circles.[51]

WHO, WHEN, AND WHERE

Here we must turn to what *Lebor Gabála* actually says about the reign of the Túatha Dé. The account of their sovereignty over Ireland falls into three sections. The first is a description of their invasion and defeat of the Fir Bolg—the 'first battle' of Moytura. The second provides a list of their kings; last comes an account of their genealogies. These three subsections look like they were originally separate tracts, and this tells us much about how *Lebor Gabála* was assembled. It suggests that the pseudo-

---

49 And which was effective; it may even have reactivated anxiety about gods as pagan figures, since Carey ('Myth and Mythography', 64, fn.57) notes that Núadu drops out as a personal name after the ninth to tenth centuries, 'perhaps due to its "remythologization"' in the saga. On the other hand, Óengus—equally once the name of a pagan god—continued to be popular.

50 Scowcroft, 'Leabhar Gabhála, Part II', 35–6.

51 This is 'The Battle of Moytura at Cong'—'Cath Maige Tuired Cunga', ed. & trans. J. Fraser, *Ériu* 8 (1915), 1–63. The name reflects a rather desperate attempt to distinguish the first and second battles by relocating the first to a different Moytura, near Cong in Co. Mayo. The belatedness of the tradition of the 'First Battle' is underscored by the fact that it is alluded to in a text called 'The Poem of the Forty Questions' (*Dúan in Chetharchat Cest*), a series of abstruse mythological posers written in the eleventh century. This seems to be the first mention of the 'First Battle' outside the *Lebor Gábala* tradition, and the whole point (tellingly) is that the answers were not mainstream knowledge. See 'Das Gedicht der Vierzig Fragen von Eochaid ua Cerin', ed. & German trans. R. Thurneysen, *ZCP* 13 (1921) 130–6, 132, 135.

historians scoured all available sources for information about the god-peoples, including glossaries and scholarly miscellanies, and that they patched these testimonia into the text more or less wholesale.

The first section ushers the gods onto the stage of Irish history. There is considerable variation in both detail and tone between the recensions, although they all agree that the god-peoples arrived and defeated the Fir Bolg in the first battle of Moytura. They arrive from the North—the most ill-omened direction in medieval thought. In some versions it is said that the sun and moon grew dark at their arrival, perhaps a disquieting pre-echo of the Crucifixion, the pivotal catastrophe of biblical history.[52] And whereas all previous peoples had reached Ireland by ship, the Túatha Dé arrive via a stagey special effect and make an aerial landing in clouds of black vapour:

> The descendants of Bethach son Iarbonél the Prophet son of Nemed were in the northern islands of the world, learning magic and knowledge and sorcery and cunning, until they were pre-eminent in arts of the heathen sages. They are the Túatha Dé Danann who came to Ireland.
>
> It is thus that they came: in dark clouds. They landed on the mountains of Conmaicne Réin in Connaught and they put a darkness upon the sun for three days and nights. Battle or kingship they demanded of the Fir Bolg. Battle was fought between them, the first battle of Moytura, in which a hundred thousand of the Fir Bolg fell. After that they took the kingship of Ireland.[53]

Conmaicne Réin, site of the Túatha Dé touchdown, is an area east of the Shannon and comprises parts of Counties Leitrim and Longford.[54] The god-peoples were meant to be descendants of Nemed, like the Fir Bolg, but this tradition makes them the medieval equivalent of eerie, technologically superior extraterrestrials.[55] Continuing in the same tone, the second recension also adds that they had been in Greece, where they had

---

52 Details of manuscripts on this point in Scowcroft, 'Leabhar Gabhála, Part I', 109–10.

53 LGE, iv., 106, 108 (text); trans. here by Carey, CHA, 252–3, slightly altered; text in Carey, 'Lebar Gabála, Recension I', 129–30.

54 E. Hogan, Onomasticon Goedelicum... (Dublin, 1910), 289–90.

55 Or demons; Isidore (Etymologiae, 8.xi, 16–17) had associated fallen angels with atmospheric murkiness and imagined them as imprisoned for all time in the 'lower air'; see below, 264.

put their knowledge to use infusing demonic spirits into corpses in order to help their Athenian allies in a war against the Philistines.[56] Curiously to modern eyes, this actually strengthens the pseudohistorians' attempt to classify the Túatha Dé as human rather than divine: that men and women might acquire the knowledge to force demons to do their will was a classic prop of the medieval explanation for magic.[57]

Other versions of *Lebor Gabála* present their arrival in a more positive light, with them travelling in ships they then burned in order to make it impossible to turn tail and flee: the clouds of inky vapour had only been their vessels going up in smoke.[58] Significantly, this rationalizing version was secondary: the motif of the Túatha Dé's supernatural arrival seems to have been the older of the two. We know this because something close to it appears in a text called *Scél Tuáin meic Chairill* ('The Tale of Tuán son of Cairell'), composed towards the end of the ninth century. The tale provides an account of the various invasions as witnessed by the ancient Tuán—the shapeshifting sole survivor of the Partholonians—and imparted by him to a saint, Finnia of Moville, who is going about converting the people of Ulster to Christianity. The text is crucial because it gives us a snapshot of an intermediate stage in the integration of the god-peoples into the synthetic history. It shows that around the year 900, the god-peoples were already thought of as one in the sequence of invaders, but that they had *not* (yet) been redefined as human descendants of Nemed in the way that had become orthodox a century or two later. Tuán speculates uneasily:

> Beothecht son of Iordanen took this island from the people that were in it. Of them are the Gáilióin, and the Túatha Dé and Andé, whose origin the men of learning do not know; but they thought it likely that they are some of the exiles who came to them from heaven.[59]

Here the Túatha Dé are still identified as fallen angels: presumably the idea of exile from heaven has influenced the uncanny motif of landing

---

56 *LGE*, iv., 138 (text), 139 (trans.).

57 See, for example, C. Saunders, *Magic and the Supernatural in Medieval Romance* (Woodbridge, 2010), 109–11.

58 See Scowcroft, 'Leabhar Gabhála, Part I', 109–10.

59 Translation by Carey, 'Scél Tuáin meic Chairill', 106; Irish text 102. For the phrase (Túatha) Dé and Andé (literally 'gods' and 'non-gods') see below, 168–9.

from the sky. A century or so later, the pseudohistorian Eochaid ua Flainn was still batting the arguments this way and that:

> Their numbers were sufficient, whatever impelled them;
> they alighted, with horror, in warlike manner,
> in their cloud, evil wars of spectres,
> upon the mountains of Conmaicne in Connaught.
>
> Without [?concealment they came] to skilful Ireland,
> without ships, a savage journey;
> the truth concerning them was not known beneath the starry
> heaven—whether they were of heaven or of earth.
>
> If from the demons, it is devils
> that comprised the troop of... famous exiles,
> a blaze [?] [drawn up] in ranks and hosts;
> if from men, they were Bethach's offspring.[60]

This looks like dithering, but it is rather a learned poet's scrupulous setting out of variant opinions, before allowing himself to reach his conclusion—the opposite to that of the 'Tale of Tuán'—and avow: 'they belong properly among mortals.' This is the first datable assertion in Irish tradition of the plain humanity of the former divinities; it was to become the standard pseudohistorical doctrine.

CITIES, SAGES, AND TREASURES

How did the pseudohistorians imagine that the Túatha Dé—apparently mere human beings—had acquired such power? Other versions of *Lebor Gabála* add more details about the arrival of the Túatha Dé, some declaring that they had learned their magical arts at the feet of four sages in four mysterious cities in the north of the world, whence they had brought four 'treasures' to Ireland.[61] This famous passage is worth quoting:

---

60 Trans. Carey, *CHA*, 254–5; text in Carey, '*Lebar Gabála*, Recension I', 133–4, with his earlier trans., 289–90.

61 The earliest surviving version of Recension I, that in the Book of Leinster, does not mention the cities or sages, and of the treasures alludes only to the Stone of Fál. The textual background to the 'four treasures' tradition is complex, though the actual data

Four cities in which they used to learn knowledge and lore and devilry: these are their names, Falias and Goirias and Findias and Muirias. From Falias was brought the Stone of Fál which is in Tara, which used to cry out beneath every king who used to take control of Ireland. From Goirias was brought the spear which Lug had: a battle would never go against the man who had it in hand. From Findias was brought Núadu's sword: no one might escape from it— from the moment when it was drawn from its battle-scabbard, there was no resisting it. From Muirias was brought the Dagda's cauldron: no group of people would go from it unsatisfied. Four sages in those cities: Mórfhesa, who was in Falias, Esrus who was in Goirias, Uiscias who was in Findias, Semias who was in Muirias. Those are the four poets (*filidh*), with whom the Túatha Dé Danann used to learn knowledge and lore.[62]

This was to become a vital part of the body of lore associated with the Túatha Dé, and it would capture the imagination of a number of writers who gave the gods their Anglo-Irish afterlife. Those set on interfusing Ireland's traditions into western hermeticism—W. B. Yeats in particular— were forcibly struck by the apparent symbolism here, which seemed to evoke the four elements of natural philosophy and esoteric doctrine.

This dimension of the gods' reception is discussed later, but the reader may wonder whether the medieval texts themselves actually point to any particular symbolism. We cannot push back the date of this tradition much before *c.*1100, for neither the four cities nor the four sages occur anywhere before *Lebor Gabála*, and only one of the four talismanic objects—the Stone of Fál—is significant in earlier texts.[63] While there is

---

involved is consistent. There are three versions. The first is that in the various manuscript versions of Recensions I (though, as said, *not* the earliest), II and III of *Lebor Gabála* itself, Scowcroft's Recensions a, b, and c; see Scowcroft, 'Growth of the Text', 110. The second account of the treasures forms the preamble to the extant Middle Irish redaction of 'The Battle of Moytura' (*CMT*, 24, 25), which clearly draws on an interpolated version of Recension I (see Carey, 'Myth and Mythography', 54). The third account is a short prose anecdote and poem found in the Yellow Book of Lecan (*c.*1400) and elsewhere. It uniquely identifies the god-peoples' northern home as Lochlann, which sometimes means Scandinavia and sometimes a more otherworldly or mythologized locale; see 'The Four Jewels of the Tuatha Dé Danann', ed. & trans. V. Hull, *ZCP* 18 (1930), 73–89.

62 This is from the version of Recension I in the fifteenth-century *Book of Fermoy* (*LGE*, iv., 106, 107). In some cases the accents are uncertain.

63 That said, the *lúin*—a legendary spear belonging to the Ulster hero Celtchair mac Uthechar—is strongly reminiscent of the spear of Lug, and may have inspired it. It ap-

always the chance that the treasures, sages, and cities represent a sounding from oral tradition, it is more likely they are late eleventh-century creations by the pseudohistorical school, which had an urgent need to invest the god-peoples with the trappings of hidden knowledge. This is because the *power* of the Túatha Dé posed a problem in exact proportion to their humanity. The key to the anecdote therefore is to appreciate that it partially explains how the Túatha Dé could have been human, as pseudohistorical doctrine had come to insist, and yet have exhibited the supranormal powers which tradition invariably accorded them.[64] It is tellingly bound up with the god-peoples' northern sojourn and descent from Nemed; there was no need for magical academies in the north when the gods were regarded as indigenous to Ireland, nor when they were seen as fallen angels, since magical expertise was intrinsic to demons. The pseudohistorians' solution to this bind was one that was particularly apt to comfort intellectuals: the assertion that knowledge itself is power.

One of the strongest arguments that the tradition is a late creation is the fact that the scenario of sages and cities closely resembles that of the educational structure of the eleventh-century Irish church. Schools were located in different monastic towns, each headed by one of the learned scholars termed *scribae* or *fir léginn* in the Annals.[65] The sages Uiscias, Semias, Esrus, and Mórfhesa would thus be reflections in a distorting mirror of those responsible for *Lebor Gabála* itself, the class of experts in biblical and native historical tradition: we saw that the version quoted above actually calls the four sages *filidh*, 'learned poets', though other accounts use the word *fissid*, 'seer', or *druí*, 'druid', emphasizing that theirs is specifically *pagan* knowledge, and that their cur-

---

pears in the originally ninth-century tale 'The Phantom's Frenzy' (*Baile in Scáil*), for which see *I&G*, 16; we are told 'it is the island of Fál from which it was brought.' Fál became an alternative name for Ireland itself, but this passage implies that Fál is somewhere else, perhaps the Fomorian-inhabited *Fál(gae)* identified with the Isle of Man in the early text 'The Siege of the Men of Fálgae' (*Forfess Fer Fálgae*) (*I&G*, 32–3). Celtchair's *lúin* is often wielded by other heroes; it is mentioned in a poem written in the mid-tenth century by Cináed ua hArtacáin and makes a vivid appearance in two tenth- or eleventh-century sagas, 'The Destruction of Da Derga's Hostel' and 'The Intoxication of the Ulstermen'. 'The Destruction' alleges that the *lúin* was discovered 'at the Battle of Moytura', which may have inspired the tradition of the spear of Lug, most prominent of the Túatha Dé in that battle; see *DDDH*, 170, 207.

64 See the comments of Charles-Edwards, *ECI*, 200–1.

65 *Cathrach*—the word used for the 'cities' in the text—is the plural of *cathair*, the normal term for a monastic town.

riculum, involving the black arts, is decidedly unwholesome.[66] The miraculous heirlooms associated with each city look like demonic—or at the very least ironic—counterparts to the venerated relics associated with major ecclesiastical foundations.[67] This is a version of the non-historical idea, attested as far back as Muirchú's seventh-century 'Life of Patrick', that Irish paganism had been Christianity's evil twin, complete with unholy, quasi-scriptural books and a learned priesthood teaching diabolical doctrine.[68] It is possible that the *-ias* endings of some of the names were concocted to echo the names inscribed on many an ogam stone: learned medieval scholars were able to read these, and though in many cases the language would have been opaque to them, they would certainly have recognized that they were looking at personal names of great antiquity.[69]

There is uncertainty behind the true meanings of the cities, sages, and treasures in the Túatha Dé (Table 4.1).[70] In theory, there is nothing intrinsically improbable about the idea that the four cities should echo the four elements, which formed part of mainstream medieval cosmology and were perfectly well known in Ireland.[71] 'Warm' and 'marine' cities and a 'watery' sage look promising for elemental correspondences;

66 See comments of E. A. Gray, '*Cath Maige Tuired*: Myth and Structure (1–24)', *Éigse* 18 (1980–1), 189.

67 Kim McCone made the brilliant observation that the inspiration behind the tradition may have been biblical: in Judges 18 the Israelite Tribe of Dan (a name reminiscent of the standard name for the Irish gods, 'Túatha Dé Danann') take four cult objects from the house of Micah, just before the invasion of the Promised Land; as they are, as a tribe, prone to lapses into idolatry, their situation closely parallels that of the Túatha Dé. See K. McCone, 'A Tale of Two Ditties: Poet and Satirist in *Cath Maige Tuired*', in Ó Corráin *et al.* (eds.), *Sages, Saints and Storytellers*, 143.

68 See *L&IEMI*, 127, for *fir léginn* and the supremacy of particular monastic institutions, and 110, fn.112 for this representation of druids.

69 *LGE*, iv., 293; -*ias* in Primitive Irish was the characteristic ending of the genitive singular of feminine -*ia* stem nouns and of the nominative of masculine -*io* stems; it was common on ogam inscriptions because '[the stone] of X son of Y' was the standard form for such inscriptions. But note also Macalister's point that biblical names in -*iah* (Isaiah, Jeremiah) ended in -*ias* in the Vulgate, so the names like *Semias* and *Uiscias* might have felt simultaneously Old Testament and archaically native.

70 Because these are invented names, none of these interpretations are definite; at best one can guess the associations the words might have set up in the minds of contemporary readers.

71 For this knowledge in Ireland, see M. Smythe, *Understanding the Universe in Seventh-Century Ireland* (Woodbridge, 1996), 47–87.

TABLE 4.1. THE CITIES, SAGES, AND
TREASURES OF THE TÚATHA DÉ

City	Sage	Treasure
Falias *fál*, 'hedge'?	*Mórfhesa* 'Greatness of Wisdom'	Stone of Fál
Goirias *gor*, 'fire, warmth'	*Esrus* *esrus*, 'means, channel, opportunity'	Spear of Lug
Muirias *muir*, 'sea'	*Semias* cf. *séim*, 'slender, transparent'?	The Dagda's Cauldron
Findias *find*, 'fair, bright'	*Uiscias* cf. *uisce*, 'water'	Sword of Núadu

but 'watery' Uiscias is not associated with the 'marine' city, Muirias, and there are other difficulties making these names fit.

In all, the balance of probabilities is that the tradition of the Túatha Dé's cities, sages, and treasures was a creation of the pseudohistorical movement itself, rather than an old—let alone pre-Christian—concept. The array of names seems designed to evoke and underscore the god-peoples' heathen knowledge, as a strategy for explaining their power after they had been humanized and historicized.[72] It is also noteworthy that it accords with a demonstrable high medieval interest in depicting the acquisition of magical learning. The pseudohistorian Geoffrey of Monmouth's mid-twelfth-century account of the magical isle of Avalon is a classic example, and provides a feminine equivalent for the cities of the Túatha Dé. He describes the island as kind of women's college headed by Morgen (Morgan le Fay), who teaches astrology to her eight sisters and who, like the god-peoples, is able to fly through the air. As with Semias, Uiscias, Esrus, and Mórfhesa, Morgen's sisters have names which smack of antiquity (phony Greek, in their case) so that we read of Moronoe, Mazoe, Glitonea, and the like.[73] As often with Irish mythology,

72 A brave attempt to find coherent symbolism behind this tradition is provided by F. Le Roux, 'Les Isles au Nord du Monde', *Hommages à Albert Grenier* (3 vols., Brussels, 1962), ii., 1051–62, at 1060.

73 Geoffrey of Monmouth, *Vita Merlini*, ed. & trans. B. Clarke, *Life of Merlin* (Cardiff, 1973), 100–3, 206–8.

apparent relics of heathen lore turn out to reflect intellectual and literary currents which were widespread in medieval Christendom.

GENEALOGIES

The second section of the Túatha Dé interlude in 'The Book of Invasions' is a chronological list of their kings with the lengths of their reigns—Núadu (seven years), Bres (also seven), Núadu again (twenty), Lug (forty), the Dagda (eighty), Delbaeth (ten), Fíachu son of Delbaeth (ten), and then the three grandsons of the Dagda, Mac Cuill, Mac Cécht, and Mac Gréine (twenty-seven, or an average of nine each).[74]

This part of the text need not detain us greatly. The earliest version is spare, though later ones stitch in a brief roll call of some of the Túatha Dé's more minor personnel at this point.[75] The regnal periods suggest symbolism: notably as the era of the god-peoples reaches its zenith, the kings' reigns double in length, not once but twice: twenty, forty, eighty. Blatantly artificial though this is, we may still discern an echo here of the Dagda's original mythological eminence as the 'supreme father': his kingship is the longest, after which things begin to fall away. It is also striking that the three longest reigns belong to figures who are all securely former gods, while those of minor and shadowy figures such as Fíachu and Delbaeth are shorter. The fundamental pseudohistorical doctrine that the god-peoples' sovereignty over Ireland was merely a phase is underscored by this numerical pattern of increase, apogee, and ebb.

The third and final subsection before the story of the Gaels resumes consists of the genealogies of the Túatha Dé, and it provides an inventory of the god-peoples with their various attributes. This part of *Lebor Gabála* has long been a happy hunting ground for those bent on excavating an Irish pantheon, because it contains some transparently old material and shows a clear relationship to the sagas. It is also fearsomely complex, and it is important to remember how fundamental the tracing of lineages was to the workings of power and hierarchy in early Ireland. There could be no nobility without the details of descent. Setting out the family tree of the god-peoples underlined their realness and provided a chain of relationships extending back into the mythical past. That said,

---

74 *LGE*, iv., 112–27.

75 Originally a separate anecdote; see 'A *Tuatha Dé* Miscellany', ed. & trans. J. Carey, *BBCS* 39 (1992), 24–45.

the gods are never identified as the ancestors of any group among the Irish—the role of forebear having been entirely usurped by the artificial figure of Míl Espáine—even though the ideal that the Gaels and the gods had intermarried had been implied by Máel Mura, and presumably represented the most ancient tradition.[76]

The gods' characters are basically consistent with their roles in the sagas, with a couple of striking exceptions. In contrast to 'The Second Battle of Moytura', there is no evidence in *Lebor Gabála* that Bres, son of Elatha, was thought to be a Fomorian, and his father is a fully paid-up member of the god-peoples. Another example of the closeness of this section to the world of the sagas is the fact that one early recension gives a précis of the story we know from the late medieval tale 'The Tragic Deaths of the Children of Tuireann' (*Oidheadh Chloinne Tuireann*), in which Lug punishes his father's killers with inventive sadism.[77]

The genealogies of the Túatha Dé form the most unstable section of the text, incorporating more fluctuations of detail than any other. A sense of long-standing debate about the identities and family relations of the gods is occasionally felt, as in this account of the divine physician, Dian Cécht:

> Dían Cécht had three sons, Cú and Cethen and Cían—and Míach was his fourth son, although many do not count him—plus his daughter Etan the poetess, and his other daughter Airmed the physician, and Coirpre the poet, son of Etan.[78]

'Many do not count him': how should variations of this sort be accounted for? This particular case strongly supports the argument in chapter 3 that Míach, son of Dían Cécht, was an artificial invention of the author of 'The Second Battle of Moytura', and that it took time for him to be integrated into the tradition. In other cases it looks as though the various recensions of *Lebor Gabála* were drawing on at least two, probably more, separate soundings from oral tradition.[79] (Tellingly, sometimes the same

---

76 Note Julius Caesar's statement that the Gauls believed they descended from the god *Dis Pater*, 'Father Dis' (P. Mac Cana, *Celtic Mythology* (London, 1968, revised edn. London, 1996), 36–9). Also note that the idea existed that some (subject) peoples were descended from the Fir Bolg, predecessors of the god-peoples—a clear sign of the gods' late integration into pseudohistorical tradition; see *L&IEMI*, 43–84, 88.

77 See discussion of this tale below, 260–8.

78 *LGE*, iv., 122 (text), 123 (trans.).

79 Scowcroft is undoubtedly right that oral tradition among the *literati* is a likely

bits of *data*—that so-and-so, the son of such-and-such, was responsible for this or that, for example—pop up in different words in different sections of the text: this is just what one would expect if the sources lay in oral tradition.) To the shapers of *Lebor Gabála*, the genealogies of the gods were not like an antique vase that had been carefully passed down; rather they resembled a series of patterned fragments which could be assembled in different ways, using different and more or less obvious kinds of glue. And while these blocks of oral material seem to have been broadly similar in outline, they clearly diverged in detail. All versions of the text agree, for example, that Coirpre 'the Poet' was the son of Dían Cécht's daughter Etan, but they vary wildly over the identity of his father.[80]

Thus the family tree of the god-peoples was clearly in a certain amount of flux—and small wonder, for the entire unwieldy edifice had become very complex by this stage, with a host of secondary figures assembled around a core of ex-divinities. New members of the Túatha Dé could materialize from many sources, not least the misinterpretation of toponyms as personal names many centuries after the demise of Irish paganism. Two of the most famous, the goddesses Ériu and Banba (both of whom give their names to Ireland itself) just might be of this type, as the names seem to mean 'abundant land' and 'plain of low hills' respectively, betraying no hint of divinity. Rather suspiciously for a supposedly ancient Irish goddess, the name Banba itself seems to be a borrowing from a late form of the British language well on its way to becoming Welsh.[81]

The densest growth was at the top of the family tree, at the artificial join where the pseudohistorians had been obliged to graft familiar figures like the Dagda into the kindred of Nemed, and so on back to Noah. This scheme predated *Lebor Gabála*, which nevertheless sets it out fairly clearly. The major grafting point was a shadowy figure named Tait son

---

source for this material, but we cannot wholly rule out a very early written tradition; as he notes, bare genealogical material of this sort looks much the same whether it is transmitted orally or in writing. See Scowcroft, '*Leabhar Gabhála*, Part I', 93–4.

80 See *CMT*, 119–21. There was uncertainly around the name *Etan*: sometimes it is found in the form *Étan*, or even *Étaín*.

81 *Ériu* comes from **(p)iweriu*, 'fat/abundant [land]', on which see G. R. Isaac, 'A note on the name of Ireland in Irish and Welsh', *Ériu* 59 (2009), 49–55; for Banba, see E. P. Hamp, 'Varia I: 4. *Banba* again', *Ériu* 24 (1973), 169–71. 'Banba' presumably referred originally to the rolling lands of northern Leinster, precisely the area in which influence from the neighbouring island was strong in the Roman and sub–Roman period.

of Taburn, supposed to have lived seven generations after his forefather Nemed and to have been the last common ancestor of all the Túatha Dé. From Tait there are still several generations before we arrive at any recognizable names. The core idea was that Tait's son Aldui (or Allae) had sired five sons, and it is from these that the various sub-branches of the god-peoples descend. The Dagda was Aldui's great-great-grandson, via Néit, Delbaeth, and Elatha; his brothers and children look like a self-contained and presumably very old unit, which groups most of the figures likely to be reflexes of genuinely pre-Christian gods.

As previously discussed, the pseudohistorians were most likely connecting blocks of orally sourced material here, which explains the blatantly artificial quality of most of the figures. Genealogically speaking, figures like Tait and Aldui are there simply to connect 'A' with 'B': they possess a merely notional existence and it seems unlikely that much in the way of narrative was ever attached to them. Nonetheless, the pseudohistorians deliberately borrowed names with mythological cachet in order to assemble the pedigree. This deliberate borrowing is most striking in the lineage of the Dagda, who is the most important member of the Túatha Dé in terms of paternity; it may be that his line of descent back to Tait son of Taburn is the earliest to be fabricated. His father, Elatha, 'Poetic Art', is not implausible as a theonym. His grandfather Delbaeth has the same name as one of the Dagda's brothers, and the name—possibly to do with 'shaping' or even 'shaping fire'—sounds archaic, so that he may reflect some lost deity.[82]

Further back is Néit, the Dagda's great-grandfather. A figure bearing this name is attested in 'Cormac's Glossary' as a war-god, husband of the goddess Nemain, associated with the Morrígan. Mythological data in early glossaries cannot necessarily be taken at face value, but in this case the entry is revealing and may well simply be true: '**Néit** i.e., a god of war among the pagan Irish. Nemain *uxor illius*, i.e., that one's wife.'[83] This is linguistically plausible, and there is no particular reason to doubt that an ancient deity underlies the figure.[84] However, the entry probably

82 S. P. MacLeod, '*Mater Deorum Hibernensium*: Identity and Cross-Correlation in Early Irish Mythology', *PHCC* 18/19 (1998/1999), 340, fn.4.

83 *Sanas Cormaic*, ed. Meyer, 82.

84 The word can just mean 'conflict, battle', from a root *nanti- 'be bold, aggressive', to do with 'living force', probably related to *nia*, 'champion, warrior'; see J. Vendryes, *Lexique étymologique de l'irlandais ancien: lettres MNOP* (Dublin, 1960), N7, and F. O. Lindeman, 'Varia VI', *Ériu* 50 (1999), 183–4.

refers to another Néit in the family tree: the Dagda's uncle. This younger Néit is indeed depicted as the husband of the three war-goddesses; the older Néit looks therefore like an artificial duplication brought in to extend the family tree upwards and backwards.[85] When hunting for the mythological core of the genealogies, doubling of names in this manner is a useful diagnostic sign of artificiality: in the pedigrees of medieval Irish nobles, a small number of common names constantly recur, but for obvious reasons this should *not* be characteristic of divine names.[86]

GODS AND POETS

It is of the first significance for the gods that the pseudohistorical doctrines were put into their authoritative form by poets. Much of the material about the gods in *Lebor Gabála* seems to have ultimately derived from the lore of the *filid*, and thus reflects their methods and preoccupations.[87] We saw that the gods could function as exemplars for the professions who made up the *áes dána* 'people of talent': the *filid*, as the most socially elevated of the *áes dána*, seem to have used the gods to conceptualize aspects of their own profession in an especially rich manner.[88]

On the surface, this might seem to entail a paradox; we saw earlier in this study that the professional poets had deeply identified with the Christian religion, and that historically their order derived from the fateful encounter between native schemes of learning and Christian literacy. According to hagiographical legend, when Patrick came before the court of Lóegaire mac Néill, supposed high king of Tara, the only people to rise in respect before the saint were a poet and his pupil. The

85 'Cormac's Glossary' records further detail under the head phrase *Bé Néit*, 'Néit's Wife', and puns on her name, *Nemain*, 'Poison', saying: '**Néit's Wife**, i.e. Néit was her husband's name; his woman was Nemain; that couple were indeed poisonous (*neimnech*)' (*Sanas Cormaic*, ed. Meyer, 17). The same source (16) tells us that the phrase *Bé Néit fort*, 'Néit's Wife [be] upon you!', was an Irish curse, perhaps much as people used to say 'To the devil with you!' There seems no reason to disbelieve this, and the expression might genuinely be very old.

86 See *ECI*, 631–2.

87 The role of the *filid* in *Lebor Gabála* has been noted; see Scowcroft, 'Leabhar Gabhála, Part II', 12; Johnston (*L&IEMI*, 138) notes that *coimgne* (perhaps 'historical synchronization') was part of role of the *filid*.

88 Useful discussion by L. Breatnach, 'Poets and Poetry', in K. McCone & K. Simms (eds.), *Progress in Medieval Irish Studies* (Maynooth, 1996), 65–78, at 76–7.

story tells us that the *filid* were concerned to represent themselves as an ancient order with roots in the deep past, but an order whose members had instantly perceived the truth of Christianity and readily accepted it.[89]

The *filid* did more than simply rehearse fables about the god-peoples in the secular storytelling for which they were responsible; rather they seem to have made them part of the way in which they imagined and transmitted their own schemes of knowledge.[90] To be a *fili* was to be a highly-trained professional, marked out by a course of study which involved (in Elva Johnston's words) 'oral knowledge, literate skills, and mnemonic training'.[91] They were expert in the grammatical analysis of the Irish language, in the highly formalized rules of poetic composition, and in training the memory to encompass the vast body of historical and legendary story, precedent, and genealogy which it was their business to know.[92]

In all these areas—both those to do with patronage and those to do with pedagogy—it is fairly easy to see how the native gods could be of use to the *filid*. A swift overview is necessary here before we look at how specific divinities were deployed. First and most important, *filidecht*—the art of the *fili*—was intrinsically secular, and because pagan gods were by definition out of place in the ecclesiastical sphere, they could function as useful markers of secularity.[93]

Secondly, it was essential to the *filid*'s identity to assert that their profession was an ancient, time-hallowed aspect of native culture, though this was not literally true.[94] The venerable and the obscure were their stock in trade, and these were spheres associated with the god-peoples, imagined to have ruled Ireland in the deep past. This was especially true in the realm of language, for the ability to speak in an allu-

89 On this anecdote, see Kim McCone's comments in *PPCP*, 90–2, 96–8.

90 On these see S. Mac Airt, '*Filidecht* and *coimgne*', *Ériu* 18 (1958), 139–52.

91 *L&IEMI*, 144.

92 I draw here on Johnston's analysis in *L&IEMI*, 134–62; T. Ó Cathasaigh, 'Aspects of Memory and Identity in early Ireland', in Eska (ed.), *Narrative in Celtic tradition*, 201–16; also L. Breatnach, 'Satire, Praise, and the Early Irish Poet', *Ériu* 56 (2006), 63–84.

93 *L&IEMI*, 156.

94 Language, especially metrics, is the classic example; a lot of *filidecht* involved what we would call linguistics, for which the medieval term was *grammatica*. The Irish language changed radically between 400 and 600, so that whatever linguistic conventions a pagan praise-poet followed at the turn of the fifth century must have differed in precise detail (though perhaps not so much in overall 'feel'), to those followed by his Christian counterpart at the turn of the seventh.

sive and cryptic form of 'poet's Irish' marked someone out as a *fili*.[95] A commentary on 'The Scholar's Primer', that crucial compendium of early Irish grammatical studies, provides a telling example. Ireland's various ancient peoples are said to have used different terminology for the grammatical genders of masculine, feminine, and neuter; it is the most obscure and archaic terms—*moth*, *toth*, and *traeth*—that are ascribed to the god-peoples.[96]

Thirdly, the art of the professional poet involved a degree of mental facility and verbal fluency that depended on a well-trained memory and long practice. Memory for medieval intellectuals was analogous to what we nowadays call the imagination: it was not just the rote cramming of facts, but a mode and precondition of artistic creativity.[97] Professional mind-training and poetic inspiration were inseparable, because their poetry was not primarily the expression of an individual poet's personality, but, first and foremost, a display of repertoire and technique. Only when that technique had been thoroughly mastered could a kind of miraculous ease be attained, an ease which underpinned the individual poet's claim to speak with authority.

It is an observable tendency for things involving inspiration to accrue supernatural tropes and personifications, which is why poets today still speak of their muse. That intellectual and artistic facility makes one godlike is a metaphor which the *filid* seem to have taken quite a long way; the name for one of the grades of their profession was *deán*, 'godling'.[98] (Compare the way we use the term 'diva'—literally 'goddess'—or the way that members of the Academie française are elevated to a pantheon of *immortels*.) Essentially, there is some evidence that the *filid* used the native gods to symbolize the more mysterious dimensions of their art, and to mark it out as an esoteric and hoarded form of knowledge

95 *L&IEMI*, 147.

96 P. Russell, '*Moth, toth, traeth*: sex, gender and the early Irish grammarian', in D. Cram, et al. (eds.), *History of Linguistics 1996: selected papers from the Seventh International Congress on the History of the Language Sciences, Oxford, 12–17 September 1996* (Amsterdam, 1996), 203–16. Russell points out that etymologically the three terms are coarsely genital—interestingly so, given some sagas' emphasis on the gods' sexuality. The observation is significantly ascribed to Amairgen, legendary proto-*fili*.

97 I owe this point to Elva Johnston, *L&IEMI*, 163.

98 For the grade of *deán*, see L. Breatnach, *Uraicecht na Ríar: the poetic grades in early Irish law* (Dublin, 1987), 33–6, 39–41, 82, 99. Useful discussion of bardic grades in P. Sims-Williams & E. Poppe, 'Medieval Irish literary theory and criticism', in A. Minnis & I. Johnson, (eds.) *The Cambridge History of Literary Criticism* (Cambridge, 2005), ii., 293–8.

that defined learned poets as a separate and special group within early Irish society.[99]

I have spent some time discussing the nature of *filidecht* in order to make it clear that it was a system of learning couched in terms defined by Elva Johnston as 'at once pragmatic and mythopoetic, especially at the intersection between learning and composition'.[100] As storytellers, the *filid* were skilled at adapting stories of the native gods to new circumstances; it should be no surprise if they also used such vivid figures to encapsulate complex abstractions in concrete terms. 'Mythopoeia'— the self-conscious making of myths—is indeed the correct term, for the *filid*'s use of the gods was no hangover from Irish paganism. Rather, it was a framing of the scholarly in terms of the supernatural, enabled by medieval scholars' intense and characteristic fondness for personification and allegory.[101] The impression that emerges—and again this echoes observations made in previous chapters—is that the professional poets of pre-Norman Ireland put versions of the pagan deities of their ancestors to work as a kind of symbolic or allegorical pantheon. Here begins—let me clearly signal—a more speculative part of my argument, though it builds on the work of others; it is detachable from what has gone before.

'THE GODS OF SKILL'

Several among the god-peoples bear names that explicitly connect them with the arts: one very obvious example is Credne, the divine bronze-worker, whose name etymologically means the 'skilled one' and is related to *cerd*, 'art, skill, artisan'.[102]

A tighter core of divinities, however, seems to have been specifically associated with the *filid*'s own arts of language (Fig. 4.3). Elatha, generally identified as the father of the Dagda, is also a noun meaning

---

99 *L&IEMI*, 162.

100 *L&IEMI*, 147.

101 Mythopoeia was to a degree always part of the learning of the *filid*; a good example is the 'Cauldron of Poesy', a text written c.700–50, which describes how poetic inspiration comes from the *síd*-mounds *and* (simultaneously) from God; see 'The Cauldron of Poesy' ed. & trans. L. Breatnach, *Ériu* 32 (1981), 45–93, at 67–9.

102 For Credne < **kride(s)nios*, 'Skilled One', see E. P. Hamp, 'Old Irish *Credne, cerd*, Welsh *cerdd*', in J. T Koch, J. Carey, & P.-Y. Lambert (eds.), *Ildánach, Ildírech: A Festschrift for Proinsias Mac Cana* (Andover, 1999), 49–51.

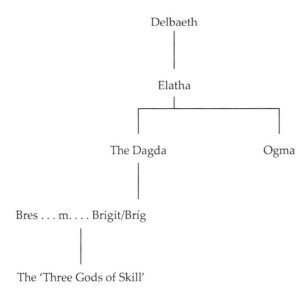

Delbaeth

Elatha

The Dagda   Ogma

Bres . . . m. . . . Brigit/Bríg

The 'Three Gods of Skill'

FIG. 4.3. Suggested view of the 'Pantheon of Skill'.

'skill, art, science, branch of learning'—particularly poetry. According to John Carey, Ogma, another of Elatha's sons, was 'associated with the literary lore of the native intelligentsia' as inventor of the ogam alphabet, supposedly named after him. Carey remarks of these figures that 'Elatha is consistently associated with Bress, Ogmae, the Dagdae, and the more shadowy Delbaeth; he is evidently another figure in what we may call the "pantheon of skill" '.[103] (It is striking that the author of 'The Second Battle of Moytura' nonetheless felt able to radically re-arrange this symbolic family, making Elatha a Fomorian for the purposes of his tale.)[104]

Within this poetic pantheon the goddess Brigit, daughter of the Dagda and wife of Bres, was apparently of considerable significance. She is a paradoxical and unique figure in the mythology, characterized by curious bifurcations of identity. Even her name has two forms, Brigit and Bríg; she seems to be both one entity and also a trio of sisters. Most famously of all she most likely bears some connection to her Christian namesake, Brigit of Kildare, Ireland's most beloved female saint. (Schol-

103 Carey, 'Myth and Mythography', 57.

104 Carey remarks that 'The notion of a "Fomorian Elatha" is due to the reinterpreta-tion of Bres in CMT' ('Myth and Mythography', 64, fn.44).

ars have found the precise nature of this connection impossible to un-ravel, and debate continues as to whether it actually exists at all.)[105] The strange split in the goddess is starkly visible in the sources. She makes one, and only one, appearance in an actual narrative, 'The Second Battle of Moytura', in which her role is to lament the killing of her son Rúadán. At the same time, 'Cormac's Glossary' lauds her divinity in the most exalted and specific terms used of any Irish goddess.[106] This famous entry is worth quoting in full; italics indicate a change from Irish to Latin.

> **Brigit**, i.e., a female poet, daughter of the Dagda. She is Brigit the female sage of poetry (or woman of poetic skill), i.e., Brigit a god-dess whom the *filid* used to worship. For very great and very splen-did was her application to the art [*frithgnam*]. *Therefore they used to call her goddess of poets, whose sisters were* Brigit the female phy-sician and Brigit woman of smithcraft, daughters of the Dagda, *from whose names almost all the Irish used to call Brigit a goddess.*[107]

This rich description articulates a special imaginative connection be-tween Brigit as supremely skilled poet and the professional poets who 'used to' worship her. The tense is significant: this bit of lore can only have come down to the glossary's compiler from the *filid* themselves, and their devotion to Brigit the goddess is clearly *not* meant to be a mat-ter of contemporary custom in the literal sense. It is also important not to overestimate the narrator's enthusiasm: two of the three explicit statements of Brigit's divine status are couched in Latin, a shift of regis-

---

105 Lucid summary of points of doubt by N. Kissane in *DIB*, under 'Brigit'. There is still another even more shadowy Bríg, identified as a female judge and counsellor in legal texts. It is not at all certain that she was imagined to be supernatural, and so she may or may not be the same as the daughter(s) of the Dagda; see Kelly, *A Guide to Early Irish Law*, 55, 187, 358.

106 *CMT*, 56, 57. The account contains a haunting line: 'Bríg came and keened for her son. At first she shrieked; in the end, she wept.' See 'A *Tuatha Dé* Miscellany', ed. Carey, 28, 30, 33–4, for Bríg/Brigit as the inventor of meaningful but non-verbal forms of speech (keening, whistling 'as a signal at night'). The same source tells us that with this act Brigit invented keening, a form of vocal lament thought to be characteristically female. One wonders if the *filid* associated this with their own responsibility for poems of lament and mourning.

107 *Sanas Cormaic*, ed. Meyer, 15. Some manuscripts of the 'Glossary' add that Brigit derives from *breoshaigit*, 'fiery arrow', but this is a typical medieval etymology and not actually true; the real origin of the name is Celtic *Brigantī*, meaning 'Exalted One'.

ter which, as previously mentioned, often indicates a desire on the part
of the glossator to put distance between himself and what is being said.
It is tellingly similar to the famous entry on Manannán mac Lir, in
which the opening description of Manannán's skill at sea as a merchant
is in Irish, while the assertion that the Irish and Britons had called him
'god of the sea' is in Latin.[108]

Therefore, it is possible that Bríg/Brigit and Bres were a highly significant pair of symbols to the *filid*, although evidence for this is indirect. It is necessary here to read against the grain of the surviving material, in which Brigit is oddly fugitive and Bres seems to have been
wrenched out of his traditional role and reshaped as the archetypal bad
king. Their importance is underlined by their children, a mysterious trio
known as the *trí dé dána* ('The Three Gods of Skill'). While the name is
resonant, they are wavering and confused figures in the tradition as it
has come down to us. Informed guesswork suggests that they began as a
kind of concentrated personification of the *áes dána*, and may originally
have been identified as the three 'craft-gods' *par excellence*: Goibniu the
blacksmith, Credne the bronze-worker, and Luchta or Luchtaine, the
wright.[109] Later, various mix-ups seem to have got in the way. The term
dána, 'of skill', was misunderstood as the name of a goddess, so that the
three gods became her sons instead of Brigit's. They also became identified—not least in *Lebor Gabála*—with another (rather nasty) threesome,
Brian, Iuchar, and Iucharba, the sons of Tuirenn. It is this trio who con-
spire to murder Lug's father Cían, and they are brutally punished for
it.[110] Despite this ambiguity, Carey astutely states that 'it is most reason-
able to see Bríg and the *trí dé* as figures belonging to the elaborate repertoire of imagery employed by the professional poets... Bres, closely
linked with them... is to be assigned to the same context'.[111] Thus we can
reconstruct a micro-pantheon of allegorical gods associated especially
with verbal skills, not as a survival of paganism, but as part of the literary lore of early Christian Ireland's secular intelligentsia.

Two minor Túatha Dé figures, Ollam and his son Aí, make the connection with poetry more overt. The father's name ('most supreme') was
the standard term for a master-poet: it remains the Irish word for 'professor'. The son's simply means 'inspired poetry', from a root **awe-*,

---

108 See below, 251–2.
109 See *CMT*, 97, and *EIH&M*, 308ff.
110 See below, 260–8.
111 Carey, 'Myth and Mythography', 56.

'breath, wind, blow', which has a very long history in Indo-European poetic vocabulary.[112] A Middle Irish birth tale about Aí provides an allegory for how the art of poetry came into existence in Ireland. Ollam, son of Delbaeth, is the brother of Fíachna, one of the Túatha Dé kings of Ireland. One day as they sit together, a 'great gust of wind'—recall the etymology of *aí*—blows over the house. The king's druid interprets this to mean that a 'wonderful art' equal in dignity to kingship will be born into Ireland, embodied in the king's unborn nephew, Ollam's son. The baby is born, and Fíachna tries to have him killed, but is prevented. The newborn infant then miraculously speaks, demanding all the rights and rewards owed to poets by kings in the name of Fíachna's honour:

> My territory, my couple,
> a cauldron of provisions with a vat;
> let division of gifts be granted by the king of Mugna;
> a vessel, a cup,
> a chariot, an ivory-hilted sword,
> thirty cows, a quern of the
> war-bands of Fíachna.

'It will be given', said Fíachna. 'What name will be given to the boy now?' 'Let him be called Aí', said the druid. It was from this that poetic craft (*aí airchetail*) was so called, that is, from Aí, son of Ollam. And that was the first poetical composition, spoken by Aí, son of Ollam.[113]

Only the *filid* can be responsible for this story, which underscores their high status and indispensible place within the social hierarchy. (Ollam,

---

112 *Elada, elatha, DIL* s.v., frequently renders Latin *ars*. *Ollam* was the standard term for the highest grade of learned poet, and literally means 'master, greatest', the superlative of *oll*, as in the Dagda's title *oll-athair*, 'Supreme Father'. *Aí* is cognate with Welsh *awen*, 'poetic inspiration', and Greek *Aiolos*, 'god of winds'—the core idea of inspiration as divine afflatus, which this story seems to underscore; on the other hand a root to do with 'seeing' has been proposed, for which see C. Watkins, *How to Kill a Dragon: Aspects of Indo-European Poetics* (Oxford, 1995), 117.

113 Trans. of the verse by J. Carey, *CHA*, 222; text and trans. of the rest from J. Carney, 'The Deeper Level of Early Irish Literature', *The Capuchin Annual* (1969), 160–71, at 169–70; quoted in J. Radner, '"Men Will Die": Poets, Harpers, and Women in Early Irish Literature', in *Celtic Language, Celtic Culture: A Festschrift for Eric P. Hamp* (Van Nuys, CA, 1990), 172–86, at 173–4.

Aí's father, is said to have *half the house* and an equal number of retainers to his royal brother: poets are placed here on an equal footing with kings.) Once again this presents a clear example of personages in the mythic time of the god-peoples being deployed to legitimize, explain, and personify elements of the poets' profession and repertoire.

The father/son pairing of Ollam and Aí raises further questions about the purposes served by the genealogies in *Lebor Gabála*. These formed a part of the text likely to have been sourced from oral tradition among the *filid*, which suggests that the pedigrees of the gods were memorized not only because the *filid* needed to be able to remember and recite stories about the Túatha Dé—crucial though that was—but also because they found family trees a useful way to visualize the branches and interrelations of native learning. Because the *filid* placed so much weight on the importance of human inspiration, the figure of Aí is again illuminating. The story of Aí's conception might be compared with a statement from an obscure Old Irish tract included within an eighth-century law text, *Bretha Nemed*, that *filidecht* subdivides into 'music' (*séis*), 'hearing' (*clúas*), and 'voice' (*guth*). These combine with 'breath' (*anál*) to yield 'inspired poetry', *aí*.[114] This is an account of the origins of inspiration in a very different vein, without personification, but it is easy to see how it could lend itself to being packaged in the form of a family tree. The implication is that metaphor—specifically personification—could allow *grammatica* to be figured as genealogy.

Further support is lent by a fascinating work from the ninth or tenth century, *Immacallam in dá Thúarad* ('The Colloquy of the Two Sages').[115] Composed by or for the *filid*, it seems to have been a text in which they took much pleasure.[116] It depicts a competition between Ferchertne, a seasoned poet, and his teenage-prodigy rival, Néde.[117] It is a rich display

114 'An Old Irish Tract on the Privileges and Responsibilities of Poets', ed. E. J. Gwynn, *Ériu* 13 (1940–2), 1–60, 220–36, at 5, 35–40, and 227–8.

115 Carey ('Myth and Mythography', 56) suggests a pre-ninth-century date; text ed. & trans. W. Stokes as 'The Colloquy of the Two Sages', *RC* 26 (1905), 4–64; this remains the standard edition.

116 *L&IEMI*, 171.

117 Important critical statements are M. Clarke, 'Linguistic Education and Literary Creativity in Medieval Ireland', *Cahiers de l'Institut de Linguistique et des Sciences de Langage* 38 (2013), 39–71; C. D. Wright, 'From Monks' Jokes to Sages' Wisdom: The *Joca Monachorum* Tradition and the Irish *Immacallam in dá Thúarad*', in M. Garrison, A. P. Orbán, & M. Mostert (eds.), *Spoken and Written Language: Relations between Latin and the Vernacular Languages in the Earlier Middle Ages* (Turnhout, 2013), 199–225; finally L. L. Patton, 'Space and time in the *Immacallam in dá Thuarad*', *Folklore* 103.1 (1992), 92–102. Note that

of the ways in which the *filid* visualized their own repertoire in the period—far richer than can be discussed here—because it presents two fictional *filid* showing off their command of the specialized jargon of their
profession.[118] Some of their exchange remains impenetrable, but the general impression is that the ability to allude to *recherché* lore and pene-
trate mythological metaphors marked one out as a qualified member of
the *filid* club.[119] Much of the lore in the 'Colloquy' is metapoetic: it is
difficult poetry about how difficult poetry is.

The pivotal moment comes when Néde, the young poet, is asked about
his ancestry. He rattles off a family tree for his professional mastery
which goes all the way back to the Túatha Dé:

> I am son of Poetry,
> Poetry son of Scrutiny,
> Scrutiny son of Meditation,
> Meditation son of Great Knowledge,
> Great Knowledge son of Enquiry,
> Enquiry son of Investigation,
> Investigation son of Great Knowledge,
> Great Knowledge son of Great Sense,
> Great Sense son of Understanding,
> Understanding son of Wisdom,
> Wisdom, son of the Three Gods of Skill.[120]

This passage can be read as an account of how learned poetry percolates
through the mind, couched in a genealogical metaphor which interfaces

---

C.-J. Guyonvarc'h's offbeat *The Making of a Druid: Hidden Teachings from 'The Colloquy of
Two Sages'* (Rochester, VT, 2002, original French edn. 1999) provides bits of useful commentary but is also seriously misleading.

118 Jargons of this kind—verbal artfoms deliberately opaque to outsiders—were a
common feature of medieval Irish privileged professions; note the title of R. C. Stacey's
book on legal performance, *Dark Speech: The Performance of Law in Early Ireland* (Philadelphia, PA, 2007), and see the remarks of J. Carey, 'Obscure styles in medieval Ireland',
Mediaevalia 19 (1996), 23–39.

119 These are reminiscent in general feel, but not in detail, of the mythological kennings characteristic of Old Norse-Icelandic skaldic verse.

120 Stokes, 'The Colloquy of the Two Sages', 30, 31. 'Great Knowledge' occurs twice
here, albeit in slightly different grammatical forms: it may not be a coincidence that the
identical phrase was a sobriquet of the Dagda's—as *Ruad rofhessa*, 'Red One of Great
Knowledge'—and this may be another sign that rhetorical personifications and mythological personages were closely aligned.

with the Túatha Dé at the top of the pedigree. We saw earlier that the 'Three Gods of Skill' are said—in a gloss on this very text, in fact—to be Bres's sons by Brigit, daughter of the Dagda, whom 'Cormac's Glossary' described as the poets' special patron.[121] Elizabeth Boyle has emphasized the degree to which the interpretion of texts on a figurative level was inculcated by the mode of education shared by ecclesiastical scholars and secular men of learning up to the beginning of the twelfth century. This mode of education may well have played a role in fostering a fondness for the use of mythological metaphors among the *filid* in the ninth and tenth centuries, flowering as vivid personifications and didactic allegories; some implications are explored below.[122]

In the 'Colloquy' it is clear that Néde intends his poetic family tree to be taken metaphorically: it describes a concatenation of mental processes proper to a mind trained in *filidecht* and he is keen to make that plain.[123] Other texts of a later date offer parallels. For example, from c.1200, *Echtra Cormaic i Tir Tairngiri* ('Cormac's Adventure in the Land of Promise') provides an elaborate description of an otherworldly well from which five streams flow. In the story the god Manannán explains to Cormac that he is looking at the 'fountain of knowledge', and the five streams are the five senses. Human knowledge amounts to drinking from the streams or from the well itself: only those who possess 'many arts'—that is, the learned classes—drink from both. Here again the workings of the trained human mind—the processes of perception, cognition, and creativity—are being allegorized through extended mythological metaphors.[124]

The overall control and influence of the *filid* on the role of the native gods in Irish culture emerges clearly, and the *Lebor Gabála* genealogies may allow us to catch an echo of the mnemonic devices which the *filid* employed to encode information. Certainly they remembered complex pedigrees for the gods; they deployed them in allegories of native

---

121 Quoted by Carey, 'Myth and Mythography', 56.

122 E. Boyle, 'Allegory, the *áes dána* and the Liberal Arts in Medieval Irish Literature', in *Grammatica and the Celtic Vernaculars in the Medieval World*, ed. D. Hayden & P. Russell [forthcoming, 2016]. This piece was kindly shown to me by the author before publication; as a result it is not possible to give page numbers.

123 The Irish habit of using the word *mac(c)*, 'son', plus a noun to express professional identity may have made this especially easy: a *mac léiginn*, 'son of reading', was a clerical student, while a *mac báis*, 'son of death', was a plunderer, and so on. See below, 254.

124 Expertly discussed in Boyle, 'Allegory, the *áes dána* and the Liberal Arts', on which I draw here.

schemes of knowledge; they emphasized their order's connection to the past in which these beings had been taken as divine; and they probably also intended certain stories to be read figuratively. But it should be stressed that the *filid* were not atavistic semi-pagans. One poem (quoted earlier) ascribed to Eochaid ua Flainn makes this ringingly clear via a long list of the god-peoples' major personages:

> It is clear that the one who wiped them from their land,
> from the royal plain, was the Son of God; I proclaim [it].
> despite the valour of their deeds in their bright division
> their race does not remain in Ireland.

> It is Eochaid, without fury of enchantments [?],
> Who arranges their fair divisions;
> Apart from knowledge of the companies we declare,
> though we enumerate them, we do not worship them.[125]

The *filid*'s habit of working individual deities or chains of deities into figurative or allegorical representations of knowledge may help to explain a well-known oddity. As we saw earlier, the late ninth- or early tenth-century 'Tale of Tuán mac Cairell' describes the arrival of the 'Túatha Dé *and Andé*' as a mysterious race of semi-demonic 'exiles from heaven'.[126] *Andé* means 'non-gods', and in *Lebor Gabála* we find the same idea: 'their men of skill (*áes dána*) were gods... but their farming people (*áes trebtha*) were non-gods.' Scholars have spilled much ink over this, positing two categories of deity in ancient Irish paganism: high gods associated with the products of culture and a group of lesser gods associated with agriculture. Some force is added to this picture because it closely resembles Norse mythology, which also features two types of god, the lofty Æsir and earthy Vanir.

But there is no need to look back into a hypothetical past. What seems more likely is that this statement represents a doctrine of the *filid*, according to which the basic division of Irish society into the skilled professionals and those involved in husbandry has been couched in terms of

---

125 *LGE*, iv., 218; trans. Carey, *CHA*, 256. This poem suggests that in the later tenth century some among the learned poets had grown touchy about the importance of ex-gods in their intellectual repertoire, in the face of critics within the pseudohistorical movement.

126 See above, 147–8.

one of their favourite metaphors: to possess a skill is to be godlike. This has then been retrofitted onto the Túatha Dé, from where the statement then comes that some of the gods were not gods at all. Far from being a relic of Irish paganism, the concept of 'gods and non-gods' is probably a development of the early Christian period, reflecting the gods' shift from divinities to members of a society imagined as similar to that of early Ireland.

'THE SEVEN PRIMARY SKILLED ONES'

As a kind of hangover of the outmoded idea that the *filid* were 'Christian druids'—a phrase guaranteed to bring the specialist out in hives—there is a tendency to imagine that the order of professional poets and men of letters remained basically the same between the sixth and eleventh centuries. Scholars have demonstrated that this was not the case, and that the role of the learned poets within the literate landscape was always changing. In short, it is possible that while the *filid* did not believe in the likes of the Dagda or Brigit as gods—'though we enumerate them, we do not worship them'—from the middle of the ninth century they became increasingly attached to them as allegories, mnemonics, and images of that within their body of learning which was *not* shared with ecclesiastical scholars.[127] The gods added to the aura of romantic antiquity which it had become convenient for the *filid* to stress, and 'pagan' supernatural tropes were invoked in order to underline their supposed roots in the ancient past and so assert their professional distinctiveness.

If this is so, then the potential ramifications are thought provoking. As noted earlier, Elizabeth Boyle has stressed that reading for non-literal levels of meaning was an essential part of the training of the learned, and that it arose directly from the way the Bible was interpreted. She makes the case that Irish men of learning wrote, on occasion, as they had been taught to read, by implanting layers of metaphorical meaning into vernacular texts. And if the gods—once the religious framework of Irish paganism had faded—were available to the literati for recycling as a stock of metaphors and personifications, then we are faced with the fundamental problem that we have no way to gauge how conservative or

---

127 See the comments of John Carey, 'The three things required of a poet', *Ériu* 48 (1997), 41–58, 47, upon which I draw here.

radical that process was for any particular divinity.[128] In other words, the fact that some among the *filid* seem to have thought in terms of a 'pantheon of skill'—including probable former deities like Brigit and Ogma—may not be a holdover from Irish paganism; instead it might be a development entirely of medieval scholarship, and thus tell us *literally nothing* about how those gods had been envisaged in the pre-Christian era.[129] Further research is needed, but this disheartening possibility must be regarded seriously.

On the other hand, there is certainly evidence that there were different schools of thought about the gods and their pedigrees among the *filid*, although it is difficult to say whether this was down to variation over time or between poetic authorities in different parts of Ireland. We find hints in two places that some *filid* thought in terms of a special group of seven or eight 'skilled' gods with whom they were prone to identify, hinting at conceptual or metaphorical structures within the patheon itself. Again, this is probably not ancient: *Lebor Gabála* is full of groups of eight, largely thanks to the biblical story of Noah in which eight human beings took ship on the Ark.[130] Seven is also a crucial number in the Bible, and in medieval Christendom: we have the seven days of creation, the seven gifts of the Holy Spirit, the seven sacraments, and so on.

In some versions of Recension II of *Lebor Gabála*, the Túatha Dé are said to have followed Bethach son of Iarbonél and 'seven subsidiary leaders'. These are termed the seven sons of Ethliu/Ethlenn, normally the name of Lug's Fomorian mother; this turns the normal genealogy into nonsense because the seven are revealed as not just Lug, but also the Dagda, Dían Cécht, Credne, Luchtaine, Núadu, and Goibnenn.[131] It is possible that the female name Ethlenn (genitive of *Ethliu*) has become

---

128 Boyle quotes R. Mark Scowcroft ('Abstract narrative in Ireland', *Ériu* 46 (1995), 121–58, at 156–7): 'Once organised paganism ceased, its *idéologie* would be rapidly dissipated by mythopoeia itself, the multiplication and variation of ancient traditions diluting (if not obscuring) their specifically religious associations, to provide the literati instead with a corpus of hidden learning and "implicit metaphor" as compelling and useful as classical mythology for the rest of medieval Christendom.'

129 Boyle makes this point about the depiction of the otherworld, but the principle works for the gods as well.

130 For Noachic octads spreading through *Lebor Gabála*, see Scowcroft, '*Leabhar Gabhála*, Part II', 22–5.

131 In Middle Irish *Goibnenn* (the genitive case of *Goibniu*) increasingly came to replace the original nominative form: they are the same figure.

confused with Elatha ('Art', genitive *Elathan*), father of the Dagda.[132] The 'seven sons of Elatha' would still be unusual in terms of the normal family tree, but not freakish.[133]

This group of eight is reminiscent of one that occurs in *Lebor Bretnach* ('The British Book'), a late eleventh-century Irish translation of the Latin *Historia Brittonum*, which (as seen earlier) contains a crucial version of the invasions-schema. Dating to the early ninth century, it attests to a time when the Túatha Dé had not yet been integrated into its structure. When medieval scholars—perhaps in Ireland, but possibly in Scotland—translated the *Historia* into Irish, they updated its version of the pseudohistory and inserted the god-peoples into what was by then their conventional place.[134] Some versions of *Lebor Bretnach* attribute the translation to Gilla Cóemáin (*fl.*1072), one of the four authoritative *Lebor Gabála* poets; the version of the god-peoples in *Lebor Bretnach* differs in significant ways from that text. Either Gilla Cóemáin was not the translator, or his views changed.

The major oddity is that *Lebor Bretnach* focuses in on a pared-down pantheon consisting of only the seven *prímelathnaig* ('chief skilled ones') among the Túatha Dé.[135] Intriguingly, the list differs slightly from that in Recension II of *Lebor Gabála*, comprising Ogma, Etan, the Dagda, Dían Cécht, Credne, Luchtaine, Lug, and Goibnenn. Etan—the only female—has been added, while Núadu had been lost. The passage is in a mixture of Latin and Irish, and is worth quoting because it is so rare to see the native gods referred to with Latin attributes:

After that the *plebes deorum* [god-peoples], i.e. the Túatha Dé Danann, conquered Ireland. Among them there were the chief skilled ones: Etan; Luchtaine *Artifex* [the Artificer]; Credne *Figulus* [the Craftsman]; Dían (Cécht) *Medicus* [the Physician]—Etan moreover was *filia eius* [his daughter], i.e., the fostermother of the poets; Goibnenn *Faber* [the Smith]; Lug son of Eithne, who possessed all the arts; the great Dagda, son of Elatha, son of Delbaeth, the king;

---

132 See comments of Gray, *CMT*, 120.

133 *Clann Eladan* (= *Elathan*), 'the children of Elatha', is used in Recension I of *Lebor Gabála* to refer to the Túatha Dé as a whole; see Carey, 'Myth and Mythography', 57.

134 T. O. Clancy, 'Scotland, the "Nennian" Recension of the *Historia Brittonum*, and the *Lebor Bretnach*', in S. Taylor (ed.), *Kings, Clerics and Chronicles in Scotland, 500–1297* (Dublin, 2000), 87–107.

135 Note that the element *elathnaig* is the plural of *elathnach*, derived from *elatha*, 'art', which we have seen used as the name of the father of the Dagda.

Ogma, the king's brother—he it was who invented the alphabet of the Irish.[136]

Putting this together, we can tentatively posit that the *filid* were prone to identify the after-images of certain gods as the patrons and personifications of the particular professional skills proper to the *áes dána*. Possibly—but by no means necessarily—they were building on genuinely ancient elements in particular cases. However, as their order increasingly risked complete assimilation into the ranks of the ecclesiastical *literati*, foregrounding the native gods may have been a strategy to bolster their archaic mystique and distinct identity. By the mid-eleventh century, and probably much earlier, there are signs that this concept had developed into the idea of an exclusive club of seven or eight allegorical gods who were specifically the prototypes and originators of the major *áes dána* professions.[137] In Recension II of *Lebor Gabála*, the list of the seven divinities is immediately followed by the statement that:

> ... they studied knowledge and the art of the *filid*, for every secret of skilful art, and every technique in medicine, and every trade-secret in poetry—all indeed derive their origin from the Túatha Dé Danann.[138]

Effectively, these figures became culture heroes for the *filid* on some level, the primordial finders-out of human resource. This reflects the general obsession of Irish men of learning with accuracy regarding origin stories. The accounts we have betray the fact that we are looking at the lore of the poets—and not other *áes dána* professions like physicians—specifically because poetic divinities are to the fore. The *Lebor*

---

136 *Lebor Bretnach: the Irish version of the Historia Britonum ascribed to Nennius*, ed. A. G. van Hamel (Dublin, 1932), §12; for a translation of the text see the older edition, *Leabhar breathnach annso sis: the Irish version of the Historia Britonum*, ed. & trans J. H. Todd, intro. & notes by A. Herbert (Dublin, 1848).

137 Also note the octad in *The Annals of Inisfallen (MS. Rawlinson B. 503)*, ed. & trans. S. Mac Airt (Dublin, 1951), §31.

138 *LGE*, iv., 164, 165. Note in particular that Macalister prints (accurately) *cach léire leghis*, 'every diligence of the physician's art' (nominative *leiges*, 'medicine'), but translates as though the last word were from *léigenn*, '(ecclesiastical) reading'. This has the effect of suppressing the ideological basis of the statement.

Bretnach octad, either written by or perhaps dedicated to Gilla Cóemáin, is bookended by two such deities, Etan the female poet and Ogma the inventor of 'the letters of the Irish'.

Might it be possible to glimpse the outline of the *filid*'s cognitive ideology here? It is striking that the eight *Lebor Bretnach* divinities can be divided into three categories: those who have to do with shaped speech (Etan, Ogma, and perhaps the Dagda, given his connection with magic, for which there were specific metres); those who have to do with crafts (Credne, Luchtaine, Goibnenn); and one who represents medicine (Dían Cécht).[139] One god—the multitasking Lug—rounds the list off as Minister without Portfolio.[140] This precisely mirrors the division embodied by the three Brigits, daughters of the Dagda, in 'Cormac's Glossary': Brigit the female poet, Brigit the female smith, and Brigit the female physician. Indeed there is a conspicuous resonance between Etan and Brigit: in *Lebor Bretnach* Etan is *muime na filed* ('the foster-mother of the *filid*'), just as in 'Cormac's Glossary' Brigit was 'a goddess whom the *filid* used to worship'. The glossary's triple Brigit and *Lebor Bretnach*'s octad of deities both seem to embody a division of the arts into three basic branches.[141] Brigit and Etan—divine women sharing a particular care for the *filid*— emerge as central to the enterprise.

This suggests that the same ideological elements recurred in different combinations, due perhaps to regional variation amongst the *filid*. This may be reflected in the entry on Brigit quoted above, for it is important to remember that Irish glossaries—not least 'Cormac's Glossary' itself— were largely Munster creations, and the accounts of mythological beings that they contain may, in some cases, reflect specifically southern understandings of these characters. Nowhere else is Brigit so richly described,

---

139 For metres associated with magic such as *díansheng* ('swift-slender'), see G. Murphy, *Early Irish Metrics* (Dublin, 1961), 21–5, and the poem 'Túatha Dé Danann fo diamair' attributed to Tanaide (*LGE*, iv., 222, 223), in which this metre is said to be a speciality of the Dagda. For medicine being associated with poetry note the term *leiccerd*, which means 'poet' but may literally be 'physician-poet' (*liaig* + *cerd*); see R. Thurneysen, *Die irische Helden- und Königsage bis zum 17. Jahrhundert* (Halle/Saale, 1921 [repnt. Hildersheim, 1980]), 71.

140 I owe the delightful suggestion that Lug's normal epithet (*sam*)*ildánach* be translated 'multitasking' to J. F. Nagy, *Mercantile Myth in Medieval Celtic Traditions* [H. M. Chadwick Memorial Lecture 20] (Department of Anglo-Saxon, Norse, and Celtic: University of Cambridge, 2011), 8.

141 See Kim McCone's argument for an underlying threefold ideology of the arts, *PPCP*, 162–5.

and in the absence of independent evidence from other texts we cannot assume that the account of her importance given there would have been universally recognized. Indeed, the entry itself seems to imply the contrary, saying that *almost all* the Irish recognized Brigit as a goddess. This may be southern overstatement, but it might be that Brigit—who embodies the threefold division of the arts, but is particularly patroness of the *filid* and sometimes also mother of the 'Three Gods of Art'—was to the poets of Munster what Etan (poetess, mother of Coirbre the poet, and 'foster-mother of the *filid*'), daughter of Dían Cécht, was further north.[142] Once again it is important to remember that in terms of medieval Irish writings, what we currently have is likely to be a fraction of what probably once existed; the possibility that our understanding of Irish mythological figures is seriously skewed by mere accidents of survival must always be reckoned with.[143]

ÓENGUS, SON OF THE DAGDA

Among all these poetic allegories, one figure is strikingly absent: another child of the Dagda, Óengus, the Mac Óc. While the reader might expect him to be numbered among the seven (or eight) 'primary skilled ones', or associated with Brigit, Bres, and Elatha as one of the *filid*'s 'pantheon of skill', he does not appear.[144] He is a notable personality in the literature: as already noted, he plays a role in 'The Wooing of Étaín', and he is the central character of one of the most mysterious of the Old Irish sagas, *Aislinge Óenguso* ('The Dream of Óengus'), perhaps composed in the eighth century.[145] There he appears as a passive figure, thrown into dazed stupefaction by a vision of a beautiful girl, whom—after much difficulty and with a lot of help—he finds once again.

There are (I maintain) important dimensions to 'The Dream of Óengus' that have not yet been fully understood, but there is no space to

142 We do not known where Gilla Cóemáin was from; the rest of his name, *mac Gilla Shamthainne*, suggests a devotion to St Samthann and thus a west-midlands origin, perhaps in the region of Clonbroney, Co. Longford.

143 It is worth noting here that Etan is actually at least as well attested a character as Bríg/Brigit: see the list of references in *CMT*, 124.

144 He is one of the eight in the *Annals of Inisfallen* octad; see above, 172, fn.137.

145 See T. Ó Cathasaigh, 'Knowledge and power in *Aislinge Óenguso*', originally in A. Alqvist & V. Čapková (eds.), *Dán do oide: Essays in Memeory of Conn R. Ó Cléirigh* (Dublin, 1997), 431–38, but reprt. in Boyd (ed.), *Coire Sois*, 165–72, at 166.

examine them here.[146] The point for our purposes is that the Óengus of the sagas undergoes a profound emotional transformation on the one hand, but is a crafty, verbally sly figure on the other; he is adept at getting other people (and himself) into, and out of, difficult scrapes. Homer's adjective for the hero Odysseus—*polutropos*, 'of many twists and turns'—would fit Óengus well. Strikingly, two of the god's schemes depend on play with literal and metaphorical meanings, which brings him into the *filid's* realm of language and figuration. He craftily gains the Bruig by insisting that 'a day and a night' means 'all time', because 'it is in days and nights that the world is spent'.[147] He also advises his father on how to kill the parasitic Cridenbél, who has been demanding daily that the Dagda hand over to him 'the three best bits' of his dinner. Cridenbél expects bits of meat, but on Óengus's advice the Dagda hides three gold coins in the food—his 'best bits' only in a rather limited sense—which clog up Cridenbél's stomach and kill him.[148]

Poetry involves play between surface and depth, the literal and the metaphorical, and Óengus appears in at least one story, perhaps others, as an allegorical personage connected with this aspect of the art. This is blatant in a Middle Irish anecdote, *Bó Bithblicht meic Lonán* ('The Son of Lonán's Perpetually-Milkable Cow').[149] In it Flann mac Lonáin—a perfectly historical poet of some distinction, who was killed in 896—meets a huge, loutish churl, to whom he ends up owing a cow.[150] The churl will

146 I hope to tackle this in an article in future, but for now I note the sheer *weirdness* of the saga, its (perhaps intentionally dreamlike) elision of normal categories. It takes place in an atmosphere of persistent ontological and chronological displacement. Óengus—a god—sees a supernatural woman as though he were a mortal hero like Connlae; and far from being located in the remote past of the god-peoples, the events take place (by implication) in the early first century AD, according to the normal timelines. The gods seem to be on familiar terms with mortals, making an alliance with Aillil and Medb and borrowing Conchobor's physician. Compare Eochaid Airem's total ignorance of who Midir is in the third part of 'The Wooing of Étaín', above, 97–8.

147 See above, 84. Note that in one (very brief) version, that in *De Gabáil in tSíde*, it is the Dagda who is tricked, whereas in the account in *Tochmarc Étaíne*, the Dagda himself advises Óengus to use this trick to obtain the Bruig from Elcmar. Translations in *CHA*, 145, 147.

148 *CMT*, 30, 31.

149 'Bó Bithblicht meic Lonán: eagrán de scéal faoi Fhlann mac Lonán', ed. & trans. D. Clifford, *Celtica* 25 (2007), 9–39 [article in Irish but English translation of the text on 22–4]. I have lightly trimmed the translation. Older edn., 'A story of Flann mac Lonáin', ed. O. Bergin, in O. Bergin, *et al.* (eds.) *Anecdota from Irish manuscripts* (Dublin, 1907), i., 45–50.

150 *L&IEMI*, 151.

only be satisfied with a cow that gives endless milk, and after a year he shows up at Flann's house with four heavies, all of them armed with woodcutting tools, to demand it. They are unpleasant guests, beating the household's women, servants, and dogs. Flann asks the churl for his name, which he gives as Fidbadach son of Fid Rúscach ('Woodsman son of Bark-Covered Wood'). In a panic—for, needless to say, no perpetually milkable cow is to hand—Flann composes a poem reflecting on his predicament. Then comes the inevitable denouement :

> It was then the churl said: '*That's* the cow always rich in milk that I have sought—for poetry is always "rich in milk", and I who have come to you am Óengus, son of Bóand, the Mac Óc, and no churl am I.'[151]

That Óengus is supposed to have some deep connection with poetry is clear in the text's relentless punning on the word *fid*, 'wood, tree', which also means 'letter of the ogam alphabet', and so stands for *filidecht* itself.[152] The churl's name, 'Woodsman son of Bark-Covered Wood', might equally be rendered as 'Man of Ogam Letters, son of Poetic Letter'.[153] Flann frets about his guest 'destroying the trees', for Óengus carries a billhook, used for cutting small branches; in fact he does quite the opposite and (metaphorically) is a guardian and tender of the letters. The lesson Óengus imparts is about *metaphor*—'poetry is a cow that is never dry'—which embodies the god's own speciality, namely the ability to exploit the gap between the literal and the figurative.

Óengus is never involved in verse-making in the sagas that survive, but there are certain striking points of similarity between his experiences in 'The Dream of Óengus' and descriptions of poetic composition from the Gaelic world. In the story of Flann's encounter with the disguised god, the poet is irked by the time his unpleasant guest spends lounging abed: '... awful his lying in his bed... fierce his length of time in the bed'.[154] Likewise, in 'The Dream of Óengus', the god languishes in bed pining for love of the woman he has so fleetingly glimpsed. From eighteenth-century Scottish sources—admittedly very late evidence—we

---

151 'Bó Bithblicht', ed. & trans. Clifford, 24.

152 An 'F' is written in the MSS when the word *fid* (or variations on it) is used, as if to underscore the double meaning.

153 Bó Bithblicht', ed. & trans. Clifford, 14, 27. *Rúscach*, 'barky' (there are no length marks in the manuscripts) might be taken as *roscach*, 'poetic', as Clifford notes.

154 'Bó Bithblicht', ed. & trans. Clifford, 24.

know that Gaelic poets habitually composed in darkness, lying on their beds for extended periods.[155] Evidence that this was the custom among the *filid* in early Ireland is lacking, though Joseph Nagy points out that 'Cormac's Glossary' describes a ritual which involves the *fili* awaiting inspiration by covering his face with his hands and lying down to sleep.[156]

It is possible that the *filid* might have interpreted (or shaped, or both) the depiction of the god's sufferings in 'The Dream of Óengus' as a metaphor for the process of poetic composition itself. There are strong points of similarity. First, the saga gives us a fugitive vision which cannot be forced to return by an act of will, followed by an intermediary period of inarticulate, bedbound stupor, plus consultation with authorities of greater knowledge. At the last comes exaltation: the god's recovery of his vision-woman and full possession of that which initially had been fleeting.[157] If the saga was not originally intended as an allegory of poetic composition, it might have been irresistible to the poets of later centuries to read it as one. This would no doubt have helped to foster an image of Óengus as a patron of their profession.

Elusive but intriguing hints that Óengus was used by the *filid* to symbolize the subjective experience of composing verse are found in other places. The best evidence for this comes from a famous anecdote in 'Cormac's Glossary'. It recounts a male 'Spirit of Poetry' appearing to the arch-*fili* Senchán Torpéist, chief *ollam* of Ireland.[158] A mysterious youth, shouting at them from the beach, insists on accompanying Senchán and his entourage of *filid* and apprentice poets on their trip to the Isle of Man. His appearance is inventively revolting:

He had a hideous shape; first of all, when he used to put his finger to his forehead a gush of foul pus would come from his ears down

155 J. F. Nagy, 'Orality in Medieval Irish Narrative: An Overview', *Oral Tradition* 1/2 (1986), 272–301, at 293–4.

156 Nagy, 'Orality in Medieval Irish Narrative', 294.

157 On stupor (*socht*) in the tale, see Ó Cathasaigh, 'Knowledge and power', in Boyd (ed.), *Coire Sois*, 168.

158 *Sanas Cormaic*, ed. Meyer, 90–4. On this story see P. Russell, 'Poets, Power and Possessions in Medieval Ireland: Some Stories from Sanas Cormaic', in J. Eska (ed.), *Law, Literature and Society* [CSANA Yearbook 7] (Dublin, 2008), 9–45, and note further major comments (plus text and translation) by M. Ní Dhonnchadha, 'The *Prull* narrative in *Sanas Cormaic*', in Carey, *et al.* (eds.), *Cín Chille Cúile*, 163–177. She notes (164) that this is a narrative deeply concerned with poets' craft and hierarchies. Note also A. Dooley, 'Early Irish literature and contemporary scholarly disciplines', in R. Wall (ed.), *Medieval and Modern Ireland* (New Jersey, 1988), 68–71.

to his neck. There was suppuration [?] from the crown of his head down to the gristle of his two shoulders. Everyone who saw him thought that it was the upper layer of his brain that had broken through his skull. Each of his two eyes were as round as a blackbird's egg, as black as death, as quick as a fox.[159]

As the whole company approach Man, they see 'a great, old, grey-haired woman upon the rock', combing the beach for seaweed. Unknown to Senchán and his retinue, she is a long-lost Irish poet. Senchán is unable to cap the riddling half-quatrain that the woman calls out to him, and instead the hideous lad answers, telling the old woman that it is him, rather than Senchán, that she should address. Thanks to the lad's intervention, Senchán realises who the old woman is and arranges for her to bathe and be dressed in finery as befits her high status. But it is the end of the brief narrative that is most significant; while all this happens the ugly lad has undergone a metamorphosis, becoming 'a youth with golden yellow hair, wavy as the scrollings on harps. He was clad in royal apparel, and had the finest appearance ever seen on any man.'[160] He circles Senchán and his retinue clockwise, and vanishes. The glossator explains, switching to Latin midsentence: '... he has never appeared since that time. Thus there is no doubt that he was the Spirit of Poetry [*poematis spiritus*].'

There are obvious similarities between this anecdote and the story of Flann mac Lonán's encounter with Óengus. Both turn on the manifestation of a loathsome man to a distinguished *fili*, in a way that puts them out or makes life difficult for them. In both, the man is revealed as supernatural and connected with poetry itself, though in neither case is this obvious to begin with. And in both tales something is achieved: in his desperation Flann composes a rather splendid poem, and the lost female poet is recognized and recovered from her exile.

On the other hand, each story has an element the other lacks: only the glossary anecdote shows us the importuning figure's transformation from hideous to divine. Likewise, the story of Flann makes it explicit that the fierce churl is Óengus, but in the Glossary anecdote the identifi-

---

159 Drawing on Ní Dhonnchadha, 'The *Prull* narrative', 166.

160 Ní Dhonnchadha, 'The *Prull* narrative', 165, 167; she notes (173–5) is part of a late Middle Irish tale *Tromdám Guaire*, in which the figure of a *lobar* ('diseased person, leper') plays the role of Spirit of Poetry: he is not identified and does not transform, though he is later said to be St Caillín.

cation is only implicit. (Máirín Ní Dhonnchadha notes that half of the manuscript versions actually identify the 'Spirit of Poetry' as Christ.)[161] That said, as far back as 1927 Robin Flower made the connection between the two anecdotes and noted the similarity between the story of the Spirit and Modern Irish tales in which Óengus lends his help in an initially disruptive or mischievous form.[162] The Spirit's great beauty—for which Óengus is famed—also fits. In short, scholars have noted that in both these anecdotes we are dealing with the mythopoetic aspects of poetry.[163] It is hard (hideous, churlish) until one attains facility; then it becomes something divine. They are stories not just about poetry but about how it feels to train as a poet.[164]

Taken together, these anecdotes may help to make sense of one of the most puzzling of all medieval Irish references to a native god. Under the year 1084, the normally laconic Annals of Tigernach contain a bizarre entry, which unsettlingly reads as though it could have been written by the Yeats of *The Celtic Twilight*.[165] In a swerve from the usual annalistic focus on battles and deaths, we learn of:

> A great pestilence in this year, which killed a quarter of the men of Ireland. It began in the south, and spread throughout the four quarters of Ireland. This is the *causa causans* of that pestilence, namely demons that came out of the northern isles of the world, namely three battalions, and in each battalion there were three thousand and thirty, as Óengus Óc, the son of the Dagda, related to Mac Gilla Lugáin, who used to frequent the *síd*-mound every year at Samain. And he himself beheld at Maistiu one battalion of them which was destroying Leinster. In the same way they were seen by Mac Gilla Lugáin's son, and wherever their heat and fury reached, there their venom was taken, for there was a sword of fire out of the gullet of each of them, and every one of them

---

161 Ní Dhonnchadha, 'The *Prull* narrative', 176.

162 R. Flower, *Catalogue of Irish manuscripts in the British Museum* (London, 1926), ii., 340.

163 P. K. Ford, 'The Blind, the Dumb, and the Ugly: Aspects of Poets and their Craft in Early Ireland and Wales', *CMCS* 19 (1990), 27–40, 40.

164 A poem by Cináed ua hArtacáin (d. 975) also exemplifies a fondness for Óengus among the professional poets. His poem on the Brugh flatteringly (and irresistibly) conflated his patron Óengus mac Ócáin with Óengus mac Óc. See 'Cinaed ua hArtacain's poem on Brugh na Boinne', ed. & trans. L. Gwynn, *Ériu* 7 (1914), 210–38.

165 See brief discussion in *A&CM*, 31.

was as high as the clouds of heaven, so that is the cause of this pestilence.[166]

That a god should convey supernatural insight to a mortal was a staple of the earliest Irish narrative prose. But on the face of it Mac Gilla Lugáin's interview with the Mac Óc seems to be accepted by the annalist as not only as a genuine occurrence, but also as contemporary. It is also accepted that the Mac Óc's intelligence is accurate—he really does identify the cause of the plague. The implications of this passage are, at first glance, startling, and commentators have on the whole not known quite how to take it, given that it seems to confirm the persistence of pagan practices in eleventh-century Ireland. Edel Bhreathnach says this passage helps us to 'begin to experience a ritual culture, replicated in so many other societies, that existed outside, and was feared by those who sought to control social and religious mores in early Irish society'.[167] The archaeologist John Waddell is impressed that Mac Gilla Lugáin 'should still apparently be a regular and persistent visitor to the otherworld mound of Óengus at the great feast of Samhain, when he evidently communed with the son of the Dagda'.[168]

Must this enigmatic passage be taken so literally? It is strange that a Clonmacnoise cleric should have unhesitatingly accepted that there were those among his contemporaries who had spoken with pagan deities; stranger still that those deities should be considered to be in some sense *on our side*. An alternative way to look at it might be as follows. The evidence examined above tells us that it was entirely possible in the Middle Irish period (*c.*900-1200) to compose an anecdote in which a famous poet encountered—and was enlightened by—the god Óengus, probably reflecting a habit of using that deity to allegorize the difficulties and rewards of the *filid*'s profession. Might Mac Gilla Lugáin—of whom nothing is known—have been a *fili*? There is nothing in the annal-entry that suggests this explicitly. On the other hand, the story depicts him as the possessor of supernatural vision (etymologically *fili* means 'seer'), inherited by his son; the practice of *filidecht* ran in families. Fur-

---

166 *The Annals of Tigernach*, ed. & partial trans. W. Stokes, *RC* 17 (1896), 416–7; *Maistiu* is modern Mullaghmast, in Co. Kildare. The name of the personage varies (Gilla Lugan, Gilla Lugán, Mac Gilla Lugáin): I have followed Donnchadh Ó Corráin, *NHI*, i., 582.

167 Bhreathnach, *Ireland and the Medieval World*, 151.

168 *A&CM*, 31. See also the comments of Ó Corráin, *NHI*, i., 582.

thermore, all of this takes place when some among the professional poets were deliberately playing up their connections with the pre-Christian past. There is no reason to think that the names of every significant medieval Irish poet are known to us, and every reason to think that they are not. Therefore, it is tempting to suggest that Mac Gilla Lugáin, whoever he was, was no half-pagan throwback, but an assertively secular *fili* who composed an account of contemporary travails within a demonstrably pre-existent subgenre which we might call 'The Poet's Encounter with Óengus'. If there was once a text called 'The Colloquy of Mac Gilla Lugáin and the Mac Óc', we will never know. Perhaps Mac Gilla Lugáin's ostentatious innovation was composing an autobiographical text, whereas for Senchán Torpéist and Flann mac Lonán, the stories of their supernatural encounters were the creation of later generations for whom they were revered figures. In short, this profoundly odd annal-entry may have a more precise cultural context than has been recognized, and its affinities should be recognized as being fundamentally literary, not literal.

It is time to pull some strands of this argument together before continuing. As the story of Mac Gilla Lugáin suggests, it is important again to emphasize that using ex-divinities in this way as symbols, rhetorical personifications, and allegories *was not paganism.* It might, in fact, have been a long way from Irish paganism as it actually had once been. Instead it was a kind of meta-mythology for intellectuals, a local analogy to the myriad ways that the classical deities were put to use by poets and thinkers throughout the Middle Ages, and beyond. Unquestionably devout Christian poets regularly used the Greek and Roman gods as figures of speech, allegories, or useful fictions, while scholars massaged Christian monotheism to find a place for the ancient gods as beings of genuine power. Invoking Apollo or the Muses is a classic example of the former process; in the latter case, one thinks of the power medieval thinkers ascribed to the planetary deities and to the goddess Natura, nature personified.[169] Irish poets, I suggest, were more than capable of similarly sophisticated strategies with their own native gods, although the measure of

169 See, e.g. Dante's splendid invocation to the god Apollo (*Paradiso* 1.13–27), right at the heart of the greatest Christian poem of the Middle Ages, and imitated by Chaucer at the opening of Book 3 of *The House of Fame*. For Natura, see *PB*, 391–6, and B. Newman, *God and the Goddesses: Vision, Poetry and Belief in the Middle Ages* (Philadelphia, PA, 2002), 51–89.

actual existence they accorded to Brigit (for example) is probably irrecoverable, and indeed may have varied between individuals.

DEAD GODS

That ends the more speculative phase of my argument in this chapter. The inclusion of the gods within the national pseudohistory—and especially within its culmination, *Lebor Gabála*—was an attempt to finally uproot an idea which clearly retained currency in some quarters, namely that the Túatha Dé were in some sense more than human, or not human at all, and were still a going concern. One of the words I have bandied about is 'euhemerism', the theory that pagan gods had merely been exceptional men and women. But the pseudohistorians left out a central prop of that theory, for while they asserted that the Túatha Dé had indeed been human, nowhere do we find the idea that ignorant pagans had mistakenly worshipped these distinguished and long-dead persons as gods.[170]

As the influence of the pseudohistorical movement grew we find attempts to distinguish the god-peoples from the pagan gods of the Irish. In the ninth-century Tripartite *Life of Patrick*, the saint casts down a great idol of the pagan Irish, known as Cenn Crúach, 'Bloody Head'; the demon who inhabits the image promptly appears, but Patrick curses him and casts him into hell.[171] There is no evidence that Cenn Crúach was once a genuine Irish deity. He is never numbered among the Túatha Dé, who (as seen) are never depicted as the recipients of human worship; this, in contrast, is Cenn Crúach's main function. In the *dindshenchas* the idol, under the variant name *Crom* Crúach ('Bloody Crookback'), is said to have stood on *Mag Slécht* ('The Plain of Prostration') in Co. Cavan, and to have been propitiated with the sacrifice of first-born children in exchange for good yields of milk and grain.[172] This sinister figure is

---

170 Note the partial exception of Manannán, 251–2.

171 *Bethu Phátraic: The Tripartite Life of Patrick*, ed. K. Mulchrone (Dublin, 1939), 55–6; an old but useful collection of references is J. P. Dalton, 'Cromm Cruaich of Magh Sleacht', *PRIA* 36 (C) (1921–4), 23–67.

172 *The Metrical Dindshenchus*, ed. & trans. E. Gwynn (Dublin, 1906), iv., 18–23; J. Borsje, 'Human sacrifice in medieval Irish literature', in J. Bremmer (ed.), *The Strange World of Human Sacrifice* (Leuven & Dudley, MA, 2007), 31–54. Hutton (*The Pagan Religions of the Ancient British Isles,* 155, 159), argues that Crom Crúach and related figures have

plainly inspired by biblical images of bloodthirsty pagan deities like Moloch, just as depictions of druids in early Irish saints' lives owe more to the biblical priests of Ba'al, opponents of the prophet Elijah, than to native tradition.[173]

In the eleventh century, not all learned poets seem to have been equally enthuasiatic about the mythopoetic tropes that their profession had embraced. Some *filid*, after all, identified closely with clerical learning and operated in a monastic milieu: it was perfectly possible to be both a *fili* and a cleric. Those who took this view emphasized the humanity of the god-peoples trenchantly. The poet Tanaide wrote:

> The Túatha Dé Donann, under concealment,
> men who did not observe the faith;
> young hounds of the territory which does not decay,
> men of the flesh and blood of Adam.[174]

In keeping with this insistence on the Túatha Dé's humanity, some learned poets described stories about how they had died out. A Middle Irish text, *Senchas na Relec* ('The Historical Lore of the Burial Grounds'), expounded the places where the various grandees of the Túatha Dé had been buried.[175] Óengus's great *síd*-mound at Bruig na Bóinne is identified as their tomb, and the otherworldly hill is re-imagined as a vast vault of ancient bones. In *dindshenchas* tradition, another of the great mounds of the Boyne necropolis, Knowth, was identified as the burial place of one Bua or Buí, Lug's wife.[176] A *dindshenchas* poem on the Bruig addresses the landscape around Newgrange itself, putting the gods—its onetime inhabitants—in hell:

---

been overlaid or inspired by the Christian Devil; he is more like the god Moloch of 2 Chronicles 28:3, 33:6, and Jeremiah 7:31, 19:2–6, but the two suggestions are not mutually exclusive.

173 See the comments of T. O'Loughlin, 'Reading Muirchú's Tara-event within its background as a biblical "trial of divinities"', in J. Cartwright (ed.), *Celtic Hagiography and Saints' Cults* (Cardiff 2003), 123–135.

174 *LGE*, iv., 220; trans. Carey, *CHA*, 256. For the spelling *Donann*, see below, 186–9.

175 Recent edn. and trans. provided by K. Kilpatrick in her 'The historical interpretation of early medieval insular place-names' [unpublished D.Phil thesis, University of Oxford, 2012], 393–404; much earlier edn. 'Senchas na relec in so', ed. & trans. J. O'Donovan, in G. Petrie, *An Essay on the Origin and Uses of Round Towers of Ireland* (1846), 97–101.

176 Ó Cathasaigh, in Boyd (ed.), *Coire Sois*, 155.

You hide a bold and kind brood,
O plain of the son of the swift Dagda [*i.e.* of Óengus],
who did not perform the worship of the great God;
it is worse for them where they are in torment.

They vanish, you remain:
every believing [i.e. Christian] band rides around you;
as for them, their wisdom has deceived them;
you shall attain a noble age.[177]

Uncompromising as this is, an even more acid statement in this direction was made by the prolific Flann Mainistrech (d.1056), a scholar-poet whom we know to have been interested in *Senchas na Relec*. A top scholar of the great monastic school at Monasterboice in Co. Louth (as we saw), his work was not one of the original sources for *Lebor Gabála*, but was soon incorporated into it.[178] Flann is a good example of a clerical *fili*, much admired for his ability to versify his immense historical scholarship.[179] He was deeply embedded within the world of the monastery, and his impatience with the pseudo-pagan trappings and mythological tropes adopted by some professional poets is palpable in his poetry. He has left us a bravura poem which details in thirty-eight stanzas how every member of the Túatha Dé came to an unpleasant end. In my view, it is one of the most peculiar things ever produced in medieval Ireland, its triumphalist vision of the defeat of the pagan gods standing as a weird pre-echo of Milton's poem 'On the Morning of Christ's Nativity', which has the demonic classical deities foisted from their temples by the birth of the saviour.[180] Flann's poem has usually been dismissed as aridly dogmatic—an attempt by a vehement euhemerist to discredit the idea of native gods—but this is to ignore the streak of black humour which runs through it. The poem is as much satire as historical scholarship: each death is ironic and depicts the Túatha Dé as doomed, spiteful, and self-absorbed.

A few examples will serve. Coirpre the Poet, son of Etan, feebly expires of sunstroke—a ray, perhaps, from Christ the 'Sun of Justice'. Flann

---

177 *Metrical Dindshenchus* ed. Gwynn, ii., 16, 17.

178 *L&IEMI*, 139.

179 *L&IEMI*, 141–3.

180 Useful discussion by E. Thanisch, 'Flann Mainistrech's Götterdämmerung as a Junction within *Lebor Gabála Érenn*', *Quaestio Insularis: Selected Proceedings of the Cambridge Colloquium in Anglo-Saxon, Norse, and Celtic* 13 (2013), 69–93.

has Dían Cécht the physician and Goibnenn the smith—both significantly named in healing charms—die 'of painful sickness', while Credne,
who deals with precious metalwork, drowns while on a mission to loot
gold from Spain. Bé Chuille and Dinann, the sorceresses of the Túatha
Dé, are hexed to death by 'the dusky demons of the air', while the unlucky Óengus drowns in the mouth of the Boyne. His own mother
Bóand, goddess of that river, is clearly powerless to save him.[181]

Flann's poem is more subtle than it sounds, partly because it includes
some stories which are otherwise unknown or obscure, although they
nevertheless are probably traditional. For example, readers will never
know why Ainge (or Áine), a daughter of the Dagda, 'died for the love
that she gave to Banba' (or, possibly, 'to Ireland'): it is a lost story. Evidence from elsewhere confirms that Flann almost certainly did not invent the story that Lug murdered Cermait Milbél, a son of the Dagda,
because of jealousy over his wife. So much for divine imperviousness; it
is difficult to imagine that anything like this was part of pre-Christian
Irish mythology, but the story may already have been of considerable
antiquity by Flann's day, and may possibly have existed in saga-form.[182]
Other textual evidence confirms that there were stories of killings
among the Túatha Dé; the tale of the sons of Tuirenn is one, as is the
burning alive of Midir's wife Fúamnach by Manannán. But Flann inten-
sifies the violence here, mockingly depicting the gods as a people in the
process of tearing themselves apart.[183] Flann makes the god-peoples into
wayward exempla of envy, rage, jealousy and lust—but most of all he
makes them *inept*, in what may be a calculated rebuke by one *fili* to his
colleagues' 'pantheon of skill'. Deeply identified with the pseudohistorical movement and given the admiring title *senchaid*, 'historian', Flann's

181 *LGE* iv., 224–239, at 229–31.

182 Though Flann's is the oldest reference to the killing of Cermait, an interesting
late Middle Irish fragment edited by O. Bergin ('How the Dagda Got his Magic Staff', in
R. S. Loomis (ed.), *Medieval Studies in Memory of Gertrude Schoepperle Loomis* (Paris, 1927),
399–406) makes it reasonably certain that the story was older; for obvious reasons Flann
leaves out the fact that the story has a happy ending, in that the Dagda is eventually able
to restore his son to life. This mythological episode was known to the bardic poet Gofraidh Fionn Ó Dálaigh (d.1385), who uses it touchingly in an elegy on the death of his
own son (Bergin, 'How the Dagda', 400–1).

183 Some deaths he may have made up; others have been spun to emphasize their
wretchedness. That the Boyne-goddess Bóand met her end in her own river is a clear
example of the latter, as the story of her drowning seems to be quite old; see G. Toner,
'Landscape and Cosmology in the *Dindshenchas*', in J. Borsje, A. Dooley, *et al.* (eds.), *Celtic
Cosmology: Perspectives from Ireland and Scotland* (Toronto, 2014), 268–83, at 279–80.

didactic agenda in the poem is to assert not only the humanity of the Túatha Dé, but also their ultimate damnation. Flann emphatically puts a Christian framework around the pre-Christian past, which is why the redactors of the 'Book of Invasions' drew on his poetry; but he did not hold back from passing judgment upon it.

DANU, DONAND, DANANN

Here we come to a major point. Aficionados of Irish mythology will have noticed that this book so far has avoided using the most famous name for the native pantheon, *Túatha Dé Danann*, 'The Peoples of the Goddess Danu'. The reason is that this name is not ancient: it is a development of the central Middle Ages, and is related to the crystallization of the gods' place in the pseudohistory. Old Irish texts had standardly referred to the kin of the Dagda simply as the 'god-people' or 'god-peoples' (*túath/túatha dé*), or sometimes as the 'god-men' (*fir dé*); there are no articles in any of these phrases. But during the 900s a new name—*Túatha Dé Donand*—came into use, which, by about 1200, had mutated into *Túatha Dé Danann*, the form familiar to us today.

It is not entirely clear what motivated the development of this new terminology. What *can* be said is that the new name was transparently the creation of the learned classes, rather than being a popular or folk usage that suddenly spread into the written record. That this new, artificial name rapidly and completely replaced the old one suggests that by the tenth century, talk of 'god-peoples' had come to seem problematic. It is likely that the old name *túatha dé* presented the learned with a double affront: not only did it underline the fact that Óengus, Midir, and so on were pagan gods—a fact the learned had never forgotten, as the glossaries testify—but *Túath Dé* was also the standard Irish term for the Israelites, the biblical 'People of God'.[184] Quite apart from the fact that it was probably a source of mental dissonance to use identical terms for both God's chosen people and the pagan divinities, the framers of the national pseudohistory had gone to great lengths to figure the Gaels, not the gods, as the counterparts of the Israelites. Like the Israelites, the story of the ancestral Gaels included both an exodus from Egypt and a meandering journey to a promised land.

---

184 The ambiguity resides in the fact that *dé* is both the genitive singular and the genitive plural of the word *día*, 'god'—so the 'People of God' and 'people of [the] gods' were formally identical.

FIG. 4.4. The Paps Mountains, Co. Kerry—the breasts of the 'mother of the Irish gods'?
Photo: Gerard Lovett.

Tacking the proper name *Donand* onto the phrase *túatha dé* seems to be a method of safely corralling the old gods in the distant past: instead of the disquieting 'god-peoples' they were now the 'peoples of the deity Donand', more circumscribed because more specific.[185] But no trace of narrative tradition about this Donand is found in any source. That the nature and identity of this personage is almost a complete blank suggests that it may have been a deliberate attempt at inducing mental estrangement, redefining the familiar *Túatha Dé* as distant and difficult. Later, in the eleventh century, Eochaid ua Flainn referred to her in passing as 'Donand, mother of the gods'; before this it is not even clear that Donand was thought to be female, even though the usual rendering of the phrase in English translates *dé*, 'deity', as 'goddess'.[186]

Where, then, did *Donand* come from, and why do we always take her to be female? The explanation is technical, and two factors are in play. Carey suggests that the 'Three Gods of Skill'—*trí dé dána*—are fundamental.[187] An original phrase like 'the people of the gods of skill' (*túatha*

185 Note the intermediary form *Túath(a) Déa*, 'people(s) of the goddess'.

186 *LGE*, iv., 216, 217 (*Donand, máthair na nDea*).

187 J. Carey, 'The Name "Tuatha Dé Danann"', *Éigse* 18 (1981), 291–4; also his 'Myth and Mythography', 56.

dé dána) seems to have hybridized with tribal names involving the element *Domnann*. This form occurs corrupted as *Donann*, and indeed occurs combined with *dé*, 'god', in the proper name *mac dé Domnand*, applied to the Fomorian king Indech in 'The Second Battle of Moytura': this explains the *o*- in the first syllable of Donand. This scenario is tentative, but its sheer untidiness lends plausibility in the context of the furiously creative redaction of tradition undertaken by learned personnel in the tenth century.[188]

This still does not tell us who this Donand was imagined to be. Celtic scholars have traditionally striven to identify her with a goddess named 'Ana', mentioned in 'Cormac's Glossary', around the year 900. This figure—*mater deorum hibernensium*, 'the mother of the Irish gods', according to the glossary—is certainly impressive: the glossary tells us that spectacular twin hills near Killarney in Co. Kerry were regarded as her breasts, 'as the story goes'—*ut fabula fertur*—quite understandably, one might add, evoking as they do the form of a vast recumbent woman (Fig. 4.4). Even more strikingly, Ana 'used to feed the gods well', though whether with her cooking or her breast milk is not clear.[189]

The air of plausibility in all this is tantalizing. Cormac's 'Ana' is clearly a latinization of a name which would have been *Anu* in Old Irish (*Anann* in the genitive case), and technically the nominative of the name *Danann* should have been the similar-looking **Danu*. Add to all this the fact that river names across Celtic Europe contain the root **dan*- (the Danube is the most famous example), and that Indian mythology has a goddess of heavenly waters named *Dānu*, and it is little wonder that scholars have enthusiastically set about reconstructing an ancient Celtic and Indo-European river-goddess of maternal bounty.[190]

However, a series of major difficulties stand in the way of this evocative picture. First, equating the glossary's Ana with **Danu* is tricky, because nowhere is Danu actually attested. The earliest form of the name

188 MacLeod, '*Mater Deorum Hibernensium*', 368, summarizes Carey's argument with great concision.

189 *Sanas Cormaic*, ed. Meyer, 3.

190 See Mac Cana, *Celtic Mythology*, 84–6, where the case is made for a Celtic goddess *Danu/Donu; a still more maximal version of the old view is W. J. Gruffudd, 'Donwy', *BBCS* 7.1 (1933), 1–4, with references to European rivers containing the **dan*- element. The reconstructed *Danu is often linked to the Welsh ancestor-figure Dôn, but J. T. Koch notes that the 'phonology of these equations has never worked' and that Danu 'must be jettisoned' ('Some Suggestions and Etymologies Reflecting upon the Mythology of the Four Branches', *PHCC* 9 (1989), 1–10, at 4–5).

attached to the Túatha Dé was plainly *Donand*, with an *-o-*; the form *Danann* was a later development. If this name were connected to Cormac's Ana we might expect the *-a-* to have been there from the start. Also our texts are unanimous that the nominative case of these names was identical to the genitive—it is always *Donand, Danann*—and not the required **Donu, *Danu*, which are reconstructions by modern philologists.[191] Finally, Ana has no connection with rivers or water in the glossary entry.

This tangle indicates two things: first, the origins and development of the mysterious *Donand* are not fully recoverable, and secondly the idea that Irish paganism knew a divine matriarch named Danu cannot now be maintained. The compilers of 'Cormac's Glossary' may have been quite correct that there had once been a goddess called Anu or Ana associated with the Paps mountains, since it beggars belief to think that the pre-Christian Irish would *not* have associated so impressively breasted a landscape with a female deity. On the other hand, it is suspicious that so important a figure as the glossary's 'mother of the Irish gods' should go unmentioned in the early sagas, teeming as they are with former gods and goddesses. This raises the possibility that Ana/Anu may have simply been a local Munster figure, less familiar or even unknown elsewhere in Ireland.

Michael Clarke goes further, and suggests that the lofty description of Ana/Anu in 'Cormac's Glossary' may itself owe more to medieval learning than to pagan religion, and result from a monastic scholar musing learnedly on the goddess Cybele, mother of the classical gods. Irish intellectuals knew of Cybele from Virgil's *Aeneid*, where she puts in a brief appearance in Book 7, as well as from other sources. Clarke says that 'it is possible to posit a precise chain of influence from Servius' Vergilian commentary and the *Etymologies* of Isidore, two texts that we know influenced the learned compilers of the Irish glossaries. Servius notes that Cybele of Mount Ida is the same as Earth, which is "the mother of the gods", *mater deorum*.'[192] He also quotes Isidore, Irish scholars' favourite source for the learning of Mediterranean antiquity, who describes Cybele in striking terms:

191 On the assumption that *Danann/Donann* are the genitives of Old Irish n-stem nouns **Danu/*Donu*; this is not unreasonable on the face of it, even though these forms are nowhere attested. The name of the smith-god Goibniu offers a potentially parallel example of the genitive form of an n-stem theonym being redefined in Middle Irish as a nominative, for by this stage he was usually referred to as *Goibnenn*.

192 Clarke, 'Linguistic Education', 52.

They imagine the same one as both Earth and Great Mother... She
is called Mother, because she gives birth to many things; Great,
because she generates food; Kindly, because she nourishes all living things through her fruits.[193]

This, as Clarke notes, is so close to the Irish glossary entry that it is
hard to avoid the suspicion that the 'personality' of the goddess Ana—
'who used to feed the gods well'—has been cooked up in imitation of the
classical deity. That Clarke's analysis may be right is suggested by a distinctive oddity in the 'Ana' entry: while traces of the activities of divine
beings are constantly detected in the landscape in Irish tradition, nowhere else is a natural feature described as part of a divinity's body. This
is rare even for the better-attested gods of classical tradition, with the
signal exception of the great mother-goddesses of the eastern Mediterranean, of whom Cybele, the 'Mountain Mother', came to be the most
prominent. Ana/Anu is simply not on the same scale or plane of representation as *síd*-beings like Midir or Óengus, and it is telling that the
Paps of Ana were imagined (by the early thirteenth century at the latest)
as a pair of *síd*-mounds, the separate and unconnected dwellings of different otherworldly rulers.[194] (It so happens that we pay a disconcerting
visit to the inside of one of her breasts in the following chapter.)[195] This
discrepancy could be accounted for by seeing Ana as a remnant of an
older, more chthonian kind of divinity, though there is no way to prove
this; equally, Clarke could be correct in arguing that she is a invention
of the early Middle Ages. It is worth noting that his view does not explain where the *name* 'Ana/Anu' comes from, however: perhaps it once
attached to some genuine legendary figure associated with the Paps, and
that this was all the compilers of the glossary knew of her. Certainly
synthesizing a mother-goddess by using information drawn from the
classical Cybele might reflect Munster scholars' desire to dignify their
province by crediting it with a grand mythological personage. Yet
again—in what is emerging as a leitmotif of this book—an apparently
plausible pre-Christian deity evaporates in front of us, just at the moment we seemed to have caught a convincing glimpse.

193 Clarke, 'Linguistic Education', 53; the Isidorian quotation is *Etymologiae*, 8.11.61.
Clarke notes that Carolingian mythographic compilations identified Cybele as 'mistress
of mountains', and the Paps are, if nothing else, two mountains.
194 See *IIMWL*, 45, and J. F. Nagy, *The Wisdom of the Outlaw: the Boyhood Deeds of Finn
in Gaelic Narrative Tradition* (Berkeley, 1985), 168–9, 216.
195 The home of the fairy-woman Créde: see below, 213.

Clarke's argument has alarming implications for the integrity of the Irish pantheon. If Irish men of learning were capable of cross-cultural mapping of this kind—and it seems clear that they were—then the possibility that the Irish gods were influenced by those of Greece and Rome during the medieval period must always be borne in mind. In other words, the more we know about early Irish learned culture, the less we can say with confidence about ancient Irish paganism. Tellingly, Ana/Anu/Anann becomes more shadowy as the Middle Ages progress: we find her identified with the war-goddesses and also with Ériu, or Ireland, as though the learned were unsure about where to place her.

The coinage *Túatha Dé Donand* distinguished the gods from the Israelites and subtly took the edge off their divinity, but at the expense of making an oddly insubstantial goddess central to the pantheon. The effect is a feeling of disconnection or lacuna. Nor does the 'Mother of the Irish Gods' ever meet her counterpart, the 'Supreme Father', the Dagda. Indeed the Dagda, vividly characterized in the sagas and certainly a genuine ex-deity, somehow contrasts with and evades the shadowy mother-goddess, attested only in the recondite, Latin-tinged lore of glossaries and the poetry of learned pseudohistorians. Bold but unconvincing attempts have been made by scholars to identify our elusive goddess with the Morrígan, with whom the Dagda is observed boisterously coupling in 'The Second Battle of Moytura'; this is presumably out of a sense that the pantheon's 'Great Mother' and 'Great Father' belong together.[196] It is preferable, rather, to resist the lure of reconstructing lost myths and instead to see their failure to connect as symbolic of the tension between the inherited and the artificial in the new mythology of the pseudohistorical school.

HUMAN, ALL TOO HUMAN

Like the unknown first compiler of *Lebor Gabála*, my role in this chapter has been to effect a synthesis out of a mass of data originally expounded by others, and it is time to consider some larger patterns.

---

196 See MacLeod, '*Mater Deorum Hibernensium*', 340–384, which accurately and usefully references all the allusions to Ana/Donand (etc.) but does so from an implicitly reconstructionist perspective that tends to smooth over the difficulties which attend these figures.

Scholars have long lamented that Irish myth is not really a mythology in the usual Indo-European way: archaic elements have been inextricably interwoven with biblical and medieval material. This mythopoetic tendency accelerated remarkably in the late tenth and eleventh centuries, with the result that in this period 'Irish mythology' actually came into existence as a distinct cultural category. The great edifice of the national pseudohistory allotted to the gods their own era of eminence in the deep past, with a list of personnel and a clear timeline; it was at this point too that they acquired their lasting name, Túatha Dé Danann.

Ecclesiastical *literati* in the period had become more and more interested in the lore of the *filid*, and as they built up a narrative of the national past, they foraged from the professional poets' genealogies, images, and ideas about the native gods. The *filid* in turn—anxious about losing their distinctiveness and being absorbed into clerical ranks—may increasingly have begun to use the gods to personify and allegorize aspects of their own intellectual curriculum, as well as to underscore the secular status of their profession.

The effect of the pseudohistory was paradoxical. On the one hand, it gave solidity to the fluid ontology of the gods by defining them as human magic-workers and tracing their descent from Noah. As intrinsically native figures, with no connection to the Bible, working the gods into the pseudohistory was a remarkable achievement; Ireland was now furnished with a new national myth that fused the natural and supernatural. On the other hand, the result was unwieldy and unstable, continuously expanding by the copious accretion of authorities.

The influence of the doctrines of *Lebor Gabála* on Irish letters, though substantial, was patchy. The idea that the gods had died out (or were among the damned) never took hold in most narrative genres, and some simply ignored it. The whole point of the synthetic history had been to connect the story of Ireland's ancient past to that of the rest of the world, but the native god-peoples were unavoidably parochial: until the nineteenth century no one outside Ireland and Scotland took any notice of the Túatha Dé Danann. A case in point is the twelfth-century Cambro-Norman cleric Gerald of Wales, who gives a rundown of the Irish account of the past in his *Topographia Hiberniae* ('Topography of Ireland'). He sensibly asks how anything could be known about the fate of Cessair, because, after all, she and all her company drowned. 'Perhaps some record of these events was found inscribed on stone or a tile, as we read was the case with the art of music before the Flood', he drily com-

ments.[197] Gerald clearly had access to a chronology of the invasions because he describes Cessair, Partholón, Nemed, the Fir Bolg, and the Milesians in full. In contrast, he passes over the Túatha Dé Danann so
quickly that one could miss them altogether: they are described as 'another branch of the descendants of Nemedius'—Nemed—and that is it.[198]
All the adventures and achievements of the god-peoples are compressed
into a single colourless clause. Gerald clearly felt the historical narrative
of the Irish past was worth recording, but it seems he could summon up
no interest in the doings of the Túatha Dé. To an outsider, the Irish gods
were so native as to be beneath notice—a pattern that prevailed for centuries to come.

197 Gerald of Wales, *Topographia Hibernie*, ed. J. J. O'Meara, *PRIA* 52 (C) (1948–50),
113–78, at 157.

198 *Topographia Hibernie*, ed. O'Meara, 160.

5

VULNERABILITY
AND GRACE

THE FINN CYCLE

Although the gods come to Cuchulain, and although
he is the son of one of the greatest of them, their
country and his are far apart, and they come to him
as god to mortal; but Finn is their equal.

—W. B. YEATS, PREFACE TO AUGUSTA GREGORY,
GODS AND FIGHTING MEN

THIS CHAPTER'S MAIN focus is upon literature written in the first decades of the thirteenth century, with a glance into the fourteenth. Historically, this means a turn from the relative stability and cultural revival which followed the end of the Viking Wars to a period characterized by momentous change in both the political and literary spheres. The twelfth century was marked by endemic violence and internal turmoil, climaxing with the advent of the Anglo-Normans in 1169 and the fateful enunciation of the English crown's claim to lordship over the whole of Ireland. If the extension of Anglo-Norman power to Ireland brought with it an English administration and an influx of English settlers, it did not immediately or straightforwardly turn the island into a colony. Over the following centuries, geographical penetration and political domination by the descendants of the Anglo-Normans was never total, even at its most extensive; by the end of the Middle Ages English authority had to a very great extent been eroded by a resurgent native tide.[1] Crucially, however, the so-called invasion inaugurated a split polity, dividing Ire-

---

1 Overview of the period and its intense historiographical controversies in F. J. Byrne, 'The Trembling Sod: Ireland in 1169', *NHI* ii., 1–42; crucial historical study by M. T. Flanagan, *Irish Society, Anglo-Norman Settlers, Angevin Kingship: Interactions in Ireland in the Late Twelfth Century* (Oxford, 1989).

land for the first time into two 'nations', two cultures, and at least two languages.

One of the features of the period is the apparent disconnection between what, with the benefit of hindsight, was clearly a social and political watershed in Ireland's history, and the relative lack of literary attention paid to it, at least in the years immediately after the Anglo-Norman invasion.[2] Conspicuous changes certainly took place in the literary sphere in the twelfth and thirteenth centuries, but these changes tended to reflect the contemporary religious reform movement, not the importation and expansion of English power. This movement transformed the internal structure and practices of the Irish ecclesiastical establishment, aligning it far more closely with the wider Church.[3] The importation of the continental monastic orders—far less interested in the production and preservation of vernacular literature than had been the case in the native monastic establishments—meant that literary production shifted from the hands of the ecclesiastical elite and became the task of secular learned families.[4]

The most famous literature of the period belongs to a hugely influential secular genre which came to prominence around the turn of the thirteenth century, namely *fíanaigecht* or 'fenian tales', stories about the warrior-poet and hunter Finn mac Cumaill and his band of fighting men, the *fíana*.[5] With *fíanaigecht* (also known as the 'Finn Cycle'), we enter a world noteworthy for lush imagination and plangent emotion, especially when compared with the pseudohistorical mythography worked through in chapter 4. Though the genre dramatically burgeoned in popularity

2 See P. Wadden, 'Some views of the Normans in eleventh- and twelfth-century Ireland', in S. Duffy & S. Foran (eds.), *English Isles: cultural transmission and political conflict in Britain and Ireland, 1100–1500* (Dublin, 2013), 13–36.

3 For the reform movement, see the major study by M. T. Flanagan, *The Transformation of the Irish Church in the Twelfth Century* (Woodbridge, 2010), and (older) K. Hughes, *The Church in Irish Society* (London, 1967), 253–74.

4 See particularly the essay by M. Ní Mhaonaigh, 'Pagans and holy men: literary manifestations of twelfth-century reform', in D. Bracken & D. Ó Riain-Raedel (eds.), *Ireland and Europe in the Twelfth Century: Reform and Renewal* (Dublin, 2006), 143–161.

5 Lucid overview by M. Ní Mhaonaigh, *CHIL* i., 57–9; for the history of Finn Cycle scholarship see the introduction to G. Parsons & S. Arbuthnot (eds.), *The Gaelic Finn Tradition* (Dublin, 2012), 9–13. As always, the focus on the gods in this study means that large stretches of important literature in which they do not feature must be passed over, especially (in this period) that from the ecclesiastical sphere. I make no pretence of giving here anything resembling an overview of Irish literary activity of the mid- to late– Middle Ages.

from the beginning of the twelfth century, written material about Finn mac Cumaill can be shown to have a much longer history.[6] The Túatha Dé Danann are ubiquitous in fenian tradition, and the genre itself represents the highpoint of their narrative proliferation outside the Mythological Cycle. It also encapsulates the considerable gulf between mythological deities and the literary Túatha Dé Danann, a distance which has bedevilled discussion of a supposed Irish pantheon. Though familiar faces appear—not least Aengus (Óengus) of Bruig na Bóinne—they are now clearly the aristocrats of a supernatural race, divested of divinity but supercharged with magic.

The authors of Finn Cycle tales clearly refused to countenance a central prop of Irish pseudohistorical doctrine, the idea that the Túatha Dé Danann had died out long ago. Instead they aligned themselves with older literary traditions about the supernatural partition of Ireland, insisting upon the Túatha Dé Danann's persistence within the world of the *síd*-mounds and thus gorgeously reasserting the cultural dream of hidden immortals. And in a number of tales—some connected with Finn and some not, but all alike in atmosphere and effect—the Túatha Dé persist long enough to encounter the Christian religion. In a few the ontological possibilities of such an encounter are taken to a dizzying extreme, with a few select members of the god-peoples becoming sincere—even saintly—converts to the faith of Christ.

FINN MAC CUMAILL AND THE GODS

Rumination upon the borderland between paganism and Christianity is characteristic of the Finn Cycle, and this is reflected in the pervasive intimacy between the world of the *fían*-warriors and that of the *síd*-dwellers. In the mature literature this is due to a desire to explain how the noble warriors of the pagan past might have attained salvation against the odds, but a productive tension between pagan and Christian seems to belong to the genre's deepest roots. These are to be found in the historical realities of Ireland between the fourth and mid-ninth centu-

---

6 Finn apparently existed as a literary figure by the ninth century, and a few stories about him had entered the canon by the tenth; see K. Murray, 'Interpreting the evidence: problems with dating the early *fíanaigecht* corpus', in Parsons & Arbuthnot (eds.), *The Gaelic Finn Tradition*, 31–49, especially references to K. Meyer's examination of the earlier material, *Fianaigecht: being a collection of hitherto inedited Irish poems and tales relating to Finn and his fíana* [Todd Lecture Series 16] (Dublin, 1910).

ries, in which *fían*-bands—gangs of roving, aristocratic youths without fixed dwellings—were a social institution.[7] Like many societies, early Ireland was faced with the problem of what to do with its combustible young men, especially those who had reached physical maturity but had not yet inherited the land and property upon which masculine social identity was founded. The solution was an accepted and temporary period of vagrancy, spent in hunting and raiding outside settled society; there is some evidence from secular texts that the existence of *fían*-bands was acknowledged—within limits—as something appropriate to a functional social order.[8]

If the secular authorities of early Christian Ireland could accommodate the *fían*-band as an institution, the same was not true of the church, which regarded it with horror and dubbed its members 'sons of death'.[9] In part this was down to the destructive violence which was integral to a *fían*. Ecclesiastical authorities typically refused to make a distinction between the activities proper to a *fían* and the violent marauding known as *díberg*, 'plundering'—and no doubt they could indeed look much the same in practice. But there is also evidence that one reason for their revulsion was that the *fían* was seen as intrinsically pagan, and that *fían*-warriors were one of the social groups (like druids) that held out for a time against Christianity. There are suggestive hints that membership of such a band involved wearing some kind of forehead mark or headgear—regularly abominated as 'diabolical' by churchmen—and the swearing of pagan *uota mali*, 'oaths of evil', to kill a man.[10] Kim McCone has shown that real *fían*-bands were still in existence as late as 850, though it seems highly improbable that actual paganism among them continued this long.[11]

7 See K. McCone, 'The Celtic and Indo-European origins of the *fían*', in Parsons & Arbuthnot (eds.), *The Gaelic Finn Tradition*, 14–30, and his earlier arguments in *PPCP*, 205–7.

8 A late Old Irish text refers to '*fían*-bands without arrogance' as an aspect of the idea social order; see *Tecosca Chormaic*, ed. & trans. K. Meyer, *The Instructions of King Cormac mac Airt* [RIA Todd Lecture Series 15] (Dublin, 1909), 8, 9. For the social benefits a *fían* might offer to the *túath* see *TEI*, xii–xiii.

9 See R. Sharpe, 'Hiberno-Latin *laicus*, Irish *láech* and the devil's men', *Ériu* 30 (1979), 75–92, and K. McCone, 'Werewolves, cyclopes, *díberga*, and *fíanna*: juvenile delinquency in early Ireland', *CMCS* 12 (1986), 1–22.

10 See E. Bhreathnach, *Ireland in Medieval Europe AD 400–1000* (Dublin, 2014), 141–3.

11 McCone, 'Celtic and Indo-European origins', in Parsons & Arbuthnot (eds.), *The Gaelic Finn Tradition*, 15; but for arguments against *fíanagecht* as a late survival of pagan-

Nonetheless, the pagan associations of the historical *fían*—as opposed to its refined literary reflections of half a millennium later—may explain why *fíanaigecht* was slow to get established in a literary culture dominated by a clerical intelligentsia. The figure of Finn himself may have needed particularly thorough decontamination, as the case can be made that he was originally a pagan god—perhaps the very deity to whom members of a *fían* swore their murderous oath.[12] If so, this being's name was probably *Vindos in Celtic (the older form of *Finn*), making him simply the 'Fair' or 'White' one. (The name of an attested Gallo-Roman god *Vindon(n)us*, identified with Apollo, suggestively contains the same element.)[13] Linguistically cognate with Irish Finn is Welsh *Gwynn*, a figure who appears in Welsh tradition as a supernatural hunter; there also seem to be common themes between stories about Finn and those about the god Lug.[14] Reconstructions of this kind are fraught and out of fashion, but the evidence for a lost god Vindos as divine patron of the institution of the warband—perhaps a hunter, and perhaps a by-form of Lugus— is at least worth considering.[15]

This begs the question of why Vindos/Finn was never absorbed into the literary edifice of the Túatha Dé Danann, unlike Óengus, the Dagda, and so on. A divine Finn, still the recipient of some kind of active cult after the conversion period, would certainly have been abhorred by the monastic men of learning who were putting old gods like Lug and Manannán to literary use in the late seventh and eighth centuries. There are also hints that a similar trajectory may have been followed by other

---

ism, see C. Etchingham, *Church Organisation in Ireland A.D. 650 to 1000* (Maynooth, 1999), 298–318.

12 See P. Mac Cana, '*Fianaigecht* in the pre-Norman period', in B. Almqvist, *et al.* (eds.), *The Heroic Process: Essays on the Fenian Tradition of Ireland and Scotland* (Dublin, 1987), 75–99, and *EIH&M*, 277–8, along with *Duanaire Finn*, ed. G. Murphy, iii. (London, 1953), xiii—xxxvii.

13 See M. Aldhouse-Green, 'Gallo-British Deities and their Shrines', in M. Todd (ed.), *A Companion to Roman Britain* (Oxford, 2004), 210.

14 See above, 20, and J. Carey's analysis of Gwynn and related figures in 'Nodons in Britain and Ireland', *ZCP* 40 (1984), 1–22. The Núadu who is Finn's maternal great-grandfather may once have been identical with Núadu Argatlám, especially as Irish Núadu corresponds etymologically to Welsh Nudd; it is significant that both Núadus have sons named Tadg.

15 Sims-Williams (*IIMWL*, 10–1) has salutary warnings on the difficulties in precisely this instance, cautioning that cognate names of supernatural beings in Irish and Welsh are '*not* proof that the reconstructed shared name, and the myth, cult, or shared story that it represents, are necessarily a common inheritance...'

figures who we know as the leaders of literary *fían*-bands. For example, Finn is not always the pre-eminent *fían*-leader in the pre-twelfth-century material: a Munster personage named Fothad Canainne sometimes occupies that position.[16] Fothad is one of three brothers—all called Fothad—who have the suggestive alternative names *Tréndia*, *Caíndia*, and *Oíndia*, 'Strong god', 'Fair god' and 'Singular god'.[17] Might this figure or figures have been a south-western variation on the pagan divinity invoked by the members of a *fían*? It seems possible.

Either way, the Finn of the literary record is a human being; if he was ever numbered among the gods, this was forgotten or obscured. It also seems that his literary reshaping occurred under ecclesiastical rather than popular impetus, and involved blending him with a Leinster literary figure called Finn *fili*, Finn the poet. This generated his distinctive composite character as both seer-poet and warrior, and may simultaneously have contributed to his increased prominence as the *fían*-leader *par excellence* and helped to disperse any lingering aura of paganism. Nonetheless, there is a curiously *embroiled* quality to the entanglements between Finn and the Túatha Dé Danann, and it is tempting to ascribe this to his having once, in some pre-literary incarnation, been divine.

ELDERS AND ANCIENTS

This brings us to the texts in which Finn appears. So far I have used the word 'genre' to describe *fíanaigecht*, but this gives a misleading impression of a lack of formal variety. Fenian literature is actually a versatile and long-lived tradition manifesting in a number of forms over the centuries, from medieval and early modern prose-sagas and poetry down to oral material collected in Ireland and Gaelic Scotland over the last two hundred years.

That said, the Finn Cycle's palpable centre of gravity is the luminous, nostalgic compendium *Acallam na Senórach*, 'The Colloquy of the Elders'.[18] Composed *c.*1200–1220, this novel-length crossweave of stories

16 See Ní Mhaonaigh, *CHIL* i., 58, on the early *fíanaigecht* poem, *Reicne Fothad Canainne*. Links between Finn and Fothad in P. McQuillan, 'Finn, Fothad and *fían*: some early associations', *PHCC* 8 (1990), 1–10.

17 *Fothad* means 'support, sustenance'; see note in *EIH&M*, 10. 'God' names in Nagy, *CWA&A*, 299.

18 As with *Lebor Gabála* in the last chapter, *Acallam na Senórach* is an instance of an elegant Irish title becoming fiddly in English translation—literally 'The Colloquy of the

within stories is framed by the encounter between Patrick, apostle of the new religion, and the doddery remnants of Finn's *fíana*.[19] Though the inset stories may be comic, tragic, or uncanny, the prevailing atmosphere might best be called autumnal: a new dispensation takes over and an era of material splendour and martial valour fades forever from human recollection.[20] (Angels tell Patrick that the *fían*-warriors to whom he speaks have forgotten fully two-thirds of their store of memory: the last third is saved against the odds by the grace of God.)[21] The *Acallam* as we have it is missing its ending and we do not know who composed it, but it clearly draws extensively on previous traditions and incorporates pre-existing poetry.[22] It also has deep connections with the genre of place-name lore, *dindshenchas*. As Caílte and Oisín—the last of the *fíana*—traverse Ireland with Patrick, their tales of the past battles and wonders embedded in the landscape are confirmed by the relics

---

Old Ones'. ('Veterans' Talk' might be another way of translating it, as *senóir*, of which *senórach* is the genitive plural, means 'seasoned elder, old hand, someone expert thanks to time and experience'.) I therefore use 'the *Acallam*' as my preferred way of referring to the text. Recent translations are A. Dooley & H. Roe, *Tales of the Elders of Ireland* (Oxford, 1999) [*TEI*], and—less well-known—M. Harmon, *The colloquy of the old men (Acallam na senórach)* (Dublin, 2001). For the dating, see A. Dooley, 'The Date and Purpose of *Acallam na Senórach*', *Éigse* 34 (2004), 97–126.

19 Bibliography on the *Acallam* is now substantial: good lists in *TEI*, xxxviii-xl, and more recently in the introduction to Parsons & Arbuthnot (eds.), *The Gaelic Finn Tradition*, 10, fn.10. Very good introductory essay by H. Roe, 'The *Acallam*: the Church's eventual acceptance of the cultural inheritance of pagan Ireland', in S. Sheehan, *et al.* (eds.), *Gab-lánach in Scélaigecht: Celtic Studies in honor of Ann Dooley* (Dublin, 2013), 103–15, and useful summing-up in M. Harmon, 'The Colloquy of the Old Men; Shape and Substance', in P. A. Lynch, *et al.* (eds.), *Back to the Present, Forward to the Past: Irish Writing and History since 1798* (2 vols., New York, 2006), ii., 123–34.

20 Good on this point is D. Schlüter, '"For the entertainment of lords and commons of later times": past and remembrance in *Acallam na Senórach*', *Celtica* 26 (2010), 146–60.

21 *TEI*, 12, W. Stokes (ed & partial trans.) 'Acallamh na senórach', in W. Stokes & E. Windisch (eds.), *Irische Texte* (4 vols., Leipzig, 1880–1909), iv (1), ll.298–9 [note that vol. 4 of *Irische Texte* is actually two volumes: the *Acallam* is in the first]. See also Schlüter, '"For the entertainment of lords"', 147. As *TEI* is an excellent and easily-available translation I have quoted from it throughout, sometimes with minor changes. The phrasing of the Irish is mentioned in fns. if significant in the argument.

22 There is also a later recension of the text, *Agallamh na Seanórach*, and also an abbreviated and significantly different version known as the 'Little *Acallam*', or *Acallam Bec*; unfortunately there is no space to address these here. For these and the MS tradition of the *Acallam*, see G. Parsons, 'A Reading of *Acallam na Senórach* as a Literary Text' [unpublished Ph.D thesis, University of Cambridge, 2007].

which they uncover, monuments which bear, as Joseph Nagy writes, 'mute witness to their stories'.[23]

The structure of the *Acallam* is immensely complex, with a frame-tale and some two hundred embedded stories; only a few relevant to the discussion of the native supernaturals can be pulled out here. The Túatha Dé Danann are presented throughout as completely synonymous with the people of the *síd*. They inhabit a series of apparently separate parallel worlds, a hidden archipelago stippling the landscape of Ireland as islands stud the sea. It is also worth bearing in mind that the Túatha Dé Danann in the *Acallam* are legion—a people, not a pantheon—especially if one is accustomed to thinking of the Dagda, Lug, and so on as a smallish group of 'Irish gods'. The author of the *Acallam* evidently imagines them as numbering in the tens of thousands. This reflects the situation in 'The Second Battle of Moytura', for example, which describes massive losses among the Túatha Dé and Fomorians. But the composer of the *Acallam* is conscious of the evocative power of names, and the sheer number of otherworld-folk named in the text gives a powerful impression of multitudinousness.

On the most basic level, they physically resemble us—or would, were we all gorgeous, splendidly dressed young adults in glowing health. Characteristic of the *Acallam*, as of much Irish medieval literature, is play with size as a marker of supernatural status, though this is intermittent and not always thought through. We find out at the beginning that the warriors of the *fiana* are around thirteen feet tall, so presumably the average man or woman of the *síd* is of similar stature.[24] Nonetheless, one winsome story early in the compendium gives us the *síd*-musician Cnú Deróil and his wife Bláthnait ('Nutlet' and 'Floret'), who are only four of Finn's handwidths in height. Their story probably existed before the *Acallam*, which may explain why they are so unlike their fellow people of the *síd*. We discover that the midget Cnú Deróil is the only son of the mighty Lug—the force of which is perhaps meant to amuse in its incongruity.

One of the text's crucial areas of innovation is the intimacy of the relationship between Patrick and the *síd*-folk, though we do have at least

23 J. F. Nagy, 'Keeping the *Acallam* together', in Parsons & Arbuthnot (eds.), *The Gaelic Finn Tradition*, 112; on temporal layers in the text see also G. Parsons, 'The structure of *Acallam na Senórach*', *CMCS* 55 (Summer 2008), 11–39.

24 *TEI*, 5, Stokes (ed.), 'Acallamh', ll.76–9; the tallest of Patrick's clerics, standing, only comes up to the shoulders of the seated warriors.

one story of an encounter between a saint and an otherworldly being from the eighth century.[25] The Patrick of the *Acallam* is an impressive figure who insists—at the prompting of angels, no less—that the stories of the *fíana* be recorded, giving ecclesiastical licence to tales of the pre-Christian past. As seen, the historical Patrick makes no mention of native gods, but the literary Patrick of the *Acallam* cuts a very different figure. His conversion mission involves the destruction of 'idols and spectres and the arts of druidry', but no imaginative connection at all is made between the people of the *síd* and the gods whom the Irish once worshipped.[26] Here Patrick enjoys hearing about the Túatha Dé Danann—including risqué tales of their erotic imbroglios—and he meets several of them, accepting them as sentient persons with souls to save or lose.[27] In a climactic moment towards the end of the text, Donn, son of Midir, lays his head in Patrick's lap in an act of formal submission, giving power over the Túatha Dé Danann into the saint's hands.[28] We are told that Patrick will soon shut the *síd*-mounds and seal the Túatha Dé Danann inside forever; the access to the numinous and imperishable which they had provided will henceforth belong to the church alone.[29] As it happens, we never do witness this momentous act of segregation in the *Acallam* as it has come down to us; possibly it formed part of the text's lost ending.

More will be said about the specific case of Patrick later, but as Caílte and Oisín's stories make plain, the relationship between (heroic) mortals and immortals in the *Acallam* exactly corresponds in most respects to that between different groups of humans. The Túatha Dé Danann strike

25 This is the mysterious 'Colloquy of St Columba and the Youth' (*Immacaldam Choluim Chille 7 int Óclaig*), in which St Columba and his monks meet a mysterious and otherworldly young man on the shore of Lough Foyle; see J. Carey, ed. & trans., 'The Lough Foyle Colloquy Texts', *Ériu* 52 (2002), 53–87, and Elva Johnston's comments, *L&IEMI*, 30–1.

26 In Irish, *idhul 7 arracht 7 ealadhan ndráidhechta; TEI*, 45, Stokes (ed.), 'Acallamh', l.1500.

27 See Patrick's well-known reaction to the story of Aillén, Uchtdelb, Manannán, and Áine—essentially a tale of wife-swapping: 'this is an intricate tale!' (*TEI*, 111, Stokes (ed.), 'Acallamh', ll.3666–7).

28 *TEI*, 150, Stokes (ed.), 'Acallamh', ll.5376–8. Stokes notes that the Bodleian Laud 610 manuscript of the *Acallam* has a marginal note at this point saying 'So it was then that the Túatha Dé Danann believed in Patrick', implying that they all become Christians; but I think this is explicitly against the grain of the text, which emphasizes the damnation of all but a few of them.

29 *TEI*, 210, Stokes (ed.), 'Acallamh', ll.7533–7.

internal alliances and nurture bitter vendettas, so that the warriors of Finn's *fíana* may simultaneously be on hostile terms with one group and the best of friends with another. The *fíana* seem able to visit the world of the *síd* with ease: there is no suggestion that the entrances to such places are difficult to find, that they only open at particular times, or that there is a time-differential between the *síd* and the human world. In one inset story, Caílte spends over a year as an honoured guest in the *síd* of Assaroe, exactly as though it were any other aristocratic residence.[30] Moreover, Finn's *fíana*, a sodality in which the sole criterion is heroic excellence, also includes a man of the Túatha Dé Danann, Ferdoman, son of Bodb Derg; he functions within the warrior-band precisely as do his mortal counterparts. Similarly, the royal household of Cairbre Lifechair, the son of Cormac mac Airt, includes a beautiful young couple as its hospitallers—we only realize they are of the *síd* when they casually let drop that they are two hundred years old.[31]

Genealogy is the key to the relationship between mortals and immortals. In one of the text's pivotal imaginative propositions, we are told that there are 'only two aristocracies of equal merit' in Ireland, the Sons of Míl and the Túatha Dé Danann.[32] Unlike the scenario in 'The Book of Invasions', the former do not displace the latter in linear time. Instead, a constant level of ambivalent interaction is the norm, so that benign and malignant manifestations seem to alternate. One alarming passage hints that the two peoples have in some mysterious way to be balanced, and that the people of the *síd* will take drastic measures if mortals overstep the mark. An Ulsterman, Dub, son of Trén, possesses to a high degree the virtue of generosity, but when a delegation of *síd*-horsemen are unwisely told that Dub is 'the most generous of the Sons of Míl and of the Túatha Dé Danann', they promptly kill him out of 'jealousy and envy', having 'no one to match him'.[33] (There is a faint echo of Greek myth here, in which mortals such as Niobe or Arachne make unwise boasts and so attract the anger of the gods.) Indeed, violence perpetrated by the Túatha Dé against mortals often has precisely this quality of uncanny disproportionality. We hear, for example, of how one Aillén son

30 *TEI*, 56, Stokes (ed.), 'Acallamh', ll.1793ff.

31 *TEI*, 58, Stokes (ed.), 'Acallamh', ll.1877–8.

32 *TEI*, 14, Stokes (ed.), 'Acallamh', l.399: in Irish, *acht dá airecht chudrama a n-Eirinn*; on this phrase see the comments of J. Carey, 'Acallam na senórach: a conversation between worlds', in A. Doyle & K. Murray, *In Dialogue with the Agallamh: Essays in Honour of Seán Ó Coileáin* (Dublin, 2014), 76–89, at 84.

33 *TEI*, 100, Stokes (ed.), 'Acallamh', ll.3310–5.

of Midgna razes Tara to the ground every year for twenty-four years: he puts the inhabitants to sleep by playing his dulcimer before incinerating them with a blast of fire from his mouth.[34] We are never given the slightest inkling why, hinting that a certain motiveless malignancy is part of the intended aesthetic effect.[35]

More reassuring is the frequency of fosterage in the *Acallam*, important because the institution involved profound emotional bonds. We hear constantly of the children of mortal grandees fostered by the people of the *síd*, and one member of Finn's *fían* has a *síd*-foster-mother, Muirenn, daughter of Derg; rather touchingly he casually pops into the *síd* to ask her advice.[36] But even in the matter of child-rearing there is a dark shadow, in the prominent story of the youth Áed, son of the King of Leinster. The boy is abducted into the *síd* and raised there for three years—a kind of enforced fosterage, and one of the earliest examples in Irish tradition of the theme of the child stolen away by otherworld-folk.[37] The story of Áed's abduction and restitution forms a common thread running through the frame-tale. It is striking that fosterage does not appear to occur in the other direction in the *Acallam*: no mortal kings in the text foster children from the *síd*, though the inhabitants of the *síd* plainly produce offspring.[38]

LOVE AND POWER

If the Túatha Dé Danann are so human (if not always humane), then what practical difference exists between them and the Sons of Míl?[39]

---

34 Aillén mac Midgna is an obscure personage outside this story; cf. T. F. O'Rahilly's suggestion that he be linked to the mysterious *(t)ellén*—a destructive three-headed monster—which emerges from the Cave of Crúachain in 'The Battle of Mag Mucrama'. The term *ellén* might be cognate with Welsh *ellyll*, 'elf, sprite, spirit, fiend', itself cognate with the Irish name Aillil; see S. Mac Mathúna, 'The Relationship of the Chthonic World in Early Ireland to Chaos and Cosmos', in J. Borsje, *et al.* (eds.), *Celtic Cosmology: Perspectives from Ireland and Scotland* (Toronto, 2014), 53–76, 67 fn.30.

35 *TEI*, 51–2, Stokes (ed.), 'Acallamh', ll.1664–70. This story is structurally crucial because the young Finn attains leadership of the *fíana* of Ireland by killing Aillén.

36 This is reminiscent of situation in some Ulster Cycle tales; in *Táin Bó Fraích* ('The Cattle-raid of Fróech') the human hero's foster-mother is Bóand, the mother of Óengus.

37 *TEI*, 121, Stokes (ed.), 'Acallamh', ll.4090–4099.

38 The theme of *síd*-children fostered by mortal grandees does occur in later texts, e.g. 'The Wooing of Treblann' (*Tochmarc Treblainne*), perhaps composed c.1300.

39 Some of my thinking in what follows was anticipated by John Carey in his il-

The author of the *Acallam* answers that lineage is ontology—a difference in nature is re-imagined as ethnic difference. So much is evident in one of the text's pervasive themes, that of romance across the border between worlds. In one story, set in the text's Patrician present, we discover that Caílte, greatest of the *fían* after Finn himself, long ago made a marriage-pledge to Scothníam ('Flower-lustre'), daughter of Bodb Derg, son of the Dagda: it is implied that they quarrelled and Caílte jilted her. Scothníam appears—a few centuries late, perhaps—to demand her bride-price, causing Patrick to marvel at the difference between her and her one-time betrothed:

> 'We find it strange to see you both thus,' said Patrick, 'she a young and beautiful woman, and you, Caílte, a withered old man, bent and grey.' 'I know the reason,' said Caílte, 'our ages and lineages are not the same. She is one of the Túatha Dé Danann, who are immortal, and I am one of the Sons of Míl, mortals with a short life.'[40]

Making plain the gulf between orders of being, snapshots such as this underline the vulnerability of unredeemed humanity, for the Túatha Dé are not subject to entropy. By the thirteenth century the theme of the otherworldly paramour was already an old one, but the composer of the *Acallam* enlarges its potential as a vehicle for poignant emotion. Plangency resides in the fact that the two races are so physically and cognitively similar that deep bonds of love can develop, but so glaringly are they destined to different fates that these bonds almost never blossom into lasting happiness. The theme of intermarriage is delicately modulated through the text, curiously taking us back to the world of the ninth-century poem 'Whence did the Irish originate?', which describes how the incoming Sons of Míl took wives from among the Túatha Dé. But in the *Acallam*, this scenario is imagined to have persisted down the centuries. Finn's own family is bound up with the folk of the otherworld: his father's first wife was of the Túatha Dé Danann, while Finn's own

---

luminating '*Acallam na Senórach*: a conversation between worlds', in Doyle & Murray (eds.), *In Dialogue with the Agallamh*, 76–89, which became available as this book was nearing completion. As sometimes happens in scholarship we had arrived at similar conclusions independently, but his publication has priority; I am grateful that he was content to allow me to put out this chapter as I had written it.

40 *TEI*, 117–8, Stokes (ed.), 'Acallamh', ll.3904–9, and see comments of Carey, '*Acallam na Senórach*: a conversation between worlds', 80–1.

mother, Muirne, was a granddaughter of Núadu; Finn's wife Sadb is a daughter of Bodb Derg, son of the Dagda. Blaí, the mother of Finn's son Oisín, is another otherworld woman, the daughter of Derg Díanscothach, and dwells in the 'síd of the Breast of Cleitech'—Cletty, on the Boyne. In both Finn and Oisín, therefore, the lineages of mortals and immortals mingle.

Another tragic vignette describes how a síd-woman, Créde, is wooed by Cáel, a mortal man and member of Finn's fíana. They marry, but after only twenty-four days Cáel is killed in battle and Créde dies of grief. Significantly this story—like a miniature *Turandot*—shows marriage provoking a transformation in moral stature in the woman: Créde begins as a haughty materialist, but ends as the fían's nurse and hospitaller, tending their wounds and dispensing healing milk.[41] The idea that erotic suffering might be redemptive is also central to the most important human-síd love-match in the *Acallam*, that of Áed and Aillenn. Áed—a confusingly common name in the text, as in Irish literature and history in general—is the young King of Connaught.[42] Towards the close of the text, while he has married the daughter of the King of Leinster, he has unfortunately fallen deeply in love with Aillenn of the síd, another granddaughter of the Dagda. Their love is genuine and painful indeed, but Patrick sternly forbids them to be together until the time Áed's wife should die. (Our text, scholars have shown, is strongly aligned with reforming currents within the twelfth-century Irish church, one imperative of which was the enjoining of strict monogamy, against what had been long-standing norms in Ireland.)[43]

When we first meet Aillenn, she has already singled herself out. Though many fairy-women become infatuated with mortal lovers in the *Acallam*, Aillenn does so for love, and in so doing makes a grand gesture of self-exposure:

> 'Well, dear woman,' said the king, 'do you wish to be seen by the nobles of the province?' 'I do indeed', she said, 'for I am not a be-

---

41 *TEI*, 25–8, Stokes (ed.), 'Acallamh', ll.742–867.

42 He is a recurring character: he owes his life to Patrick, who brings him back to life after he has been accidentally killed in a game of hurley. Áed was the name of the son of the King of Connaught ruling at the time of the *Acallam*'s likely composition, Cathal Crobhdearg (who died in 1224); for contemporary resonances of this kind and the text's likely western bias, see Dooley, 'Date and Purpose', especially 102–3.

43 See *TEI*, xxviii-xxx.

witching woman of the *síd*. Though I am of the Túatha Dé Danann, I have my own body about me.' Aillenn showed herself to the host, and never had they seen before or after a lovelier woman.[44]

Her transparency works on two levels. First, given the Túatha Dé Danann's fondness for hiddenness and invisibility, she is brave to appear to a host of nobles openly; and secondly, she appears as she is, unenhanced by otherworldly glamour. She has already stepped beyond the borders and the ethos of her people.[45]

Her self-display also involves a significant—if less than convincing—ontological discrimination: though she is one of the Túatha Dé, as she admits, she is not a 'bewitching woman of the *síd*'. As 'bewitching' suggests, 'not a woman of the *síd*' simply means 'not deploying magic at the moment', accompanied by the hint that naturally she could do so if she desired.[46] The idiom used—that she has her own body 'about' her—is normally applied to clothing; it implies that changing appearance, for the people of the *síd*, is as easy as changing garments.

This is her own assessment; more interesting is Patrick's subsequent sizing up of Aillenn's nature, and his understanding of *what* she is, as well as who she is. He has no truck with her attempt to differentiate herself from the rest of her people. With a mixture of compassion and sternness he treats her as a fallen being and sends her on her way to await the natural death of her beloved's wife.

'Well, my dear woman', said Patrick, 'good are your appearance and condition. What has kept you in such a perfection of shape and form?' 'Each one of us that has been at the drinking of the Feast of Goibniu', she said, 'is not afflicted with disease or sickness. Well now, my dear and holy cleric', said Aillenn, 'what is your judgment on me and the King of Connaught?'... 'The king has pledged to God and to me' [said Patrick,] 'that he would be bound to a single wife, and we may not go against that pledge.' 'And I then', she said, 'what shall I do now?' 'Go home to your *síd*-mound',

44 *TEI*, 179, Stokes (ed.), 'Acallamh', ll.6378–83.

45 See the comments of A. Dooley, 'Pagan Beliefs and Christian Redress in *Acallam na Senórach*', in J. Borsje *et al.* (eds.), *Celtic Cosmology: Perspectives from Ireland and Scotland* (Toronto, 2014), 256.

46 The word is *sirrachtach*, Old Irish *sírechtach*, 'full of longing, wistful, entrancing, transporting', used especially of music.

said Patrick, 'and if the daughter of the King of Leinster should die before you, then you may thenceforth be the only wife of the man you love and cherish. But if you bring harm, by day or by night, to the king or to his wife', said Patrick, 'I shall disfigure you so badly that your mother or your father or your foster-father would not wish to see you.'[47]

Patrick is a realist: he has already listened to many tales of the malice of the otherworld. He never loses sight of Aillenn's innate capacity, almost despite herself, for vindictiveness. Firmly in control, the saint insists on spiritual purification through suffering: Aillenn must not give in to her envy by bringing harm upon an innocent. When he calls upon her to take his blessing and go in peace, the blessing resembles a curse, despite its moral force. We sense that Patrick is speaking to Aillenn in language that she understands. Can she remain true to her better feelings, to her own sense of difference from the rest of the Túatha Dé? It is telling that the punishment, should she fail, would be disfigurement: it strikes at the heart of what it means to be 'of the *síd*' in the *Acallam,* namely radiant beauty no matter what ugly acts one perpetrates. If Aillenn transgresses, Patrick threatens to make the outer and the inner match. But she succeeds, and there is—eventually—a happy ending. The frustrated lovers are married by Patrick in the first wedding he performs in Ireland, and Ireland's 'two aristocracies' are joined once again.

The people of the *síd* also differ from mortals in a second, more ambiguous manner, and that is their capacity for direct actualization of the will—that is, for magic. Aillenn claimed to be in, or wearing, her own body, and the implication is that the otherworld-folk are intrinsically able to change their physical appearance, though this is importantly nuanced as the text unfolds. The idea does occur in earlier literature: in the *Táin* the Morrígan famously changes herself into various animals to entrap Cú Chulainn, while Lug impersonates the hero in battle as he recovers from his wounds. But in the *Acallam* (and the Finn Cycle in general) this becomes a richly elaborated theme, so that instability of shape becomes a major marker of otherworldliness. *Síd*-women in particular seem fond of transforming themselves into animals, and even in human form seem curiously interchangeable. At one point an otherworld woman challenges the *fiana* to a race; when they are entertained

---

47 *TEI*, 180 (with minor changes of phrasing), Stokes (ed.), 'Acallamh', ll.6400–14.

afterwards in the *síd* of the Hill of Howth, Finn thinks he spots the woman in the crowd:

> 'She is not at all the one who was there with you', said Áed Ucht-gel, the king of the *síd*... 'Who was with us then?', asked Finn. 'Bé Mannair, the daughter of Aincél', said Áed Uchtgel, son of Aengus, the son of the Dagda, the messenger of the Túatha Dé Danann. 'It is she who goes in the shape of the water-spider or a whale, who transforms herself into the shape of a fly or a person's best friend, whether male or female, so that the secrets of all are entrusted to her...'[48]

This unsettling personage—her name means 'Woman of Destruction, daughter of Ill-Omen'—embodies the Túatha Dé Danann's penchant for transmogrification. This specifically magical and implicitly feminine power seems to be particular abominated by the *fíana*. Elsewhere, Finn has a lover from the *síd* named Úaine ('Green'), whom he is forced to reject because of her intolerable habit of constantly changing herself into different animals.[49]

Less extreme but more insidious are the hints throughout the *Acallam* that otherworldly beings use magic to enhance their glamour and éclat. Indeed there is a hint—without looking for the literal in the literary—that the author imagined that one of the *síd*-people's powers was the projection of a phantasmal body. Caílte explains that Patrick will soon confine the Túatha De Danann within their hollow hills forever, 'unless someone doomed to die should see an apparition visiting earth'.[50] This is terrestrial, rather than astral, projection: the Túatha Dé Danann may appear to sight and sense, but are not really there.

The *síd*-woman Aillenn—as Patrick and the nobles of Connaught acknowledge—is gorgeously beautiful even without magical enhancements of this kind. Her youth and health derive, as she says, from drinking at the Feast of Goibniu, the Irish equivalent of Greek nectar and ambrosia. It appears that even mortals can benefit from the same regimen. When Áed, the abducted son of the King of Leinster, is restored to his parents

---

48 *TEI*, 159, Stokes (ed.), 'Acallamh', ll.5675–81.

49 *TEI*, 74, Stokes (ed.), 'Acallamh', ll.2400–03.

50 *TEI*, 210, Stokes (ed.), 'Acallamh', ll.7535–7; Carey, '*Acallam na senórach*: a conversation between worlds', 86, corrects the trans. in *TEI*.

after his years of captivity in the *síd*, Patrick removes the magic of the Túatha Dé Danann from him, so that 'he shall get the death that the King of Heaven and Earth has ordained for him'.[51] The implication is that he would otherwise have shared the immortal life of his abductors, and that this would have been against the will of God.

In a striking late episode, Caílte illustrates similar discrimination, the fundamental principle—akin to Patrick's hard-headedness with Aillenn—which the *Acallam* enjoins when dealing with the powers of the *síd*. He is decrepit and badly injured, and the Túatha Dé—who owe him a great debt—possess expert healers. They tell him:

> '... we shall change your shape for you so that you may be vigorous and fully active. You shall likewise have the noble youthfulness of the Túatha Dé Danann.' 'Is is sad', said Caílte, 'that I should take on a magical shape. I shall not have any shape but that which my Maker and my Creator and the golden True God gave to me, with the faith of belief and piety of the Adze-Head [= Patrick], he who has come into Ireland.'[52]

Caílte accepts healing with gratitude but refuses cosmetic enhancement; far from being offended, his otherworldly hosts admiringly salute his stoicism. The implications are subtle. For the mortal and now-Christian Caílte, it would deny the will of the Creator to take on a 'shape of druidry'—theologically, a disavowal in himself of the *imago Dei* in which, according to the Book of Genesis, mankind was created. Shape-changing enchantment also ceases to be appropriate for any *síd*-being who, like Aillenn, desires to migrate into the human world. What is less clear, however, is whether such enchantment is intrinsically sinful for the folk of the otherworld themselves. As ever, the implications of the word 'druidry' (*draídecht*) are difficult. It may mean 'enchantment'—*draídecht* is the normal word for magic—but it clearly carries pagan and unclean connotations: when Aillenn marries Áed, her joining the mortal world is also a religious conversion, a forsaking of 'false and druidical belief' for the Gospel.[53] The ex-gods are so thoroughly humanized that they are represented as pagans, though we are given

---

51 *TEI*, 137, Stokes (ed.), 'Acallamh', ll.4926–9.

52 *TEI*, 197, Stokes (ed.), 'Acallamh', ll.7037–44; see also Carey, 'Acallam na senórach: a conversation between worlds', 85.

53 *TEI*, 217, Stokes (ed.), 'Acallamh', l.7828.

no insight in the *Acallam* as to the nature of the gods they are imagined as worshipping.

OTHERWORLD CULTURE

The lack of bodily affliction germane to the people of the *síd* is also characteristic of what one might call their culture—or, less grandly, their lifestyle. William Sayers aptly describes the Túatha Dé Danann as 'privileged but, in a sense, quarantined beings', and in this period their realm is a clear locus of human wish fulfilment, characterized—with a few exceptions—by its abundant wealth and beauty.[54] The same themes constantly recur: precious and reflective substances, exquisite music, and advanced knowledge. The *síd*-mounds of the *Acallam* noticeably lack the unsettling dimension common to otherworld(s) elsewhere in medieval Irish literature—the undermotivated shifts between helpfulness and hostility, the surreal, dreamlike décor, the uncanny timeslips—and the key idea seems to be, in fact, that the *síd* is the source of both material and aesthetic pre-eminence.[55]

On the material level, the otherworld stories in the *Acallam* make it possible to build up a detailed picture of what the author imagines life within a *síd*-mound to be like. Firstly, the palaces of the Túatha Dé in the text are all contained within hills and mounds—there is no sign of the overseas otherworlds of other early Irish texts.[56] (One apparent exception, Rathlin, the *síd* of Áed son of Áed na nAmsach, is indeed an island—but one which is *explicitly a hill*.)[57] As Sayers astutely notes, going into a *síd* brings with it no sense of going downwards; rather there is a sense of moving *through* a single entrance, though this tends to be passed over almost without comment. In one important exception, Caílte spends some time cautiously peering in through the open door of the *síd* hidden within Slievenamon in Co. Tipperary—a place which we see inside sev-

54 W. Sayers, 'Netherworld and Otherworld in early Irish Literature', *ZCP* 59 (2012), 201–30, at 210.

55 On the misleadingly unitary quality of the term 'otherworld', see P. Sims-Williams, *IIMWL*, 59, who underscores how protean such dimensions are in the literature.

56 See Sayers, 'Netherworld', 222. The gigantic Bé Binn (one of two women of that name in the *Acallam*) and her murderous betrothed Áed Álaind do come from mysterious lands over the sea to the west; but they are clearly not people of the *síd*. See *TEI*, 166–70, Stokes (ed.), 'Acallamh', 5917–6081.

57 *TEI*, 15, Stokes (ed.), 'Acallamh', ll.417–8.

FIG. 5.1. Slievenamon, Co. Tipperary, *síd*-mound (or rather mountain) of the twenty-eight sons of Midir. Photo: Trounce/Wikimedia Commons.

eral times in the *Acallam*. Within he can see splendid drinking vessels sparkling.[58] The straightforward ease with which the *fíana* can enter the *síd* may be due to their intimacy with the inhabitants, for (as seen) at least one member of Finn's *fíana* is fully of the Túatha Dé and Finn and Oisín are of mixed parentage.[59] The implication is that an upshot of being fostered in the *síd* as a mortal is that one can afterwards enter it easily, rather in the way that people who have acquired a language in childhood are often baffled by others' difficulty with it. This can backfire on the people of the *síd* themselves. We find that for one mortal amazon the secrets of all the mounds of Ireland are laid so bare that she can raid them mercilessly, simply because she was raised by 'an enchanted woman of druidry'—a woman of the *síd*.

Paradoxical internal brightness is characteristic of such dwellings. The absence of reference to candles, fires, and other sources of light is perhaps one token of the otherworldliness of the *síd*-mounds: everything feels sharply seen, although we are never told how this is achieved.[60] Ad-

58 *TEI*, 140, Stokes (ed.), 'Acallamh', ll.5017–9.

59 One might compare Mongán mac Fíachnai, the hero sired in legend by Manannán, who has deep links to Finn and the *síd*; in one story he is able to send a scholar into the *síd* to recover treasures on his behalf, assured of good reception. See *Compert Mongáin and Three Other Early Mongán Tales*, ed. & trans. N. White (Maynooth, 2006), 38, 49–50.

60 The *síd* of Ilbrecc of Assaroe does have at least one 'golden window', however; *TEI*, 51, Stokes (ed.), 'Acallamh', ll.1630–1.

ditionally, the Túatha Dé seem fond of chairs made out of crystal, which sparkle in and reflect the mysterious light source. Furthermore, it is not clear to what degree those within a given *síd* are aware of the outside world: sometimes messengers seem required to shuttle in and out, whereas at others the *síd*-folk seem clairvoyantly informed. Once inside, one typically finds a royal house, and that of Créde, under the Paps Mountains in Co. Kerry, is a hundred paces square, with a doorway twenty paces wide.[61] It is not at all clear whether the door of a *síd* admits one directly into its built structure—the equivalent of the *tech*, 'house' within a *ráth*, 'ringfort'—or into a wider space in which a house stands, corresponding to the *les*, the enclosed area around the house. Inside the house there are typically racks for weapons and an armoury.[62] The weapons may be hung on the walls of the drinking hall, the heart of the *síd* and of any Irish noble residence, and which also contains vats filled with drink and a 'warrior platform', a kind of dais upon which the most important persons present are seated and where musicians perform. Additionally, there are only the shadowiest hints of (agricultural?) land—we hear of cattle taken into the *síd* and of rooted apple-trees brought out of it—but typically a *síd* exhibits a curious lack of spatial depth.[63]

Who lives there? The notables of the Túatha Dé Danann seem to have one each, but in many cases their children seem to be more cramped.[64] The twenty-eight sons of Midir all live in Slievenamon (Fig. 5.1), while Aífe, Fergus, and Étaín, three children of the Dagda, share the '*Síd* of the Ridge of Nemed' in Connaught.[65] Otherwise, the social hierarchy exactly mirrors the human one: one inset story lists great nobles, boys, girls, women, and poets.[66] Those at the top of the tree have a wealth of retinue—several noblewomen in the *Acallam* are said to have one hundred and fifty female retainers with them—but, intriguingly, the world of

61 *TEI*, 26, Stokes (ed.), 'Acallamh', ll.804–5.

62 *TEI*, 200, Stokes (ed.), 'Acallamh', l.7146.

63 For the apple-trees of the Bruig, see *TEI*, 15, Stokes (ed.), 'Acallamh', ll.437–9, clearly echoing those of the coda to the brief mythological anecdote 'On the Seizure of the *Síd*-mound' (*De Gabáil in tSíde*), perhaps a later addition; for nine cows driven off into the *síd* of Crúachain, see *TEI*, 211, Stokes (ed.), 'Acallamh', ll.7625–8.

64 See above, 91, fn.61.

65 Unromantically, the latter is probably the prehistoric mound near the present Forthaven housing estate, Coolaney, Co. Sligo.

66 *TEI*, 201, Stokes (ed.), 'Acallamh', ll.7184–5.

the *síd* also contains both male and female slaves, mirroring early Irish social reality.[67]

TOO MUCH AND NOT ENOUGH

Apart from the slaves, the *síd*-folk pass the time in an idealized and prodigal version of medieval Irish aristocratic life. Everything from drinking vessels to clothing and weapons is materially abundant, and ordinary objects are curiously enhanced. In one sequence the exhausted Caílte has laboured heroically for the *síd*-folk of Ilbrecc of Assaroe. As a token of their appreciation he is given a beautiful cloak that will cause anyone to fall in love with him, along with a fish hook that will always come up with a fish attached.[68] The objects embody the blessings of *síd*-life: a dazzling and potentially manipulative allure, coupled with the easy and guaranteed gratification of physical needs.

Nights in the *síd* are spent in drinking and feasting, with everything provided unstintingly to guests. In one inset story, four hundred warriors and four hundred boys, with their dogs, enter the *síd* of Slievena-mon. There 'a true song of welcome was sung to them, without guile and without deceit. All sorts of fresh food and fine wine were brought to them, and they were there three days and nights before they mentioned their errand.'[69] The inhabitants seem to venture out as they wish, especially for games of hurley; there is even a hint that a kind of champions' league is held every seven years between the boys of the various *síd*-mounds. In one splendid sequence at the *síd* of Assaroe, the boys of the *síd* are playing a match, as they apparently do every Samain Eve, and the spectators amuse themselves betimes with music and board-games:

> Then the Túatha Dé Danann went off to watch the hurling. A *fidchell*-set was brought along for every six of them, a *brandub*-board for every five. A dulcimer was played for every twenty, harps for every hundred of them, and shrill, overpowering flutes for every nine.[70]

---

67 *TEI*, 202, Stokes (ed.), 'Acallamh', ll.7221–2.
68 *TEI*, 204, Stokes (ed.). 'Acallamh', ll.7266–72.
69 *TEI*, 85, Stokes (ed.), 'Acallamh', ll.2793–8.
70 *TEI*, 198, Stokes (ed.), 'Acallamh', ll.7053–7.

Later, in an example of the delightful, sunlit specificity characteristic of the *Acallam*, the people of the same *síd* all decide to go for a dip, diving into the River Erne.[71]

William Sayers has an interesting but tendentious theory on this aspect of the life within the *síd*-mounds. Because of the Túatha Dé's banishment within the earth and their material superabundance, he connects them to the third of the 'three functions' detected by many scholars of Indo-European mythology—the function of economic and agricultural productivity.[72] But in the *Acallam* at least, agricultural harvesting is hardly mentioned and seasonality is expressly denied. The three apple trees transplanted from the Bruig are simultaneously each at a different stage of ripeness, and the *síd*-mounds seem equipped with magical devices that convert water into mead and wine; there is no need for beekeeping or viticulture. (Similarly, the pigs of Manannán, which can be eaten one day, are ready to be cooked up again the next.) Rather than third-function earthly productivity, the world of the *síd* instead depends upon replication without growth. It is therefore, in a sense, a vision of culture floating free of any dependence on nature.[73]

Some of the earliest Old Irish literature we have expresses the idea that one source of creative inspiration lies in the otherworld; our text glosses this dramatically with the idea that *síd*-beings are capable of perfect artistic and professional skill. This includes healing: some emphasis is placed on the physicians of the *síd*-mounds, who seem to be expert in herbalism and battlefield medicine. In one startling scene the exhausted Caílte is dosed with powerful emetics, before two slaves suck the 'bad blood' from his body through primitive venous catheters.[74]

The artistic skill of the people of the otherworld is principally embodied in Cas Corach, one of the most important figures in the *Acallam*. A minstrel of the *síd*, he befriends Patrick and Caílte within the frame-tale. Cas Corach's situation reminds us that the world of the *síd* replicates human social hierarchies with a particular emphasis on the crises and ambitions of youth:

71 *TEI*, 202–3, Stokes (ed.), 'Acallamh', ll.7226–8.

72 Sayers, 'Netherworld', 215. The elaborator of the trifunctional hypothesis was the celebrated mythographer Georges Dumézil, though, as Sayers rightly notes, the theory has been largely neglected by Celtic scholars; see also above, 109, fn.113.

73 I thus completely disagree with S. Ó Cadhla's comments in his (nonetheless stimulating) 'Gods and Heroes: Approaching the *Acallam* as Ethnography', in Doyle & Murray (eds.), *In Dialogue with the Agallamh*, 132.

74 *TEI*, 201–2, Stokes (ed.), 'Acallamh', ll.7221–2.

He wore a fair, green cloak with a pin of silver in it, a shirt of yellow silk next to his skin, and a tunic of soft silk on top of it. He had a choice dulcimer on his back with a valuable linen covering about it. 'Where do you come from, young man?' asked the King of Ulster. 'From the *Síd* of Bodb Derg, son of the Dagda, in the south of Ireland.' 'What brought you from the south and who are you?' asked the king. 'Cas Corach, son of Caincinde, the Sage of the Túatha Dé Danann, and I aspire to be a sage myself.'[75]

The word *ollam*, translated as 'sage', refers to the highest grade of poet and indeed to the top practitioners of any learned profession. The detail that his father is an *ollam* is important, because this eminence could only be attained by those whose fathers were similarly qualified: skill without heredity was not sufficient.

In due course Cas Corach's ambitions are richly fulfilled, but as Ann Dooley and Harry Roe have noted, we discover that he has left the *síd* for a significant reason. Driven by the knowledge that his repertoire is incomplete, he has ventured into the mortal world because he does not yet know the stories of the great deeds of Finn's *fíana*. His departure acts a symbol of the validity of the new fenian literature, and of the ambitions of the secular learned families who were becoming the powerhouses of literary production in the period of religious reform. As Dooley and Roe note, this must have involved a considerable struggle between the old eulogistic modes and new paradigms of creativity, and it is significant that Patrick warns Cas Corach that he may not always get a warm reception—at least until he begins to perform. The composer of the *Acallam* seems to favour artistic risk and to be familiar with envy, suspicion, and rivalry. Even the extraordinary skill of the miniature musician Cnú Deróil has, we are told, made him an object of jealousy for the other musicians of the Túatha Dé Danann.[76]

This is perhaps the resentment often attracted by the conspicuously gifted, but it is also a sign of something overheated and unbalanced in the responses of the people of the otherworld; often they seem not quite able to appreciate what they have. The composer is sly enough to suggest (once) that life in the *síd* might eventually induce ennui, and tellingly puts this sentiment into the mouth of Derg Díanscothach ('Swift of Speech'), a former member of the *fíana* and half-human hybrid: his

---

75 *TEI*, 101, Stokes (ed.), 'Acallamh', ll.3346–53.
76 *TEI*, 21, Stokes (ed.), 'Acallamh', l.618.

mother is of the *síd* but his father is not. Derg openly confesses that 'we have no lack of food and clothing... but I would rather be living the lives of the three who had the worst life in the *fían*... than the life I live in the *síd*.' He is immortal, but in a constant state of nostalgia for past days of human glory: 'Although I dwell within the *síd* ... my mind is upon the *fiana*.'[77]

If touches such as these suggest something missing in the *síd*, there is an insistent sense of overplus about its music. The *Acallam* features many scenes of otherworldly music, typically described as technically perfect but also mysteriously 'beguiling' or 'soothing'. An idea commonly found in medieval Irish literature is that music—and not just fairy-music—can dull pain, provoke laughter, or induce sleep. However, the *Acallam* is perhaps the first text to both analyse and critique this magical capacity to overwhelm. Often such music is beneficial, and is an indispensible accompaniment to the exquisite mode of living enjoyed within the *síd*-mounds. But its effect on consciousness is profound and can be horrifying: the malevolent Aillén was able to use his dulcimer to chloroform the inhabitants of Tara before burning them alive.

Cas Corach's appearance halfway through the *Acallam* allows Patrick to directly interrogate the moral status of the music of the *síd*. When the apprentice minstrel strikes up, Patrick's clerics find they have 'never before heard anything as melodious, except for the praise of the service of the Lord and the praise of the King of heaven and earth'. Patrick's own response—in dialogue with one of his own clerics, Broccán—mingles high praise with measured insight:

> 'Good was the art that you have performed for us,' said Broccán. 'Good it was,' said Patrick, 'were it not indeed for the magical melody of the *síd* in it. If it were not for that, there would be nothing closer to the music of the King of Heaven and Earth than that music.' 'If there is music in heaven,' said Broccán, 'why should there not also be music on earth? Thus it is not proper to banish music.' 'I did not say that at all,' said Patrick, 'but one should not put too much stock in it.'[78]

Music is here a metaphor for the totality of Irish culture. There is nothing in Cas Corach's music—that is, in native culture and tradition—which

---

77 *TEI*, 49, Stokes (ed.), 'Acallamh', ll.1571–6, 1583. See also the comments of Carey, 'Acallam na senórach: a conversation between worlds', 84.

78 *TEI*, 106, Stokes (ed.), 'Acallamh', ll.3481–6.

is not compatible with Christianity, *except* for the 'magical melody of the *síd*'. It possesses a kind of timbre, a thread of supersensual ornamentation that must be expunged for the performance to benefit from full, albeit cool, ecclesiastical sanction. That magical melody may stand for the *síd* itself—the continuing allure of pagan themes and imagery, with its sensual delight and danger, in a Christian literary culture. This passage is prefaced by Cas Corach's conversion and assurance of salvation, and it is easy to forget, given the *Acallam*'s apparently harmonious rapprochement between pagan and Christian, that the future it predicts for the Túatha Dé Danann is a wretched one. Quarantine is in store for almost all, ending with damnation. A very few will be converted, but at the price of permanent exile from a realm at once atavistic and utopian.[79]

BODB THE RED AND HIS KIN

So far we have looked in general terms at how the Túatha Dé Danann function in the *Acallam*; it is now time to turn to specific otherworldly personnel. The author's treatment of tradition is often startlingly free and fluid—making people and places up, rearranging well-known genealogies—and this is eye-catchingly clear in his handling of the *síd*-folk.[80] It is this fluidity surrounding the *Acallam*'s Túatha Dé that would have surprised its first audiences.

Some of the figures already met—Scothníam, Aillenn, Créde—are basically unfamiliar: others seem to have been created wholesale for our text. Allusions to the classical mainstays of the literary tradition—the Dagda, Dían Cécht, Núadu, Lug, and so forth—are scattered throughout the *Acallam*, but as characters in the action they are by and large avoided in favour of their children. Sociologically, the *síd* in the *Acallam* is curiously modern: it is a world in which those who strove at Moytura and Tailtiu have died, leaving political power in the hands of their offspring.

It seems that we are indeed to suppose that within the world of the text the Dagda and his ilk are dead, although this is a very different model of death to that in 'The Book of Invasions'. In the pseudohistorical

---

79 It will be apparent that I find the text less cheerful on this point than (for example) H. Roe, in 'The *Acallam*: the Church's eventual acceptance of the cultural inheritance of pagan Ireland', in Sheehan, *Gablánach in Scélaigecht*, 103–115.

80 On this dimension of the author's creativity, see Carey, '*Acallam na senórach*: a conversation between worlds', 76–8.

tradition, the Túatha Dé are ultimately eradicated. In the *Acallam*, they are still extant within the hollow hills, but a new generation has partially succeeded the old. But because the Túatha Dé in the text do not die of sickness or old age—they must die by violence or injury—it seems that that process has been much slower than it would be for mortals; only one or two generations of the otherworld-folk have passed for many generations of the human Sons of Míl. Even Lug, we discover, is dead: one of Ireland's 'four greatest losses', along with Conn, Conaire, and Finn himself.[81] The *Acallam's* composer furnishes Lug with a special treasure, a magical chain or net, which may be another invention as it is referred to nowhere else in Irish tradition.[82] Its power is that it can simultaneously bind eight hundred warriors, and the first cannot be released until the last is freed. Recovered from the grave-mound of the *fían*-warrior Garb Daire, Caílte delivers it to Patrick.[83] As someone with the apostolic commission to bind and loose—a mandate which he enacts confidently throughout the text, as elsewhere in Patrician tradition—the literary Patrick is indeed the rightful inheritor of Lug's chain.[84]

The Dagda's generation evidently acts as the point of reference for the evaluation of Túatha Dé Danann nobility. In another of the compendium's mortal-immortal pairings, Échna, daughter of the King of Connaught, falls in love with none other than Cas Corach, that new Christian, handsome minstrel, and apprentice sage of the Túatha Dé Danann. Échna—who resembles a Jane Austen heroine by being beautiful, clever, and good, but also much concerned with the social suitability of the marriage—frets about his ancestry:

'Who is that minstrel who is with you, and who are his mother and father?', [said Échna.] 'He is Cas Corach', [said Caílte] 'son of Caincinde, the son of the Sage of the Túatha Dé Danann, and he himself is a sage of the Túatha Dé Danann. His mother is Bé Binn,

---

81 *TEI*, 147, Stokes (ed.), 'Acallamh', ll.5275–8.

82 *TEI*, 63–4, 73, Stokes (ed.), 'Acallamh', ll.2057–9, 2373–9.

83 I do not follow Dooley and Roe's commentary on this episode at *TEI*, 236, n.60, where they refer to 'the chain *and skull* of Lug'; the mighty skull excavated from the grave-mound belongs to the *fían*-warrior Garb Daire, not to the god. On the idea that the idea of the binding chain might be inspired by a cultural association—perhaps very old—between the god *Lug* and the word *lugae*, 'binding oath' (older *Lugus* and **lugiom*), see J. T. Koch, 'Further to *tongu do dia toinges mo thuath &c*', *ÉC* 29 (1992), 249–61.

84 The allusion is to Matt. 18:18: 'Whatsoever ye shall bind on earth shall be bound in heaven; and whatsoever ye shall loose on earth shall be loosed in heaven.'

daughter of Elcmar of the Bruig.' 'What a shame then', said Échna, 'that he is not a son of Bodb Derg, son of the Dagda, or of Aengus, or of Tadg, son of Núadu.'[85]

Noble ancestry means descent from the Dagda, or from Núadu, the original king of the Túatha Dé. Strikingly, the ornate Nemedian ancestry given to the god-peoples in 'The Book of Invasions' seems to be irrelevant in the *Acallam*: there is no interest in shadowy persons such as Tait, son of Taburn, Aldui, son of Tait, or the Dagda's own forefathers, Elatha, Delbaeth, and Néit. 'The Book of Invasions' introduced elaboration at the top of the genealogy of the Túatha Dé, but the composer of the *Acallam* prefers to embroider the base.

In general the *fíana*'s dealings are with a younger generation of the Túatha Dé Danann, and with their children, and their children's children, in a way that runs counter to the text's preoccupation with the timeworn and venerable. This works two ways: sometimes the Túatha Dé seem young, even adolescent, in a way that chimes with the youthful strength of the *fíana*, but poignantly contrasts with them in their latterday decrepitude. But there is something unexpected here. The most prominent of the Dagda's sons *in narrative* had always been the shrewd, handsome Aengus—as his name was spelled by this stage—and given this generational shift we might have expected him to be the central personality of the Túatha Dé Danann in the *Acallam*, as he is in other tales in the Finn Cycle. In the late medieval *Tóruigheacht Dhiarmada agus Ghráinne* ('The Pursuit of Díarmait and Gráinne'), for example, he is the hero Díarmait's foster-father, and intervenes prominently as a *deus ex machina* to rescue the tragic lovers; at the end of the tale, he spirits away Díarmait's corpse to Bruig na Bóinne.[86]

And yet it seems the composer of the *Acallam* has made a deliberate effort to keep Aengus at arm's length. Instead, we repeatedly meet the family of Bodb Derg, 'the Red', another son of the Dagda and thus brother to—and substitute for—Aengus. Bodb is both the first of the Túatha Dé

---

85 *TEI*, 210, Stokes (ed.), 'Acallamh', ll.7525–30.

86 *Tóruigheacht Dhiarmada agus Ghráinne*, ed. & trans. N. Ní Shéaghdha [ITS 48] (Dublin, 1967). See also discussion of this tale in Irish by T. Ó Cathasaigh, 'Tóraíacht Dhiarmada agus Ghráinne', originally in *Léachtaí Cholm Cille* 25 (1995) 30–46, but reprt. in Boyd (ed.), *Coire Sois*, 449–65; English trans. in the same volume, 466–83. The date of the tale is uncertain: it might date to the fourteenth century at the very earliest, but given the lateness of the manuscripts and the language it could well have been composed as late as the sixteenth.

Danann to be mentioned in the text and the first to appear. His inaugural epiphany amounts to a programmatic statement about the nature of the *síd*-folk within the *Acallam*'s imaginative world:

> He had a brown, two-forked beard and lovely curly hair of light-yellow gold coming down over his shoulders. His long golden hair was held by fastenings of thin gold thread, lest the stormy coastal wind blow it before his face or eyes. He had a sandal of bright silver on his foot, and his sandalled foot, where it touched the ground, did not disturb the dewdrops on the ends of the blades of grass.[87]

Bodb is handsome, hyper-cultivated, and wealthy. This could describe any idealized Irish king, were it not for the arresting detail of his tread: as his footsteps do not disturb the dew, he is in some sense both there and not there. He is perturbing but imperturbable, just as the threads of gold keep his hair from being stirred by the wind.

But why Bodb? A second-division figure in the earlier sagas that survive, he has a cameo role as king of the *síd*-mounds of Munster in 'The Dream of Óengus', a crucial fore-tale to the *Táin* in which he is famed for his wisdom.[88] In *Airne Fíngein* ('Fíngen's Night-Watch'), written *c*.900, he is one of the four *síd*-protectors of Ireland, along with the Morrígan, Midir, and the Mac Óc; together they hunt down Fomorian renegades after the Second Battle of Moytura.[89] But he is consistently the most important of the Túatha Dé Danann in the *Acallam*, although his brother Midir, here likewise a son of the Dagda, is also significant. According to a late tradition for which the *Acallam* provides the earliest evidence, Bodb becomes the ruler of the Túatha Dé Danann after they are defeated by the Sons of Míl and withdraw into the *síd*-mounds. In this entirely new account of the Túatha Dé's political configuration, Bodb is their

---

87 *TEI*, 14, Stokes (ed.), 'Acallamh', ll.380–6.

88 In 'The Dream of Óengus', §7, Bodb identifies Cáer Iborméith for whom his brother is languishing lovesick. In *De chophur* [or *chobur*] *in dá muccida* ('On the ?Quarrel of the Two Swineherds') his swineherd falls out with that of the king of the Connaught *síd*-mounds: transforming themselves into the forms of different animals, the two swineherds end up as the White Bull and the Brown Bull of the *Táin*—the ultimate cause of vast destruction. He may well be an afterimage of a genuine ancient deity; given the frequency of Celtic war-gods, his name—perhaps <*bod*ʷ*os*, 'strife'—is plausible, especially given the epithet *derg*, 'blood-red'.

89 *Airne Fíngein*, ed. J. Vendryes (Dublin, 1953), §9; see also J. Borsje, 'Bodb', in J. T. Koch, *et al.* (eds.), *The Celts: History, Life, and Culture* (Santa Barbara, CA, 2012), i., 100–1.

lynchpin and patriarch, although as the reader soon discovers, his rule locks him into internecine strife with his own brother and nephews.[90] It is far from clear how old this tradition is; it may have been the invention of the author of the *Acallam*. But by the late Middle Ages the tradition of Bodb's kingship over the Túatha Dé had decisively crystalized, though often with allusions to rivalry and dissent.[91]

In the passage above Bodb has emerged from Bruig na Bóinne. In the *Acallam* the Bruig seems to function as a centre of power and a gathering place for the Túatha Dé; specifically it was famous as the home-*síd* of Aengus. This fact, in addition to the description of a lordly young man, generates a certain surprise when the reader learns that the otherworldly visitor is instead the Mac Óc's brother. (The *Acallam* is inconsistent on the question of whether Bodb possesses the Bruig or is merely a visitor in it.) Aengus was a byword for beauty, and the composer of the *Acallam* clearly wants to depict his Túatha Dé as radiant glitterati. Something of Aengus's charisma, therefore, seems to have been deliberately transferred to Bodb, perhaps as an attempt to compromise with earlier sources: Aengus is the most charismatic of the Dagda's sons, but Irish tradition never has him wield political power. The audience would be surprised to find Aengus, though alluded to from time to time, so conspicuously sidelined; significantly, he is given only one line of dialogue in a dialogue-heavy text.

Bodb is emphatically the central figure in the genealogy of the Túatha Dé in the *Acallam*. An extraordinary number of the otherworldly figures named in the text are his children and grandchildren. We have met his daughters Aillenn and Scothníam, but other daughters include Sadb, Slat, Mumain, Dairenn, and Findine; his son Ferdoman is a member of Finn's *fíana*, and other sons mentioned include Derg, Artrach, Áed the Fair, and Aengus. Bodb's triumphant fertility replicates that of his father the Dagda, but also elevates it to a higher level of sophistication: there is in him none of the comic earthiness which earlier sagas had imputed to his father.

The tension between the Túatha Dé as a pantheon on the one hand and as the population of a parallel, permeable world on the other—a shift partly historical and partly of perspective—has already been discussed. Spotlighting the family of Bodb Derg as a kind of micro-pantheon allows the composer of the *Acallam* to have the best of both worlds, so that

---

90 As described by one of Midir's sons, *TEI*, 141, Stokes (ed.), 'Acallamh', ll.5067–88.
91 See below, 257.

members of a single dynasty are repeatedly met within a large and con-fusing population. Crucially, it is a family connected by marriage to the *fíana*: Bodb is the father of Sadb, wife of Finn.[92] But there is also a kind of deliberate haziness here, because of the sheer *unfamiliarity* of the sons and daughters of Bodb: mostly they are just names. The aesthetic effect—brilliantly—is to trope the gradual evanescence of the Túatha Dé Dan-ann: little-known personages proliferate even as they elude our grasp. Furthermore, family ties in no way prevent otherworldly victimization: at one point Dairenn, another daughter of Bodb, poisons Finn when he sexually refuses her. In his nightmarish delirium he vilifies the *fíana*, nearly driving away his comrades. Only Caílte's heroic efforts are able to keep them together until the poison wears off.[93]

DROPPING OUT, DROPPING IN

Issues addressed so far—the pre-eminence of Bodb, the utopianism of *síd*-culture, the emotive similarity-in-difference of humans and otherworld-folk—are all prominent in the first Túatha Dé Danann narrative in the *Acallam*. This is the inset story of the three sons of the mythical King of Ireland Lugaid Menn, young men who devise a novel method of ensur-ing their fortune and standing in the world: it forms the context of the epiphany of Bodb already quoted. As Caílte tells it, it is a crucial episode in that it showcases the world of the Túatha Dé for the first time in our text, exemplifying their role in relation to mortals.

The three youths have a problem. Their period of fosterage is over, and they approach their father in order to ask for land and territory—that is, to inherit, and so take up their identity as adult grandees. But Lugaid flatly turns them down. He was the author of his own success in life, and he informs his sons that they would be well advised to do like-wise.[94] Scholars have rightly emphasized that this story's concern with the inheritance of royal youths foregrounds the deeper cultural back-ground of the *fían*-band as a historical institution.[95] But for our purposes

92 *TEI*, 184, Stokes (ed.), 'Acallamh', ll.6552–4.

93 Excellent reading of this incident by J. F. Nagy, 'Keeping the *Acallam* together', in Parsons & Arbuthnot (eds.), *The Gaelic Finn Tradition*, 113–5.

94 Nagy calls Lugaid's attitude 'a remarkably modern-sounding sentiment'; see his 'Keeping the *Acallam* together', in Parsons & Arbuthnot (eds.), *The Gaelic Finn Tradition*, 111–121, at 116.

95 See for instance A. Dooley, 'The Date and Purpose of *Acallam na Senórach*', *Éigse* 34 (2004), 97–126, at 105–6.

it is more important that the three young men turn to the Túatha Dé Danann, settling themselves outside Bruig na Bóinne and fasting until the people of the *síd* agree to supply the territory and wealth their father has refused them.[96]

To this proposal, rather surprisingly, the Túatha Dé Danann accede; it is clearly part of their equivocal nature in the *Acallam* to alternate between exorbitant generosity and equally exorbitant viciousness. At this point we pass around the interior of the *síd*, with the greatest notables present bestowing gifts upon the three young men to establish them in their adult lives. The position of this detail at the beginning of the text allows the composer to unveil a kind of portrait gallery of the Túatha Dé at their most gracious. There are, we find, 'one hundred and fifty kings' sons' gathered in the hollow hill: these are not human fosterlings but refer to the Túatha Dé themselves, for the sons of Lugaid—luckily for them—have clearly arrived at festival time, when the rulers of many *síd*-mounds have gathered at the Bruig.[97] First Midir, then Bobd, then Áed son of Áed na nAmsach, then Lir, then Aengus Óc—his only speaking line in the whole *Acallam*—and then Áine daughter of Modarn bestow valuable commodities upon the three boys. They are presented with wives, gold, fine clothes, objects which provide endless mead and wine, a cache of weapons, magical apple trees, a first-rate chef, an otherworldly musician, and—best of all—a spectacular fort, Ard Ruide. Their hunger strike has been emphatically successful.

Two things are notable in the account of the gift-giving. The first is the atmosphere of ritual solemnity, as we behold the world of the *síd* at its most dignified and beautiful:

> Bodb then arose with a goblet of smooth buffalo horn in his hand and said, 'Let all be silent.' All the people in the mound fell silent, holding in their hands cups and horns and goblets of bright gold and silver.[98]

Part of the dignity in this scene lies in its horizontality, the way one immortal face is highlighted after another as though on a single level. This timeless inaugural vision of the Túatha Dé Danann contrasts sharply

---

96 Abstention from food was a recognized method of distraint, termed *troscad* in Irish; see F. Kelly, *A Guide to Early Irish Law* (Dublin, 1988), 182–3.

97 *TEI*, 15, Stokes (ed.), 'Acallamh', ll.411–2.

98 *TEI*, 14–5, Stokes (ed.), 'Acallamh', ll.402–5.

with the roll call of 'The Book of Invasions', with its complicated vertical lineages branching like coral.

The second important thing to note is that the pecking order among the assembled Túatha Dé is suggestive of the political tensions that later explode into violence. We are told that 'the noblest and most exalted' personage present is Midir Mongbuide ('Yellow-mane'), and he bestows the crucial first gift, his three daughters, upon the mortal brothers. But his brother Bodb Derg speaks a great deal more, for not only does he meet the three young men outside on the lawn of the Bruig, he is also the only figure to speak twice and to bestow two separate gifts.[99] Within this apparently irenic and politically harmonious world, the theme of rivalry between Midir and Bodb has been subtly introduced.

One of the issues raised in this intricately layered tale is the familiar ontological question of how far intimacy between noble mortals and the people of the *síd*—Ireland's *other* aristocracy—can progress before the mortals no longer count as fully human. Furnished with otherworldly riches and real estate, the lives of the three brothers seem prolonged beyond the natural span: they live in their fort for a hundred and fifty years. When an unspecified 'destruction' visits them, 'because of their kinship and their alliance, they returned to the Túatha Dé Danann and remained there ever after'.[100] They become 'honorary' people of the *síd*, travelling in the opposite ontological direction to the likes of Créde and Aillenn. We are to take it, I imagine, that the brothers have agreed to the kind of magical rejuvenation to which we saw Caílte make a principled refusal.

All this would count, one might think, as conspicuous success for the sons of Lugaid Menn, and it serves to introduce the pivotal theme of the intimacy between the mortal and immortal worlds. And yet there is something provocatively immature here. It is tempting to forget that what Lugaid says to his sons is quite true, and their response—not pausing to question their own entitlement—is to expect another party to fulfil their requests. And when duly endowed, they sequester themselves, first partially and then completely, from the world of mortal Ireland. The Túatha Dé Danann here savour of adolescent fantasy, functioning as an idealized solution to the problems of aristocratic youth. They are both patrons and substitute parents, presiding over a dreamlike economy in which the magical endlessly disgorges the material. Although almost all

---

99 Aengus gives trees, but in reported speech.
100 *TEI*, 15, Stokes (ed.), 'Acallamh', ll.440–2.

the Túatha Dé who bestow gifts in this story are male, their parentalism is nevertheless symbolically maternal: they emblematize a world of unearned wealth and unstinting supply, generous, opulent, and feminine. Its motto is supplied by Midir, the boys' first benefactor: 'fortune, good or ill, comes from women.'[101] Though no apparent self-interest is involved on the part of the *síd*-folk, the mobile and energetic realm of the father, who achieved his kingship through 'good fortune and brilliance', is held at arm's length. If this is indeed a tale about the crises of youth, then its protagonists, in a sense, never achieve adulthood. As we are told so often, the Túatha Dé Danann look young, and the three sons of Lugaid Menn are ultimately absorbed into their endlessly prolonged adolescence.

As I have already had occasion to remark, critics have unanimously thought that this story is of programmatic significance within the *Acallam*. What has been noticed less often is that its themes are conspicuously inverted in a second inset tale later in the text. A kind of mirror image of the first story, this second perhaps suggests we are meant to think back and consider; it too is told by Caílte, though not this time to Patrick, and again it is stimulated by a question about a fort.

As before, the story tells of three youths whose economic will is blocked by their father; but this time the youths are not mortal, but of the *síd*. The three sons of Bodb Derg, Artrach, Aengus, and Áed, dwell with him in the 'sun-dappled Bruig.' They quarrel with their father, who instructs them to leave the Túatha Dé Danann and take themselves off to Cormac mac Airt, the mortal King of Ireland. The tale does not state explicitly at the outset that this is again an altercation over patrimony, but this emerges as the story proceeds. In a complete contrast with the *síd*'s material superabundance in the first tale, Bodb Derg's sons are bleeding him dry with their conspicuous consumption: 'The people here', he tells them, 'do not have enough territory to support themselves, let alone the wealth that the well-loved Artrach has, and moreover Aengus, son of Bodb, has more servants and warriors than all of the Túatha Dé Danann, and Áed Álaind of the Poets has more poets here than the poetic bands of Ireland and Scotland have.'[102] It is important to note that each of these markers of prosperity rests in turn on something more basic: wealth (which means cattle) depends on grazing land, servants and warriors need feeding, and poets require not only board and lodging, but also generous patronage.

---

101 *TEI*, 15, Stokes (ed.), 'Acallamh', ll.408–9.
102 *TEI*, 83, Stokes (ed.), 'Acallamh', ll.2721–25.

In the earlier story of the sons of Lugaid Menn, the wealth of the Bruig had seemed infinite, hence the harmonious beauty that characterizes the Túatha Dé Danann: when capital is infinite and produced without labour or lack, then politics itself is moot and is reduced to pure aesthetics. In this second story, things have clearly changed, and there is glaring evidence of economic crisis. Still more unexpected is Cormac's response to the arrival from the otherworld of these habitual sybarites, who say:

> 'Our own father has banished us from the Túatha Dé Danann, and we have come to seek land from you.' 'You shall have it then', said Cormac, 'I shall give you four cantreds of rough land, that which is now called Tirconnell.' Artrach, the eldest son, had a public guest-house with seven doors, and welcomed thrice a year all that came there. Aengus Ilchlessach 'of Many Feats' dwelt in the fort of Mongach, and the sons of the Kings of Ireland and Scotland came there to study the art of spear-throwing. Áed of the Poets dwelt in the Enclosure of the Poets and the poetic bands of Ireland and Scotland dwelt there with him. For thirty years they enjoyed the sovereignty of Cormac, the descendant of Conn, until he died at the fort of Spelán in Brega.[103]

With kingly generosity, Cormac is able to re-route the talents of the three supernatural youths in ways that are viable and productive in the human realm. Though the word is not used, Artrach clearly becomes a *briugu*, a hospitaller, a position of considerable dignity; Aengus coaches noble youths; and Áed patronizes the professional poets of the entire Gaelic world.

How can this be so? Mirrors both replicate and reverse, and the world of the *síd* works in an analogous way in this pair of stories; the two superficially similar anecdotes are full of subtle inversions. Where the sons of Lugaid Menn have nothing, the sons of Bodb Derg begin with an unsustainable surplus, each in a different arena—wealth, retinue, and men of art. But the generosity of the Túatha Dé towards the three mortal youths ultimately has a coddling, stymieing effect, one that diverts their youthful energies from the realm of human productivity. (Their fort is spectacular, there is never any mention of the brothers actually *achieving* anything; it may be significant that their musician's speciality is put-

---

103   *TEI*, 83–4, Stokes (ed.), 'Acallamh', ll.2727–36.

ting people to sleep.) But Cormac's less prodigious generosity—his gift is only a measure of 'rough land'—enables the three sons of Bodb Derg to become otherworldly patrons and providers in turn, to Ireland's profit. Cormac here exhibits one of the primary qualities required in a literary king: the ability to remain on shrewd good terms with the otherworld. As Eve Sweetser writes, dealing with the world of the *síd* involves 'the risks of major loss and the opportunities for major gain'.[104] In particular, the message of these twinned tales seems to be that what is oppressive or problematic in one realm can be turned to good use in the other.

VIOLENCE AND VULNERABILITY

Both these stories end with almost identical verbal formulae, describing how the two trios return into the maternal matrix of the *síd*. But this absorbency is only one facet of the otherworld in the *Acallam*, and we must now look squarely at its unexpectedly violent and unstable politics. The otherworld-woman in the early saga 'The Adventure of Connlae' famously punned on her realm and the homonym *síd*, 'peace', but the *síd*-mounds in the *Acallam* are prone to massive bouts of bloodletting. (Immortal beings can only meet death by violence: interestingly, we find that the people of the *síd* care for the bodies of their dead as mortals do.)[105]

The *Acallam* features two major internal conflicts among the Túatha Dé, both of which have an important role in exhibiting the world of the *síd* to the audience. Members of the *fíana* play a robust role in both. The first is the simmering but essentially local war between two northern *síd*-mounds, the one ruled by Ilbrecc and Áed at Assaroe, near Ballyshannon in what is now Co. Donegal, and the other being *Síd Finnachaid*, up in the Fews Mountains in Co. Armagh, which is ruled by Lir.[106] The second conflict, near the end of the *Acallam* as we have it, is on a more global scale; it sees the forces of Midir's sons, helped by Finn and Caílte,

---

104 E. Sweetser, 'Cognate Formulas for a Welsh and Irish Topos of Otherworldly Ambiguity', in G. Henley & P. Russell (eds.), *Rhetoric and Reality in Medieval Celtic Literature: Studies in Honor of Daniel F. Melia* [CSANA Yearbook 11–12] (Hamilton, NY, 2014), 191–4, at 194.

105 *TEI*, 144, Stokes (ed.), 'Acallamh', ll.5184–92.

106 *Síd Finnachaid* ('The Fairy-Mound of the White Field') is probably Deadman's Hill, near Newtownhamilton, Co. Armagh.

make a last stand against the combined might of the rest of the Túatha Dé Danann, now ruled by Bodb Derg.

When considering these clashes, it is crucial to understand that the complex structure of the *Acallam* means that three narrative arcs are intercut, and because each puts the Túatha Dé Danann in a subtly different light it is worth clearly establishing their timelines at this point.[107] The first is the Patrician frame-tale, which (in chronological order) describes Patrick's encounter with the remnants of the *fíana*, the introduction of *síd*-beings such as Aillenn and Cas Corach, the submission of Donn, son of Midir, to Patrick, the geriatric Caílte's exhausting exertions in the *síd*, the marriage of Áed and Aillenn, and finally—beyond the text itself—the permanent isolation of the Túatha Dé Danann within the *síd*-mounds.

The second timeline is that of the embedded fenian stories, set two to three hundred years before the frame-tale. This is harder to clarify, because the triumphs and disasters of the *fíana* jump about in time; only rarely are we given a secure sense of when particular events occurred in a linear sequence. That said, we do have a rough pair of bookends: Finn's killing of Aillén son of Midgna—as a result of which he becomes leader of the *fíana*—must be early, while the *fíana*'s rescue of the sons of Midir from the rest of the Túatha Dé is explicitly their final venture into that dimension. 'Since that time', as Caílte says to the King of Leinster, 'the *fíana* of Ireland have had no more dealings with the settlements of the Túatha Dé Danann.'[108]

Thirdly and last, there is the surface *textual* sequence—the *Acallam*'s continual flow of happenings—formed by intercutting past and present and often arising directly from the topography encountered and the recollections it sets off in the surviving warriors.

A series of observations can be made about the relationship between strife and the Túatha Dé Danann within these three timelines. Firstly, within the time of the frame-tale, their power catastrophically declines. The very emergence of *síd*-beings such as Cas Corach, Aillenn, Scothníam and Donn, son of Midir, represents a kind of dying fall: the *fíana*'s dealings with the Túatha Dé Danann ended long ago, and so we meet a series of exceptional figures, all of whom submit themselves to Patrick's authority.

---

107 Note John Carey's parallel emphasis on three frames/timelines in the text in 'Acallam na senórach: a conversation between worlds', 83–4.

108 *TEI*, 149, Stokes (ed.), 'Acallamh', ll.5366–70.

At two points in the frame-tale we see Caílte accomplish great deeds on behalf of the people of the *síd*. The first is when he lends his aid to Ilbrecc and Áed of the *síd* of Assaroe, who (as mentioned above) have been fighting a year-long war with Lir of Síd Finnachaid.[109] Caílte is required not only to take charge of the battle and to kill Lir personally—which he does—but also to steel the mettle of the Assaroe contingent. Áed Minbrecc—a son of the mighty Dagda!—gets increasingly flustered as the forces of Lir surround the *síd*:

> 'It's my bad luck', said Áed Minbrecc, 'that which shall happen to us now, our own death and destruction, and the seizing of our dwelling by the Children of Lir of Síd Finnachaid.' 'Do you not know, Áed,' said Caílte, 'that the strong, wild boar escapes from hounds and packs, and when the bellowing stag leaps he likewise comes away unscathed from the hounds.'[110]

This suggestion amounts to a polite way of telling the dolorous Áed to buck up: one of the running jokes of the *Acallam* is that the *síd*-folk of Assaroe are delightful but useless in a crisis. It is easy to understand why Lir has decided they are a soft target.

So much is reinforced in Caílte's second and final visit to the *síd* in the frame-tale, where the Túatha Dé are in a sorry state. The events that ensue form one of the great comic sequences in the *Acallam*. In it, Cas Corach and the ancient Caílte meet Cas Corach's half-brother, the handsome Fer Maisse ('Man of Beauty'), and all three enter the '*Síd* of Mounds' in Leyny in Connaught. Its inhabitants are in a condition of military collapse, and are initially so embarrassed that they cannot tell Caílte directly what is wrong. The great *fían*-warrior and his sidekicks from the *síd* are obliged to solve one problem after another for their hosts, first at the *Síd* of Mounds and then once again back at Assaroe. First, the Túatha Dé are being plundered year on year by raiders under the command of the King of Lochlann—here, as usual, vaguely identified with

---

109 *TEI*, 51, Stokes (ed.), 'Acallamh', ll.1640–1. Useful comments on the symbolism of Caílte's contribution here in J. F. Nagy, 'Compositional Concerns in the *Acallam na Senórach*', in D. Ó Corráin *et al.* (eds.), *Sages, Saints and Storytellers: Celtic Studies in Honour of Professor James Carney* (Maynooth, 1989), 152–3.

110 *TEI*, 55, Stokes (ed.), 'Acallamh', ll.1783–89. Áed's first phrase—in Irish *pudhur leamsa*—is hard to translate: 'I regret it' or 'I think it a misfortune' would be literal, but more idiomatically something like 'just my luck' would better capture his characteristic whininess.

Scandinavia, but often with otherworldly associations in fenian tales.[111] Not only are the people of the *síd* being thoroughly clobbered by mortals, but the chief warrior of the men of Lochlann is female, the formidable Bé Dreccain, 'Dragon Woman'.[112] Caílte, Cas Corach, and Fer Maisse meet the enemy forces near Assaroe and send them packing. Cas Corach—mocked as a 'little boy' by Bé Dreccain—delivers her the coup de grâce in single combat.

The wit lies in the fact that we are continually reminded that Cas Corach is a musician, and not, as he nervously admits, 'raised for valour'; neither is his half-brother Fer Maisse. Even worse, poor Caílte—already decrepit at the start of the frame-tale—is by this stage very creaky indeed. In spite of these hurdles, the unlikely trio manages more military success in a morning than the Túatha Dé Danann have achieved in years. More amusing still are Caílte's repeated, piteous requests for the healing promised him by the people of the *síd* of Assaroe, even as they fob him off with a laundry list of problems to solve. The valiant three-some have to destroy three man-eating ravens, negotiate a settlement with the three sons of the King of Ulster (who have been raiding *síd* after *síd*), and finally destroy three hungry does that eat the Túatha Dé's grass down to bare rock.[113] At this last, Caílte splutters, not unreasonably, 'What is all this?!'[114]

Eventually, the people of the *síd* of Assaroe, their difficulties resolved, heal Caílte of all his wounds and infirmities. It is clear, nonetheless, that the coming of Patrick has begun to end their power; they are touchingly helpless and seem barely competent to run their own affairs. The coda to this story—the final sojourn in the *Acallam* of a mortal in the *síd*—ends with a kind of love-in, with Caílte blessing them and blessing them again as he departs:

> Caílte and Cas Corach then bad farewell to the people of the *síd*, and went to the Hill of the Sound. The people of the *síd* made a great sound when Caílte parted from them, so that it has been called the Hill of the Sound ever since. Caílte said: 'I shall not re-

111 See M. Ní Mhaonaigh, 'Literary Lochlann', in W. McLeod, *et al.* (eds.), *Cànan & Cultar/Language & Culture: Rannsachadh na Gàidhlig* 3 (2006), 25–37.

112 Her nastiness is underscored by making her daughter of Irúath, Irish for 'Herod'.

113 It is not unheard of in earlier texts for mortals to attack the *síd*-folk; in the eighth- or ninth-century 'Dream of Óengus' Medb and Aillil of Connaught are able to thoroughly clobber the *síd* of Ethal Abual.

114 '*Créd sut iter?*'; *TEI*, 200, Stokes (ed.), 'Acallamh', l.7132.

turn to this place before the judgment of the destruction of the world.'[115]

The last shout of the Túatha Dé: a melancholy, magnificent sound that represents the *síd*-strain in the 'music' of Ireland's culture, dying away in valediction. Over time, the Túatha Dé become vulnerable, and their presence in the text reduces to a haunting diminuendo.

So much for the Túatha Dé Danann in the *Acallam*'s frame-tale. Despite the jumbled chronology in the timeline of the *fíana's* inset tales, a complex political scenario is still discernable. The starting point seems to be a state of harmony, with Midir, son of the Dagda, as the acknowledged first amongst equals. This mirrors the situation found in the story of the sons of Lugaid Menn, in which Midir, though the noblest of the Túatha Dé Danann, is not quite described as their king, and his brother Bodb Derg seems to be muscling in—a hint of the archetypal story of a mild brother displaced by an ambitious one.

But as Caílte's tales unfold, it becomes clear that at some point during the fenian age radical political change swept the world of the *síd*. Bodb Derg was made king 'by election and muster', by implication ousting his brother Midir from his pre-eminent position. (Sinisterly, Midir is never mentioned again in the text—has he been murdered?) Our information comes from those who lost most in the change of regime, Midir's twenty-eight sons. Bodb, like any Irish king during a takeover bid, demands that Midir's sons (and *only* they) be handed over to him as hostages, and threatens to raze Midir's *síd* to the ground over them if met with a refusal. The youths evacuate their father's home—presumably meaning Brí Léith, Midir's dwelling in 'The Wooing of Étaín'—and eventually set up home secretly in Slievenamon.[116] The irenic, uncanny Bodb we meet at the beginning of the *Acallam* has been replaced with a figure of savage *Realpolitik*. We saw earlier that the mortal Cormac—the archetype of the wise king in Irish tradition—was able to handle Bodb Derg's sons with an insight of which their father was incapable, and the story of the last stand of Midir's sons is designed to further bolster the sense that Bodb is a bad and maladroit king. We think back to the story of Bodb's three

---

115 *TEI*, 204, Stokes (ed.), 'Acallamh', ll.7279–83.

116 An irony, and another illustration of the author's freedom with tradition: some sources identified this very mountain with *Síd Buidb* or *Síd ar/ol Femun*, 'the síd on/beyond the plain of Femen'—Bodb's own home-*síd*. See F. J. Byrne, *Irish Kings and High-Kings* (Dublin, 1973), 166.

sons, in which Bodb had no sooner taken over the Túatha Dé than their capital suddenly seemed to be limited. This was not linked explicitly to Bodb's accession, but it does echo the standard conception of Irish kingship: the good king, favoured by the otherworld, has a realm and reign of fruitful plenty. Here that is short-circuited—for the equation surely should not apply *within* the otherworld itself. Instead it has clearly become a mere convention, severed from its older ideological roots.[117]

What is striking here is the degree to which the Túatha Dé in this story no longer appear as 'exemplary' figures, embodiments of the cultural ideal of how things should be done; Bodb in fact comes quite close to being the opposite.[118] Thanks to him, the Túatha Dé Danann become a house divided against itself. The sons of Midir refer to their enemies as 'the Túatha Dé Danann', pointedly excluding themselves, and no wonder: they have been assailed three times a year for many years, and have lost twenty-eight thousand men. The green outside their *síd* is pockmarked with 'graves and tombs.'[119]

Finn and five other members of the *fíana* lend their aid to the sons of Midir, though—in a gulp-inducing moment—even the fearless Finn knows the odds against them surviving are steep. The ensuing battles are on a far larger scale that that between Ilbrecc and Lir: it is a vision of civil war, with thousands of fighters from *síd*-mounds from all over Ireland converging on a last, beleaguered enclave. The sense of vast scale is crucial: the sequence contains the most extensive 'epic catalogue' in the *Acallam*, listing the various lords of the *síd*-mounds with the tally of their mustered forces. Bodb alone has a retinue of one thousand, two hundred and ten men.[120] The responsibilities of Finn and the *fíana* are not clear in this particular instance: the story illustrates the axiomatic quality of the world of the *síd*—that you always get more than you bargained for. (Two of the *fíana*, Oscar and Díarmait, are grievously injured.) Finn certainly owes the sons of Midir for their hospitality, but we are told that the same sons had deliberately lured Finn and his compan-

117 The theme of resentment over Bodb's lordship crops up frequently in later works; see below, 257.

118 For an exploration of a Middle Irish shift away from handling the Túatha Dé as 'exemplary' figures and towards their deployment as antitypes—'awful warnings', in other words—see C. Breatnach, '*Oidheadh Chloinne Tuireann* agus *Cath Maige Tuired*: dhá shampla de mhiotas eiseamláireach', *Éigse* 32 (2000), 35–46.

119 *TEI*, 142, Stokes (ed.), 'Acallamh', l.5113.

120 This may be a formula; it is the same as the number of the Túatha Dé's losses in the first battle.

ions to Slievenamon because they were in desperate need of their help. The extremity of the story is embodied in the long time period it covers: three battles are fought, and Finn and his followers are missing from the 'real world' of Ireland for over a year, during which the rest of the *fíana* conclude that they are dead and grieve for them.

Needless to say, Finn and the sons of Midir win, but the composer slyly passes over the victory almost in parentheses. 'We fought three battles against them', relates Caílte, 'and Conn Cruthach "the Shapely", the son of Midir, was our only loss.'[121] Equally, he refuses to spell out the political implications, though they are easy to grasp when we are told that Finn and his companions remain in the *síd* 'until we got hostages from the Túatha Dé Danann for Donn, son of Midir'.[122] Thanks to Finn, Donn becomes the ruler of the Túatha Dé; Bodb's fate is unknown. From a startlingly extreme flash-forward to the Patrician present, the reader gathers that this state of affairs lasts for centuries. The moment Caílte finishes his tale

> … they saw a warrior approaching, with a shirt of royal silk against his skin, and a tunic of soft silk over it. He wore a fringed purple mantle, with a pin of gold in it above his breast, and a gold hilted sword in his hand, and a helmet of gold around his head. It was Donn, son of Midir, who had come there. He put his head in Patrick's lap, and gave him power over the Túatha Dé Danann, and all did homage to Patrick.[123]

Patrick embodies true authority as Bodb Derg could not, and so it is to him that Donn can reverently and joyfully submit.

THE GOSPEL ACCORDING TO EITHNE

In the frame-tale of the *Acallam*, the Túatha Dé Danann become gradually enfeebled, with the exception of Cas Corach, the convert to Christianity, who finds his powers augmented. That humanity's potential is greater than that of the Túatha Dé is intensively thematized in another

---

121 *TEI*, 144–5, Stokes (ed.), 'Acallamh', ll.5197–8.
122 *TEI*, 149, Stokes (ed.), 'Acallamh', ll.5367–8.
123 *TEI*, 150, Stokes (ed.), 'Acallamh', ll.5373–8.

text, the fourteenth-century saga *Altrom tigi dá medar* ('The Fosterage of the House of Two Vessels').[124] Although this text does not belong to the Finn Cycle, its skilful interlacing of hagiography and mythology places it in a similar imaginative world to that of the *Acallam*, with which it shares some major themes.

The plot is as follows. Manannán is over-king of the Túatha Dé Danann, imagined here as a race of pagan magicians, while Bodb Derg (once again) is their king. Through the machinations of Manannán, Aengus acquires the *síd*-mound of Bruig na Bóinne by displacing his own foster-father, Elcmar. The steward of the Bruig has a daughter named Eithne; she becomes one of Aengus's many foster-daughters. She grows up beautiful and admired, although she is not the most noble of Aengus's fosterlings. Aengus's brother Finnbarr visits in order to inspect the famed women of the Bruig. In doing so, he makes a lewd remark to Eithne, and she, desperately ashamed, undergoes an unexpected and catastrophic change of nature that dislodges her from the Túatha Dé altogether. She can no longer eat their food, and manages to sustain herself on the milk of a pair of wonderful cows brought by Aengus and Manannán from India.

Eithne endures in this manner for centuries, until the time of Patrick. One day, while she and Aengus's other foster-daughters swim in the Boyne, she accidentally slips out of the haze of invisibility that keeps the Túatha Dé Danann hidden from mortals. She meets and befriends a cleric, Cessán—Patrick's chaplain in the *Acallam*—who instructs her in the Christian faith and recognizes her as a holy person. Meanwhile, her foster-father Aengus seeks for her throughout Ireland with genuine grief and anxiety; he finds her at the tale's dramatic climax, even as Patrick himself arrives on the scene. Patrick sternly dismisses Aengus and all the Túatha Dé Danann, who go on their way lamenting their lost sister bitterly. Patrick can perceive the folk of the otherworld directly, whereas Cessán—whose spiritual charisma is lesser—cannot. Patrick baptizes Eithne and forgives her sins; she dies with her head cradled in his lap.

---

124 Editions are 'Altromh tighi da medar', ed. & trans. M. C. Dobbs, *ZCP* 18 (1930), 189–230; and 'Altram Tige Dá Medar', ed. & trans. L. Duncan, *Ériu* 11 (1932), 184–225. Mc-Cone (*PPCP*, 149) argues that the tale could be older than the version we have. A recent important study of this story—which alas I only saw as this book went to press—is C. [Dahl] Hambro, 'Waiting for Christian Fish and Milk from India: A Textual and Contextual Analysis of *Altram Tige Dá Medar* ("The Nourishment of the House of Two Milk Vessels")' [unpublished Ph.D dissertation, University of Oslo, 2011].

The great folklorist Máire MacNeill aptly described this tale as 'self-evidently the product of a gracious mind and imagination', and with its vivid dialogue scenes it blends speculative theology and domestic drama, centring on the state of Eithne's soul.[125] It has something in common with 'The Wooing of Étaín': it too is about the identity and status of a woman of the *síd* as she lurches between the otherworldly and human realms. Interestingly, there is some evidence for the existence of a sovereignty goddess named Eithne in pre-Christian Ireland, and after-images of her appear in the literature as the mothers of saints and kings, and as various supernatural women.[126] 'Eithne' was a sobriquet of the river-goddess Bóand in 'The Wooing of Étaín', for example, and elsewhere it is a variant of Ethliu, mother of the god Lug.[127] But in 'The Fosterage' she and the other Túatha Dé are explicitly *not* gods, so to describe Eithne's story as the 'transition from pagan deity to Christian saint', as Kim Mc-Cone does, may well be true on the level of the history of religions, but it goes against the grain of the text's literal sense.[128]

'The Fosterage' poses a crucial question which resonates throughout this book: how human are the Túatha Dé Danann? On one level the answer given by our text is simple, theologically speaking. Eithne is saved and goes to heaven: it is a fundamental of the Christian doctrine of salvation that redemption is only possible for that which was taken on ('assumed') by Christ at the Incarnation, meaning full humanity, including body, soul, and mind. 'That which Christ has not assumed is not re-

125 M. Mac Neill, 'The Legend of the False God's Daughter', *JRSAI* 79 (1949), 100–9, at 101.

126 I remain unconvinced by Séamus Mac Mathúna's comment in 'The Relationship of the Chthonic World in Early Ireland to Chaos and Cosmos', in Borsje, *et al.* (eds.), *Celtic Cosmology*, 53–76, 70–1, that Eithne was 'in origin an otherworld goddess who had a close association with the waters'.

127 The etymology of 'Eithne' is obscure: the–*ne* may be an agental suffix (as in the name of the craftsman-god Cred*ne*), while the first element might be connected to the verb *ethaid*, 'to make one's way, go, go for, get', making Eithne 'the Wender'—a good name for a river-goddess. Alternatively, given the sovereignty connection, the element may be that seen in *etham*, 'fertile land.' Hambro ('Waiting for Christian Fish and Milk from India', 132) quotes Garrett Olmsted's view that the ancient form of the name, which would have been *Eitonia*, may have implied a drink of milk or a milch cow. For the sovereignty goddess Eithne Thóebfhota, 'the long-sided', specifically identified with the Tara kingship, see T. Ó Cathasaigh in Boyd (ed.), *Coire Sois*, 23 and 502, fn.20.

128 *PPCP*, 149–51; McCone is here alluding to C. Dagger, 'Eithne ban-dia agus ban-naomh', *Léachtaí Cholm Cille* 15 (1985), 61–78. Dagger surveys the evidence for Eithnes great and small in 'Eithne: the sources', *ZCP* 43 (1989), 84–124.

deemed' is the classic formulation.[129] If Eithne were not fully human by the end of the story, she could not be saved.

The wider context of this dimension of the tale is to be found in the upsurge of interest among medieval thinkers across western Christendom in questions of essence, selfhood, and supernatural transmogrification. As Caroline Walker Bynum has shown, this was a phenomenon of the twelfth and thirteenth centuries, and the proliferation of theological anxieties was in part a response to the rediscovery of Ovid's *Metamorphoses*, a labyrinthine game of snakes and ladders disrupting the ordered Chain of Being.[130] In that poem, gods, humans, animals, trees, and stones interchange in a manner profoundly disturbing to the medieval mind, and part of the response was an imaginative willingness to explore the relationship to Christian truth of human-like, hybrid, and mutated beings.

Despite the prominence of supernatural races, long-lived transmigrants, and ontological prodigies in Irish tradition, we still lack a full consideration of how thinkers in Ireland responded to this intellectual trend.[131] One observation is that the increasing humanization of the Túatha Dé Danann in the thirteenth and fourteenth centuries can be seen in this context, and in particular the sudden development of narratives in which they convert to Christianity, precisely because such narratives foreground questions of ontology. Aillenn, Cas Corach, and Eithne herself are only a few examples among many: a particularly germane figure is Lí Ban ('Beauty of Women'), a fairy woman and sometime mermaid who has a cameo in the *Acallam*, although she is known from elsewhere as well. In one story she is baptized after three hundred years in her aquatic form and immediately dies; startlingly, that text hails her as a 'virgin saint' (*náemóg*).[132] It is worth emphasizing how decisively this

129 Gregory of Nazianzus, *Epistle* 101.32, in J. P. Migne (ed.), *Patrologia Graeca* (161 vols., Paris, 1857–86), vol. xxxvii., col. 177–80.

130 See her classic study *Metamorphosis and Identity* (New York, 2001).

131 This is particularly odd given that the story that leads off Bynum's exploration is an Irish one recorded by Gerald of Wales in the twelfth century, which climaxes with a pair of werewolves receiving the Eucharist. The whole area will form part of the study of magic and transformation in Irish and Welsh literature with which I intend to follow this study.

132 There is no room here to dwell on the fascinating figure (or figures) of Lí Ban/Lí Bán, but see H. Imhoff, 'The Themes and Structure of *Aided Echach maic Maireda*', *Ériu* 58 (2008), 107–131, and R. de Vries, 'The Names of Lí Ban', in J. F. Nagy (ed.) *Myth in Celtic Literatures* [CSANA Yearbook 6] (Dublin, 2007), 39–54. See too the comments of Carey, '*Acallam na senórach*: a conversation between worlds', 77–8.

new pattern reverses that of that early and inaugural text, 'The Adventure of Connlae', examined in chapter 2. There, joining the people of the *síd* seemed to be a metaphor for interior Christian conversion, perhaps even for redemption itself. But half a millennium later, the otherworld-folk are clearly damned, apart from a very few prepared to travel in the opposite direction and throw in their lot with suffering humanity.[133]

In the case of Cas Corach and Aillenn, we considered the question of whether the composer of the *Acallam* visualized an essential commonality of nature between humanity and the Túatha Dé Danann, a shared bedrock which would allow for redemption and intermarriage, if and when the latter's immortality, agelessness, and magical powers were let go. 'The Fosterage' imagines how this might work at a deeper level, and at this point we must turn to the crucial scene. Finnbarr, the lord of Síd Meda (Knock Ma, near Tuam in Co. Galway) and elder brother of Aengus, comes to the Bruig in order to ogle its women:

> ... Finnbarr looks intently at Ethne daughter of Dichu, and asked: 'Who is that sitting on her heel? And though I am asking you', said Finnbarr, '[I say] it is the steward's daughter who is doing it, and I almost called her "Heel-Sitting" ', and he spoke the stanza:
>
> > 'The royal daughter of the steward,
> > dear is the gentle stately swan,
> > it is one of the children of a proper person
> > who has sat upon her heel.'
>
> And from that moment the lovely face of the maiden went white, and green, and red, and she went wretchedly, anxiously, wet-cheeked, her face scarlet, to the sun-room in which she normally lived...[134]

Eithne is subjected here to a particularly aggressive form of the male gaze: she is singled out from the other women for lubricious appraisal.

---

133 These stories have something in common with the hagiographic topos of the 'good pagan'; in Adomnán's *Life of Columba* there is an example of a just pagan baptized on the point of death (see *ECI*, 199) but later medieval writers took this further and had long-dead pagans saved by a miracle. One instance is the late medieval English poem *St Erkenwald*, and it was also said, not least by Dante, that the prayers of Gregory the Great had gained salvation for the emperor Trajan.

134 *Altram*, ed. & trans. Duncan, 193, 213.

There is a difficulty here in that the precise import of Finnbarr's remark is now unclear, but in the context in seems plain that it was a joke of astonishing crudity, made worse by the way he turns it—typical manoeuvre of the bully—into a nickname. He may be implying that Eithne has one leg crossed under her—the pose of a very young girl—in order to stimulate herself sexually with her foot.[135] Eithne's response to this degrading treatment is dramatic. The colours of her face register shock, nausea, and shame; but they are also an important sign to the reader of the operation of divine grace, reminiscent as they are of the 'three martyrdoms'—white, green, and red—of the early Irish church.[136] Themes of exile and sanctity are already being sounded.

The sequence which follows establishes that Eithne can no longer eat the food of her people and must be nourished on the milk of a pair of cows brought from India—imagined here as a 'righteous' country, perhaps because according to medieval geography it lay near to the earthly paradise in the east. The milk is a marker of a change of state, because to live on milk alone is to be a newborn: it has the flavour of honey, associating it with the Promised Land, and the power of wine—a subtle Eucharistic touch.[137] Here there is an echo of the *Vita Prima* of St Brigit, in which the infant saint is unable to keep down the unclean food of her pagan foster-father, a druid.[138] There is a further subtle miracle: the Feast of Goibniu and the pigs of Manannán are supposed to ensure the immortality of the Túatha Dé, but Eithne endures unaged for centuries while abstaining from both.

---

135 It is difficult to discuss this passage without laying oneself open to the charge of having a dirty mind; Anton van Hamel thought (using a reconstruction of the text which cannot be sustained) that Eithne is being accused here of having made 'a dirty mess', for which see Hambro, 'Waiting for Christian Fish and Milk from India', 123–7, who thinks Finnbarr is satirizing Eithne's proto-Christian modesty, out of place among the aristocratic Túatha Dé.

136 C. Stancliffe, 'Red, White and Blue Martyrdom', in D. Whitelock, *et al.* (eds.), *Ireland in Early Mediaeval Europe: Studies in Memory of Kathleen Hughes* (Cambridge, 1982), 21–46. The difference between 'green' in the text and 'blue' in Stancliffe's title is not significant: it is the same word in Irish, *glas*.

137 See D. M. Wiley, 'Baptizing the Fairies: The Christian-Conversion Typescene as a *Rite de Passage*', *PHCC* 15 (1995), 139–146. Hambro ('Waiting for Christian Fish and Milk from India', 150) sees this as an allusion to 1 Corinthians 3:1–2, in which Paul refers to new Christians as 'infants in Christ' who must be 'fed… with milk'.

138 *Vita Prima S. Brigitae*, ed. J. Colgan, *Triadis Thaumaturgae… Acta* (Louvain, 1647), 527–42; trans. S Connolly, Journal *of the Royal Society of Antiquaries of Ireland* 119 (1989), 14–49, ch.10.

Eventually Manannán divines the reason, and again the passage is crucial for our understanding of what is going on:

'She is not of the people of Aengus at all, nor of our people either. For when Finnbarr gave the insult to that girl, her accompanying demon (*a deman comuidechta*) went from her heart and an angel took its place, and that does not allow our food into her stomach, and from now on she will put no faith in magic or devilry, and therefore she drinks the milk of that cow... and it is the... Trinity in three persons which will be the God whom that maiden will worship', he said.[139]

Staggeringly, this is a Christian anthropology of the people of the *síd*. In Christian theology, the human person is formed of both body and soul, both of which are essential: at the Last Judgment souls will be reunited with their transfigured but nonetheless fully physical bodies. Hence, this is why *nourishment* in 'The Fosterage' is important, because it is about what gives the body substance. Additionally, from a number of biblical hints, the idea emerged early in the history of Christianity that each human being is accompanied from birth by a guardian angel, though this has never in fact been doctrinally defined.[140] Sinful human beings might be assailed by devils—Patrick finds that even the noble *fíana* are attended by hordes of them, promptly exorcized—but the situation here is different.[141] The implication of Manannán's words is that each of the Túatha Dé Danann have a single accompanying demon 'bolted on' as part of their inner configuration, in place of the guardian angel which a human being would have. Now in other texts taking a severe line on the Túatha Dé Danann, they are imagined *as* demons; not so here. Eithne clearly has both a body and a soul, and when her demon is supplanted by an angel she becomes, in terms of spiritual potential, wholly human. This is the author's conceptualization of the Túatha Dé

139 *Altram*, ed. & trans. Duncan, 196, 216.
140 Though the concept of the guardian angel can be traced back to Jerome's commentary on Matthew's Gospel in the fourth century, it was formalized in Honorius Augustodunensis's very popular *Imago mundi* in the twelfth; the Honorian scheme may have come to Ireland with the ecclesiastical reform movement (indeed he is sometimes argued to have been Irish), and may be reflected in our text's imaginative concern with guardian angels (and devils). See Flanagan, *The Transformation of the Irish Church in the Twelfth Century*, 14, fn.62.
141 *TEI*, 5, Stokes (ed.), 'Acallamh', l.67–8.

Danann's potential for shifts in being. The change occurs deep within: elsewhere Manannán glosses his own words to say that Eithne 'parted from her magic, so that an angelic spirit *came into the place of her mind* [or *nature*]'.[142] The nature of the Túatha Dé can evidently be rebooted, so to speak: on the hardware of their bodies and souls, new spiritual software can apparently be installed.

The question of the baseline spiritual state of the Túatha Dé is addressed with cunning. They are explicitly described as magicians and the worshippers of pagan gods: once again ex-gods are troped as their votaries. In the Middle Ages, magicians were generally believed to traffic with evil spirits, but the Túatha Dé clearly have a one-to-one relationship with a personal devil. The fall of Lucifer and his angels is described early in the text: other Irish texts had identified the Túatha Dé with 'half-fallen' angels, held in suspension upon the earth. The composer of the saga may be expanding on this doctrine here, explaining the close relation between fallen angels and Túatha Dé as one of spiritual parasitism rather than identity.[143]

In short, the Túatha Dé Danann are clearly fallen beings—again a stark contrast to some earlier attempts to explain them as a mysteriously sinless branch of humanity.[144] Finnbarr's insult seems, formally, to function analogously to the medieval paradox of the *felix culpa*, the 'fortunate Fall', because it is through his sin that Eithne is redeemed. She says as much, declaring:

A blessing from me to that Finnbarr;
my love for God came about thanks to him.[145]

Medieval people could and did bless Adam and Eve for their primal sin in Eden, because that sin made redemption necessary and thus, in a sense, brought Christ into the world.[146] The Church Father Ambrose of

---

142 *Altram*, ed. & trans. Duncan, 197, 217, emphasis mine.

143 Their situation is thus reminiscent of that in in the twelfth-century parodic tale 'The Vision of Mac Conglinne' (*Aislinge meic Con Glinne*), in which king Cathal mac Finnguine is afflicted by a 'demon of gluttony' stuck in his throat: but Cathal's situation is not one of ontological fusion.

144 See above, 59–60, 87–9.

145 *Altram*, ed. & trans. Duncan, 201, 221 (trans).

146 Good summary in D. L. Jeffrey (ed.), *A Dictionary of Biblical Tradition in English Literature* (Grand Rapids, MI, 1992), 274–5. A classic instance of the *felix culpa* theme in English is the exquisite and famous late medieval lyric *Adam lay ybounden*.

Milan thought that the sin of eating the forbidden fruit had brought more good into the world than would have come to pass had humanity remained in a state of unfallen innocence.

But Eithne's fallen spiritual state undercuts the formal resemblance here. If one had to tie down precisely what that state is, one might say that the Túatha Dé Danann are clearly fallen, but fallen *further* than humanity. Fallen humans still have guardian angels, but the people of the *síd* enjoy no such benefit; indeed, it is quite the reverse. The idea of an 'accompanying devil'—presumably preventing the angel standing ready from rushing in to fill the gap—is a clever solution to the theological conundrum posed by the Túatha Dé.[147] In order for us to empathize with them on the narrative level, they must be culturally similar to humans, and cannot be overtly depraved. (It is worth mentioning that the question of whether truly wicked beings such as demons might be redeemed was on the extreme edges of Christian thought, and the composer wisely avoids it.)[148] The opening of the text lays out their degree of fallenness for our moral evaluation, and focuses it through the figure of Manannán. The political structure of the Túatha Dé Danann is represented unusually here: Bodb Derg again is king, but Manannán is their over-king, and it is he who parcels out the *síd*-mounds to the various eminences of the Túatha Dé—the role of the Dagda in other texts—while he himself dwells apart with his people in an overseas realm all his own.

Manannán is not by any means a wholly wicked character in the tale, but in our terms he is a materialistic opportunist with a disturbing line in Ayn Randian rhetoric. Unexpectedly, he is also the interior designer for the Túatha Dé, all of whom are keen to replicate the aesthetic ostentation of his realm: the Bruig, fitted out to his specifications, is entirely floored in inlaid bronze.

147 The idea that humans had both a guardian angel and a tempting devil goes back to the second-century Christian text *The Shepherd of Hermas*, but did not become common until the late Middle Ages.

148 Famously, the early Church Father Origen wondered if even the Devil might one day repent and be saved; so did Gregory of Nyssa. If the theological speculations of this chapter seem convoluted, it is worth noting that aspects of it have been the subject of serious Christian enquiry since the ninetheeth century: the recent term is 'exotheology', meaning hypotheses about the ontological status of sentient aliens. If human beings were to encounter such beings tomorrow, would they have souls? Could they be baptized? Would they need redemption in Christ, and would that be possible? See T. F. O'Meara, O.P., 'Christian Theology and Extraterrestrial Intelligent Life', *Theological Studies* 60 (1999), 3–30, and M. J. Crowe, *The Extraterrestrial Life Debate, 1750–1900: the idea of a plurality of worlds from Kant to Lowell* (Cambridge, 1986).

The tale gives us yet another version of how Aengus gains possession of the Bruig, and this time it is Manannán who urges him to violate all ties of loyalty to his foster-father Elcmar and to simply eject him and all his people using an irresistible spell. Aengus is troubled by his conscience, but Manannán brooks no argument:

'Stop that', said Manannán, 'for a king is better than a knight (*ridiri*), and a prince is nobler than one second-in-line, and ability (*comus*) is better than cooperation, and the safe course is better than pity...'[149]

Thus upbraided, Aengus uses the spell to drive Elcmar out. But when the heartbroken Elcmar assures Aengus that he would have gladly *given* him the Bruig, if only he had asked, the reader is forcibly made to attend to the anti-Christian import of Manannán's code, which conspicuously reverses the Beatitudes. In Manannán's triumph-of-the-will world, the meek shall certainly not inherit the *síd*. Aengus is an apt pupil, though a more sympathetic figure than his teacher, despite his attacks of temper and poor judgment.[150] Most disturbingly of all, Manannán, and later Aengus too, are shown to be in possession of genuine theological truth. Manannán knows about the Trinity, and elsewhere he indicates that he is well-informed about the fall of the rebel angels. Yet both repeatedly show themselves left unmoved by the knowledge, in what may be a pointed reversal of John 20:29: 'Blessed are they who have not seen, and yet have believed.' It could also be a direct allusion to James 2:19, which points out that intellectual belief in God is not sufficient, for demons believe in just this way but are nonetheless damned ('The devils believe, and tremble.')[151] Such biblical twists make an important point. Even as Manannán concentrates the reader's sense of what the Túatha Dé Danann's fallenness entails—a taste for opulence, might-makes-right politics,

149 *Altram*, ed. & trans. Duncan, 191, 210.

150 See for example his murderous rage against Finnbarr, and the wonderful detail that the womenfolk approach him 'timorously' (*cu hedana*, i.e. *go hédána*) to tell him that Eithne has been lost: they are afraid of his temper. (*Altram*, ed. & trans. Duncan, 200, 220).

151 See, for instance, Aengus's impassive response to Patrick's plea to him to convert and be baptized: 'That is not the cause for which we came from our house' (*Altram*, ed. & trans. Duncan, 201, 221). I gratefully acknowledge that the source of the second biblical reference was one of Princeton University Press's two anonymous reviewers.

and a stony indifference to spiritual truth—we are forced to confront the question of how redemptive change might enter such a system.[152]

The answer is, and can only be, grace. Eithne's transformation is a study of divine favour that is, precisely, gratuitous, and invites analysis as such. The initial impulse of grace must come entirely from God: it is this which gives her an internal jolt sufficient to allow her to feel *pudicitia*, or shame, a very Christian virtue. The state she achieves thanks to this operative grace is analogous to that of Adam and Eve immediately *after* the Fall—they are pervasively corrupted in their nature and thus drop down an ontological rung, whereas Eithne arrives at the same place by going up one. This is why her access of reticence and *pudeur* is so reminiscent of the moment in Genesis 3:7 in which Adam and Eve realize that that are naked, and then feel shame for the first time. It is important for me to stress that I am talking here about sinfulness of *nature*, rather than *person*. In the case of humans, medieval theologians thought there was sin in both: original sin inheres in human nature, while the sins committed by each individual accrue in their person. Eithne does not perform any act of personal sin in the course of the story, but as one of the Túatha Dé Danann her nature is intrinsically corrupted to a degree below even that of a fallen human being.[153]

Her sense of shame, the ousting of her demon, and the entrance of a guardian angel all happen in a flash, with divine grace as the galvanic spark. Subsequent grace allows her to persist in goodness, as symbolized by her inability to take anything from the world of the Túatha Dé Danann into her body. This is one of a sequence of typical hagiographical motifs that begin to appear at this point. Eithne's diet of milk aligns her with the host of female saints in the Middle Ages whose sanctity manifested through dietary outlandishness, not least the ability to live on

152 Note that I read Manannán very differently from Cathinka Hambro, who regards him as a John the Baptist figure, whose 'druidical powers have undergone a process of conversion and are now prophetic rather than druidic and performed in the service of God' (Waiting for Christian Fish and Milk from India', 114).

153 My terms here are drawn from the theology of Anselm of Canterbury, but space prevents further detail here: a close reading of the whole saga, currently in preparation, explores Eithne's predicament in terms of Anselm's (and Augustine's) theory of regenerative grace. Shifts in theological thinking in the period may have affected images of virtuous pagans, so that they were regarded with more compassion; see the comments of M. Ní Mhaonaigh, 'Pagans and holy men: literary manifestations of twelfth-century reform', in D. Bracken & D. Ó Riain-Raedel (eds.), *Ireland and Europe in the Twelfth Century: Reform and Renewal* (Dublin, 2006), 143–61, at 152–3.

nothing but the Eucharistic bread and wine.[154] Though she lives in this way for centuries, among the Túatha Dé but no longer of them, this period is passed over quickly. Once she has crossed the Boyne and encountered Christianity for the first time, the markers of sanctity multiply. Her first food in hundreds of years, for example, is a shared salmon, caught for her by the cleric Cessán. He catches only one small fish, and Eithne instructs him to return to the water and try again: he promptly catches a second specimen so big he can hardly carry it. Boldly this story echoes John 21, in which the risen Christ tells the apostles, despondent because of their empty net, to cast it again on the other right side of their boat: this time the net comes up so filled with fish that they cannot haul it in. Both sequences end by the waterside with a shared meal of grilled fish. Eithne, like Christ, is both divine and human; she has risen to new life after a sojourn in the world below. The effect is to dramatically underscore her holiness as she joins the human world. She becomes a kind of monastic postulant, blessed with hyperlexia—the gift of instinctive, voracious reading.

As I also observed about the *Acallam*, here again ontology is imagined as ethnicity: Eithne's change of metaphysical state is repeatedly described as a change of kin-group. 'She is of no other people', observes Manannán's daughter Curcóg, 'but of the true people of the omnipotent High King.'[155] At Eithne's death her soul ascends to heaven. Her trajectory in 'The Fosterage' shows that this poignant and unusual saga shares a sense of the fundamental interchangeability of the Túatha Dé Danann and humanity with the *Acallam*—ultimately we are, so to speak, the same species. Both texts make the people of the *síd* out to be pagans, but their innate capacity for magic makes them tricksier and more dangerous than other pre-Christian figures. 'The Fosterage' attempts to imagine this state of affairs theologically with a striking intensity and coherence. As they stand, the Túatha Dé Danann seem more than human, but are instead rather lesser—they are unclean on some deep structural level. Both the *Acallam* and 'The Fosterage' draw on contemporary intellectual preoccupations with the status and implications of human-like beings, and on the extent of God's salvific plan. It was only possible to use the Túatha Dé Danann in this way because by the high Middle Ages texts such as the *Acallam* had ferried them so far from their original status as

---

154 See C. W. Bynum, *Holy Feast and Holy Fast: the Religious Significance of Food to Medieval Women* (Berkeley, Los Angeles, & London, 1987), especially 59–60.

155 *Altram*, ed. & trans. Duncan, 197, 217.

pagan divinities. The depth of this transformation is clear if we think back to 'The Adventure of Connlae', from the turn of the eighth century; in that pivotal early saga (as I argued) the people of the *síd* stand for the souls of the redeemed. In 'The Fosterage' they are quite the reverse: doomed to hell and subject to demonic contamination from within.

FINAL THOUGHTS

So rich are the texts examined in this chapter that it may be helpful to restate some ideas in conclusion. Both the *Acallam* and 'The Fosterage in the House of Two Vessels' meditate on the ontology of the people of the *síd*. Together they represent the end of a bleaching process, so that hardly a trace of divinity is left in the Túatha Dé Danann. Their immortality and mercurial fluidity of form are given explanations other than divinity. In both texts they are explicitly pagans; 'The Fosterage' mentions the false gods the Túatha Dé Danann worship. Furthermore, they are not even the exemplary figures of the learned and skilled classes which they were in some Old Irish texts and the pseudohistorical tradition of 'The Book of Invasions.' They are instead a fundamental part of an Ireland which is self-estranged: one thinks of Joep Leerssen's shrewd, if now overworked, term, 'auto-exoticism', used to describe certain typical strategies of Anglo-Irish literature. The very intimacy of the *síd* reinforces this sense of defamiliarization: the *fíana* live in a world in which the enticingly and alarmingly uncanny is always close by, simultaneously within and beyond. The characteristic metaphor used in the *Acallam* for this quality is the beguiling strain of *síd*-music, which can foster both health and harm.

Both texts also agree that the final fate of the Túatha Dé is an unhappy one. Though the people of the *síd* represent everything one might envy and feel reduced by (and yet eroticize), their beauty and immortality clearly pay no eschatological dividend. In the fenian age, heroism can elevate a mortal to the heightened level of the people of the *síd*, albeit those of a callow, second-generation kind. Later, Christianity raises the sons of Míl far beyond the Túatha Dé Danann. On this point, it is worth stressing how hard the *Acallam*, often said to be a text about the sunny reconciliation of pagan and Christian values, actually is on the people of the *síd*. In the eyes of Patrick, the hypnotic music of Cas Corach was so powerful as to blemish something otherwise admirable. The Túatha Dé themselves seem to occupy the same position within culture, embodying an excess of allure that must be radically pruned. What Caílte says of Cas Corach applies also to Aillenn, and to Eithne: ultimately they are among the best off of all the people of the *síd*, because they alone of all their kind will taste the bliss of heaven.

6

DAMAGED GODS

THE LATE MIDDLE AGES

The houses are all gone under the sea.
The dancers are all gone under the hill.

—T. S. ELIOT, 'EAST COKER'

WITH THIS CHAPTER we arrive at an intermezzo. The second half of this book looks at the modern reception of the Irish gods, and it thus far has investigated the bulk of the sources which mythologically minded writers reworked in English from the nineteenth century onward. Magnetized by the archaic, such writers excavated the earliest layers of material they could find, with the result that the Irish gods were retrieved from the Old Irish sagas, interwoven with the highlights of the Finn Cycle, the *dindshenchas*, and high medieval learned pseudohistory. The existence of late medieval stories about the Túatha Dé Danann was generally ignored, giving the impression that interest in the gods had petered out in Ireland around the turn of the fifteenth century. This was in point of fact quite false, and we will examine some characteristically late-phase manifestations below. It is true, however, that new additions to the mythology were rare after about 1400: culturally there was a pervasive backwards look towards pre-Norman Ireland, with a strong tendency to revisit and revise earlier tales.[1] Bardic poetry, for example, which was composed in Ireland down to the turn of the seventeenth century, frequently alluded to the events of the Mythological Cycle.[2]

---

1 See K. Hollo, 'Later medieval Ireland, 1200–1600: Part II: Prose literature', *CHIL* i., 114.

2 For example the poet Fearchar Ó Maoilchiaráin alludes to the skills of the smith-god Goibniu in a poem about what kind of brooch his beloved deserves (see *CHIL* i., 98, and *Dánta Grádha: an anthology of Irish love poetry (A.D. 1350–1750)*, ed. T. F. O'Rahilly

We know that bardic poets were involved with the composition of late prose-tales, and in this period sagas from the Ulster Cycle and King Cycles were recast.[3] So were tales about the gods: we have, for example, a late version of 'The Second Battle of Moytura' from *c*.1400, which tells the same story as the better-known ninth-century text but excises the less dignified elements—including the Dagda's sordid sexcapades.[4] Another late story, *Eachtra Thaidhg meic Chéin* ('The Adventure of Tadg son of Cían'), racily revists 'The Adventure of Connlae', written seven hundred years earlier. It describes how the hero Tadg visits the otherworld where he meets Connlae, son of Conn of the Hundred Battles, along with the mysterious woman who had drawn Connlae away. We saw in that earliest of Irish stories that she had personified the Christian Church, blurring pagan goddess and unfallen (or redeemed) human being. The author of 'The Adventure of Tadg' plays on this gulf between orders of being by giving her name—with marvellous incongruity—as 'Venusia, daughter of Adam'.[5]

This is indicative of how innovation in this period tended to be local and to take place on the level of style, with the emergence of the so-called 'romantic tales', termed *rómánsaíocht* in Irish. Scholars of Irish literature have tended to look askance at these, dismissing them as formulaic and derivative in comparison to the complex splendour of the earlier sagas.[6] Nonetheless, attention is being increasingly drawn to their literary value, as well as to the fact that research into their context, structure, and style is at present at an early stage.[7] They form a stepping stone between the earlier medieval sagas and the later folk tales collected in Ireland and Gaelic Scotland; one crucial difference between

---

(Dublin, 1926), 18); Gofraidh Fionn Ó Dálaigh used the story of Lug's arrival at Tara in a praise-poem from the mid fourteenth century, for which see 'A Poem by Gofraidh Fionn Ó Dálaigh', ed. & trans. O. Bergin, in E. C. Quiggin (ed.), *Essays and Studies presented to William Ridgeway* (Cambridge, 1913), 323–33.

3 Hollo, *CHIL* i., 114.

4 See, e.g. M. Hoyne, 'The Political Context of *Cath Muige Tuireadh*, the Early Modern Irish Version of the Second Battle of Magh Tuireadh', *Ériu* 63 (2013), 91–116.

5 *Eachtra Thaidhg meic Chéin*, ed. & trans. S. H. O'Grady, *Silva Gadelica: A Collection of Tales in Irish* (2 vols., London, 1892), i., 350, ii., 392.

6 G. Goss, 'Women, Gender, and Sexuality in Late Medieval Irish *Rómánsaíochtai*', in S. Sheehan & A. Dooley (eds.), *Constructing Gender in Medieval Ireland* (New York, 2013), 153–170, at 153; see too A. Bruford, *Gaelic Folk-tales and Medieval Romances: A Study of the Early Modern Irish 'Romantic Tales' and their Oral Derivatives* (Dublin, 1969).

7 The opening salvo was fired by J. F. Nagy, 'In Defence of *Rómánsaíocht*', *Ériu* 38 (1987), 9–26.

them is that the romances survive in manuscript, whereas the folk tales were taken down from oral performance. No consensus has emerged as yet on the question of how far these tales draw on non-written tradition: Alan Bruford argues that they are dependent on manuscript versions, while Joseph Nagy is prepared to think in terms of a continuing drip-feed from and interaction with oral performance.[8] Such 'romantic tales' about the Túatha Dé Danann were only one strand in an elaborate web of story. Typically entertaining and told with panache, they are more accessible than the complex narratives of earlier centuries—narratives which we should remember continued in many cases to be copied. And because we have met most of the characters and scenarios already, this short chapter can focus on what is distinctive in the period in question.[9]

It is ironic that the most famous of all Irish mythological tales happens to belong to this most belated phase of medieval Irish writing about the gods: this is the tragic story of the Children of Lir, transformed into swans by their jealous stepmother. While writing this book I repeatedly found that people who were unaware of Ireland's native pantheon of deities nonetheless often knew this narrative. This reflects the fact that, though a very late addition to the Mythological Cycle, the tale developed a conspicuously rich cultural afterlife, endlessly alluded to, retold, and re-imagined in many media.[10]

Oidheadh Chloinne Lir ('The Tragic Deaths of the Children of Lir') is the first of three prose-tales examined here, in order to set out the ways that they present the gods and highlight how these were typical of the times. The second tale is often found paired with 'The Tragic Deaths of the Children of Lir' as one of the famous 'Three Sorrows of Storytelling': this is *Oidheadh Chloinne Tuireann* ('The Tragic Deaths of the Children of Tuireann'), an entertainingly gruesome story of vengeance and vendetta.[11] The third is a fenian tale, *Cath Finntrágha* ('The Battle of Ventry'),

8 An example might be 'The Journey of the Two Bands of Nine Men' (*Imtheacht an Dá Nonbor*), a fenian tale composed in east Ulster in 1700s: it is a classic 'romantic' tale in that it recycles tired tropes about Manannán and Aengus, who appear alongside Finn's *fíana*; see C. W. MacQuarrie, *The Biography of the Irish God of the Sea from Immram Brain (c. 700) to Finnegans Wake (1939): the Waves of Manannán* (Lewiston, NY, 2004), 315.

9 See Hollo, *CHIL* i., 111.

10 Oisín Kelly's dramatic 1964 sculpture *The Children of Lir* in the Garden of Remembrance in Dublin is only the most famous of these. It configures the moment of transformation as a swirling vortex of upward motion, imaginatively fusing the moments of curse and release from curse to make a profound political statement.

11 The third of the 'Three Sorrows' is the story of the sons of Uisnech, for which see

one section of which describes how the Túatha Dé Danann ride to the rescue of Finn mac Cumaill and his *fíana* when they are Ireland's sole defence against the invading armies of Dáire Donn, 'King of the Great World'.

THE KINDRED OF THE SEA

Lir, father of the swan-children, must be considered first before we move on to the tale itself, because his family furnishes an excellent example of the ways in which the Irish pantheon could bud and branch centuries after the end of Irish paganism.

The first thing to note is that there is a fundamental disjunction in the texture of the mythology between Lir (or Ler)—a shadowy cipher who only begins to coalesce in the thirteenth century—and his putative son, Manannán. There is a pervasive oddness about Manannán, and debate continues as to his precise relationship with the medieval Welsh literary character Manawydan; as the names are not fully cognate it seems likely that the Welsh one is an adaptation of the Irish.[12] Both contain an element relating to the Isle of Man—as Patrick Sims-Williams notes, 'Manannán' means 'one born in or having the nature of the Isle of Man'—and there is no problem in theory with the concept of a native marine god associated with the largest island in the Irish sea. As noted in chapter 2, some (unclear) quality in the original pagan Manannán allowed an early medieval *literatus*, working in an Ulster monastery around the turn of the eighth century, to use the sea-god to allude to or allegorize Christian epistemology. He may well have been the first example from Ireland of a pre-Christian deity being thus experimentally re-purposed. Equally exceptionally, he is the only god in the entire history of the pantheon to benefit from an explicitly euhemerist reading, found in 'Cormac's Glossary'. The fabulist Euhemerus had argued that the Greek gods had simply been noble mortals, and this is a rationalizing manoeuvre that we have seen deployed in Ireland at various points in the Middle Ages.[13] But Euhemerus added that Zeus, Athena, and so on

---

Oidheadh Chloinne hUisneach: The Violent Death of the Children of Uisneach, ed. & trans. C. Mac Giolla Léith (London, 1993).

12 *IIMWL*, 11–12.

13 See D. C. Feeney, *The Gods in Epic: Poets and Critics of the Classical Tradition* (Oxford, 1991), 31–2.

had been mistakenly taken to be divine by their grateful subjects because of their conspicuous excellence in particular spheres: the 'Glossary' states that Manannán was a merchant and mariner, 'the best at sea in the west of the world', whence 'the Irish and the Britons called him god of the sea' (*Scoti et Brittones eum deum uocauerunt maris*).[14] The fact that only Manannán is treated this way suggests there was something intrinsically exceptional about him.[15] Part of this, surely, was his clear association with one particular realm of nature, the sea, purviews of this kind being rare indeed among the Irish gods. (Patrick Sims-Williams notes that the anecdote may have been intended to undermine 'a popular idea that Manannán could create and calm storms, as he does in modern Irish folklore'.)[16] Though 'Cormac's Glossary' is not an early text, even in its first, shorter version, there is likely to be something very old here, because Manannán's divine status is explicit; there is no attempt to pigeonhole him as one of the people of the *síd*-mounds.

Manannán's exceptionalism is remarkably persistent. He is repeatedly depicted as the ruler of an otherworld over the water, from the mysterious double or overlayered space of 'The Voyage of Bran'—in which the sea in one sense *is* the otherworld—to the paradisial lake island found in the Ulster Cycle saga 'The Wasting Sickness of Cú Chulainn'. It is easy to discern how his odd-man-out quality might derive from and reflect his unique association with a particular area, the Isle of Man. Although it was not geographically part of Ireland, it nevertheless came within its sphere of cultural and (often) political influence: accordingly, Manannán is always half-removed, with one foot in and one foot out.

Two texts discussed in the previous chapter showcase this ambivalence. As William Sayers points out, Manannán's stock rises during those phases in Irish literature in which otherworlds across the sea, rather than within hills, are of pre-eminent imaginative significance.[17] In the *Acallam*, the only two stories about Manannán are found very close together, and in both his overseas island is called by its conventional name *Tír Tairngire*, 'the Land of Promise'.[18] The first is an anec-

---

14 *Sanas Cormaic*, ed. Meyer, in Bergin, *et al.* (eds.), *Anecdota from Irish Manuscripts* iv., 78; [reprnt. Llanerch, 1994]; on this passage see comments above, 61, 81, 162–3.

15 D. Spaan, 'The Place of Manannan Mac Lir in Irish Mythology', *Folklore* 76 (1965), 176–95, points out the god's exceptional status but the analysis is now a little outdated.

16 *IIMWL*, 13.

17 W. Sayers, 'Netherworld and Otherworld in early Irish literature', *ZCP* 59 (2012), 201–30, at 218.

18 Originally a Latin, biblical term, *terra repromissionis*, for which see L. Bieler, 'Two

dote of knowing erotic sophistication, in which Manannán falls in love with a woman named Áine, while his wife, here called Uchtdelb, falls in love with Áine's brother, Aillén. Husband and wife cheerfully agree to change partners without mutual rancour.[19] The author implies that love among the Túatha Dé is not like mortal love. One is reminded that stories about the god-peoples fulfilled the purpose of all good fantasy writing, in that by depicting characters who differ ontologically from mere mortals, they enabled ironic commentary on what human nature and society is actually like.

The same note recurs in the second story in the *Acallam* over which Manannán presides. Riding over the sea on his horse, he rescues three princes from shipwreck—one Irish, one Greek, one Indian—and conveys them to *Tír Tairngire* itself, apparently the haunt of a questionable *demimonde*.[20] There the princes meet the three daughters of Manannán's physician. In a sequence that is clearly meant to be amusing, no sooner are we told these young women are 'the three storehouses of chastity and celibacy of the Túatha Dé Danann' than they leap enthusiastically into bed with the young men and decide 'to elope with them on the first fine day'.[21] The overall impression given by these depictions of Manannán and his kingdom is of enigmatic power allied with amoral impulsiveness—an unsettling combination. (In 'The Fosterage of the House of Two Vessels', we recall, Manannán's code of behaviour involved an anti-Christian contempt for weakness, for all his status as an over-king of great wisdom.) In short, it seems that Manannán came to personify the ambivalences which were part and parcel of the late medieval view of the Túatha Dé Danann: his knowledge is deep, his interventions unpredictable, and his morals dubious. This view is even more pronounced in the late romantic tales, in which he becomes an out-and-out trickster. In one of the most famous, the late sixteenth-century *Eachtra an Cheithearnaigh Chaoilriabhaigh* ('The Adventure of the Narrow-Striped Kern'), Manannán appears as a grubby rogue who wreaks havoc

---

Observations Concerning the *Navigatio Brendani'*, *Celtica* 11 (1976), 15–7, reprt. in J. M. Wooding (ed.), *The Otherworld Voyage in Early Irish Literature: An Anthology of Criticism* (Dublin, 2000), 91–3.

19 *TEI*, 111, W. Stokes (ed & partial trans.) 'Acallamh na senórach', in W. Stokes & E. Windisch (eds.), *Irische Texte* (4 vols., Leipzig, 1880–1909), iv (1), ll.3649–71.

20 Manannán's attitude to the youths in this entire episode is never really clear: is he rescuing them or humiliating them?

21 *TEI*, 115, Stokes (ed.) 'Acallamh na senórach', ll.3815–7.

amongst the Irish petty gentry of the early 1500s, before transforming and becoming helpful.[22]

Manannán mac Lir is a good example, therefore, of an Irish god tracing a sharply incised trajectory over many centuries, albeit one at a tangent to that of the rest of the pantheon. The same cannot be said of Lir, his nebulous father, although this has escaped notice until recently. Joseph Nagy points out that Lir never appears as a figure of story in any Irish text written before the mid-thirteenth century, and that his 'role in general is limited to that of an unseen parent or genealogical figure'.[23] Lir may in fact have only coalesced as a character in the high Middle Ages. Readers may object that from the very first Manannán is identified as *mac Lir*, 'son of Lir' (more correctly 'Ler'), so there must have been a Lir to have fathered him. But my suspicion is that *mac lir* began as a metaphor, not a patronymic; the glossary entries on the god point in this direction, and additional support is given by the frequency in Irish of figures of speech taking the form '*mac(c)*-of-X', to mean 'man who has professionally to do with X'. In Old Irish a *macc légind*, 'son of reading', is a clerical student, while a *macc báis*, 'son of death', is a reaver or wicked person, and so on.[24] The word *ler* was a less common but not exceptional synonym for *muir*, 'sea', and would have been understood as such by speakers of Old Irish.[25] Therefore the phrase *mac lir*, 'sea's son',

22 *Silva Gadelica*, ed. & trans. O'Grady, i., 276–88, ii., 311–23; see too MacQuarrie, *Biography of the Irish God of the Sea*, 289, 311. It is an interesting story because it shows a pagan god interfering in the life of a recently deceased historical person, Aodh Dubh Ó Domhnaill (d.1537), and other early sixteenth-century lords, a theme that takes us all the way back to the early Mongán tales; see E. M. Slotkin, 'What Allows Fixed Texts to Enter Gaelic Oral Tradition?', in H. C. Tristram (ed.), *(Re)Oralisierung [ScriptOralia 84]* (Tübingen, 1996), 64, on the relationship between oral and literary versions of this tale.

23 J. F. Nagy, 'Some strands and strains in *Acallam na Senórach*', in A. Doyle & K. Murray (eds.), *In Dialogue with the Agallamh: Essays in Honour of Seán Ó Coileáin* (Dublin, 2014), 90–108, at 103. Tale-lists which predate the *Acallam* point to the existence of a tale of destruction (*togail*) known as 'The Triple Assault on the House of Lir' (*Trechúairt Tigi Lir*); this seems likely to be related to the inter-*síd* war fought in the *Acallam*, suggesting that Lir may already have been in existence as a literary character by c.1000; see P. Mac Cana, *The Learned Tales of Medieval Ireland* (Dublin, 1980), 41, 57.

24 See *DIL* s. v. *mac (macc)*, 1 iii. (a) and (b); see A. Rees & B. Rees, *Celtic Heritage: Ancient Tradition in Ireland and Wales* (London, 1978), 31, 39; for *mac* in kennings, see P. Russell, '"What was best of every language": the early history of the Irish language', *NHI* i., 405–50, at 435.

25 Sims-Williams (*IIMWL*, 11) traces the word back to Celtic *li-ro-*. The root-meaning had to do with the ocean's multitudinousness: a distant cognate in English (via Latin) is the word *plural*.

may originally have been nothing more than an idiom for 'seaman, sailor': it need not imply that Lir/Ler was thought to be a personage at all, still less a pre-Christian god. Sims-Williams adduces strong evidence for this scenario when he notes that when Manannán's father is referred to in the earlier literature—not least in 'The Book of Invasions'—his name is always given as some variation on 'Alloid', not Lir/Ler.[26]

None of this, however, explains why an idiomatic expression should suddenly morph into a literary character around the turn of the thirteenth century. Nor is he minor: Lir-the-character first appears in the *Acallam*, around 1220, where (as we saw) he is identified as the possessor of Síd Finnachaid and as a principal personage and patriarch among the Túatha Dé, named fourth after Bodb Derg, Óengus, and the shadowy Finnbarr of Síd Meda. Tellingly Finnbarr is another high medieval addition to the Túatha Dé, and like Lir he became an important fairy king in later folklore—sometimes being understood as the king of all the Irish fairies.[27] (As a result, nineteenth-century enthusiasts often identified him as an ancient Irish god, which he had transparently never been.) It is not at all clear that the author of the *Acallam* identified this Lir with Manannán's father, or even that he took Manannán's sobriquet *mac Lir* to be a patronymic.[28] But he does tell us that Lir is the eldest of the Túatha Dé, and the most skilled in battle. As he is killed by the human warrior Caílte in the course of the story, part of the purpose of bringing Lir in seems to have been to re-emphasize the extraordinary valour of the warriors of the *fíana* by pitting one of them against a formidable— but ultimately disposable—figure.[29]

I have lingered on Lir because of a historical irony about his afterlife. He went on to capture the imagination of a whole troop of Anglo-Irish mythographers and mystics, who—thinking perhaps of his claim to be the oldest of the Túatha Dé Danann—retroactively installed him as a

---

26 *IIMWL*, 13. The Welsh, who seem to have borrowed the name Mannannán mac Lir from Ireland as *Manawydan fab Llŷr*, could easily and independently have taken the second element to be a patronymic, as I am arguing the Irish did, and thus created their own character Llŷr, who became an important if shadowy figure in Welsh genealogies. That *mab Llŷr* and *mac Lir* are exact cognates does *not* prove that there was an inherited figure predating both the Welsh and Irish attestations: on the dangers here see *IIMWL*, 11.

27 *Síd Meda* (*Síuil*) is Knockmagha/Knock Ma, near Tuam in Co. Galway. For *Síd Finnachaid* see above, 228, fn.106.

28 See Nagy, 'Some strands and strains', 103.

29 *TEI*, 144, Stokes (ed.) 'Acallamh na senórach', ll.5185–6.

major divinity in the pantheon as they understood it. How this was accomplished is discussed later in this study. A further contributing factor in the late–Victorian enthusiasm for Lir was his supposed link with Shakespeare's King Lear, via Welsh tradition and English chronicles.[30] The connection—if there is one—is indirect at best, and Lir and Lear have next to nothing in common, the only banal point of resemblance being that both famously suffer with their children.

That brings us to 'The Tragic Deaths of the Children of Lir', which was composed during the fifteenth century, probably (as Caoimhín Breatnach has persuasively argued) in the Franciscan monastery of Multyfarnham in what is now Co. Westmeath.[31] The monastic context is telling, for this most famous of Irish 'myths' is not, strictly speaking, a myth at all, though it certainly uses mythological characters. Rather it is a religious anecdote used to epitomize a moral truth, in this case the Christian virtue of fortitude, the patient bearing of suffering. The story

---

30 The link is as follows. The Welsh cognate of Irish *Ler* is *Llŷr*, and this was certainly understood to be a person, the father of a number of important Welsh literary characters. Then, in the twelfth century, the pseudohistorian and chronicler Geoffrey of Monmouth identified *Leir* as a one-time king of Britain and the father of three daughters; Geoffrey might have invented the name independently from a false etymology of Leicester as the 'city of Leir', but, on the other hand, he was familiar to some degree with Welsh tradition and his imagination may have been sparked off by stories of the travails among the family of Llŷr. (Certainly thirteenth-century translators of Geoffrey into Welsh rendered his Leir as Llŷr). Geoffrey's story of Leir and his daughters then reached Shakespeare through a number of later chroniclers, a process discussed in *King Lear*, ed. R. A. Foakes (London. 1997), 92–100. Earlier Celtic and Shakespearean scholars were more confident of direct links between Lir/Ler and Llŷr, and between Llŷr and Leir/Lear, than present scepticism allows. See Sims-Williams, *IIMWL*, 11, 13, and *Trioedd Ynys Prydein: The Welsh Triads*, ed. & trans. R. Bromwich [4th edn.] (Cardiff, 2014), 421.

31 C. Breatnach, 'The Religious Significance of *Oidheadh Chloinne Lir*', *Ériu* 50 (1999), 1–40. For such a famous story there has been surprisingly little critical assessment and there is no modern edn. Text in 'The *Tri Thruaighe na Scéalaigheachta* (i.e. the "Three Most Sorrowful tales") of Erinn, ii., The fate of the Children of Lir', ed. E. O'Curry, *Atlantis* 4 (1863), 113–57; also R. O'Duffy, *Oidhe Chloinne Lir; The fate of the children of Lir* (Dublin, 1883, 1897); see also Breatnach's article, fn.11. Discussion of the tale in relation to 'The Frenzy of Suibhne' (*Buile Shuibhne*) in J. Carney, *Studies in Irish Literature and History* (Dublin, 1979), 129–64; a recent cultural history which touches on the story, J. Beveridge, *Children into Swans: Fairy Tales and the Pagan Imagination* (Montreal & Kingston, 2014), is not really concerned with the details of the Irish text. That the tale's author was the same as that of *Oidheadh Chloinne Tuireann* and *Oidheadh Chloinne hUisneach*—as Thurneysen and Robin Flower thought—is as yet unproven; see *Oidheadh Chloinne hUisneach (The Violent Death of the Children of Uisneach)*, ed. & trans. C. Mac Giolla Léith (London, 1993), 22–5.

of the Children of Lir offers perhaps the most blatant example of a theme sounded throughout this book: that the Irish gods, as we know them, owe at least as much to Christianity as they do to paganism.

It begins with Bodb Derg, son of the Dagda, embroiled, once again, in political dispute. He has been elected king of the Túatha Dé Danann, much to the annoyance of Lir, who seems on the verge of occupying the same oppositional role as the sons of Midir in the *Acallam*, holding out against Bodb's pre-eminence. But any potential feud is circumvented via a marriage alliance: to appease Lir, Bodb gives him one of his foster-daughters, Aobh.[32] Aobh bears two sets of twins to Lir—a girl, Fionnghuala, and a boy, Aodh, plus two further boys, Fiachra and Conn. Aobh dies giving birth to the latter two, in what is to my knowledge the only explicit example in the whole of Irish tradition of a woman of the *síd* dying in childbirth.[33] Wanting to keep Lir happy, Bodb dispatches another daughter, Aoife, to marry the widowed Lir. But in the manner of the classic wicked stepmother, Aoife resents the affection in which her sister's children are held and plots to murder them. En route with her stepchildren to the house of Bodb, she orders her servant to kill them, but he refuses. Enraged, Aoife first tries to kill the children herself, but lacking the courage forces the children into a lake and uses her magic to transform them into swans. When Bodb hears of this, he punishes Aoife and turns her into a 'demon of the air' for all eternity—an interesting ontological change of direction. The children then spend nine hundred years as swans, forced to sojourn for three sets of three hundred years in three different locations. Throughout, Fionnghuala nobly fortifies her brothers with her example, even as their miseries continue. At the end of nine hundred years—during which time Ireland has been converted to Christianity—the swans encounter a saintly monk, Mochaomhóg, who blesses them. The spell is broken and they revert to their human form, now decrepit and near death. The saint baptizes them, and their souls ascend to heaven.

---

32 This is an Early Modern Irish spelling for a name which would have been *Áeb* in Old Irish: I use the Old Irish spelling here for now-familiar figures such as Bodb Derg to avoid confusion, though the text in fact uses the later form *Bodhbh Dearg*.

33 Macha, wife of Crunnchu mac Agnomain in the mid-ninth-century saga 'The Debility of the Ulstermen' (*Noínden Ulad*), is sometime said to have died giving birth to twins; her status as an otherworld woman is only implied, and the text does not actually say that she dies. See *Noínden Ulad: The Debility of the Ulidians*, ed. & trans. V. Hull, *Celtica* 8 (1968), 1–42, 29, 38.

There are many points of contact with what had gone before in this problematic tale. Most obviously, as in the *Acallam* and 'The Fosterage of the House of Two Vessels', this is a story about the conversion of members of the Túatha Dé Danann to Christianity through the agency of a saint. And as with Lí Ban—another example of that theme—stress is laid upon the length of time the characters spend languishing in transformed form. As with Eithne and Lí Ban, the virtues of the Christian faith are appreciated and upheld by a female figure—it is Fionnghuala who encourages her brothers—and the focus is on her suffering and spiritual transformation. Fionnghuala mysteriously comes to believe in God before the coming of Christianity to Ireland—another act of grace, like that of Eithne's conversion in 'The Fosterage'—and he explicitly intervenes:

> 'My brothers', said Fionnghuala, 'have faith in the most splendid true God of truth, who created heaven with its clouds, and earth with its fruits, and the sea with its wonders, and you shall receive help and full relief from the Lord.'
>
> 'We do believe', they said.
>
> 'And I believe with you', said Fionnghuala, 'in the faultless true God, the truly all-knowing one.' And they believed in the proper hour and received help and protection from the Lord after that. And neither tempest nor rough weather affected them from that time onwards.[34]

The 'proper hour' is implied here, perhaps, to be the time of the Crucifixion, for it is explicitly the very worst night of snow and cold that the Children of Lir experience, the freakish weather reflecting the cosmic calamity of Christ's death.[35]

But what is distinctive in our tale is the fact that the transformed figures are all children. The two older children may be on the edge of adolescence, but the other two are clearly very young. (One suspects that this story was taken up so enthusiastically in the nineteenth century because it resonated with that era's notorious mixture of exploitative and sentimental attitudes towards children.) Nowhere else do we find an

---

34 *Oidheadh Chloinne Lir*, ed. & trans. E. O'Curry, 'The Fate of the Children of Lir', 144, 145.

35 We might compare the various versions of the Old Irish saga *Aided Conchobuir* ('The Violent Death of Conchobor') in which the Crucifixion is accompanied by darkness and 'a great trembling over the elements'; analysis in Williams, *Fiery Shapes*, 18–19.

emphasis on the suffering children of the Túatha Dé Danann. It has been suggested that this story is an adaptation to theological morality of an older mythological tale, but there is no particular need to posit an original that has been altered; rather, it should be seen as a late medieval religious parable using a native mythological setting.[36] This explains the prominence of Lir. Because he was the most papery and undeveloped figure in the whole pantheon, he provided a convenient hook in the tradition upon which the author could hang a new story. Lir's four children are likely to be the author's own invention, and Fionnghuala in particular is too good to be true; she is an idealized character with whom the author perhaps unconsciously identifies. For all that, he does not seem very interested or invested in traditions about the god-peoples *per se*. It is tellingly difficult to square the winsome children of Lir with the ambiguous and imposing Manannán, theoretically their older half-brother. They are incommensurate.

Why did the author chose to set his story among the Túatha Dé Danann at all? It was not unusual for the writers of late medieval pious fables to turn to figures from Greek and Roman antiquity, such as Xerxes or Cleopatra, for vivid illustrations of moral truths; as famed personages in the national pseudohistory the Túatha Dé occupied a local version of the same role. A further answer lies in the author's preoccupation with the passage of time, so insistently harped upon. In our tale, the Túatha Dé find it impossible to imagine that death is inevitable, and in this they suffer from the same existential conundrum as humanity, albeit in a more attenuated form. They seem to believe themselves nearly immortal (as they actually are in the Fenian Cycle, for example), but the story belies this and death seems merely deferred. Even though they are full members of the Túatha Dé Danann, the children of Lir are *old* when they recover their human forms. The author seems to have imagined that the people of the *síd* enjoy lifespans much greater than those of normal humans, but not unending or unageing, very much in the manner of the biblical patriarchs, some of whom (significantly) are also said to have lived for more than nine hundred years.[37]

As the story ends, Lir's *síd* lies empty and choked with nettles, while the Túatha Dé seem to have been wiped from the face of the earth. It is

36 See Breatnach, 'The Religious Significance', 11–14.

37 Adam lives for 930 years, Seth for 932, Noah for 950, and Methuselah 969. The two sets of twins (speaking impressionistically) seem to have been transformed when aged around twelve and eight respectively.

telling that this happens just after the Children of Lir are mysteriously inspired to believe in the true God: if my suggestion that their moment of conversion is coincident with the Crucifixion holds, Christ's death and resurrection seems to have exorcized the Túatha Dé. As a result there exists a poignant contrast between temporary and permanent happiness, for all happiness in time—even if supernaturally long-lasting—is a mere eyeblink compared with eternal bliss. The story is a kind of *memento mori*, and harmonizes with the themes of much early modern Irish religious literature: hell, torment, Christ's passion, and the joy of heaven.[38] And by being given a mythological setting, a familiar homiletic theme has been imbued not only with local colour, but with an unfamiliar kind of scale and sweep.

SOCIAL COLLAPSE

The second tale to be examined also criticizes the society of the Túatha Dé Danann, but in a less theological and more disturbing vein. In 'The Tragic Deaths of the Children of Tuireann' we find a society buckling under internal pressure because, for all its antique splendour, it lacks basic Christian virtues.[39] It is probably a composition of the 1500s.[40]

An inset episode within the larger story of the second battle of Moytura, the tale begins with the familiar story of the replacement of Núadu's arm and the arrival of Lug at Tara as the Fomorians begin their onslaught. But at this critical juncture internal rivalry bedevils the Túatha Dé. The three sons of Tuireann (older *Tuirenn*)—Brian, Iuchar,

---

38 Breatnach ('The Religious Significance', 29) points out that the fifteenth and sixteenth centuries saw the enthusiastic translation of continental devotional literature into Irish.

39 This is a view which has been put forward by Caoimhín Breatnach, '*Oidheadh Chloinne Tuireann* agus *Cath Maige Tuired*: Dha Shampla de Mhiotas Eiseamlaireach', *Éigse* 32 (2000), 35-4.

40 The tale goes back to eleventh century at least, and is summarized in *Lebor Gabála*; see R. Thurneysen, 'Tuirill Bicren und seine Kinder', *ZCP* 12 (1918), 239-50. Text in '*Oidhe Chloinne Tuireann: The Fate of the Children of Tuireann*, ed. & trans. R. J. O'Duffy (Dublin, 1901) [henceforth *OCT*]. Note that there is a bizarre Latin adaptation from *c*.1600 of part of the story in BL MS Harleian 5280, the only Latin translation of any part of the Mythological Cycle known to me. Lug is renamed 'Mundulius' ('Elegant One'), Tuireann becomes 'Turnus'—evoking Virgil's *Aeneid*—while the Fomorians are historicized as Vikings. See '*Oidheadh Chloinne Tuireann*: A Sixteenth Century Latin Fragment', ed. & trans. R. B. Bhreathnach, *Éigse* 1 (1939/40), 249-57.

and Iucharba—are locked in a feud with the sons of Cáinte, who are named Cú, Cethen, and Cían.[41] The last named is Lug's father. The sons of Tuireann encounter Cían alone and resolve to murder him; he attempts to escape by changing himself into a pig and hiding amongst a herd of swine. But the trio sees through Cían's magical disguise, and he changes himself back into human form just before they beat him to death. When the murderers try to bury the mangled remains, the earth refuses six times to receive the corpse.

Lug knows instinctively that his father has been killed and immediately suspects the sons of Tuireann. The eldest brother, Brian, barefacedly lies about the murder in front of Lug and the assembled Túatha Dé Danann ('we have not killed your father'), but nonetheless announces his willingness to pay Cían's *éric*, the legal compensation for homicide.[42] Lug details a series of tasks to be achieved, largely consisting of the collection of a series of precious objects from far away or inaccessible places. One of them, the pigskin of Tuis, King of Greece, is a magical panacea which heals all injuries while life remains in the wounded person: this object plays a prominent role in the denouement of the tale. The brothers set off, and when they have acquired most of the treasures—thanks to an unlovely combination of cunning and thuggery—Lug magically makes them forget the last, so that they return and present him with the *éric*. He then reminds them of their uncompleted task, which is to give three shouts upon the hill of Modhchaoin in Lochlann (here meaning Scandinavia). Modhchaoin and his children are under a solemn obligation not to allow anyone to shout upon that hill (it is never explained why). The three brothers succeed in giving the shouts but are cut to pieces in the process. More dead than alive, they crawl back to Ireland and beg Lug for the magical pigskin, which would heal their wounds in an instant. He coldly refuses, and as they expire, he has his revenge.

It will be plain that the story is essentially—indeed deliberately—an ugly one. The rot in the society of the god-peoples runs deep, and is not merely expressed in the relationship between the sons of Tuireann and Lug. It is also visible in the way the gods quake beneath the Fomorian jackboot. Núadu, who as their king should protect them, is spineless; only the newcomer, Lug, is able to see what must be done. Shortly after he comes to Tara with his retinue, he observes the Túatha Dé Danann

---

41 Cáinte, Cían's father in this text, replaces the more usual Dían Cécht; see *CMT*, ed. Gray, 126.

42 *OCT*, 93.

standing up before the team of Fomorians who have been sent to extract tribute:

'Why did you stand up before that surly, ugly band, but did not stand up before us?' [said Lug].
'We have to do that', said the king of Ireland [Núadu], 'for if one of us were a child only a month old [and stayed] sitting before them, they would not think it too small a reason to kill us.'
'I swear', said Lug, 'that a desire to kill them has come upon me.'[43]

And when the Fomorians (here termed 'foreigners') come ashore and begin plundering Bodb Derg in Connaught, Lug rushes to the king for aid. 'I will not give you assistance', Núadu says, 'for I will not go to avenge a deed that has not been done upon me.' Núadu, the noble, humble king of 'The Second Battle of Moytura', is now depicted as a coward ruling over an enfeebled race. It is not difficult to detect criticism of the political policies pursued by some native lords here, given the waxing and waning in Ireland's domination by the English in the likely period of the text's composition.[44] As Caoimhín Breatnach notes, the tale's caustic portrayal of the Túatha Dé stands in sharp contrast to that in texts of the pre-Norman period, in which they functioned (sometimes at least) as exemplary figures.[45]

The problems of Túatha Dé society are made flesh in the sons of Tuireann, and in particular in the memorable Brian, a rare medieval portrait of a psychopath.[46] Although he is conspicuously brave and intellectually accomplished, he is also a shameless liar and manipulator of the sympathies of others. He leads his brothers into acts of brutal vio-

43 *OCT*, 73.

44 Classic account in K. W. Nicholls, *Gaelic and Gaelicised Ireland in the Middle Ages* (Dublin, 1972), and see also P. Duffy, D. Edwards, & E. FitzPatrick (eds.), *Gaelic Ireland, c.1250-c.1650: land, lordship and settlement* (Dublin, 2001).

45 C. Breatnach, '*Oidheadh Chloinne Tuireann* agus *Cath Maige Tuired*', 35–46. A certain *froideur* between Lug and Núadu is typical of the late sagas, also appearing in the late version of 'The Second Battle of Moytura'; see *CMT*, ed. Gray, 126.

46 He might be usefully compared with the Welsh character Efnisien in *Branwen uerch Lyr*, the Second Branch of the *Mabinogi*, written c.1100. He has much also in common too with Gwydion fab Dôn in the Fourth Branch: both disguise themselves as poets in order to obtain supernatural pigs; both are accompanied by a clearly junior brother (or brothers, in the case of Brian); both are magicians; both are conspicuously skilled as poet-storytellers.

lence and deception that ultimately result in their deaths. Their murder of Cían is representative:

> It was not long until all the swine fled, except for one; and it saw a stand of trees and headed towards it, and as it passed through the wood Brian hurled his spear at it, so that he put it through the thick part of its chest. And the pig screamed, and said: 'You have done evil to cast at me, when you knew me.'
>
> Then Brian said, 'I think that is human speech'.
>
> 'In origin', said the pig, 'I am a man, and I am Cían, the son of Cáinte; spare me!'
>
> 'We will indeed', said Iucharba and Iuchar, 'and we are sorry about what has happened to you.'
>
> But Brian said, 'I swear by the gods of the air, if life returned to you seven times, I would deprive you of it.'
>
> 'Well', said Cían, 'grant me a favour'.
>
> 'We shall', said Brian.
>
> 'Allow me to transform back into my own shape', said Cían.
>
> 'We will allow it', said Brian, 'for I often think less of killing a man than a pig.'[47]

It is clear that while Iuchar and Iucharba—the archetypal dim henchmen—are thugs, they lack the chilling malice of their brother. (Later the two of them want to confess to the murder, but are overruled by Brian.) The horror of the deed is encapsulated in the earth's rejection of Cían's corpse: six times it refuses to receive and so conceal the body. The earth itself acts a character in the drama: it speaks to Lug, telling him that the sons of Tuireann have killed his father. To my knowledge, this semi-personification of the earth (*an talamh*) is unprecedented in Irish tradition. It would be interesting to know how the saga's original audience visualized this sequence as they heard it—presumably a voice (of what gender?) speaking from the ground.[48]

In this tale, the society of the Túatha Dé Danann is infused with tension and hatred. Significantly, the origin of the feud between the sons of Tuireann and the sons of Cainte lies in the fact that both trios are 'equally high in degree'.[49] Internal rivalry tears the body politic asunder,

---

47 *OCT*, 13–4, 80–1.
48 *OCT*, 19, 87.
49 *OCT*, 21 (*cómhárd a cóimhchéim*), 89.

and Cían's murder is described as a kind of origin-legend for kin-slaying in Ireland: Lug says 'evil will come to the Túatha Dé Danann from this deed, and long shall kin-slaying (*fionghal*) be done in Ireland after it.'[50] Although Cían is clearly an innocent victim, in the context of such rivalry could the act of murder, one wonders, have happened just as well the other way around? Even Cían's magical transformation into a pig rooting about in a herd is less than reassuring. Possibly the audience would have thought of the Gadarene swine in the Gospels of Mark and Luke, in which Jesus casts out demons who then drown themselves in the sea of Galilee—for the social order of the Túatha Dé is clearly bent on self-destruction in the same way.[51]

Nor is Lug without inner tensions of his own. In this tale he is more disquieting—harsher and more vindictive—than anywhere else in the corpus. He is closely associated with Manannán, who in the tale is referred to but never seen. Manannán's purpose is to act as an alternative centre of Túatha Dé power within the story's political landscape. Lug comes to Tara from fosterage in Manannán's overseas kingdom, and his confident agency derives directly from his foster-father, who supplies him with magical weapons and accoutrements. Manannán's power contrasts with Núadu's hopeless weakness, and a new spin is put on the old idea of the sea-god's overseas otherworld, here clearly envisaged as an enclave in which the Túatha Dé Danann have retained their dignity and independence.

Lug appears to be a kind of natural monotheist, a traditional designation for virtuous pagans in medieval literatures.[52] Not so the sons of Tuireann; above we saw Brian swear by 'the gods of the air', which implies that his gods are demons, conventionally supposed to build themselves bodies of vapour.[53] Lug in contrast cries aloud to 'God, whom I adore!'

---

50 *OCT*, 22, 90.

51 Mark 5:11–13; Luke 8:30–33. In the oldest attested précis of the story, from the eleventh century, the animal into which Cían transformed himself seems to have been a 'lapdog' (*oirce*); this was very similar to a word for pig (*orc*) and this misunderstanding—if it is such—thus entered the tradition. See P. A. Bernhardt-House, *Werewolves, Magical Hounds, and Dog-headed Men in Celtic Literature: A Typological Study of Shape-Shifting* (Lewiston, 2010), 226–8, and *LGE*, ed. Macalister, iv., 134, 135.

52 *Beowulf* is the classic example: like Lug, the noble characters in the Old English poem believe in one God, the omnipotent creator of all, who watches over the world and punishes transgression. We hear of the worship of demons (i.e. pagan deities) only as a response to terrible circumstances.

53 See Williams, *Fiery Shapes*, 51–2, for airy demons in Augustine, and L. Barkan,

when he learns of his father's killing.[54] (The modern reader thus enjoys the irony of hearing a figure whom we know to reflect an ancient pagan divinity pray to the Christian God, but this would not have been perceptible to the tale's author or audience.) And while he shows mercy to the thoroughly undeserving Fomorian Bres, his virtue is combined with a capacity for implacable coldness and calculation: he uses magic to trick the sons of Tuireann out of the means with which to heal themselves. He is curiously Achilles-like, embodying the tale's atmosphere of brightly lit violence. It is worth noting that it is only with this tale—very late indeed in the tradition of Irish mythology—that any association enters between Lug and the sun. Nineteenth-century writers tended to identify him as a sun-god; the association may have come about thanks to two moments in our tale in which the radiance of Lug's countenance is said to rival the sun.[55] This is, however, the kind of hyperbole typical of the late 'romantic tales', and has no bearing on the character of the pre-Christian Lug.

In overview, the story's conspicuous virtues include it being well-plotted and intensely dramatic. We find ourselves in a world akin to that of international medieval romance—the most protean of all high medieval European secular genres—and a long way from native Irish mythology. For a time the merely national is left behind as the sons of Tuireann travel through an exotic, semi-classical version of the Mediterranean and Near East, mounting a raid on the orchard of the Hesperides before brutalizing Persia, Greece, and Sicily. (The connection with the Hesperides brings in a deliberate parallel to the Labours of Hercules, of which this is a dark reflection.) There are delightfully imaginative moments, typical of the romantic tales. The horses of the king of Sicily, for example, come back to life if killed, 'provided their bones are found to be collected', while Manannán's magical self-propelling boat has the peculiar property that it is forbidden 'to be grumbled at': perhaps it refuses to budge until its hurt feelings have been soothed.[56] One of the brothers' tasks involves scuba-diving, for which the wily Brian has come prepared:

The Gods Made Flesh: Metamorphosis and the Pursuit of Paganism (New Haven, CT, & London, 1986), 99–100, for Augustinian views of demonic illusions more generally; see above, 146, for Isidore's view that demons dwell in regions of damp vapour.

   54 *OCT*, 20, 87.

   55 *OCT*, 15, 82–3.

   56 *OCT*, 97, 101.

Then Brian donned his diving suit and put his transparent glass helmet on his head, and plunged into the water; it is said that he was a fortnight walking in the salt water...[57]

Far-flung Mediterranean and Middle Eastern regions only really entered the world of Irish storytelling in the eleventh century (we recall that one recension of *Lebor Gabála* described the Túatha Dé Danann's alliance with the Athenians); it is notable that in the précis of this tale in *Lebor Gabála* the brothers' itinerary is less explicitly exotic and classical in flavour. Sicily is mentioned, but the magic apples which the brothers have to collect belong not to the Hesperides but to a magical region under the Irish Sea.[58] The increase in lush exoticism on display in the version we have aptly illustrates the change in Irish literary fashions between 1100 and 1500.

Also effective is the modulation of tone, whereby the sombre and the comic are interplaited. So much is clear in the story's opening, which begins with a version of the story of the replacement of Núadu's arm. The author makes several telling changes to the conventional version. First, he introduces a comic parallel. Núadu is missing an arm, but his doorkeeper is missing an eye, and the physicians showcase their skill by transplanting that of the doorkeeper's pet cat into his eye-socket: 'that was both convenient and inconvenient for him, for when he wanted to sleep or rest, then the eye would start at the squeaking of the mice... but when he wanted to watch a host or an assembly, then it would be in deep sleep and slumber'.[59] But soon things become more disturbing. The theme that there is something deeply wrong with the Túatha Dé Danann is sounded when we find that Núadu's side is blackened by a *daol*, literally a 'beetle', but here imagined as a parasite that burrows into human flesh. Still less savoury is the physicians' harvesting of an arm for transplant:

And Míach looked for another arm of the same length and thickness to give to him [Núadu], and all the Túatha Dé Danann were examined, but no arm was found which would suit him, except that of Módhán, the swineherd.

---

57 *OCT*, 127, 57; 'diving suit', *earrad uisge*, lit. 'water-apparel'; 'transparent glass helmet', *léasbaire gloine*, lit. 'light-(admitting) helmet of glass'.

58 *LGE*, iv., ed. Macalister, 134–7.

59 *OCT*, 2, 68.

'Would the bones of his arm suit you?', everyone asked.

'That is what we would prefer', they replied.

And accordingly a man set out for the arm, and brought it back with him to Tara, and it was given to Míach.[60]

One wonders what the unfortunate Módhán made of the commandeering of his arm, and perhaps the reader is meant to sense that Núadu, who cannot defend his people, is nonetheless prepared to exploit their bodies in the most literal fashion imaginable.

Similar play with tone (and with a modulation between comedy and violence) is apparent in the adventures of the three brothers. Brian's penchant for spectacular brutality is matched by his skill, intelligence, and ready wit. Twice the brothers have to disguise themselves as poets, and the two younger brothers fret that they cannot compose verse. When in the court of Tuis, King of Greece:

… the king's poets stood up to sing their poems for the people. Brian son of Tuireann spoke then to his brothers, [asking them] to sing a poem for the king.

'We don't *have* a poem!' they answered, 'and do not ask us to do anything apart from that which we are used to—taking whatever we want by force of arms, if we are stronger, and if they are more powerful, falling at their hands.'

'That is not a happy method of composing a poem', said Brian.[61]

In both cases Brian effortlessly produces a finely turned piece of subtly threatening bardic verse, before unleashing an orgy of violence; the amiable King of Persia, for example, has his brain smashed out through the back of his skull. The author masterfully balances repetition against the subversion of expectation: in my favourite incident in the story, Brian comes (in his diving gear) to the underwater home of 'a company of women engaged in needlework and embroidery', from whom he has to steal a magic cooking spit. The reader shudders at the thought of the monstrous acts Brian may be about to perpetrate upon these defenceless ladies. But—completely unexpectedly—they catch sight of him and fall about. Their leader says:

---

60 *OCT*, 3, 69.
61 *OCT*, 36–7, 106–7.

'Bold is the deed that you have put your hand to, for if your two brothers were along with you, the least valorous in prowess or valour of the one hundred and fifty women here would not let either you or them take the spit! Even so, take one of the spits away with you, since you are so undaunted, so courageous, and so brave as to try to carry it off with you despite us.'[62]

This incident in particular manipulates the audience's perception of the brothers, just as the cruelty of Lug's revenge makes us pity them, even though we know they are thoroughly nasty pieces of work. Amid the story's brutal symmetries, in the end it is not easy to distinguish heroes from villains.

VENTRY

Are the gods of Ireland actually Irish? Such a question might seem an impertinence—but we remember the pseudohistorical doctrines of 'The Book of Invasions', which insisted that Túatha Dé Danann had been invaders from outside. The gods' 'national identity' is one of the things which our last text, 'The Battle of Ventry', asks us to consider.

The story belongs to the Finn Cycle, and in its extant form it was composed in the second half of the fifteenth century, though it is clear that versions of the story existed as early as the twelfth century.[63] The theme is an 'endless battle', lasting a year and a day, between the *fíana* and the rest of the world, a battle supposed to have taken place upon the long sandy beach at Ventry, Co. Kerry. ('Ventry' is an anglicization of medieval Irish *fionn tráigh*, 'white strand'.) Much of the text consists of long descriptions of single combat. (The story of the love of Cáel and the *síd*-woman Créde in *Acallam na Senórach* fits into the story of the battle.) The tale begins with Ireland threatened by Dáire Donn ('the Brown'), 'the King of the Great World', who wants to take revenge upon Finn for an amatory indiscretion involving both the wife and the daughter of the king of the Franks. Dáire gathers a fantastical armada, including Vulcan, king of the Franks, Lughman, king of the Saxons, as well as the king (*rí*) of the Greeks—curiously named Margaret. The last member of

62 *OCT*, 57, 129.

63 *Cath Finntrágha*, ed. & trans. C. O'Rahilly (Dublin, 1962); the older edn. is *Cath Finntrága*, ed. & trans. K. Meyer (Oxford, 1885).

the invasion force is Margaret's daughter, the amazon Ógarmach.[64] Finn and the *fíana* face disastrous odds, and this is where the Túatha Dé Danann come in, although they only have a limited role. In dire need, the *fíana* send a messenger to the people of the *síd* to ask for their help defending Ireland:

> Then Bran son of Febal went to gather and muster the Túatha Dé Danann, and he went to Dún Sesnáin Sengabra in Conaill Gabra, and there was a feast being held there, and a great number of the young men of the Túatha Dé Danann were there, and there were three noble sons of the Túatha Dé Danann, namely, Ilbrecc the son of Manannán, and Némannach ('the Pearly') the son of Óengus, and Sigmall the grandson of Midir, and they made Bran son of Febal welcome and desired that his feet should be washed. 'Youths!', said Bran, 'we have a need more urgent than that'. And he began to tell them his story and to relate to them the strait that his son Conn Crithir was in. 'Stay with me tonight', said Sesnán, 'and my son, Dolb son of Seasnán, will go to Bodb Derg, the son of the Dagda, and he will bring together the Túatha Dé Danann to us.'
>
> And they did thus, and Dolb son of Sesnán went to Síd Ban Finn above Mag Femen (Slievenamon, Co. Tipperary), and it was there that Bodb Derg son of the Dagda was at that time, and Dolb relayed that news to him. 'Young man', said Bodb Derg, 'we are under no obligation to help the Irish out of that trouble.' 'Do not say that', said Dolb, 'since there is no king's son nor prince nor leader of one of Ireland's *fían*-bands whose wife is not of the Túatha Dé Danann, or whose mother or fostermother or sweetheart is not from among you; and they have given you a great deal of help every time *you* were in trouble.' 'Indeed I give our word of honour', said Bodb Derg, 'that it is right to answer you, thanks to your excellence as messenger.'
>
> And they sent off messengers to the Túatha Dé Danann wherever they were, and they all came to the place where Bodb Derg was, and they came to Dún Sesnáin. And they were there that

---

64 *Bolcán rí na Fraingci ⁊ Marghairéd rí na Gréigi*: the author surely cannot have thought *Margairéd* was a male name, though why he did not describe her as a *banfhlaith*, 'woman sovereign', is obscure to me. Perhaps he wanted to suggest that she should be imagined as the ruler of the Greeks in her own right, or—given the woman-warrior Ógarmach—to hint that the Greeks were a race of amazons.

night, and the next day they arose early and put on their noble shirts of silk and their decorated richly-embroidered tunics of many colours, and their thick, long-sided, resplendent coats of mail, and their ornamented helmets of gold and gems, and their protective green shields, and their heavy broad-sided strong swords, and their whetted spears with their broad, flat heads.[65]

This passage is full of surprises. As king of the Túatha Dé Danann, Bodb Derg—an instinctive isolationist—has to decide if the people of the *síd* have more in common with the Gaels than with the invaders: his dismissive use of the word *Éireannaigh*, 'Irishmen', has real force. After all, it was by the agency of the Gaels that the god-peoples—themselves once termed the 'men of Ireland' in 'The Second Battle of Moytura'—were dispossessed.[66] But ancient bad blood is transfigured by love: we saw that intermarriage between the Túatha Dé and the warriors of the *fíana* is characteristic of the Finn Cycle, and here it has the effect of instantly changing Bodb's mind and bringing the Túatha Dé 'into the war'.

The Irishness of the Túatha Dé Danann is cleverly stressed later in the story, when—for the first time within an Irish text—there is a non-Irish assessment of the native god-peoples. The world-king Dáire Donn notices that the *fíana* have been reinforced, and unsurprisingly, he wonders who these magnificently armed people are. He turns to his pet Irishman, the treacherous Glas:

'Glas, my friend... those people over there, are they the *fíana* of Ireland?'

'They are not', said Glas, 'but another group of the men of Ireland, who do not dare be on the surface of the earth, but live in *síd*-palaces (*sídhbroghaibh*) under the ground, that is to say, the

---

65 *Cath Finntrágha*, ed. & trans. O'Rahilly, 11–12.

66 The idea that the Túatha Dé Danann loathe the Irish is expressed most forcefully in *Eachtra Airt meic Cuind* ('The Adventure of Art son of Conn'), a late tale found in the fifteenth-century Book of Fermoy. There earthly, mortal Ireland is represented as a place especially despised by its former rulers and therefore suitable as a place of exile for the adulterous fairy-woman Bécuma. We are bluntly told that 'the Túatha Dé Danann hated the sons of Míl after they had been driven out of Ireland by them'—an inconvenient detail quite forgotten by the nineteenth-century romantics examined later in this book. See *Eachtra Airt meic Cuind ocus Tochmarc Delbchaime ingine Morgain*, ed. & trans. R. I. Best, 'The Adventures of Art son of Conn, and the Courtship of Delbchæm', *Ériu* 3 (1907), 152, 153.

Túatha Dé Danann, and I have come to announce battle from them.'[67]

Not only are they intermarried, but to an outsider's glance, the immortal Túatha Dé Danann and the mortal *fíana* are hard to tell apart. Glas includes the god-peoples in precisely the shared identity as 'men of Ireland' which Bodb Derg had aloofly disclaimed. In the context of the mid-to late fifteenth century the assertion that Irishness is not mere ethnicity surely had distinct political resonances, which Caoimhín Breatnach has persuasively set out.[68] The intervention of the Túatha Dé Danann in the story suggests an inclusive concept of Irish identity, and Breatnach sees this as applicable to the relationship between the Anglo-Norman and native Gaelic aristocracies in the fifteenth century. In this period, the word *Éireannaigh* ('Irishmen')—the favoured term in 'The Battle of Ventry' for Ireland's defenders, both the *fíana* and the Túatha Dé—begins to be used to refer to individuals from both backgrounds, and to mixed groups. The theme of intermarriage is also suggestive, echoing the frequency of marriage alliances between aristocratic families of natives and incomers. Indeed the tale may actually have been composed for a female patron of aristocratic Gaelic stock, Sadhbh Ní Mháille, who may have been married to a member of the Anglo-Norman Bourkes of Mayo; she certainly had close connections with the Anglo-Norman nobility.[69]

By implying that Irish identity is conferred by shared habitation, not racial lineage, the author of 'The Battle of Ventry' was using the traditional invasion narrative of Irish pseudohistory to a radical end. In 'The Book of Invasions', any people aspiring to become 'the men of Ireland' were obliged to wrest the island away from its current inhabitants, but here our author suggests that the dispossessed and the conquerors can both be 'Irishmen' on the same basis simultaneously. Within the world of the story, such a thing could only be possible because of the Túatha

---

67 *Cath Finntrágha*, ed. & trans. O'Rahilly, 13.

68 C. Breatnach, 'Cath Fionntrágha', *Léachtaí Cholm Cille* 25 (1995), 128–41 [in Irish]; see also his 'The Historical Context of *Cath Fionntrágha*', *Éigse* 28 (1994–5), 138–55, and *Patronage, Politics and Prose* (Maynooth, 1996), 8–12. Also useful is K. Simms, 'Bards and Barons: The Anglo-Irish Aristocracy and the Native Culture', in R. Bartlett & A. MacKay (eds.), *Medieval Frontier Societies* (Oxford, 1989), 177–97.

69 Breatnach's argument has been usefully summarized in English by Kaarina Hollo in *CHIL* i., 117–8. On Sadhbh Ní Mháille see *Cath Finntrágha*, ed. O'Rahilly, viii–x; our earliest text of 'The Battle of Ventry' is dedicated to her, which does not prove that it was composed for her, but is nonetheless suggestive.

Dé's immortality and withdrawal to the *síd*-mounds. In the real world, such an implication presumably reflected a pragmatic desire for a policy of peaceful accommodation between Gaelic and Anglo-Norman lords.[70]

The role of the Túatha Dé Danann in 'The Battle of Ventry' is therefore compressed but of great significance. In terms of personnel, Bodb Derg is in charge (as is normal in tales of the Finn Cycle), and the major figures belong to the second and third generations of the god-peoples, if we imagine the Dagda at the centre: we meet Ilbrecc son of Manannán, Némannach son of Óengus, and Sigmall grandson of Midir. But as individual figures the Túatha Dé reach an apogee of vagueness here, for no attempt is made to differentiate them or invest them with any complexity of character. Instead we are given a long alliterating roll call of their warriors as they set off to fight at Ventry, and while some of the names are borrowed from a version of *Táin Bó Cúailnge*, many seem to have been simply made up to add to a onrushing wave of evocative and resonant, but essentially spurious, fairy names. We hear of Donn from Síd Becuisce ('Smallwater'), Dreagan Dronuallach, Fer an Bérla Bhinn ('The Man of the Sweet Speech'), and Dolb 'of the Bright Teeth', among many more. Apart from their wealth and underground dwellings, these figures seem barely supernatural; and while there *is* one vivid description of uncanny beings in the story—in which we hear of the cries of airy beings and demon women, even of the earth itself—these entities are in no way associated with the Túatha Dé Danann.

FADING OUT

At this point we can make some final reflections to round off the first half of this book. By the end of the Middle Ages there were a number of figures among the Túatha Dé Danann in possession of very long trajectories, a small number of whom reflected pre-Christian deities, at least to some degree: Lug, Núadu, the Dagda, and Bóand are secure examples. Then there were various figures who probably had no roots in Irish paganism but had entered the tradition during the high Middle Ages, Lir being a likely example. Beyond these there was a crowded periphery of minor figures, some of whom had defined and consistent roles, such as

70 Breatnach ('The Historical Context', 140–54) relates this in detail to the settlement between Richard MacWilliam Bourke and Aodh Ruadh Ó Domhnaill in 1469; Aodh Ruadh may well have been Sadhbh Ní Mháille's husband.

Abcán, Lug's harper; many, however, were probably invented off the cuff by storytellers for particular tales.

There is a substantial chance that accidents of survival may mean that we have little knowledge of Túatha Dé figures that medieval Irish poets and storytellers might well have regarded as important. In particular it is clear from the *dindshenchas* and other sources that there was a rich body of tradition about some of the children of the Dagda—Cermait, Ainge, perhaps Brigit as well—which has only come down to us in the form of summaries or compressed allusions. A classicist friend once remarked to me how odd it is that no *literary* account of the career of the hero Perseus has survived from antiquity; we know his story only from allusions and mythographies. In Irish mythology equivalents to this state of affairs are common, and to a worse degree: often we can barely even guess at what we have lost. It is important to grasp just how *big* the Túatha Dé Danann was imagined to be: if a database of every member named in Irish medieval literature were compiled it would (I suspect) run to several hundred names. We are dealing not with a pantheon, but with an imagined people.

If the stories of the Children of Tuireann and the Children of Lir are anything to go by, it is difficult to avoid the general sense that from the fourteenth century uncanniness ceased to be among the aesthetic aims in writing about the Túatha Dé Danann. (It is still there, however, in the stranger and more poignant episodes of the *Acallam*.) The late stories about them are moralizing and melodramatic. As Irish culture changed dramatically, the god-peoples progressively lost touch with their role in pre-Norman literature as exemplary figures and ideological symbols. Two of the stories we have looked at suggest that the Túatha Dé Danann should be seen as profoundly inadequate, whether religiously or politically.

In short, a long chain of cultural developments ensured that, by the early modern period, writers in Irish had lost all awareness that some among the Túatha Dé Danann had once been their island's native gods and goddesses. A telling example is the priest and historian Geoffrey Keating—one of the most learned Irish writers of the early seventeenth century. When he wanted to depict ancient Irish paganism, it was the Bible and hagiography to which he turned, and not to the stories we know as the Mythological Cycle. Keating's Irish pagans bow down before a golden calf—replicating the most prominent instance of Israelite idolatry in the Bible—and he identified only two native deities: one was the spurious god Bel (or Ba'al) of 'Cormac's Glossary', now promoted to the status of primary god, and the other was Crom Crúach, the 'chief idol' supposedly cast down by Patrick.[71] Members of the Túatha Dé Danann simply did not register on Keating's radar as reflexes of ancient deities, and in this he was typical of his times.

Neither does any English writer associated with Ireland in the period show any awareness of native gods, though one of them, the Elizabethan poet Edmund Spenser, managed to hint at them in a characteristically disturbing way. Though Spenser was infamously up to his neck in the brutal imposition of English rule in Ireland, the country seemed to get under his skin. Much of the last complete book of his colossal poem *The Faerie Queene* (1593, 1596) is set in Ireland, so that his national epic seems to morph progressively into a colonial romance. In the final fragment of the poem he describes a gathering of the classical gods on 'Arlo hill' (Galtymore, a low mountain on the border between counties Limerick and Tipperary), and weaves an intricate Ovidian account of the punishment wreaked by the goddess Diana upon an Irish river nymph and the god Faunus.[72] Spenser may have been aware of native traditions of the *dindshenchus* type, but these are not Irish deities: the Túatha Dé Danann have been displaced in their own landscape by the international pantheon of Greece and Rome. Nonetheless, it as though the gaps where they should be can be seen through Spenser's English poetry: the gathering of deities on a notable hill half-echoes the *síd*-mounds of native tradition, and the personification of rivers takes us back to Bóand, goddess of the Boyne, and to Loigodēvā, enigmatic calf-goddess of the Corcu Loígde.[73]

And with that, the Irish gods fade; it was to be nearly three centuries before they re-emerged and took up divine shapes again.

---

71 G. Keating, *Foras feasa ar Érinn: the history of Ireland*, ed. & trans. D. Comyn & P. S. Dinneen (4 vols., London, 1902–14), ii., 346–7; ii., 246, 247 (for Bel); and ii., 122, 123 (for Crom Crúach, here Crom *Cruaidh*).

72 See Book 7, canto 6 in *The Faerie Queene*, ed. A. C. Hamilton (London, 1980), 714–24, and see T. Herron, *Spenser's Irish Work: Poetry, Plantation and Colonial Reformation* (Aldershot, 2007), 160–2, for the political and ideological context of these deities.

73 Important discussion of the interaction between languages in Tudor Ireland in A. Doyle, *A History of the Irish Language from the Norman Invasion to Independence* (Oxford, 2015), 40–50.

PART TWO

7

THE IMAGINATION OF THE COUNTRY

TOWARDS A NATIONAL PANTHEON

I saw gods rising up from the earth.

—1 SAMUEL 28:13

THE SECOND HALF of this book represents a fresh point of departure in two ways. Firstly, it turns from a complex range of texts to a complex range of persons. Secondly, it turns from writing in Irish to material written for the most part in English.

The sagas, pseudohistories, and poems examined hitherto had all been part of a developing literary tradition, one in which the Túatha Dé Danann and the people of the *síd* had been major players. That tradition had certainly been responsive to outside influences and to internal cultural realignments, but it had nevertheless been essentially continuous, and—at least until the beginning of the seventeenth century—confident of its own value.[1] Nearly three decades after the Flight of the Earls in 1607—often regarded as the moment of apocalypse for the native Gaelic order—Geoffrey Keating felt able to set down the traditional framework of 'The Book of Invasions', including the Túatha Dé Danann, as part of his panoramic narrative of Irish history. And even in the late eighteenth century the poet Brian Merriman could play with the conventions of the native otherworld and its inhabitants in his exuberant masterpiece *Cúirt an mheon-oíche* ('The Midnight Court'), at a time when Irish-language culture was undergoing a period of contraction and decline.[2] That de-

1 See M. Caball & K. Hollo, 'The literature of later medieval Ireland, 1200–1600: from the Normans to the Tudors', in *CHIL*, i., 74–139.

2 A consideration of Merriman's poem—and Aoibheall, its splendid fairy queen—

cline was nevertheless all too real, and it continued catastrophically, with power under English rule being diverted further and further from those whose language was Irish. Part and parcel of the same process was the loss of the native linguistic disciplines, so that old manuscripts could no longer be fully understood and access to the treasures of the medieval past was cut off.[3] After the failed rebellion of 1798, the turn of the nineteenth century brought with it one kind of nadir for a planted and colonized country, when the 1800 Act of Union officially absorbed the island into the United Kingdom.

BACKGROUND MOVEMENTS

At this point, therefore, history compels a radical shift in direction, and it is worth beginning with three orienting observations. The first is that the recuperation of the native gods by English-speaking Ireland was a phenomenon of the last quarter of the nineteenth century, and was associated with currents of preoccupation within the Irish Protestant bourgeoisie of that period. While an enterprising reader in the year 1800 might have turned up brief mentions of the Túatha Dé Danann in the works of Irish antiquarians, a century later the ancient divinities could be found thronging the poetry, mythography, academic scholarship, art, and spiritual speculation of the age. In a single century, the gods spilled into the vanguard of Irish culture; this chapter and the next set out to investigate and explain this spectacular growth.

Secondly, a signal feature of the gods' proliferation was that they were redefined as spiritual entities. By the end of the Middle Ages, the literary Túatha Dé Danann figured in the literature as supernatural beings, but they were not regarded as divine, mystical, or cosmic. The conspicuous importation of those qualities was largely down to two literary writers—the poet W. B. Yeats, and his youthful friend the mystic George Russell, also known as 'Æ'. Others have set important precedents, but fundamentally it was their creativity between 1885 and 1905 that shaped the ways in which the Irish gods were imagined by modernity.

---

was cut from the final version of this book; discussion in S. Ó Tuama, 'Brian Merriman and his *Court*', *Repossessions: Selected Essays on the Irish Poetic Heritage* (Cork, 1995), 63–77.

3 K. McCone, 'Prehistoric, Old, and Middle Irish', in K. McCone & K. Simms (eds.), *Progress in Medieval Irish Studies* (Maynooth, 1996), 7–54, at 9.

Thirdly, it is important to stress that the late nineteenth century's version of the Irish pantheon was far from a direct hand-me-down from the Middle Ages: it had to be reconstituted from the ground up. There were three currents of influence in this process. The oldest and most comprehensive of these three was the upsurge of interest in the pagan deities of Greece and Rome which had been an aspect of the international Romantic movement since the late eighteenth century. This tendency took on a more specific inflection from the middle of the next century, as one European writer after another imagined the ancient gods returning to reinvigorate a stuffy Christianity with a strain of ecstatic pantheism.[4] In the background, therefore, there was a wide cultural movement which had already called one pantheon of ancient gods down from their niches in literary rhetoric and resuscitated them as living spiritual symbols.

The second set of influences was closer to home. The development of the Celtic as a cultural category in this period in Ireland (as in Wales and Scotland) was reflected in the appropriation and even fabrication of a picturesque 'native' past, and by a growing interest in each country's medieval literature, history, and language on the part of both dilettantes and serious scholars. This in turn was to feed into a bewilderingly complex landscape of cultural and political nationalisms; the more fashionable the concept became, the less clear its outline and implications seemed to be.[5]

If this revived Celticism would go on to affect the fate of nations, the third current was more subterranean. This was the late Victorian groundswell of interest in the occult—a series of irrationalist castings-about in the wake of a Christianity beleaguered by scientific developments and the new biblical criticism. For some—not least Yeats and Russell—explorations of hermetic thought, ritual magic, and gussied-up versions of eastern wisdom plugged the gap left by the decline of Christian dogma.[6]

---

4 This mode of thinking and writing was inaugurated by the German poet Schiller's *The Gods of Greece*, which was published in 1788; see R. Jenkyns, *The Victorians and Ancient Greece* (Cambridge, MA, 1980), 174–191.

5 See J. Leerssen, 'Celticism', in T. Brown (ed.), *Celticism* (Amsterdam, 1996), 1–20 (the main collection of essays on the topic), and two crucial articles by P. Sims-Williams, 'The visionary Celt: the construction of an "ethnic preconception"', *CMCS* 11 (1986), 71–96, and 'Celtomania and Celtoscepticism', *CMCS* 36 (1998), 1–36.

6 See A. Butler, *Victorian Occultism and the Making of Modern Magic: Invoking Tradition* (Basingstoke, 2011).

DIVINE IMAGES

From the start, the project of working the Irish divinities into a new language and a new literature faced a major stumbling block: it was wholly unclear what the gods looked like. They seemed to lack imaginative distinctness. This state of affairs had urgent political resonance, for as Declan Kiberd emphasizes, 'Ireland after the famines of the mid-nineteenth century was a sort of nowhere, waiting for its appropriate images and symbols to be inscribed within it.'[7] Towards the end of the century, this was particularly true of its threadbare native pantheon, which became the very symbols that some writers and artists aimed first to imagine, and then to inscribe.

But why did the gods—as recovered by writers in English—suffer from this pervasively hazy silhouette? A glance back to the ancient and medieval worlds may cast suggestive light here. In the second century AD, Lucian of Samosata described an image of the Gaulish god Ogmios, identified with Roman Hercules, and in so doing he recorded one of the most famous accounts of a Celtic deity from antiquity.[8] The classical Hercules was a musclebound strongman, but Lucian was puzzled to find that the Gauls depicted the god as bald, elderly, and sun-blackened, leading a troop of followers by means of golden chains attaching their ears to his tongue. A handy Gaul explains this strange image as a symbol of Ogmios-Hercules's spellbinding eloquence—a power superior to brute strength and more often found in the old than the young.[9]

This report anticipates some of the themes already picked out: that the Celts might have their own subtle teachings about the gods, and that their deities might stand in a peculiar relation to those of the Graeco-Roman world, being simultaneously akin but distinct. It further hints, suggestively, that the powers of the Celtic gods might be keyed in some way to the spoken word, or to the potency of poetry. But there is clearly nothing intrinsically vague about 'Celtic' iconography here: quite the reverse. The very crispness of Lucian's description echoes the precision of the symbols possessed by deities in Romanized areas of the Celtic

7 D. Kiberd, *Inventing Ireland: the literature of the modern nation* (London, 1995), 115.

8 See P. Mac Cana, *Celtic Mythology* (London, 1970), 35–6, and M. (Aldouse-)Green, *A Dictionary of Celtic Myth and Legend* (London, 1992), 165–6.

9 Experts agree that Ogmios is likely to be connected to Irish Ogma, son of the Dagda and inventor of the ogam alphabet, though the equation of the names is linguistically problematic unless one presupposes an earlier form *Ogomios or *Ogumios. See *CCHE*, 1393.

world, symbols which formed part of the apparatus of each god's cult: the goddess Rosmerta's vat and dipper, for example, or the ram-horned serpent of the antlered god Cernunnos.[10]

The Irish gods were different, because—crucially—the medieval material failed to provide individualized verbal descriptions. Such descriptions as there are of the Túatha Dé Danann simply depict them as idealized versions of early medieval Irish aristocrats, men and women both physically beautiful and sumptuously dressed. Verbal accounts are the beginning and end of what we have; no Irish manuscript provides visual images of the gods in the way that some splendid codices from Iceland do for the Norse deities.[11] Likewise, no Irish god is described in the medieval literature in terms which point to a purview in the external world, even in the rare cases when they do apparently possess something along those lines. Marine Manannán is a telling example, for while 'Cormac's Glossary' labelled him a god of the sea, even in his epiphany in 'The Voyage of Bran', he does not look like (say) the classical god Neptune. In fact, he is hardly described in visual terms at all, even in that sumptuously visual tale: 'the man in the chariot' is all we get.[12]

Sticking with watery examples, it is not surprising to find that the appearance of Bóand—quite clearly in origin the eponymous goddess of the River Boyne—is nowhere described. We might contrast another literary river deity, Tiberinus, god of the River Tiber, who appears in Virgil's *Aeneid* as a half-submerged figure dressed in grey-green and crowned with sedge.[13] This illustrates how weak in the medieval Irish sources is the sense of elemental specificity—of the gods as responsible for and visually echoing facets of nature. In the nineteenth century, writer after writer grappled with this deficiency in the pantheon, eventually leading to the development of a new iconography; by the turn of the twentieth century the reader was in a position to tell the Irish gods apart. The face of the god Lug came to stream sunlight in a way that echoed the classical Apollo, while Aengus Og (the Revival's favoured spelling for Óengus,

10 For these see P. Mac Cana, *Celtic Mythology*, 23–4, 39–42; for a suggestive take on Rosmerta, see *I&G*, 353–4, 357.

11 The classic example is a seventeenth-century paper manuscript, AM 738 4to or 'Edda oblongata'; even better (but a century or so later) is SÁM 66, which shows the Norse gods going about their business in early modern dress. Both are held in the Árni Magnússon Institute for Icelandic Studies, Iceland.

12 *Immram Brain: Bran's Journey to the Land of the Women*, ed. S. Mac Mathúna (Tübingen, 1985), 38.

13 *Aen.* 8. 31–4.

the Mac Óc) morphed into a Celtic Cupid, singing birds circling around his head to represent his kisses.

This chapter and the next, therefore, form a pair. We look first at the background to the pre-Yeatsian resuscitation of the Túatha Dé: my purpose is to show how the process of imagining the gods *as gods* in English-language writing in Ireland was begun, producing a provisional visual system during the nineteenth century. Then chapter 8 analyses how two crucial writers—Yeats and George Russell—inherited that system and re-shaped it at the end of the century, furnishing the Irish divinities with an iconography tied to their own spiritual and aesthetic fixations.

ANTIQUARIAN ACCOUNTS

Recovering the Túatha Dé Danann as a pantheon came about slowly, and we begin with the cultural activities that prepared the intellectual ground. The recuperation of the gods fitted into the wider awakening of interest in Irish mythology and folklore which led up to and into the Literary Revival towards the end of the nineteenth century.[14] As noted earlier, the first accounts of the Túatha Dé Danann to be found in English are found in the work of patriotic antiquarian scholars, who combed through the Irish past in a spirit of broad-gauge if unsystematic inquiry from the late seventeenth to the early nineteenth centuries.[15]

The first foray was made by a Catholic, the Galway aristocrat and historiographer Roderick O'Flaherty (1629–1718). While he was still a child, the bulk of his family's landholdings were confiscated under the brutal Cromwellian land settlement.[16] It is remarkable that despite a life of some travail he managed to publish *Ogygia*, his celebrated and sprawling 1685 chronology of Irish history, written in Latin. Displaying knowl-

---

14 The focus is on heroes (Cú Chulainn and Finn) rather than the Túatha Dé, but for further background see A. T. Seaman, 'Celtic Myth as Perceived in Eighteenth- and Nineteenth-Century Literature in English', in C. J. Byrne, *et al.* (eds.), *Celtic Languages and Celtic Peoples: Proceedings of the Second North American Congress of Celtic Studies held in Halifax August 16–19* (Halifax, 1992), 443–60.

15 See C. O'Halloran, *Golden Ages and Barbarous Nations: antiquarian debate and cultural politics in Ireland, c. 1750–1800* (Cork, 2004); R. Foster, *Paddy and Mr Punch: Connections in Irish and English History* (London, 1993), 1–5.

16 Leaving him, nonetheless, with a substantial amount of land; a recent useful way in is the introduction to *Roderick O'Flaherty's Letters To William Molyneux, Edward Lhwyd, and Samuel Molyneux, 1696–1709*, ed. R. Sharpe (Dublin, 2013).

edge of an impressive range of manuscript sources, in the classic anti-quarian manner he was content to rationalize the details of the medieval synthetic history, considering its stories of ancient migrations and set-tlements to contain significant truths about the island's remote antiq-uity in symbolic form. He shrank the geography—complaining that the mazy peregrinations of the Milesians were far-fetched—and had both the Túatha Dé Danann and the Fomorians hail from what we would call Scandinavia, thus making the two races closely related and disconcert-ingly insisting that they spoke German (meaning Norse). The very name 'Tuath Dee' arose, he asserted, because they had paused on their journey by the River Dee in Yorkshire; the term 'Tuatha de danan' derived from their veneration of their ancestress 'Danan' as a deity.

Ogygia is a vital witness to the world of native Irish learning in the seventeenth century, but it attests to how marginal a position the Túatha Dé Danann had come to occupy within that intellectual framework. In this it reflected the single most crucial source for antiquaries to use in attempting to grasp the shape of their island's ancient past. This was Geoffrey Keating's great nationalist account *Foras Feasa ar Éirinn* ('A Groundwork of Knowledge concerning Ireland'), mentioned earlier, which had reached its final form around 1634, half a century before *Ogy-gia*'s publication. The *Foras Feasa*—circulating solely in manuscript—rep-resented one kind of culmination to the medieval synthetic history. Ke-ating's history drew on (and superceded) Mícheál Ó Cléirigh's 1631 recension of 'The Book of Invasions', the final version of that compendi-ous text.[17] Thanks to Keating, the complex welter of Irish pseudohistory took on lastingly cohesive and monumental form. Because he structured his smoothly-flowing narrative around who was in the sovereignty over several millennia from the creation through to the Norman conquest of Ireland, a limited place for the Túatha Dé was ensured in the narrative.[18] In one eye-catching passage, Keating remarked that he could not under-stand how details of the invasions before the Flood could have been passed down to later generations, 'except it be the aerial demons gave them to them, who were their fairy lovers during their time of being

17 For the sense in which Ó Cléirigh's recension can be seen as the culmination of *Lebar Gabála*'s development, see R. M. Scowcroft, '*Leabhar Gabhála* I: The Growth of the Text', *Ériu* 38 (1987), 88.

18 The major study is B. Cunningham, *The world of Geoffrey Keating: history, myth and religion in seventeenth-century Ireland* (Dublin, 2000), but see also P. Ó Riain, *Geoffrey Keating's* Foras Feasa Ar Eirinn: *Reassessments* [ITS Subsidiary Series 19] (London, 2008).

pagans'.[19] There is no need to take this literally and assert that Keating believed that Irish prehistory had been transmitted by fairies: he was using a typically ironic metaphor to draw attention to the blend of history and mythology in material he nonetheless felt obliged to set down, highlighting the fact that so much of the historical Gaelic past was being thrust into oblivion as he wrote.

Several English translations of his history emerged, the earliest published version being that of Dermod O'Connor in 1723; though his translation was criticized for numerous inadequacies, it nonetheless went on to be influential and much consulted.[20] Keating had incorporated the poem from the Yellow Book of Lecan on the four treasures of the Túatha Dé into his account; to my knowledge O'Connor's blank-verse rendering represents the first time the Túatha Dé Danann had appeared in printed poetry in the English language.[21] A distinctive feature of the medieval poem is that the Túatha Dé sail to Ireland from *Lochlann*—Scandinavia—instead of the more usual vaguely imagined 'northern islands'. O'Connor followed this and the poem's list of the Túatha Dé's talismanic treasures—the Stone, Sword, Spear, and Cauldron:

> The kind Norwegians receiv'd the strangers,
> And hospitably lodg'd them from the cold.
> But, when they saw their necromantic art,
> How they had fiends and spectres at command,
> And from the tombs could call the stalking ghosts,
> And mutter words, and summon hideous forms
> From hell, and from the bottom of the deep,
> They thought them gods, and not of mortal race,
> And gave them cities, and ador'd their learning,
> And begg'd them to communicate their art...
> The towns wherein they taught their magic skill

19 G. Keating, *Foras feasa ar Érinn: the history of Ireland*, ed. & trans. D. Comyn & P. S. Dinneen (4 vols., London, 1902–14), i., 146, 147.

20 There were at least two earlier translations, including one made in 1635, immediately after Keating's own text was finished; they exist only in manuscript. For these see M. Caball & B. Hazard, 'Dynamism and declicine: translating Keating's *Foras Feasa ar Éirinn* in the seventeenth century', *Studia Hibernica* 39 (2013), 49–69; also Caball's 'Lost in translation: reading Keating's *Foras feasa ar Éireann*, 1635–1847', in M. Caball & A. Carpenter (eds.), *Oral and printed cultures in Ireland, 1600–1900* (Dublin, 2010), 47–68.

21 For this poem and the recensions of *Lebor Gabála* in which the data appears, see above, 148, fn.61, and V. Hull, 'The Four Jewels of the Tuatha Dé Danann', *ZCP* 18 (1930), 73–89.

Were Falias, Finias, Murias, Gorias.
Four men, well read in hellish wickedness,
Moirfhias the chief, a wizard of renown,
And subtle Erus, Arias skilled in charms,
And Semias fam'd for spells—these four presided
In the four towns, to educate the youth.
At length these strolling necromancers sail'd
From Norway, and landed on the northern slope
Of Scotland; but perfidiously convey'd
Four monuments of choice antiquity,
From the four cities given them by the Danes:
From Falias, the stone of destiny;
From Gorias they brought the well-try'd sword
Of Luighaidh; from Finias, a spear,
From Muirias, a cauldron.[22]

Ghoulish apparatus of this sort—spectres, tombs, eerie muttering—was
well ahead of its time. In tone it anticipated Thomas Gray's 1768 *Norse
Odes*, which kick-started a vogue for Northern mythology in English
verse three decades later. Even more strikingly it foreshadowed James
Macpherson's faux-Gaelic *Ossian* material, which was to be so influential
in Romantic constructions of the Celtic.[23] But the governing stylistic
debt here is clearly to the darker episodes of Milton's *Paradise Lost*, to
the extent that O'Connor seems to be angling his poem as a fragment
of an unwritten Miltonic epic. It is overwhelmingly clear, however, that
O'Connor disliked the Túatha Dé, imagining them as malevolent and
macabre: no one else ever suggests, as he does, that their four treasures
did not belong to them, but had been 'perfidiously' swiped from their
Scandinavian hosts.[24] In this it is noteworthy that the Túatha Dé Dan-

---

22 D. O'Connor, *Keating's General History of Ireland, Translated from the original Irish,
with many curious Amendments* (Dublin, 1841 [translated in 1723]), 89–90.

23 I do not mean to sound over-condemnatory by labelling Macpherson's work in
this way; certainly the truth claims he made for his poems' origins were wildly misleading, but recent scholarship has stressed that they should be viewed as *real* epics, albeit in
rhythmic prose rather than verse and nowhere near as close to Gaelic sources as
Macpherson maintained. The foundational revisionist study was D. Thomson, *The Gaelic
Sources of Macpherson's Ossian* (Edinburgh, 1952); see too the more recent essays in F. J.
Stafford & H. Gaskill (eds.), *From Gaelic to Romantic: Ossianic Translations* (Amsterdam,
1998).

24 O'Connor himself seems to have been a rather sketchy type, accused at one point
of embezzlement; see Caball & Hazard, 'Dynamism and declicine', 66.

ann occupied precisely the same position in Irish antiquarianism that druids did in the British equivalent in the period: both were imagined as black magicians engaged in gruesome rites, embodying an example from the past to be resisted.

In 1789 a Church of Ireland clergyman named Thomas Campbell took the northern connection a stage further. Clearly attempting to map Keating's version of the synthetic history onto the more secure contours of the Irish past, he made the Túatha Dé not just temporary lodgers among the Danes but themselves a race of 'Danish-Gothic' invaders.[25] And in the same decade, Sylvester O'Halloran, a renowned Catholic surgeon from Limerick, published a pair of similarly demythologizing, but more cheerful, accounts. He followed Keating in giving a completely spurious interpretation of the name 'Túatha Dé Danann' as an encapsulation of their 'three classes':

[T]he nobility, who were so called from *Tuatha*, a lord; the priests from *Dee*, God, as devoted to the service of God; and the Danans who composed hymns, and sung the praises of the Supreme, from *Dan*, a poem.[26]

The quintessentially rationalizing tone of the antiquarian occasionally had disconcerting effects: O'Halloran followed Keating in identifying the Fomorians, legendary enemies of the Túatha Dé Danann, as Africans, 'who still held some places in the north', while the Fomorian leader Balor becomes 'Bale Beimionach, general of the Africans'.[27]

In O'Halloran's histories many of the myths of the Irish pantheon are found in English for the first time. Here is his account of Balor's defeat by Lug and the foundation of the Fair of Tailtiu (*óenach Tailtenn*):

Luigha, surnamed Lamh-fhada, or of the Long-hand, a descendent of Neimheidh's, was the next monarch. Besides his blood, the uncommon intrepidity he displayed in the last battle (having with his

25 See O'Halloran, *Golden Ages and Barbarous Nations*, 63.

26 S. O'Halloran, *A General History of Ireland* (London, 1775), i., 11. To those familiar with twentieth-century theories of mythology, there is a curious anticipation of Dumézil's 'three functions' here; see above, 109, 111, 215.

27 See T. Comerford, *History of Ireland from the Earliest Accounts of Time to the Invasion of the English under King Henry II* (London, 1751), 4, where the unnamed Fomorians appear, Keating-style, as 'a fleet of pyrates from Africa'.

own hand slain the African chief) seemed to call him to this dignity. He ruled with great prudence; and, sensible of the utility of public shews and amusements, especially to a fierce military people, he instituted the Aonach-Tailtean, so celebrated in every subsequent period of Irish history.[28]

O'Halloran clearly approved of the Túatha Dé a great deal more than Keating and O'Connor had: neither gods nor wizards, they were to him the very model of martial virtue as well as 'a commercial and maritime people'.

He did not, however, lack ideas about the deities worshipped in Ireland in ancient times, and it is telling how completely unconnected these were to the Túatha Dé Danann.[29] To him the ancestral Gaels had been animists, and had venerated 'their river and mountain deities; those who presided over hills, and these who ruled the valleys'. He asserted that 'next to the sun and moon, Neptune was their principle deity'.[30] This idea ultimately derived from a fragmentary late-medieval account of the arrival of the sons of Míl, which, influenced by classical epic, had depicted the Milesians as sacrificing to the Roman god Neptune before setting sail for Ireland; the detail had been picked up by Keating, where O'Halloran had found it.[31] 'Neptune', it should be noted, does *not* refer here to the native sea-god Manannán mac Lir, whom O'Halloran praised as the human conqueror of the Isle of Man, notable for his 'extensiveness in trade'—a distant echo of the euhemerized Manannán of 'Cormac's Glossary'. Additionally, O'Halloran's idea that the ancient Irish had worshipped the sun as a divinity named 'Bel'—hence the Mayday festival of *Bel*-tane, Bel's fire—ultimately derived from one of Cormac's false etymologies, albeit via Keating. (He did not realize that the 'Glossary' had

28 O'Halloran, *General History*, 13–4. For *óenach Tailtenn*, see above, 23–6.

29 In the first of his two considerations of Irish antiquity O'Halloran in fact blundered closer to the truth, making the connection between Lucian's Ogmios and the ogam alphabet, and even wondering if 'Ogma Grianan, who was married to Aethna, a celebrated poetess, and who, on account of his superior talents, was called *Grianan*, or the Shining, might be the person alluded to.' This was as close as he came to recognizing that the Túatha Dé had in some sense been Ireland's pre-Christian gods, but he immediately spoiled the insight with a preposterous free-association between *ogam* and the medieval philosopher William of *Ockham*, of razor fame.

30 O'Halloran, *General History*, 114.

31 *Tochomlad mac Miledh a hEspain i nErind*, ed. & trans. M.E. Dobbs, 'Tochomlad mac Miledh a hEspain i nErind: no Cath Tailten?', *ÉC* 2 (1937), 50–91, at 52, 69.

in fact been alluding to the Canaanite god Ba'al.)[32] O'Halloran was a tidy-minded man, however, and took the connection between deity and festival a stage further; looking to the winter feast at the opposite end of the year to Beltane, he loftily pronounced that among his forebears the moon had been 'undoubtedly worshipped by the name of Samhain'.[33] This last was a singularity never taken up by any other writer, but it does emphasize the vulnerability of Irish mythology at this stage in history, when the errors and eccentricities of an individual scholar had a good chance of permanently entering the tradition.

ATTEMPTED EPIC

Taken together, the foregoing gives a representative sense of the tensions of the Irish antiquarian tradition in relation to the Túatha Dé Danann. Keating had left enough ambiguity for them to be viewed positively or negatively, but the important point is that neither O'Flaherty, nor O'Connor, nor O'Halloran made them ontologically supernatural. For O'Connor, fully in the tradition of 'The Book of Invasions', they had been humans with malign magical powers, but these were an acquired skill. For O'Halloran, the no-nonsense medical man, they had been a race of busily imperial entrepreneurs.

The first influential and original *literary* work to feature members of the pantheon heavily stressed a negative view, but also innovated by making the Túatha Dé into a race of explicitly supernatural (yet still not divine) beings. *Congal*, a five-book poem by Sir Samuel Ferguson (1810–86), was published in 1872 but begun some thirty years earlier.[34] A leading light of the Protestant Ascendancy, Ferguson's antiquarian interest in the preservation and 'translation' of early Irish literature was deeply bound up with his unionist political motivations. Sinéad Garrigan-Mattar sums these up in a shrewdly suggestive study: 'Ferguson was anxious that the value of Ireland's native literature should be seen as equivalent to England's, without disturbing the cultural "umbrella" of the Union. Secondly, Ferguson wanted to inspire and inform the Irish

---

32 See above, 81, fn.35.

33 O'Halloran, *General History*, 113.

34 See R. O'Driscoll, *An Ascendancy of the Heart: Ferguson and the Beginnings of Modern Irish Literature in English* (Dublin, 1976), and T. Brown & B. Hayley (eds.), *Samuel Ferguson: A Centenary Tribute* (Dublin, 1987).

Protestant Ascendancy... so that they would have the requisite tools...
to maintain their position of power.'[35]

Ferguson's *Congal* is an antiquarian epic set in ancient Ireland, and its
basic plot is drawn from the Middle Irish saga *Fled Dúin na nGéd* ('The
Feast of the Fortress of the Geese'). It concerns the lead-up to the battle
of Mag Rath (Moira) in 637, in which Congal Cáech, king of Ulster, was
done to death.[36] It features only two beings whom we would now recognize as gods: the 'Washer at the Ford', a grisly hag associated with the
war-goddess, and the sea-god Manannán mac Lir.

In a memorable scene Congal finds Manannán prowling round his
encampment, a 'monstrous Shape' who sends the king flying with 'a
mighty blast of wind' from under his cloak. Here Ferguson attempted
the uncanny but achieved the absurd. While Manannán seems to have
regained the colossal size possessed by the Túatha Dé in 'The Second
Battle of Moytura', Fergusonian gigantism seems more Swiftian than
medieval—it is hard to escape the impression that Congal has been flat-
tened by an almighty fart. But what *is* Manannán? As seen, medieval
texts had vacillated for centuries between supernatural and euhemeris-
tic ontologies for the Túatha Dé. Ferguson also hedged his bets: Congal's
bard identifies Manannán as both a demonic being and *simultaneously*—
in the tradition of the synthetic history—as a member of a race long-
vanquished by the Gaels:

'King, thou describest by his bulk and by his clapping cloak
A mighty demon of the old time, who with much dread and fear
Once filled the race of Partholan, Manannan Mor Mac Lir,
Son of the Sea. In former times there lived not on the face
Of Erin a sprite of bigger bulk or potenter to raise
The powers of air by land or sea in lightning, tempest, hail,
Or magical thick mist, than he; albeit in woody Fail
Dwelt many demons at that time: but being so huge of limb,
Manannan had the overward of the coast allotted him,
To stride it round, from cape to cape, daily and if a fleet
Hove into sight, to shake them down a sea-fog from his feet

---

35 S. Garrigan-Mattar, *Primitivism, Science, and the Irish Revival* (Oxford, 2004), 14–5.

36 Ferguson's direct source was John O'Donovan's 1842 edition and translation, *The Banquet of Dun na n-Geadh and the battle of Magh Rath, An Historical Tale* (Dublin, 1842). Useful overview of Ferguson, and *Congal* in particular, in C. Graham, *Ideologies of Epic: Nation, Empire, and Victorian Epic Poetry* (Manchester & New York, 1998), 73–122.

Or with a wafture of his cloak flap forth a tempest straight
Would drive them off a hundred leagues; and so he kept his state
In churlish sort about our bays and forelands, till at last
Great Spanish Miledh's mighty sons, for all he was so vast
And fell a churl, in spite of him, by dint of blows, made good
Their landing, and brought in their Druids: from which time forth,
The brood of Goblin people shun the light; some in the hollow sides
Of hills lie hid; some hide beneath the brackish ocean-tides;
Some underneath the sweet-well springs. Manannan, Poets say,
Fled to the isle which bears his name, that eastward lies halfway
Sailing to Britain; whence at times he wades the narrow seas,
Revisiting his old domain, when evil destinies
Impend o'er Erin: but his force and magic might are gone...'[37]

Dermod O'Connor had given the Túatha Dé 'spectres at command', but here, amid the gothic shadows of the nineteenth century, they have themselves become spectralized, a diminished 'brood of Goblin people'. Later in the poem, the Washer of the Ford announces that she comes from 'the Tuath de Danaan line of Magi', which superficially aligns her with O'Connor—but again, like Manannán and in contrast to O'Connor's idea of the Túatha Dé, she too is in fact eerily and explicitly more-than-human.

These pared-down Túatha Dé represent a failed experiment. Their presentation is inconsistent: Manannán is a 'demon', but one who nevertheless protects Ireland. His magic is apparently gone, but that magic consisted of circumambulating the island and releasing blasts of wind—precisely what Congal finds him doing. Ferguson avoids deciding whether his Túatha Dé are a going concern or not, so that in a manner reminiscent of certain Old Irish sagas they occupy a place between divine epiphanies and spectral revenants.

There is a theoretical point to be made about Congal and Manannán's failure to connect, for it mirrors Ferguson's difficulty in working supernatural beings into his poem. This difficulty reflected long-standing eighteenth- and nineteenth-century debates about whether heathen gods and goddesses should feature in modern attempts at epic poetry.[38]

37 S. Ferguson, *Congal: a poem, in five books* (Dublin & London, 1872), 55–6. The phrase 'hollow sides' may contain a pun on the Irish word *síde*, as Ferguson used the word in his 1880 poem *Conary* ('this slavery of gaysh or sidh').

38 T. Gregory, *From Many Gods to One* (Chicago, 2006) gives a useful overview of

Could sublimity be achieved without them? Should they be replaced with Christian saints and angels? Pagan deities and the heroic poem had gone together since Homer, and not just in the sense that 'divine machinery' was a traditional feature of the epic genre. It can be argued that the tie between gods and epic is more intimate, because what mythology does on the level of culture—encapsulating everything of importance and furnishing an overarching system of meanings—epic, as the most capacious and serious genre, does on the level of literature. Epic and mythology therefore share the capacity to act as symbols of entire cultures. The Homeric poems, for example, functioned as both the canonical source of Greek mythology and something like the Greeks' internal image of their own cultural greatness. Epic without myth is therefore symptomatic either of some catastrophic cultural disintegration—there are no gods in the Roman poet Lucan's bitter *Civil War*, for example—or, less disastrously, of a culture's withdrawal of energy from a shared idea of itself, towards merely private forms of aesthetic expression to be shared within coteries of the like-minded. Hence too the historically close link between the stirrings of nationalist sentiment, mythology, and epic: shaping a national culture requires an epic, and epic requires a pantheon and a myth-world.

That some theorists felt this to be the case did not, however, make it any easier for eighteenth- and nineteenth-century poets, beset by a sense of their historical distance from the ancient world, to render a set of pagan gods aesthetically persuasive. More often than not divinities were simply dropped; James Macpherson's Ossianic epics, for example, made no attempt to introduce Gaelic deities hovering over the action.[39] In the preface to *Fingal*, Macpherson had explicitly emphasized that Ossian does not bring down the gods to aid his heroes in the way that Homer does: the literary story of the Túatha Dé Danann might have been rather different if he had.[40] In contrast to Macpherson, Ferguson once again

---

issue in the earlier period; for later debates see H. F. Tucker, *Epic: Britain's Heroic Muse 1790–1910* (Oxford, 2008), 94–5.

39 See S. Dentith, *Epic and Empire in Nineteenth-century Britain* (Cambridge, 2006), which does not tackle the problem of divine machinery directly but usefully lays out the background cultural politics.

40 The possibility was there as Macpherson does make some use of Highland fairy-beliefs; but they were not divinities. The one pagan god in his work comes in 'Cathloda', where Starno and Swaran consult the 'Spirit of Loda'—supposedly the Norse god Odin. See F. Stafford, *The Sublime Savage: a study of James Macpherson and the poems of Ossian* (Edinburgh, 1988), 54–5, and especially 156.

wants to have it both ways. He simultaneously gestures towards and forecloses the possibility that an ontologically supernatural Túatha Dé might be installed as the divine machinery of a new body of heroic Irish literature, written in English but on ancient, native themes.[41] As we shall see, other creative writers were soon to attempt the same manoeuvre and find it similarly stymieing.

'CELTOLOGY' AND COMPARATIVE MYTH

On one level Ferguson's *Congal* looked back to the antiquarianism of the late eighteenth century. But it also reflected the coming together of the cultural forces which would bring to birth the Literary Revival towards the end of the nineteenth; these had been gathering pace since the 1830s and were deeply bound up with the period's shifting politics.[42] Against the background of a burgeoning vogue for the collection of folk and fairylore, learned societies devoted to Gaelic texts were founded and the work of translating the medieval king-tales was begun; this was coupled with a tendency to begin condensing all these into literature.[43] Critics have tended to highlight the proprietorial aspects of this kind of Celticism, seeing it as a way of writing and thinking that allowed Anglo-Irish Protestants—increasingly pushed to the sidelines by a growing Catholic bourgeoisie—to feel less estranged.[44] A significant dimension of this process was the tendency for writers of the time to represent Ireland as a repository of mystery and uncanniness, as strange to itself as to outsiders, and as a result, the search for Irish identity in the literature of the period often quarries the unusual and the phantasmagoric.[45] Originally this tendency spotlighted the nearer rather than more distant past as a

41 See J. W. Foster, 'The Revival of Saga and Heroic Romance during the Irish Renaissance: The Ideology of Cultural Nationalism', in H. Kosok (ed.), *Studies in Anglo-Irish Literature* (Bonn, 1982), 126–36.

42 See in particular S. Deane's influential *Strange Country: modernity and nationhood in Irish writing since 1790* (Oxford, 1996).

43 J. Leerssen, *Mere Irish and Fíor-ghael: Studies in the Idea of Irish Nationality* (Amsterdam, 1986), 435.

44 M. Pittock, *Scottish and Irish Romanticism* (Oxford, 2008), 74, quoted by R. Foster, *Words Alone: Yeats and his Inheritances* (Oxford, 2011), 39.

45 Joep Leerssen coined the splendid term 'auto-exoticism' for this way of thinking; see his *Remembrance and Imagination: patterns in the historical and literary representation of Ireland in the nineteenth century* (Cork, 1996), 35, 225.

way to negotiate a contested and recently traumatic history: when at mid-century writers went in for ancient Irish subject matter, they turned to kings and not to gods. That said, it is likely that the pervasive super-naturalism identified here did help to open the way for a recovery of the divinities towards the end of the century—the very phenomenon cum-bersomely anticipated in Ferguson's Manannán.

Irish antiquarians had turned to historiographical texts in which the Túatha Dé Danann appeared in euhemerized guises; they had not exam-ined the sagas in which their supernatural status was impressively obvi-ous. The spur to excavate the supernaturals from the medieval sagas came from outside Ireland, with the emergence from the 1850s of com-parative mythology, a new scholarly discipline which was itself an out-growth of the development of philology (or linguistics). The horizon of European scholarship had been dizzyingly expanded in the late eigh-teenth century when the connection between Sanskrit and the classical languages of Europe was discovered, and by midway through the fol-lowing century the comparative study of the Indo-European tongues had been placed on a highly technical footing.[46] Hopes ran high in en-suing decades that mythology might turn out to be similarly amenable to a comparative analysis. There were a number of superficially impres-sive parallels, especially between Greek and Indian myth—the Greek sky-god *Ouranos* looked suspiciously like the Hindu deity *Varuna*, for example—and these raised hopes that an ancestral Indo-European pan-theon might be uncovered via the philological method.[47]

As a result, thinking about the 'Celtic' in the period fissured and went in two different directions.[48] 'Celticism' gradually transformed itself from a hobby for Ascendancy gentlemen (and a few gentlewomen) of antiquarian tastes and various kinds of romantic politics into a serious academic discipline, one aligned with the agreed standards of interna-tional scholarship. The new scholars tended to see this as a coming of age, with (bad, old) romantic Celticism morphing into (good, modern)

46 See R. H. Robins, *A Short History of Linguistics* (New York, 1997); for the European encounter with Indian languages, see A. Amaladass, 'Jesuits and Sanskrit Studies', *Jour-nal of Indo-European Studies* 30 (1992), 209–31.

47 See Garrigan-Mattar, *Primitivism*, 6; early hopes were dashed, but the more mod-est contemporary claims of the field are best represented by J. Puhvel, *Comparative My-thology* (Baltimore, MD, 1987). Ironically the Ouranos/Varuna correspondence is not now accepted.

48 This transformation has been traced by Garrigan-Mattar (*Primitivism*, 38), to whose discussion I am indebted here.

'Celtology'—from *Keltologie*, the German term for the new discipline, nowadays called Celtic Studies. Writers moved by romantic visions of the ancient Irish past could thus be dismissed as muddle-heads who would not, or could not, keep up with developments. For romantic Celticists, on the other hand, it felt more like a partition, with themselves on one side and a group of dogmatists on the other; the latter might have some interesting ideas, but they privileged scholarly pedantry over the Celtic soul.

By the 1850s 'Celtology' had been placed on a secure basis and a body of scientifically edited texts began to flow from learned societies.[49] Progress in Ireland, although spasmodic, was gathering pace.[50] The scholar Eugene O'Curry (1794–1862) provides a useful example. He was a transitional figure, part Celtologist, part old-fashioned antiquarian, and part representative of traditional native scribal learning. His most striking achievement was his unrivalled knowledge of the Irish manuscript tradition which allowed him to introduce the reading public to the kinds of material that Irish manuscripts contain. To this end, in 1861 he produced *Lectures on the Manuscript Materials of ancient Irish History*; this was followed posthumously twelve years later with *Lectures on the Manners and Customs of the ancient Irish*, a general introduction to traditional Gaelic culture, including a pioneering look at Irish law.[51] O'Curry was genuinely breaking new ground here in making texts accessible to scholars who could not read them in Irish themselves, but it must be said that the degree to which he was prepared to credit saga narratives sometimes seems rather credulous to the modern reader. It was partly for that very reason, however, that his works were to exert a significant hold upon the imaginative writers of the Revival; not himself a colourful writer, in literary terms—both his books are a turgid read—O'Curry was the cause of colour in other people.

---

49 A convenient (if essentially symbolic) date for the beginning of modern Celtic Studies might be the appointment of Johann Kaspar Zeuss to a Chair in philology at Munich in 1847; the fourteen years between 1844 and 1858 saw the birth of no fewer than four masterly German-speaking scholars—Ernst Windisch, Heinrich Zimmer, Kuno Meyer, and Rudolf Thurneysen—who were to develop and dominate the field into the twentieth century.

50 For an overview of the introduction of comparative philology to Ireland itself, see the short account in McCone, 'Prehistoric, Old and Middle Irish', 9–16, and now P. Moran, 'Their harmless calling: Stokes and the Irish linguistic tradition', in E. Boyle & P. Russell, (eds.), *The Tripartite Life of Whitley Stokes, 1830–1909* (Dublin, 2011), 175–84.

51 See P. Ó Fiannachta, 'Eoghan Ó Comhraí, file traidisiúnta', in Ó Corráin, *et al.*, (eds.), *Sages, saints and storytellers*, 280–307.

O'Curry's account of ancient Irish culture was compendious but un-selective, and he was disinclined to investigate questions of religion and mythology. His comments on the beliefs of the pre-Christian Irish are limited to the blander sort of Victorian speculation about druidism, and he expended five times as many words on Ireland's ancient music as he did on its religion. The Túatha Dé Danann are sparingly acknowledged in both his works, but in a rationalizing manner as the pre-Milesian in-habitants of Ireland about whom supernatural traditions had accrued, and whose 'magical skill' was of course 'in reality... scientific supe-riority'.[52] The crucial point here is that it was entirely possible, as late as the early 1860s, for a scholar to immerse his mind in the oldest records of Ireland's past and yet for it not to occur to him that the Túatha Dé had been Ireland's pagan gods.

A few decades later this would have been unthinkable, and the turn-ing point came in the decade after O'Curry's death, when comparative mythologists began to investigate the Irish data. The key publication from this time was the *Revue celtique*, the first scholarly journal devoted to Celtology.[53] Its first issue emerged in 1870, and over the next two de-cades its issues showed a significant bias towards mythological material. The journal's role in the change of approach to the Celtic past described above is illustrated by the fate of one David Fitzgerald, who published his thoughts on Irish myth and its gods in the 1883–5 volume. Fitzger-ald's assertions were unwisely expressed—he pronounced recent Celtic scholarship 'more arid than the sands of the Libyan desert'—and his views were memorably savaged in the same volume by the learned Whitley Stokes, one of the greatest Celtic scholars of the era. Stokes re-sponded with sufficient ferocity to make it clear that the field was no longer one for romantic amateurs, and indeed Fitzgerald seems never to have made a second foray.[54] As it happened, the most 'romantic' aspect of Fitzgerald's article was his impatience with the piecemeal way in

52 E. O'Curry, *Lectures on the Manuscript Materials of ancient Irish History* (Dublin, 1861, 250.

53 The influence and importance of the journal is explored by S. Garrigan-Mattar, 'Reviewing the Celt: The *Revue Celtique* and Irish Celticism', *Bullán: an Irish Studies Jour-nal* V.2 (Winter/Spring 2001), 55–74, and in her *Primitivism*, 26–40.

54 D. Fitzgerald, 'Early Celtic History and Mythology', *RC* 6 (1883–5), 193–259; W. Stokes, 'Remarks on Mr Fitzgerald's "Early Celtic History and Mythology"', 358–70 in the same volume. Stokes condemned 'this farrago of bad Irish, doubtful English, mythologi-cal guesswork and impossible etymology'; while he was a very great scholar, not even his conclusions about the gods were invariably correct (e.g. his mistaken etymology of the name *Dagda* on 369). See also B. Maier, 'Comparative philology and mythology: the let-

which the new scholarship was making its conclusions available; he declared that the mythology of ancient Ireland should be recovered whole and placed before the public in English translation. To want this was to understand the nature of neither translation, nor scholarship, nor ancient Ireland, but it was a desire which would be shared by many literary writers over the following decades.

As luck would have it, the Stokes-Fitzgerald spat came shortly after the publication of the first genuinely authoritative statement on Irish mythology to derive from the comparative method, the 1884 *Cycle mythologique irlandais et la mythologie celtique* by the French historian and philologist Marie-Henri d'Arbois de Jubainville. This was to become *the* scholarly handbook on the meaning of Irish myth and its divinities for the Literary Revival; in it d'Arbois de Jubainville analysed the traditions relating to the Túatha Dé Danann and retold their narratives in crisp paraphrase. Little in it would pass muster today without modification, and much was simply wrong; but upon publication it laid the foundation for all future scholarship on the subject, quoting in Irish and giving dates and references. Crucially its author tackled 'The Book of Invasions', revealing it as an elaborate medieval structure one corner of which concealed a disguised pre-Christian pantheon. Ancient Greece was his main point of reference as a comparative mythologist—representative subsections included 'Lug and Hermes' and 'Balor and Poseidon'—and while many of his parallels were thoughtful many more now seem far-fetched. In particular he regularly pronounced Greek and Irish deities of opposite sexes equivalent, something which modern awareness of the fundamental significance of gender in mythology would probably now prevent.

Furthermore, he over-emphasized one of the observations made by early comparative mythologists, which was that Indo-European peoples often have a story of a primordial clash between the gods and a race of antigods, who resemble the former in power and immortality but are often older or more primitive. He was the first person to point out that 'The Second Battle of Moytura', in which the Túatha Dé Danann defeat the Fomorians, precisely fits this pattern.[55] Many scholars would still accept this, but d'Arbois de Jubainville turned an episode in the corpus into a structural principle, a pervasive dualism setting 'the good gods, those of Day, of Light, and of Life' against 'the gods of Death and Night,

ters of Whitley Stokes to Adalbert Kuhn', in P. Russell & E. Boyle (eds.), *The Tripartite Life of Whitley Stokes, 1830–1909* (Dublin, 2011), 119–33.

55 See above, 95.

the wicked gods'.[56] *Le Cycle mythologique* overstated its case here, and its author's relentless assertion that the fundamental theme of ancient Irish myth had been Good Túatha Dé Danann vs Bad Fomorians contributed more than anything else to limiting the work's lasting value.

Its significance, however, lay both in its status as the first study to systematically make the case for the Túatha Dé as Ireland's native pantheon, and in its being the first to make a series of reasoned judgments about where in the medieval literature myth ended and pseudohistory began. One effect of its publication was to make it more difficult for Irish literary writers to ignore the fact that a body of scientific scholarship devoted to their native mythology now existed. It also helped that it contained cameos of some of the major figures—in order, the Dagda, Óengus, Lug, Ogma, Goibniu, Midir, Étaín, and Manannán—in a way that seemed calculated to help those wanting to include them in their own creative work. The problem, of course, was that the book was written in French, which limited its accessibility in Ireland until a translation was published in 1903. (Yeats, who did not know the language, finally 'read' the book in the late 1890s by having Maud Gonne—his great love of the period and a fluent French speaker—translate parts of it out loud.)[57]

Comparative mythology had shown how Ireland's medieval literature was a crucial source for the country's pagan pantheon. Simultaneously another nascent discipline—anthropology—was making possible a new, more empirical view of fairylore, the other major source for images of native supernatural beings.[58] Anthropology encompassed the study of how human societies and beliefs function, and it developed theories of the growth of culture, including religion.[59] One of its most important (and self-congratulatory) proposals in the era was that cultures evolve from a more primitive state to a more developed one, with a correspond-

56 In this he was betraying the partial influence of the 'solar' theories of Max Müller which reduced all deities to natural phenomena, often related to the course of the sun through the year or the day.

57 S. Putzel, *Reconstructing Yeats: The Secret Rose and The Wind Among the Reeds* (Dublin, 1986), 219.

58 Stimulating discussion of the background to nineteenth-century investigations of Irish fairylore in Leerssen, *Remembrance and Imagination*, 159–70. As wellsprings of data, medieval mythology and fairylore were strikingly polarized. The one was written, learned, and dependent on international elite scholarship, within which it was discussed among peers; the other was oral, popular, and local, often recorded by individuals possessing far higher social status than their informants.

59 A useful one-volume survey is G. W. Stocking, *Victorian Anthropology* (London & New York, 1987).

ing shift on the religious level from a belief in a spirit-world to a pantheon of deities, leading eventually to monotheism. Its key proposal for our purposes was the suggestion that folklore was debased myth, a residue of old beliefs left clinging, barnacle-like, to the flanks of a culture as it hauled itself up the shore to a higher stage of development. Irish scholars influenced by anthropological thought now had a tool with which to tackle fairylore on an apparently rational basis. Collectors of fairy traditions in the 1820s–30s often wrote to entertain and intrigue middle-class English and Irish readers, but the new science brought the supernatural beings of folklore to the attention of an intellectual elite. The literary Túatha Dé and the sheeogues of the rural poor alike could now be seen as the after-images of lost divinities—preserved in very different mediums and adulterated by time and transmission—but both providing evidence for the beliefs of the pagan Irish.[60]

BARDIC HISTORY

The foregoing has traced the evolution of a series of distinct intellectual frames within which, by the mid-1880s, a national pantheon could be contemplated. There was a broad shift from antiquarianism to Celtology (the latter accompanied by its handmaidens, anthropology and comparative myth), each with a different take on the native supernaturals. Significantly, all the individuals we have looked at so far thought of themselves as scholars—albeit amateur scholars—rather than as imaginative writers. Samuel Ferguson looks superficially like an exception, but though *Congal*'s epic scale indicated his literary ambition, in its own way that poem too was an exercise in scholarship, as its copious apparatus of notes made plain.[61]

---

60 Here perhaps more than anywhere else I have greatly compressed the work of others. The above is to say nothing, at this stage, of the attractions which this anthropological model offered to literary writers, for it held the capacity to imbue Irish fairylore with a primordial dignity, even to see it (turning cultural evolutionism on its head) as a necessary corrective to a materialist present. See R. Hutton, *The Triumph of the Moon* (Oxford, 1999), 112–7; Foster, *Words Alone*, 97–102, 115–22; S. Garrigan-Mattar, 'Yeats, Fairies, and the New Animism', *New Literary History* 43.1 (Winter 2012), 137–57; and the still essential M. H. Thuente, *W. B. Yeats and Irish Folklore* (Dublin, 1980), 32–73.

61 The accuracy of these was commended by the *Revue celtique*—evidence that at least some neo-Celtic literature could be sanctioned by a publication which was to be-

In this, Ferguson's poem prefigured a tension between the empirical analysis of myth on the one hand and the need of an emerging creative literature to mine it for imagery and matter on the other; this tension was to become acute for Yeats. By their nature, scholarly conclusions invite correction, and in a new field like comparative myth provisional facts were about the best that could be hoped for. This was not necessarily of much comfort for the cultural nationalist of literary inclinations, who—enthused by the excavation of a pantheon of native deities parallel to those of Greece and Rome—instead found a mass of instabilities. One year's consensus about Lug, or the Fomorians, or the 'Three Gods of Skill' could be overturned by new research the next. In short, the last quarter of the nineteenth century saw the ground of Irish mythology become exceedingly treacherous underfoot, and in the distance the odd donkey—such as poor David Fitzgerald—could be heard braying helplessly as it was sucked into the mire.

In the right hands, of course, tension of this kind could galvanize creative impetus. So much is embodied in the work of a man who, from 1873, was to channel his considerable energies into the glorification of Ireland's antique past, but who seemed unable to reconcile himself to either scholarly historiography or poetic romance. This was the polemicist Standish James O'Grady (1846–1928), thanks to whom ancient Irish paganism and the Túatha Dé Danann became firmly established as part of the imaginative furniture of the Literary Revival.[62] The son of a Church of Ireland rector in County Cork, O'Grady was a life-long upholder of aristocracy in general and of the British monarchy and Ascendancy landlordism in particular. His early discovery of Sylvester O'Halloran's *History of Ireland* and translations of Ireland's medieval literature inspired furious productivity, which resulted in his two-volume *History of Ireland: The Heroic Period* (1878 and 1880), followed by *The History of Ireland: Critical and Philosophical* (1881). These exerted an influence out of all proportion to their lack of commercial success on an entire generation of young Anglo-Irish writers, some of whose politics evolved in entirely different directions to O'Grady's own.[63]

---

come known for its fastidious hostility to romantic Celticism. See Graham, *Ideologies of Epic*, 97.

62 See E. A. Hagan, *'High Nonsensical Words': A Study of the Works of Standish James O'Grady* (Troy, NY, 1986), now supplemented by M. McAteer's searching reassessment, *Standish O'Grady, Æ and Yeats: History, Politics, Culture* (Dublin, 2002).

63 Standish *James* is easily confused with his cousin Standish *Hayes* O'Grady, who was also deeply involved in Irish antiquities and produced a celebrated two-volume set

O'Grady's combination of interests may seem idiosyncratic—much later Lady Gregory, Yeats's friend and collaborator, was to term him a 'Fenian Unionist'—but he was really using the language of radical romanticism to a conservative end. His works took the aristocratic heroes of an imagined Gaelic past and held them up for emulation by an increasingly eclipsed Ascendancy class, to the end of reclaiming their social and political dominance in perpetuity. 'The translation of that exemplar into a reality', as Garrigan-Mattar has written, 'depended on the capacity of the Anglo-Irish not only to "know" the primitive Irish but also to identify with them, since their culture apparently provided a model of chieftainship and right-rule that might be renewed in a newly-feudal Ireland.'[64] Hence the significance of his heroic Ireland being *pagan*: locating his ideal political system in the pre-Christian past allowed the peremptory cancellation of sectarian tensions in the present—though, as we shall see, O'Grady's ancient Ireland occasionally seemed to contain Protestant pagans and Catholic ones.

O'Grady's importance for this study lies in the central place he ascribes to the divinities. The inhabitants of his ancient Ireland explicitly worship the Túatha Dé Danann as the focus of their religion. While O'Grady had ransacked Keating and O'Curry, this was an idea drawn directly from the new comparative mythologists and Celtic scholars, here making its debut in imaginative literature. In a vividly lyrical passage, we hear of 'the children of Dana, a divine race':

> ... they were immortal, and travelled upon the wind, and... had power over the elements, and were very glorious to look upon; Lear, whose dominion was over the sea, and his son Mananan, whose home was in Muirnict and Loch Oribsen in the west, beyond the great stream in which dwelt Shenâne, Yeoha the Ollav with his sons... Eadane the poetess, and many others; ...the descendants of the Fir-bolgs were subservient to them, paying them tribute and reverence; ...they were now assembled together in the centre of the island, for it was the custom of the Tuatha Eireen to gather together from time to time, like men, to each other's fairy

of translations entitled *Silva Gadelica: a collection of tales in Irish with extracts illustrating persons and places* (London, 1892). See Garrigan-Mattar, *Primitivism*, 38 for early scholarly reviewers boggled by the misapprehension that such different works could stem from one and the same man.

64 Garrigan-Mattar, *Primitivism*, 16.

habitations ... but for the rest, they dwelt upon their hills over Eiré, delighting themselves with infusing subtle influences into the winds and waters, the earth and the sea, and into the souls of men, having magic power over all things.[65]

This was the language of romantic paganism ultimately traceable to eighteenth-century Germany, in which ancient divinities had been envisioned as animating an organically unified nature and culture. O'Grady had studied Divinity for a time at Trinity College, but abandoned Christianity in his youth for the personal pantheism reflected here; in this the English critic and thinker John Ruskin had been a formative influence upon his sensibility.[66] O'Grady wrote that 'legends represent the imagination of the country; they are that kind of history which a nation desires to possess. They betray the ambition and ideals of the people, and, in this respect, have a value far beyond the tale of actual events and duly recorded deeds, which are no more history than a skeleton is a man.'[67] In his view mythology was a kind of emanation stirred up from a country's psychic depths.

CLASSICAL CORRELATIONS

This conception of mythology as unconscious cultural fantasy also owed much to another well-established language through which ancient paganism could be imagined, that of deep respect for the achievements of Greece and Rome.[68] O'Grady's innovation was simply to reinvent pre-

---

65 S. J. O'Grady, *The History of Ireland* (2 vols., London, 1878–80), i., 65. Some of O'Grady's spellings may need unpacking. Muirnict is Modern Irish Muir nIocht, the English Channel, though O'Grady actually meant the Irish Sea; Loch Oribsen [*sic*] is Loch Oirbsen, now Lough Corrib, with Oirbsen (really *Oirbsiu*) a sobriquet of Manannán mac Lir according to *Lebor Gabála*; Shenâne is Sinand, eponymous goddess of the River Shannon; Yeoha the Ollav may be the Dagda ('Eochaid Ollathair'), or Ollam Fódla, a legendary Nemedian king of Tara, here wrongly included among the Túatha Dé; Eadane is Étaín, or possibly Etan the poetess, daughter of Dían Cécht.

66 O'Grady would have agreed with Ruskin's lament in the 1870s about the inexplicable lack of pantheism among Victorian Welshmen, exposed as they were to magnificent natural landscapes—'Holyhead mountain is your Island of Aegina' (Ruskin wrote), 'but where is its Temple to Minerva?' See Jenkyns, *The Victorians and Ancient Greece*, 181.

67 O'Grady, *History of Ireland* i., 22.

68 For these 'languages' of paganism, and the terms in which they are discussed, I am indebted to Hutton's magisterial *Triumph of the Moon*, 3–31.

Christian Ireland as an alternative version of classical, and especially Greek, antiquity, and here he owed a great deal to his Trinity training in ancient literature.[69] His *History* began with a survey of references to Ireland by Graeco-Roman authors, placing early Ireland and ancient Hellas on an equal footing as parallel civilizations. This idea was in a sense a reflection of a medieval one, as the synthetic history had persistently ascribed a Greek connection to the Nemedians—ancestors of both the Fir Bolg and the Túatha Dé Danann—and to the Milesians. Bardic poets could thus in a stock expression refer to the 'Gaels of the Greeks' (*Gaedhil na nGrég*), and closer to O'Grady's own time, antiquarians had obdurately defended the historicity of the Greek link. That the idea was profoundly attractive is suggested by the way that romantic writers over the ensuing decades pounced on the wholly coincidental similarity between the Túatha Dé *Danann* and the *Danaoi*, one of the most frequent names for the Greeks in Homer. That Homer's translators had sometimes rendered *Danaoi* as 'Danaans' served to enable this apparent connection, and explains why erroneous spellings such as 'Tuatha de Danaan' soon became ubiquitous in the Revival (and beyond).

O'Grady's own blending of Ireland and ancient Greece was more elegant. 'The Tuatha of Ancient Erin'—the chapter of his *History* devoted to the gods—showed how his comparativism and his classical scholarship could dovetail, often with subtle political undertones. The chapter was headed with an untranslated epigraph from Sophocles' tragedy *Oedipus at Colonus*, in which the self-blinded hero asks to what god the place he has reached is dedicated. The reply comes:

' "The Kindly Ones, who see all things", we call them hereabouts;
but in other lands other names will suit.'[70]

On the surface, the point was simply that Ireland was also sacred ground, inviolably consecrated to divinities familiar under other names elsewhere in Indo-Europe. But in the very next line of the play, which O'Grady omitted, Oedipus recognizes Colonus as the place in which he is destined by the gods to abide forever. Oedipus's acceptance by native divinities held an obviously providentialist implication for Anglo-Irish

---

69 For O'Grady's youthful skill as a classicist and indeed as a composer of Greek verse, see Hagan, *'High Nonsensical Words'*, 13–4.

70 Sophocles, *Oed. Col.*, 44 (my trans.); O'Grady, *History* i., 65.

Protestants, whose powerbase it was O'Grady's avowed aim to bolster. Oedipus comes from his home into a foreign land, where he is nonetheless ordained to stay by fate and the will of the local divinities; he embodies a historical curse that, if welcomed, will transmute—in some tactfully unspecified way—into a blessing.[71] The Greek was not quoted, but the allusion hovered meaningfully.

A further facet of O'Grady's Hiberno-Hellenism was his philological style, suggestive of an anxious need to underscore the seriousness of his work. This was in part a further imitation of the classics—indeed of classical philology and textual criticism—but it was also an attempt to emulate the new Celtic scholarship on the typographic level. In a pastiche of the *Revue celtique* his prose was studded with technical terms in untranslated medieval Irish, foraged from O'Curry's *Manners and Customs*. Additionally, his idiosyncratic theonyms bristled with diacritics, tellingly including two—the circumflex and the macron—which belonged solely to the realm of the scholarly edition; thus the Dagda Mór, the 'Great Father', charmingly became the *Dâda Mōr*.

On one level, O'Grady's *History* can be seen as an attempt to overgo Ferguson and produce a national epic, but it suffered from an unresolved crisis of generic identity; its author could never truly make up his mind about the relationship between history and imagination. On the one hand, O'Grady felt the urge to pen a didactic historical epic. In this he was inspired by his great model Thomas Carlyle, the eccentric Scottish philosopher and historian: for Carlyle, the purpose of history was to inform the present and he held historiography, therefore, to be the noblest form of art.[72] But on the other, the haunting pull of myth was strong, and it constantly drew O'Grady towards a mythological epic in the Homeric mould. This was a tension never to be resolved and the Irish gods were thus caught between two stools.

The same tension was clear in the invocation in which O'Grady trumpeted his epic ambitions, and which struck again that Miltonic note:

71 There are many of these allusive epigraphs. O'Grady's negative view of Queen Medb/Maeve is signalled when the description of her palace at Crúachain is prefaced by Milton's Satan on his 'throne of royal state'; a nifty piece of comparative myth is worked in when the chapter on Macha, one of the war-goddesses, begins with an allusion from *Macbeth* to the Roman battle-goddess Bellona.

72 Carlyle—notorious for aggressive anti-Irish sentiment—might seem an odd choice of model for O'Grady; Foster (*Words Alone*, 46–7, 49–50) makes a strong case for his having held a more nuanced position on Ireland than has usually been thought.

Spirits of the ancient bards, my ancestors, and ye sacred influences that haunt for ever the soil and air of my country, nameless now and unworshipped, but strong and eternal, be with me and befriend, that in circles worthy so glorious singing their praise upon whom nations looked back as upon their first and best, with a flight unfailing I may rise to regions where no wing of laborious ollav or chanting shanachie ever yet fanned that thinner air.[73]

In this bizarre passage several of the contradictory positions identified above come together in a moment of startling generic instability. The prose threatens to turn into blank verse, even as historiography seems on the verge of morphing into mythological epic. The Túatha Dé—those 'sacred influences'—are part of a contraband of poetic images, pressed into service here as the epic's muses and machinery. They are identified in a significantly awkward clause as both 'eternal' (in other words, supernatural immortals) and as the historically specific 'first and best' of the nation's past (that is, long-dead heroes). The curious syntax mirrors the intellectual fudge.

But the really important thing was the gods' indigenous permanence, as that Sophoclean quotation had implied: they might indeed be known by other names elsewhere, but in Ireland they had particular, inalienably local identities. In contrast, English poetry written in the spirit of romantic primitivism had long peopled the landscape of Britain with the international deities of classical antiquity, imagining them as vibrantly present in the countryside and embodying a radically anti-urban and antimaterialist set of values. A few English poets had worried that mediterranean divinities might be out of place in northern drizzle—'Her foot the Cumnor cowslips never stirr'd!' wailed Matthew Arnold of the goddess Proserpine—but they were in the minority. O'Grady's *History* opened the way to installing the Túatha Dé Danann in an equivalent role in an emergent national literature, and thus succeeded where Samuel Ferguson had failed. In place of Jove there would be the Dadga (or even the Dâda). Instead of Neptune, one could bring on Manannán, the mist-cloaked son of the sea. These 'gorgeous unearthly beings that long ago emanated from bardic minds' might now serve as divine machinery for unwritten epic, and their worship could be imagined as embedded in the very landscape. Emain Macha became 'the sacred heights of Macha, the

73 O'Grady, *History* i., 48–9.

War Goddess of the Gæil'; the Hill of Uisnech, at the very centre of the island, was 'where men were accustomed to worship Fohla', the tutelary goddess of Ireland. Bardic literature itself was, according to O'Grady, a product of the landscape, and 'still lingers in the mountains which gave it birth'—geography generating theography.

PERCEPTIBLE PRESENCES

It is with O'Grady's *History* that a coherent iconographic system began to condense around the various members of the Túatha Dé Danann. Before they could be invested with individual imagery and paraphernalia they first had to be recovered *as gods*, in the course of which some considerable intellectual manoeuvring had been necessary. In the first volume of the *History* they were somewhat vague and phantasmal, but in the second they came into sharper focus. At the climax of the first volume, the injured Cú Chulainn (or *Cuculain*, as O'Grady spelled it) is treated to a vision of the 'blessed Shee', and as they parade before him the prose becomes a kind of litany:

> From the Shannon, where the hills are dark above the waters of the Red Lake, came Bove Derg, endlessly grieving for his grand-children, the cruelly transformed.... Came Lear of the Shee Fio-naháh, on Slieve Few, whose were the sweet children. His domin-ion was over the sea, and he lorded it over the lawless sea. Came Mananán, the son of Lear, from his isle, eastward in Muirnict, tra-versing the soft waves in his chariot, drawn by fairy steeds that brake not a bubble nor severed the wave-crest. Came the warrior queens of the Gæil, Bauv and Macha, and Moreega, relaxing their stern brows about the couch of Cuculain, and the three sweet sis-ters Eire and Fohla and Banba, whose gentle names are upon Inis Fail. ... Came Brihid, adored by the singing tribe, and Angus-an-Vroga, dazzling bright, round whom flew singing birds, purple-plumed, and no eye sees them, for they sing in the hearts of youths and maidens. Came Goibnenn, the father of craftsmen, and Yeoha Mac Erc, surnamed Ollav Fohla, and the Dâda Mōr, who ruled over all the Tuatha De Danan, from his green throne above the waters of the Boyne. Came Ogma, the inventor of letters, and Coirpry Kin Kæth, surnamed also Crom and Cruag, "the stooping one" and

"the stern" whose altar was upon Mah Slact when the Talkend, cross-bearing, with his clerics, came to Inis Fail, and many more of the Tuatha De Danan...[74]

One could draw them. The divine chorus line, one god filing on after another, was to become a formal cliché (which I call the 'enumerative topos') over the next two decades: in terms of O'Grady's Homeric ambitions it was really a kind of subset of the epic catalogue, a classic feature of that genre.[75] It was a transparently useful device for introducing the reader to a series of unfamiliar deities—deities upon whom the reader's eye is not allowed to linger too long lest they begin to look insubstantial.

At this point we must confront a fundamental issue, namely Catholicism. From the passages above, it is clear that the 'bardic' side of O'Grady's *History* came to develop a distinctly mystical air: the figuration of the Túatha Dé Danann as spiritual powers finally became overt in his writings. This reflected a distinctive Irish Protestant subculture, for Protestant fiction writers had long shown themselves to be conspicuously fascinated by occult and supernatural themes. This has been explained as the response of an increasingly marginalized Ascendancy class to a creeping sense of political and religious precariousness, and it was a strategy both anxious and escapist.[76] In fact, the recovery of the indigenous divinities presented a particularly extreme example of this phenomenon: it reinforced Anglo-Irish claims to nativeness, and by appealing to pre-Christian divine powers, Catholicism could (rhetorically at least) be bypassed altogether.

Nose-thumbing at Catholic pietism disguised a degree of unacknowledged envy, and this too is visible in O'Grady's work.[77] In Cuculain's vi-

---

74 O'Grady, *History*, i., 265–6.

75 The texture of this passage is distinctly classical, but there seems to be no direct model in ancient literature, though there are glancing similarities to the councils of the gods in *Iliad* 20 and *Odyssey* 1, and (especially) to the gods arriving as guests at the marriage of Peleus and Thetis in Catullus 64.

76 A phenomenon analysed by R. Foster in the chapter 'Protestant Magic: W. B. Yeats and the Spell of Irish History', in his *Paddy and Mr Punch: Connections in Irish and English History* (London, 1993), 212–32.

77 Later O'Grady introduces one 'Ayha Coelshanig', a character of his own devising, simply to illustrate a superstitious and slavish clericalism (Ayha) getting in the way of national energy and aspiration (symbolized by Cú Chulainn's charioteer Laeg). Ayha's druid—for which read Catholic priest—teaches him 'the observances due to the Shee that they might be favourable to him' (*History* ii., 253). See also Hagan, 'High Nonsensical Words', 86–7.

sion of the Shee, the iconography and the quasi-liturgical form cause the gods to resemble the saints in a Catholic church, each one gentled by candles and clutching their symbol or instrument of martyrdom. O'Grady's gods reflected a displaced attraction to the iconographic multiplicity and closeness to the landscape of Irish Catholicism. Startlingly, parts of the *History* can be read as questioning the very value of Ireland's conversion, from a standpoint that blended Protestant anxieties about Catholicism with the romantic freethinker's embrace of a divinized natural world. The supremely villainous representative of Romish priestcraft was—needless to say—St Patrick, and in this connection O'Grady deployed some of his most unabashed, if second-hand, pro-pagan rhetoric. In a passage which would later feed directly into Yeats's 1889 *The Wanderings of Oisin*, O'Grady had the aged Oisín, son of Finn and the last of the *fiana*, revile Patrick and the new faith:

> Withered trees are ye, blasted by the red wind. Your hair, the glory of manhood, is shaven away; your eyes are leaden with much study; your flesh wasted with fasting and self-torture; your countenances sad. I hear no gleeful laughter; I see no eyes bright and glad; and ever the dismal bells keep ringing, and sorrowful psalmody sounds.[78]

This was the classic romantic rejection of Christianity as thin-lipped and world-denying, contrasting with paganism as a religion of joy, pleasure, and natural beauty. Taking the whole thing even further over the top, O'Grady introduced an unmistakable verbal echo of Swinburne, then the most famous contemporary poet to write in this louche, antiauthoritarian vein, having Oisín lament: 'How, then, hast thou conquered, O son of Calpurn!'[79] The allusion was to a memorable line of the English poet's 1866 'Hymn to Proserpine', which notoriously adapted the apocryphal last words of Julian the Apostate, the Roman Emperor who had tried to restore pagan worship:

> Thou hast conquered, O pale Galilean; the world has grown grey from thy breath.[80]

78 O'Grady, *History* i., 37.
79 O'Grady, *History*, i, 38.
80 A. C. Swinburne, *Poems and Ballads & Atalanta in Calydon*, ed. K. Haynes (London, 2000), 57.

The phrase also illustrates the fact that O'Grady's affinities were with European, and not merely British, writers: in 1873 Ibsen had made this theme the basis of an entire play, *Emperor and Galilean*, translated into English in 1876.

O'Grady seemed unable to make his several *Histories* stabilize generically. They listed between mythological epic and providentialist history, between bardic romance and scientific sobriety. This was partly down to forces ambient in the culture, for the picture of early Ireland available at the time was in such flux that it could still be used to represent almost any set of values. This tellingly resembled the state of contemporary scholarship on the ancient Greeks (who could be invoked to justify anything from primitivism to pederasty), and for O'Grady the study of ancient Erin formed a kind of parallel world to the classical studies of his early youth, in which familiar Attic contours could be mirrored and transformed. He used it to defend government by a self-perpetuating aristocratic elite, anti-commercialism, and the inevitability of a fixed world order, urging his system on his Anglo-Irish contemporaries for implementation.

There was one final, specifically Protestant, dimension to the recovery of the gods. In a stimulating set of observations on the politics of fairylore, Joep Leerssen notes that both the Túatha Dé Danann and the fairies of folklore were 'ousted' beings, 'withdrawing into the nether fringes and the upper fringes of existence, *under*ground and into the *super*natural. From the wild and uncivilized parts of the landscape they threaten the settled order and rational plausibility of the victors' existence: changing babies in the cradle, luring people away from hearth, home and family.'[81] For the Protestant Ascendancy, the native supernaturals—beings that had been pushed under and pushed out—possessed an unsettling imaginative resemblance to a troublesome and potentially dangerous Catholic peasantry: both were the aboriginal inhabitants of Ireland and had been displaced by incomers whose security they might still undermine and overwhelm.

This precisely explains why the O'Gradyian retrieval of the gods—and the pattern which he established—involved attempts to extract them from the synthetic history. By downplaying or cancelling the traditional narrative of invasion and displacement, the disturbing link between the native supernaturals and the Catholic peasantry was uncoupled. Beings dispossessed by incomers were re-imagined as tutelary divinities who

81 Leerssen, *Remembrance and Imagination*, 166.

had never been away, to whom classically educated Anglo-Irish Protestants—like O'Grady himself—might have privileged imaginative access. As such, they could now be seen as analogous to the divinities of other places and peoples, and were similarly capable of being deployed to the ends of a national literature. Thus the major story of this chapter—the retrieval and spiritualization of the native gods—emerges as, in part, a strategy to assuage certain strands of specifically Protestant paranoia.

It is also worth noting that O'Grady's assertion that the native gods were 'nameless now and unworshipped' was especially disingenuous: they were being named in an increasing stream of publications, not least his own.[82] And it was not only their names which were becoming familiar, but their forms as well—forms which he himself had an important role in originating. Luminous, usually beautiful, and amiably disposed, his Túatha Dé can be observed stiffening into characteristic poses: take Angus, with his psaltery and circling birds, or Bove (Bodb) Derg, 'endlessly grieving'. We must therefore ask if O'Grady *believed* in the gods that his pen helped to shape. The question is not quite as ridiculous as it appears. Even as O'Grady published his final work on ancient Ireland, his hero John Ruskin, whose own writings had helped to turn him as a youth from Anglican Christianity to Romantic pantheism, was about to assert 'literally and earnestly' his belief in the existence of 'spiritual powers... genii, fairies, or spirits'. These, he emphatically insisted, should be termed 'gods'. This astounding statement came in the final chapter of Ruskin's autobiographical *Praeterita*, the last of his writings, and he continued: 'No true happiness exists, nor is any good work done... but in the sense or imagination of such presences.'[83] O'Grady did not quite go that far; but the thought, for the first time in nearly a thousand years, was now available.

---

82 One example might be Sophie Bryant, the remarkable Anglo-Irish mathematician and feminist, who simply channelled O'Grady in her 1889 *Celtic Ireland*, representing the island as a blatant transplantation of an idealized Victorian Hellas. Its religion, she asserted, had been marked by 'respect for the dead... reverence for the Tuatha... observance of the great feasts, [and] the periodical celebration of games in the sacred places'.

83 J. Ruskin, *Praeterita*, ed. F. O'Gorman (Oxford, 2012), 360.

8

DANAAN MYSTERIES

OCCULT NATIONALISM AND
THE DIVINE FORMS

Difficult are gods for mortals to see.

—HOMERIC HYMN TO DEMETER

WE COME NOW to the Literary Revival proper, and thus to W. B. Yeats
and George Russell (Fig. 8.1), whose creativity between 1885 and 1905—
when both were in their twenties and thirties—forms the subject of this
chapter. The focus is again on imagery, specifically the ways in which
both men came to crystallize an iconography for the indigenous gods. To
do this they built on the work of Standish O'Grady in particular, who
had sought with indifferent success to persuade a Protestant landed class
to acknowledge a direct connection between Gaelic antiquity and contemporary Ireland. For Yeats in particular iconography was crucial, as
he subscribed to a complex personal philosophy of the image; looking
back from later life at his youthful immersion in Irish myth, he was to
identify the generation of a coherent system of images as both the point
and the pre-condition of his early work—and the place where it had most
spectacularly run aground.

Thus far in this book there have been few household names among
the individuals discussed, but Yeats's fame, in contrast, threatens to
overwhelm. Many scholars have touched upon the gods as a facet of the
poet's occult interests and of his use of Irish folklore, but the results
have been curiously diffident, so I think something remains to be said.
Perhaps the main problem has been that critics have tended to imagine
that the Irish gods were fixed, with distinct identities and meanings,
and thus that in dealing with Irish mythology Yeats was mastering a
body of empirical data. However, as this book shows, the pantheon itself
was a moving target, and Yeats himself was a central player in the pro-

cess of retrieval and imaginative reshaping.[1] Russell's contribution—for
he wrote about the Túatha Dé Danann at snooze-inducing length—has
received less scrutiny, but was of
similar importance.

ESOTERIC INVESTIGATIONS

Both Yeats and Russell can be thumb-
nailed as irrationalizing intellectuals, and in both cases, their view of
the native gods was a redemptive
one: any focus on what the gods had
represented in the ancient past was
subordinate to the ways in which

FIG. 8.1. George Russell, 'Æ', c.1890.

they might be persuaded to intervene in a conflicted present. The crucial
background to this redemptive vision was the longstanding predisposition to doctrinal eccentricity and spiritual exploration among Ireland's
Protestant bourgeoisie. At the more avant-garde end of the spectrum in
the 1880s, this manifested as an openness to eastern wisdom and to the
occult, and both of these were to influence each of the two men. However, in what has long been a truism to specialists, they were to develop
those influences in different directions, Russell as a mystic, and Yeats as
a magician.[2]

Russell's mysticism took the form of a fervent idealism, a sense of the
phenomenal world as a veil impalpably penetrated by divine beauty.[3] In

1 It is this failure to understand the plasticity of the Irish gods which scuppers the
one relevant study so far, Peter Alderson Smith's loopy *The Tribes of Danu: Three Views of
Ireland's Fairies* (Gerrards Cross, 1987); see reviews by C. Holdsworth, 'Yeats and Ireland',
English Literature in Transition, 1880–1920 32.1 (1989), 108–10, and B. O Hehir, 'The Passing
of the Shee: After Reading a Book about Yeats and the Tribes of Danu', *Yeats: An Annual
of Critical and Textual Studies* 6 (1988), 245–65.

2 Useful comments by J. Hutchinson (*The Dynamics of Cultural Nationalism: the
Gaelic Revival and the Creation of the Irish Nation State* (London, 1987), 145–6) who points
out that Yeats and Russell soon attracted distinct constituencies 'to become rival poles of
the literary revival'.

3 Like much of Russell's oeuvre: his most recent investigator, Nicholas Allen, finds
'his poetry invisible, his prose unrecognisable, his paintings in the vault' (*George Russell
(Æ) and the New Ireland, 1905–1930* (Dublin, 2003), 14). The best single-volume biography

this he was influenced by his adherence to Theosophy—a fashionably syncretistic pseudo-religion that interwove strands of western science and esotericism with elements of Hindu and Buddhist thought.[4] While its emphasis was on eastern cosmology and symbolism, as a system it could also find a place for the pagan divinities of Europe as personifications of natural forces.[5] In just this way, Russell the mystic could avow simultaneous belief in a boundless original deity and in a mass of spiritual beings that had emanated from that primordial One.

The impact of Indian philosophy on Yeats's complex metaphysics was also considerable, although he never found Theosophy as satisfying as Russell, for whom its doctrine at least would provide a lifelong spiritual berth. Like Russell, Yeats believed in the continual interpenetration of the physical and spiritual worlds, and for him occult practice held out the possibility of developing spiritual knowledge—and more-than-usual powers—by deploying the rational intellect in the service of the irrational.[6] Occultism had undergone a significant late-Victorian revival; Ronald Hutton aptly characterizes its appeal, noting that it 'offered the thinkers of the age a middle way between a defensive Christian orthodoxy and a science which threatened to despiritualize the universe and question the special status of humanity'.[7] Yeats soon directed his search for spiritual development to the Hermetic Order of the Golden Dawn, founded in 1888, which became the most active and influential magical order in the last decade of the century.[8] Progress up through the grades of the Golden Dawn was via a series of initiations and examinations, each of which required the initiate to master aspects of occult symbol-

---

is still H. Summerfield, *That Myriad-Minded Man: a Biography of George William Russell, 'A.E.', 1867–1955* (Gerrards Cross, 1975); the course of Russell and Yeats's friendship is traced in P. Kuch, *Yeats and A.E.: the antagonism that unites dear friends* (Gerrards Cross, 1986). Useful overview by J. Nolan, 'The Awakening of the Fires: A Survey of AE's Mystical Writings 1897–1933', *ABEI Journal: The Brazilian Journal of Irish Studies* (2001), 89–99.

4 The history of the Theosophical Society is concisely summarized by R. Hutton, *The Triumph of the Moon* (Oxford, 1999), 18–20, and its doctrines by Foster, *TAM*, 50, and N. Allen, *George Russell (AE) and the New Ireland, 1905–30* (Dublin, 2003), 16–7.

5 See Hutton, *Triumph of the Moon*, 19.

6 For Yeats's views of Madame Blavatsky and his own earlier break with the Society, see Foster, *TAM*, 102–4; for the impact of Hindu imagery and thought on him, see 47–8 in the same volume; details now set out at length in K. Monteith, *Yeats and Theosophy* (London, 2008).

7 Hutton, *Triumph of the Moon*, 72.

8 Lucid overview of the Golden Dawn in fin de siècle occultism in A. Owen, *The Place of Enchantment: British Occultism and the Culture of the Modern* (Chicago, 2007).

ism and philosophy—a system of considerable intellectual complexity. As several scholars have observed, for Yeats the autodidact this training was the equivalent of university, and he was to remain a member of the Golden Dawn until 1923.[9]

Russell and Yeats had met at art school in Dublin in 1884. Both were Protestants drawn to the irrational and the idea of perfect, unchanging spiritual essences, but they cut very different figures. Russell—slim, unworldly, a tad dishevelled—could already be found ignoring the flesh-and-blood model in front of him to paint pictures of ethereal beings. Yeats, the Sligo bourgeois and apprentice poet, suffered from a more earthly sense of dislocation: as Roy Foster points out, he was deeply conscious of the Irish Protestant identity denied him by straitened historical and familial circumstances, and therefore was inclined to overcompensate by striking ostentatiously 'Celtic' poses.

The nature of the difference between Yeats the magician and Russell the mystic can best be explained by returning to the concept of images. Russell beheld and—as a painter—created images, while Yeats placed them at the centre of his early-career quest to spiritualize the Irish imagination. But each man conceived of the nature of the inner image-making or image-beholding faculty differently, reflecting their preoccupation with different esoteric spheres, and it is worth setting out these differences schematically.

For Russell, the key word was *vision*. Rather like O'Grady's Cuculain, he enjoyed near-continual visions of divine beings. His accounts of these beatific irradiations do not suggest (say) temporal lobe epilepsy—which can produce phenomena of this kind—but that, like William Blake, he possessed the capacity to give himself eidetic images: vivid inner pictures which take on an independent life of their own and can be followed with open eyes.[10] The plumed titans who crowd his paintings

9 Foster, *TAM*, 103–7. The study which broke the ground on Yeats the ceremonial magician is G. M. Harper, *Yeats's Golden Dawn* (London, 1974); his occult thought is condensed with astonishing clarity by G. Hough, *The Mystery Religion of W. B. Yeats* (Brighton, 1984). Further detail is to be found in the essays in G. M. Harper (ed.), *Yeats and the Occult* (London, 1976); the field will undoubtedly be transformed by the publication of Warwick Gould's forthcoming edn. of the poet's magical notebooks. S. J. Graf's *Talking to the Gods: Occultism in the Work of W. B. Yeats, Arthur Machen, Algernon Blackwood, and Dion Fortune* (Albany, NY, 2015) came too late to be used in this study.

10 See the account 'An Irish's Mystic's Testimony', in *The Descent of the Gods: The Mystical Writings of George Russell-A.E.*, ed. R. & N. Iyer (Gerrards Cross, 1988), 377, in which Russell (in his early forties at the time) makes it clear that 'mystical beings... are

assert the fact of Russell's vision, but originally he did not consider these to be in any sense especially 'Irish': his initial interpretative scheme was a theosophical one, with its cosmopolitan aura of the east. It was only in the mid-1890s that Russell, increasingly fired up by mystical nationalism, began to understand his hazy visitants to be figures from Irish mythology.[11]

For Yeats, on the other hand, the key word was *symbol*. He handled the Túatha Dé Danann by slotting them into an occult symbol system that was under continual revision. The core of what magic offered Yeats was a system for organizing his thought, and it was a system that crucially entailed an active process of shaping rather than mimeographic transcription. 'Symbol' had a specific sense within the world of *fin de siècle* esotericism. Yeats believed that any given symbol possessed an intrinsic, living potency, which the magician might access through invocatory meditation. Thus each true symbol functioned as a pass-key with which the adept might mount a raid on the spiritual world, bringing himself into an increasing inner alignment with that realm.[12] In terms of Yeatsian occult theory, therefore, each of Ireland's ancient gods could be seen as such a symbol: the task was to identify the core image, the centre of gravity that held together the complex of meaning embodied by the deity.

IMMORTAL MOODS

Yeats's symbol theory, coupled with what Declan Kiberd calls his 'interrogative cast of mind', was to inspire a taxonomic approach to the Túatha Dé Danann, the urge to pigeonhole and classify. This was an illustration of the poet's tendency to cross-pollinate his studies in Irish folklore and the occult with the fruits of scientific enquiry, even as he loftily inveighed against the rationalizing approach.

What, precisely, did Yeats think he was taxonomizing? Mary Helen Thuente has explored the shape of his thought on the issue, and its es-

---

never seen with the physical eyes' and that seership requires a particular 'mood'—meaning, I take it, mental quiescence. For Blake and eidetic images, see P. Ackroyd, *Blake* (London, 1995), 24–5.

11 Hutchinson, *Dynamics of Cultural Nationalism*, 142.

12 The literature on the role of the symbol in Yeats's occult thought is vast: the place to start is his essay 'Magic' (published 1901 but reprinted in Yeats, *Ideas of Good and Evil* (London, 1903)), and see the discussions in Hough, *The Mystery Religion of W. B. Yeats*, 48ff.

sence can be distilled into a three-way equation: the literary Túatha Dé Danann = the ancient gods of Ireland = the fairies or Sidhe of folklore. This might seem a simple enough set of equivalences, but in fact it took an elaborate series of steps over half a century to become intellectually available—antiquarianism, anthropology, comparative mythology, historiography, primitivism, and both scientific and romantic Celticism all had a role in this process. Up to about 1890, writer after writer more or less gets there, but fails to foreground the thought; by Yeats's early twenties the idea that the Túatha Dé were the ancient Irish gods, who in turn were also in some sense the fairies, had the odd status of a miscarried cliché.

Yeats's innovation in the 1890s was to yoke this three-way equation to a set of personal and national agendas, with occultism as the licensing factor. Once again, others had tacked in a similar direction; at the beginning of the decade Lady Wilde, Oscar's mother, had begun a collection of Irish folklore by asserting that 'all nations and races' had held a belief 'in mystic beings... all around them'.[13] This was to blend folklore with the Anglo-Irish taste for the supernatural, then spice the whole with a dash of anthropology, according to which the fairies could be interpreted as the shrunken after-images of pagan gods. Wilde failed to identify the fairies with the Túatha Dé Danann, but Yeats would later find her animist conception useful.[14] He experimented with replacing the idea that the gods had dwindled over time into fairies with the proposal that, in the Ireland of his own day, the fairies were actually still gods. Ireland's rural, Catholic poor could thus be made out to be atavistic semi-pagans in a world still thronged with the beings that their ancestors had once worshipped, beings whose divine status was continually on the point of reasserting itself.[15] Unsurprisingly, considerable offense was taken in Catholic quarters at this skewed vision of rural piety.[16]

---

13 Lady Wilde, *Ancient Cures, Charms, and Usages of Ireland* (London, 1890), 1; see also M. H. Thuente, *W. B. Yeats and Irish Folklore* (Totowa, NJ, 1980), 32–73.

14 See S. Garrigan-Mattar, 'Yeats, Fairies, and the New Animism', *New Literary History* 43 (Winter 2012), 137–157.

15 See S. Garrigan-Mattar, *Primitivism, Science, and the Irish Revival* (Oxford, 2004), 46–7.

16 Yeats's pronouncements on fairylore were criticized in the press coverage of a notorious 1895 murder trial, in which a Tipperary farmer named Michael Cleary was revealed to have burned his wife to death in the belief that she was a fairy changeling. Cleary seems to have been mentally unbalanced, but Angela Bourke's extraordinary microhistory of the tragedy, *The Burning of Bridget Cleary* (London, 1993), superbly inves-

Nonetheless, statements like these were the end result of a decade-long process of intellectual accommodation by Yeats towards the folklorists and Celtologists. It is clear that the groundwork for that accommodation was in place by 1888. A passage in the first of Yeats's two famous folklore collections, *Fairy and Folktales of the Irish Peasantry*, published in that year, began by directly addressing the issue of fairy ontology, setting before the reader the three alternatives: gods, fairies, or Túatha Dé Danann. Tellingly these three were not yet confounded:

> Who are they? 'Fallen angels who were not good enough to be saved, nor bad enough to be lost,' say the peasantry. 'The gods of the earth,' says *The Book of Armagh*. 'The gods of pagan Ireland,' say the Irish antiquarians, 'The Tuatha Dé Danann, who, when no longer worshipped and fed with offerings, dwindled away in the popular imagination, and now are only a few spans high.'[17]

Yeats had been sifting through a great deal of mixed material, both for himself and his readers, and the passage hints at the central importance of occultism as a unifying intellectual frame. The central option, 'gods of the earth'—a reference back to Tírechán's seventh-century definition of the men of the *síd*—is the only one of the three that Yeats picks out for expansion, and he glosses it with reference to the elemental spirits of occult philosophy: 'behind the visible are chains on chains of conscious beings, who are not of heaven but of the earth, who have no inherent form but change according to their whim...' Strikingly, he failed to reach for a far more obvious analogy to 'gods of the earth'—the demigods of classical religion which were ubiquitously visible in contemporary English poetry in the form of nymphs, fauns, and pans. The idea, too, that deities might dwindle if not 'fed by offerings' is an antiquarian metaphor which Yeats was nudging in the direction of an occult reality: by implication, it was a process which might be run in reverse.

Two years later, in 1890, he published 'Invoking the Irish Fairies' in the *Irish Theosophist*, which described an attempt by him and his Golden Dawn *consœur* Florence Farr to induce visions of the fairies. A far more ephemeral piece, it was nevertheless significant because it developed the

---

tigates the actual role that fairylore and 'fairy-doctors' played in a rapidly modernizing late Victorian Ireland—a useful antidote to Yeatsian mystifications.

17 W. B. Yeats (ed.), 'The Trooping Fairies', in *Fairy and Folktales of the Irish Peasantry* (London, 1888), in *Prefaces and Introductions*, ed. W. O'Donnell (Basingstoke, 1988), 10.

idea that the fairies were occult forces but without aligning them (yet) with figures from ancient Irish mythology. The deliberately offhand frame—Yeats and Farr are idly passing the time while waiting for the kettle to boil—sets off the impinging strangeness of the ensuing phantasmagoria. The good spirits, dressed in petals, have the teeming prettiness of late Victorian fairy paintings: 'a great multitude of little creatures... with green hair like sea-weed... after them another multitude dragging a car containing an enormous bubble.' The evil fairies, on the other hand, are chimerical horrors straight out of Goya, centred on a monstrous serpent called 'Grew-grew': '[a]bout him moved quantities of things like pigs, only with shorter legs, and above him in the air flew vast quantities of cherubs and bats.'[18] The division into two orders, good and bad, displayed Yeats's fondness for categorization, but much closer was the world of western occultism: the Irish fairies were very obviously the elementals of that tradition, to the extent of being divided into fiefdoms of earth, air, fire, and water. This was quite a distance, aesthetically and in other ways, from the Túatha Dé Danann, who had not yet incarnated in the imagery.

The process of interlinking folklore and ancient mythology was anticipated as early as 1893 but became increasingly important during the later 1890s.[19] Its effect was a cumulative increase in the fairies' stature—in both senses—in Yeats's writings: they get physically bigger and loom larger intellectually. The end result of this equation was explicit in 'Dust Hath Closed Helen's Eye', first published in *The Dome* in 1899, in which Yeats tells of a woman who 'died young because the gods loved her, for the Sidhe are the gods...'[20] Such beliefs, Yeats argues in the same piece, place the peasantry 'many years nearer to that old Greek world... than are our men of learning'. This was of course precisely the kind of Hiberno-Hellensim which had characterized Standish O'Grady's writings, and it brought to the fore once again the epistemological gulf between scholar and peasant.[21]

---

18 *WIFL&M*, 66.

19 Once again, Thuente sets out the basic movement, *W. B. Yeats and Irish Folklore*, 143–6.

20 This was later included in the 1902 second edn. of *The Celtic Twilight*, from which I quote ('Dust hath closed Helen's Eye', *Mythologies*, ed. W. Gould & D. Toomey (Basingstoke, 2005), 18).

21 This is even clearer in 'The Hosting of the Sidhe' in *The Wind Among the Reeds* (1899), in which the difference between the Sidhe and the Túatha Dé is explained (uniquely) as a *class-based* difference in terminology: 'The powerful and wealthy called

One aspect of the divinization of the Sidhe was a radical reduction in their number. In 1888, Yeats had remarked that '[y]ou cannot lift your hand without influencing and being influenced by hoards'; the ensuing decade saw undifferentiated multitudes condense into increasingly iconicized personalities. This manifested as constant lists of the divinities, a literary tic the origins of which lay in O'Grady's epic catalogues. This is apparent as early as 1894 in Yeats's bleakly ironic story 'A Crucifixion', which, lightly revised, appeared as 'The Crucifixion of the Outcast' in the first edition of *The Secret Rose* (1897). The suspicious and eventually murderous medieval clerics of the story feel a particular hatred for poets, because of their lingering paganism. As one brother says:

'Can you name one that is not heathen in his heart, always longing after the Son of Lir, and Aengus, and Bridget, and the Dagda, and Dana the Mother, and all the false gods of the old days; always making poems in praise of those kings and queens of the demons, Finvaragh, whose home is under Cruachmaa, and Red Aodh of Cnoc-na-Sidha, and Cliona of the Wave, and Aoibheal of the Grey Rock, and him they call Donn of the Vats of the Sea...?'[22]

And in one of Yeats's most plushly hallucinatory short stories of the period, 'Rosa Alchemica' (first version 1896), the conditional return of the native divinities is anticipated:

A time will come for these people also, and they will sacrifice a mullet to Artemis, or some other fish to some new divinity, unless indeed their own divinities, the Dagda, with his overflowing cauldron, Lug, with his spear dipped in poppy juice lest it rush forth hot to battle, Aengus, with his three birds on his shoulder, Bodb and his red swineherd, and all the heroic children of Dana, set up once more in their temples of grey stone. Their reign has never ceased, but only waned in power a little, for the Sidhe still pass in every wind, and dance and play at hurley, and fight their

---

the gods of ancient Ireland the Tuatha Dé Danaan, or the Tribes of the goddess Danu, but the poor called them, and still sometimes call them, the sidhe, from aes sidhe or sluagh sidhe, the people of the Faery Hills, as these words are usually explained.' This U and non-U distinction has no authority in medieval tradition, and was simply—as the shift of tense suggests—a back-projection of the contemporary shibboleths of middle-class scholars and dilettantes.

22 *Mythologies*, ed. Gould & Toomey, 101–2.

sudden battles in every hollow and on every hill; but they cannot build their temples again till there have been martyrdoms and victories...

The contextual ironies of these catalogues are complex, and 'Rosa Alchemica' is examined in more detail below. But the point here is that these two passages, one anti- and one pro-paganism, use comparable formulae: in both cases there is a shift from great personages of the Túatha Dé Danann to the Sidhe, though in the first passage some of the Sidhe are actually named and not very well distinguished, except by sentence structure, from the divinities. In the second, there is a kind of pulling back from close-up (Túatha Dé) to long-shot (Sidhe), cleverly implying simultaneous difference and sameness.

What Yeats had taken from d'Arbois de Jubainville and O'Grady was permission to give iconic identities to the deities. In both excerpts the light only catches on a single suggestive detail for each god—the Dagda's cauldron, Donn's mysterious 'Vats of the Sea', Aengus's three birds—as though describing a painting. Elsewhere in *The Secret Rose*, the 'ancient gods' appear in tenebrous form as 'tall white-armed ladies who come out of the air, and move slowly hither and thither, crowning themselves with the roses or with the lilies, and shaking about them their living hair, which moves... with the motion of their thoughts...'[23] The god-fairies here have been aligned to the shadowy world of spirits, ghosts, and dhouls—the whole Yeatsian spectropia—but they have nonetheless acquired a certain glinting individuality.

This was rooted in Yeats's most hermetic theological idea, the doctrine of gods as 'moods' or 'signatures of the divine imagination' that threads through the stories, poems, and plays he wrote during the 1890s. This was a strategy for asserting the reality of the invisible and ideal: it was also in a sense a new theory of divine or fairy ontology more fundamental and more personal than the three he had set out at the beginning of *Fairy and Folk Tales* in 1888. The key idea was a hermetic twist on Plato's theory of forms. To Yeats, 'immortal moods'—clusters of mingled thought and feeling, rather like a musical chord—existed in the divine mind, eternal and disembodied. They become incarnate in the visible world and in time by means of human emotions, which they govern and in which they participate, but they can also be consciously invoked by the occultist. This is why symbols were significant to Yeats in both his

23 'The Heart of the Spring', *Mythologies*, ed. Gould & Toomey, 115.

poetry and occult practice: to Yeats, a well-chosen symbol should resonate like a tuning fork with a particular discarnate, immortal mood, consciously drawing its influence across into the human world.

Typically, he ironized his own theory in *The Celtic Twilight* (1893), in the story 'Regina, Regina Pigmeorum, Veni.' In an example of the blend of folklore collection and occult reportage that characterized that volume, Yeats dramatized an evocation of the queen of the fairies which he, his uncle George Pollexfen, and his cousin Lucy Middleton had undertaken in Sligo. When the queen appears, the speaker questions her just as a Victorian anthropologist, notebook in hand, might investigate an uncontacted tribe:

> I then asked her whether she and her people were not 'dramatisations of our moods'? 'She does not understand,' said my friend, 'but says that her people are much like human beings, and do most of the things that human beings do.' I asked her other questions, as to her nature, and her purpose in the universe, but only seemed to puzzle her.[24]

This brilliant moment of self-parody simultaneously invited and held back the uncanny by demonstrating the gap in understanding between human observer and supernatural observed. It also stressed that the occult theory of the fairies—or divinities—as immortal moods does not reduce them to a merely subjective existence: they live with a life of their own which is as real, perhaps more real, than that of human beings. In 'Rosa Alchemica', Yeats placed a more extreme and unsettling form of this in the mouth of his fictional theurgist Michael Robartes, who refers to 'the power of the old divinities, who since the Renaissance have won everything of their ancient worship except the sacrifice of birds and fishes, the fragrance of garlands and the smoke of incense':

> The many think humanity made these divinities, and that it can unmake them again; but we who have seen them pass in rattling harness, and in soft robes, and heard them speak with articulate voices while we lay in death-like trance, know that they are always making and unmaking humanity, which indeed is but the trembling of their lips.'[25]

24 *Mythologies*, ed. Gould & Toomey, 37.
25 *Mythologies*, ed. Gould & Toomey, 181.

THEOSOPHY AND THEOLOGY

From about 1890 Yeats was able to put his ideas about the Túatha Dé Danann before the public through a number of channels, and this mirrors his cautious control over perspective and ironic parcelling out of positions among fictional personae like the just mentioned Michael Robartes. The first channel comprised his occult fictions and poetry, and particularly the apparatus of explanatory glosses with which early editions of *The Wind Among the Reeds*, for example, were supplied. His two folklore collections, both of which were prefaced with significant essays, constituted the second. Those collections gave him the status of perceived expert on Irish folklore, which led to invitations to write reviews and other occasional pieces for a range of periodicals: these made up the third avenue. A more intimate perspective is granted by the drafts of his various plays, especially the perennially unfinished *The Shadowy Waters*, which was full of Celtic and occult themes. Very frequently Irish deities who appeared in the drafts were edited out of the published versions; since the drafts are now available to scholarship it is possible to use them to watch Yeats's thought developing.[26]

Yeats's views about specific divinities will be examined shortly, but first we must turn to George Russell. In the 1890s he too began to grapple with the nature of the native gods, and his views were a major influence on Yeats. His favoured mode was frenetic journalism on mystical and nationalist themes, though in the last decade of the nineteenth century he had not yet started his influential career as an editor.[27] From 1895, his rate of publication gathered pace, turning a peppering into a fusillade. Article after article emerged (often in the *Irish Theosophist*) and it is these articles, rather than his poetry or fiction, which provide the best guide to Russell's growing thought about the Túatha Dé.

Repetitiousness was the inevitable result of such a rate of production, and week after week Russell's Celto-theosophical sermons turned to the

---

26 The crucial book here is H. C. Martin, *W. B. Yeats: Metaphysician as Dramatist* (Gerrards Cross, 1986), which uses the drafts of the drama to reconstruct Yeats's metaphysical system at the turn of the century; a good example of how rich the versions of a drama can be is *Druid Craft: The Writing of 'The Shadowy Waters'* [Manuscripts of W. B. Yeats I], ed. D. R. Clark, M. J. Sidnell, *et al.* (Amherst, 1971).

27 Russell was to edit two influential journals, *The Irish Homestead* and *Irish Statesman*, weekly for twenty-five years, keeping up an extraordinary rate of work; see Allen, *George Russell and the New Ireland*, 9.

same stock of themes and images. In tenor these owed much to his love for O'Grady's *History*, a text which seems to have fixed the form taken by Russell's visions of Irish spiritual beings.[28] (Many of Russell's paintings could be aptly captioned with phrases drawn from O'Grady, so closely is his visionary aesthetic anticipated by the older man's 'gorgeous unearthly beings', and 'mighty forms of men and women seen afar upon the sides of the mountains'.)[29] That aesthetic remained basically unchanged for most of Russell's life, but his theoretical take on the Túatha Dé seems to have undergone at least one significant shift. His initial position in the mid-1890s looked back to the antiquarians of over a century before, with a mystical twist:

> [T]he Tuatha De Dannans who settled in Eire... were called Gods, differing in this respect from the Gods of ancient Greece and India, that they were *men who had made themselves Gods* by magical or Druidical power... Superhuman in power and beauty, they raised themselves above nature; they played with the elements; they moved with ease in the air.[30]

Here again are Samuel Ferguson's 'race of magi', or even—with a more positive spin—Dermod O'Connor's 'strolling necromancers'. Magic here is hermetic wisdom, and the gods are supreme occultists. A corollary of this idea for Russell was the possibility that strenuous spiritual exercises might allow the modern seeker to undergo the same process and so become a god: many of Russell's visions, related at length in his articles, involve a human being brought before the gods—cloudy, luminescent colossi—to be enthroned among them.[31] The idea was drawn from the psychic evolutionism of Theosophy, according to which individuals might

28 See M. McAteer, *Standish O'Grady, Æ, and Yeats: History, Politics, Culture* (Dublin, 2002), 104, 123, 136, for O'Grady's influence on Russell, and also R. Foster, *The Irish Story: Telling Tales and Making It Up in Ireland* (London, 2001), 13, 16–7.

29 O'Grady, *History*, i., 28, 61, with which compare plate 19 in O. Nulty's rare catalogue, *George Russell–Æ.... at The Oriel's 21st Anniversary* (Dublin, ?1989), 15, which shows a woman climber surprised by a luminous, purple-plumed mountain-goddess or spirit. See also Allen, *George Russell and the New Ireland*, 18–9, for O'Grady's impact.

30 'The Legends of Ancient Eire', *The Irish Theosophist* 3 (March-April, 1895), reprinted in Iyer & Iyer (eds.), *Descent of the Gods*, 342.

31 See e.g. Russell's painting of a human being before a semicircle of huge, enthroned spirits reproduced on the seventh page of plates in Kuch, *Yeats and A.E.* [no page numbers in plates]; Kuch relates the painting to passages in *The Avatars* featuring 'many immortals shining... in majesty, each on their thrones...'

attain spiritual perfection and become immortal; but it also could be made to dovetail with the native concept of the man or woman enticed away to the deathless otherworld of the *síd*. It is a conspicuous irony that by taking the gods to have once been mortal magicians—in precisely the manner of 'The Book of Invasions'—Russell ended up emphasizing the most obviously *non*-pagan element in the medieval mythography.[32]

The idea that spiritual illuminati might swell the ranks of the native divinities remained a lasting feature of Russell's thought. Nevertheless, the concept that the Túatha Dé Danann themselves had begun as divin-ized magicians was gradually jettisoned around the turn of the century, in favour of ascribing them innate divinity; at this point we must look at the pantheon's internal structure as he imagined it. By 1902, Russell was downplaying the distinction he had drawn between other Indo-European pantheons and that of Ireland, and the orientalist strain in his thinking, long encouraged by Theosophy, became more marked. Theosophy, to him, was an ancient truth, and he expected to find its doctrines reflected in Irish mythology. This aprioristic way of working was, in typically theosophical fashion, a distorted reflection of Victorian science, in this case comparative philology and mythology. (In a similar way, evolution was an important concept in Theosophy, but one shunted from the bio-logical to the spiritual plane: karma replaced natural selection, and rein-carnation took the place of reproduction.)[33] Comparative mythology at the time pointed to parallels between deities from different Indo-European cultures and suggested that a proto-pantheon might be recon-structed: Russell took this to mean that there was no essential difference between Irish and Indian divinities, licensing him to take Hindu my-thology as a framework into which Irish elements might be slotted as he saw fit.

---

32 It is worth noting the curious return here to an idea which we saw in 'The Ad-venture of Connlae', written twelve hundred years before, in which going to be with the people of the *síd* served as metaphor for the idea of 'divinization', or theosis (see above, 54–6). But in that story the idea was clearly drawn not from paganism, but from Christian theology; it is a persistent oddity of Irish mythology that many of its themes persist over centuries but have grown to look *more* pagan, not less, with the passage of time.

33 A precisely similar instance is his borrowing of the idea of linguistic 'roots' from philology to create—or, in his view, reconstruct—a primordial divine language in which the relationship between sound and meaning would be non-arbitrary. The results were, alas, ludicrous ('The root which follows Y is W, the sound symbol of liquidity or water. Its form is semilunar ☽ and I think its colour is green.') See 'The Language of the Gods', in Iyer & Iyer (eds.), *Descent of the Gods*, 139.

An instance of how this worked in practice is offered by Russell's response to Irish mythology's notorious lack of a creation myth. Shortly after the turn of the century he borrowed from theosophical doctrine in order to furnish Ireland with an 'ancient' cosmology. The task he faced was to show how an infinite, impersonal, and ineffable deity could have given rise to the many spiritual beings which he saw in visions. His solution was two parts Hinduism to one part Kabbalah, with a dash of Neoplatonism.[34] From the infinite primordial One (thought Russell) two beings emanate: the unmanifest male Logos, or Divine Mind, and the female World-Soul, which becomes both matter and the spiritual substance out of which matter supposedly coagulates. This primal couple then eternally mingle and from them proceed myriads of manifest beings (including human souls) which fall into increasingly coarse grades of embodiment. Their most important emanation, however—their child, in a sense—is the so-called 'Light of the Logos', a universal shaping force of divine energy in the form of love.[35]

The difficulty lay in mapping this scheme onto the figures of the medieval literature, and in March 1902 Russell tackled the process in two instalments in the strongly nationalist weekly, the *United Irishman*. His title for the piece, 'The Children of Lir', was sly, for it led the reader to expect a version of the story of the transformed swan-children (Fig. 8.2), long a maudlin favourite of the Revival; instead, Russell provided a theosophical theogony crowded with wafty abstractions. Lir himself appeared, not as an anguished father, but as the transcendental meta-deity of Hindu thought:

> In the beginning was the boundless Lir, an infinite depth, an invisible divinity, neither dark nor light, in whom were all things past and to be.... The Great Father and the Mother of the Gods mingle together and heaven and Earth are lost, being one in the Infinite Lir. Of Lir but little can be affirmed, and nothing can be revealed.... It is beyond the gods and if they were to reveal it, it could only be through their own departure and a return to the primeval silences.[36]

34 'That Myriad-Minded Man', 61–2; Summerfield gives a longer account of theosophical cosmogony than I can here.

35 Martin (*W. B. Yeats: Metaphysician as Dramatist*, 37–8) gives a lucid account of this aspect of Russell's thought.

36 'The Children of Lir', *The United Irishman* (15th March 1902), reprinted in Iyer & Iyer (eds.), *Descent of the Gods*, 156.

FIG. 8.2. J. H. Bacon, A.R.A., *Lêr and the Swans*, in Charles Squire, *Celtic Myth and Legend* (London, 1905); a roughly contemporary but more conventional Lir/Ler than Russell's transcendental Source. Photo: The Stapleton Collection / Bridgeman Images.

By making Lir into the primordial and boundless sea of divinity, Russell simply attached a Celtic name to a Hindu concept, the frail connecting thread being the meaning of the word 'Lir'—really *ler*—'ocean'.[37] But as I suggested in chapter 6, it is possible that Lir was not originally a proper name but part of an idiomatic epithet of Manannán, only appearing as a personage in the tradition in the thirteenth century. As a result, it may be that he underwent probably the most extreme transformation of any figure traced in this book, moving in under a millennium from an ordinary noun meaning 'sea', to a literary character, and later to 'an infinite being, neither spirit nor energy nor substance'.[38] Lir is thus emblematic of the radical instabilities which are characteristic of the Irish pantheon.

Russell's Celtic cosmogony maintained the link between Manannán and Lir, having the former arise from the latter as 'the Gaelic equivalent of that Spirit which breathed on the face of the waters'. Manannán was thus his Logos and represented the divine imagination, 'the most spiritual divinity known to the ancient Gael'—perhaps a distant harking back to 'The Voyage of Bran' in which the sea-god articulates a double layered vision of reality, though the phrase itself was a quotation from O'Grady.[39] Russell continued that as Manannán separated from Lir, Lir seemed to him to be obscured by a 'veil': that veil was the World-Soul personified as 'Dana, the Hibernian Mother of the Gods', 'the primal form of matter, the Spirit of Nature'. From Manannán all the other deities then ramified, beginning with seven whom Russell does not name but who presumably include Bodb Derg, Ogma, Lug, Goibniu, and so on.

To readers not familiar with Theosophy, the Vedas, or the Upanishads, all this was no doubt mightily cryptic. Neither conviction nor clarity were added when Russell commented offhandedly that the Irish

37 Iyer & Iyer (*Descent of the Gods*, 715), aptly point to hymn 10.129 of the Rigveda, the oldest layer of Hindu scripture, which is a famously baffling account of creation, piling up questions. Many of them imply a primordial ocean: 'Was there water, bottomlessly deep? …Darkness was hidden by darkness in the beginning; with no distinguishing sign, all this was water.' This was clearly in Russell's mind when he conceived his Lir-as-theosophical divinity: see Kuch, *Yeats and AE*, 141 for Russell quoting this very hymn at Yeats to justify the vagueness of his poetry.

38 See above, 254–5.

39 O'Grady, *History*, i., 110: 'Manánan, the son of Lir. He was the most spiritual and remote of all the mysterious race. We never hear of him engaging in wars, but as educating youth, giving advice, bringing to his weird palace favourite kings and heroes, to teach them wisdom…'

names did not in fact matter—the Dagda would do just as well for Lir, 'Boan for Dana, Fintan for Mananan, and others again might be interchangeable with these'.[40] Clearly all this cannot really be described as 'myth'—it is too exasperatingly shapeless—but Russell's basic point was nonetheless clear: Theosophy, with its Indian trappings, offered a congenial cosmogony, and Irish mythology could and should be massaged into harmony with it.

This, needless to say, was not what the comparative mythologists had had in mind, and the interest of the article lies not so much in its turbid theology as in the excuses Russell makes for his method. The *United Irishman* was a significant nationalist newspaper and Russell could probably expect less indulgence from its readers than from those of a fringe publication like the *Irish Theosophist*. This made no initial dent on his style, however, and the article opens with his characteristic tropes—the waters of faery, the call of the Sidhe, the tinkling bell-branch—and goes on to make a bold plea for an imaginative polytheism. This was at the time quite usual for a certain type of radical poet, being germane to the escapist and anti-materialist strand in nineteenth-century English verse, which called for a revival of the (classical) divinities and the veneration of nature; it was to project on, essentially unimpeded, into the Edwardian era.[41] Russell's cosmological articles were very much in this vein; he predicted an imminent return to 'ancient sweetness', and asked, of God, '... is the nature He has made nobler in men's eyes because they have denied the divinity of His children and their invisible presence on earth?'

What *was* unusual, but well-judged for a nationalist publication, was the specifically Irish inflection which Russell plied throughout, along with his adoption of the Yeatsian idea of the native gods as moods—dense nuclei of meaning, energized by a single emotion:

> The gods are not often concerned with material events. They build themselves eternal empires in the mind through beauty, wisdom, or pity: and so, reading today the story of Cuculain, we do pay reverence by the exaltation of our spirits to the great divinity, Lu the sun-god, who overshadowed the hero.[42]

40 Iyer & Iyer (eds.), *Descent of the Gods*, 160.
41 See Hutton, *Triumph of the Moon*, 21–30 for an array of examples.
42 'The Children of Lir', *The United Irishman* (15th March 1902), in Iyer & Iyer (eds.), *Descent of the Gods*, 155.

Readers of the *United Irishman* might have been surprised to find that their bedtime reading was in reality a way of doing obeisance to the god Lug. But Russell continued, prefacing his account of Lir, Manannán, and Dana with an unusual apologia that went some way to acknowledging his audience—a subliminal acceptance of the fact that many of his fellow countrymen would judge his cosmogony to be twaddle:

> I am mindful that these names which once acted like a spell in the secret places of the soul are no longer powerful.... They do not interpret moods, but require themselves an interpreter; and here I propose, not with any idea of finality or fullness, and without pretence of scholarship, to speak of Druid Ireland, its gods and its mysteries. Let no one who requires authority read what I have written, for I will give none. If the spirit of the reader does not bear witness to truth he will not be convinced even though a Whitley Stokes rose up to verify the written word. Let it be accepted as a romantic invention, or attribution of divine powers to certain names to make more coherent to the writer the confusion of Celtic myth.[43]

On one level this was apotropaic, but its tone betrayed a personality who found it difficult to accept that there might be other ways of seeing the world than his own. Did even Russell really believe that theosophical free-association could recover the lost mysteries of Irish mythology? That there had been such mysteries was to him an article of faith. Since 1895 he had sought to demonstrate how these mysteries lay concealed within the medieval literature, attempting to recuperate the sagas of the Middle Ages as druidical scripture. But in the present article one can detect his (rather belated) awareness of the shift in the meaning of Celticism which had been going on for twenty years. It is difficult not to see Russell's intransigent truth-claim for his cosmology as driven by anxiety—the realization that intellectual control of the native gods had been wrested from the seer-poet by the Celtic philologist, of whom the wholly remarkable Whitley Stokes was his exemplar.[44]

---

43 'The Children of Lir', in Iyer & Iyer (eds.), *Descent of the Gods*, 155–6.

44 Stokes was one of the greatest and most prolific Celtic scholars of the age. Born in Ireland, much of his scholarship was conducted from India where he was a jurist in the colonial administration. (It is an irony that he knew the culture of India far more

EPIPHANY AND REPRESENTATION

As we have seen, Russell's Túatha Dé were remodelled from native ma-hatmas into Irish reflexes of Indian divinities. There was no equivalent iconographic shift to match the philosophical one: his depictions of the gods, in both verbal and visual media, remained consistent throughout his life.[45] The spiritual entities of his paintings are invariably larger than human and glow from within in various hues, mainly yellow, pink, and (especially) purple.[46] They appear nude or in vaguely classical drap-ery in twilit rural landscapes—rising from water or amongst trees or on a mountainside—and usually to one or more human figures. The latter may be taken aback or apparently unaware: often Russell's pastel phan-tasms seem to be tenderly bending towards some oblivious human, per-haps inspiring them with vision. So much is exemplified by the painting reproduced here in which a small child is being led away by three self-radiant fairy-women (Fig. 8.3). The painting also illustrates another of Russell's characteristic motifs, namely the plumes or rays that rise from the women's heads. Like a halo in Byzantine art these always face for-ward flatly in his paintings, even when the being's head is not in profile. These had struck Yeats early on, who included them in his account of the art of a 'Visionary'—a thinly-disguised Russell—in *The Celtic Twilight*, de-scribing paintings of 'spirits who have upon their heads instead of hair the feathers of peacocks'.[47]

---

intimately than Russell, and at first hand). See E. Boyle & P. Russell (eds.), *The Tripartite Life of Whitley Stokes 1830–1909* (Dublin, 2011).

45 Art historical resources on Russell are limited, but see D. Beale, 'Landscapes and faery', *Apollo* (December, 2004), 70–75, and there is also an exhibition catalogue from the Model Arts and Niland Gallery, Sligo, which is H. Pyle, M. Beale, &. D. Beale (eds.), *The Paintings of George W. Russell (AE)* (Sligo, 2006). An earlier and difficult to obtain cata-logue is O. Nulty, *George Russell–Æ... at The Oriel's 21ˢᵗ Anniversary* (Dublin, ?1989).

46 Russell's fondness for the latter was maliciously sent up by the dramatist Sean O'Casey, who ridiculed his 'purple mountains, lilac trees, violet skies, heliotrope clouds, and amethyst ancestral selves...' (Kuch, *Yeats and Æ*, 98).

47 'A Visionary', *Mythologies*, ed. Gould & Toomey, 9. In fact Russell's spirits usually have both plumes *and* hair, but this neatly illustrates Yeats's knack for borrowing some-one else's idea and improving on it. Russell's plumed beings are never *eerie*, but in 'The Wisdom of the King' in *The Secret Rose* Yeats created supernatural women 'of a height more than human' with 'the feathers of the grey hawk instead of hair'—an altogether more unsettling because more concrete image (*Mythologies*, ed. Gould & Toomey, 110).

FIG 8.3. *The Stolen Child* (date unknown), pastel by George Russell, Armagh County Museum Collection. Reprinted by the permission of Russell & Volkening as agents for the Estate of George Russell.

Russell later explained that these plumes were simply what he saw, and that their presence or absence denoted an internal division within the world of spirits. The lower orders of Sidhe-beings were shining and plumeless, but the upper echelons were opalescent and lit from within (Fig. 8.4). He described his first vision of one of these:

> ... there was first a dazzle of light, and I saw this came from the heart of a tall figure with a body apparently shaped out of half-transparent or opalescent air, and throughout the body ran a radiant, electrical fire, to which the heart seemed the centre. Around the head of this being and through its waving luminous hair, which was blown all about the body like living strands of gold, there appeared flaming, wing-like auras.[48]

He went on to identify the presence of plumes as a sign that these beings were 'Aengus, Manannan, Lug, and other famous kings or princes among the Tuatha De Danann'. The division shows that he too was facing the

---

48 'An Irish Mystic's Testimony', Iyer & Iyer (eds.), *Descent of the Gods*, 378.

FIG. 8.4. George Russell, *A Spirit or Sidhe in a Landscape* (date unknown), oil on board, National Gallery of Ireland. Reprinted by the permission of Russell & Volkening as agents for the Estate of George Russell.

old problem that Yeats had tackled by means of the divine catalogue: the many undifferentiated Sidhe of folklore were hard to square with the limited number of individualized Túatha Dé, each of whom has a specific narrative trajectory.

His paintings bespeak a struggle to evolve a visual language to fit this distinction: it was difficult for him to individualize the Túatha Dé Danann crisply when 'trembling on the verge of no form' was the highest compliment he could give.[49] By 1897 Yeats's fairy divinities had become shadowy but iconographically *precise*; Russell's rainbow smudges, on the other hand, tended to a sunlit non-specificity. The same problem continued to dog his poetry: May 1900 found Yeats mildly remonstrating with him that 'vast and vague' was a poor choice of words to use about Dana, mother of the Túatha Dé Danann—a criticism the obdurate Russell refused to take on board.[50]

THE CELTIC RITUALS

Russell's conception of the genesis of the gods was a strong influence on Yeats, and it is time to look in more detail at how the two men imagined specific divinities. The focus of operations was Yeats's attempt between 1896 and 1902 to develop an Order of Celtic Mysteries, his most well-known, though abortive, attempt to fuse Irishness and occultism. It was also the Túatha Dé's most famous modern outing, and one long familiar to scholars of the Literary Revival, though the material which Yeats produced towards it (in collaboration with others, including Russell) is more often alluded to than investigated.[51] Many of the texts discussed previously here emerged during the years that the Celtic Mysteries were being planned out, especially the stories of *The Secret Rose* (1897), the verse-play *The Shadowy Waters*—which had a particularly close relationship to the Mysteries—and the collection *The Wind Among the Reeds* (1899), not to mention most of Russell's more delphic pronouncements on Irish legend.

49 Summerfield, '*That Myriad-minded Man*', 64.

50 Yeats wrote: 'I avoid every kind of word that seems to me either 'poetical' or 'modern' and above all I avoid suggesting the ghostly (the vague) idea about a god, for it is a modern conception. All ancient vision was *definite and precise*.' See Kuch, *Yeats and A.E.*, 141.

51 See S. J. Graf, 'Heterodox Religions in Ireland: Theosophy, the Hermetic Society, and the Castle of Heroes', *Irish Studies Review* 11.1 (2003), 51–9.

The Celtic Mysteries were to be the poet's hermetic 'dissertation', a distinctively Celtic hermetic order which would have involved, in Roy Foster's words, a Golden Dawn-style 'ascent by stipulated "paths" from the world of material consciousness to that of the transcendent archetypes'.[52] From the Golden Dawn too was borrowed a great deal of the physical and mental structure which was projected for the Mysteries—the idea of a lodge of adepts, for example, as well as the use of symbolic gestures, colours, images, and invocations, and of the four elements as markers of grades of initiation. These last were inevitably identified with the four treasures of the Túatha Dé Danann, partly because the symbolism of the latter seemed to Yeats to evoke the four suits of the Tarot: swords (like that of Núadu), wands (Lug's spear), cups (the Dagda's cauldron), and pentacles (the stone of Fál).[53]

The occult nature of these secondhand fixtures and fittings stresses that the project, as Yeats conceived it, was always more magical than religious, no matter that part of the plan was to waft incense about while intoning invocations to Midir, Aengus, and so on. Its goal was *not*, in other words, to reinstate Irish paganism as it had once been (or even as Standish O'Grady thought it had once been); rather it was an attempt, nationalist in spirit, to solder Irish symbolism onto the template of international occultism. As Ronald Hutton remarks of the parent order, 'the ceremonies... were not acts of worship; their focus was the celebrant.'[54] As we shall see, this was once again to bring to the surface Yeats's differences with Russell, not least because it was essential to Yeats that his Mysteries be hybridized with Christian imagery.

Inventing tradition from a magpie range of sources came easily to Yeats, despite the disjunctions identified above. He began developing the idea for the Mysteries in the mid-1890s, and initially planned to base it in a castle on an island in Lough Key, which he and Douglas Hyde had seen on a trip in April 1895. Appropriately enough the lake had mythological associations: according to the *dindshenchas* it was named after Cé (whence *Key*), a daughter of Manannán, who had drowned in it, or alternatively after a male Cé, Núadu's druid. This piece of fantasy real estate

---

52 *TAM*, 104. There is no space here to discuss how the Celtic Mysteries project was reflected in Yeats's endlessly unavailing attempt at an autobiographical novel (eventually known as *The Speckled Bird*), drafted simultaneously with the Celtic Rituals, and whose protagonist also tries to 'bring back the gods'; see the comments of Foster, *TAM*, 174–6.

53 See M. C. Flannery, *Yeats and Magic: The Earlier Works* (Gerrards Cross, 1977), 42–3; for the treasures, see above, 148–52; 284–5.

54 Hutton, *Triumph of the Moon*, 79.

never came to pass, and the idea itself was not original: Yeats had come across it in a book by Nora Hopper years earlier.[55] Looking back in 1915, Yeats went into classicizing mode, recalling that he had sought to 'establish mysteries like those of Eleusis or Samrothace'; but the idea of a grand (or grand enough) building to which a self-marginalized and self-identified esoteric elite might repair from an uncomprehending Catholic populace had obvious Anglo-Irish resonances—it was to be a kind of equivalent on the spiritual plane of Coole Park, the Galway seat of Yeats's friend and patron, Augusta Gregory. In this connection, one wonders too about the Protestant overtones of the Túatha Dé's 'temples of grey stone' projected for restoration in 'Rosa Alchemica'. These recalled the Ascendency 'Big Houses', which Yeats himself had dismissed as 'granite boxes', before a change of heart: such temples would house another kind of marginalized elite, for after all the fairies were also termed 'Gentry'. Once again we see the Túatha Dé Danann functioning subliminally as a form of anxious Anglo-Irish self-representation.

After some two years of intermittent work, the Celtic Order and its rituals seem to have been framed by late November 1898, followed by another burst of activity in 1901. Working divinities so bereft of cult into a series of ceremonies was an uphill task. Lucy Kalogera, who has investigated Yeats's papers on the subject in depth, writes that Irish mythology has 'strong ritualistic associations': but in fact this is the element in which it is most signally lacking. Thus the whole process entailed a conspicuous irony, for it required the Túatha Dé Danann to be equipped with two things that they had never possessed in the whole course of Irish literature—a detailed iconography and a ritual context—at the same time as it excised the one area in which that literature made them splendidly rich, that of dramatic narrative. The mythological tales which d'Arbois de Jubainville among many others had recovered could therefore only find a place in the rituals as allusions in litanies of invocation, which took the form of a frieze-like resumé of each god's career. Here is Midir:

> Midir dweller at Bri Leith I invoke you.
> Midir father of Blathart I invoke you.
> Midir foster father of Aengus I invoke you.
> Midir mast[er] of the fairies I invoke you.
> Midir Husband of Etain I invoke you.

55 Foster, *TAM*, 186.

Midir loser of Etain I invoke you.
Midir builder of the way in the bog I invoke you.
Midir builder of Lam rad in the bog I invoke you.
Midir the clearer away of the stone out of Meath I invoke you.
Midir the planter of Tethba with rushes I invoke you.
Midir master of the three cows I invoke you.
Midir master of the three herons I invoke you.[56]

This invocation does acknowledge, in a rather clumsy way, that members of the Túatha Dé such as Midir were embedded in a web of complex story; but as we have seen repeatedly in this book, such a web is not quite a mythology. Mythology furnishes a culture with a total world-view, interpreting and mirroring back everything that that culture finds significant. For traditional peoples mythology has a role in explaining everything: the configuration of their landscape, the nature of truth, the dealings of the gods with each other and with humans, all the way down to gender relations, social customs, art, and technology. Ireland's monastic early literature certainly had strands of mythology in it, but it was not in itself a full mythology in this sense. Hence, for Yeats, the tremendous value of occult philosophy, which provided a substitute context within which the native gods, orphaned of their mythology by Christianity, might be productively incubated.

IMAGES AND EVOCATIONS

This brings us to the actual processes by which Yeats invented tradition about the Túatha Dé Danann for his projected order. The single most crucial activity was the generation of vivid inner images of the gods which were then recorded. Recalling this period in his life in 1924, Yeats dismissed his activities as 'willful phantasy': he meant this self-disparagingly, but it was in fact an accurate description of the psychic state required for occult visualization. For this he needed his old companion Russell, whose sensibility seemed permanently tuned to the cor-

56 L. S. Kalogera, 'Yeats's Celtic Mysteries' [unpublished PhD dissertation, Florida State University, 1977], 284–5. *Lam rad*: this strange form looks like a copying error, perhaps a variant of the previous line: the reference is surely to the task of building a causeway across the bog of the Lámraige, *Móin Lámraige*, imposed upon Midir in 'The Wooing of Étaín'.

rect ethereal frequency; the Celtic Mysteries were the last time the magician and the mystic would actively collaborate. By laying bare their differences of opinion the process resulted in a cooling of relations. Nevertheless, Russell was an essential contributor to the shaping of the god images, along with the Scottish writer William Sharp—whom we shall encounter at length in the next chapter—and a number of Golden Dawn initiates, not least MacGregor Mathers, the peremptory and authoritarian head of that order. Others included Yeats's maternal uncle George Pollexfen, plus a husband and wife team, Edmund and Dorothea Hunter, the last of whom had an Irish background.[57] Investigation should not be imagined as taking place in a physical group: Yeats had long resided in London (as did the Hunters), Mathers was in Paris, Russell in Dublin, and Sharp in Scotland, and so work on the Mysteries was usually carried on by correspondence, or consisted of Yeats plus one other person.

The technique for generating images of the gods—'building up the divine forms', in the jargon—was simple, and was part of the training imparted by the Golden Dawn. Usually one person—typically Yeats himself—would enter a state of loosely focused concentration upon a deity until imagery began to flow unimpeded before his mind's eye. All that had to be done was to keep steering one's mental focus back to the figure until a clear and detailed picture had been built up; this was described to the other person present, who wrote it down.[58] The obvious problem with this photofit approach was the absence of a control against which to calibrate the results, as the medieval saga-writers had failed to provide a gazetteer. Ultimately there was nothing to reassure the seer that any given image was 'correct' beyond gut instinct, or the protocols internalized from other mythologies and from the works of romantic and scholarly Celticism. The effect was a pervasive sense of forcedness: details transparently derived from a personal, conscious reading of d'Arbois de Jubainville and O'Grady can be observed floating to the sur-

57 Foster, *TAM*, 186; for Mathers, see Hutton, *The Triumph of the Moon*, 74–8; for Dorothea Hunter, see W. Gould, ' "The Music of Heaven": Dorothea Hunter', *YA* 9 [= *Yeats and Women*] (2nd edn., Basingstoke, 1997), 73–134.

58 More elaborate tactics involved several people meditating on the same deity and then comparing their visions, or the tracing of complex inner journeys though symbolic or elemental landscapes. At one point the aim was to create shortcuts of a sort in the form of talismanic 'glyphs'—logo-like symbols for each deity—which could act as a kind of hotline to their essence. The finding of these talismanic forms was initially assigned to Moina Mathers, MacGregor Mathers' wife, with limited success. See Flannery, *Yeats and Magic*, 90.

face, to be announced as pre-conscious—and also in an important sense defensively *pre-aesthetic*—emanations from the collective.

Yeats's magical notebooks contain descriptions of the 'forms' of Lug, Étaín, Ogma, the Dagda, Manannán, Lir, Núadu, Danu, and Bodb Derg, which all emerged out of the studious aimlessness of inner vizualization and were noted down by Dorothea Hunter.[59] Lug led off:

> Entering into the presence of Lug it is impossible for some time to discern any distinct form, because of the dazzling light which proceeds from him, but after a little while the light becomes less overpowering. His hair is like yellow wool, his eyes red, revolving with a terrible rapidity; above his head are radiations of light in the colours of the prism. His under robe is red, his mantle yellow. From his eyes, mouth, and hands pour streams of light.[60]

It is clear that Lug has become a deity of solar fire here, for which medieval literature gave no warrant. Standish O'Grady's Lug had been radiant but at considerably lower wattage, and was cloaked in decidedly non-solar green—the last a detail drawn directly from his appearance to his son Cú Chulainn the *Táin*. It is difficult to pinpoint the source for Lug's Victorian transformation from multi-skilled warrior into the sun-god exemplified here. Several factors were in play; the simplest was that as a young, handsome deity associated with the arts, Lug was the nearest match for the Graeco-Roman Apollo. Initial etymologies of Lug's name linked it to an Indo-European root meaning 'light', though later research has shown this was certainly wrong.[61] Furthermore, we saw that the Early Modern Irish version of 'The Tragic Deaths of the Sons of Tuireann' had averred that 'the appearance of his face and his forehead was as bright as the sun on a dry summer's day', though this was conventional literary exaggeration typical of its times and not a relic of ancient solar cult.[62] Finally, d'Arbois de Jubainville had repeatedly stressed that the Fomorian king Balor was a god of night, and that alone might have been reason enough for Yeats and others to associate his slayer with sunlight.

59 Foster, *TAM*, 164.

60 Kalogera, 'Celtic Mysteries', 271.

61 See *CCHE*, 1202; P. Schrijver, *Studies in British Celtic historical phonology* (Rodopi, 1995), 348.

62 See above, 265.

More surprising was the 'form' of the god Ogma, who came

> ... dancing a curious barbaric measure in which he gesticulates much. He is naked and carries under his left arm a bunch of fruit, in his right hand he waves an apple bough. Laying down the fruit and placing a reed pipe between his lips, he dances round the fruit, forming figures of intricate circles, playing meanwhile weird wild music on his flute.[63]

This was superficially an exception to the general rule of the over-apt image; note that one of Ogma's genuine medieval attributes—the epithet *gríanainech*, 'sun-faced'—had been noted by d'Arbois de Jubainville but failed to make it into Yeats's consciousness, perhaps because its basic import had been used up by Lug. But secondhand associations from classical mythology have flowed in to fill the gap: Ogma is half-satyr, half-male maenad. Yeats went on to say that Ogma 'represents the natural impulse in action, as opposed to any Art expression', showing that at this stage he clearly did not know Ogma's traditional role as inventor of the ogam alphabet or Lucian's account of the cognate Ogmios, since 'Art expression' would in fact have been an excellent description of the latter's role as patron and personification of eloquence.

Superficially, Manannán proved less baffling:

> The form of Mahanon [*sic*] rises from the depths of the ocean on a chariot formed of the crests of two meeting waves; this chariot is drawn by two swans. His face is old and calm; and over it ceaseless shadows flicker. His under robes are formed of calm sweeping waters, his mantle of broken tossing waters; above his head is a winged sun.[64]

This peaceable description of the god is compatible with Russell's, in which he was the 'Logos', the primordial male emanation of Lir. But Manannán clearly refused to settle, as elsewhere in Yeats's writings the sea-god cuts a more ambivalent figure. In the prototypes of his 1907 play about the Ulster Cycle heroine Deirdre, Yeats seems to have thought of

---

63 Kalogera, 'Celtic Mysteries', 270.

64 Kalogera, 'Celtic Mysteries', 270; 'Mahanon' for Manannán, like 'Lur' for 'Lir', was probably Hunter's mishearing of Yeats's words.

Manannán as a god of fate, and as basically inimical to human beings. He noticed—as had others—that by virtue of his dominion over the sea, Manannán was aligned with the realm of the Fomorians, whom he envisaged as marine deities of watery darkness, the opponents of the Túatha Dé Danann as gods of life and light. In manuscript drafts of *Deirdre*, he went so far as to make Manannán Deirdre's father—a blatant alteration of medieval tradition—and thus the source of the fateful tragedy which overtakes the Ulstermen. One (rather good) version described the god appearing in the court of king Conchobor with the infant Deirdre, before prophesying disaster:

> … 'this weakling shall grow up a woman
> So coveted by the proud kings of the world
> They shall blow up all to quarrel and in that quarrel
> Your country and all the countries of the west
> Shall go to rack and ruin'; and thereon
> He folded his sea green cloak upon his head
> and vanished.[65]

Typically, Yeats removed Manannán as god of fate from the final version of the play, perhaps out of anxiety that the god was locked into a personal symbolic language that could not be successfully conveyed to a general audience.

Looking over the notes of the esoteric visualizations, the overall impression conveyed by these deities—kitted out with branches, tridents, and chariots—is classical pastiche. The 'forms' were not intended, of course, as art in themselves, but as the archetypal background against which a national art might be made. This, however, was to deny the aesthetic debts which the figures so obviously proclaimed: the attempt at the primordial and pre-aesthetic feels second-hand. Because the point was to find the eternal essence which underlay each god's narrative, the shaping of the god-forms involved the concentration and condensation of information drawn from an eclectic range of medieval sources. The god-forms were thus abstracted from mythic narrative and so locked into an endless automatic motion.

Yeats read the medieval sources in translation, but he accessed most through the summaries in the works of Celtic scholars. The quirks of the

---

65 Quoted in Flannery, *W. B. Yeats: Metaphysician as Dramatist*, 39.

transmission process could not always be evaded, and sometimes deter-mined the whole shape of the image. Nowhere was this clearer than in the case of the triple-goddess Brigit:

The Three Bridgets guard the entrance to the land of the Gods. This entrance consists of 3 gateways, formed of heavy beams of wood, inlaid with small ornaments of silver and brass.

Bridget the Smithworker stands strong and alert at the left hand gate. She is very dark, with black wiry hair, and restless black eyes. Her tunic is of blue and purple. Her bratta purple; a bronze broach clasps her bratta and on her head is a bronze band; beaten bronze work adorns her leather belt and sandals. She governs all handi-works and represents the hard, laborious and painful side of life.

Bridget of Medicine stands at the right hand gate. She has a fair and gentle face. Her robes are light blue embroidered with silver thread, clasped by a silver winged broach, another winged orna-ment rests on her head. She represents the happy and sympathetic side of life, and so becomes the healer of that which is bruised and broken by the hammer of the Bridget of Smithwork.

Bridget of Poetry. Over the central gateway stands Bridget of Poetry, her robes are more sombre, and cloudy. They are of dull blue grey and white; her face is neither fair nor dark, she has soft blue eyes which sadly look out upon the world, feeling the joys and sorrows that work therein. She combines the forces of the other two, being both active and passive, receptive of impressions, and possessing the power of producing form.

Her right arm rests upon a silver harp, her left is extended as though to emphasize some spoken words. She says 'expand, ex-press, dispose from the centre, then rest and draw in. Old force must be thrown away or it becomes unhealthy.' She gives as her sign the drawing of the hands inwards towards the heart, then throwing them open outwards.

While she rests the vegetation grows; she blows the blast from her trumpet during the dead months of winter. The waves of the sea flow towards her when she is at rest, and are driven back when she becomes active.

Behind the posts of the gateway are two hounds, that on the side of B the Smithworker is black, the other is white. They represent Life and Death, Joy and Sorrow. Whosoever would enter through this gateway should know the secret of one of these hounds, for a battle takes place between them, and that hound which is known grows stronger through that knowledge, and when the stronger has devoured the weaker, it becomes the servant of him who knows its nature.[66]

This was the longest and the most icon-like of all the god-forms, for reasons that are revealing. Brigit was unique in medieval tradition because she combined a clear and intriguing purview with a minimal narrative presence, hardly appearing in the Mythological Cycle. This was (perhaps) a pure accident of transmission: we know the likes of Midir, Lug, and Aengus thanks to saga-narratives, but our knowledge of Brigit's character comes not from a tale, but from 'Cormac's Glossary'. The factuality of the glossary form invested her with exactly the kind of timeless stillness Yeats was trying to achieve in the Celtic workings, identifying her first as the daughter of the Dagda, and then, in triplicate, as a female poet, female smith, and female healer, worshipped by the professional poets 'for very great and famous was her application to the art'.[67]

Yeats's figure is essentially a thoughtful expansion of the glossary entry, and the idea that Brigit the poetess mediates between the harsh and the tender sides of life that her sisters represent was an inspired allegorical touch of a kind that went unachieved elsewhere. His imagination was clearly compelled by the idea of a native goddess of poetry, and it was significant that the three Brigits 'guard the entrance' to the land of the gods: they seem to be initiatory figures embodying the opposites inherent in life, as well as the reconciliation of those opposites in art. (It is worth noting that the two antithetical hounds are Yeats's invention, and a telling one.) As such they anticipate the dynamic equilibrium of antinomies in *A Vision*, that much later Yeatsian system—but they also echoed the initiation ceremony for the second grade of the Golden Dawn, which involved a complicated visualization of a divine woman, Isis-Urania.[68] Given Brigit's position at the gateway to the land of the gods, Yeats may have intended this elaborate 'form' to perform a similar function in his Celtic order.

66 Kalogera, 'Celtic Mysteries', 268–9.

67 For Brigit outside 'Cormac's Glossary', see *CMT*, 56–7, 119; also J. Carey, 'A *Tuath Dé* Miscellany, *BBCS* 39 (1992), 24–45. Also see above, 161–3.

68 Hutton, *Triumph of the Moon*, 79.

THE GODS RETURN

So far our analysis of the iconography of the Celtic Mysteries has necessarily focused on Yeats as prime mover, but we must now turn to Russell's contribution. The project brought the two men into collaboration, albeit one charged with mutual frustration. Ultimately, it foundered on the intrinsic contradictions which that collaboration crystallized.

The rise of Russell's Celtic interests in 1895 preceded the groundwork for the Mysteries by about a year, but the advent of Yeats's project supplied tremendous additional energy. On the simplest level, Russell's visionary faculty could be used as a kind of digital enhancement for the god-forms seen by others. (A letter to Yeats in June 1901 saw him imitating the latter's quasi-scientific tone, informing him that '[t]he colour of the ring in the Nuada symbol is gold or yellow, not blue'.)[69] But it became obvious that Russell imagined the role the ancient gods would play in the Ireland of the future to be wholly different from the one Yeats had in mind. Yeats himself was later to write, famously, that he had in his youth sought to create an 'aristocratic esoteric' literature, and this very typical phrase also characterizes the basic bias of his Celtic order. Its ceremonies were projected to be for an elite group of initiates, and were to fuse pagan and Christian imagery in an occult rather than devotional mode.

Russell, on the other hand, remained fired by the evangelistic tenor of Theosophy, which held itself to be the restoration of a universal and enlightened religious system. The important difference was that he had come to see 'druid Ireland' as one of the places where that system had been preserved in uncorrupted form, and one which might yet enlighten the rest of Europe.[70] (Atlantis—inevitably—was invoked as the source of the ancient doctrine.) His articles from 1895 connecting Theosophy with Irish myth were propelled by a conviction that the Irish should return *en masse* to this idealized, imagined paganism. This belief system would have the advantage, to Russell's way of thinking, of being rooted in the land of Ireland (and thus nationalist), while also being a local version of theosophical doctrine (and thus true). It was also historically determinist, because Madame Blavatsky—Theosophy's formidable foundress—had prophesied that a new age would dawn at the end of the 1890s, and this prophecy made a profound impression on Russell. Yeats's call to create a

---

69 Quoted in Kuch, *Yeats and A.E.*, 123.

70 See J. W. Foster, *Fictions of the Irish Literary Revival: A Changeling Art* (Syracuse, NY, 1987), 58.

Celtic mystical order seemed to him like the first glimmerings of that new dawn, for it echoed an 1896 decision by the International Theosophical Convention to begin founding temples and mystery schools, including one in Ireland.[71]

The psychological effects of all of this on Russell—a kindly, shy, and still young man—were tinged with the uncanniness of religious mania. By 1896 he had initiated a period of frenetic public campaigning, famously writing to Yeats in June of that year that the new age had already arrived:

> The Gods have returned to Erin and have centred themselves in the sacred mountains and blow the fires through the country. They have been seen by several in vision, they will awaken the magical instinct everywhere and the universal heart of the people will turn to the old druidic beliefs. I note through the country the increased faith in faery things. The bells are heard from the mounds and soundings in the hollows of the mountains.[72]

Russell's mobilizing rhetoric was oddly dissociative, since the 'several' visionaries alluded to seemed to mean Yeats and himself; the reader is further disconcerted by the recurrent paramilitary note in his letters during that year ('The hour has come to strike a blow... Let us be hopeful, confident, defiant!'; 'What am I to understand? Am I to tell my men to go ahead?').[73] Millenarian excitability was pushing him in the direction of mental breakdown; he began accosting Catholic priests and on one occasion was observed preaching to Sunday strollers on the esplanade at Bray, near Dublin, about the return of the native gods. (By surreal coincidence, among his bemused audience was none other than Standish O'Grady.)[74] By 1900, Yeats had become seriously concerned by the suicidal imagery which had begun to appear in his friend's visions, particularly the recurrent urge to drown himself.[75]

---

71 Kuch, *Yeats and A.E.*, 110–11.

72 Kuch, *Yeats and A.E.*, 110.

73 Kuch, *Yeats and A.E.*, 109, 110.

74 D. Kiberd, *Inventing Ireland: the literature of the modern nation* (London, 1995), 196.

75 See Foster, *TAM*, 186. Russell may have had this turbulent episode in mind when he asserted, in 1911, that he always dreaded seeing the Sidhe-beings associated with water, 'because I felt whenever I came into contact with them as great drowsiness of mind and, I often thought, an actual drawing away of vitality' (Iyer & Iyer (eds.), *The Descent of the Gods*, 380).

The crucial point is that both men anticipated the return of Ireland's pagan divinities, but from very different underlying ideological positions. Russell saw Yeats's projected order as the nucleus of a spiritual revolution that would mould collective Ireland and usher it into the New Age. Yeats's own plan was for something on a more homeopathic scale—not to mention the fact that one of his major concerns for the order was to capture Maud Gonne, his great if unavailing love of the period, who would act as its High Priestess. Russell was not incapable of putting his involvements in this period into an ironic perspective, but of the two, Yeats possessed the mind far more able to stand back, scrutinize, and aestheticize occult and mystical experience.

As Peter Kuch has pointed out, the story 'Rosa Alchemica' can be seen as a clearing house for the anxieties stirred by the recuperation of the gods. Michael Robartes, the leader of the neo-pagan theurgical order in the story, can be seen as a chiaroscuro portrait of Russell: the gods of this little cosmos are eerie, hallucinatory presences who are enemies to personality. At one point Robartes boasts (wrongly) that he and his adepts can come to no harm from ordinary mortals, 'being incorporate with immortal spirits'. This was a heavily ironic version of Russell's theory that human beings might become gods, but for the narrator the process—accomplished through a disorientating *grand pas* of adepts and immortals—has more in common with the pleasures of being vampirized:

> ... [A] mysterious wave of passion, that seemed like the soul of the dance moving within our souls, took hold of me, and I was swept, neither consenting nor refusing, into the midst. I was dancing with an immortal august woman, who had black lilies in her hair, and her dreamy gesture seemed laden with a wisdom more profound than the darkness that is between star and star...; and as we danced on and on, the incense drifted over us and round us, covering us away as in the heart of the world, and ages seemed to pass, and tempests to awake and perish in the folds of our robes and in her heavy hair.
>
> Suddenly I remembered that her eyelids had never quivered, and that her lilies had not dropped a black petal, nor shaken from their places, and understood with a great horror that I danced with one who was more or less than human, and who was drinking up my soul as an ox drinks up a wayside pool; and I fell, and darkness passed over me.[76]

76 *Mythologies*, ed. Gould & Toomey, 190.

This was an ironic version of Yeats's own doctrine of the gods as eternal signatures or moods, fused with suspicion of Russell's woozy deprecation of ego and outline. The mysticism of Michael Robartes (and by implication, Russell) depends on the cancellation of individuality, human and divine. This may be the reason that in later versions of the story Yeats excised the passage quoted below on page 394, which listed the individual gods of the Túatha Dé Danann. Iconographic precision was out of place in a narrative in which becoming 'incorporate' with immortal spirits entails a horrifying exsanguination of the self.

'Rosa Alchemica', therefore, implicitly criticized Russell's hopes for a pagan renaissance as formless and fanatical, and by extension inimical to art. (In a telling moment, the narrator regains consciousness at dawn to find that the exquisite symbolic icons of individual divinities that he had seen the night before are in reality only 'half-finished', and that the decorations of the temple are botched.) Developing the Celtic Order demonstrated that the two men's polytheological positions were irreconcilable. For Yeats, the gods had individual identities and trajectories, each a facet of the divine imagination. His hierarchic desire to control and examine spiritual experience led him to see them as gateways to the ultimate, unknowable divinity. For Russell, in contrast, the gods were less distinguished and individualized. He emphasized the Many at the expense of the One, approaching them all with oceanic feelings of sweeping, all-purpose reverence. It is telling that Yeats's writings tend to introduce the Túatha Dé separately, one by one, whereas Russell's bring the reader before assemblies of indistinguishable beings.

In both cases, the gods were extracted from the stories about them and reconfigured as unchanging principles that had always underpinned the inner Ireland. But the very indistinctness of Russell's divinities made them languorous; when they were also divorced from their narratives the effect was a catastrophic loss of imaginative force. But as seen in the case of the god-forms, Yeats's need to focus in on each deity could attract similar problems. Recovering the native gods implied energy and movement, but the creation of individual iconographies necessitated first fixing each god into a lifeless pose, like a daguerreotype; as such they were opposed to the passionate experience out of which Yeats felt art should come.

Much later in life the poet asserted that a great poet's role was to be 'the subconscious self' of his people, capable of uttering the 'truths they have forgotten, bringing up from the depth what they would deny'.[77]

---

77 Quoted in Foster, *TAP*, 658.

This was to see the poet as the mouthpiece of the collective unconscious of the nation. Something very like this was implied by a mysterious passage in Yeats's *Autobiographies*, which posited 'a nationwide multiform reverie, every mind passing through a stream of suggestion, and all streams acting and reacting on one another, no matter how distant the minds, how dumb the lips'.[78] In the late nineties, Yeats seems rather to have imagined the role of the magus-poet as activator and accelerant, bringing into consciousness the archetypes—the 'primordial images'—buried deep in the country's unconscious psyche.[79] John Hutchinson stresses the top-down rather than bottom-up dimension of this project: 'Yeats believed in the creation of a nation from above, from an injection of a unified body of images into society, which, diffused by journalists, would bind the different social strata into a community of sentiment.'[80] What is clear is that one source of the disillusionment which the Celtic Mysteries produced was the basic contradiction inherent in delving into the national unconscious while having pre-existing expectations about what would be found there: in this case the paralyzing expectation was that the 'unified body of images' that emerged would correspond to the gods of ancient Ireland.

THE ANGLO-IRISH AENGUS: A CASE STUDY

The final part of my argument widens out again from the abortive Celtic Mysteries to make some points about broader currents within the Revival, looking now at how a single deity was re-imagined in the period.

The Homeric poems have a formula: 'which god was it who...?' If we were to ask which member of the Túatha Dé Danann was the presiding deity of the Revival, the answer could only be Aengus Óg (Óengus, the Mac Óc). Aengus, in short, was the Irish divinity most complexly projected into modernity, and his very ubiquity in the poetry, prose, drama, and visual art of the period requires explanation. What are the forces that propelled him—and not Lug, or Brigit, or the Dagda—into the minds of so many writers and artists? How and why did Aengus become the

---

78 W. B. Yeats, *Autobiographies* (London, 1955), 263.

79 Here, as elsewhere, there is a curious overlap between the thought of Yeats and that of C. G. Jung, the only study of which is J. Olney, *The Rhizome and the Flower: The Perennial Philosophy: Yeats and Jung* (Berkeley, CA, 1980).

80 Hutchinson, *Dynamics of Cultural Nationalism*, 145.

'subtle-hearted' god of love, when the Túatha Dé tended, precisely, to lack purviews of that kind? Unlike almost every other member of the pantheon, the revived Aengus has also enjoyed a long career as a literary figure, persisting well into the afterglow of the Celtic Twilight and beyond—the most recent mainstream fiction in which he features, by the popular Scottish novelist Alexander McCall Smith, was published in 2006.[81] What follows therefore is the first of two case studies of the Mac Óc in this book, divided partly by theme and partly by chronology: this initial investigation takes us up to the turn of the century, while the god's more recent career is examined in the penultimate chapter.

A superficial reason for Aengus's prominence is that he was simply the most pleasant member of the Irish pantheon in the medieval literature. As we saw in earlier chapters, he appears therein as a byword for physical beauty and as a wily, youthful trickster, remarkable for his rich emotionality. He exhibits a range of humanly recognizable responses— reverie, love-longing, and suffering—and displays warmth to mortals. Restless desire and the propulsive force of visionary beauty were immediately appealing in the context of an idealist literary movement.

A second reason is to be found in the subject matter of the Irish texts that early scholars chose to edit and publish. One of the most important of the fissiparous learned fraternities established to rescue Irish traditional literature was the Ossianic Society, founded in Dublin in 1853. As the name suggests, its *raison d'être* was to collect and publish poems and tales about Oisín, Finn, and the *fíana*—partly out of a long-simmering resentment that cultural ownership of the material had been so spectacularly claimed by the Scots, for whom Ossian, thanks to Macpherson's epics, had become a cultural totem. And in that copious Ossianic material Aengus had the status of recurring special guest star, appearing in tight situations as a *deus ex machina* to rescue the lovers Díarmait and Gráinne. *The Transactions of the Ossianic Society* had the double effect of highlighting Aengus's significance and of underscoring his role as the protector of a pair of human lovers, especially as its third volume consisted of a translation of the canonical version of the story, *Tóruigheacht Dhiarmada agus Ghráinne* ('The Pursuit of Díarmait and Gráinne').[82] Of course, traditionally speaking, Aengus's sympathies were a function of his role as Diarmaid's foster-father, and in rescuing his foster-son he was

---

81 A. McCall Smith, *Dream Angus: The Celtic God of Dreams* (London, 2006).

82 *Tóruigheacht Dhiarmada agus Ghráinne*, ed. & trans. N. Ní Shéaghdha (Dublin, 1967); see above, 220, fn.86, for the problems involved in dating this tale.

acting entirely within the norms of the traditional Gaelic mores upon which the stories depended. But this was a subtle point, and it is easy to see how, in the imaginations of those who read the *Transactions*, Aengus could begin to acquire a romantic penumbra as the supernatural patron of lovers.

Two more steps were now required before he could be identified as the god of love, and these happened concurrently. The first was the recognition that the Túatha Dé Danann were Ireland's pagan deities, as already detailed. It helped that in one early saga, the poignant 'Dream of Óengus', the god appeared as a lover himself, thus reinforcing Ossianic perceptions to nineteenth-century readers. The second step was to expand his role from protector of two specific literary lovers to the guardian spirit of lovers in general. Standish O'Grady was once again the crucial figure here, and at the end of the 1870s Aengus appeared in his work as a fully fledged native divinity of love.[83] O'Grady's formula 'Angus an Vrōga, the Eros of the Gæil' was the first instance of his conflation with the classical love-god—a motif which soon became conventional.[84]

O'Grady's imagination was clearly attracted by Aengus, and he equipped him with the halo of circling birds which were the most distinctive feature of his modern iconography, the equivalent of Apollo's lyre or Neptune's trident. There was a tendency to multiply the number of these over the next decade, but—typically—their origin was obscure, being originally drawn from a puzzling *dindshenchas* story, where they were four in number. The story tells of Aengus shaping four of his kisses into two pairs of birds, 'so that they might entice the nobles of Ireland'.[85] *Dindshenchas* material is often elliptical—because it alludes to stories that the reader or audience probably already knew—and so the significance of Aengus's action is unclear to us. The rest of the story makes it obvious that it was something mischievous at best and sinister at worst, because the four birds act as the supernatural equivalent of nuisance callers for the unlucky Cairbre Lifechair, son of the legendary king Cor-

---

83 It may have helped that there was a family connection here: Standish James's cousin, Standish Hayes O'Grady, had been one-time president of the Ossianic Society and was the editor of 'The Pursuit of Díarmait and Gráinne.' Note also that O'Grady could access an accurate text of 'The Dream of Óengus' as it had been edited and translated in the third volume of the *Revue celtique* (1876–8) by Edward Müller.

84 'Angus an Vrōga' = *Aengus an Bhrogha*, 'Aengus of the Brugh', meaning his great *síd*-mound, Newgrange.

85 'The Prose Tales in the Rennes Dindshenchas', ed. & trans. W. Stokes, *RC* 15 (1895), 68–9.

mac mac Airt. They appear at his dwelling, Ráth Cairbri, where one pair chirrups 'Come here, come here!' while the others cry 'I go, I go!' They follow Cairbre wherever he goes for almost a year, incessantly carolling this peculiar mantra.

There was no scholarly edition of this anecdote until 1895, but Eugene O'Curry had mentioned Aengus's birds, and this was probably O'Grady's source.[86] Fashioned from kisses and with a mysterious song that hinted at unattainability, Aengus's birds could be taken to gesture towards the erotic. O'Grady enthusiastically took up the theme: Aengus/Angus made numerous appearances in the *History*, and the birds were repackaged both as his permanent accessories and as metaphors for the impalpable force of romantic love which he had come to personify in O'Grady's mind. At one point the god appears to Cormac mac Airt accessorized 'with a shining tiompan in his hands'—a *tiompán* being a stringed instrument, perhaps a psaltery.[87] Even more typical was the following passage:

> ... and Lara observed her, and she observed him, for in the minds of both there sang the immortal birds, children of the breath of Angus of the Brugh, the beautiful son of Yeoha, and their minds trembled towards one another, and a strong compulsion led them on to love.[88]

Accounting for human behaviour and emotion in terms of the actions of gods was very rare in medieval Irish tradition, as a direct consequence of its 'post-pagan' character.[89] When an ancient Greek thinker wanted to

---

86 E. O'Curry, *Lectures on the Manuscript Materials of Ancient Irish History* (Dublin, 1861), 478–9.

87 O'Grady, *History* i., 51.

88 O'Grady, *History* i., 83. 'Yeoha' = Eochaid, i.e. the Dagda.

89 I know of only two exceptions. The first is the Book of Leinster version of the Middle Irish saga 'The Intoxication of the Ulstermen' (*Mesca Ulad*), in which Delbaeth son of Ethlenn and Óengus and Cermait sons of the Dagda mingle with an army to invisibly foment conflict among mortals; see *Mesca Ulad*, ed. J. C. Watson (Dublin, 1941), ll.575–80, on 25. The second comes in the perhaps twelfth-century 'Battle of Mag Rath' (*Cath Maige Rath*) in which the hero Congal's excited mental state is directly attributed to the machinations of the war-goddesses as 'guardian demons' within his mind—rather in the manner of Eithne's 'accompanying demon' in 'The Fosterage of the House of Two Vessels'. Michael Clarke has related this to a wider learned tradition of equating classical and native deities, and of allegorizing both as mental states ('Demonology, Allegory and Translation: the Furies and the Morrígan', in R. O'Connor (ed.), *Classical Literature and Learning in Medieval Irish Narrative* (Cambridge, 2014), 101–22). Note that Clarke draws on

rationalize his divinities he could call upon philosophy to recast them as poetic labels for inner or outer phenomena—such as the atmosphere, or sexual desire—and this was a persistent, respectable current within the intellectual mainstream of antiquity, the roots of which could be traced back as far as Homer.[90] But in a Christian culture like that of medieval Ireland, the idea that pagan gods might inwardly interfere with human beings was not a welcome one—so rationalization had to take place upon the plane of history, not upon that of philosophy.[91] The Anglo-Irish Aengus, then, began as a particularly vivid example of Standish O'Grady's fondness for taking a well-attested figure from medieval Irish tradition and wresting it into a new, Hellenic shape.

The result was an old-yet-new deity who had come sharply into focus—bird-haloed, *tiompán*-toting—by the early 1880s, and over the next twenty years other writers continued to refine him. Both Yeats and Russell found Aengus compelling—perhaps the most compelling of all the Túatha Dé Danann—and this has been recognized by scholars in passing but not fully accounted for.[92] It is clear that he chimed with their esoteric (and, for Yeats, erotic) preoccupations, and could be keyed to the ways in which those preoccupations shifted over two decades. 'The Dream of Óengus' in particular set forth themes that seemed tailor-made to appeal to the younger Yeats, not least supernatural vision and the relationship between transcendence and desire.[93] It is also likely, given the poet's thwarted love life, that the elusive nature of consummation in that tale stirred him deeply. Its hero, who seems every bit as ado-

---

J. Borsje, 'Demonising the enemy: a study of Congal Cáech', in J. E. Rekdal, et al. (eds.), *Proceedings of the Eighth Symposium of Societas Celtologica Nordica* (Uppsala, 2007), 21–38.

90 Compare *Iliad* 19, ll.86–9, in which Agamemnon tries to explain why he has compensated himself for the loss of a mistress by robbing Achilles of his: 'Not I was the cause of this act, but Zeus and my lot and the Fury that walks in the dark; they it was who in the assembly put wild madness in my wits, on that day when I myself took Achilles' prize away from him.' The point is that the two kinds of causation—that of Agamemnon's ego-self ('I myself') and that of the divinities—function here as alternative languages for human motivation, operating in parallel.

91 See D. C. Feeney, *The Gods in Epic: Poets and Critics of the Classical Tradition* (Oxford, 1991), 6–14, 31–2.

92 See for example L. O'Connor, *Haunted English: the Celtic Fringe, the British Empire, and De-Anglicization* (Baltimore, MD, 2006), 69, 70, 204, n.15.

93 The impulse to see pervasive allegory in the tale is still with us, though Christianity rather than paganism is now in fashion: see B. Gray, 'Reading *Aislinge Óenguso* as a Christian-Platonist Parable', *PHCC* 24 (2004), 16–39.

lescent as his sobriquet 'the Young Lad' would imply, is charged with eros but seems to lack genital sexuality. And when Óengus and his beloved are united, instead of falling into one another's arms they turn into swans and fly off together—desire sublimated by a seemingly symbolic metamorphosis.

But in Yeats' case, the concept of Aengus as divine lover was down, in part, to sheer misinformation. Aengus played an important role in the saga 'The Wooing of Étaín' (as discussed in chapter 3), a work which excited Yeats deeply. By virtue of involving reincarnation and shifts between orders of being, it seemed to embody some profound statement of pre-Christian Irish spirituality. Unfortunately, the only text known at the time was in fragments, leaving huge holes in the plot. (The full saga was not restored until the 1930s.) This made it necessary for scholars and littérateurs to reconstruct the story. Inevitably, major misapprehensions came in, the most serious being that Étaín had left her husband Midir in order to elope with Aengus, an idea which clearly—and with circular reasoning—drew on the latter's recent 'recovery' as the Irish god of love.[94]

As it happened, this conjecture was utterly wide of the mark, but the idea that Aengus and Étaín had been a pair of wandering, passionate lovers shaped Yeats's conception of the god from the first.[95] He later recorded that, in 1897, 'while I was still working on an early version of *The Shadowy Waters*, I saw one night with my bodily eyes, as it seemed, two beautiful persons, who would, I believe, have answered to their names'.[96] Yeats's reconstructed version of 'The Wooing of Étáin' mirrors the the exquisite fable of Cupid and Psyche, whose sufferings are recounted in Apuleius's late antique novel *The Golden Ass*. That tale—transparently an allegory of the growth of the soul (*psyche*, in Greek) through love—was highly regarded by Symbolist writers and artists.[97] Yet again, it seemed impossible for Irish figures to avoid being lensed through perceived clas-

---

94 Thus, in 1884, d'Arbois de Jubainville averred that 'Etain, after her separation from Mider, *became the wife of Oengus...*' (*The Irish Mythological Cycle*, trans. R. I. Best (Paris, 1884 [Dublin & London, 1903]), 176–7, emphasis mine).

95 Brendan O Hehir has set out this process of misunderstanding in detail, showing that the folklorist Alfred Nutt was probably Yeats's source; see 'Yeats's Sources for the Matter of Ireland, I. Edain and Aengus', *Yeats: An Annual of Critical and Textual Studies* 6 (1989), 76–89.

96 *The Variorum Edition of the Poems of W. B. Yeats*, ed. P. Allt & R. K. Alspach (2nd edn., New York, 1966), 817.

97 See below, 392–3, where a related equation to Orpheus and Eurydice is made explicitly by Yeats's Scottish collaborator in the Celtic Mysteries, William Sharp.

sical equivalents, and in this way Aengus's reputation as Ireland's esoteric Eros grew. The significance of this process lay in the fact that the
elements required to repackage Aengus as god of love derived from the
new Celtic scholarship (comparative mythology, the editing and translation of Gaelic texts), while their actual synthesis was effected by creative
writers.

Aengus made a number of appearances in Yeats's early poetry. The
most influential was 'The Wanderings of Oisin' (1889), in which he featured—in a weird innovation—as the father of Niamh, the fairy-maiden
who lures the hero Oisin away.[98] A 'beautiful young man', he is a narcoleptic figure, a divine lotus-eater. One suspects that this removed sleepi-
ness was Yeats's attempt to accommodate the contradiction of a love-
deity who seemed somehow pre- or suprasexual. If so, the effect was
knowingly decadent. Yeats even gave the god a phallic sceptre which
attracts the dainty devotions of both sexes:

> One hand upheld his beardless chin,
> And one a sceptre flashing out
> Wild flames of red and gold and blue,
> Like to a merry wandering rout
> Of dancers leaping in the air;
> And men and ladies knelt them there
> And showed their eyes with teardrops dim,
> And with low murmurs prayed to him,
> And kissed the sceptre with red lips,
> And touched it with their finger-tips.[99]

Such ministrations awaken the god sufficiently for him to rhapsodize on
the island's antinomian and paradisiacal delight, climaxing: 'joy is God
and God is joy.' He then lapses back into (post-orgasmic?) slumber, after
'one long glance for girl and boy' in a manner suggestive of a languorous
bisexual responsiveness. Discussion of the ways in which the Anglo-
Irish Aengus destabilized sexual norms will be held back for the final
chapter of this book, but it should be emphasized in passing that 'The
Wanderings of Oisin' launched a version of the god characterized by
passivity and ephebic loveliness, and these would soon become major

---

98 Niamh had been made up by the eighteenth-century poet Mícheál Coimín; see O
Hehir, 'Yeats's sources for the matter of Ireland: I', 77.

99 *Variorum Poems of W. B. Yeats*, ed. Allt & Alspach, 17–8.

motifs in his imagery across the works of several writers and artists. For the most part, however, these did not again include Yeats himself, nor Russell, both of whom developed Aengus in esoteric rather than androgynous directions.

From the mid-1890s Aengus entered a second phase of importance in Yeats's thought, and the poet returned to him with greater sophistication. This is visible in the poetry, in the notes and letters pertaining to the Celtic Mysteries, and in the earlier versions of some of the drama. George Russell led the way in 1895, giving Aengus a central position as 'the master magician of all, sailing invisibly "on the wings of the cool east wind"', whose 'palace... remains to this day at New Grange, wrought over with symbols of the Astral Fire and the great Serpentine Power'.[100] By 1901, 'Angus the Young' had become firmly embedded in his cosmogony as the native form of the 'Light of the Logos', meaning that emanation of the original godhead impelled to pass outwards and downwards into the material world as 'an eternal joy becoming love, a love changing into desire, and leading on to earthly passion and forgetfulness of its own divinity'. This was another strategy for getting around Aengus's relative sexlessness: in his primordial or refined form the god represented divine ecstasy, gradually degrading itself into energetic love, and thence into desire, finally sinking into the 'spiritual death' of sexual passion. For Russell, Aengus was like the little girl in the nursery rhyme: when he was good, he was very, very good, but when he was bad, he was horrid.

As Russell himself noted, '[t]he conception of Angus as an all-pervading divinity who first connects being with non-being seems removed by many aeons of thought from that beautiful golden-haired youth who plays on the tympan surrounded by singing birds.'[101] In fact, both conceptions of the god detailed here were unmistakably the imaginative creations of the late nineteenth century, one O'Grady's, the other Russell's own; far from being 'aeons of thought' apart, they were separated only by two decades and a few miles of metropolitan Dublin. But a certain amount of attraction is surely necessary for anything to exist at all, and Russell went on to identify the god with 'every form of desire', from the child's instinctive urge to draw near to beautiful things all the way down to 'chemical affinity'—that is, molecular bonds.[102] This was an

---

100 Russell, 'Legends of Ancient Eire', in Iyer & Iyer (eds.), *Descent of the Gods*, 342.

101 Russell, 'The Children of Lir', in Iyer & Iyer (eds.), *Descent of the Gods*, 158.

102 Russell meant it literally: it follows that the god Aengus (in one of the weirdest

exalted (if diffuse) role, and one echoed by Yeats, for when the latter began work on the Celtic rituals, Aengus soon emerged as chief deity in the divine apparatus, 'the Spirit of Life' who embodied 'eternal desire which is a reflection of divine love in a fallen world'.[103] Yeats also identified him with Hermes and Dionysus, both sons of the father-god and envisioned as young, attractive men.[104] Sometimes it appears that the god had taken on so strong a shape in the poet's mind that he felt free to flatly contradict the medieval sources—stating that Aengus had been the king of the Túatha Dé Danann, for example, a role which in the sagas he explicitly refuses.

IMAGINATION AND DESIRE

What these versions of Aengus seem to share is a conception of the god as mediatory and mobile, making him the divinity that descends, who moves between things and joins them together. This was clear in Russell's cosmogony, in which Aengus circulated between the realms of formless divinity and manifest matter, and it also tallied with his role in Yeats's verse-drama. It seemed to derive from direct inner experience: George Pollexfen, followed by Yeats himself, enjoyed an astral vision of Aengus as a radiant colossus connecting heaven and earth, his head and shoulders lost among the clouds.[105]

But Yeats also described Aengus as the 'god of ecstatic poetry', and—in short—it seems he came to identify him with the poetic imagination itself. Strikingly, this meant that the Celtic Mysteries recuperated and emphasized *two* divinities of poetry, Aengus and his triple sister Brigit, whose complex 'divine form' was examined above. It may be objected that this is hardly surprising in a system developed by a poet, but what is significant is the schematic difference between the two gods. Aengus moves; Brigit is still. The three Brigits stand in a row, with the central Brigit of Poetry interblending the harshness of the Brigit of Smithwork and the sweetness of the Brigit of Medicine, being both 'receptive of impressions, and possessing the power of producing form'. It is as though

---

modulations of any medieval literary character) is to be identified not only with covalent bonds inside molecules, but also with gravity (!) because it is attraction, or 'desire'.

103 Martin, *W. B. Yeats: Metaphysician as Dramatist*, 38, 41.

104 For the identification, see O'Connor, *Haunted English*, 204, n.15.

105 Martin, *W. B. Yeats: Metaphysician as Dramatist*, 41.

FIG. 8.5. George Russell, *A Landscape with a Couple, and a Spirit with a Lute* (date unknown), oil on canvas laid on board, National Gallery of Ireland. Reprinted by the permission of Russell & Volkening as agents for the Estate of George Russell.

they are on different axes: Brigit's poetry is a horizontal transmutation of experience, and that of Aengus a vertical plunge in search of it. The distinction is between the conscious mixture of rigour and sensitivity necessary for a command of poetic form on the one hand, and the ecstatic quest for inspiration on the other. This recalls Declan Kiberd's observation about the precedence of style over content in a colony: Aengus is the rhapsodic flash that intuits and innovates a style, but Brigit the smith-goddess is the alchemical process of integration necessary to have something worth expressing—in Yeats's own famous phrase, the hammering of thoughts into unity. In a crucial sense, then, the brother and sister deities of the Celtic Mysteries represented the twin poles of Yeats's maturing poetic.

The 'divine form' of Aengus is not recorded, perhaps because Yeats and Russell felt they knew what he looked like: his iconography had been more or less fixed by O'Grady. Tellingly, Russell's visions and images of Aengus accordingly showed an uncharacteristically confident use of detail: the being in Figure 8.5, although typically undated and untitled, answers so closely to Russell's description of Aengus in 1901 that that is surely who it depicts. (Similar figures—again almost certainly representing Aengus—appear in a number of Russell's surviving paintings.)[106] It seems that in this period Russell came to identify Aengus retrospectively as the focus of one of his earliest and most important visions. The actual date of this experience is unclear: he did not acknowledge it in print as a vision of his own until 1918, but had worked it into a short story entitled 'A Dream of Angus Oge', published in 1897. (It may well have been the occasion he recalled in 1911 as the first time he had seen one of the 'opalescent' beings whom he identified with the Túatha Dé Danann.) The iconographic accessibility of the Anglo-Irish Aengus is clear from Russell's account of his vision, because he expected the reader to be able to identify the god:

> ... I saw the light was streaming from the heart of a glowing figure. Its body was pervaded with light as if sunfire rather than blood ran through its limbs.... It moved over me along the winds, carrying a harp, and there was a circling of golden hair that swept across the strings. Birds flew about it, and... [o]n the face was an ecstasy of beauty and immortal youth.[107]

It is likely that Aengus would have been the only member of the Túatha Dé that Russell could have counted upon being identifiable in this way.

All this merely confirms that Aengus, much more than the other members of the Túatha Dé, had reached an extreme point of individualization and precision. But as Yeats and Russell worked him into the Celtic Mysteries, something unique happened, consonant with his exceptional position: he hived off a secondary form, a new being. The context was another attempt by Yeats, once again with Pollexfen, to get a vision of Aengus's divine form. The attempt was made at the very end of December 1898, prefaced by an invocation to the god. A surviving litany from the Celtic Mysteries probably gives a good idea of what this was like (and may be the actual one which was used):

Aengus chief of the young we evoke thee
Master of the four winds we evoke thee

---

106 See for instance the harp-strumming, golden-haired youth in the painting entitled (though not by Russell) 'The Glory and the Dream', in O. Nulty's catalogue, *George Russell–Æ. . . . at The Oriel's 21st Anniversary* (Dublin, ?1989), 8; I would have reproduced this painting but (as with much of Russell's art) its current whereabouts have proved untraceable.

107 From *The Candle of Vision* (London, 1918), but vision recorded (and fictionalized) in 1897; see below, 447.

Guarder of Grainne we evoke thee
Sojourner with Mider we evoke thee
Sojourner in [the] Brugh we evoke thee
Lover of Fame we evoke thee.[108]

But instead of the expected radiant youth, the image of a jester or a fool appeared before Yeats's inner eye. He described the figure as a 'medieval fool… in a cap of pale violet with two ears of pink & a cap of the same colour & pointed shoes. He held a long staff of… mountain ash… surmounted by a kind of caduceus shape… when asked [he indicated] that he was only a messenger of the true Aengus.'[109] Yeats and Russell undertook intense visionary work on the fool over the next two years, during summer sojourns with Lady Gregory at Coole Park; soon Russell began to glimpse him lurking in Coole's Georgian corridors, dressed in white. Yeats was to frame these experiences in the third person in one of the stories included in the revised second edition of *The Celtic Twilight*:

I knew a man who was trying to bring before his mind's eye an image of Ængus, the old Irish god of love and poetry and ecstasy, who changed four of his kisses into birds, and suddenly the image of a man with a cap and bells rushed before his mind's eye and grew vivid and spoke and called itself 'Aengus' messenger.' I knew another man, a truly great seer, who saw a white fool in a visionary garden, where there was a tree with peacocks' feathers instead of leaves, and flowers that opened to show little human faces when the white fool had touched them with his coxcomb, and he saw at another time a white fool sitting by a pool and smiling and watching images of many fair women floating up from the pool.[110]

But where had the image come from? A fool had been the subject of one of Yeats's poems earlier in the decade; and of course medieval tradition made Óengus/Aengus a trickster—providing a further link with Hermes, god of thieves—because in the first part of 'The Wooing of Étaín' he wangles Newgrange by sheer sophistry. The main source for the image, however, was the folklore collection that had become Lady Greg-

108 This invocation is found on a folded sheet inserted into one of the magical notebooks (NLI MS 13574), quoted in Putzel, *Reconstructing Yeats*, 194.
109 NLI MS 13574–5, quoted in Yeats, *Mythologies*, ed. Gould & Toomey, 295.
110 *Mythologies*, ed. Gould & Toomey, 76.

ory's passion, and in which Yeats intermittently collaborated. One of her discoveries was a set of traditions about 'the fool of the fort(h)'—*amadán na bruidhne* in Irish—a supernatural being whose very touch, like a blasting dew, brings disablement or death.[111] The fool had a reputation for being the only fairy from whose malevolence one cannot recover: paralysis and loss of speech were seen as evidence of the *amadán*'s touch. As with much fairylore, it is clear that his role was to provide an explanation for unpredictable losses and disasters—in this case the suddenness of a stroke or aneurysm.

At this point Yeats had a problem. Vision had associated the fool with Aengus, the most affable of Irish divinities, yet the *amadán* of folklore was clearly not a being one would care to meet. Various strategies were tried: he and Russell privately experimented with the theory that there might be *two* fools, a 'white' one (Aengus's messenger) and a 'dark' or 'black' one (the malevolent *amadán*). In *The Celtic Twilight*, however, Yeats implied that there was only one, whom he acknowledged was indeed deadly from an earthly perspective—but (he weakly continued) '[w]hat else can death be but the beginning of wisdom and power and beauty?'[112] In many anecdotes collected by Gregory, the touch of the *amadán* brought not death but catastrophic mental impairment (again the relationship of such stories to the consequences of a stroke are obvious); this allowed Yeats to associate the fool with the dubious insights of delirium, thus bringing him back—by a circuitous route—into the ambit of Aengus, god of ecstasy.[113]

At some point during this process Yeats passed on Lady Gregory's findings about the *amadán* to William Sharp, his Scottish collaborator in the Celtic Mysteries. To Gregory's great annoyance Sharp promptly published them, working the figure of the sinister 'faery fool' into his own misty Celtic verse.[114] In particular, Sharp gave the 'dark fool' a name—'Dalua'—and he inserted this being into his version of the Gaelic pantheon as the personification of madness. This process is examined in detail in the following chapter, and it was not the only occasion on

111 See D. Hyde, 'Amadán na bruidhne', *Gadelica: A Journal of Modern-Irish Studies* 1 (1913), 271.

112 *Mythologies*, ed. Gould & Toomey, 77.

113 'The self, which is the foundation of our knowledge, is broken in pieces by foolishness, and is forgotten in the sudden emotions of women, and therefore fools may get, as women do get of a certainty, glimpses of much that sanctity finds at the end of its painful journey.' (*Mythologies*, ed. Gould & Toomey, 77).

114 See *Mythologies*, ed. Gould & Toomey, 295.

which the magpie-like Sharp would lift an idea from Yeats, publish it, and then try to pass it off as a parallel and meaningfully coincident recovery of ancient tradition.[115] The result was that Aengus in the 1890s produced not one but two new beings, the white fool and the black; thanks to Sharp, the latter took on a life of its own now wholly unrelated to the medieval Aengus.

This was a by-product of a process which had seen Aengus become, for Yeats, the deity who presided over and personified the intersection of sex, magic, and poetry, and who gave access to the creative energy of euphoria. I suspect his importance lay in his ability to act as a kind of projected divine double for Yeats himself during *fin de siècle* uncertainties, and that he should be seen as one of the poet's many personae, alter egos, and anti-selves. To use the metaphor of 'Rosa Alchemica', Aengus was the immortal mood with which the poet was most eager to become incorporate, and this reminds us that the Celtic Mysteries were intended in part to claim Maud Gonne, and so represented an intertwining of the poet's occult and erotic aims.

Yeats's correspondence during the shaping of the Celtic Mysteries and his 'therapeutic' invocations to Aengus—the adjective is Foster's—present the odd sight of Yeats and Gonne speaking to one other using the gods as metaphors for their own affective ambitions.[116] If this seems far-fetched, one must remember that this was precisely what the training of the Golden Dawn had taught them, though Gonne was only briefly a member of the order. Yeats, the passionate and preoccupied lover, figured himself as a votary of the Eros of the Gael. Gonne, the English-born Fenian separatist, explicitly chose to place herself under the aegis of the god Lug, the potent and masculine divinity who rejected his mixed inheritance in order to lead the Túatha Dé Danann in throwing off Fomorian oppression. It was an easy step to substitute 'Irish' and 'British' for the mythological races, and for Gonne to feel that she was herself flinging slingshots into the eye of the colonial Balor.[117] (The myth of Lug was given

115 The most famous is the 'Archer vision', seen by Yeats at Tulira Castle in 1896; he told Sharp about it in a letter, and the latter immediately rushed out a closely similar story under his *alter ego*, the Hebridean seeress Fiona Macleod. See Foster, *TAM*, 165–6.

116 *TAM*, 204.

117 For Gonne's ambiguous devotion to and cross-gendered identification with Lug, see Foster, *The Irish Story*, 13, 16; also *The Collected Letters of W. B. Yeats, Volume 2: 1896–1900*, ed. W. Gould, J. S. Kelly, & D. Toomey (Oxford, 1996), 320. For the (rare but attested) identification of the English with the Fomorians in bardic verse, see J. Radner, 'The Combat of Lug and Balor', *Oral Tradition* 7.1 (1992), 143–9.

precisely this anti-colonial spin by revivalist poetasters such as Alice Milligan.)[118] According to Yeats, in December 1898 Gonne claimed that she had dreamed that Lug had married them: 'I saw my body from outside it—& I was brought away by Lug & my hand was put in yours & I was told we were married. Then I kissed you & all became dark.'[119] She had been lecturing intensively on Irish mythology at this point, and—if Yeats's account of her words is at all accurate—her unconscious mind seems here to have uncannily projected herself and the poet into the medieval tale 'The Phantom's Frenzy', casting Yeats as Conn of the Hundred Battles and herself (majestically) as the nubile Sovereignty of Ireland.[120] It was certainly of a piece with other aspects of the vehement Gonne persona, and shows how deep the saturation in mythological images went.[121]

Ultimately, however, the introjection of Aengus availed Yeats little, and there seems to be a link between his erotic disappointments and the increased ambivalence the god took on after the turn of the century. (The version of his play *The Countess Cathleen* produced in 1900 involved a misleading vision sent by Aengus, for example.)[122] The Anglo-Irish Aengus emerges as an ambiguous product of individual and collective influences, arising from but also obscuring the Óengus of early Irish saga. In the hermetic circles in which Yeats moved, he came with great rapidity to personify everything that was best in the native mythology, and in particular by morphing into a god of love he emphasized delicate feeling in a mythology which was not short on bloodthirsty or sordid moments. He became in a sense a partial counterweight to the hero Cú Chulainn, important to so many writers of the Literary Revival, Yeats not least; the two figures personified the polarized self-images of a nation beginning to de-anglicize. Poetic, ecstatic, delicate, occult and sometimes half-feminine, Aengus mirrored an Arnoldian version of the supposed Celtic character, and so became, for a time, the personification of Ireland's imagination.

118 See, *inter alia*, her crude political allegory 'The Return of Lugh Lamh-fada', *Hero Lays* (Dublin, 1908), 10–13, discussed by J. F. Deane, *All Dressed Up: Modern Irish Historical Pageantry* (Syracuse, 2014), 63–5. Deane's work came to my attention just as I finished this study and could not be incorporated, but note her important discussions of various staged representations of Lug, 63–8.

119 Crucial discussion in D. Toomey, 'Labyrinths: Yeats and Maud Gonne', *YA* 9 (1992), 95–131.

120 For this text, see above, 26–7.

121 *The Collected Letters of W. B. Yeats, Volume 3: 1901–1904*, ed. J. S. Kelly & R. Schuchard (Oxford, 1994), 315.

122 See Foster, *TAM*, 230.

9

HIGHLAND DIVINITIES

THE CELTIC REVIVAL IN SCOTLAND

> Not the wretchedest man or woman but has a deep
> secretive mythology with which to wrestle with the
> material world and to overcome it and pass beyond
> it... We are all creators. We all create a mythological
> world of our own out of certain shapeless materials.
>
> —JOHN COOPER POWYS

AS THE NINETEENTH century drew to a close, awareness grew among
Scottish writers and artists of the mythological dimension to the Gaelic
heritage their nation shared with Ireland.[1] This was, in a sense, no surprise: Ireland and Gaelic Scotland had been part of a single cultural and
linguistic zone in the Middle Ages, and thanks to James Macpherson's
Ossianic poems, Scotland had been the fountainhead of romantic Celticism in English for more than a century.[2] From the mid-1890s Scotland
developed a parallel Celtic Revival of its own, an anti-industrial aesthetic movement centred in Edinburgh but that looked to Ireland for an
example. In highlighting the difference in tone between Irish and Scottish fairylore, Yeats had once archly chided the Scots for 'souring the
disposition of their fairies'; now, in a striking counter-movement, a Scot-

---

1 On a much more modest scale, the same phenomenon can be also observed in
relation to the Isle of Man, a significant area because of its small size and the fact it possessed a distinct Gaelic tradition and language, but was not a nation; uniquely it also had
a strong and genuinely ancient association with a single god, Manannán mac Lir, a characteristic now conspicuously incorporated into the island's cultural identity (a major
museum of Manx maritime history in Peel is named 'The House of Manannan', for
example).

2 For a challenge to the single culture-zone consensus, see W. McLeod, *Divided
Gaels: Gaelic Cultural Identities in Scotland and Ireland, c.1200-c.1650* (Oxford, 2004).

tish artistic elite laid claim to the Túatha Dé Danann as a pan-Gaelic pantheon every bit as native to the Highlands as to Ireland.[3]

GAELIC FOLKLORE AND *CARMINA GADELICA*

The second half of the nineteeth century saw the systematic collection of oral folklore undertaken in Gaelic Scotland. As in Ireland, it was the far west where the Gaelic language was strongest that was envisioned as a well of immemorial tradition, where customs which had died out elsewhere were supposedly retained.[4]

But here two opposed sets of contemporary expectations were at work, and these influenced the kind of material collected and the way in which it was packaged for the reading public. Contemporary fashion painted the Gaels as innately spiritual, and folklore gatherers satisfied the public appetite by presenting short poems full of dignified spirituality, seeming to evoke the pristine dawn of Christianity in Scotland. But this Christian piety clashed with another set of expectations, this time supplied by Victorian theories about the nature and origin of folk customs. As Gillian Bennett and others have observed, the folklorists of the age were fixated on the idea that the customs of rural communities represented survivals of pagan religion, embedded in a supposedly timeless countryside like fossils in the cultural shale.[5] Scotland's native Gaelic tradition largely failed to provide the ex-divinities so prominent in Irish literature and folklore, but that did not deter late-Victorian folklore collectors, whose hankering after a pantheon of Gaelic deities was so strong that it did not preclude making them up them if necessary.

The first Gael—indeed the first Scotsman—to put out a scholarly account of the Túatha Dé Danann was named Alexander MacBain. He had

---

3 For Yeats on Scottish and Irish fairies, see *WIFL&M*, 26–9.

4 There is some evidence that Scottish collectors were particularly interested in mythological tales but failed to obtain them: see D. U. Stiùbhart, 'Alexander Carmichael and *Carmina Gadelica*', in D. U. Stiùbhart (ed.), *The Life and Legacy of Alexander Carmichael* (Port of Ness, 2008), 6. In the same volume, see R. Black, 'I Thought He Made It All Up: Context and Controversy', 57–61, for the background to the golden age of Gaelic folklore collection.

5 The literature here is large: for a brisk summary see R. Hutton, *The Triumph of the Moon* (Oxford, 1999), 112–4, and for more detail, see G. Bennett's influential essay, 'Geologists and Folklorists: Cultural Evolution and the Science of Folklore', *Folklore* 105 (1994), 25–37.

been publishing Gaelic charms since 1888 and would later find fame as a lexicographer and philologist, areas in which his contributions have proved of lasting value. On mythology he was less secure: his purpose was 'the reconstruction of the Gaelic Olympus' and by 1885 he had claimed the gods for a wider Gaeldom by giving his material a Scottish inflection. The county of Angus took its name (he averred) from Aengus Óg, while the Aberdeenshire town of Banff memorialized the Túatha Dé woman Banba.[6] He was also a pagan survivalist who believed that Gaelic society had been Christianized in the relatively recent past, and then only superficially. Gaelic charms were his primary evidence for this theory, and he wrote that '[s]uperstition is nearly all a survival of Paganism into Christian times; and in the incantations the names of Christ, his apostles, and the Virgin Mary took those of the old heathen gods'.[7]

The contribution of the indefatigable folklorist Alexander Carmichael (1832–1912), a contemporary of MacBain's, was both more restrained and more influential. Carmichael produced the quintessential work of the Celtic Revival in Scotland, the exquisite body of charms, prayers, and blessings known as *Carmina Gadelica*, which he had collected between 1855 and 1899.[8] After decades in the Hebrides he had settled in Edinburgh in 1882, where he became a pillar of that city's Gaelic establishment and came to play a supporting role in the Celtic scene centred there.

Only the first two volumes of the *Carmina*, which appeared in 1900 accompanied by Carmichael's pellucid translations, are relevant for our purposes here.[9] The relationship between the *Carmina* as published and the actual traditions which he encountered is problematic. Since the 1970s research has revealed that Carmichael, a perfectionist with a romantic streak, polished up the material he collected in order to make the best possible impression; a consensus has emerged that *Carmina Gadel-*

---

6 A. MacBain, *Celtic Mythology and Religion* (Inverness, 1885 [Stirling, 1917]), 131–2.

7 A. MacBain, 'Incantations and magic rhymes', *Highland Monthly* 3 (1891–2), 223; see Stiùbhart, 'Alexander Carmichael', in Stiùbhart, (ed.), *Life and Legacy*, 36. A scholar of the stature of Martin West has been prepared to see something of Indo-European antiquity in Gaelic charms, comparing some of their phraseology with the Rigveda; but the case is not strong. See M. L. West, *Indo-European Poetry and Myth* (Oxford, 2007), 216.

8 D. U. Stiùbhart, 'The Making of a Charm Collector: Alexander Carmichael in the Outer Hebrides, 1864 to 1882', in J. Kapaló, É. Pocs, & W. Ryan (eds.), *The Power of Words: Studies on Charms and Charming in Europe* (Budapest, 2013) 25–66.

9 The edn. is *Carmina Gadelica, ortha nan Gaidheal: hymns and incantations with illustrative notes on words, rites, and customs, dying and obsolete*, ed. & trans. A. Carmichael (6 vols., Edinburgh, 1928–71), but note that only vols. 1 & 2 were edited by Carmichael himself, and were originally published in 1900.

ica should be understood as a literary, not literal, version of the charms and prayers imparted to him by Highland people. In this he was a man of his time, his work part of a grand project to demonstrate to the outside world that a belittled and beleaguered Gaelic culture was worthy of respect.[10]

This was propaganda in a noble cause, but it is clear that Carmichael was torn between his primary desire to stress the Christian piety of Highland people and a secondary need to report the pagan survivals which contemporary folklorists told him ought to exist.[11] To pull this off, he was required to ignore the centuries that separated Victorian Gaels from paganism, no matter how incongruous the effect. This is most apparent in his prose—precisely the part of his work now identified as the least reliable.[12] In a telling purple passage in the introduction to the *Carmina*, nameless native divinities appeared as symbols not only for the Gaels themselves, but also for a surviving paganism—and indeed for an entire dimension of Gaelic culture felt to be on the verge of vanishing:

> Highland divinities are full of life and action, local colour and individuality. These divinities filled the hearts and minds of the peoples of the Highlands, as their deities filled the hearts and minds of the people of Greece and Rome. The subject of these genii of the Highlands ought to be investigated and compared with those of other lands... Though loving their haunts and tenacious of their habitats, the genii of the Highlands are disappearing before the spirit of modernism, as the Red Indian, once bold and courageous, disappears before the white man. Once intrusive, they are now become timid as the mullet of the sea, the shrew of the grass, the swift of the air... They are startled at the crack of the rifle, the whistle of the steamer, the shriek of the train... Their homes are invaded and their repose is disturbed, so that they find no rest for their weary feet nor sleep for their heavy eyes; and their native

10 For a witty summation of thirty years of debate, see again Black, 'I Thought He Made It All Up', in Stiùbhart, (ed.), *Life and Legacy*, 57–81. At the end of his article, Black advances a crucial series of criteria for identifying which of the *Carmina* are likely to have been tinkered with the least.

11 There was a noteworthy vogue for these in Scottish journalism in the 1880s: representative are L. Sands, 'Survivals of Paganism in Foula', *Glasgow Herald* 17th November 1884, 8, and R. Munro, 'Some Survivals of Paganism in Scotland', *Good Words* 30 (1889), 333–7.

12 Black, 'I Thought He Made It All Up', in Stiùbhart, (ed.), *Life and Legacy*, 73.

land, so full of their love, so congenial to their hearts, will all too soon know them no more.[13]

One would have little idea from this passage that Christianity had arrived in Scotland thirteen hundred years before, but laments about the vanishing of nature spirits in the face of industrialization were widespread in antiquarian writing about fairy traditions in nineteenth-century Britain.[14] That Carmichael's rhetoric reflected a literary convention is underscored by the fact that these divinities—who apparently only stir from pre-Raphaelite drowsiness in order to bolt like startled fawns—are notable for their near total absence in the material Carmichael collected. Overwhelmingly, the figures actually invoked in the *Carmina* are Christ, Mary, and the angels and saints of the medieval church. Even in the wider oral literature of Gaelic Scotland, much of it consisting of lays about Finn mac Cumaill, Óengus/Aengus was really the only member of the classical Túatha Dé Danann to play a prominent role.

Carmichael must therefore have known that the charms and prayers that he took down were not full of relics of pre-Christian religion. Nevertheless we find him making the occasional nod in that direction, describing St Michael the Archangel, for example, as 'the Neptune of the Gael'—the implication being that he was a disguised substitute for the sea-god Manannán mac Lir.[15] Manannán in fact appears only very briefly in the *Carmina*, in a charm to be said over a cow with bloody urine:

The nine wells of Mac-Lir,
Relief on thee to pour,

---

13 *Carmina Gadelica* i., ed. Carmichael, xxxiii-iv.

14 For the topos, see C. Silver, *Strange and Secret Peoples: Fairies and Victorian Consciousness* (Oxford, 1999), 185ff, esp. 203–5, and N. Bown, *Fairies in Nineteenth-Century Art and Literature* (Cambridge, 2001). This passage quoted is rich, with revealing anthropological and proto-ecological dimensions, and its language is extraordinary coming from a Gael only fifty years or so after the last large-scale Clearance, especially one who, like Carmichael, had seen evictions in action on his native island of Lismore in the 1830s.

15 *Carmina Gadelica* i., ed. Carmichael, 198. Carmichael's translation of Michael's epithet *brian* as 'god' is disingenuous: the normal sense would be the orthodox '(arch) angel', and tellingly Carmichael himself is given as the sole source for the sense 'god, divinity' in Dwelly's *Dictionary* (s. v.). See Black, 'I Thought He Made It All Up', in Stiùbhart (ed.), *Life and Legacy*, 68, for the suspect nature of words in Dwelly drawn from Carmichael alone.

Put stop to thy blood,
Put flood to thy urine,
   Thou cow of cows, black cow.[16]

The prayers in the first two volumes of the *Carmina* are thought by scholars to have been tinkered with the least, so there is a good chance this allusion to the sea-god may be genuine; but in the absence of other allusions to Manannán in the corpus it is impossible to be sure. Dòmhnall Uilleam Stiùbhart, the leading contemporary expert on Carmichael, notes that he was prone to adding 'esoteric references' when polishing up his material, and 'the nine wells of Mac-Lir'—presumably an elaborate kenning for the ocean, invoked to flush out the animal's bladder—may be one such.

SHONY AND ST BRIDE

Carmichael alluded elsewhere to what seemed on the surface to be another pagan survival—a ritual libation made to a god of the sea on the island of Lewis.[17] This has become a famous and widely reported piece of Scottish folklore; if true, it would be a spectacular and probably unique instance of a pre-Christian deity continuing to be honoured in the British Isles more than a millennium after the introduction of Christianity.

But things are not so simple. Carmichael was drawing, not on oral tradition, but on a text that was already two centuries old, Martin Martin's *A Description of the Western Islands of Scotland*, published in 1703. One of the first English accounts of the Hebrides to be written by a native Gael, Martin's book described how the inhabitants of Lewis:

> ... had an ancient custom to sacrifice to a sea-god called Shony, at Hallow-tide, in the manner following: The inhabitants round the island came to the Church of St. Malvay, having each man his provision along with him; every family furnished a peck of malt, and this was brewed into ale; one of their number was picked out to wade into the sea up to the middle, and carrying a cup of ale in his

16 *Carmina Gadelica* ii., ed. Carmichael, 122, 123. A slightly different version, immediately before, also mentions Manannán in almost identical words.

17 See the deft recent discussion by Hutton, *PB*, 380–1, who comes (independently) to the same conclusions as myself.

hand, standing still in that posture, cried out with a loud voice saying, 'Shony, I give you this cup of ale, hoping that you'll be so kind as to send us plenty of sea-ware for enriching our ground for the ensuing year'; and so threw the cup of ale into the sea. This was performed in the night time. At his return to land they all went to church, where there was a candle burning upon the altar; and then standing silent for a little time, one of them gave a signal, at which the candle was put out, and immediately all of them went to the fields, where they fell a-drinking their ale, and spent the remainder of the night in dancing and singing, &c.[18]

This anecdote was to be endlessly recycled as evidence for lingering paganism in the Hebrides—we will meet it again several times in this chapter—but its historical value is dubious.[19] Martin Martin was neither approving nor an eyewitness: his informant was one John Morison of Bragar, whose own description points to the yearly libation to 'Shion' or 'Shony' having ceased around the 1630s.[20] The most likely interpretation is that it was a survival not of paganism, but of pre-Reformation Catholicism; its context was clearly the custom of visiting and keeping up chapels on the feast days of the saints to whom they were dedicated.[21] On the other hand, the detail of the drink offering is odd, though the making of offerings in gratitude at saints' shrines was a major part of Catholic piety, often done for healing on an individual level, for example, or more collectively, as here, for agricultural bounty. (Seaweed was used as fertilizer.) Perhaps the custom of pouring ale into the sea—interpreted by a hostile observer as a heathen act of propitiation—arose when there had ceased to be a priest in the community to receive the offering on the saint's behalf.

18 M. Martin, *A Description of the Western Islands of Scotland* [1703] (Edinburgh, 1999), 29.

19 Its most recent appearance may be in Robin Hardy and Anthony Shaffer's novelization of their cult 1973 horror film *The Wicker Man*, which of course took the idea of Hebridean paganism to a new and lurid extreme.

20 The major recent discussion, upon which I draw here, is D. U. Stiùbhart, ' "Some heathenish and superstitious rites": a letter from Lewis, 1700', *Scottish Studies* 34 (2000–6), 205–26; he gives an edition of John Morison's account of this custom (among others).

21 The church in question is almost certainly Teampall Mholuaidh, 'The Chapel of St Molua(g)', one of the major centres of worship on Lewis during the late medieval period and now used by the Scottish Episcopal Church. It is in the village of Eoropie, in the parish of Ness, in the very north of Lewis.

All this would help to explain the name of the mysterious supernatural being in question, as Martin Martin's informant specifically stated that *Shion* was a word he did not know. Various etymologies have been suggested, but it is probable that it is simply a Gaelicized form of the name 'John'; as the region of Lewis in question is remote, it may be that we have here evidence that the cult of one or other St John had survived the Reformation—probably John the Baptist, given the custom of wading into the water.[22] If so, it tellingly bespeaks the complex history of Christianity in the British Isles that an older form of Christian worship could look so convincingly like paganism to the learned commentators of subsequent centuries.

Carmichael's version generalized Martin's highly local account ('people in maritime districts made offerings... to the god of the sea') and ignored his testimony that it had long been extinct.[23] He also gave a Gaelic version of Martin Martin's invocation which looked so suspiciously like a verse from one of the *Carmina* that it may well have been his own back-translation from Martin's English. If this is so, he inserted another significant hedge, replacing the outlandish 'Shony' with the tactful *A Dhè na mara*, which he translated 'O God of the sea.' The difference between the 'God of the sea' and the 'god of the sea' exactly encapsulates the tension between piety and paganism that Carmichael was negotiating.

In all this it is obvious that Carmichael had no desire to deceive, and accounts of his life stress his integrity. It is simply that the notion of pagan survivals was integral to contemporary thinking about folk customs, and an underconfident Carmichael found what he expected to find. He never implies that his sources themselves were wholly cognizant of the supposedly non-Christian nature of some of their customs, as

22 This was Ronald Black's suggestion, made in editorial comments on the Rev. John Gregorson Campbell's *Superstitions of the Highlands and the Islands of Scotland* (1900) and *Witchcraft and Second Sight in the Highlands and Islands* (1902), republished together as *The Gaelic Otherworld*, ed. R. Black (Edinburgh, 2005), 332 fn.181, 548–9, 590–591 fn.114, though he takes a less sceptical view than I of the possibility of surviving Manannán-worship. Stiùbhart ('"Some Heathenish"', 217) notes that the Shion/Shony word may be connected to a rare Gaelic term *sionn* and its derivatives, meaning 'supernatural, of the otherworld', or to the Norse *sjon*, meaning 'sacrifice'; but in the context it seems clearly to be a name. On the other hand, John the Baptist and John the Apostle were known as *Eòin* in Gaelic; if 'Shony' (= *Seonaidh*) refers to one of them it must presumably be via a Gaelicized version of Scots 'Johnny', for reasons that are unclear to me.

23 *Carmina Gadelica* i., ed. Carmichael, 162–3.

another prop of folklore research at the time was the idea that only scholars, and not the folk themselves, were in a position to recover the 'real' (pagan) significance of their behaviour.

This tendency is most clearly visible of all in his lengthy commentary on the numerous prayers addressed to Gaeldom's most popular female saint, the complex figure of Brigit of Kildare, or Bride, of whom more will be said later. Astonishingly we seem to lack a full study of the Gaelic cult of Brigit and its cultural afterlife, but by Carmichael's day it was well known that Highland devotions to the saint had a number of un-usual features, including an association with the hearth, serpents, and the spring, plus the pious legend that she had acted as Christ's foster-mother—a deeply Gaelic concept.[24] Celtic scholarship in the late nine-teenth century had also begun to stress a putative continuity between the pre-Christian Brigit or Bríg, daughter of the Dagda, and the Chris-tian saint. None other than Maud Gonne had lectured on Brigit's double-ness in Dublin in 1899, emphasizing the imaginative primacy of the god-dess over the saint. It quickly became *de rigueur* to explain the quirks of popular devotion to Bride as relics of her once-divine status. Carmichael termed her 'the Mary and Juno of the Gael', thus fusing the primary feminine figures of three traditions.[25]

This inevitably entailed a degree of circular reasoning, as Bride's sta-tus as a goddess was extrapolated from some of the peculiarities of her saint's cult, but then those peculiarities themselves were explained in terms of her supposed pre-Christian origins. As with the debatable Shony, the cult of Bride therefore seemed to confirm contemporary theo-ries by providing a patent example of a pagan survival, and while recent scholarship has done much to cast doubt on the whole idea, it is ubiqui-tous in the apparatus to the *Carmina*. In particular Carmichael can be observed allowing an air of rhetorical paganism to attach to the pious lore he recorded about the saint:

Bride is said to preside over the different seasons of the year and to bestow their functions upon them according to their respective

24 The nearest approach so far is S. Ó Catháin, *The Festival of Brigit* (Dublin, 1995), supplemented by A. Bourke, 'Irish Stories of Weather, Time, and Gender: Saint Brigit', in M. Cohen & N. J. Curtin, (eds.), *Reclaiming Gender: Transgressive Identities in Modern Ire-land* (London, 1999), 13–32, and C. McKenna, 'Apotheosis and evanescence: the fortunes of Saint Brigit in the nineteenth and twentieth centuries', in J. F. Nagy, (ed.), *The Individ-ual in Celtic Literatures* [CSANA Yearbook 1] (Dublin, 2001), 74–108.

25 *Carmina Gadelica* i., ed. Carmichael, 164.

needs... Bride with her white wand is said to breathe life into the mouth of the dead Winter and to bring him to open his eyes to the tears and the smiles, the sighs and laughter of Spring.[26]

Bride's saint's day traditionally marked the end of winter, and what we have here is the pupation of metaphor into myth by a kind of folklorist's sleight-of-hand.[27] Note that the seasons are personified: had they been given the names of Gaelic deities then the image of Bride giving mouth to mouth resuscitation to 'the dead Winter' would clearly evoke (for example) the goddess Isis reviving the corpse of Osiris. This was precisely the step which later myth-makers were to take.

WILLIAM SHARP—'FIONA MACLEOD'

In 1891, Alexander MacBain had (inaccurately) praised hymns collected by Carmichael for their location on the 'indefinable borderland that separates Christianity and Paganism'.[28] This was the territory to which our next writer, William Sharp (1855–1905), was to stake his creative claim (Fig. 9.1). We have already met Sharp briefly as a collaborator in Yeats's Celtic Mysteries; he became Scotland's pre-eminent theorist of the Túatha Dé Danann, and was responsible for importing the pantheon prominently into the country's literature. Sharp's writings in this vein began to appear in 1894, invariably characterized by a hazy atmosphere of spiritual beauty. For the Paisley-born Sharp, Gaelic Scotland embodied a shimmering fantasy-land on the horizon in a way that it had not for Carmichael, the Gaelic speaker and native Highlander. Sharp was also quick to see that the folklorists and charm collectors had developed a new literary form: dignified, quasi-liturgical verse yoked to a prose apparatus of folklore, personal anecdote, and mythological speculation, liberally studded with Gaelic. It was this characteristic fusion of anthropology and incantation that he adopted.

His career featured one notorious oddity. Sharp—a red-faced six-footer in plus-fours—published all his most commercially successful

26 *Carmina Gadelica* i., ed. Carmichael, 172.

27 That myths were in origin mistaken extensions of metaphor was, precisely, the theory of the influential nineteenth-century mythologist Max Müller; see W. G. Doty, *Mythography: The Study of Myths and Rituals* (Tuscaloosa, 2000 [2nd edn.]), 11.

28 A. Macbain, 'Incantations and magic rhymes', 232.

FIG. 9.1. William Sharp, 'Fiona Macleod' (1855–1905).
Photo © National Portrait Gallery, London.

work in a female persona, that of a self-sequestered Hebridean visionary by the name of 'Fiona Macleod.' Before we look at the use he made of the gods there is the question of how this pseudonym (his most famous and sustained) should be interpreted.

Pronouns inevitably cause problems here, especially as the secret of Sharp's dual identity was not officially revealed until his death in 1905, though Yeats and Russell had had shrewd suspicions long before. For

371

simplicity's sake, I will from now on refer occasionally to Sharp, writing as Macleod, as 'she', 'her', and 'Macleod', and the reader must bear in mind that Macleod was an imaginary personage, albeit an alarmingly insistent one. More than an alias, she escaped into Sharp's daily life as something between a literary framing device and a secondary personality.[29] She replied to fan mail—Sharp had his responses copied out by his sister lest masculine handwriting give the game away—and received at least one offer of marriage.

Inevitably the adoption of a feminine alter ego has been a source of fascination for critics, with Sharp's three biographers divided on its significance. Of the three, Flavia Alaya's acute psychoanalytic portrait from 1970 is sensitive to the inner needs which the Macleod persona may have satisfied for Sharp.[30] A more circumscribed study by Terry Meyers takes the creation of Macleod as evidence for a specifically sexual crisis in Sharp's identity.[31] Finally, a recent biographer, Steven Blamires, has richly rounded out the picture of Sharp's life story by using the full range of unpublished primary sources. This renders his study invaluable, but as an esoteric account of Sharp's life written by a devotee of the 'faery tradition', its presuppositions about Fiona are not my own.[32] Blamires's view is that Fiona was a 'faery contact', meaning a disembodied spiritual being who intermittently wrote through Sharp. One can only counter that transcribing the words of an impalpable inner female, the Muse, is in fact the West's oldest metaphor for literary creation. Granted, Sharp's sense of Fiona's separate existence could border on the eerie: in a letter to his wife, he once told her 'it is with me as though Fiona were asleep in another room. I catch myself listening for

---

29 The latter phrase was Yeats's, in a letter to Maud Gonne after Sharp's death; see T. L. Meyers, *The Sexual Tensions of William Sharp: A Study of the Birth of Fiona Macleod* (New York, 1996), 19.

30 F. Alaya, *William Sharp—"Fiona Macleod"* (Cambridge, MA, 1970). The archive of correspondence on which Alaya drew has subsequently been expanded, so that her work—still valuable—is perhaps less nuanced than it would be if undertaken today.

31 Meyers, *The Sexual Tensions of William Sharp*, makes a persuasive case for a homoerotic element to Sharp's make-up. See especially (on page 20) the fascinating account by Yeats of a version of the advent of 'Fiona' which Sharp had apparently vouchsafed to Lord Killanin, in which Fiona appeared in the 'sidereal body' of a beautiful young *man*, and then 'lay with him [Sharp]... as a man with a woman.' Sharp said his breasts physically swelled after the astral encounter, making him 'almost the physical likeness of a woman'.

32 S. Blamires, *The Little Book of the Great Enchantment* (Arcata, CA, 2008).

her step sometimes, for the sudden opening of a door.'[33] But I resist Blamires' esoteric explanation of Macleod because finding this kind of self-dissociation unusual would imply a certain naiveté regarding artistic creativity.[34] Male pseudonyms were common among women creative writers in Sharp's lifetime, and no one suggests that Marian Evans (say) was channelling a logophiliac phantasm calling itself George Eliot.[35] The reverse is admittedly perhaps more unusual, but male novelists had long been aware of and identified with an inner contrasexual persona when creating women characters.[36] *Madame Bovary, c'est moi*, Flaubert had insisted, and although Macleod was somewhere between a character and a pseudonym, her creator might similarly have murmured in Gaelic, *'S mise, Fionnghal NicLeòid.*

For Blamires, Fiona's writings are so uncannily inexplicable that only a supernatural description can do them justice. (When contemplating this faery theory it is salutary to remember that Sharp furnished Fiona with a rich husband, a classical education, and a penchant for yachting.) Nevertheless, Blamires's biography reflects an understandable and telling desire on the part of the many who feel a connection with Macleod's work to rescue Sharp from the charge of bad faith. By shunting Fiona 'upstairs' onto the spiritual plane, her creator can be made to seem less parasitic on contemporary sensibility. It should be stressed, however, that Sharp's sense of self-identification with Fiona seems to have been quite genuine, and it may be that with our sophisticated contemporary vocabularies for sexuality and gender identity we find ourselves better placed than previous generations to understand this aspect of his writ-

33 Letter to Elizabeth A. Sharp, 20th February, 1895, The William Sharp Archive, ed. W. F. Halloran, http://www.ies.sas.ac.uk/research/current-projects/william-sharp-fiona -macleod-archive/william-sharp-fiona-macleod-archive, section XII, 25 [accessed 12th April 2015].

34 Indeed, the Portuguese poet Fernando Pessoa (1888–1935) spectacularly outdid Sharp with over seventy 'heteronyms', each with a distinct personality and imagined relationships.

35 Though like many creative writers Eliot sometimes suggested this herself, as it happens; see J. W. Cross, *George Eliot's Life as related in her Letters and Journals* (Edinburgh & London, 1885), iii., 421–5.

36 Gaye Tuchman and Nina Fortin have found evidence that male writers in the 1860s and 70s were in fact more likely than women to use a cross-gendered pseudonym; see their *Edging Women Out: Victorian Novelists, Publishers and Social Change* (London, 1989), 53–4. In a short story published in 1894—the year of Fiona's 'birth'—entitled 'The Death of the Lion', Henry James juxtaposed a woman writing as 'Guy Walsingham' with a man writing as 'Dora Forbes'.

ings. That said, it must also be admitted that there were also sound commercial reasons for maintaining the secret, for Fiona was consistently more critically admired and successful a writer than Sharp himself; by publishing under her name Sharp cannily concretized the contemporary fashion for seeing the 'Celt' as intuitive, visionary, and feminine.[37] My own preference would be to see her as an extreme blending of a literary phenomenon (the contrasexual authorial persona) with a set of artistic themes (the exteriorized soul, the daemonic double). Both of these had a long history and numerous parallels in nineteenth-century literature, and in Sharp's case it all seems to have been undergirded and powered by some deep psychic need.[38]

GENERATING GODS

For Sharp, the pagan-Christian blend of his imagined version of Gaelic culture was more precisely a pagan-Catholic one, with relics of the 'beautiful old cults' surviving in the Catholic heartlands of South Uist and Barra, where they were protected from the sterilizing effects of Calvinism.[39] This was a standard assertion of the folklorists, but Sharp's identification went deeper. His fictional biography for Fiona expressly made her a Roman Catholic, even though this was apt to alienate Protestant Scots his alter-ego might otherwise have been expected to flatter.[40] For Sharp, the key attraction of Catholicism was the prominence it gave to Mary, which drew him because of the centrality of the feminine to his imagination. The Virgin is a constant figure in the Macleod writings, and one of Sharp's mystic pronouncements was that Christ's second coming would take place upon the island of Iona, and involve him becoming incarnate as a woman.[41]

Furthermore, the ecumenical nature of this imagined Hebridean Catholicism allowed the spiritual correction to flow both ways in his writ-

37 On this point, see Meyer, *Sexual Tensions*, 21–2.

38 My conclusion echoes that of C. Lahey-Dolega, 'Some Brief Observations on the Life and Work of William Sharp (Fiona Macleod)', *Ball State University Forum* 21:4 (Autumn, 1980), 20, who sees Fiona as 'an autopsychic identification with an imagined female self'.

39 'The Gael and his Heritage', *The Works of 'Fiona Macleod'*, arr. E. Sharp (7 vols., London, 1913), v., 235.

40 See Alaya, *William Sharp*, 167–8.

41 'The Gaelic Heart', *Works of 'Fiona Macleod'*, v., 199.

ing: Christianity could be imagined to reveal the deeper truth, while paganism more fully expressed the meaning of the natural world and the feminine spirit. Once again, St Bride (Brigit) seems to have been the crucial symbol of that spirit, echoing her genuine prominence in folk tradition. When Sharp's writings on the gods are taken together, Bride emerges as the only divine or quasi-divine figure to rise above a kind of misty shapelessness, shining instead with iconographic brilliance as mother-goddess, divine virgin, saint, and Gaelic redemptrix. In a hallucinatory short story published in 1896, Macleod transplanted the infant Bride to Iona to be reared by druids, who recognize the girl as 'an Immortal'. Indeed, as a girl Bride is so visibly filled with 'strange piety' that 'the young Druids bow before her as though she were a bàndia'—a goddess—neatly explaining how she might be simultaneously saint and divinity.[42] One of the story's most striking episodes—a druidic fire ceremony lifted straight from Muirchú's seventh-century 'Life of Patrick'—takes this reconciliation of Christianity and paganism even further:

> ... as the three Druids held their hands before the sacred fire there was a faint crackling... and soon dusky red and wan yellow tongues of flame moved to and fro. The sacrifice of God was made. Out of the immeasurable heaven He had come in His golden chariot. Now in the wonder and mystery of His love, He was reborn upon the world, reborn a little fugitive flame upon a low hill in a remote isle... Bride could no longer bear the mystery of this great love... The beauty of the worship of Be'al was upon her as a golden glory. Her heart leaped in a song that could not be sung. The inexhaustible love and pity in her soul chanted a hymn that was heard of no Druid or mortal anywhere, but was of the white spirits of Life.[43]

Here Macleod's druids are illuminated by natural grace, and the (bogus) Gaelic deity Be'al, incarnate in the sun and fire, is revealed as a foreshadowing of Christ.[44]

42 Correctly *ban-dia*; Sharp's Gaelic was erratic.

43 F. Macleod, 'Mary of the Gael', *The Evergreen, A Northern Seasonal: The Book of Autumn* (Edinburgh, 1895), 130.

44 Macleod's 'Be'al' is a mirage ultimately derived from the definition of the word Beltane, 'May-day', in 'Cormac's Glossary' (c.900) which explained the word as 'the fire of Bil', meaning the Canaanite deity Ba'al, whom early Irish scholars knew from scrip-

Interspersed among these rhapsodic visions of ancient theological harmony Macleod duly reported the expected survivals of paganism:

> To this day, there are Christian rites and superstitions which are merely a gloss upon a surviving antique paganism. I have known an old woman... who on the day of Beltane sacrificed a hen: though for her propitiatory rite she had no warrant save that of vague traditionary lore, the lore of the *teinntean*, of the hearth-side—where, in truth, are best to be heard the last dim echoes of the mythologic faith of our ancestors... A relative of mine saw, in South Uist, less than twenty-five years ago, what may have been the last sun-sacrifice in Scotland, when an old Gael secretly and furtively slew a lamb on the summit of a conical grassy knoll at sunrise.[45]

This passage may simply be fantasy; needless to say it can in no way be taken as evidence for persistent paganism in the Hebrides.[46] That said, there is nothing obviously disingenuous about it, and it has been pointed out to me that we have no way of knowing whether one of Sharp's siblings or in-laws actually did visit South Uist and (wilfully or not) misinterpreted something nasty seen behind the woodshed.[47] If so, it amounts to yet more evidence that the problem with the theory of pagan survivals was that investigators simply found what they expected to find.

In 1902 Sharp depicted pagan water rites by quoting directly from Carmichael's *Carmina*. Inevitably he lighted upon the very anecdote which Carmichael had derived from Martin Martin, demonstrating in the process the way in which he was prone to boost Carmichael's paganizing rhetoric:

> Offerings of honey-ale or mead... were given to the god of the sea. As... Mr Carmichael relates in his beautiful *Carmina Gadelica*, the man deputed by the islefolk would walk into the sea up to his waist, and then, while he poured out the offering, would chant

---

ture. Modern scholarship regards the existence of an ancient Irish deity called Bel as spurious. See above, 81, 288.

45 F. Macleod, *The Washer of the Ford and other legendary moralities* (Edinburgh, 1896), 7.

46 Fiona's characteristic imagery was precisely recycled on the small screen in Starz network's 2014 adaptation of Diana Gabaldon's best-selling *Outlander* romances; in the first episode, 1940s Inverness features stone-circles, eerie dancing druids, animal sacrifice at Samhain, and references to the mysterious doings of early Gaelic saints.

47 I owe this point—including its phrasing, which I could not better—to one of the anonymous pre-publication reviewers of the book.

A Dhe na mara
Cuir todhar 's an tarruin
Chon tachair an talaimh
Chon bailcidh dhuinn biaidh.

'O god of the sea,
Put weed in the drawing wave
To enrich the isle-soil,
To shower on us food.'

'Then those behind the offerer took up the chant and wafted it along the seashore on the midnight air, the darkness and the rolling of the waves making the scene weird and impressive.'

That I have not seen; and now I fear the god of the sea has few worshippers and knows no scattered communes of bowed chanters at night.[48]

Carmichael had insinuated—without openly stating—that the extinct custom had represented an offering to Manannán mac Lir, and here Sharp dramatized his statement while adding in a note of acute nostalgia for a vanished world of pagan ritual.

As it happened, Sharp returned often to the subject of sea-gods, and indeed Manannán mac Lir was clearly one of his favourites. In the lyrical 'Sea-Magic', Fiona reported, at supposed first hand, an aged Gael's vision of that deity; the god's wavering plumes tell us that the source of the imagery lay less in immemorial Gaelic tradition than in the frenetic journalism of George Russell:

For who can doubt that it was Manan, in the body or vision, he the living prince of the waters, the son of the most ancient god, who, crested as with snow-white canna with a blueness in it, and footcirct with cold, curling flame—the uplifted wave and wandering sea-fire—appeared to the old islander?[49]

And in the short story 'Mäya', she recounted a dream-vision of Manannán as a titan formed of salt water, 'most ancient of the gods, the greatest of the gods', who throws a wave into her heart:

48 F. Macleod, 'Sea-Magic and Running Water', *Contemporary Review* 82 (1902), 570.
49 Macleod, 'Sea-Magic', 575.

Then I knew that I was made of the kinship of Mânan, and should never know peace, but should have the homeless wave for my heart's brother, and the salt sea as my cup to drink, and the wilderness of waters as the symbol of all vain ungovernable longings and desires.[50]

Sharp recycled the motif of the wave in the heart several times, making it clear that he was attracted by the literary seascape's potential as a vehicle for a supposedly 'Celtic' melancholia and emotional turbulence. ('Moananoaning'—James Joyce's superb pun on the sea-god's name—comes irresistibly to mind.)[51]

What the passages quoted so far make plain is the contradiction between the purported and actual processes by which Sharp generated images of the Gaelic gods. His favourite form was the first-person anecdote, in which Macleod appears as a visionary folklorist pondering the spiritual meaning of supernatural encounters vouchsafed to her by Gaelic speakers—an adoption of the mode Yeats had developed in *The Celtic Twilight* in 1893. Quasi-religious doctrines are expounded in evocative prose, often interspersed with chant, and if this fused Carmichael with early Yeats, significantly it also harked back to the prose-poetry of Macpherson's Ossianic epics. Macleod was thus shrewdly positioned, with extensive commercial success, as both an earnest inquirer into Gaeldom and a voice emanating from its secret heart. Her mystical ruminations on Gaelic tradition were thus fed back into the culture, and indeed it was not until more than a decade after Sharp's death that public doubt was cast upon the authenticity of Macleod's Gaelic folklore.[52] Something of the tension inherent in this double pose is apparent in the way that Sharp was not above making his alter-ego sound rather grand—the old fellow visited by Manannán in 'Sea-Magic' addresses her as *Bàn-Morar*, 'm'lady'—and Fiona's supposed informants are expressly depicted as her inferiors in class and education.[53]

Sharp purported to be transcribing from Gaelic oral tradition, but a significant source for his imagery was the periodical literature of Dublin and the world of Celtic research, which he read shrewdly. (In communi-

50 'Mäya', Works of 'Fiona Macleod', v., 162–3.
51 J. Joyce, *Finnegans Wake* ([1939] Oxford, 2012), 628.
52 G. G. King, 'Fiona Macleod', *Modern Language Notes* 33 (1918), 352–6.
53 Macleod, 'Sea-Magic', 115. Sharp's wobbly Gaelic again: it should be *bana-mhorair*, 'Lady, countess'.

cation with Celtic experts, 'Fiona' tended to adopt a 'feminine' and submissive tone, posing as the amateur collector yielding to the expertise of established scholars.) Significant does not mean only, however, for Sharp gathered information about the superstitions of Hebridean fisherfolk from conversations with an Iona man in and around Kilcraggan, and he stayed several times on Iona itself in order to immerse himself in the atmosphere of the place.[54] The upshot was a romanticized mixture of fact and fiction, akin to much late Victorian travel writing, with its anti-industrial strain. This was the mode which Sharp, writing under his own name, pursued for much of his life, and the reader familiar only with Fiona's diffuse Hebridean pastels may be startled to find how crisp and concrete Sharp could be when writing about Sicily or Lucca. Common to both modes was an anecdotal manner and a belletrist knack for capturing place, framing the search for traces of a spiritually edifying antiquity in the present.

NEW MYTHS AND NEW GODS

This fondness for the dim, the shadowy, and the evanescent powerfully determined how Sharp responded to Gaelic myth as a body of material.[55] Like George Russell he was a transcendental idealist, believing that a veiled divine beauty animated the world. To such an individual it was hardly necessary that Gaelic mythology or its gods be coherent or consistent, and there was no attempt at synthesis: he preferred to stitch eclectic scraps together, hinting at connections and allowing allusions to hover.

In fairness, it must be pointed out here that Sharp and his alter-ego have long been held in contempt by Gaels, precisely because this combination of interests meant that for Sharp the continuing fragmentation of Gaelic tradition was an essential part of its appeal. Stiùbhart labels Sharp a 'Symbolist poetaster', while Murdo Macdonald has excoriated him for 'cultural necrophilia' on the grounds that he evidently preferred

---

54 Information I owe, once again, to one of the anonymous readers of the book.

55 Important new essay by Michael Shaw, 'William Sharp's Neo-paganism: Queer Identity and the National Family', in D. Dau & S. Preston (eds.), *Queer Victorian Families: Curious Relations in Literature* (Abingdon, 2015), 77–96, which tackles the gender-roles in Sharp's mythology, noting how he stressed passivity and reflectiveness in the male deities.

Gaelic culture and its language fetchingly doomed. Both find the Macleod writings essentially distasteful and exploitative. Macdonald is salutary on the matter, alluding to Sharp's 'fantasy yearning for the death of the Gael' and determination 'to claim the future of Celtic culture for English speakers like himself'—a future in which Gaelic was 'to be subjugated by English rather than a language to be presented in its own right'.[56]

It is no surprise therefore to find that when Sharp *does* narrate a myth at any length it tends to be one of his own devising: these I term *neomyths*. They could be powerful and evocative; one of the most beautiful took the only two Gaelic divinities to be mentioned in the apparatus to the *Carmina*, Manannán and Brigit, and—in defiance of all tradition—repackaged them as a version of the incestuous brother-sister pairing popular among late Romantic English writers. Tellingly, Sharp gives two versions of this neomyth within a few pages. The first is a footnote, couching the innovation in terms of comparative myth:

> That earlier Brighid was a goddess of poetry and music, one of the three great divinities of love, goddess of women, the keeper of prophecies and dreams, the watcher of the greater destinies, the guardian of the future. I think she was no other than a Celtic Demeter—that Demeter-Desphœna born of the embrace of Poseidon, who in turn is no other than Lir, the Oceanus of the Gael; and instead of Demeter seeking and lamenting Persephone in the underworld, it is Demeter-Brighid seeking her brother... Manan (Manannan), God of the Sea, son of Oceanus, Lir—and finding him at last in Iceland... Persephone and Manan are symbols of the same Return of Life.[57]

This was Macleod as self-scholiast, a device for drawing attention away from the neomyth's manufactured nature. As a result, when it reappears

56 M. Macdonald, 'The Visual Dimension of *Carmina Gadelica*', in D. U. Stiùbhart (ed.), *The Life and Legacy of Alexander Carmichael* (Port of Ness, 2008), 143. Macdonald speculates fascinatingly on the reasons behind Sharp's vicious reaction to an image by John Duncan of Alexander Carmichael's daughter, Ella, which featured prominently in the first volume of *The Evergreen* under the title 'Anima Celtica'. The threat posed by a real-life Gaelic-speaking young woman to a middle-aged man whose career depended on moonlighting as one can be easily imagined.
57 'The Gaelic Heart', 196–7.

in more lyrical guise in the main text Macleod can present it as a glean-
ing from living folk tradition:

> It was years afterward that I heard a story of a woman of the di-
> vine folk, who was called the Lady of the Sea, and was a daughter
> of Lîr, and went lamenting upon the earth because she had lost her
> brother Manan the Beautiful, but came upon him at last among the
> hills of Iceland and wooed him back with songs and flowers and
> brought him back again, so that all the world of men rejoiced, and
> ships sailed the seas in safety and nets were filled with fruit of the
> wave.[58]

The reunion of Brigit and Manannán was far from the only neomyth
Sharp devised, but it was perhaps the most poignant and dignified; there
are others that are only sketches, without named deities or with half
fleshed-out personifications in the process of turning into deities. On the
other hand, Sharp's longest neomyth, 'The Birds of Emar' from 1899, goes
to the opposite extreme in its elaboration. It is a Gaelicized version of the
first and third stories of the *Mabinogi*, the great quartet of medieval
Welsh prose-tales. Though the core plotline has been preserved, every
detail has been rendered indistinct and portentous.

One quotation will serve to give the flavour. Just prior to the following passage, Ailill, Emar's newborn son, has been snatched away by a
supernatural wind. He returns the next morning miraculously fully
grown, in order to explain to his mother (who, like the medieval Étaín,
has forgotten that she was once an immortal) the nature of their connection to the gods:

> 'You have forgotten much,' he said: 'since you ask me why that I
> have my comely manhood upon me when you bore me only last
> night.'
>   'I asked as a woman, Ailill. I bore you.'
>   He smiled.
>   'If, last night, you had put dew in your hand, and let a ray of the
> Secret Star fall into it, you would have known. I was a long way
> from here when I heard you calling. As I came, the wind wore me
> to a shadow. When I was beside you, I was a little eddy of air. Then

58 'The Gaelic Heart', 198–9.

the Haughty Father breathed, and I was in his breath, and the breath quickened that which was within you. When Balva snatched me away he flung me at the feet of Him who is the mystery of the Red and White and Black: and my mortal clay was like the old wax of bees: and that you have Ailill for son is because Angus and Midir, who loved you long, long ago, and ever love you, came between me and the wind.'

'I remember,' said Emar softly.

'Angus lifted me. "He is mine," he said, "because he is the child of love, that is all in all because it is love. And he is mine, because those who die young are mine. And he is mine, because I am the Dart-thrower."'

'Midir, who wore a cloak of green leaves, with the veins under his earth-brown skin filled with white sap, lifted the ash-staff he carried. At the end of it was a little moonwhite flame. This he put to the clay that was as the old wax of bees: and I felt the sap rise and the blood flow, and I was on my feet, leaning against the tree into which Midir had gone, as the wind goes into grass, and looking into the sky where I saw Angus the Helmsman sitting in the Great Galley, and singing as he sailed along the shining coasts of the stars.'

Emar leaned and kissed Ailill.

'Then you came to me, my dream?'

'Yes. And because we are of the kin of Angus, the dream that we dream is beyond the thrust of the spear.'[59]

Myth is being invented and amplified with cheerful abandon here, as happens so often in the literature examined in this book; in chapter 5, for example, we saw that the composer of the *Acallam* had no compunction about inventing new members of the Túatha Dé Danann when it suited him. Here Emar, Ailill, and Balva are characters of Sharp's own devising, although they do correspond in a general way to the figures of Rhiannon, Pryderi, and Gwawl in the Welsh tales. There is no 'Secret Star' in Irish mythology, nor is there a 'Haughty Father', unless this is a coy reference to the Dagda. Perhaps because his Emar vaguely resembles Étaín, Sharp has imported the two deities most prominent in the medieval 'Wooing of Étain', Midir and his foster-son Óengus/Angus. Angus's three purviews here have no obvious medieval forerunners: as seen in

59 F. Macleod, 'The Birds of Emar', *The Dominion of Dreams* (London, 1899), 267–8.

the previous chapter, Anglo-Irish mythography had made him a god of love, but nowhere is he the patron of those who die young, and the title 'Dart-thrower' has been borrowed from the Greek god Apollo.[60] But all this is to labour the point, and a generous critic might assert that here we have Sharp the Symbolist, working in the manner of that artistic movement to generate a personal vocabulary of resonant images with which to point beyond the earthly. A less generous critic might observe that he could clearly write this kind of thing by the yard.[61]

One of the most important contributions made by 'Fiona' was the introduction of new divinities to the pantheon. In a review of *The Dominion of Dreams*, published in 1899, Yeats paid her a backhanded compliment for precisely this capacity: '... Miss Macleod has recovered the art of the myth-makers, and gives a visible shape to joys and sorrows... It was minds like hers that created Aphrodite out of love and the foam of the sea, and Prometheus out of human thought and its likeness to leaping fire.'[62] This was exactly right, mingling praise with an acknowledgement of the synthetic nature of Macleod's gods. Sometimes Christianity was simply paganized: in one story we are told that the god Angus has a brother, 'Airill Ail na'n Òg', both being 'beautiful lords of life and youth'.[63] But Airil—to spell it more correctly—was simply the Gaelic version of the archangel Ariel, a rare but attested figure in Christian angelology. Sharp had found him invoked in *Carmina Gadelica* and decided to insinuate that he had been a Celtic god.[64]

On other occasions, Sharp would borrow a mythological figure created by someone else and allow his own imagination to work upon it. One example was the goddess Orchil, apparently an original invention of Standish O'Grady, who had envisioned her as 'a great sorceress who ruled the world under the earth'; soon Orchil had begun appearing as a

---

60 As god of archery, Apollo was called both *hekebolos* and *hekaërgos* in Greek, 'the far-shooting'; Macleod was prone to identifying Óengus/Angus with Apollo. The link with those who die young probably suggested by Aengus's role in fenian literature as the foster-father of the tragic Díarmait ua Duibne, who elopes with Finn's wife Gráinne.

61 In this same story Sharp curiously and for the only time doubled Manannán, creating 'Manànn, son of Manànn mac Lir' who nevertheless seems to be a sea-god indistinguishable from his father.

62 W. B. Yeats, review of F. Macleod, *The Dominion of Dreams*, in *The Bookman* (July, 1899), in *The Collected Works of W. B. Yeats Volume IX: Early Articles and Reviews*, ed. J. P. Frayne & M. Marchaterre (New York, 2004), 440.

63 'The Lynn of Dreams', *Works of 'Fiona Macleod'*, v., 150.

64 *Carmina Gadelica*, ii., 223.

sensual demoness in drafts of Yeats's play *The Shadowy Waters*.[65] But Sharp's spiritual feminism demanded a Gaelic version of the 'Great Goddess' beloved of Victorian and Edwardian radicals, and in his hands Orchil was soon rendered all the more memorable and impressive as 'the dim goddess', a chthonian *magna mater* weaving the strands of fate in a cave beneath the earth, 'patient, abiding, certain, inviolate, and silent ever'. In Sharp's hands O'Grady's infernal queen morphed into a Gaelic mother-goddess: she appeared in a number of Fiona's works and was pronounced equivalent to Hera and Isis.[66] So effectively did Sharp promote his version of Orchil in the Macleod writings that Yeats made no further use of the figure, writing dismissively in 1899, 'I forget whatever I may once have known about her'.[67] He may have been irritated that Sharp's borrowing had been passed off as an independent sampling from the Celtic folk soul, despite the fact that he had himself originally borrowed Orchil from O'Grady.

DALUA

Some deities Sharp simply invented. In *The Immortal Hour*, a verse-drama based on 'The Wooing of Étaín' and first published in 1900, Sharp, still *en travesti*, turned from borrowing gods to breeding them: Orchil was paired off with a mysterious god 'Kail' to become 'mother and father of the earth-wrought folk', that is, the Sidhe. Dictionary thumbing was

---

65 O'Grady, *The Coming of Cuculain: a Romance of the Heroic Age* (London, 1894), 62, 102. For the emergence of the 'great goddess', see Hutton, *Triumph of the Moon*, 32–42; for Orchil, see also Macleod's collection of 'prose rhythms', *The Silence of Amor: prose rhythms* (Portland, Maine, 1902), 30, which contains an allegory about her weaving; she gets a speaking part in the story 'The Awakening of Angus Òg', *Works of 'Fiona Macleod'*, v., 91–99.

66 O'Grady's source for the name was probably the Irish noun *oirchill*, 'readiness', which can mean 'providence' or 'store', in the sense of the portion that 'lies in store' for a person (cf. the phrase *trí oirchill Dé*, 'through God's providence'). This is probably another instance of O'Grady's Hiberno-Hellenism: he may have been trying to calque the Greek word *moira*, literally someone's 'allotted portion', but also (in the plural) the term for the goddesses of fate, the *Moirai*. This became exactly the role played by Orchil in the Macleod writings.

67 See M. J. Sidnell, G. P. Mayhew, & D. R. Clark (eds.), *Druid Craft: the Writing of 'The Shadowy Waters'* [*Manuscripts of W. B. Yeats*, i.] (Dublin, 1971), 34–5; for Yeats's annoyance with Sharp—and suspicion that Sharp and Macleod were one and the same, which was dawning at precisely this point—see Foster, *TAM*, 196–7.

probably to blame for this one: it looks as though Sharp—casting around for a name suitable for a father-god—selected the Scottish Gaelic word *càil*, 'life, mettle, strength', originally a borrowing of Latin *qualitas*, 'quality'.

A more meaningful part in the drama is played by another invented deity, 'the Faery fool'. This was a genuine figure of Irish folklore, the sinister *amadán*, who—as seen in the previous chapter—had been investigated by Lady Gregory. Yeats had privately shared Gregory's findings with Sharp in the context of Russell's visions at Coole; he was embarrassed when 'Macleod' promptly published them as meaningfully coincident recoveries of great spiritual significance.

The Dark Fool became Sharp's grandest and most sinister new divinity: an alienated being not unlike a Celtic Loki, he appeared in several places in his work and was clearly of considerable imaginative significance. In *The Immortal Hour* Sharp/Macleod hugely amplified the importance of the arbitrary *amadán* of folklore, and retrofitted him into the essentially medieval, literary structure of the Túatha Dé Danann. Sharp also gave him a name, 'Dalua'—which is an uncommon variant of 'Lua' or 'Molua', the early Irish saint who gives his name to Killaloe in Co. Clare. (In naming his new god thus, the luckless Sharp had lit upon one of the few early Irish names which announced by its very form that it could only belong to a monk.)[68] He may have felt that it vaguely evoked the word *dall*, 'blind'—metaphorically 'dark, misled, false'—which fits Dalua's nature well.[69]

Importations such as Orchil and Dalua are useful for showing up where gaps were felt to exist within the texture of the pantheon. Fortunately, Sharp left detailed thoughts on Dalua in the preface to the play, giving us a keener sense of what this absence was felt to be:

> ... [Dalua] is at once an elder and dreadful god, a mysterious and potent spirit, avoided even of the proud immortal folk themselves: and an abstraction, 'the shadow of pale hopes, forgotten dreams,

68 Briefly, *Molua* (Mo Lua) and *Dalua* mean 'My Lua' and 'Your Lua' respectively: affectionate pet names of this form were apparently unique to monks between the sixth and ninth centuries. There were lots: Do Bécóc, Mo Dímmóc, etc. See *ECI*, 5.

69 *Dalua* is preserved in the Irish name of Killaloe, *Cill Dalua*, 'the Church of St Lua', with the second person singular possessive, 'your Lua', instead of the more common first, 'my Lua'. Lua itself is a by-form of *Lugaid*. Possessive nicknames such as these are very frequent, and any account of Irish saints or placenames could have given Sharp the name.

and madness of men's minds.' He is, too, to my imagining, madness incorporate as a living force.[70]

'Macleod' concluded this piece by squarely acknowledging that she had fabricated a new divinity. Well, yes, she says; her whole interpretation of the saga on which the play is based is in a sense an innovation, and so is Dalua. Or is he?

> This is new, perhaps: though what seems new may be the old become transparent only, the old in turn being often the new seen in reverse... Nor has Dalua part or mention in the antique legend. Like other ancient things, this divinity hath come secretly upon us in a forgetful time, new and strange and terrible, though his unremembered shadow crossed our way when first we set out on our long travel, in the youth of the world.[71]

The metaphor Macleod uses here for concocting new Gaelic gods is making the tradition limpid, as though waiting for muddy water to settle. It is typical also that she speaks of Dalua—significantly lapsing into antique diction—as a real and primordial being which has bided its time before manifesting. There is a dim prefiguring here of Yeats's great 1919 poem 'The Second Coming', with its gnostic 'rough beast, its time come round again', on the point of incarnating into a shattered world; but one is also put in mind of the lurking horrors of H. P. Lovecraft. The connection may seem unexpected, but is direct: Lovecraft drew on Macleod's writing via an anthology of 'psychic tales'.[72]

---

70 F. Macleod, *The Immortal Hour: A Drama in two Acts* (Edinburgh & London, 1908), ix.

71 Macleod, *The Immortal Hour*, xi.

72 See S. Joshi, *A Subtler Magick: The Writings and Philosophy of H. P. Lovecraft* (Gilette, NJ, 1982), 97–8, for evidence that Lovecraft had read and was influenced by Macleod's gloomy story 'The Sin-Eater'. Lovecraft and Macleod have more in common than one might think—Lovecraft's Cthulhu, who lies in the watery depths, is a kind of nightmare obverse of Macleod's 'Manann of the Dividing Wave'—though the American writer was only fifteen at the time of Sharp's death. Had the latter lived longer, one doubts that he would have been pleased by the comparison. A further connection is provided by the work of the Anglo-Irish fantasy-writer Lord Dunsany, whose writings were strongly influenced by Sharp and were in turn an influence on Lovecraft. Useful discussion by T. Scott, 'The Fantasy of the Celtic Revival: Lord Dunsany, Fiona Macleod, and W. B. Yeats', in C. Younger (ed.), *Border Crossings: Narration, Nation and Imagination in Scots and Irish Literature and Culture* (Newcastle, 2013), 127–141.

In *The Immortal Hour* itself, Macleod explains Dalua's order of being. In the opening scene, one of a chorus of 'Voices in the Wood' addresses the Dark Fool thus:

Brother and kin to all the twilit gods,
Living, forgot, long dead; sad Shadow of pale hopes,
Forgotten dreams and madness of men's minds:
Outcast among the gods, and called the Fool,
Yet dreaded even by those immortal eyes…[73]

The Chorus's mocking laughter echoes through the wood—but titter ye not, Dalua warns. The *other* gods find him nothing to joke about:

For Lu and Oengus laugh not, nor the gods
Safe set above the perishable stars.
They laugh not, nor any in the high celestial house.
Their proud immortal eyes grow dim and clouded
When as a morning shadow I am gathered
Into their holy light…[74]

Sharp seems to be angling Dalua as a Gaelic Lucifer here, for there is an echo of the first chapter of the Book of Job, in which Satan appears among the 'sons of God' presenting themselves before the Almighty. Dalua goes on to inform the Chorus that he is a being both kin to and yet in some sense beyond the Túatha Dé Danann, as the agent of 'Shadow, eldest god', who appears to be a kind of nameless demiurge. (That Lovecraftian note recurs.)[75] In Dalua, it seems that Sharp gives us a new deity who incarnates everything Irish tradition had tended to exclude from the otherworldly realm: mortality, sorrow, delusion, and decay. In furnishing the Túatha Dé with a grim deity of fate, Sharp reveals an internal notion—characteristic of the decades either side of the turn of the century—that a crucial component of the 'Celtic' (along with an immaterial aestheticism) was a brooding sense of destiny.

Elsewhere, Sharp had recourse to obscure names drawn from medieval Irish tradition, which afforded him an imaginative free hand and the savour of antiquity. The three divine brothers 'Seithoir', 'Teithoir',

73 Macleod, *The Immortal Hour*, 5.
74 Macleod, *The Immortal Hour*, 6.
75 Macleod, *The Immortal Hour*, 5.

and 'Keithoir' fall into this category: the names are in fact *recherché* aliases of the Túatha Dé Danann chieftains Mac Gréine, Mac Cécht, and Mac Cuill from 'The Book of Invasions'.[76] In the dedication to his Highland romance *Pharais*, published in 1894, Sharp had introduced Keithoir as a nature-god. And if Orchil was Gaeldom's Isis, Keithoir explicitly served as its Pan:

> In the mythology of the Gael are three forgotten deities, children of Delbaith-Dana. These are Seithoir, Teithoir, and Keithoir. One dwells throughout the sea, and beneath the soles of the feet of another are the highest clouds; and these two may be held sacred for the beauty they weave for the joy of eye and ear. But now that, as surely none may gainsay, Keithoir is blind and weary, let us worship at his fane rather than give all our homage to the others. For Keithoir is the god of the earth; dark-eyed, shadowy brother of Pan; and his fane is among the lonely glens and mountains and lonelier isles of 'Alba cona lingantaibh.' It is because you and I are of the children of Keithoir that I wished to grace my book with your name.[77]

The dedicatee of *Pharais* was Edith Wingate Rinder, with whom Sharp had had an affair (or had come close to having one) during one of his Italian journeys. Placing the two of them under the auspices of Keithoir—neurasthenic deity of anti-industrial melancholia—allowed Sharp not only to bridge the gap between himself and Rinder, but also, perhaps, to delicately excuse his own failures of erotic initiative. It amounted to a weighty role for a figure which had begun as a medieval gloss.[78]

---

76 *LGE*, v., 36. The edited text says (in Macalister's translation) 'The three kings of Ireland, Mac Cuill, Mac Cécht, and Mac Gréine, were there', but one manuscript (now split into two parts, Stowe D 3.1 and the Book of Fermoy), inserts at this point the phrase *Setheor 7 Cetheor 7 Tetheor a n-anmann*, 'they were called Setheor, Cetheor, and Tetheor.' A little later (*LGE*, v., 52–3) the names appear in the main text, but as *Ethor, Cethor,* and *Tethor.* They were picked up by Geoffrey Keating and thus found their way into Sylvester O'Halloran's *History*. Steve Blamires (*The Little Book*, 101–2) is baffled by Macleod's Keithoir, which underscores the obscurity of the three names; that they *are* obscure does not mean (*pace* Blamires) that they had to be channeled from ethereal beings.

77 F. Macleod, *Pharais: A Romance of the Isles* (Derby, 1894), viii. *Alba cona lingantaibh:* 'Scotland with its lochs.'

78 See Alaya, *William Sharp*, 124–7.

In 'The Awakening of Angus Òg', a neomyth published in 1896, Keithoir reappeared as 'the god of the green world', now attempting to wake the Mac Óc whom Orchil has plunged into an endless slumber. His brothers retain their elemental associations with sky and sea but now bear more familiar names: Seithoir appears as Manannán and—in a rather arbitrary touch—Teithoir is now the Gaulish deity Esus (or Hesus), who seems to have been a stellar figure in Macleod's personal pantheon. His ethereal fire certainly overcooked Macleod's prose:

> 'He will awake no more,' murmured Hesus; and the unseen god, whose pulse is beneath the deepest sea and whose breath is the frosty light of the stars, moved out of the shadow into the light, and was at one with it, so that no eyes beheld the radiance which flowered icily in the firmament and was a flame betwixt the earth and the sun, which was a glory amid the cloudy veils about the west and a gleam where quiet dews sustained the green spires of the grass. And as the light lifted and moved, like a vast tide, there was a rumour as of a starry procession sweeping through space to the clashing cymbals of dead moons, to the trumpetings of volcanic worlds, and to the clarions of a thousand suns.[79]

I suspect the hectic style here may hint that Sharp, as Macleod, was overcompensating for some dimension of the story felt to be dissatisfying; perhaps it was the timeworn plot, for this neomyth is a simply a gender-reversed version of 'Sleeping Beauty', with Manannán, Hesus, and Keithoir as the good fairies.

MYTH AND SYMBOL

From one perspective, the Macleodian vision of the Gaelic gods can be seen as a specialized version of ideas which were shared by a whole generation. That rural traditions were essentially pagan and should be interpreted as such was a dogma of the folklorists and the emerging discipline of anthropology; a contemporary, Jessie Weston, was to argue that

---

79 F. Macleod, 'The Awakening of Angus Òg', originally published as 'The Snow-Sleep of Angus Ogue', *The Evergreen, A Northern Seasonal: The Book of Winter* (1896–7), 120. Esus might have made a better god of the green world than Keithoir, as Gaulish iconography represented him as a woodcutter; see Mac Cana, *Celtic Mythology*, 35.

another genre of medieval literature—in her case, the Arthurian cycle—embodied the teachings of a pre-Christian Celtic mystery religion. Even as Alexander Carmichael wrote that 'Highland divinities' were soon to be forgotten, Sharp was energetically advancing them as the mystical vaccine that would inoculate British culture against industrial materialism—long after the Gaels and their language had passed into the oblivion he so blandly contemplated.

This view had something in common with the 'new paganism' of many Victorian and Edwardian writers, who were preoccupied with the numinous associations of landscape and invoked classical deities to chafe against the constraints of Christianity. In his youth, Sharp had been editor of the short-lived *Pagan Review*, the attempt showing that he had once shared his contemporaries' concern with sexual freedom and the joyful liberation of the body. Startlingly, these priorities vanished when Sharp became Macleod. Macleod's gods, like her Gaels, stand on ceremony; they tend to be weirdly immobilized and erotically remote. An emphasis on the gods' chaste dignity was something Sharp shared with George Russell, and while the latter reconfigured various members of the Túatha Dé Danann to suit his purposes, Sharp was one of relatively few writers who actively created new deities. It is worth noting, however, that he was not unique and had precursors, albeit at the opposite end of the literary spectrum. One example is James Bonwick, an English schoolteacher and émigré to Australia, who produced *Irish Druids and Old Irish Religions* in 1894. This mixed Celtic scholarship with a large measure of barmy free association, for his book listed screeds of Irish gods and goddesses—the god '*Ti-Mor*', '*Ceara*, goddess of nature', '*Creeshna*, the sun', and '*Bidhgoe, Nanu*, and *Mathar*'—whom he seems simply to have made up.[80]

Ultimately the themes and images examined here belonged to Sharp's personal mythology, not that of Gaeldom. An assessment of his achievement must therefore be couched less in terms of precedent and retrieval than in metamorphosis and mythopoeia, processes which can be clearly traced in the overarching structure of the Macleodian pantheon. It seems that Sharp came to distinguish between three families of divinities. The least powerful are the 'homeless, sad, bewildered gods' who seem to be the offspring of the mother goddess Orchil and the mysterious Kail.[81] An 'earth-wrought' race, they are greater than humans but

---

80 *Creeshna* (= Krishna?) looks like an orientalizing touch.
81 Quotations here from Macleod, *The Immortal Hour*, 3–4.

spend their time drifting about disconsolately. In the middle come the 'sleeping gods', who have passed into the hills and about whom Macleod has little to say. Most powerful are the 'strong, immortal gods', titanic beings with a celestial aspect. They are the elite children of a primordial couple, Dana or Ana, 'ancient mother of the gods', and Delbaith—the medieval Delbaeth, whom Sharp may have thought to be the same as the Dagda, though 'The Book of Invasions' makes him the latter's grandfather. This division of the gods into these three ranks simply literalized their different manifestations across the history of Irish literature: the 'earth-wrought' race echoes Tírechán's 'earthly gods'; the 'sleeping gods' are akin to the people of the *síd* in the *Acallam*, sealed into their hollow hills by St Patrick for all time; and the powerful immortals correspond to the classical Túatha Dé of the Old Irish sagas.

Among the children of the 'strong, immortal gods' is a trio of brothers composed of a deity of starry heaven, a sea-god, and a doleful divinity of wild nature, all of whose names vary. As seen, the last is usually called Keithoir, although the leaf-cloaked Midir of 'The Birds of Emar' seems to be another version of the same figure. Other children include 'sky-set' Lu (Lug), apparently another stellar deity; Angus, at times a limp ephebe and at others an Apollo-like sun-god; and finally Brigit, goddess of fire and poetry. Brigit's lover (or brother, or both) is Manann or Manannán, who sometimes has an identically named son, perhaps because it is not clear where his father Lir, 'the Oceanus of the Gael', should fit in to this scheme. Off to the side there appears to be an ancient and demiurgic 'Shadow' who is of uncertain relation to the other gods. As seen his son is Dalua, who plays much the same role in the divine economy as the malcontent in a Renaissance tragedy.

It seems improbable that Sharp ever held in his head a theogony as compartmentalized as this—there are too many inconsistencies and changes in the portrayals of individual gods between one text and another. However, it is greatly to his credit that he attempted to address the disparity between centre and periphery in the medieval Túatha Dé by distinguishing the core pantheon from the less differentiated people of the *síd*.

A fondness for and facility with images that suggest some profound meaning was also a key aspect of Sharp's myth creation, in that they deepen a sense of mystery by virtue of being offered without context or interpretation. From passages already quoted we might choose the images of Angus's star-galley, the 'mystery of red and white and black', the identity of the 'three great deities of love', and Keithoir's blindness: a knowledge of medieval Irish literature will shed no light on any of these. Ironically, however, this was a technique which Sharp may have learned from the colloquy texts of that literature, many of which gain stylistic traction by showcasing obscure mythological allusion. One is reminded of the poet Ferchertne in the tenth-century 'Colloquy of the Two Sages', who boasts that he has come 'by way of the *síd*-mound of the wife of Nechtán, down the forearm of Núadu's wife, via the land of the sun, via the dwelling of the moon, along the umbilical cord of the Young One'.[82] It seems highly likely that these images point to a treasury of lore which professional poets would have understood, but in Sharp's case we are dealing more with the equivalent of costume jewellery: designed to be evocative, his allusions have no actual myth behind them.[83]

At the same time as he bolstered the impression that Gaelic tradition contained deep reserves of spiritual mystery, Sharp was keen to make its folklore and mythology transparent to current anthropological interpretation. The story of Brigit wooing Manannán back from Iceland is an example: 'Persephone and Manan are symbols of the same Return of Life', Macleod opined, thus immediately thrusting readers into the realm of Frazer's *Golden Bough*—the greatest work of Victorian anthropology—in which every myth turns out to be about the seasonal renewal of fertility. The analysis of *The Wooing of Étaín* in the preface to *The Immortal Hour* is in the same vein, making the saga symbolize

the winning of life back to the world after an enforced thralldom: the renewal of Spring: in other words, Etain is a Gaelic Eurydice, Midir a Gaelic Orpheus who penetrated the dismal realm of Eochaidh, and Eochaidh but a humanised Gaelic Dis.... To the Gaelic mind... the myths of Persephone and Eurydice might well be identified, so that Orpheus sought each or both-in-one, in the gloomy underworld. And the tale suffered no more than a seachange when, by the sundown shores, it showed Eurydice-Persephone as Etain being wooed back to sunshine and glad life by the longing passion of Orpheus as Midir. For in the Gaelic mythology, Midir, too, is a son of light, a servant of song, a son of Apollo, being of the divine

82 See Carey, *A Single Ray*, 4, and *Immacallam in Dá Thuarad*, ed. & trans. W. Stokes, 'The Colloquy of the Two Sages', *RC* 26 (1905), 18 (Irish), 19 (trans).

83 It is possible, at least theoretically, that a medieval Irish writer might also have invented recondite allusions in order to add prestige to a composition, given how highly obscurity was valued as a poetic skill, but no examples are certainly determinable.

race of Oengus the Sun God, Lord of Life and Death. By his symbol of the dew he is also the Restorer, the Reviver.[84]

One might regret the way that a multilayered medieval story has been invested with a monolithic Frazerian meaning here, but in this Sharp was entirely typical of his era, and it is important to remember too that his intense engagement with mythological themes produced works that caught the imagination of a wide audience, in Ireland as much as in Britain. And though (personally speaking) I find Fiona's ecstatic transports lend themselves to selective quotation, in writing in this way Sharp was emphatically not a charlatan peddling a sham mythology. Rather, his neomyths and neodivinities exemplified a crucial and enduring aspect of the story told in this study: Gaelic myth itself has never simply been an assemblage of tradition handed down through the generations, but has always grown via unpredictable—and often unrepeatable—acts of individual creativity.

JOHN DUNCAN'S GAELIC GODS

The gods of the Scottish Celtic Revival's leading writer can been seen more fully when set next to those of its most distinguished artist. John Duncan (1866–1945) contributed numerous images to the *The Evergreen*, a series of four seasonal 'books' published between 1895 and 1897 by Sharp and the polymathic Sir Patrick Geddes, and which formed the key publishing venture of the Celtic movement in Scotland. Sharp (writing both as himself and as Macleod) contributed lavishly, and in several cases Duncan's images were juxtaposed to his words. The relationship between their idioms was symbiotic: both shared a love of the Hebrides and a preoccupation with Celtic myth as a wellspring of spiritual beauty lacking in the modern industrial world. Both, in their different ways, were Symbolists. John Kemplay, the most recent scholar to assess Duncan's work, has stressed that Duncan had much in common with painters of that movement such as Moreau and Klimt, particularly their fondness for imagining pagan divinities with a high decorativeness. By focusing on the gods of the Gael, he further resembled Sharp/Macleod in giving a local inflection to a wider movement. It was less important to him than to Macleod to present himself as an actual seer: though he

---

84 Macleod, *The Immortal Hour*, vii-viii.

enjoyed episodes of hallucinatory inner vision, he thought of himself as a spiritual artist or craftsman bodying forth the mystical vision of others. Duncan plies a hard, shadowless line; his gods characteristically have a kind of stilled fixation (Fig. 9.2). That other painter of Gaelic mythological beings, George Russell, had experimented with a lower-wattage version of this iconicizing style (as indeed had a number of other Irish artists), but it was Duncan who brought it to perfection.[85]

All these features are splendidly manifest in the 1911 painting which has a claim to being Duncan's masterpiece, *The Riders of the Sidhe* (Fig. 9.3). The composition combined one motif best represented in Irish folklore, the hosting of the fairy-folk, with another that had been confined to the medieval literature, that of the gods' four treasures. By 1911 both were already clichés of the Celtic Revival. The supernatural company of folklore provided a useful means with which to parade the gods of an unfamiliar pantheon: not only had Yeats written an early poem, 'The Hosting of the Sidhe', on the topic, but (as discussed in chapter 8) he had made delineating the gods—as though in solemn procession—into a habit. Duncan's picture is the precise equivalent of the passage from 'Rosa Alchemica' (1896)—later excised—in which is prophesied the return of 'the Dagda, with his overflowing cauldron, Lug, with his spear dipped in poppy juice lest it rush forth hot to battle. Aengus, with his three birds on his shoulder, Bodb and his red swineherd, and all the heroic children of Dana...'[86]

The treasures too were a Yeatsian theme; two—the cauldron and the spear—appeared in the list just quoted, and along with the sword and the stone they had symbolized the grades of initiation of Yeats's abortive Celtic Mysteries. Sharp had worked them and their elemental associations into a late Macleod poem, 'The Dirge of the Four Cities', prefacing

85 The Irish painter Beatrice Elvery's 1907 painting *Éire* is a good example: it depicted the sovereignty goddess as a green-cloaked Madonna, haloed by a Celtic cross. For Russell in this mode, one need look no further than his portrait of the famously dumpy Madame Blavatsky, showing her as a hieratic Celtic goddess in a solar headdress. For Elvery's painting, see J. C. Steward (ed.), *When Time Began to Rant and Rage: Figurative Painting from Twentieth-Century Ireland* (London, 1998), 130–1; Russell's paintings are all too often undated, but the mystical nature of the image suggests it was produced after Blavatsky's death in 1891.

86 See comments on this passage in W. B. Yeats, *Mythologies*, ed. W. Gould and D. Toomey (Basingstoke, 2005), 387, and *The Secret Rose, Stories by W. B. Yeats: A Variorum Edition*, ed. W. Gould, *et al.* (2nd edn., London, 1992), 139v.

FIG. 9.2.
Fairy Enthroned,
by John Duncan;
date and location
uncertain. © Estate
of John Duncan.

FIG. 9.3. John Duncan, *The Riders of the Sidhe* (1911), tempera on canvas,
Dundee City Council (Dundee's Art Galleries and Museums).

the poem with a 'quotation' from one of the imaginary Gaelic books he
was fond of referencing:

> There are four cities that no mortal eye has seen but that the soul
> knows; these are Gorias, that is in the east; and Finias, that is in
> the south; and Murias, that is in the west; and Falias that is in the
> north. And the symbol of Falias is the stone of death, which is
> crowned with pale fire. And the symbol of Gorias is the dividing
> sword. And the symbol of Finias is a spear. And the symbol of
> Murias is a hollow that is filled with water and fading light.[87]

Duncan's own explanation of his painting drew on both Macleod's idealism and hermetic Yeats, in that the face of each rider is meant (he recorded) to embody the symbol which they carry. The cup, for example,
represents love, and the rider who carries it wears an expression of beatific tenderness; the stone, 'symbol of the will in its passive form', has
become a crystal sphere affording visions of the past and future, its
holder sternly patient; and so on. To Duncan, it was this aspect of his

---

87 'Poems and Dramas', *Works of 'Fiona Macleod'*, vii., 224.

painting that lifted it 'from being merely an ingenious allegory to being a symbol of the better kind'.[88] But from the medieval point of view each of Duncan's four treasures is, in a sense, a symbol of a symbol. The Dagda's cauldron or the Stone of Destiny could scarcely be lugged past on horseback, while one (the spear) had been altered beyond recognition into a flowering branch, representing wisdom.

The Riders of the Sidhe represents the endpoint of the Revival's transformation of the four treasures from social into psychic symbols. The same process also impersonalized the gods. The medieval sources associated each treasure with a specific member of the Túatha Dé Danann, but Duncan (following Macleod) makes the deities of his painting radiantly non-specific. For example, near the front of Duncan's divine cavalcade rides a pre-Raphaelite androgyne in mushroom-coloured jodhpurs, holding a golden vessel: if this is intended to be the Dagda, he and his cauldron have both been utterly transmuted since 'The Second Battle of Moytura'. Their idealized faces tellingly fail to live up to Duncan's own description of the figures that passed before the inner eye of his imagination, 'living people with quick eyes and strange solemn gestures who move as if in some ritual'.[89] Even in apparent motion his Sidhe seem to possess splendour without velocity. This somehow allows the painting to hint that the cultural appetite for neo-Gaelic mysteries was fading, just as World War One was about to kill off the Edwardian vogue for the Greek god Pan. The gods' drapery—of which Duncan was especially proud—is flaccid, as though the winds of history have already dropped.

The medium of most of Duncan's paintings was egg tempera, which underscored the neo-medieval, icon-like quality of his art. In *Aoife* (*c.*1913) Duncan turns to a trecento palate of gold, blue, and Venetian red to model a luminous fairy-woman, caught like his *Riders* in radiant freeze-frame (Fig. 9.4). *Aoife* also shares with *Riders* Duncan's characteristic combination of reduction and ornamentation, strangely analogous to Fiona Macleod's prose style. As Macleod, Sharp imbued his writing with poetic resonance by adding Gaelic curlicues to simple, elemental terms— wave, water, sea, fire, stone, wind, white. Duncan's figures also possess a basic, idealized simplicity cluttered by ornament—the swordbearer's la Tène shield, for instance, or Aoife's Art Deco crown.

---

88 Quoted in J. Kemplay, *The Paintings of John Duncan: A Scottish Symbolist* (Warwick & Petaluma, CA, 2009), 51.

89 Quoted in Kemplay, *The Paintings of John Duncan*, 50.

FIG. 9.4. John Duncan, *Aoife* (*c.*1914), oil on panel, City Art Centre, Edinburgh Museums and Galleries. © Estate of John Duncan. All rights reserved, DACS 2015.

For all their aesthetic proximity, the relationship between Duncan and Macleod's work could be quite subtle. In another massive composition of multiple figures, *A Masque of Love* (1921), the Greek figure of Semele (Fig. 9.5) (incinerated by Zeus when she asks to see him in his true form) immediately recalls Macleod's iconic Brigit-Bride. The large (5' x 2') chalk and watercolour rough draft could be an icon of the goddess-saint, blessed (Macleod wrote) by 'every poet, from the humblest wandering singer to Oisin of the Songs, from Oisin of the Songs to Angus Òg of the rainbow or to Midir of the Under-world… because of the flame she put in the heart of poets as well as the red life she put in the flame that springs from wood and peat'. She continued, with piercing lyricism:

> None forgot that she was the daughter of the ancient God of the Earth, but greater than he, because in him there was but earth and water, whereas in her veins ran the elements of air and fire. Was she not born at sunrise? On the day she reached womanhood did not the house wherein she dwelled become wrapped in a flame which consumed it not, though the crown of that flame licked the high unburning roof of Heaven?[90]

Duncan, familiar with Macleod's oeuvre, was well aware of the importance of Bride in her version of Gaelic tradition, and indeed left two pictures explicitly on the topic. I think it possible, though unprovable, that Duncan's *Semele* started out as a sketch of Macleod's favourite goddess, later adapted to fit another composition. If this is so, it is an irony that Duncan's most rhapsodic image of a Gaelic divinity may lie hidden under a Greek name in the corner of one of his least Celtic paintings.

SUCCEEDING FIONA

All of Duncan's mythological paintings—as opposed to his book illustrations—were produced after Sharp's death in 1905. Sharp/Macleod, as the Scottish Celtic Revival's literary centre of gravity, seems to have had an inhibiting as well as an inspiring effect on his imagination. It is striking that no Scottish writer overtly laid claim to the legacy of Fiona Macleod; 'her' influence was simultaneously potent and diffuse. It is possible that

---

90 F. Macleod, 'St. Bridget of the Shores', *Where the Forest Murmurs: Nature Essays by Fiona Macleod* (London, 1906), 76–86.

FIG. 9.5.
John Duncan, *Semele*
(before 1921), chalk and
watercolour, The Robert
Gore Rifkind Collection,
Beverly Hills. © Estate of
John Duncan. All rights
reserved, DACS 2015.

as a visual artist Duncan could negotiate with her example more boldly than those who made their living by the pen; all attempts seem curiously depleted.

So much is visible in Duncan's sole return to book illustration, a series of images produced post-*Evergreen* for one of the most prominent of Macleod's successors, Donald Alexander Mackenzie. Mackenzie's *Wonder Tales from Scottish Myth and Legend* was published in 1917, and his collaboration with Duncan sheds light on the uneven reverberations that Macleod's writing continued to set up in Scottish culture.[91] Mackenzie, a journalist and a minor but highly productive folklorist, took many of the prevailing ideas of that nascent discipline to an extreme, specializing in placing them before the general public in an accessible form. He believed, as did many more eminent contemporaries, that the worship of a single great goddess had once prevailed over prehistoric Europe; more eccentrically, he also held that Buddhism had likewise at one time been spread across the far west, including ancient Britain. He was also, needless to say, keen on pagan survivals. Thus in the introduction to Mackenzie's collection we find Martin Martin's sea-god Shony (again), and the *Carmina* is quoted as evidence for a nameless pagan deity called 'the god of the elements'. This was either ignorance or an outrageous sleight of pen: the phrase was in fact one of the most frequent Gaelic titles for the Christian God, richly attested from the early Middle Ages onwards.

Mackenzie's *Wonder Tales* was also the most obvious of all attempts after Sharp's death to occupy Macleod's niche in the market and furnish Scotland with a mythology, the existence of which was boldly asserted by the title. Although he lacked Sharp's literary gift, he had evidently learned the art of the neomyth from his model. Indeed, he invented a miniature pantheon: 'Beira', a cantankerous mother goddess and 'Queen of Winter', along with cut-price versions of the Mac Óc and Brigit, who appeared respectively as 'Angus-the-Ever-Young', and Bride, 'a beautiful young princess.' Mackenzie identified Bride only as a goddess of spring and summer, and stripped away the associations with fire and poetry that made her such a solemn and hieratic figure for Sharp.

91 An interesting contrast with Duncan is the Scottish Colourist J. D. Fergusson (1874–1961) who came to associate the 'Celtic Spirit' with the feminine spark of life. So much is visible in his 1952 painting 'Danu, Mother of the Gods' (The Fergusson Gallery, Perth and Kinross Council), the only prominent artistic depiction of that divinity. In it the goddess—looking like a voluptuous 1930s Hollywood starlet—strides forward against a background of moutains and water.

Beira, on the other hand, was an oddity. Her name was based on that of a Gaelic folk-figure of genuine importance, the Cailleach Bheur (or, in Ireland, the 'Caillech Bérri'), 'the Hag of Beare' (Fig. 9.6), who appeared in oral folklore as a giantess associated with winter weather and mountainous uplands, amongst several other guises.[92] Some of Mackenzie's details about Beira—the iron hammer, for example, which she uses to bring the frost—were drawn directly from the description of the Cailleach in John Gregorson Campbell's *Witchcraft and Second Sight in the Highlands and Islands*, published in 1902.[93] Furthermore, Mackenzie gave Beira a piece of doggerel which clearly evokes the Cailleach's most famous literary appearance, in the Old Irish poem known as 'The Lament of the Old Woman of Beare':

O life that ebbs like the sea!
I am weary and old, I am weary and old—
Oh! how can I happy be
All alone in the dark and the cold.[94]

This was an act of violence to one of the most subtle of all medieval Irish lyrics, one of a piece with the name 'Beira' itself: Beara is a West Cork placename, so its use as the personal name of the goddess was a barbarism. To be congruent with Gaelic folklore, Mackenzie should simply have called her 'the Cailleach', but he may have worried that this would be found unpronounceable by his target audience.[95]

This trio of gods—Beira, Bride, and Angus—was as far as Mackenzie's Scottish pantheon went. *Wonder Tales* followed the Victorian and Edwardian folklorists in imagining a paganism which bore scant resem-

92 See G. Ó Crualaoich, *The Book of the Cailleach: Stories of the Wise-Woman Healer* (Cork, 2003), and E. Hull, 'Legends and traditions of the Cailleach Beare', *Folklore* 38.3 (1927), 225–54; also D. Ó hÓgáin, *Myth, Legend, and Romance: An Encyclopedia of the Irish Folk Tradition* (London, 1990), 67–8.

93 See *The Gaelic Otherworld*, ed. R. Black (Edinburgh, 2005), 544 [= edn. with commentary of J. G. Campbell's *Superstitions of the Highlands and Islands of Scotland* (1900) and *Witchcraft and Second Sight in the Highlands and Islands* (1902)].

94 D. A. Mackenzie, *Wonder Tales from Scottish Myth and Legend* (London, 1917), 25. For an interpretation of the (remarkable) Old Irish poem, see J. Carey, 'Transmutations of Immortality in "The Lament of the Old Woman of Beare"' *Celtica* 23 (1999), 30–7. The relation between the *Caillech Bérri* of the poem and the Cailleach of later folklore is a vexed question.

95 Other poems show that Mackenzie wince-makingly thought 'Bride' to rhyme with 'ride'—not at all the Gaelic pronunciation.

FIG. 9.6. *Beira*, from D. A. Mackenzie, *Wonder Tales from Scottish Myth and Legend* (1917), by John Duncan. Photo: Bodleian Library.

blance to the religions of the ancient world, focusing instead (as Ronald Hutton has noted) on 'great primal forces—Earth, Sky, Corn, Vegetation, Nature, Mother, Father.'[96] Mackenzie's other deities are saccharine powers and seasonal personifications of the Jack Frost variety, such as 'Father Winter.' And as in Macleod's neomyths there was a heavy emphasis on the renewal of life: 'blue-faced' Beira keeps Bride imprisoned until Angus rescues her, thus bringing the spring. They then marry, becoming—according to the classical family tree of the Túatha Dé—another incestuous brother-sister pair, like Macleod's Brigit and Manannán. If Bride had been 'Demeter-Desphœna' for Macleod, here she has been transformed into Demeter's daughter, Persephone.

Had Mackenzie gone further in this vein he might have succeeded in taking over Macleod's large following. But the whole enterprise was riven by confused thinking; the release of Bride, for example, serves no practical purpose because it is Beira who personifies the year:

> Beira always visited the island on the night before the first lengthening day—that is, on the last night of her reign as Queen of Winter. All alone in the darkness she sat beside the Well of Youth, waiting for the dawn.... As soon as Beira tasted the magic water, in silence and alone, she began to grow young again.... Then she went to and fro through Scotland, clad in a robe of green and crowned with a chaplet of bright flowers of many hues. No fairer goddess was to be found in all the land, save Bride, the peerless Queen of Summer. As each month went past, however, Beira aged quickly. She reached full womanhood in midsummer, and when autumn came on her brows wrinkled and her beauty began to fade. When the season of winter returned once again, she became an old and withered hag, and began to reign as the fierce Queen Beira.[97]

If Mackenzie's new mythology evoked the folksiness of a Russian ballet, this was simply because its basic outline had, in fact, been lifted from that country.[98] Considering that Mackenzie's previous book, published

96 *Triumph of the Moon*, 130–1.
97 Mackenzie, *Wonder Tales*, 23–4.
98 The conflict between Bride and Beira was startlingly—and very beautifully—brought to life by the Edinburgh artist and singer Hanna Tuulikki as this book went through the press. Tuulikki dramatized the story as *Women of the Hill*, an outdoor ritual drama for three female dancers and vocalists, first performed on the Isle of Skye in No-

in 1916, had been *Stories of Russian Folk-Life*, the connection between Beira and Baba Yaga, the sinister hag of Slavic folklore is obvious; Bride in turn is Vasilissa the Beautiful, the young woman imprisoned by Baba Yaga and set impossible tasks; and finally 'Prince' Angus is Prince Ivan, the hero who rescues Vasilissa. Other tales in the collection offered more genuinely Scottish material drawn from medieval legend—the story of Thomas the Rhymer, for example—but Mackenzie's starting mythology was a makeshift and borrowed affair. That notwithstanding, John Duncan appears to have felt sufficiently inspired as Mackenzie's collaborator to illustrate several episodes in the book, including a picture of Beira rather obviously modelled on Michelangelo's blocky Cumaean Sibyl. The quality of the illustrations themselves was low and their ornamental borders perfunctory, both perhaps expressing signs of an aesthetic ennui which presaged the end of Celtic Revivalism in Scotland.

Sharp and Duncan snagged on the same issue around the tension between personal and collective vision in their work with Gaelic myth; authorship and myth do not go together. In this they had much in common with Yeats's unavailing struggle with the 'god-forms' of his Celtic Mysteries. The idea of 'private myths'—in Joseph Campbell's famous phrase—is oxymoronic: the author plies a personal, shaping consciousness while myth is a collective cultural product generated unconsciously. For Sharp, the attempt to write myth evolved into a persistent psychic fissure. 'Fiona Macleod' gave him access to a submerged part of the self, and I agree with Steve Blamires that some of the Macleod writings have the air of having welled up compulsively from somewhere beneath ego-control, though perhaps there is a subjective sense in which the dignity and sinew of genuine mythology was not often attained. Nonetheless there was another side to the picture, in that the attempt to tailor a bespoke mythology for Scotland effected a permanent cultural change, and it was, in that sense, a conspicuous success. Mythological divinities had been of negligible importance in the culture of Gaeldom in Scotland, but in the Macleod writings Sharp made a virtue of the gods' obscurity. In this endeavour he was so successful that the Túatha Dé Danann became permanently integrated into the country's sense of its own Celtic inheritance and identity.

---

vember 2015. No one involved seems to have known that Bride and Beira are not genuinely ancient deities from Scotland's pagan past, but the effect was clearly haunting. Account at https://broadly.vice.com/en_us/article/summoning-celtic-goddesses-on-a-remote-scottish-island [accessed 31st December 2015].

10

COHERENCE
AND CANON

THE FAIRY FAITH AND THE EAST

Tradition is always the same. The earliest poet of
India and the Irish peasant in his hovel nod to each
other across the ages, and are in perfect agreement.

—W. B. YEATS, 'IRISH WONDERS'

AT THIS POINT we must return from Scotland in order to consider Irish
attempts to make sense of the Túatha Dé Danann in the early decades of
the twentieth century. A crucial contribution was made in 1904 by Augusta Gregory, Yeats's collaborator and confidante, when she put before
an international audience a full English version of the Mythological
Cycle. As indicated by its title, *Gods and Fighting Men*, this famous volume retold most of the sagas about the native pantheon before segueing
into the Finn Cycle. It was a sequel to Gregory's 1902 account of the Ulster Cycle, *Cuchulainn of Muirthemne*, and in both she stitched together
lively semi-translations of the medieval sources to make a smoothly
flowing narrative.[1] In doing so she furnished Ireland with the first account of its pagan gods with palpable aspirations to literary canonicity
since Standish O'Grady.[2]

---

1 A. Gregory, *Cuchulainn of Muirthemne* (London, 1902), and *Gods and Fighting Men:
The Story of the Tuatha De Danaan and of the Fianna of Ireland* (London, 1904); the most
recent biography is J. Hill, *Lady Gregory: an Irish Life* (Stroud, 2005), but see earlier M. L.
Kohlfeldt, *Lady Gregory: the Woman behind the Irish Literary Renaissance* (London, 1985).

2 As opposed to scholarship; see M. Tymoczko, *Translation in a postcolonial context:
early Irish literature in English translation* (Manchester, 1999), 122–145, for incisive discussion of the split between scholarly and literary modes of translating the medieval literature; 72–3, 126–30 give detailed accounts of Gregory's method, the second discussing her
treatment of the Dagda's difficulties in 'The Second Battle of Moytura' (see above, 118–25).

The Túatha Dé Danann section of Gregory's book falls into two parts. In the first, she traces a single narrative line, basically following 'The Book of Invasions' from the moment of the arrival of the god-peoples until their eventual defeat. From the conquest of the Fir Bolg—the first battle of Moytura—we move swiftly through Fomorian oppression and into the second battle. Typically, the saga of Lug's revenge upon his father's killers—the sons of Tuireann—is spliced with great skill into the narrative of the Túatha Dé's victory over their enemies, in which Lug's part is pivotal; Gregory then relates versions of Lug's manifestations to later figures, Conn and Cú Chulainn. Foregrounding the charismatic, ruthless Lug as the protagonist of the Túatha Dé ascendancy gives a much-needed clarity and coherence to a story woven from many parts, boosted by a swift, racy style. The account of the cycle ends with a return to 'The Book of Invasions' and the defeat of the Túatha Dé Danann by the incoming sons of Miled (Míl), and their retreat behind 'hidden walls... that no man could see through, but they themselves could see through them and pass through them'.[3]

At this point Bodb Derg becomes king of the Túatha Dé Danann, and the second section of Gregory's account begins. She sketches the major personages one by one, using them as heading under which to gather mythological anecdotes which had not featured in the first section. The account of Bodb Derg is the first of these and draws skillfully on the *Acallam* and the fore-tales to the *Táin*; then come the Dagda, Óengus (Angus), the Morrígan, Áine, Aoibheall, and—as a diptych—Midir and Étaín. This display-case of stories about individual figures culminates with a long section on Manannán, collecting together very early accounts ('The Voyage of Bran') with very late ones ('The Adventure of Tadg mac Céin'). Thus, Manannán dominates the second half of Gregory's account of the gods, as Lug does the first.

Throughout she was remarkably faithful to the grainy detail of medieval tradition, extracting anecdotes from the *dindshenchas*, for example, which remain little known, even to aficionados. (Thus we find a story about the theft of a magical tub belonging to Ainge, a rather shadowy daughter of the Dagda, and obscure details about the early amours of the Mac Óc.) It is greatly to Gregory's credit that she—the amateur folklorist and littérateur—could tolerate the basic idiosyncrasy of the god-peoples and so convey an accurate impression of the medieval material. Her es-

---

3 Gregory, *Gods and Fighting Men*, 73; this is a detail drawing on the Old Irish anecdote 'On the Seizure of the Hollow Hill', for which see 91, fn.61, and 175, fn.147 above.

sentially transcriptional attention to her sources thus became a kind of originality. In refusing to reduce the Túatha Dé to classical caricatures or pigeonhole them as spiritual principles, she stalwartly resisted O'Grady, her own closest forerunner, but she also managed simultaneously to evade Yeatsian occult nationalism and the comparativist theories of Celtic scholarship. Despite her book's title, it is telling that Gregory's only references to the Túatha Dé Danann as 'gods' come in the book's first paragraphs, in passages which reel the reader in with a few well-placed but otherwise atypical O'Gradyisms.

If Gregory's approach seemed calculated to sidestep hermetic speculations, Yeats tacked in the opposite direction in his preface to the book, asserting (characteristically) that the reality of the gods was 'confirmed by apparitions among the country-people to-day'.[4] But the mythology, he wrote, was in 'fragments', its deeper meaning jumbled up with 'fantastic history' and with much 'altered or left out'. Although he acknowledged that the Túatha Dé were anthropomorphic reflections of the ancient Irish themselves—'their own images in the water'—he suggested that they might 'have been much besides this', subtly alluding to his own surveyings of the astral plane. In a sense his words further underscore the failure of the Celtic Mysteries: they hint that the structural problems besetting the national pantheon remained essentially unsolved after years of work, though (as we saw) the gods' visual shape at least had come into greater focus. Yeats still allowed for the possibility of some deep spiritual significance, but before that might be laid bare the pantheon stood in need of straining and amplification.

Russell continued to make efforts in this direction, but Yeats's interest in imaginative polytheology had tailed off by this point. Nevertheless, in some quarters the refusal of the Irish pantheon to constellate satisfactorily continued to be a perceptible source of cultural anxiety. In response, a second wave of writers emerged who attempted to put the mythographic house in order, and the remainder of this chapter will be devoted to examining three of them. The first, Walter Evans-Wentz (1878–1965), was an American anthropologist and full-bore romantic enthusiast, while the second, the Belfast-born James Cousins (1863–1956), made his living as a writer, poet, critic, and playwright. The third, James Stephens (1882–1950), born in Dublin, was, like Cousins, a poet and critic, but he was also a significant novelist, and for his work in all three guises he

---

4 Yeats, 'Preface', to Gregory, *Gods and Fighting Men*, 15.

merits a place in the second division of great modern Irish writers.[5] All three were in their own way remarkable, but the life stories of Evans-Wentz and Cousins share certain similarities, meaning that they can be compared. Stephens, as a more considerable literary figure, stands slightly apart.

THE 'FAIRY FAITH'

Both Evans-Wentz and Cousins began as theosophists, and both contributed significant, systematizing books to the discussion of the Irish gods; both men then strikingly literalized the orientalism of the Revival and abandoned Celticism for the East. Evans-Wentz took himself off to Darjeeling in 1919 and became the first translator of *The Tibetan Book of the Dead*, devoting the rest of his life to the study of Asian religions.[6] Cousins emigrated to India with his wife in 1915, cheerfully announcing his conversion to Hinduism.

Evans-Wentz was the first of the two to publish on the Túatha Dé. In 1911 he brought out *The Fairy-Faith in Celtic Countries*, based on the Oxford doctoral thesis on which he had worked under Sir John Rhŷs, at that time the most distinguished Celtic scholar in Britain.[7] The thesis had been framed as folklore research, inflected with anthropology and academic 'Celtology', but when the book emerged it had been expanded in an eccentric direction.[8] It made a single crucial assertion, that a van-

5 W. A. Dumbleton, *James Cousins* (Boston, MA, 1980); crucial recent discussion in chapter eight of J. Lennon, *Irish Orientalism: a Literary and Intellectual History* (Syracuse, NY, 2004).

6 Closest approach to a life of Evans-Wentz is D. S. Lopez, *The Tibetan Book of the Dead: A Biography* (Princeton, NJ, 2011), where the focus is on the orientalist's adventures; the background to anthropological investigations in Ireland in the period is given by S. Guinness, 'Visions and Beliefs in the West of Ireland: Irish Folklore and British Anthropology, 1898–1920', *Irish Studies Review* 6:1 (1998), 37–46.

7 Wentz came to Britain in 1915 specifically to study under Rhŷs; during his time in Oxford he added 'Evans', his Welsh mother's maiden name, to his surname.

8 One of the many individuals there has not been space to discuss is Evans-Wentz's contemporary, the Scottish journalist Lewis Spence (1874–1955), also an anthropologist and folklorist. The two could be usefully compared: in a series of well-written but wild books Spence attempted to reconstruct the mystery traditions he believed to lie behind Celtic mythology. *The Mysteries of Britain: Secret Rites and Traditions of Ancient Britain Restored* (London, 1905) is representative; discussion in R. Hutton, *The Pagan Religions of the Ancient British Isles* (Oxford, 1991), 141–2.

ished pan-Celtic religion—the so-called 'Fairy-Faith'—could be reconstructed by scholarship and sensitive inquiry.

Rhŷs had published his *Celtic Heathendom* in 1886, and by theorizing about the lost paganism of the Celtic peoples, Evans-Wentz was following in his mentor's footsteps. Like Rhŷs, his ambitions were pan-Celtic, although his view of Celticity was of a more stereotyped and essentialist stripe. Their approaches differed, however, in that Evans-Wentz insisted on citing metaphysical evidence as part of his argument, for it was a key hypothesis of his book that fairies actually exist.[9] In arriving at this position, Evans-Wentz engaged with all the discourses that contemporary scholarship had to bring to bear upon the matter: psychology, comparative mythology, and the then-prevalent anthropological theory that belief in fairies arose from memories of a dark, diminutive Bronze Age people—'pygmies'—who had been displaced by Iron Age invaders.[10]

Evans-Wentz was not reconstructing ancient Celtic religion so much as the spiritual reality out of which he felt sure that religion had grown. But there were only three potential sources for such a reconstitution: the medieval literature, modern Gaelic folklore, and spiritual vision. Evans-Wentz's strategy was simply to regard the first two as transcriptions of the third. His account of the literature, for example, was fundamentally ahistorical, in that he treated its sagas and poetry not as the products of medieval culture, but as mimeographic accounts of pagan tradition or some metaphysical faery reality. (The tendency to collapse the two is characteristic of the book.) This he termed the 'recorded Fairy-Faith', which he contrasted with the 'living Fairy-Faith', his equally naïve interpretation of folklore collected at first hand from the Celtic regions and countries in a series of expeditions, supplemented with older reports from the researchers of the previous century. If the accounts of fairy beings in medieval literature and modern folklore could be shown to harmonize, then the only rational explanation (felt Evans-Wentz) was that such beings must genuinely exist.

He prefaced discussion of the medieval texts with a display of the training which he had received in Oxford, summarizing contemporary scholarship. His argument was that the ancient Irish had worshipped the Sidhe, that the latter were more or less identical with the literary

9 *FFCC*, xvi.

10 A classic example is provided by A. MacBain, *Celtic Mythology and Religion*, 27, discussed above, 362–3; for the pygmy-theory, see C. Silver, 'On the Origin of Fairies: Victorians, Romantics, and Folk Belief', *Browning Institute Studies* 14 (1986), 141–56.

Túatha Dé Danann, and that both therefore corresponded to the Indo-European pantheons of Greece, Rome, and India. As discussed, this was at the time the standard model in the academy and one with a kernel of truth to it, even if time—as this book has endeavoured to show—has crucially qualified that truth. On the whole Evans-Wentz made a decent fist of summarizing the Celtological consensus, although he and the academy parted company over his literal belief in the fairy beings of legend. He quoted O'Grady with approval on the idea that paganism had never really ended in Ireland, and was prone to florid rhapsodies on the country's ancient mystery rites—rites, however, which existed entirely in his own imagination.[11] He hypothesized, for example, that the spectacular Iron Age fortress of Dun Aengus (Dún Aonghasa) on Inishmore had been the site of 'pagan mysteries comparable to those of the Greeks', where the god Óengus had been honoured with 'mystic assemblies' conducted in a 'sun-temple'. This kind of intense attraction to an imagined ancient paganism was more frequently found among the literary writers of the period than among Evans-Wentz's fellow anthropologists, whose work tended to reveal a mixture of attraction and repulsion towards the beliefs which they studied.[12] Evans-Wentz's feelings were less conflicted in that he frankly preferred his putative mysteries to Christianity, the advent of which had seen, he said, 'the Sacred Fires... buried in ashes, and the Light and Beauty of the pagan world obscured with sackcloth.'[13]

Evans-Wentz was thus a particularly extreme pagan survivalist, but with a crucial difference that set him apart from most of his contemporaries. Collectors of folklore in rural England tended to exhibit, in Ronald Hutton's words, 'a crushing condescension' towards their informants, but Evans-Wentz's exorbitant Celtophilia led him to the opposite extreme.[14] To him, Celtic communities—supposedly unchanged and unchanging—were 'unconventional and natural', and he persistently idealized the individuals he encountered. 'Let us, then, for a time' (he wrote) 'forget that there are such things as libraries and universities, and betake ourselves to the Celtic peasant for instruction, living close to nature as he lives, and thinking the things which he thinks.'[15] This sounds as if Evans-Wentz, true to his anthropological training, was advocating an

---

11 *FFCC*, 283.

12 See Hutton on Jane Harrison, in *The Triumph of the Moon* (Oxford, 1999), 124–5.

13 *FFCC*, 13.

14 Hutton, *Triumph of the Moon*, 127.

15 *FFCC*, 19.

early form of participant observation, implying the investigator's self-immersion in a world of archaic belief.

If this was his aim, it foundered for two reasons. Firstly, the individuals that he interviewed were considerably more self-aware than he had been led to expect (some of them must have been pulling the leg of their earnest, fairy-fixated visitor), but he was also oblivious to the stratifications of class and education in the communities from which he gathered material. As a result, a reading of his book reveals that a number of his informants in Ireland and Scotland were not, in fact, mouthpieces of pristine Gaelic folk tradition, but rather were thoroughly conversant with the paradigms within which Evans-Wentz himself was operating. In Ireland in particular Celtological and revivalist understandings of the supernatural beings of native lore had become widely diffused. For example, despite dismissing the academy at the beginning of his book, Evans-Wentz quotes 'a professor in a Catholic college in West Ireland'—hardly an untutored peasant—who opined:

> The fairies of any one race are the people of the preceding race—the Fomors for the Fir Bolgs, the Fir Bolgs for the Dananns, and the Dananns for us. The old races died. Where did they go? They became spirits—and fairies. Second-sight gave our race power to see the inner world. When Christianity came to Ireland the people had no *definite* heaven. Their ideas about the other world were vague. But the older ideas of a spirit world remained side by side with the Christian ones, and being preserved in a subconscious way gave rise to the fairy world.[16]

This excerpt ingeniously combines pagan survivalism (naturally), psychology, a version of the then-current 'pygmy' theory, spiritual speculation, and the skeleton of the medieval synthetic history. All this was to fail to distinguish the folklorists from the folk, and whenever this kind of mixture was taken as evidence for living fairy beliefs there was a real risk of naïve circularity of argument. Many of Evans-Wentz's informants fed him ideas which owed less to the lore of the shanachie than they did to O'Curry, O'Grady, and the Dublin periodical press.

An acute instance of this circularity is offered by a section of Evans-Wentz's book entitled 'An Irish Mystic's Testimony'. That unnamed mystic was transparently none other than George Russell, to whom, along

---

16 *FFCC*, 70.

with Yeats, the book was dedicated. (Yeats was also a major source for Irish material in the book.)[17] Considerable prominence was given by Evans-Wentz to these visions, and his spiritual crush on Russell manifested as a duplication of the latter's style:

> Of all European lands I venture to say that Ireland is the most mystical, and, in the eyes of true Irishmen, as much the Magic Isle of Gods and Initiates now as it was when the Sacred Fires flashed from its purple, heather covered mountain-tops and mysterious round towers, and the Greater Mysteries drew to its hallowed shrines neophytes from the West as well as from the East, from India and Egypt as well as from Atlantis; and Erin's mystic-seeing sons still watch and wait for the relighting of the Fires and the restoration of the old Druidic Mysteries... until this mystic message is interpreted, men cannot discover the secret of Gaelic myth and song in olden or modern times, they cannot drink at the ever-flowing fountain of Gaelic genius, the perennial source of inspiration which lies behind the new revival of literature and art in Ireland, nor understand the seeming reality of the fairy races.[18]

It is the sheer belatedness that is remarkable here: with its 'Fires' and 'Druidic Mysteries', this recycled the rhetoric that Russell had plied in the mid-1890s. In contrast, the actual interview shows how strikingly Russell's ideas about the relationship between his visions and the mythology had shifted:

> I saw many of these great beings, and I then thought that I had visions of Aengus, Manannan, Lug, and other famous kings or princes among the Tuatha De Danann; but since then I have seen so many beings of a similar character that I now no longer would attribute to any one of them personal identity with particular beings of legend; though I believe that they correspond in a general way to the Tuatha De Danann or ancient Irish gods.[19]

By uncritically recording Russell's words as part of the 'living Fairy-Faith', Evans-Wentz was allowing the theosophically inflected vision of

---

17 H. Martin, *W. B. Yeats: Metaphysician as Dramatist* (Waterloo, Ontario, 1986), 50, fn.37.

18 *FFCC*, 59.

19 *FFCC*, 61–2.

a single remarkable individual to guide his interpretation of an entire tranche of Irish and Scottish folklore.

The same feedback loop was clearly operative in Scotland, in that Evans-Wentz's informants repeatedly show evidence of familiarity with *Carmina Gadelica* and the works of the inescapable Fiona, which seemed now to be shaping the way in which Gaelic folklore was conceived on a local level. The reader will by now be able to anticipate the nature of the 'pagan survival' that one Protestant minister in the Hebrides reported to Evans-Wentz:

> In Lewis libations are poured to the goddess [or god] of the sea, called *Shoney*, in order to bring in seaweed. Until modern times in Iona similar libations were poured to a god corresponding to Neptune.[20]

By this stage Martin Martin's anecdote had clearly taken on a life of its own, becoming an instance of the phenomenon that the American folklorist Richard Dorson called 'fakelore'.[21] It is symptomatic that while even William Sharp acknowledged that the custom of making offerings to the sea-god was extinct, here (in 1911!) it is reported as a going concern. Furthermore, we saw Carmichael had alluded to 'the Neptune of the Gael', and the verbal echo here suggests that Evans-Wentz's source had simply been reading *Carmina Gadelica* and passing on what he found there—supplemented perhaps by Fiona Macleod's story 'Cuilidh Mhoire.' Evans-Wentz, who was accompanied on several of his Scottish jaunts by Carmichael, seems to have been blithely unaware of the possibility.

There was a poignant quality to Evans-Wentz's insistence that both medieval literature and modern folklore gave access to a spiritual plane of reality, a proposition which he set himself the task of justifying in the long concluding section of *The Fairy-Faith*. The Celtic countries were merely a laboratory for his ultimate goal, which was no less than to enlarge the scientific consensus about the nature of reality, so that a place might be found within it for the real existence of ethereal beings. If he could demonstrate that the Celtic belief in fairies was scientific, then

---

20 *FFCC*, 93.

21 This is a convenient term, though it has been challenged as over-condemnatory. It corresponds to the German term *Folklorismus*, meaning the appropriation and reworking of folklore, often for commercial purposes; see V. J. Newall, 'The Adaptation of Folklore and Tradition (Folklorismus)', *Folklore* 98:2 (1987), 131–51.

materialism itself would be overturned. The wider context of such speculations was the then-fashionable field of psychical research, in which investigators, many of them spiritualists, laboured to show that a non-material dimension to reality could be shown to exist by scientific means.[22] A decade later no less a figure than Sir Arthur Conan Doyle would publicly argue in precisely this vein for the fairies' existence, and like Conan Doyle, Evans-Wentz longed to *experience* the beings he obsessively catalogued. Hence the embarrassingly invocatory tone for a work that began as an academic thesis: Evans-Wentz described Lough Gur, for example, as surrounded by 'a circle of low-lying hills on whose summits fairy goddesses yet dwell invisibly', and the transition from the Isle of Man to Wales in his book was accompanied by a rhetorical prayer to the island's tutelary god, Manannán mac Lir, requesting that he ensure 'safe passage across his watery domain'.[23]

This last was a rare moment of focus on a particular member of the Túatha Dé Danann, and may therefore serve to introduce some conclusions about Evans-Wentz's view of the gods. A kind of cryptozoologist of the spirit, Evans-Wentz's interest lay in establishing the *reality* of ethereal beings, rather than exploring their individual identities or relationships to one another. This had consequences for the political affiliations of his work, in that his engagement with earthly Ireland could be extraordinarily clumsy—perhaps unsurprising in a man so attuned to the abstract and unearthly. '[T]o-day', he averred, 'Ireland contains two races,—a race visible which we call Celts, and a race invisible which we call Fairies. Between these two races there is constant intercourse even now; for Irish seers say that they can behold the majestic, beautiful *Sidhe*, and according to them the *Sidhe* are a race quite distinct from our own, just as living and possibly more powerful.'[24] Published five years before the Easter Rising in a climate of nationalist ferment, racial discourse of this kind betrayed a personality astonishingly blind to political realities.

It was all an idiosyncratic exercise, to say the least, and a number of the authorities who contributed to *The Fairy-Faith*—who included major figures such as John Rhŷs and Douglas Hyde, founder of the Gaelic League and later Ireland's first President—sounded distinctly discom-

---

22 See J. Oppenheim, *The Other World: Spiritualism and Psychical Research in England, 1850–1914* (Cambridge, 1985).

23 *FFCC*, 78, 115.

24 *FFCC*, 284.

fited by its author's transcendental divagations. In a strange way the monomania of the project is underscored by the despatch with which, after publication, Evans-Wentz jettisoned the mysteries of the West in favour of those of the East. It is certain that he did later researchers a service in that he recorded some genuine Celtic folklore which might otherwise have vanished, but ultimately his naiveté ensured the book was received as a crank piece.

WESTERN MYSTERIES

As previously noted, James Cousins makes a revealing comparison with Evans-Wentz. The life stories of the two men may have been similar, but that kinship was not for the most part reflected in their understanding of the divinities. Cousins focused on the gods as individual entities and thus drew near to becoming the 'polytheologian' the Irish gods so badly needed. His contribution consisted of a short book, *The Wisdom of the West*, published a year after Evans-Wentz's *Fairy-Faith*, and also a series of long narrative poems which emerged between 1906 and 1912.

Much light is shed on his development by the double autobiography he wrote with his wife, Margaret ('Gretta'), entitled *We Two Together*, a title which underlines her influence on his thinking. The Cousinses' interminable account of their spiritual adventures, unbending moral fibre, and social and political radicalism paints them (not altogether unappealingly) as a pair of good-natured narcissists. In terms of our three sources from which a pantheon might be configured, Cousins' primary focus was the medieval literature, and the Mythological Cycle in particular. In a complete contrast to Evans-Wentz, he brusquely dismissed folklore as 'vague suggestions... preserved in grotesque stories... around the fires of the peasants'. The third source, spiritual vision, was represented by the inner experiences of Margaret Cousins, who seems to have excelled at esoteric visualization.

Unlike Evans-Wentz, Cousins was interested only in Ireland. He set his ideas out with great clarity in *The Wisdom of the West*, which began as a series of lectures to esoteric and Irish nationalist societies.[25] Its title reversed the theosophical emphasis on the wisdom of the East, although this remained Cousins' crucial interpretative paradigm. Indeed, Theosophy's attraction lay in the fact that it offered a way to uncover a spiritual

---

25 *WOTW*, 19.

heritage common to both East and West. As Joseph Lennon argues, theo-sophical theories of race dovetailed well with the comparative mythol-ogy then in vogue in the academy. One was rooted in hermetic philoso-phy and the other in linguistics, but both hypothesized 'that a unified Indo-European race and culture had once spanned East and West', with the result that Ireland and India shared a number of essential similari-ties: both could be depicted as 'untouched by Roman civilization and modern culture', and as 'ancient and remote'.[26] Evans-Wentz's lofty pro-nouncement that the country was still the 'Magic isle of Gods and Initi-ates' is a classic example of this kind of language.

Theosophy would also shape the entire direction of Cousins' life, as it was Annie Besant, by then leader of the movement, who arranged the position which took the Cousinses to India in 1915. There he befriended a number of key figures—including the mystic Aurobindo, the poet Rabindranath Tagore, and even Gandhi—and India became the site of his mature work, work not conducted for the most part along Irish themes.[27] Being Irish in India gave him, Cousins felt, an instinctive af-finity with Indian culture and its anti-colonialism.[28] He was, in other words, beginning with a predisposition towards grandiose theories of cultural synthesis.[29]

In *The Wisdom of the West* Cousins probed the Mythological Cycle with the aim of reconstructing a suppressed spiritual system—'the lost religion or philosophy of ancient Ireland'—which he believed would be revealed as akin to Hindu Vedanta.[30] A decade later he summed up the theory when he wrote that a primeval Indo-European inheritance had always been latent in Irish culture; when Hindu religious doctrine reached Ireland in the form of Theosophy, it had simply reactivated a submerged but kindred element in Ireland's soul. Russell and Yeats were,

---

26 Lennon, *Irish Orientalism*, 329–30.

27 See Lennon, *Irish Orientalism*, 351–2.

28 See Lennon, *Irish Orientalism*, 332.

29 This was reflected in his consciousness of his own mixed heritage, as a Belfast-born Protestant with English, Irish, Scottish, Welsh and Huguenot ancestry: his identifi-cation with Ireland and Celticity was therefore partly in the nature of a deliberate choice. See Lennon, *Irish Orientalism*, 342–3, and also T. Foley & M. O'Connor (eds.), *Ireland and India: Colonies, Culture and Empire* (Dublin, 2006), especially essays by Guinness and Len-non; also, on Margaret Cousins, see K. O'Malley, *Ireland, India and Empire: Indo-Irish Radi-cal Connections, 1919–64* (Manchester, 2009), 58–60. Also useful is J. Nolan, 'The Hindu Celticism of James Cousins (1873–1956)', *ABEI Journal: The Brazilian Journal of Irish Studies* (2005), 219–32.

30 *WOTW*, 12.

he wrote, only two among many who had recognized 'the spiritual truths that Asia had given to the world reflected in the old myths and legends of Ireland'.[31] From a contemporary viewpoint all this resembles finding shapes in shifting clouds, but this is to benefit from hindsight: in 1912 it was fashionable even in academe to assert archaic parallels between India and Ireland.[32]

Cousins had little interest in Cú Chulainn or Finn, the figures that had compelled so many of his literary predecessors. Instead he zeroed in on the Túatha Dé Danann, and professed that '[t]he existence in former times of an Irish Pantheon, crowded with personifications embodying all the characteristics which have given to the gods and heroes of Greece a classical immortality, is being slowly but surely forced upon the recognition of students of comparative mythology'.[33] For all its ambition, *The Wisdom of the West* was a much smaller book than *The Fairy-Faith* (only sixty-one pages), with an analytic edge the breezy Evans-Wentz lacked. Intervening in various academic debates about the nature of myth—he dismissed the then-fashionable 'solar' theories of Max Müller, upon which comparative mythology had snagged—Cousins found the abstract texture of mythology profound in itself, 'shadowings forth of the deepest truths of the soul'.

AVATARS AND EMANATIONS

Cousins focused squarely on the major problem posed by the Túatha Dé for the comparativists, which was that they *do* form a pantheon of sorts in the medieval texts, but its borders are vague and, in comparison to the clarity of the Greek gods, its personalities are bafflingly indeterminate

---

31 Lennon, *Irish Orientalism*, 330, quoting Cousins' *The Cultural Unity of Asia* (Adyar, Madras, 1922), 7–8.

32 This tendency was a prop of 'nativist' scholarship; a representative volume is Myles Dillon's posthumous *Celts and Aryans* (Simla, 1975). Kim McCone attempted to demolish the whole basis for the exercise in *PPCP*, 13–15, but this has not been final, not least because McCone used Indian parallels in later chapters of the same work. Some contemporary Celticists continue to explore Celtic-Indian connections, albeit with a methodology utterly different to that of Cousins; rigorous examples include C. Doherty, 'Kingship in Early Ireland', in E. Bhreathnach (ed), *Tara: A Study of an Exceptional Kingship and Landscape* (Dublin, 2005), 3–31, and M. Fomin, *et al.* (eds.), *Sacred Topology in Early Ireland and Ancient India: Religious Paradigm Shift* (Washington, DC, 2010).

33 *WOTW*, 19.

and continually multiplying. The children of the Dagda, theoretically the top god, are a good example, for earlier texts number them as Óengus, Bodb, and Brigit, and these have a good chance of having genuinely pre-Christian prototypes. But later we hear of Cermait and Ainge—she of the magic tub—and in the early thirteenth century, we find the author of the *Acallam* rather spuriously adding in a Fergus and an Étaín. Cousins saw an opportunity in this very vagueness, and recorded in *We Two Together* how he initially recoiled from the bloodthirstiness of Irish mythology, and would have shifted allegiance to the classical gods had they not been 'too solid and clear-edged for my taste. I had no use for divinities... that could not been seen through.'[34]

He picked this lock with a Hindu key, one provided by Marie-Henri d'Arbois de Jubainville. According to d'Arbois de Jubainville, the very features in Irish myth which seemed to be aesthetic flaws from the Greek point of view would stand revealed as signs of antique profundity if seen from an Indian perspective.[35] Cousins took this as his cue to construct a theological system based on divine emanations, in which the vagueness and contradiction of the Túatha Dé Danann could be explained using the Hindu concept of the *avatar*—a particular manifestation of a deity. The idea of a family tree of divinities—a hopeless tangle in the case of the Irish pantheon—could then be seen as a metaphor for a set of metaphysical relationships between abstract divine principles. In this way for Cousins the sagas put us 'in the presence of elemental representations of vast ideas whose phases are embodied in multiple personifications held together by the fundamental human relationships of parent, consort, or offspring.'[36]

This scheme relied on a cosmology which was not monotheist but monist—'the idea that the universe and the gods of both chaos and order... proceed from one unknowable principle which lies behind yet permeates phenomena.'[37] It began with a primordial divine being emanating pairs of opposites from itself (dark and light, masculine and feminine), which then in turn produce triads, heptads, and further subdivisions, which all ultimately condense back into unity.

---

34 J. Cousins & M. Cousins, *We Two Together: A Duo-Autobiography* (Madras, 1950), 572.

35 The phenomenon recalls the Sanskritist Maurice Bloomfield's description of the 'Vedic haze'—the envelope of bewildering ambiguity characteristic of early Hindu scripture.

36 *WOTW*, 25.

37 *WOTW*, 33.

The idea is stated most clearly in Cousins' 1906 poem 'The Setting Forth of Dana', which amounts to a neomyth in the mould of Fiona Macleod, deriving directly from one of Margaret Cousins' inner visions.[38] The poem declared that at the beginning of time souls had been 'sown' by the Dagda and Dana, as the masculine and feminine emanations of the nameless and primordial God. Cousins wrote:

One for the Seed and for the Sowing Twain:
But for the Ripening Three, for Reaping, Seven,
And seven times seven for the garnering.[39]

This was a pseudo–Hindu vision of a proliferating pantheon of deities emerging from a single ineffable divinity, and it owes much to the influence of George Russell. It is worth noting that the medieval texts offered no explicit justification for pairing the Dagda with Dana, apart from the fact that scholars had identified the latter with the mysterious 'Ana' Cormac had called 'Mother of the Irish Gods', and that the Dagda's traditional designation was the 'Supreme Father'.[40] Fiona Macleod had also yoked them together, but Cousins' scheme was more thoroughly worked out.

In another of Cousins' long poems, *Etain the Beautiful* (1912), we find the union of the Dagda and Dana given a more overtly Indian flavour. A druid orders king Eochaidh to take a wife, saying:

For when of old the deathless Lord of Life
Dagda came forth, and knew the immortal need
That burned within his heart, he took to wife
Dana the Mother of all human seed.
In her his breath found music and a name.
In her his fire has blossomed into flame.[41]

As there can be no speech or song without breath, and no flame without fire, the impacted imagery here thus carries an unmistakeable nuance of

38 Cousins wrote of this poem and the later *Etain the Beautiful*, 'she… communicated to me, as from some higher consciousness, the mythological stories that I later put into poetical form…'

39 J. Cousins, *The Quest* (Dublin, 1906), 7.

40 By Cousins' day Ana and Dana (Danu) were regularly identified in the literature. See above, 187–91, for the complexities of these names.

41 J. Cousins, *Etain the Beautiful* (Dublin, 1912), 3.

the Hindu male and female principles, Shiva and Shakti, often described in precisely these terms. But less abstractly Cousins' marital devotion is also in evidence here, and it is clear that his Dagda and Dana are a thumbnail portrait of himself and Gretta, collaborating in the work of gathering souls to spiritual truth. (*We Two Together*, indeed.) The Dagda's transformation into a supportive husband in the mould of an Edwardian socialist radical is particularly bizarre in the light of his wayward carnality in the medieval literature.[42]

The Wisdom of the West afforded Cousins an opportunity to articulate ideas which he had previously framed in verse and to bring them into dialogue with Celtic scholarship. He gives us, as Russell and Sharp had not, a key to his own mythology. And if he failed to delineate precisely which god went where in his scheme of divine emanations—the reader is forced to make diagrams—nevertheless the overall idea was a brilliant one. By substituting a vertical line for the sideways sprawl of the medieval Túatha Dé Danann, it neatly made a virtue of the overlap of identities that makes Irish mythology so bewildering for the modern reader.

Cousins also followed Evans-Wentz in rhetorically exalting his own imagined and impressionistic Celtic mysteries over Christianity. But his genuine knowledge of Indian thought enabled him to mount a more open challenge, setting out a religious system which was to rival or exceed the Christian religion in sophistication, particularly by acknowledging female divinities and replacing monotheism with monism—the belief that God is one, but may manifest in many forms. He wrote that Ireland's mythology offered '... a unique theology setting forth in quaint personifications and symbols a theogony as rich as any known, and a view of the universe, and man's relationship thereto, which in its essentials and implications has not been surpassed by the most advanced thought of modern times'.[43] This was the language of Theosophy on the wisdom of the East, which Cousins' title had geographically reversed. It also strikingly contrasted with Yeats, Russell, and William Sharp, all of whom had seen the putatively pagan wisdom of the Gael (under various complexions) as hybridizable with Christianity. Cousins in contrast saw 'a fundamental difference' between the two, with Irish paganism as an ancient and profound system which *should* have survived to the present

---

42 In Terence Brown's judgment, Cousins was a poet 'whose occasional attraction is a pleasing painterly exoticism, mediated in rhythms of mellifluous banality'. (*Northern Voices: Poets from Ulster* [Dublin, 1975], 67).

43 *WOTW*, 21.

in a textual form, as Indian scriptures had.[44] The Christian centuries and the vagaries of oral transmission had (he argued) disinherited Ireland of a body of native Vedas or druidical Upanishads, an archaic ritual form that he hoped modern Ireland might reinvent.[45]

INNER VISIONS

Cousins' objective tone in *The Wisdom of the West* seems largely to have been down to audience awareness: he was, after all, making a public claim for the intellectual and spiritual gravitas of his endeavour. But the actual process of developing his neomyths seems to have been more excitable, and owed less to medieval manuscripts than to modern mediumship. In theosophical Dublin the Cousinses were, in Lennon's phrase, 'occult trendsetters', summoned by Madame Blavatsky herself to be representatives of a neo-Celtic spiritual sensibility. This was a role which brought them some social status and which they seem to have taken as an instruction to put the mythology into order—or, in their own terms, to bring its latent order and meaning to light. In practice this had odd effects. In one myth-poem, 'The Marriage of Lir and Niam', medieval tradition was transformed beyond recognition. Cousins turned Lir, father of Manannán and the unfortunate swan-children, in a restless king-turned-quester reminiscent of Tennyson's Ulysses: seeking over the sea for a wife, he wins the divine Niam (*sic*). But the otherworldly Niamh 'of the Golden Head' was in no way a goddess in the tradition; she is normally the wife of Oisín, son of Finn, and had in fact been made up for precisely that purpose by the eighteenth-century poet Mícheál Coimín.[46] Yet again a new deity can be observed entering the pantheon.

As it happened, the Cousinses had an untrumpable card to play in the face of any such pedantry, for the story had the distinction of having been dictated to an entranced Gretta Cousins by none other than the goddess Niam herself.[47] In *We Two Together* James recorded a sequence of

---

44 *WOTW*, 46.

45 *WOTW*, 51.

46 See above, 254–6, for Lir; for Niamh as the creation of Coimín, see M. Ó Briain, 'Some material on Oisín in the Land of Youth', in Ó Corráin *et al.* (eds.), *Sages, Saints and Storytellers*, 192–3. Coimín's poetry was the proximate source for Yeats's 'The Wanderings of Oisin'.

47 This is therefore an early instance of the phenomenon which modern Pagans call 'unverified personal gnosis' (UPG); for modern Paganisms, see below, 477–82.

these inner visions, in which the goddess gratified his wife with a series of stupefyingly platitudinous revelations. The following is typical:

> Gretta told me of having reached the plain on which the Irish Deities, the De Dananns, dwelt. Each enthroned God was accompanied by his Goddess. One of the latter came towards her carrying something like a casket in her hands. As the Goddess came near, Gretta knelt in reverence. The Goddess told her to rise and look in the casket. Side by side were a ruby and an equally large pearl. Gretta asked the goddess to open her understanding. The Goddess said: 'The ruby is my husband, Lir. The pearl is myself, Niav. Remember this when you return to your world, and tell it to Jim: he will understand.' ... Symbolically the pearl was the inner spiritual core of life; the ruby the executive mind.[48]

In all, James Cousins' most significant achievement—significantly aided by Gretta—was to take the bewildering surface texture of the medieval mythology at face value. Slotting the Irish gods into a Hindu theological structure might look today like the effusions of a crank, but it was not without parallels in the mainstream Celtic scholarship of his day. It allowed him to raise a vast and, in a sense, obvious question, one which—despite thirty years of mythological revival—had yet to be adequately theorized: what aesthetic work might be done with the gods as the medieval literature actually presented them? Despite the importance of Margaret's visions to his poetry and their shared idealism, James Cousins was unlike almost every other Irish revivalist writer by virtue of being a respecter of the medieval text; in *The Wisdom of the West*, at least, he read the sagas in an almost midrashic manner.

This was the potential which the Cousinses' work held out—an Irish esotericism that would genuinely engage with the medieval inheritance—but their emigration to India ultimately led to a retreat from Celticism. There are signs that James was aware of the disintegration and increasing insularity of the Revival in the years immediately prior to the Easter Rising, and it is this that may have prompted so dramatic a change of life; there is no doubt that the primary interest for both the Cousinses was the Indian dimension of theosophical thought. But it is interesting to note that while Evans-Wentz never glanced back at the Celtic West and its fairies, apparently losing interest entirely, Cousins continued to

---

48 Cousins & Cousins, *We Two Together*, 123.

refer to the Irish gods intermittently until the end of his life. In his fifties, he seems to have considered writing 'a meditation on the realities expressed through the Irish myths', although it was never published, if indeed ever actually begun; nonetheless, James reported to Gretta in the late 1930s that he had sighted the Túatha Dé Danann in the foothills of the Himalayas, as an ornithologist might spot a flock of windblown birds.[49] A late poem, written in 1940 and thus in the period in which Cousins' mind turned back towards his homeland's mythology, shows him reconsidering his own juvenilia:

> These unto me Their hands will reach
> Over the archway of the sun,
> Speaking the single spirit-speech
> From the heights where East and West are one.
>
> Before the blinding morning breaks
> I shall step out behind a star
> And seek the quiet haunted lakes
> Where my De Dananns are.[50]

Two things are worth highlighting here. Firstly, Cousins' comparative religion mirrored his polytheology—in both, a lofty and ineffable 'one' undergoes primordial division into duality—light and dark, male and female, East and West, Hindu and Druidic—which, though sundered, ultimately condense back into each other and fuse. Secondly, this grand vision modulates into a sudden personal note in the final stanza: the 'blinding morning' is death, at which Cousins imagines his spirit returning to an Ireland which is invisibly inhabited and whose divinities are somehow inalienably his. Here the Túatha Dé Danann have become both an internal pantheon—one form of a universalist spiritual hierarchy—and symbols of Ireland itself, totems of the émigré's nostalgia.

COSMIC FANTASIES

This brings us to the final figure to be considered, James Stephens, whose famous capacity for linguistic mischief and mythological esprit was un-

---

49 Cousins & Cousins, *We Two Together*, 568, 628.
50 J. Cousins, 'To Ireland', *Collected Poems (1894–1940)* (Madras, 1940), 360.

derlined when Joyce famously asked him to complete *Finnegans Wake*, should he die leaving it unfinished. So mercurial a figure is difficult to categorize, and accordingly I want to discuss only one segment of his oeuvre here, leaving his most famous work—the effervescent fantasia *The Crock of Gold*—for the following chapter.[51]

Stephens was preoccupied with the ways in which ancient pre-colonial and modern post-colonial Ireland might be imaginatively yoked together. His innovation with regard to the gods lay in the way that he combined retelling the mythology with a form of systematization reminiscent of Cousins. Indeed, the two men shared spiritual and orientalist sympathies, and in a review of *The Wisdom of the West* he found himself sharing Cousins' vexation with an out-of-focus pantheon:

> The enlightened savage of Macaulay may wring his brows before he is satisfied that Our Lady of Paris is also Our Lady of Lourdes, of Geneva, of Milan, and of everywhere else; and so the reconstructor of the myths has to seek if Dana and Brigit, or Angus Og and Lugh of the Long Hand, or Mananaan Mac Lir and Midir may not be the same persons in a two-fold or three-fold presentation.[52]

The question of 'reconstructing' the myths takes us back to Yeats's preface to Gregory's *Gods and Fighting Men*, and one of the salient features of her retelling was its insistence upon a certain decorum. (The Dagda's excremental adventures from 'The Second Battle of Moytura' are dropped, for example.)[53] Like O'Grady before her, Gregory had excluded the exaggeration characteristic of many of the medieval tales, but the marvelous and grotesque formed an element very much to Stephens' liking. Indeed he found that the medieval literature chimed with many of his own preoccupations—casual transitions between planes of reality, sexual love, war, magic, and the differing states of the human soul. This happy conjunction of man and material explains how Stephens' versions of Irish saga, and its gods, remain perhaps the freshest.

---

51 Critical background in A. Martin, *James Stephens: A Critical Study* (Dublin, 1977) and P. McFate, *The Writings of James Stephens: Variations on a Theme of Love* (London, 1979).

52 J. Stephens, 'The Wisdom of the West' [review of Cousins, *WOTW*], *The Irish Review* 2:14 (April, 1912), 101.

53 There were a number of other 'full' retellings in the period: e.g. including Eleanor Hull's *The Cuchullin saga* (London, 1898), Standish Hayes O'Grady's set of translations *Silva Gadelica* (2 vols., London, 1892) and A. H. Leahy's *Heroic Irish Romances* (2 vols., London, 1905–6).

By 1919 Stephens was widely read in both the medieval literature and Celtic scholarship, and he had developed a fair proficiency in Old and Middle Irish.[54] After reworking fenian material in *Irish Fairy Tales* (1920)—a misleadingly winsome title foisted upon Stephens by the publisher—he projected a five-volume prose epic that would retell the entire *Táin*, integrating its fore-tales into a total structure. Only two parts, *Deirdre* (1923) and *In the Land of Youth* (1924) ever emerged, and Stephen's project remains a kind of torso; nonetheless *In the Land of Youth* in particular showcased his fondness for the elaborately interconnected plots, psychological realism, and intricate angles of narration which would certainly have characterized the finished work.

His approach to the material had several aspects. The first was a deliberate and thoroughgoing de-Christianization of the sagas, which he grounded in an idyllic and vividly imagined pagan Ireland. The second was an intriguing contrast between conversational language and a complex interlocking structure reminiscent of high medieval texts such as the *Acallam*: stories are nested within stories, there are narrative flashbacks and flashforwards, and characters often take on the role of narrator. It was therefore consciously a project both medieval and modernist in its affinities.[55] Such complexities did nothing to derail the momentum of his writing, and indeed the overriding characteristic of his approach is its propulsive narrative energy. This was an innovation: much of the revival's mythography had been characterized by diffuseness and inertia. In sharp contrast, Stephens' retellings were intended to defibrillate the collective unconscious of the nation, and—in his words—to 'hit the country a thump on the head' which would awaken it from torpor. Stephens' love of precision and energy meant that his gods are figures in purposeful motion, both physically and psychologically. He was adept at holding the tension between imbuing them with the capacity for dramatic change and needing them (as children need adults) to be, once met, defined in character forever. The interest in the emotional and mental interiority of the Túatha Dé is unique to Stephens, and his work abounds in acute psychological detail. When Midir, for example, tracks down the

---

54 A 1919 letter finds him thanking the great Celtic scholar Richard Best for the loan of his copy of *Silva Gadelica*. See *The Letters of James Stephens*, ed. R. J. Finneran (London, 1974), 241.

55 Describing the work of recasting the sagas as 'easily the best things I have ever written', Stephens wrote to Jame Pinker in November 1918 that 'the treatment, in each case, is so modern that modernity itself is put out of date by it' (*Letters of James Stephens*, ed. Finneran, 240–1).

lost Étaín, Stephens wrote that '[h]e cast about to see how he might re-gain his wife; and, as those who can think are happy while they are thinking, he was not unhappy'.[56]

Narrative energy was allied with tonal versatility. Capable of depict-ing suffering with considerable skill, Stephens nevertheless made amusement a key feature of his project. In particular the world of the gods becomes the site of social comedy, even farce. This is one factor that sets Stephens apart from Cousins: the latter's ponderous lucubra-tions on the Túatha Dé Danann are conspicuously devoid of wit. The burlesquing of myth went on to become a significant part of the tradi-tion of Irish experimental prose, but at the time, critics felt that this as-pect of *In the Land of Youth* in particular approached self-parody. Occa-sionally, the effect resembles an exuberant fusion of Flann O'Brien and E. F. Benson, and can put the reader in mind of Somerville and Ross's social comedies, with the Anglo-Irish 'big houses' re-imagined as other-worldly fairy-mounds.

Stephens' version of 'The Dream of Óengus' is especially rich in such moments. At one point the Dagda conjures up a magical slide show of women in order to track down the girl whom Angus (Óengus) has seen in a vision and for whom he is languishing. So far, so like the medieval saga; but Stephens typically injects farce by having the women parade *in order of weight*, 'from the wild young fawn of fifteen years to the massive and magnificent dame of forty'. It is all too much for Angus's mother, Stephens' histrionic, Lady Bracknellish Bóand, who announces: 'I wish to see legs! ... I wish to look ... on hard and angular and uncomfortable things, for my mind is clouded and there is a bad taste in my mouth from the sight of those endless females.' Even the Dagda finds his spirits drooping, and he asserts—evidently from experience—that 'something female and depressing comes on the mind when it has been too exten-sively occupied with that sex'.[57]

Tonally, this was something quite unprecedented in the adaptation of Irish myth, and Stephens can also be observed ironically reflecting on the challenges inherent in depicting divine beings. For example, how is it possible for the god of love to be lovesick, when—as the exasperated Bóand cries—'love is his normal condition!'[58] Elsewhere the gods need to weep, but find, by virtue of the otherworld's endless bliss, that they

56 J. Stephens, *In the Land of Youth* (London, 1924), 248.
57 Stephens, *In the Land of Youth*, 85, 89.
58 Stephens, *In the Land of Youth*, 72.

have quite forgotten how. (Fergne, the Dagda's physician, improvises with an onion.) Comedy of this kind requires a capacity for ironic detachment, and this quality I think is the main reason why Stephens' recreations live when so many others have failed.

But any deeper discussion of Stephens' Túatha Dé entails examining the influence of his own spiritual beliefs. Hilary Pyle has written that 'Stephens's fantasies vividly reflect the mental and spiritual climate of a literary movement which was alive with doctrinal eccentricity', and for all his humorous irreverence his work—especially the poetry—possessed a strong mystical dimension.[59] In this, as in his anti-colonial and nation-building agendas, his model was George Russell, his lifelong patron and supporter. Every bit as steeped as Russell and Cousins in Indian scripture, Theosophy, and Vedanta, Stephens briskly summed up his position in a 1927 letter to Stephen MacKenna, the translator of Plotinus: 'I like the Veda, and I don't like Christianity.'[60] In fact his saga-redactions depended on a world-view borrowed from classical Indian thought, but which he treated, as Lennon has observed, 'as if it were a native Irish philosophy and spirituality that he was merely recovering'.[61] India provided Stephens with resources from which a pre-Christian and pre-colonial Ireland might be imagined; and when Yeats inquired about the spiritual system underpinning his recreations, Stephens sent him a copy of the Upanishads, prompting Yeats to remark that he had read the *Táin* in the light of the Veda.[62]

Stephens therefore resembled Russell in treating the medieval tales as a kind of secular corroboration of sacred scripture. The main concept that he borrowed from Hinduism—via Theosophy—was that of different planes of being, which he fused in a remarkably tidy way with the otherworlds of the medieval literature. In *The Candle of Vision* (dedicated to Stephens) Russell had identified the 'overworld' of Theosophy with the Irish otherworld, but Stephens' spiritual cosmology was greatly more precise, taking the form of an intricate nesting of worlds like Chinese boxes. In the section of *In the Land of Youth* corresponding to the early saga *Echtrae Nerai* ('The Adventure of Nera'), the hero's otherworldly sweetheart explains:

---

59 H. Pyle, *James Stephens, his Work and an Account of his Life* (London, 1965), 14.
60 *Letters of James Stephens*, ed. Finneran, 350.
61 Lennon, *Irish Orientalism*, 303.
62 Lennon, *Irish Orientalism*, 302.

This world is called Tir na n-Óg, the Land of the Young. It is within the world you have left, as an apple is within its skin, and all who die in your world come to this one. But within this world is another called the Land of Wonders, and those who die here, or who can wish to do so, go to the Land of Wonders. Within the Land of Wonders there is yet a world called the Land of Promise, and those who die in the Land of Wonders are born into the Land of Promise, but they cannot die there until they can wish to do so.[63]

After the Land of Promise one arrives back at the earth again. The Shí—Stephens' preferred spelling for *síd*—further resembles the theosophical overworld in that it is realm of mental desires, 'the first world of the mind', in which events must occur on an initial, spiritual level before they can be actualized in the earthly world, just as the will is prior to its expression.[64] Furthermore, one of Stephens' boldest systematizing strokes was to impose clarity upon the time differential between the worlds—that ancient literary theme—by ingeniously gearing Shí-time to earthly time. One year on earth equals one minute in Tir na nÓg, explaining how the beings of the various nested otherworlds might live for spans analogous to the *kalpas*, the unimaginable aeons of Indian thought. (A year in the Shí would correspond to half a million earthly years.) Thus poor Étaín lives in human form in Ireland for eighteen years, but when her husband Midir comes in search of her, she has only been gone, in his terms, for eighteen minutes.

The divinities were also coloured by Stephens' fondness for Indian concepts. On the theological level, he shared with Cousins a 'Hindu' sense of the importance of dynamic movement within the divine sphere, contrasting with the static attitudinizing of the gods of Fiona Macleod and John Duncan. There was a Blakean dimension to this cast of mind: Blake was a crucial early influence, and in his review of Cousins' book Stephens explicitly made the analogy between the Irish myth system and the bewildering allegorical personages of the London poet's prophetic books.[65] Stephens intermittently treats the Túatha Dé as grand

63 Stephens, *In the Land of Youth*, 39.
64 Stephens, *In the Land of Youth*, 40.
65 The long influence of Blake on the tropes of self-consciously 'Celtic' writing is underestimated—Macpherson's Dar-thula and Fingal might be fruitfully compared with Blake's Luvah, Tharmas, and Urthona, for example.

personifications like Blake's Luvah, Tharmas, or Urthona, as had Cousins. Queen Maeve says of Angus:

> When he went abroad there accompanied him a cloud of birds that wheeled and sang about his head, so that when we see a cloud of wheeling and singing birds, all frantic with energy and exultation, we know that the son of the Dagda is passing, and we make obeisance to Youth and Beauty and Magic.[66]

Like Cousins' scheme of emanations, Stephens' gods seem to divide into paired principles, ultimately destined to reunite; but his system depends more explicitly upon conflict, and he borrows its confrontational overarching aphorism from Blake: 'without contraries is no progression.'[67] Cousins gave us the evidently bourgeois marriage of the Dagda and Dana, and while marriage is a key image in Stephens' work it is seldom depicted as happy, the integration of warring principles being achieved only with vast effort and in cosmic time.

Stephens' gods are beings in perpetual motion; as king Eochaid says, fatally underestimating them, 'They can behave just like little boys... They are delightful.'[68] The concept of childlike divine play—*lila* in Sanskrit—was another Hindu idea applied to the Túatha Dé Danann. In one passage the god Midir explains to the reincarnated Étaín what has happened to her, and here we see how subtle Stephens' cross-colonial Hindu-Hibernian fusions could be, for Midir's words, though simple, combine the concepts of divine play and karma:

> 'It was not a dream,' said Midir; 'it was a game.'
> '... it was unprofitable.'
> 'You have not had to pay,' he said, 'and the adventure has been saved for you in your mind. Thus you have gained, and you will never be the same person again.'
> 'Indeed, I never shall,' she affirmed.
> 'And that is part of the eternal game,' said Midir, 'for all that is only in a game.'[69]

---

66 Stephens, *In the Land of Youth*, 66–7.
67 See Pyle, *James Stephens*, 42.
68 Stephens, *In the Land of Youth*, 243.
69 Stephens, *In the Land of Youth*, 235.

A still more striking example occurs when Étaín describes her encounter with Midir (whom she knows to be divine but whose name she cannot recall) to her human husband:

> 'He showed himself to me in his god-form.'
>   'Ah!'
> 'He could have plucked down clouds. His hair was all a-whistling of golden flame. His eyes were bright as sunlight. He was more powerful than a winter storm, and gentler than a flower. He could not be looked at for more than an instant. He was a blazing, blinding loveliness.'[70]

Again the language is luminously simple, deceptively so: a lot depends, for example, on Eochaid's 'Ah!', which signals the hubristic complacency about the gods which is about to lead him into disaster. But the encounter also recalls the most famous theophany in all Hindu scripture—namely that moment in the *Bhagavad Gita* when the disguised god Krishna reveals himself to Arjuna as the single embodiment of all the infinite forms of divinity. Stephens knew the *Gita* intimately, and here Étaín beholds what in India would be called Midir's *viśvarūpa*, his 'universal form'. There is thus a significant level here on which Étaín, like Arjuna, is being given mystical instruction: 'The Wooing of Étaín' was the saga which the Revival most persistently took as a spiritual allegory, but Stephens' distinctiveness lies in the way that he successfully prevents the transcendental dimension of his story from impeding the onward momentum of its plot.

In 1921 Stephens remarked that 'the new religion may have much to do with the old mythology', placing him in the sizable company of radical writers and thinkers in the early years of the twentieth century who anticipated the birth of a new religious era whose principles would be rooted in a revived antiquity. The mythology to which he referred was Irish, but even so it is in a sense a pointless question to ask whether Stephens 'believed' in the Túatha Dé Danann. He was a spiritually serious man, for all his mythic subversions; and he certainly believed in a divine reality eternally at play, unmanifest as ineffable unity and manifest as bewildering multiplicity. The Irish gods were as good images of the latter as any, and were all the more important because they were inalienably

70 Stephens, *In the Land of Youth*, 241.

native to Ireland, which they could assist in the task of reimagining itself after the break from Britain. But unlike his mentor George Russell, Stephens seems never to have reported seeing the gods in vision, nor does he invoke them: the single exception is his elegiac poem 'Spring, 1916', in which he called upon the sea-god to guide the unlaunched ship of state through the confused politics and treacherous aftermath of revolution:

> Uncharted is our course! Our hearts untried!
> And we may weary ere we take the tide,
> Or make fair haven from the moaning sea.
>
> Be ye propitious, winds of destiny!
> On us at first blow not too boisterous bold!
> All Ireland hath is packed into this hold!
>
> Her hope flies at the peak! Now it is dawn,
> And we away—Be with us Mananán![71]

Though a vastly better writer than Cousins, Stephens clearly shared the latter's belief that a spiritual philosophy identical to the Vedanta was discernable in Irish mythology, albeit heavily overlaid and degraded—much as one might glimpse through shallow water the outlines of buildings long swallowed by the sea. For these two Irishmen, the Túatha Dé Danann were one key to revivifying Ireland's racial imagination, as they had been at one point to Yeats. In contrast to the likes of Fiona Macleod, whose aesthetic had depended upon keeping Gaelic myth in evocative pieces, Cousins and Stephens shared a regenerative ideal which required the mythology to be theologically coherent. Their hope was a cross-colonial restoration of the pantheon dependent on an Orientalist set of images of ancient India. (Ironically, of course, there was an obvious colonial dimension to this manoeuvre: Stephens evinced little interest in contemporary India, so that Cousins' deep investment in the country is greatly to his credit.) This quasi-Hindu vision of divinity—all lush proliferation—allowed both Stephens and Cousins to imbue their Túatha Dé with suppleness and energy.

Turning to the East to remodel Celtic gods may seem like an esoteric move, but behind the spiritual idiosyncrasies of individuals were

---

71 *The Poems of James Stephens*, ed. S. S. Mulligan (Gerrards Cross, 2006), 294.

deeper cultural and social shifts; most particularly, anti-colonial dissent from imperialism was reflected in dissent from Christianity. The political unionism of Scots such as William Sharp and John Duncan was accompanied by the firm insistence on Christian themes in their work: both saw the gods of the Gael as complemented and indeed completed by Christian revelation. Cousins and Stephens, in contrast, rejected that inheritance, turning eastwards to create a restored and imaginatively alive mythology which would fuse Ireland's present with its imagined past. Evans-Wentz and Cousins were, it should be emphasized, belated figures, part of a melancholy group who personified the dimly burning fag end of the Celtic Twilight.[72] While Stephens, on the other hand, shared some spiritual positions in common with Cousins, his wit and modernist sympathies saved his Túatha Dé Danann from ponderousness, and in so doing he turned their faces decisively towards the future.

72 See Foster, *Paddy and Mr Punch*, 231.

11

GODS OF THE GAP

A WORLD MYTHOLOGY

No apter metaphor having been
found for certain emotional colours.
I assert that the Gods exist.

—EZRA POUND

THIS PENULTIMATE CHAPTER takes the story of the Irish pantheon on-ward to the present. That story is framed by two movements: on the one hand a gradual but near-universal loss of interest in the Túatha Dé Danann among Irish writers, and on the other the wide uptake of the my-thology by creative individuals outside Ireland.

Within this picture three general trajectories can be observed, each in a different area of culture. In high culture we find the continuation of a swerve away from seriousness and towards irony, parody, and anarchy. This arc is traced below by looking again at a single god, the Mac Óc, and then by turning to an examination of the poet Austin Clarke, the most important mid-century Irish writer to engage imaginatively with the Túatha Dé Danann. In popular culture, heroic fantasy drew on Irish myth, and this is echoed and mirrored by children's literature, some of it of remarkable power. And finally, spiritual approaches to the Irish di-vinities burgeoned in the counter-culture, with many localized examples of the spontaneous invention of tradition. One of the curiosities of the story is that George Russell's dream of the return of the gods to Ireland and the revival of their worship—that cliché of the *fin de siècle*—had, by the end of the twentieth century, been thoroughly actualized by Celtic Pagans in Britain and the United States.

MYTHOLOGICAL OPERA

We must begin, however, by turning to another sphere of cultural creativity entirely. The Irish gods began to appear in classical music in the second and third decades of the last century, but no matter how avant-garde the composer, the aesthetics of the Celtic Twilight exerted a backward pull. Nowhere is this more apparent than in grand opera.

A number of operatic versions of Irish legend were composed between 1900 and 1930; all have proved resolutely minor.[1] They usually took as their focus the heroes of the Ulster and Finn Cycles, very much in the manner of the nationalist drama upon which they were based.[2] The Mythological Cycle was prudently avoided, partly, one suspects, because Richard Wagner's monumental mythic tetralogy *Der Ring des Nibelungen* could be neither imitated nor evaded.

Mention of that work instructively illustrates the difference in cultural potency between the Irish and the Germanic pantheons. Like the Irish gods, the gods of Norse myth featured in a superb medieval literature, but unlike their Irish equivalents, they achieved cultural ubiquity throughout north-western Europe during the nineteenth century. They could be framed as the indigenous, ancestral gods not only of Scandinavia and German-speaking parts of Europe, but also as those of the English-speaking world, and thus the British Empire. They were represented on the stage, offered vivid subject matter to creative writers, and their images were painted and sculpted in both Europe and the United States. The gods of the Gael shared none of this prestige and familiarity. They were associated only with Ireland and with the poorest and most remote areas of Scotland, and so seemed vague and outlandish in comparison.

As Wagner's theoretical writings show, Germanic myth had certain innate advantages. It held out the possibility for opera of a cleverly telescoped cosmic scale, entailing a narrative extending over generations. For Wagner, the most valuable quality of 'true' myth—which in his eyes

1 See A. Klein, 'Stage-Irish, or The National in Irish Opera 1780–1925', *Opera Quarterly* 21.1 (2005), 27–67.
2 See A. Klein, 'Celtic Legends in Irish Opera, 1900–1930', *PHCC* 24/25 (2004/5), 40–53; related efforts in Scotland are described in J. Purser, *Scotland's Music: a History of the Traditional and Classical Music of Scotland from Earliest Times to the Present Day* (Edinburgh, 1992).

meant Greek or Norse material—was that the depths of its meaning could never be plumbed. And exactly like the legends of the Greeks, Norse mythology offered titanic personalities, lit from within by archetypal symbolism. The incompatible claims of these beings could suffuse his art with irresoluble tensions and charged family dynamics.[3]

This was precisely where the Irish gods fell down: we have already examined the general diffuseness of relationship which is characteristic of Irish mythology and its gods' tendency to lack archetypal purviews in the natural world. A good example is offered by the goddess Brigit, often treated as a fire deity by late Victorian Celtic scholars. Because the stories about her in the medieval sources are brief and elliptical—the most important being the famous entry in 'Cormac's Glossary'—she fails to stand in any obviously dramatic relationship to the other gods, even the Dagda, her father. (She is theoretically the sister of the Mac Óc—but how difficult to imagine them speaking to one other!) Like a noble gas, she is unreactive.

It is noteworthy, therefore, that of all attempts at Irish legendary opera the most commercially successful was also the only one to manage the nearly impossible feat of putting Irish gods upon the stage. The English composer Rutland Boughton's *The Immortal Hour* (first performed in 1914) was based—for the title will by now be familiar—upon William Sharp's turbid 1900 reimagining of 'The Wooing of Étaín'. The libretto stuck closely to Sharp's text, relieving him of the need to depict any member of the Túatha Dé apart from the disguised Midir, along with Sharp's own invented deity, the sinister Dalua. The quasi-demonic Dalua dominates Boughton's opera just as he does Sharp's play; photographs of the second production in 1921 show him literally costumed as a 'dark fool', clad in black rags and a cap and bells (Fig. 11.1).[4]

Boughton's politics put him on the radical Left, where the younger Wagner—then pro-democracy and anti-absolutist—had placed himself

3 Few composers have ever theorized the principles behind their own work more than Wagner; for his use of Germanic myth in the *Ring* see E. Magee, *Richard Wagner and the Nibelungs* (Oxford, 1990), on which I draw here. See also O'Donoghue, *FATV*, *passim*, but especially 132–44.

4 To my knowledge no photographs of the 1921–2 production's Midir survive; there are however several of the soprano Gwen Ffrangcon-Davies, costumed in a bizarre five-horned headdress and trailing, Celtic knotwork gown, which can be seen on the website of the Rutland Boughton Music Trust, http://rutland-boughton-music-trust.blogspot .co.uk (accessed 3rd July 2014).

FIG. 11.1. Dalua, the 'Faery Fool' in Rutland Boughton's opera *The Immortal Hour* (second production, 1921). Photo: The Rutland Boughton Music Trust.

early in his career.[5] Wagner's mythic method was the English composer's most important touchstone and he felt the comparison acutely, to the extent that just after the end of the First World War he dreamed of founding in Glastonbury an English rival to Wagner's Bayreuth. Boughton's shift away from his Germanic sympathies and towards Celtic material was a prudent response to the outbreak of hostilities between Britain and Germany.[6] The Celticity of his music may therefore be ascribed to British patriotism, and this is not the last time in this chapter that we will find Irish myth being pressed into the service of a specifically British agenda.

Boughton had considerable talent: *The Immortal Hour* was phenomenally successful in its day, still holding the record for the longest continuous commercial run of any serious opera written by an Englishman. Though the concept of mythological music drama was clearly influenced by Wagner, in *The Immortal Hour* Boughton did not attempt to fuse words and music in a continuous stream of sound in the revolutionary Wagnerian manner. Other 'Celtic' operas of the period were more obviously

5 See R. Young, *Electric Eden: Unearthing Britain's Visionary Music* (London, 2010), 93–4. See also M. Hurd, *Immortal Hour—the Life and Period of Rutland Boughton* (London, 1962); musical analysis by A. J. Sheldon, *Notes on Rutland Boughton's The Immortal Hour* (Birmingham, 1922)

6 Young, *Electric Eden*, 94.

Wagnerian in this respect, and some—such as Granville Bantock's *The Seal Woman* (1924)—made lavish use of traditional Hebridean airs, accompanied on the harp. Boughton himself was in fact celebrated in his day for the ability to invent plausibly 'traditional' melodies, as is apparent in *The Immortal Hour*'s climactic aria, known as the 'Faery Song' or 'How beautiful they are, the lordly ones', which is sung by Midir as he attempts to remind Étaín of otherworldly bliss and lure her away from her human husband.[7] The words are Sharp's replacement for the ravishing Old Irish poem which occurs at the equivalent point in the original saga; Boughton's jaunty setting is the only part of his opera still occasionally performed.[8]

Other members of the Túatha Dé Danann are alluded to in the libretto, but do not appear onstage. As the divinities whom the human characters worship, they nonetheless have an impact on the mortal world, and Ronald Hutton has noted that one of the opera's few divergences from Sharp's play is the inclusion of a chorus of druids, who call upon them liturgically.[9] As such, we find in Boughton's opera something studiously avoided in the entire sweep of medieval Irish literature, even when set in the pre-Christian past—the explicit invocation of the Túatha Dé as a pantheon of pagan deities. The druids chant:

> Sky-set Lu, who leads the host of stars,
> And Dana, ancient Mother of the gods,
> Dagda, Lord of Thunder and Silence,
> Moon-crowned Brigid of undying flame,
> Mananaan of innumerable waters,
> Midir of the Dew and the Evening Star,
> Flame-haired Œngus, Lord of Love and Death,
> Shadowy Dalua of the Hidden Way.[10]

These were phrases drawn from Sharp's writings, rearranged by Boughton; once again they show how often the Revival's fleshing out of the Irish pantheon took cues from classical mythology and literature. Sharp ignored the fact that Old Irish literature does actually give the Dagda

---

7 I am grateful to one of the book's anonymous pre-publication reviewers for information on this point.

8 *The Immortal Hour* is available on CD from Hyperion Records (CDD22040, conducted by A. G. Melville).

9 Hutton, *Blood and Mistletoe*, 330–1.

10 Boughton, *The Immortal Hour*; II.1 on CD libretto.

something like a set of titles (in particular *ollathair*, 'Supreme Father'), instead bestowing upon him one of his own devising which assimilates him to Zeus, god of thunder.[11] Mananaan (so spelled) has 'innumerable waters', as one would expect, but Midir—who in a brilliant stroke original to Boughton's opera is present to hear himself prayed to—has become a vesperal deity of 'the Dew and the Evening Star'. A bright phrase on the trumpet drives home the irony. Next comes the Mac Óc and finally the 'shadowy' Dalua—Sharp's made-up god—who seems cast more or less in the role of Hades. The music darkens dramatically at the mention of his name.

Boughton's *Immortal Hour* is an important testament to the real poetic—perhaps even 'mythic'—power of Sharp's original play. His words, characters, and plotline were a crucial dimension of the opera's success, while the streamlining and enhancement offered by musical treatment probably helped to concentrate the work's powerful effect. Certainly for a composer an adaptation of 'The Wooing of Étaín' was a wise option, given its love theme and poignant exploration of the boundary between divine and human; indeed it is difficult to think of another Mythological Cycle saga that might have lent itself to operatic treatment, with the possible exception of 'The Dream of Óengus'. An eye-catching if improbable success, Boughton's opera remains of enduring value.

SEA MUSIC

In the same period, two of Boughton's fellow composers, an American and an Englishman, handled the gods in a less directly representational manner. The first was Henry Cowell (1897–1965), who in his bohemian life and adventurous creativity fulfilled a number of stereotypes about his home state, California.[12] A tireless enthnomusicologist and experimenter, he became a notable figure in the American musical avant-garde. His father was Irish, and his interest in Irish mythology and musical themes was stoked early by acquaintance with the world of Dublin Theosophy.[13] Cowell was thus aware of George Russell's esoteric investiga-

---

11 See above, 124.

12 See M. Hicks, *Henry Cowell, Bohemian* (Urbana, IL, 2002), and J. Cleary, 'Introduction', in J. Cleary (ed.), *The Cambridge Companion to Irish Modernism* (Cambridge, 2014), 5–6.

13 The key figure here was a writer and theosophist a generation older, John Osborne Varian, himself an émigré from Ireland to the West Coast of the United States, who

tions of the Irish pantheon, and the 'myths' imbibed by Cowell came imbued with a theosophical tint; it seems likely that he neither knew nor cared that they were ersatz. So much is clear to see in Cowell's best-known 'mystic' piano works, collectively entitled *Three Irish Legends*, which were complete by 1922 and are still widely performed. Each of the three component pieces had a brief preface explaining its mythological inspiration in precisely the Russellian vein. All three were free-associations in response to the absence in Irish mythology of a creation myth; as for being 'legends', not one was more than thirty years old.

Cowell was proudest of the first piece, 'The Tides of Manaunaun', as he kept attempting to augment his own reputation for precociousness by pushing back its date of composition. It is a brief work, little over a minute long, and it takes as its core a melody evocative of the Irish folk tune 'Slane', best known from the hymn *Be Thou My Vision*.[14] But Cowell's interest in tonal clusters—a term he coined—led him to blur that melody with dissonant textures and percussive gongings in a manner evocative of primeval chaos; the result is strange and majestic. The preface described the debt the piece owed to Manannán mac Lir—but to a Manannán redolent not of brine but of the Dublin Theosophical Society:

> Manaunaun was the god of motion, and long before the creation, he sent forth tremendous tides, which swept to and fro through the universe, and rhythmically moved the particles and materials of which the gods were later to make the suns and worlds.[15]

The preface to the third piece, 'The Voice of Lir', went straight back to Russell's writings in *The United Irishman* from the turn of the century, in which Lir appeared as the primordial divinity:

---

had known George Russell in the early 1890s and had clearly hero-worshipped him. (The photograph of Varian in Hicks, *Henry Cowell, Bohemian* [unnumbered plate] shows a man strenuously attempting to *look* like Russell: the beard, mackintosh, and unworldly gaze are the same.) He wrote long mythological poems in the same vein as James Cousins.

14 This pageant or poetry-cycle was to be called *The Building of Banba*. The 'opera'—for so Cowell termed it later, though it seems to have been less a grand affair than the term implies—has never apparently been recorded, and to my knowledge was only performed twice, once in 1917, on the beach in a theosophical commune near Oceano in California, and once a few years later; vivid description in Hicks, *Henry Cowell*, 85–7, which also has a list of pieces based on Irish myth on 166. The misspellings are wild: e.g. *Oma* for Ogma, *Eldana* for Ildánach (i.e. Lug), *Dagna* for Dagda.

15 H. Cowell, *Piano Music: Volume Two* (Associated Music Publishers, New York, 1982), 59.

Lir of the half tongue was the father of the gods, and of the universe. When he gave the orders for creation, the gods who executed his commands understood but half of what he said, owing to his having only half a tongue; with the result that for everything that has been created there is an unexpressed and concealed counterpart, which is the other half of Lir's plan of creation.[16]

One wonders if Cowell knew of Cousins' *The Wisdom of the West*, with which this kind of myth synthesis has something in common.[17] Cowell continued to compose piano pieces on Irish mythological themes into the mid-1920s; many of these have been recorded.[18]

Far better known than Cowell was Sir Arnold Bax (1883–1953), who was born and educated in London, and was of Dutch descent. For Bax, as for Boughton, the Celtic countries (Ireland especially) functioned as an alternative realm marked out by imaginative freedom, in which repressed and anti-imperial feelings could be explored. Unlike Boughton, Bax managed a partial act of self-transculturation: Boughton encountered Gaelic mythology through Sharp's less politically problematic Scottish take on the material, but Bax went physically and metaphorically to Ireland itself, rather than treating Gaelic culture as a spiritual holiday camp to satisfy English escapism.[19] As a result, for many years he and his music were more generously recognized in Ireland than in his native Britain. The Irish portion of Bax's oeuvre (which took up the first fifteen or so years of the century) is characterized by Debussy-like

16 Cowell, *Piano Music: Volume Two*, 64.

17 The eclectic use that could be made of medieval source-material is apparent in the story of Lir 'of the half tongue.' Its roots are not in any Irish story about Lir (or Ler) but rather in a legendary medieval Welsh ancestor-figure *Llŷr Llediaith*, 'Llyr Half-Speech', different from the more famous *Llŷr* of the Four Branches of the *Mabinogi*. *Llŷr* and *Ler* are linguistically equivalent but as a supposed divinity Llŷr Llediaith is an even more doubtful figure than Irish Ler/Lir. The epithet reflects the idea of broken speech or perhaps mixed parentage: Welsh *iaith* 'language, nation', cannot refer to the physical tongue, and Varian's portentous creation-story is a modern invention, probably inspired by Charles Squire's *The Mythology of Ancient Britain and Ireland* (London, 1906). See too *IIMWL*, 11–13.

18 'The Tides of Manaunaun', 'The Voice of Lir', and a sprightly piece written between 1918 and 1924 entitled 'The Trumpet of Angus Og' are all available on the CD *Henry Cowell; Piano Music* (Smithsonian Folkways Recordings, 1993).

19 See L. Foreman, *Bax: a Composer and his Times* (Aldershot, 1983, 1987; 3rd edn, Woodbridge, 2007).

washes of sound with 'Celtic' touches.[20] As with Henry Cowell, the most relevant mythological work from his pen has a marine theme, but it deals not with the sea-god Manannán, nor Lir his father, but with his wife, the otherworldly beauty Fand.

The Garden of Fand was composed 1913 and orchestrated in 1916. Fand appears most prominently in the tenth- or eleventh-century saga 'The Wasting Sickness of Cú Chulainn', in which she initiates an affair with the Ulster hero, despite the fact that he is married to the mortal Emer and she herself is the wife of Manannán.[21] Because of the medieval saga, the Celtic Revival tended to figure Fand as a sensuous ensnarer of mortal men, and interest in her was not new; the nationalist poet and folk-tale collector William Larminie, for example, had published a collection *Fand and other poems* in 1892. The poem that gives Larminie's influential collection its title retells the story of 'The Wasting Sickness', depicting the island of Fand as every bit as gorgeous as its mistress: a humid bower in which Cú Chulainn drowses in-between bouts of sexual exertion. Larminie's poem is likely to have been a major inspiration for Bax's work: a composer so steeped in the poetry of the Literary Revival was undoubtedly familiar with the collection.

For Bax, Fand's garden is double, simultaneously a magical island and the ocean itself. The depiction of the immortals in the piece is thus one of the most abstract of all those produced in the Revival, eschewing any attempt at conveying drama in favour of an impressionist seascape. Bax insisted that the piece was not to be taken as evoking any specifically literal images, but he later contradicted himself. The piece (he wrote) depicts a ship on a calm sea, which is thrown up on a magic island; celebrations ensue—a feature which Bax regarded as especially 'Celtic'—but ultimately an enchanted ocean engulfs all, and the piece ends with an evocation of the immortals gliding over the waves into the dusk. We are not told which immortals, but presumably they are Fand and Manannán. The theme was one of the oldest in Irish literature and art, going back as far as Manannán in his sea-chariot in the early medieval 'Voyage of Bran'; equally it was as as recent as John Duncan's near-contemporary painting *Fand and Manannán* (Fig. 11.2), which depicts a similar scene.

---

20 S. De Barra, 'Into the Twilight: Arnold Bax and Ireland', *The Journal of Music in Ireland* 4/3 (March–April 2004), 25–9.

21 The relevant medieval text is *The Sickbed of Cú Chulainn and the Only Jealousy of Emer*; see *Serglige Con Chulainn*, ed. M. Dillon (Dublin, 1953), and (translation) *EIM&S*, 155–78.

FIG. 11.2. John Duncan, *Fand and Manannán* (*c.*1913), oil on canvas, McLean Museum and Art Gallery / Inverclyde Council. © Estate of John Duncan.

These musical appropriations form a minor contribution to the Europe-wide vogue for nationalist musical responses to particular mythologies that had taken hold in the late nineteenth century. Wagner's achievement has already been mentioned, but closer in spirit was the work of Jean Sibelius in the 1890s, which was inspired by Finnish poetry and legend. The composers discussed are the most prominent to have drawn on Irish mythology in the early decades of the century, though none was actually Irish, and today all—even figures such as Boughton and Bax—continue to be on the fringes of mainstream music history.[22] Additionally, in all cases the Irish gods from which they took inspiration had already been percolated through the poetry and esoterica of the *fin de siècle*. Music therefore affords an early example of a pattern we will come across throughout this chapter, in which ersatz versions of 'Irish' myths, massaged or mutated out of all recognition, came to captivate audiences outside Ireland.

THE ANGLO-IRISH AENGUS:
A SECOND CASE STUDY

At this point a change of focus is necessary. I noted earlier that this chapter also discusses a turn by Irish writers towards toward less portentous handlings of the Túatha Dé Danann, and this process is best examined by tracing the shifting presentation of a single deity.

In chapter 7 we saw how Óengus (Aengus, Angus) gradually came into aesthetic focus in the last thirty years of the nineteenth century, as a beautiful youth equipped with a psaltery and a halo of birds. Anyone perusing the afterglow of the Celtic Revival in the first third of the twentieth century would rapidly notice that his imaginative allure persisted. Dazzling epiphanies proliferate: he turns up in visual art, poetry, novels,

---

22 Though note Hamilton Harty (1879–1941), born in Hillborough, Co. Down, whose orchestral tone poem *The Children of Lir* was composed in 1938, plus—in terms of opera—Thomas O'Brien Butler's critically panned *Muirgheis*, and Robert O'Dwyer's 1909 *Eithne* (not, despite the name, an adaptation of 'The Fosterage of the House of Two Vessels'). Neither features the Túatha Dé in any overt way. In the last seventy years a number of Irish composers have handled native mythological themes, among them John Buckley (b.1951). The British composer Tarik O'Regan (b.1978), who has Irish ancestry on his father's side, has recently created *Acallam na Senórach/An Irish Colloquy* (2010), a complex piece for sixteen voices, guitar, and bodhrán, setting parts of the *Acallam*. A recording by the National Chamber Choir of Ireland has been released on Harmonia Mundi.

short stories, classical music, drama, and one disquieting piece of literary erotica. In short, he became a literary and artistic cliché.

To begin with, we must turn back briefly to Yeats and George Russell. In chapter 8 we looked at the early Yeatsian Aengus—the louche, narcoleptic figure of *The Wanderings of Oisin* from 1899. Based on that poem and on the later invocations, I suggested there that for the young Yeats the god had come to personify the ecstatic and intoxicating side of the poetic imagination.[23] This was intensified in one of his most famously beautiful early poems, 'The Song of Wandering Aengus', published in the last year of the nineteenth century, in which 'Aengus' stands for imagination exalted by a nationalist fervour both irresistible and elusive. Yeats was at the time in his most Fenian phase, and he plays in the poem with the conventions of eighteenth-century *aisling* poetry, in which a vision-woman personifies the nation, crying out for rescue and redemption. But another *aisling* is in the mix too, the enigmatic eighth-century saga 'The Dream of Óengus'. There Óengus languishes after a year of nightly visions of a beautiful woman, who is only found in waking life after a search undertaken by Bodb Derg, his brother.[24]

Yeats takes the building blocks of the tale but subjects them to a mysterious rearrangement. The causal relationship between the vision of the girl, Aengus's mental anguish, and the search for her is turned on its head: Aengus *begins* the poem in mental turmoil, which the vision seems to answer. And the final stanza sees the search stretching out into infinity:

> Though I am old with wandering
> Through hollow lands and hilly lands,
> I will find out where she has gone,
> And kiss her lips and take her hands;
> And walk among long dappled grass,

---

23 In 'The Harp of Aengus', one of Yeats's earliest overtly 'Irish' poems, Aengus makes a harp of 'Druid apple-wood' and strings it with his own hair; see H. Vendler, *Our Secret Discipline: Yeats and Lyric Form* (Oxford, 2007), 156. The sonnet fitted into the story of Midir and Étaín: as seen, Yeats thought Aengus and Étaín had been lovers, a widespread misunderstanding at the time owing to the fact that the text of 'The Wooing of Étaín' then extant was missing part of the middle of the story. See B. O Hehir, 'Yeats's Sources for the Matter of Ireland: I. Edain and Aengus', *Yeats: An Annual of Critical and Textual Studies* 6 (1986), 76–89, and his 'Yeats's Sources for the Matter of Ireland: II. Edain and Midhir', *Yeats: An Annual of Critical and Textual Studies* 9 (1991), 95–106.

24 See above, 174–5.

And pluck till time and times are done
The silver apples of the moon,
The golden apples of the sun.[25]

In the first line quoted, the force of 'am'—rather than a subjunctive such as 'grow'—is tremendous: between stanzas time has uncannily dilated. Were it not for the title, we would have no idea that the speaker was a god, and the force of 'old with wandering' cuts against Aengus's traditional epithet *Mac Óc*, 'Young Lad'. But the phrase is eloquently mysterious, as the vision-girl is transparently immortal and it is left unclear whether 'old' refers to human ageing or to the span of years expended from an immortal life upon a lovelorn search (a god may be ancient and yet unaged). Yeats's poem is a characteristically oblique and politically charged response to the medieval tale, its Aengus a metaphor for the poet's own consciousness galvanized by the national ideal. But he is also spiritual intelligence, concretized yet intangible. This was the force Aengus was to have represented in Yeats's abortive Celtic Mysteries, in which he was to have served as the main god.

In fact, Yeats's poem remembered and revised an 1897 short story by Russell, entitled 'A Dream of Angus Oge', which—typically—managed to be both less concrete and more literal. Its frame was a standard cliché of the Revival, the reading of Irish legends to children. As the story opens, little Con has listened to his sister singing about an otherworldly shepherd, about whom he ruminates as dozes off. Lo and behold Con has invoked Aengus unknowingly, for the god promptly appears in a vision as 'a tall golden-bearded man standing by his bed':

Wonderfully light was this figure, as if the sunlight ran through his limbs; a spiritual beauty was on the face, and those strange eyes of bronze and gold with their subtle intense gaze made Con aware for the first time of the difference between inner and outer in himself.[26]

The god once enervated by an *aisling* in 'The Dream of Óengus' here appears as one, and he takes Con away with him. The focus of an *aisling* is

---

25 *The Collected Poems of W. B. Yeats*, ed. R. J. Finneran (New York, NY, 1996), 59.

26 G. Russell, 'A Dream of Angus Oge', *Imaginations and Reveries* (Dublin, 1915), 195–201, at 197.

normally a supernatural woman, so that Russell's story hints at a homo-erotic or double-sexed quality in the god—present as far back as Yeats's *The Wanderings of Oisin*—which subsequent writers and artists picked up. Russell's is also the only explicitly bearded version of the god I have come across, so that one wonders if he felt the need to butch his Angus up, dimly conscious of the Ganymedic overtones of the abduction of a boy by a male deity.

When the pair reach Angus's *síd*-mound of Bruig na Bóinne, the god transforms into the kind of hazy, plumed energy-being which Russell delighted in painting:

> As he spoke he seemed to breathe the brilliance of that mystical sunlight and to dilate and tower, so that the child looked up to a giant pillar of light, having in his heart a sun of ruddy gold which shed its blinding rays about him, and over his head there was a waving of fiery plumage and on his face an ecstasy of beauty and immortal youth.
>
> 'I am Angus', Con heard; 'men call me the Young. I am the sun-light in the heart, the moonlight in the mind; I am the light at the end of every dream, the voice forever calling to come away; I am the desire beyond you or tears. Come with me, come with me, I will make you immortal...' And in the child's dream he was in a palace high as the stars, with dazzling pillars jeweled like the dawn, and all fashioned out of living and trembling opal. And upon their thrones sat the Danann gods with their sceptres and diadems of rainbow light, and upon their faces infinite wisdom and imperishable youth.[27]

Politically metaphorical and spiritually literal, 'A Dream of Angus Oge' here puts a rhetorical passage of self-identification and self-praise into the love-god's mouth. The technical term for this is an *aretalogy*, and it was a feature that soon became a commonplace in writings about the gods in general and Aengus in particular.[28] The reason is not far to seek: given the general obscurity of the Irish divinities, such spotlit moments

27 'A Dream of Angus Oge', 200.

28 Aretalogies—utterances of self-praise in the mouth of a deity—are typically first-person and contain a number of 'I am' statements; Wisdom's great self-lauding poem in Ecclesiasticus 24 and the long speech of the goddess Isis at the end of Apuleius' late an-tique novel *The Golden Ass* are two celebrated examples.

were a device for conveying their identity to a general audience, who might otherwise have no clue who they were.

Three artworks serve to shed light on the mixture of flexibility and convention that determined how the god was imagined in the period. For the first we must revisit John Duncan, who unsurprisingly was far from immune to the Mac Óc vogue. In 1908 he completed the sublimely camp *Angus Og*, which was exhibited at the Royal Scottish Academy in 1909. The painting's connection to the protagonist of 'The Dream of Óengus' is slight. Winged like an outsize butterfly, Duncan's Angus is poised on a cliff-edge against a sky and seascape (Fig. 11.3), the beautiful rendering of which nevertheless fails to prevent the painting being the kitschest serious image of an Irish divinity.[29]

A piquant contrast is provided by an image of Óengus in Violet Russell's *Heroes of the Dawn* from 1913, a volume of Irish legends aimed at children.[30] Beatrice Elvery—a significant Irish figurative painter—provided pen and ink sketches for the volume. Haloed in doves, her Angus is a muscle-bound poser in a leopardskin loincloth (Fig. 11.4), liable to bring Tarzan into the modern reader's mind.[31] While the two pictures are different in tonal quality, their poses are strikingly similar. Both gods are *contrapposto*, with arms raised in the so-called *orans* position and faces full-on or slightly angled. Their solo stance is the visual equivalent of the textual aretalogy, a form of self-annunciation.

The god's androgynous quality is pronounced in a more ambiguous enamel plaque, now in the National Museum of Ireland, by Letitia Hamilton (1878–1964).[32] Completed in 1912, it depicts the epiphany of a larger-than-human divinity to an astonished artisan, who kneels in reverence upon a field of flowers (Fig. 11.5). Hamilton did not identify the figure,

29 The kitschest *non*-serious one might be the famous Max Beerbohm cartoon from c.1904, captioned 'Mr W. B. Yeats, presenting Mr George Moore to the Queen of the Fairies', in which Yeats, contorted with self-ingratiation, introduces Moore to a tiny Tinkerbell figure in a pink frock. One of the books on the shelf behind Yeats is entitled *Short Cuts to Mysticism*.

30 V. Russell, *Heroes of the Dawn* (Dublin & London, 1913), between pages 4 and 5. Violet, the author, was George Russell's wife. Useful overview of the visual culture of the Revival in J. Sheehy, *The Rediscovery of Ireland's Past: the Celtic Revival 1830–1930* (London, 1980); perhaps because of its semi-nudity, this image was not reproduced in the 1922 'school edition' of Russell's book.

31 Direct influence is not out of the question, as it happens, given that Edgar Rice Burroughs's *Tarzan of the Apes* was published in 1912 to immediate success.

32 See H. Pyle, 'The Hamwood ladies: Letitia and Eva Hamilton', *Irish Arts Review Yearbook* 13 (1997), 123–34.

FIG. 11.3. John Duncan, *Angus Og, God of Love and Courtesy, Putting a Spell of Summer Calm on the Sea* (1908), oil on canvas, The Scottish National Gallery.

FIG. 11.4. 'Wherever he went a number of white birds flew with him', pen-and-ink illustration in Violet Russell, *Heroes of the Dawn* (1913), by Beatrice Elvery, reproduced by kind permission of Brigid Campbell. Photo: Bodleian Library.

FIG. 11.5. *Inspiration* (1912), enamel and copper plaque, by Letitia Marion Hamilton,
reproduced by kind permission of Nikki Hamilton.
Photo: The National Museum of Ireland.

entitling the image 'Inspiration', the very quality which Yeats and Russell had associated with Aengus. It is clearly a nationalist statement, using a pagan deity to embody the energizing force of patriotic feeling—but is this the goddess Éire, or is it Aengus? The circling birds which halo the divinity suggest the latter; but facially the gender is hardly clear, and the art nouveau ornament on the being's gown frames its swelling breasts and pubic delta.

It is clear that, in Aengus, Irish mythology's claim upon the present was being powerfully activated and that he generated certain tensions, not least the treacherous sexual ambiguities prompted by a male deity of love. Just as King Conchobor could be figured as the Irish Agamemnon and the hero Cú Chulainn as the Irish Achilles, on the divine level the Graeco-Roman gods were the first interpretative port of call for writers dealing with the native pantheon.[33] In the Anglo-Irish Aengus, they found themselves faced with a male Venus: via the usual rules of allegory, deities of love must be supremely desirable, and one can observe writers and artists struggling for the appropriate note to strike. One route was to bestow upon him something of the allurements of both sexes. Hamilton's Aengus—if it is Aengus—is an out-and-out androgyne. If Russell's seems older than the norm (before becoming safely non-corporeal), it may be because the tweedily heterosexual mystic was made notably anxious by sexual nonconformity.[34] Duncan's trilling twink, on the other hand, is barely adolescent, with a haughty Maud Gonne face attached to an ephebic male body. While Duncan's visual model is clearly a mannerist Cupid such as Bronzino's—images of Cupid as a youth providing an obvious solution to the problem of visualizing a love god—it is striking that a female artist such as Elvery seems to have found it easier to give us an Aengus who actively invites the desiring gaze.[35]

---

33 This was not simply a topos of revivalist writers attempting to make an unfamiliar mythology available to their audiences by likening it to a more familiar one; the high medieval intelligentsia were quite capable of seeing analogies between the Ulster Cycle and the classical story of Troy, for example. See B. Miles, *Heroic Saga and Classical Epic*, 49–50, for a famous twelfth-century instance.

34 See H. Summerfield, *That Myriad-Minded Man: A Biography of George William Russell "A.E."*, *1867–1935* (Gerrards Cross, 1975), 276; Anthony Burgess's decision to depict Russell as a pederast in his novel *Earthly Powers* (1980) is an oddity, perhaps designed to underscore the unreliability of his narrator.

35 Duncan's Angus is winged to evoke his swan-transformation at the end of *The Dream of Óengus*, but as he is never semi-avian in the traditional sources the effect is to

SEX AND DEATH

Two powerful prose depictions of the Mac Óc also call for comment. James Stephens we have already met as a witty reteller of the medieval sagas, but here we need to look at the earlier work which secured his reputation. In 1912 he published *The Crock of Gold*, a magically clever comic novel which featured Angus in a major role.[36] *The Crock of Gold* provides a striking example of a member of the Túatha Dé Danann being taken up and invested with a new transcendental symbolism. At its climax, Angus—here a symbol of tender, spiritual love—repels the Greek god Pan, representing man's 'sensual nature', from the shores of Ireland.[37] This had a nationalist dimension, as English writers of the Edwardian era were in thrall to Pan, who seems to appear everywhere, not least in Kenneth Graeme's *The Wind in The Willows*.[38] By squaring off the native deity of love against the Greek goat-foot god, Stephens was enacting on behalf of Ireland a resounding rejection of lower instinct in favour of the imagination; the gesture also represented the disentanglement from the Irish psyche of a strand of specifically English vulgarity.

Angus's manifestation in *The Crock of Gold* again contains an utterance of self-praise. Angus laments that humans have abandoned the gods:

'I want you', said Angus Og, 'because the world has forgotten me. In all my nation there is no remembrance of me. I, wandering on the hills of my country, am lonely indeed. I am the desolate god forbidden to utter my happy laughter. I hide the silver of my speech

---

syncretize him visually with the classical Cupid. Cupid was of course the Roman version of Greek Eros; if Eros was one of the forces which Sharp's Angus had mediated, it is striking how precisely Duncan's image resembles the iconic 1892/3 statue of Eros on the Shaftesbury Memorial in Piccadilly Circus.

36 The novel climaxes with a splendid example of the 'enumerative topos' (*The Crock of Gold* (London, 1912), 169–70), including the longest and most gorgeous appearance of Dana as an Irish version of the great mother-goddess of contemporary radicals ('Her breath is on the morning, her smile is summer').

37 Thus Stephens: 'In this book there is only one character—Man—Pan is his sensual nature, Caitlin, his emotional nature, the Philosopher his intellect at play, Angus Óg his intellect spiritualized', quoted in B. Bramsbäck, *James Stephens: A Literary and Biographical study* (Uppsala, 1959), 134.

38 See P. Merivale, *Pan the Goat-God: His Myth in Modern Times* (Cambridge, MA, 1969).

and the gold of my merriment. I live in the holes of the rocks and the dark caves of the sea. I weep in the morning because I may not laugh, and in the evening I go abroad and am not happy. Where I have kissed a bird has flown; where I have trod a flower has sprung. But Thought has snared my birds in his nets and sold them in the market-places. Who will deliver me from Thought, from the base holiness of Intellect, the maker of chains and traps? Who will save me from the holy impurity of Emotion, whose daughters are Envy and Jealousy and Hatred, who plucks my flowers to ornament her lusts and my little leaves to shrivel on the breasts of infamy?'[39]

Here, as elsewhere, the god laments that he has been forgotten; in fact, as seen, he was inescapable. He goes on in this Blakean vein for some pages, as the embodiment of a reborn Irish culture ('my nation') simultaneously filled with desire and prudishly high-minded. Like Yeats's Aengus, Stephens' Angus represents pure imagination, unadulterated by rationality, intellection, or feeling. And just as Russell's Angus was a bearded shepherd, Stephens' deity also has a Christlike dimension, not only in the Eucharistic 'remembrance of me', but also in the way that he closely approaches Blake's 'Christ the Imagination', the embodiment of creative potential not yet brought down to earth.

Strikingly, in all the texts we have looked at so far, the god's language is patterned in dualities. Repeatedly we find a series of paired metaphors: silver and gold (Yeats's 'apples', Stephens' 'speech' and 'merriment'), moonlight and sunlight (Russell, Yeats again), heart and mind (Russell once more). One unexpressed pair is clearly male and female, but nevertheless they are implicit in the recurrent suggestions of divine androgyny; another—a layer deeper in the nationalist rhetoric—was Irish and English. It seems that in our period Aengus acted as a symbol for the inner fusion that a certain kind of Protestant intellectual hoped could be accomplished deep within the national psyche—an amphibious mode of existence incorporating the best of both worlds. Like an alchemical androgyne, the love-god was an obvious metaphor for cultural wholeness, and the transcendence of what Declan Kiberd has termed Anglo-Irish 'spiritual hyphenation'.[40]

Ireland's catastrophic descent into civil war in 1922 was to make this hope look desperately naïve, and this is reflected in the last appearance

39 *The Crock of Gold*, 88.
40 Kiberd, *Inventing Ireland*, 317.

of the god that I want to explore in this context. In 1931, Liam O'Flaherty (1896–1984), a native Irish-speaker from the Aran Islands, published *The Ecstasy of Angus*, which was billed as a mythological 'fantasia'—an unexpected direction for a writer best known for gloomy realism.[41] But the volume was printed in London for private circulation only, and the ecstasy in question is *sexual* ecstasy; before long O'Flaherty's little book turns out to be shot through with the disillusionment of the post-independence generation.

Set in a mythological dreamtime, the text is another neomyth that reveals O'Flaherty as a shrewd reviser of previous versions of the Mac Óc. His Angus is, like Duncan's, a male Venus, a divine spirit of desire in the earthiest sense: young women fantasize about him during intercourse, but (more unexpectedly) so do young men. His divine energy is so all-impelling that he causes a Malthusian population explosion in Ireland, and he has to visit Manannán to ask for some more land to be reclaimed from the sea—a very dark joke indeed in the context of the famines and mass emigration of the previous century. The sea-god's playground turns out to be disturbingly reminiscent of the Emperor Tiberius's villa in Capri, with suggestions that Manannán—here a podgy erotomane—might have equally *recherché* sexual inclinations. Manannán and Angus promptly fall out, and Fand, Manannán's evidently unsatisfied wife, attempts to seduce him. It is here that O'Flaherty introduces his boldest twist to the medieval Óengus tales. His Angus must remain chaste: the Dagda has cursed him so that he must never copulate, *even as the spirit of fertility and sexual delight*. As he tells Fand, if they make love even once, then the world will be swiftly overrun by contraception, lesbianism, abortion, impotence, prostitution, effeminacy, and venereal disease. Clearly at this point his seduction is inevitable.

O'Flaherty's Angus retains his characteristic passivity as a half-feminine *ingénu*. Fand bears him away wrapped in her cloak, and with enormous relish O'Flaherty then gives us a twenty page love scene worthy of D. H. Lawrence. Says Angus:

'Terrible queen, my only fear is that you might vanish from my sight or become indifferent to my love before my body's juices reach your womb and close its doors upon my generating image. You are terrible like the blazing sun, before whose brightness every

---

41 Best discussion is still P. Costello, *The heart grown brutal: the Irish revolution in literature from Parnell to the death of Yeats* (Dublin, 1977).

eye must fall in adoration; but as the sun's warmth gives life and strength to every growing thing, so does the warmth of your beauty cause my life's bud to rush springing from its shell and point its daring head at the portals of your love.'[42]

This gives an idea of the style of O'Flaherty's steamy tableaux, in part a parody of O'Grady's breathless *History of Ireland*. The luscious Fand—evidently the Túatha Dé Danann's answer to Anaïs Nin—emerges as a mistress of the erotic arts. At the crucial moment Angus finds himself impotent, and crisis is only averted when both he and Fand are orally pleasured by troops of female fairies, naked except for diamonds in their navels, while others prance around brandishing 'mysterious instruments, suggestive by their shapes of potent love-making'.[43] The effect upon the reader used to either the medieval tradition or to the dim pastels of the Celtic Twilight is startling.[44]

The Ecstasy of Angus climaxes accordingly, and Fand instantly conceives. So miraculous is their orgasm that the reader is briefly convinced that Angus's curse was a delusion—but at this point the tale fills with dark and unintelligible menace: Angus wakes to find himself sucked dry and dying, an 'old man, trembling, ribbed like a hungry horse'.[45] As Fand groans in accelerated childbirth, the ruined god encounters a malevolent 'Genius of Unrest' and a 'Tree of Knowledge', neither of which had been there before. The Genius is a sinister and implacable figure, significantly not unlike the Dalua of Sharp's *Immortal Hour*. Angus's transgression has caused the death of all the gods, and the Genius taunts him with it: 'They are all dead. You are no longer god but an old man, weak and near your death. All gods ceased to be when your seed entered Fand's womb and came to life. She shall bring forth a godless son, born in your image but of the earth's substance. And his seed shall conquer the universe through the dual agency of this tree's knowledge and my

42 O'Flaherty, *The Ecstasy of Angus* (London, 1931), 23.

43 O'Flaherty, *The Ecstasy of Angus*, 31.

44 I note in passing that O'Flaherty's story makes boldly explicit—in every sense of that word—the eroticism which had been left implicit in Victorian fairy painting, which had enjoyed such a vogue between twenty and forty years earlier. Fairy painting had been a distinctively English genre, and one is tempted here to see O'Flaherty—the Irish speaker and bitter realist about human nature—reclaiming the fairies for Ireland via an arch return of the repressed.

45 O'Flaherty, *The Ecstasy of Angus*, 39.

genius.'[46] Angus curses his progeny to remain under the spell of Fand forever:

'Let her be a foil to his genius and let my curse go with her and her daughters. With my last breath I curse this land of Banba which shall henceforth be poisoned to its deepest layer, so that continual war shall desecrate its beauty. With my last breath I curse the children of Banba, unless they rise and slay this son of mine, who has denied and slain his father. Lo! The sky grows dark and the godless sea does roar in mourning for the death of Mananaan, and from all the corners of the firmament the ungoverned winds unloose their fury. The earth shakes. I die. My breath is waning. I curse, I curse with my last breath, man, whose blood shall be salt and who shall forever languish in desolate pain.'

Then Angus died amid a tumult of all the elements, and the cry of a new-born babe came from the tree and the spirit struck his spear upon his shield and cried:

'Hail! Genius is born.'[47]

It will be immediately apparent that O'Flaherty's disturbing fable represents the most radical re-envisioning of the internal life of the Túatha Dé Danann that we have encountered so far. The literary cliché of the gods' return is here decisively reversed. O'Flaherty also precisely inverts the conventional Aengus of the Revival. As we have seen, on the traditional level that deity could be taken as a symbol of the freshness of love, and more deeply he could stand as the personification of the creative fusion of inner opposites; O'Flaherty's Angus, on the other hand, is entrapped by lust and destroyed by poisoned sex.

Upon closer inspection, the story can be taken as an allegory of the relationship between imaginative literature and politics in the preceding decades. O'Flaherty correctly settled upon Angus as the key figure to symbolize the aspirational manoeuvres of the Revival, considered retrospectively at the end of the tumultuous and disillusioning decade that had seen both independence and civil war. The style was a satirical takedown: writing about the national gods in such a rococo manner drew attention to the fact that the Celtic trappings of the Revival were no

---

46 O'Flaherty, *The Ecstasy of Angus*, 41.
47 O'Flaherty, *The Ecstasy of Angus*, 43.

more authentic. *The Ecstasy of Angus* can be seen not so much as a parody of the mythology itself as of bowdlerized and sentimental versions thereof. I note in passing that a sense of what O'Flaherty was writing against can be obtained by opening *Celtic Wonder Tales* (1910) by Ella Young (1867–1956)—mythologist, *confidante* of Maud Gonne, and third-rate poet—which consists of manically proliferating 'Irish' myths of Young's own devising.[48]

The climate of post-independence Ireland for writers was notoriously unhappy. As Declan Kiberd has observed, by the late twenties, 'War and civil war appeared to have drained all energy and imagination away: there was precious little left with which to re-imagine the national condition.'[49] Angus, moribund and sapped of vigour, stands for the Literary Revival: impelling the sexual drive in men and beasts but forbidden from coupling himself, he represents that movement's idealism, doomed in the attempt to actualize it in political reality. The armed 'Spirit of Unrest' therefore represents political revolution itself, and its unintended consequences, including the retreat from revolution that occurred in the 1920s as the sternly autocratic new state identified itself with a rigid Catholicism. But why does the Spirit preside over the birth of 'Genius', born from two members of the national pantheon, but killing off the gods in the process? With the censorship of films (1923) and publications (1929), Ireland became an increasingly inhospitable place for creative artists, many of whom (including O'Flaherty himself) fell foul of the state's reactionary censoriousness.[50] The result was a notorious exodus of Irish writers and intellectuals: not just Joyce, but Russell too, and others by the dozen.[51] O'Flaherty himself spent years outside Ireland, mainly in Europe but also settling for a period in Hollywood in the

---

48 Young is one of a number of figures who had to be cut from the final version of this chapter. Her writing was sunk by oracular glibness, but her life was an adventurous one: she emigrated to California, alone, at the age of fifty-six, and became a lecturer in Celtic myth at Berkeley. My views on her writings on the Túatha Dé Danann are in 'Ella Young and Ross Nichols: Sourcing the Irish Gods', *Abraxas: the International Journal of Esoteric Studies* 6 (2014), 72–82; Dorothea McDowell manages to summon greater enthusiasm in *Ella Young and Her World: Celtic Mythology, the Irish Revival and the Californian Avant-Garde* (Bethesda, 2014).

49 Kiberd, *Inventing Ireland*, 263; see also T. Brown, *Ireland: A Social and Cultural History 1922–79* (London, 1981), 42.

50 In 1928 the newspaper *An Phoblacht* execrated the writings of O'Flaherty and Sean O'Casey as 'sewage'; see D. Ferriter, *The Transformations of Ireland 1900–2000* (London, 2004), 311.

51 See Kiberd, *Inventing Ireland*, 264.

1920s. The ambivalent Spirit is, in part, a symbol for the incubatory pressures of exile.

While this is one possible interpretation, O'Flaherty's morbid fable could admit of a number of readings. But its core message is that the obfuscations of the Revival—riven, like Angus, by internal contradiction—had to be expunged for a more hard-headed Irish writing to emerge.[52] *The Ecstasy of Angus* uses myth-making to condemn mythification.

In chapter 8 we saw that it was Aengus, of all the Túatha Dé Danann, whose qualities had been most insistently delineated in the *fin de siècle*. This was partly down to his pleasantness as a character and the appealing quality of the stories in which he appeared. But he was also a god dominated by dreams the meaning of which he cannot fathom, and who—in 'The Dream of Óengus'—spends a year lying on a couch with what look distinctly like hysterical conversion symptoms. There is something Freudian in the way his mythology centred upon mysterious inner drives, a libido searching for sublimation, and not least, the process of growing up—another reason, I think, for his relentless self-articulation in several of the texts examined here. The medieval literature allowed him to be presented as loving in an idealized manner, without being explicitly sexual: a quality which Stephens exploits and O'Flaherty explodes. The god was therefore available for bolstering Ireland's moral *amour propre*, even as his youth allowed him to serve as a flexible symbol for cultural renewal. This was also why he had to be killed off by O'Flaherty when disillusion set in in the decade or so after the Easter Rising: political trauma, doctrinal rigidity, and cultural sclerosis had destroyed the taste among Irish writers for sentimental epiphanies of the native gods.

AUSTIN CLARKE AND PROSE ROMANCE

There was one major exception. The Túatha Dé Danann in general and Angus in particular continued to play a significant role in the work of

---

52 O'Flaherty's religious commitments were complex—he loathed organized religion but spent several years studying for the priesthood—and he was for much of his life an ardent Communist. It is striking that the Spirit speaks in the idiom of a futuristic atheism, describing himself as 'part of universal space, of which neither gods nor humans have yet gained comprehension', and dismissing the gods as 'but the barbarous predecessors of human genius'.

Austin Clarke (1896–1974)—an exact contemporary of O'Flaherty—who was the last major Irish writer to undertake an imaginative immersion in the pantheon. His importance for the present study is as a bridge between the generation of Yeats and Russell (both of whom he knew) and the later twentieth century. Clarke was disappointed by the turning away from the Irish past by intellectuals and imaginative writers after 1916 and much of his varied body of work—early 'epic' poems, mid-career prose romances, plays, a substantial body of lyrics—draws on native literature and myth.[53]

Clarke was a nervous and conflicted man, a consequence of the harsh brand of Catholicism in which he was brought up. But he used the native gods to interrogate the psychic scars of this inheritance in himself: suffocating guilt, a puritan distrust of sexuality, and a fear of intellectual freedom. There is a huge gap between this interior situation and that of Russell, Yeats, and Sharp: all raised as Protestants, they were able to develop idiosyncratic spiritual syntheses with less constraint by an internalized clerical authority. Indeed, in midlife Clarke was able to look back at Russell's heterodoxy with envy:

> … [R]eligious fervor and utter faith are not usually associated with literary paganism. But in a country of intensely organized and militant Christianity the unfailing strength of A.E.'s paganism was to the young a highly attractive and informative experience. All the paganism of the past still lingering in vestigial tradition in remote parts of Ireland seemed to be concentrated and living when he spoke on his favourite themes, and his eyes twinkled with general heresy.[54]

This was generous, as in 1922 Russell had penned a bitchy review of Clarke's mythological poem, *The Sword of the West* (1921), dismissing his gods and heroes as 'heavy with dream… spirits of the dream landscape made self-conscious and thinking of nothing but their own atmosphere'.[55] This was rich, coming from such a quarter, and one suspects Russell may have found his own stylistic tics reflected back at him rather

---

53 The best discussion so far is M. Harmon, *Austin Clarke 1896–1974: A Critical Introduction* (Dublin, 1989).

54 Review of John Eglinton's *A Memoir of A.E.*, in *The New Statesman and Nation* (1937), quoted in G. A. Schirmer, *The Poetry of Austin Clarke* (Dublin, 1983), 80–1.

55 Quoted in Harmon, *Austin Clarke*, 260.

too faithfully in Clarke's volume, which in places was cherishably bad. (One line ran: 'When the far light of sunset lingers in the dew... Lugh comes as otters through the starlight'.)[56]

Despite early false starts of this sort, Clarke developed a vigorous and accomplished voice in maturity, and *The Sword of the West* is in fact a prime example. Its two sections were designed to frame a verse retelling of *Táin Bó Cúailnge*, describing the lead-up to Cú Chulainn's birth and death respectively. One section relates a vision of the Túatha Dé Danann and the Fomorians clashing at Moytura, hence its significance for our purposes: it is a kind of epic fragment. Clarke revised it repeatedly, however, first in the thirties and then again in the last years of his life. The second revision was so radical as to constitute wholescale rewriting: only a handful of lines from the 1921 version survive unaltered in the 1974 *Collected Poems*. *The Sword of the West* is thus in effect both an early and a late work in Clarke's canon, but because the voice of the final version is noticeably more individual, it is discussed with his later poetry below.

In the thirties and forties Clarke composed a trio of 'prose romances'— his own term—all of which drew on Irish myth and were set in the world of the medieval Irish church. Below I examine the first and third of these, *The Bright Temptation* (1932) and *The Sun Dances at Easter* (1952, but written 1947–8), which deal directly with legendary source material derived from the Finn and Mythological Cycles.[57] As discussed in chapter 5, several narratives from both these cycles had thematized the contrast between pagan and Christian values, and this was a topic close to Clarke's heart. As seen, the early thirteenth-century *Acallam na Senórach* was framed by the friendly encounter between St Patrick and the remnants of the *fíana*, while 'The Fosterage of the House of Two Vessels' ended with the conversion and baptism of Eithne, a woman of the Túatha Dé Danann.[58] Clarke returned to this second tale several times in his career, and it is key to his subversive exploration of the clash between pagan and Christian imaginative worlds, and between individual freedom and moral rigidity.

---

56 A. Clarke, *The Sword of the West* (Dublin, 1921), 28.

57 The second, the bleak 1936 *The Singing-Men at Cashel*, focuses on the tragic Gormlai (Gormfhlaith), daughter of the tenth-century Uí Néill king Flann Sinna; it has little to do with the gods but is of considerable interest. See the major recent study of Clarke's three prose romances in J. Lanters, *Unauthorized Versions: Irish Menippean Satire, 1919–1952* (Washington, DC, 2000), 105–72.

58 See above, 234–46.

The Bright Temptation is Clarke's earliest attempt in this vein, and is something of an artistic failure, although it is not without its powerful moments. Set in the early Middle Ages, it narrates the falling in love of Aidan, a young monastic student, with the beautiful Ethne (Clarke's spelling), and their separation and reunion after various picaresque adventures. Aidan, who suffers with guilt at his natural feelings of love and desire, shows how one may suffer at the hands of an unenlightened church; Ethne, whose feelings have a natural clarity and delicacy, represents joy in earthly life. Their eventual blissful reunion is stage-managed by an unnamed supernatural force whom the reader realizes in short order is none other than the god Angus, in yet another of his appearances.

That the heroine of *The Bright Temptation* is named Ethne alerts us to the relationship between Clarke's first prose romance and 'The Fosterage of the House of Two Vessels'; but the third and best of Clarke's three novellas, *The Sun Dances at Easter*, includes a more overt and radical retelling of that tale. Once again Angus plays a major role, his last appearance in high literature; the general tone is subdued and elegiac.[59] In the frame-tale, a young woman makes a pilgrimage to the holy well of St Naas to attempt to conceive a child; on the way she meets a handsome clerical student who tells her two inset stories. Angus appears in both: the second tells how the god disguises himself as a portly cleric in order to reveal to king Congal More that his boast of his wife's chastity is premature. Angus transforms the unfortunate king into a goat—a change of status in which he comes to take a cheerful sensual pleasure—and in this form Congal witnesses his wife's adultery. The Mac Óc here is a figure of carnivalesque chaos, as well as an initiating wisdom-deity akin to the goddess Isis of Apuleius's *Golden Ass*, which this inset tale resembles. But from the perspective of a discussion of Clarke's manipulation of medieval sources, the first inset tale in *The Sun Dances at Easter* is of greater importance.

'The Fosterage of the House of Two Vessels' staged a clash between paganism and Christianity. We saw that in the saga the Túatha Dé have heard tell of the one God, and the beautiful Eithne, foster-daughter of Óengus, wanders from the otherworld into the world of early Christian Ireland. There she meets a monk, Cessán, and is converted by St Patrick

---

59 Clarke's preferred spelling was actually *Aongus*, which I have silently changed to *Angus* in discussion to avoid introducing yet another version of the name into the chapter.

to Christianity; as the waters of baptism run over her head, she is sundered forever from Óengus and the pagan world of the Túatha Dé. The movement is one-directional, but in Clarke's rewriting, the otherworld woman and the hermit-monk are contrapuntally magnetized by one another's worlds, with the Boyne acting as the barrier between Christian Ireland and the bliss of the otherworld.[60]

Clarke's Ceasan (so spelled) is entranced not only by Eithne's loveliness but also by the evidence she embodies for the existence of the immortal beings of legend: 'Were there many worlds, each with its own order of beings, known in dream or delirium by the different races of men?'[61] (Russell and Evans-Wentz would have answered in the affirmative.) In a manner reminiscent of Stephens' mutually enfolding otherworlds, Clarke's inset tale gives an authentically late medieval Irish world of non-Christian immortal beings who exist but who are not evil, and who can long for Christian revelation. Ceasan has tried not to believe in the Túatha Dé, but there they are: '… reason was failing him and ancient superstitions were beating through his veins. He could struggle no longer, yet Eithne was resisting their power, and her body was rigid with suffering.'[62] Attracted by, but also as a Christian profoundly opposed to, Angus's power, Ceasan gives Eithne a brave message about human ontology to carry to the love god, whose existence he has been forced to acknowledge: 'We, too, are immortal, though we must choke into another world, though our remains must stink in earth through slow rottenness.'[63]

The climax comes with Eithne's baptism in the Boyne, by which Ceasan hopes to save her soul from her divine foster-father, even as he himself conflictedly longs for the bliss of the otherworld. Clarke has Ceasan—not Patrick—perform the ritual, concentrating the clashing currents from which the tale is woven:

> He laid his hand gently on the crown of her head and the light of her coming grace shone round her so that she did not seem mortal. Her flesh was glorified, her smile so joyful that he closed his eyes

---

60 See J. Lanters, 'Carnivalizing Irish Catholicism: Austin Clarke's *The Sun Dances at Easter*', in P. I. Barta *et al.* (eds.), *Carnivalizing Difference: Bakhtin and the Other* (London & New York, 2001), 191–208.

61 A. Clarke, *The Sun Dances at Easter: a romance* (London, 1952), 111.

62 Clarke, *The Sun Dances*, 105.

63 Clarke, *The Sun Dances*, 112.

from such a wonder and began to pronounce the words of the ancient rite. But scarcely had he uttered a syllable when the chill of
horror held him. His fingers touched nothing and he knew that he
was alone. He sprang back and stared at the spot where Eithne had
been, stared at the rushing waters, and then, from the cliff-wood,
came, in echo, his own cry of disbelief.[64]

Clarke utterly reverses the ending of the medieval saga: Angus triumphs
in place of Christianity.[65] The ironies of the passage underscore the way
that Ceasan has misread events: though Eithne can long for baptism, it
will not 'take' on her because by nature she is not mortal. This was a
radical reversal of the medieval saga, in which a member of the god-
peoples could, by the intervention of divine grace, be transformed into a
human being. The bouncing 'echo' of Ceasan's cry suggests spiritual
narcissism behind his attempt to define the cosmos within Christian
certainties; indeed, his faith atrophies after this glimpse of a wider and
more mysterious universe, in which non-Christian powers operate. On
this level, the romance is a parable about loss of faith, and because the
tempting god of love is an indigenous figure, it is also a satire on contemporary Irish bishops' tendency to ascribe lax sexual morals to foreign
influences.[66] The critique of moral censoriousness is characteristic of
Clarke, as is the way that otherworldly elisions of time and space undermine authority and the Church.

Depicting the pagan divinities as actively taking part in the early
Christian world is an important reweighting of the medieval inheritance. Active in both the frame-tale and the sub-tales in *The Sun Dances
at Easter*, Clarke's Angus is in many ways the ideological opposite of
Stephens' in *The Crock of Gold*; here he ensures that the lower instincts
for desire and consummation will not be neglected. He is associated
with a constellation of imagery representing joyousness of spirit, a subversive and comic sensuality being brought into dialogue with Christian rigour. In this manner he is triumphant, but there is no doubt that
the Eithne-Ceasan sub-tale retains its elegiac edge.

64 Clarke, *The Sun Dances*, 131.

65 Discussion of Clarke's Angus in G. C. Tapping, *Austin Clarke: A Study of his
Writings* (Dublin, 1981), 137–8.

66 See J. Lanters, 'Carnivalizing Irish Catholicism', in Barta *et al.* (eds.), *Carnivalizing Difference*, 193. The Boyne in Clarke's romance is oddly like the otherworldly river
in the Middle English dream-poem *Pearl*: an ontological divide between a male and female character, the crossing of which breaks the dream.

POETRY AND SATIRE

I mentioned above that the final 1974 version of Clarke's *The Sword of the West* stands as the most recent substantial poem by an Irish writer to feature the Túatha Dé Danann. Clarke's view was that medieval Irish literature had been classical, objective, and concrete—quite the opposite of fairy vagueness. This explains why he tried his hand at a fragment of epic poetry when he came to depict the great battle between the Túatha Dé and the Fomorians. Celtic tradition carefully avoided the telling of stories in poetic form, so Clarke's desire to replicate a native monumentality drove him to use a strikingly non-native form.[67]

The depiction of pagan gods was, however, an area in which Clarke's desire for classical objectivity let him down.[68] In the vision of the battle of Moytura his desire to find a new cliché-free idiom for the gods was palpable, but weird tonal misfires tended to undermine the effect. Here the gods appear through the chaos of battle:

> I saw in confusion
> The Battle of Moytura. I heard a clamour
> Of shoring waters surge below me: a King
> Passed, mantling the tide, tip of his spear,
> A sea-green star. Within my vision, appeared
> The demi-gods, Midir the Proud, Iuchar,
> Bore Derg, clapped in thunder, Diancecht,
> Erc, Len. I counted the assembly of those heroes
> In wars, too terrible for the annals of men, as
> Leaning on sword-hilts, their great paps dark as warts
> Within the gleam of breast, their scrota bulged
> in shadow.[69]

---

67 Since the victory of the gods at Moytura is the central event of the Mythological Cycle, one would have expected Clarke's poem to have had significant precursors; the only one known to me is 'Moytura' by William Larminie (1849–1900), who had retold it in lengthy heroic style as a 'mystic battle' between the forces of good and evil, back in the 1890s; see W. Larminie, *Fand and other poems* (Dublin, 1892), 60–149.

68 Maurice Harmon has witheringly called him 'over-responsive to Irish mythology' ('*The Sword of the West* (1921, 1936, 1974)', *Études Irlandaises* 10 (December, 1985), 102).

69 *Collected Poems of Austin Clarke*, ed. L. Miller (Dublin, 1974), 76. *Bore* Derg is an error for *Bove* Derg, as the 1921 edn. shows; the 1974 *Collected Poems* is full of such quirks. The obscure 'Len' was perhaps a poor choice, poetically, but Lén *Línfhíacalach*, 'of the full complement of teeth', is a supernatural smith associated with Killarney Lakes and men-

Scrota?! The reader's eyes widen. Perhaps mention of the divine balls was meant to have the same effect as the sexual explicitness of O'Flaherty's *Ecstasy of Angus*, putting distance between these gods and theosophical waftiness. But here it serves also, less than successfully, as a metonym—like those jutting nipples—for the gods' hyper-masculinity: no fey androgynes allowed.

The opponents of the gods, the Fomorians, appear here in their belated guise as sea-beings, and naturally the only deity who can combat them effectively is Manannán:

> As when our fishermen are blown
> With the last light of day towards a fiord
> Of Lochlinn, tossed on the billow tops, they see
> Between the storm-rents of sails and cordage
> A headland loom from the east, the blue-haired god
> Walked through the waves; he held in readiness
> A brace of javelins and on his forearm
> A shield of copper like a blood-red moon
> Clotted in sea-fog. At every stride of his,
> The shore changed to brine and the Fomors became
> A raft of tern, a row of rocks.[70]

The beginning of this passage is, precisely, a Homeric simile, illustrating the way in which Clarke's attempt at epic inevitably brought with it an intense Graeco-Roman penumbra. When Clarke sharpened up the language in this final version of the poem, one effect was to bring the diction close to that of Richmond Lattimore in his vastly successful translations of the Homeric poems from the 1950s and 1960s, with their briskly vernacular idiom, predominantly Anglo-Saxon vocabulary, and flexible six-beat line.[71] Yeats had once urged 'We must go where Homer went', and the dogged Clarke did just that. The resultant poem reads like a translation of some lost Hiberno-Homeric work, and Clarke's epic style emerges as most indebted exactly where it aimed to be most original.

---

tioned in the *dindshenchas*; Clarke no doubt learned of him from Lady Gregory's *Gods and Fighting Men*. (See *The Metrical Dindshenchas*, ed. & trans. E. J. Gwynn (Dublin, 1903–35, 5 vols.), ii., 260.18). 'Erc' is normally one of the Fir Bolg, but the name is a common one.

70 *Collected Poems*, 79.

71 The clear model is Homeric, even if the indistinct opacities are more obviously Virgilian.

In the main study so far published on the poet, Maurice Harmon observed that in his later years Clarke attemped to put his conflicts behind him and celebrate the 'merry sins', without necessarily being temperamentally suited to the task.[72] In one late poem, 'Phallomeda', published in 1968, Clarke turned again to the mythology of Moytura, but this time he focused on the Dagda's sexual misadventures, which he thoroughly and successfully re-imagined.[73] Far freer and more ironic than his 'epic' narratives—in any of their versions—the poem does not fret about faithfulness to native lore. It begins:

> Aeons ago, before our birth,
> The Irish gods, who were coarse and mirthful,
> Held their annual sessions on earth.[74]

The first line contains a formal joke: this poem about the gods begins, as in a sense the gods themselves had done, with George Russell, whose pseudonym, Æ, stood for 'Aeon'. And yet how different Clarke's gods are to Russell's, 'coarse and mirthful' instead of vague and solemn. 'Aeons ago': how far we have come, Clarke implies, since the days of dear old Æ. (Clarke's late style is full of homonyms and etymological puns of this kind: the nature of these 'annual sessions'—the sitting of a court, but with a hint of drink, music, and sex—can only be guessed if one knows that the word *session* ultimately comes from the same root as *síd*.)[75]

The poem dramatizes the Dagda's attempts to copulate with an attractive woman, despite impotence owing to the consumption of a gargantuan helping of porridge. As seen in chapter 3, in the medieval source the woman was a Fomorian princess, but here she has become a Greek goddess, clearly Aphrodite herself. ('Phallomeda' is the goddess's pseudonym whilst on the prowl in Ireland.)[76] This symbolic innovation tells us that we are no longer in the realm of pristine retellings of medieval saga, but are operating within a freer and more intellectually sophisticated poetic.[77] Events, however, turn cheerfully crude:

72 Harmon, *Austin Clarke*, 135.

73 See above, 118–25.

74 'Phallomeda', *Collected Poems*, 453.

75 See Sims-Williams, *IIMWL*, 59–63.

76 All sense of narrative time is removed from the mythic world. Elsewhere in the poem Clarke calls Phallomeda 'that paradigm, who immortalised the glance of Paris', identifying her as Aphrodite. The name would mean, roughly, 'she who knows what to do with a penis'—ironic, in the circumstances.

77 See Seamus Deane's observation that Clarke turned from 'a deliquescent aes-

> She fumbled
> To fire his godhead while he clumsied,
> Till she could hear the porridge mumble,
> Slapdash as foreign speech.[78]

The presence of a Greek goddess and the pun on 'head'—for the Dagda is struggling both to draw his divine energies together and to get an erection—serves to underscore how far the Irish 'Supreme Father' is from Zeus in potency; and as an unprepossessing symbol of Irishness, the crapulous divinity only manages to achieve congress in a dream, waking up at the moment of penetration. Once again Irish myth has been spliced with Homer, but in a less portentous way. The Túatha Dé Danann tittering at the spectacle echo the Olympians convulsed by the sight of Aphrodite and Ares trapped *in flagrante* in Homer's *Odyssey*:[79]

> Peering from doorway, portico,
> The gods were laughing at such sport,
> Until Phallomeda transported
>   Herself, in tears, to Greece.[80]

The correspondence is precise: in Homer, the Greek gods also crane their necks 'from the doorway', the classical 'portico' underlining the connection.[81] Here the Irish gods once again behave exactly like their Graeco-Roman counterparts, but such rewriting of the tradition alerts us that the poem's narrative is symbolic as well as physical. After all, despite the spasmodic grunting and clambering, Greek goddess and Irish god fail to unite. The coupling was always bound to be grotesque, and 'Phallomeda' emerges as a wry backward look from Clarke's maturity upon what Len

---

thetic to the higher pungencies of satire and self-discovery', and that he affords 'a startling example of the salutary effects which flow from the abandonment of unexamined and therefore misunderstood myths and systems.' ('Literary myths of the Revival: a case for their abandonment', in J. Ronsley (ed.), *Myth and Reality in Irish Literature* (Waterloo, Ontario, 1977), 322–3.

78 *Collected Poems*, 454.

79 See *Odyssey* 8.266–366, especially 325ff.

80 *Collected Poems*, 455.

81 Thus *Odyssey* 8.325–7: 'The gods, the givers of good things, stood in the doorway; and unquenchable laughter arose among the blessed gods as they saw the craft of wise Hephaestus.'

Platt has called the 'Hellenist obsession of revivalist Ireland', visible in so much of the literature.[82]

The native tradition itself is identified with earthy freedom:

> So in the words of the Great Mahaffy,
> Annalists frolicked with the pen and laughed
> At what they saw in the Hereafter,
>   Forgetting their horn-beads.
> Anticipating Rabelais,
> They wrote of the god who lay
> With loveliness. I copy that lay,
>   Applaud their disobedience.[83]

Clarke has hardly 'copied' any medieval Irish text, but the ingenuous assertion points to his determination to locate the subversive and the life-affirming in the medieval inheritance, gods included, as a qualification to present rigidity.[84] The poem may be artificial, but it is also one of the most original attempts to deal with the mythological material; even if the coupling fails to come off, Greece and Ireland have certainly drawn closer together than when James Stephens' Angus dismissed Pan from Ireland.

Clarke's satirical exposure of hypocrisy puts him in contact with others who were engaged, often from exile, in attempting to free up some of the tensions in the national psyche. He can be seen as deploying the Túatha Dé Danann to precisely the same moral end as many English Romantic and Victorian poets had done with the Graeco-Roman gods, between fifty and a hundred and fifty years before: grounding and physicalizing the divinities, he used them as symbols for the joyous, anti-

---

82 L. Platt, *Joyce and the Anglo-Irish: A Study of Joyce and the Literary Revival* (Amsterdam, 1998), 114. Chapter 3, 'Corresponding with the Greeks' is an incisive study of this cultural project with all its ideological excesses.

83 *Collected Poems*, 455. The pun on 'lay' is typical; 'Great Mahaffy' is the polymathic Anglo-Irish classicist, wit, and sometime Provost of Trinity, John Pentland Mahaffy (1839–1919).

84 Clarke identifies the tone of the medieval episode as proto-Rabelaisian, but the model of his own poem is classical; the witty, bibliofocal burlesque of mythological tradition is reminiscent of nothing so much as the eleventh *Idyll* of Theocritus, in which the physically grotesque Cyclops pines for the love of a beautiful nymph.

authoritarian, sexually frank, and creative side of human personality, closely identified with the natural world.[85]

CHILDREN'S LITERATURE AND FANTASY

At this point we shift away from high literature, although there remain intermittent things to admire. Phases of Celtic enthusiasm tend to be brief, and Irish literary writers since Clarke (under the influence of the internationalizing Joyce and Beckett) have had little use for the Túatha Dé Danann, even in parodic or allusive handlings.

We have seen that after about 1920, literary intoxication with themes of Irish myth manifested in the creation of secondary worlds, of which the pastoral idyll of Stephens' *The Crock of Gold* and Clarke's supernaturalized medieval Ireland are two examples.[86] Both deploy irreverence and parody in the service of renewed life, and in one sense this was absolutely true to native tradition, in which there is certainly a powerful strain of the comic and fantastic. And while there had long been a relation between children's literature and didactic themes, from the latenineteenth century one can observe the repackaging of pre-Christian mythology as imaginative literature for children. This could bring problems. On the one hand mythology involved a rich store of fantastic beings and events, and could potentially be pressed into service for the inculcation of approved values; on the other, the sexual element of much ancient mythology had to be downplayed.

Irish mythology was no exception, and early retellings often had both a young audience in mind and a political purpose—the de-anglicization of the imagination, not least in the adult who might be reading the text aloud. Indeed the re-imagining of the 'fairies' in these retellings served to replace one inner image of Irishness with another: dignified, wise, and powerful divinities took the place of the capricious and ungovernable fairies of folk tradition, who had mirrored colonial stereotypes so perniciously. It is striking that even in children's literature this was

85 Hutton (*The Triumph of the Moon* (Oxford, 1999), 20–31) has elegantly anatomized this romantic, celebratory discourse among English and German writers.

86 Though it does not feature the gods, also in this category is Eimar O'Duffy's satirical *Cuanduine* trilogy, *King Goshawk and the Birds* (New York, 1926), *The Spacious Adventures of the Man in the Street* (London, 1928) and *Asses in Clover* (London, 1933), which do feature (hilariously) the hero Cú Chulainn.

sometimes associated with the possibility of worshipping the Túatha Dé once more, because the 'return of the gods' was such a powerful contemporary trope, at least initially. Children are often depicted as closer to the gods: we saw that George Russell's 1897 *Dream of Angus Oge* gave us a bedtime story that comes true, accompanied by an idealization of children's visionary acuity. And at the start of Violet Russell's *Heroes of the Dawn* (1910) a little boy asks why the Túatha Dé Danann are no longer around; the reply comes that it is probably because not many people pray to them anymore. The child immediately begins to invoke Angus devoutly. (Curiously, it is nowhere suggested that praying to pagan deities might be incompatible with Christianity.)

Such winsomely nationalist retellings petered out in the aftermath of political revolution. More sophisticated and more individual were the responses to Irish myth, decades later, by two of the most significant children's writers of the twentieth century, Pat O'Shea (1931–2007) and Alan Garner (1934-). Both turned to the darkest—and most fascinating—female member of the Túatha Dé Danann, the Morrígan.[87] Garner took his place as the leading British author of fantasy for children in the 1950s, and was to turn to Celtic myth repeatedly in the decades to come. His youthful success was confirmed with the publication in 1960 of *The Weirdstone of Brisingamen*, in which the Morrígan appears not as a goddess, but as a shape-shifting witch among a ragbag of mythological beings drawn from Norse and Welsh tradition, leavened with inventions of Garner's own.[88] (In this, if not in tone, Garner's *Weirdstone* resembled *The Crock of Gold*, but the mixing of mythologies is less successful.)[89] The novel is set in and around Macclesfield in Cheshire, and as the Morrígan is the only character drawn from Irish mythology, her ethnic otherness helps to mark her out as an important antagonist.

Detached from the body of Irish mythology, the significance of the Morrígan in Garner's novel is difficult to gauge. In contrast, his contemporary Pat O'Shea, who was born in Galway but spent her adult life in Manchester, placed the goddess in a native Irish context in her 1985 *The Hounds of the Mórrígan*.[90] Though O'Shea published little else, the novel is

---

87 *Morrígan* is the older form, later *Mórrígan*.

88 A. Garner, *The Weirdstone of Brisingamen: a Tale of Alderley* (London, 1960).

89 This has been seen as one of the novel's major flaws; see N. Phillips, *A Fine Anger: a Critical Introduction to the Work of Alan Garner* (London, 1981), 33–4.

90 The spelling varies in the title: some editions have *Mórrígan*, with accents, others do not.

regularly spoken of as one of the most unforgettable children's novels ever written; its thorough rootedness in Irish tradition suggested that for O'Shea a certain nostalgia was at the root of creative invention. As in Garner, a boy and girl are pitched against the Mórrígan (so spelled), here uncompromisingly the 'Goddess of Death and Destruction' who 'feeds on the miseries of humankind', although her identity is only gradually revealed.[91] Idyllic and dark moments alternate in O'Shea's novel in a manner that makes clear that her prime model was Stephens, whose *Crock of Gold* she answers and equals. Flashes of carnivalesque wickedness indicate—more surprising in a children's novel—a debt to Bulgakov's great Russian fantasy, *The Master and Margarita*. Set in Tír na nÓg and an idyllic and poignantly dated Connemara, it gives us a world in which the Túatha Dé Danann are still at work, even if unremembered by mortals.

The plot is notable for its simultaneous absorption in and creative freedom with the medieval inheritance. O'Shea's Mórrígan—a sinister, sadistic, and eventually terrifying figure—wants to take over the world by absorbing the evil power of the serpent Olc-Glas and reclaiming one of the drops of her own blood which Cú Chulainn had spilt in the *Táin*. As 'The One who is Three, She who is also They', she is aided by Macha and Bodbh (meaning the Badb, another war-goddess), who appear on a motorbike and cause gleeful chaos. O'Shea's control of language and tone is remarkable. The reader hoots at the goddess of slaughter's verdict on Tolstoy—'Too much Peace; not enough War'—but other passages chill: ' "When mankind cries 'mercy', my ears are shells of granite", said The Mórrígan. "My child is the blow-fly, the mother of maggots." '[92] With her two doubles, the Mórrígan is exactly opposed by the forces of good: the Dagda, who never appears but who is described as Life to the Mórrígan's Death, together with Angus Og (of course) and Brigit, who help the two children as forces of joy and kindness. It is striking to see them paired up as representatives of new life: if Angus was the most significant member of the pantheon in the early years of the twentieth century, that role was taken over by Brigit in later decades, and we will turn to her trajectory below.

All the gods in O'Shea's novel initially appear in disguise and gradually become more recognizably themselves. The passage in which the

---

91 P. O'Shea, *The Hounds of the Mórrígan* (Oxford, 1985), 122.
92 O'Shea, *The Hounds of the Mórrígan*, 183, 365.

gentle, kooky 'Boodie' reveals herself to be the goddess Brigit showcases O'Shea's delicacy and control:

> Then there was a lovely moment when Boodie tended her fire with a stick. There was a hallowed feeling, like being in church. There was something about her movements and the expression on her face that was noble and full of grace, as if she were a very great lady. The fire glared and was pale yellow, bright orange and flame red.[93]

To the reader in the know, the phrase 'tended her fire' is enough by itself to out the mysterious woman as Brigit: here O'Shea echoes Gerald of Wales's famous twelfth-century account of the holy fire at Kildare. There are (said Gerald) nineteen nuns, and each tends the fire for one night; on the twentieth, the departing nun says: 'Brigit, guard your fire; this is your night', and in the morning it is found miraculously tended and still alight.[94]

O'Shea's Mórrígan deviates from but also echoes that of the medieval texts, in which she is in no way a purely, or even predominantly, evil figure. In 'The Second Battle of Moytura', she is a sibylline being who copulates with the Dagda and aids the Túatha Dé (of whom she is one) against their Fomorian enemies. In O'Shea's novel, the Dagda is her implacable enemy, as Life against Death: ironically in the medieval *dindshenchas* tradition he is explicitly her husband. The good divinities never boast of their identity—it is revealed subtly—but a number of terrifying self-praises are placed in the mouth of the Mórrígan. The climax reveals her, Macha, and Bodbh in their full horror:

> All around the battle raged, while the Goddesses shouted with savage joy. They slobbered and they didn't try not to, and they were crying out that even the trees would tremble and bleed and the stones of the earth would weep. They walked through the fighting mass, saying words of sly sweetness like flowers of poison. Dropping their voices to a deep and artificial huskiness, they fawned over the warriors and said old words that incite men to murder. It

---

93 O'Shea, *The Hounds of the Mórrígan*, 394.

94 Gerald of Wales, *The History and Topography of Ireland*, trans. J. O' Meara (London, 1951, revised 1982), 82; useful discussion of the 'perpetual flame' in C. Harrington, *Women in a Celtic Church, Ireland 450–1150* (Oxford, 2002), 27–8.

was the whispering of death to life, of old bones to warm flesh, a deadly mist of words sprayed out of their mouths...[95]

This is a dramatic and sympathetic response to the medieval sagas, sharply contrasting with Garner's somewhat clumsier handling. Their depictions contrast in another way also: Garner puts the Morrígan in England, but O'Shea puts Englishness in the Morrígan. Part of the fun for the adult reader is the disguise adopted by Macha and Bodbh when scouting out a base of operations—a pair of uppercrust English witches, taken by the locals to be artists or bohemians and described with persistent hints of lesbianism.

The Hounds of the Mórrígan is now thirty years old. More recently, children's adventures about the internal doings of the people of the *síd* have been revived by the Scottish writer Gillian Phillip, to critical acclaim. Her novel *Firebrand* (the first of a trilogy) gave teenage readers a glimpse into a disquietingly brutal fairy world, although it operates under three of the usual conventions: it is ruled by a powerful queen, time passes differently there, and it is hidden from our own by a 'veil'.[96] But in a brilliant twist of narrative perspective, Phillip's fairies—referred to by the Scottish Gaelic term *Sithe*—regard *our* world as 'an occult and dangerous otherworld', peopled by 'despised creatures'. They are not divinities but impulsive, sexual beings, dangerously out of place in the human world, who for all practical purposes feel themselves to be more or less immortal. In this they are, of course, a brilliant encapsulation of what it feels like to be a teenager, a quality which has no doubt contributed to the novel's success. At the same time, the novel represents a decisive break with both the Túatha Dé Danann and the tradition of Scottish fairy-writing that originated with Fiona Macleod, not least by being—ironically—more adult in its themes.

Like all the best children's fantasy, the novels discussed here can be enjoyed by adults, and, like Austin Clarke's romances, they invoke the marvellous—including the gods or *síd*-folk—not for escape but for imaginative and moral exploration. Adult fantasy literature, on the other hand, reads notoriously often as though it might perhaps be aimed at adolescents, a charge which has been levelled at the novel which contains the most famous, and most oblique, of all resonances of the Túatha Dé Danann in twentieth-century literature. This is J. R. R. Tolkien's *The*

---

95 O'Shea, *The Hounds of the Mórrígan*, 421.
96 G. Phillip, *Firebrand* (Glasgow, 2010).

Lord of the Rings, in which the Túatha Dé are disguised as the immortal elves; as such they hide in plain sight in one of the most perennially popular of all works of imaginative literature.

Tolkien's elves reflect different currents within his taste and reading as a medieval scholar. On the one hand he affected distaste for the Irish sagas, finding their complexity confused and so playing into the Victorian stereotype of the rational Anglo-Saxon unsettled by 'Celtic' craziness. He reacted with defensiveness when a correspondent wrote to him in 1937 wondering innocently if the strange names in his work might not be Celtic: 'Needless to say, they are not Celtic! I do know Celtic things, often in the original languages... there is bright colour but no sense.'[97]

This pronouncement should not, however, be understood as a definitive statement but rather as a specific response to a specific questioner, almost two decades before the publication of *The Lord of the Rings*. At other times Tolkien was perfectly prepared to acknowledge the role that Celticity played in his conception of the elves—not least in the languages he invented for them, one of which amounts to a philologist's elaborate (and to many people very beautiful) homage to Welsh.[98] Echoes of Irishness, in contrast, were avoided on the linguistic level but are visible everywhere on the level of theme, for his elves resemble nothing so much as an elegant compromise between the Túatha Dé Danann of 'The Book of Invasions' and those of the *Acallam*.[99] They have little in common with the shadowy elves of Norse mythology who give us the English word.[100] Like the people of the *síd*-mounds, Tolkien's elves are immortal and preternaturally beautiful, immune to ageing and natural death but capable of being slain in battle, and they can under exceptional circumstances intermarry with mortals; the wedding of the mortal Áed and the immortal Aillenn at the climax of the *Acallam* (as we have it) is one of the literary models for Tolkien's Aragorn and Arwen.

Furthermore, the complex series of wanderings and voyages he imagined for sub-groups of elves—from Middle Earth to the 'Undying Lands'

---

97 *The Letters of J.R.R. Tolkien: a selection*, ed. H. Carpenter (London, 1990), 26.

98 See C. Phelpstead, *Tolkien and Wales: Language, Literature and Identity* (Cardiff, 2011).

99 For Tolkien's contradictory attitudes to the 'Celtic', see D. Fimi, '"Mad" Elves and "elusive beauty": some Celtic strands of Tolkien's mythology', *Folklore* 117.2 (2006), 156–70, and now the same author's *Tolkien, Race and Cultural History: From Fairies to Hobbits* (Basingstoke, 2008).

100 It was not uncommon in the Celtic scholarship of Tolkien's day to translate *síd* as 'elfmound' and to refer to the people of the *síd* as 'elves'.

and back again, and then back *again*—echo the tangled trajectories of the peoples of Nemedian descent in 'The Book of Invasions'. And as has often been noticed, the story of the most skilled branch of his elves, the Noldor, echoes that of the Túatha Dé Danann at several points, not least their association with learning and the arts, their arrival over the sea from magical cities, and the burning of their ships.[101] Like the Túatha Dé, the elves are poignantly poised on the cusp of fading from the world altogether, either about to depart for a realm of existence (an overseas otherworld in the west) never again accessible to mortals, or to diminish into invisibility. It is ironic that the elves were clearly Tolkien's favourite creation, present in his thinking (originally as 'fairies') from his early twenties until his death; he spent many thousands of hours elaborating and revising their histories in a way that would have seemed familiar to the likes of Flann Mainistrech or Gilla Cóemáin, back in the eleventh century.

Tolkien invented a genre—heroic fantasy, or, more loosely, 'sword and sorcery'—which soon attracted a slew of imitators. He had transmuted his sources in a way that succeeded magnificently in capturing the imaginations of millions, and one way for his successors to evade his overpowering influence was to turn more directly to medieval Celtic material, and in particular to the Túatha Dé Danann. The genre has been pursued most prominently by writers outside Ireland and Britain. The most faithful has been Kenneth C. Flint, a native of Nebraska, who during the 1980s and 90s made a valiant effort in two series of novels to return to the whole body of the medieval tradition and repackage it as heroic fantasy for an American audience.[102] He did this by blending the Mythological Cycle with science fiction and echoes of Tolkien, so that (to take one example) the Fomorians—otherwise more or less forgotten after about 1920—appear as beings horribly mutated by the misapplication of industrial technology. His work represented an attempt to rework the texture of the material creatively in order to meet the expectations of a new audience, while still maintaining its essential shape. In contrast, the New Zealand author Juliet Marillier's *Daughter of the Forest* harked

101 See M. Burns, *Perilous Realms: Celtic and Norse in Tolkien's Middle-Earth* (Toronto, 2005), 24–5, 66, 69–70.
102 The 'Sidhe' Series comprises *The Riders of the Sidhe* (1984), *Champions of the Sidhe* (1985) and *Master of the Sidhe* (1985), which taken together retell 'The Second Battle of Moytura', after a fashion. 'The Gods of Ireland' series, despite the title, is about the Nemedians; it includes *Most Ancient Song* and *The Enchanted Isles* (both 1991), written under the pseudonym Casey Flynn.

back to the nineteenth-century retellings of O'Grady in its depiction of the Túatha Dé as luminous and unearthly beings, possessed of wisdom and inscrutable goals of their own. And in the American Stephen Lawhead's *The Paradise War*, they appear in a more human guise (thus seeming less like Tolkien's elves), and inhabit an otherworld tightly bound to our reality. In both Marillier and Lawhead's work the Túatha Dé are tangential to the action rather than central characters, and this was a solution to a problem Tolkien had also encountered: unearthliness is a quality hard to maintain in characters one has to look at squarely. Taking children's literature and fantasy together, it is a historical irony that from the 1980s the Túatha Dé have been safely corralled into genre fiction, in much the same way that the literary mythographers of the eleventh century had cordoned them off in the pseudohistorical past.

CELTIC PAGANISM

In the final part of this chapter we turn to countercultural manifestations. As the focus of this book is essentially literary I am not proposing to make a contribution to the sociology of religion; nevertheless, no history of the Irish gods would be complete without mentioning modern Paganism.[103]

As Ronald Hutton has shown, the complex of modern religious traditions grouped together under the heading 'Paganism' can be seen as a late offshoot of Romanticism.[104] Romanticism had insisted on the value of that which had traditionally been feared or deprecated in the Christian West: the feminine, the night, wild nature, sexuality, and the phantasmagoric power of the human imagination. Invocations to pagan gods and goddesses—especially those of Greece and Rome—and vivid notions of their power abounded in the writings of nineteenth-century literary radicals. This upswell of pagan feeling can be observed over a century coalescing around two divine figures, the Great Goddess and a horned god, usually identified as Pan. In Britain, literary and intellectual currents of this kind formed the matrix for the emergence in the first half of the twentieth century of a self-conscious new Paganism,

---

103 I follow the emerging convention in Religious Studies that modern Pagans and Paganism as spiritual identities are capitalized; I retain the lower-case form for ancient paganism.

104 Hutton, *Triumph of the Moon*, 3–51.

based on ancient themes and images, as a religious identity in place of Christianity.

Why did the same process not occur in Ireland? Superficially the ground seemed well prepared. Russell and Yeats had given, as we have seen, a nationalist spin to the Europe-wide idea of a return of, and to, the pagan gods as living powers. But Austin Clarke, looking back, had cherished Russell's '*literary* paganism' (emphasis mine), and various factors caused that paganism to fail to cohere in Ireland into a religious tradition. Yeats's efforts to create an Irish hermeticism ran out of steam, and though Russell went through phases of intense, apparently serious, belief in the native divinities, ultimately his investment in the ideas of Asian religion siphoned off his energies in the direction of a more universalizing, eastern-tinged spirituality. The same was true of James Cousins, and (to an extent) of James Stephens; all were grappling with a mythology as slippery and diffuse as it was alluring.

Nor was the climate of the twenties, thirties, and forties conducive to the development of the heterodoxies of previous decades. The hold of Christianity on the British was (arguably) weakening, but in Ireland a powerful Catholicism was bound up with the fabric of the new state.[105] That state defined its identity against the former colonial power in a way that only underscored the two nations' entanglement. The gods could not be assimilated to the institutional fetishizing of all things Gaelic characteristic of the period after independence. The likes of Finn mac Cumaill—as ancient hero turned quasi-Christian—were one thing, but the native gods had been in large measure the concern of a Protestant avant garde, some of whose activities now attracted open condemnation in the intensely conservative and Catholic state. A final factor should not be overlooked, and this was the difference in the scale and pace of urbanization between Britain and Ireland. Industrial guilt and pastoral nostalgia contributed powerfully to the development of Paganism in mid-century Britain, partly because this sense of retrospection and loss in relation to the countryside had become characteristic of the country's

---

105 But note that the overall decline in church attendance in the twenties and thirties in Britain was not, it has been suggested, a sign of a substantial loss of Christian faith; Catholicism grew numerically in Britain into the fifties (partly thanks to immigration from Ireland) and the forties saw a major church revival among Anglicans and other Protestant groups; on this see C. Brown, *The Death of Christian Britain: Understanding Secularisation 1800–2000* (London, 2009 [2nd edn.]). The major turning away from Christianity came in the fifties and sixties, when—not coincidentally—Paganism in Britain began to emerge into the public eye.

culture in a more general way; this impulse was not at work at anything like the same pitch in Ireland after independence, where industrialization was limited and rural poverty and depopulation still a major problem.[106]

This explains why the emergence of postmodern spirituality based on Irish myth has taken place largely outside Ireland, either in Britain or the United States, the home of expatriate nationalism. At the start of this chapter we met the composer John Cowell, who exemplified how Russellian idealism about the Irish gods could persist in New Age California, even as it dwindled in Ireland. It is no coincidence that in 1923 the poet Ella Young—Russell's exact contemporary—transplanted herself to that state and there lived out a successful old age as a Celtic mythographer and mystagogue. (When the United States immigration authorities discovered her literal belief in the beings of Irish legend she was nearly denied entry on psychiatric grounds.) So far as I am aware, Young is responsible for establishing the earliest Pagan or quasi-Pagan gatherings based on Irish myth, for in the 1930s she established 'The Fellowship of Mount Shasta', which met at the Celtic quarter days for ceremonies including chanted invocations to the Túatha Dé Danann.[107]

In Britain the scene centred rather upon the integration of Irish deities into the rituals and philosophy of Druidry, a re-imagined tradition with its roots in romantic strains of Welsh cultural nationalism and the friendly societies of the eighteenth century. In the course of the twentieth century Druidry gradually reconstituted itself into a Pagan religious tradition looking back to the images and ideas of the ancient Celtic world for inspiration. The influential figure of Phillip Ross Nichols (1902–75), Chief of the Order of Bards, Ovates, and Druids, was responsible for the importation of Gaelic material into Druidic ceremonies. An Englishman and (oddly) a lifelong Anglican, he nevertheless felt a deep connection to the pseudo-Gaelic world of the Celtic Revival—'Fiona' was a particularly powerful influence—and he was convinced that pre-Christian deities were symbols carrying religious truth. Irish, Welsh, and Egyptian gods rub shoulders in the evocative and often beautiful syncretic hodgepodge of his writings; he established the convention among British

---

106 See R. Foster, *Modern Ireland, 1600–1972* (London, 1989), 577ff for a survey of economic policies and resultant effects in the period.

107 See R. Murphy, *Ella Young: Irish Mystic and Rebel* (Dublin, 2008), 113, and C. Clifton, *Her Hidden Children: The Rise of Wicca and Paganism in America* (Lanham, MD, 2006), 112–13; also above, 458.

Pagans that Irish gods were essential in any attempt to retrieve a truly 'Celtic' spirituality.[108]

The willingness to deal directly with Irish sources varies widely among contemporary Pagan writers. The remarkable R. J. Stewart has remained consciously close to Sharp and Russell. As a Scotsman like Sharp, a composer like Boughton and Bax, and ceremonial magician like Yeats, Stewart continues to make the case for (and, in doing so, embody) the spiritual profundity of the first Celtic Revival. He has also acted as a popular mythographer, retelling stories of the Túatha Dé Danann in a number of attractively illustrated volumes.[109] In 1914, W. K. Magee had observed that the 1890s had made 'gods of the "fairies"', a trajectory which Pagan writers have maintained; R. J. Stewart is the salient exception, for in his writings the fairies are living beings of a different order to humanity and explicitly not divinities.[110] Gaelic fairy lore is reworked in his publications into a whole system of 'initiation', involving travelling via inner journeys into the world of the *síd*, or 'faery', in his preferred spelling; such journeys tend to be 'underworldly' rather than otherworldly, and the ends include personal and spiritual transformation and environmental healing.[111] It will be apparent that Stewart stands in a direct line of inheritance from Walter Evans-Wentz.

The prodigiously productive and popular Caitlín and John Matthews have turned to a far greater extent to the medieval sources than most Pagan writers; in doing so, they became in the 1980s and 90s the prime interpreters of those sources to Celtic-leaning Pagans.[112] Their work quotes from medieval texts but the revolution in medieval Irish Studies of the 1970s and 80s seems to have passed them by. With good reason: the current consensus is sceptical about the extent to which aspects of pre-Christian myth or religion can be retrieved from medieval Irish texts, and such retrieval is precisely the project upon which their livelihood as writers depends. Nevertheless, their charms and prayers for a renewed 'Celtic Tradition' showcase a pellucid and often beautiful house style intended for spiritual uplift, which owes much to *Carmina*

108 See Hutton, *Blood and Mistletoe*, 405–6.

109 R. J. Stewart, *Celtic Gods, Celtic Goddesses* (London, 1990); *The Living World of Faery* (Glastonbury, 1995).

110 Quoted in Foster, *TAM*, 89.

111 See his *Power within the Land: the Roots of Celtic and Underworld Traditions* (Shaftsbury, 1992).

112 See the detailed analysis by Ronald Hutton, *Witches, Druids, and King Arthur* (London, 2002), 244–8.

Gadelica, Fiona Macleod, and Ross Nichols, whose *Book of Druidry* John co-edited.[113] They are both explicitly conscious of the debt their approach owes to the first Revival, and John has edited two useful collections of Celtic Twilight and neo-Celtic writing; more recently he published a selection of Ella Young's work, underscoring her status as a major progenitrix of Irish-inflected Paganism centred on the Túatha Dé Danann.[114]

A second current in Celtic Paganism has made contemporary academic research more fundamental. This is Celtic Reconstructionism, which originated in the 1980s and has been vastly fostered by the growth of the web. It aims to recreate an approximation of ancient tribal religion—in the forms relevant to the present work, that of Iron Age Ireland.[115] Its practitioners turn their back on the eclecticism of modern Druidry, also rejecting the heritage of ritual magic that formed a vital strand in the genesis of modern Paganism as well as offering a direct connection back to Yeats.[116] In many ways it is a form of Paganism more calculated to appeal to intellectuals, especially those interested in language and identity. Where Druids like Nichols had looked to the past for romantic wisdom, Celtic Reconstructionists have tended to ally subjective feelings with thoughtful investigations of the writings of classical authors, archaeology, and comparative Indo-European mythology, thus creating a self-consciously innovative religious tradition drawing on scholarly interpretations of ancient materials.[117]

---

113 A representative sample of their work with an Irish dimension would include Caitlín's *The Elements of the Celtic Tradition* (Shaftesbury, 1989), John's *The Celtic Shaman* (Shaftesbury, 1991), and their joint *The Encyclopedia of Celtic Wisdom* (Shaftesbury, 1994).

114 See J. Matthews (ed.), *From the Isles of Dream: Visionary Stories and Poems of the Celtic Renaissance* (Melksham, 1993); *Within the Hollow Hills: an Anthology of new Celtic Writing* (Guildford, 1994); and with D. Sallee (eds.), *At the Gates of Dawn: A Collection of Writings by Ella Young* (Cheltenham, 2011).

115 There are multiple forms of Pagan Reconstructionism, one for most of the ethnic groups of the ancient European world. It should be noted that in the vast majority of these, a corresponding ethnic affiliation or ancestry is *not* a criterion for practising the spiritual path.

116 Published material on the subject of Celtic Reconstructionism is limited, as most discussion tends to be online; but see A. Kondratiev, *The Apple Branch: A Path to Celtic Ritual* (San Francisco, CA, 1998).

117 See for example the online mission statement at www.imbas.org, and especially the conspicuously learned http://www.tairis.co.uk/introduction/celtic-reconstructionism [accessed 30th September, 2015].

The development of Celtic Paganism has shifted the spotlight onto particular members of the pantheon. As discussed earlier, in the first decades of the twentieth century Aengus was *the* Irish divinity; and while he was still of interest to Nichols in the early 1970s, contemporary Pagan writing and ritual seem to have forgotten about him.[118] An impressionistic survey reveals that at the turn of the twentieth century, Aengus, Manannán, Lug, and the Dagda were the deities most frequently referenced; by the turn of the twenty-first, only Lug retained his importance, trailing behind Brigit, the Morrígan, and the Cailleach—the last a folk figure now commonly identified by Pagans as an ancient divinity.[119] Lug's persistence is to be ascribed to his strong association with the Gaelic seasonal festival of *Lugnasad* at the beginning of August, repopularized by Pagans as a major point in the ritual year.[120] Accompanying this shift was a process of winnowing; Pagan writing about the Túatha Dé Danann has jettisoned the framework of 'The Book of Invasions' and has reversed the medieval process that turned a small nucleus of former divinities into an otherworldly race. To judge by Pagan publications, only the most distinctive members have retained popularity: the likes of Airmed and Bodb Derg—and even major gods such as Núadu, Midir, and Dían Cécht—have suffered something of an eclipse.

THE GODDESS BRIGIT: A CASE STUDY

What has replaced them is a decisive alteration in the gender balance of the gods, reflecting the rise of second-wave feminism and Goddess spirituality from the 1970s onwards. Of the female members of the Túatha Dé Danann, Brigit in particular underwent an explosion in popularity in

118 An impressionistic survey of material published since 1990 finds him playing a major role only once, being invoked in the script for a Druid wedding ceremony in P. Carr-Gomm, *The Druid Way* (Shaftesbury, 1993), 151–5.

119 *Cailleach* (Old Irish *caillech*) simply means 'old woman' (originally 'nun'). A single line in a famous Old Irish poem, 'The Lament of the Old Woman of Beare', names her as *Buí*, which elsewhere is the name of one of the wives of Lug; it is possible but not certain that they should be identified. But as the Cailleach was an important figure in Irish and Scottish folklore, experts in that field have tended to bolster her putative divinity while scholars of medieval Irish literature have tended to dispute it. See G. Ó Crualaoich, *The Book of the Cailleach: Stories of the Wise-Woman Healer* (Cork, 2003), and contrast McCone, *PPCP*, 154, who detects the influence of biblical models upon the figure.

120 For the history of the festival, see R. Hutton, *The Stations of the Sun: A History of the Ritual Year in Britain* (Oxford, 1996), 327–31.

the final third of the twentieth century. Long taken by Celtic scholarship to be a peculiar, if not unique, amalgam of Christian saint and pagan goddess, like Lug she was strongly associated (thanks to her saint's day) with another seasonal festival, that of Imbolc, at the beginning of February.[121] According to Catherine McKenna, the first scholar to examine Brigit's cultural role during the modern era, the goddess Brigit became increasingly prominent from the second half of the nineteenth century, but before that point, had been completely lost to sight since the early Middle Ages.[122] As discussed in this study, the goddess is one of the most static figures among the Túatha Dé; the famous description in 'Cormac's Glossary' identifies her as the daughter of the Dagda and then, in triplicate, as a female poet, female healer, and female smith, who used to be worshipped by the professional poets.[123]

If Cormac's definition manages to be as numinous as ever a glossary entry could—or at least has struck modern readers as being so—it serves to highlight how low-key Brigit's other appearances in the textual record are. In 'The Second Battle of Moytura' she—under the name Bríg, generally assumed to refer to the same personage—utters the first keening in Ireland for the death of Rúadán ('Little Red-Haired One'), her son by the half-Fomorian king Bres.[124] Elsewhere she is associated with particular animals and with various types of cry, including whistling.[125] Brigit's role as originator of vocal grieving—clear as day in medieval tradition—has been largely ignored by Pagans, as have her husband and son. Austin Clarke, however, did describe the death of Rúadán, and Bríg's keening, in *The Sword of the West*, but there he called Bríg/Brigit 'Brifé', a deformation—if not simply a misprint in a text full of errors—perhaps intended to evade uncertainties about the goddess's ambiguous identity.[126]

By the 1970s Brigit's unique duality was beginning to render her accessible to 'Celtic' Christians, for many of whom the idea of feminine imagery and a limited rapprochement with pre-Christian tradition was

---

121 See Hutton, *Stations of the Sun*, 135–8.

122 'Apotheosis and evanescence: the fortunes of Saint Brigit in the nineteenth and twentieth centuries', in J. F. Nagy, (ed.), *The Individual in Celtic Literatures* [CSANA Yearbook 1] (Dublin, 2001), 74–108.

123 See above, 162–3, 341.

124 Significantly or not, *rúadán* was also the word for a kind of cereal crop.

125 For Brigit outside 'Cormac's Glossary', see *CMT*, ed. Gray, 56–7, and (for further references) 119; also J. Carey, 'A *Tuath Dé* Miscellany', *BBCS* 39 (1992), 24–45.

126 *Collected Poems*, 78. He was quite aware of these; see below, 485–7.

attractive. At the same time, she became increasingly central to Celtic Paganism, via the wholesale transferal of the saint's characteristics to the goddess. In one well-known episode in a medieval Life, the saint hangs her cloak to dry over a sunbeam; but in Ella Young's 1910 *Celtic Wonder Tales* the cloak had become the primary attribute of the goddess and the means by which she created the world out of chaos. Most often, however, Brigit was pigeonholed as a fire deity, thanks to the fire imagery in hagiographical tradition and Gerald of Wales's account of the perpetual flame at Kildare. In fact, such fiery imagery was far from unusual in early medieval saints' lives, and the tradition of the undying flame likely reflected a situation of no great antiquity. It is telling that 'Cormac's Glossary'—our major source for the goddess's characteristics—describes Brigit as a female deity, but makes no connection with flame; in theory there should have been no problem with the latter concept, since the same text's entry on the Roman deity Vesta plainly terms her 'a goddess of fire' (*bandēa tened*).[127] As a result, the most likely reason why Brigit is not described as a fire-goddess in the 'Glossary' is simply that she wasn't one.

But cavils of this kind did not stop the upward trajectory of Brigit as combined goddess and saint.[128] The groundwork for this remodelling had been laid by many of the writers we have met in this book, although no one seems to have identified the saint and the goddess before d'Arbois de Jubainville in 1880. William Sharp—as Fiona—offered an epiphany of the goddess, reinterpreting the historical confusion of divinity and holy woman as a revelation of Brigit's true nature. Brigit appears in a vision to an old woman who identifies her immediately as the saint, before being gently corrected (I have inserted translations of the Gaelic phrases):

> I am older than Brighid of the Mantle, Mary, and it is you that should know that. I put songs and music on the wind before ever the bells of the chapels were rung in the West or heard in the East. I am Brighid-nam-Bratta (*Brighid of the Mantles*), but I am also Brighid-Muirghin-na-tuinne (*Brighid conception of the waves*), and Brighid-sluagh (*Brighid of hosts*), Brighid-nan-sitheach seang (*Brighid of the slender Shee*), Brighid-Binne-Bheul-lhuchd-nan-trusganan-uaine

---

127 *Sanas Cormaic*, ed. K. Meyer, *Anecdota from Irish Manuscripts*, ed. O. Bergin, R. I. Best, K. Meyer, & J. G. O'Keefe (Halle, 1912), iv., 4 [reprnt. Llanerch, 1994].

128 Note the objections to the identification raised by P. Ó Riain, 'Pagan Example and Christian Practice: A Reconsideration', in D. Edel (ed.), *Cultural Identity and Cultural Integration: Ireland and Europe in the Early Middle Ages* (Dublin, 1995), 144–56, at 154–5.

(*Brighid sweet mouth of the people of the green garments*), and I am older than Aona (*Friday*) and am as old as Luan (*Monday*). And in Tir-na-h'oige (*Land of Youth*) my name is Suibhal-bheann (*Mountain-goer*); in Tir-fo-thuinn (*the Land under Wave*) it is Cù-gorm (*Grey Hound*); and in Tir na h'oise (*the Land of Old Age*) it is Sireadh-thall (*Seek yonder*). And I have been a breath in your heart. And the day has its feet to it that will see me coming into the hearts of men and women like a flame upon dry grass, like a flame of wind in a great wood.[129]

Sharp's rhapsodic prose poem anticipated the feminist adoption of Brigit later in the century, but the passage was all the stranger as there is no evidence for the pre-Christian Brigit in the literature and folklore of Gaelic Scotland, although the saint was of tremendous importance. The incantatory aliases of Sharp's archaic Brigit paint her as an active and mobile being in a universe of different realms or dimensions. While the epithets are in Gaelic, it is nevertheless clear that she is in a sense as synthetic as Sharp's other 'neo-divinities' such as Dalua and Orchil.[130]

Some decades later, Austin Clarke also also drew attention to the changing face of Brigit, but he located it in his imagined medieval Irish past rather than Sharp's purported Hebridean present. His 1932 poem 'Wandering Men' is another epiphany of Brigit, but also an altogether more mysterious and complex work. It begins with the familiar themes of Brigit's hagiography: a band of lost, weary men find themselves at Kildare, its monastic bell house illuminated by a 'momentary flame',

---

129 F. MacLeod, *The Winged Destiny: studies in the spiritual history of the Gael* (London, 1904), 195. 'Fiona' does go on to give renderings of these Gaelic names, but—as usual—the grammar, orthography, and translations are a bit dubious; Sharp may well have concocted some of the Gaelic phrases himself. The last three, certainly, are the names of fairy hounds mentioned in the apparatus to *Carmina Gadelica* (ii, 266–67), where they occur with the two otherworldly realms alluded to; one gets the impression Sharp had simply thumbed through Carmichael's text looking for plausible phrases to pull out. I have tried to be more literal in the translations; for 'Muirghin-na-tuinne' I have followed Fiona's 'Conception of the Waves', but Dwelly's *Dictionary* (which includes the phrase) suggests a more accurate translation might be 'mermaid'. Perhaps Sharp was aiming at the title 'Lady of the Sea' which he gives to Brighid/Bride elsewhere.

130 John Duncan painted Brigit several times but kept the pagan and Christian Brigits distinct. In his 1913 *St Bride*, the prepubescent saint is carried over the sound of Iona by angels, whose rich vestments locate us firmly in the world of the early Irish church. His 1917 *The Coming of Bride*, on the other hand, shows Brigit as a wistful nature-goddess attended by a train of youths and children.

which seems simultaneously—and metaphorically?—to be the flaming forehead of the abbess herself:

> Among her women on the threshold
> Great Brigid gave us welcome.
> She had concealed in colder veil
> Too soon the flaming of her forehead
> That drew our eyelids in the wood.[131]

Given board and lodging for the night, the speaker beholds mysterious apparitions which hint that the monastery has a dimension beyond the Christian:

> And all that night I was aware
> Of shapes no priest can see,
> The centaur at the house of prayer,
> The sceptred strangers from the east.
> Confined in dreams we saw again
> How Brigid, while her women slept
> Around her, templed by the flame,
> Sat in a carven chair.

This has become a syncretic revelation, both mythological and Christian, symbolized by the 'centaur in the house of prayer': on the literal level this alludes to a famous twelfth-century carving in Cormac's Chapel at Cashel, but it also points to Brigit's hybrid nature as saint and goddess, as well as suggesting something uncontrollable that fuses the animal with the human, instinct and intellect. The dream vision is of a feminine space ('no priest'), with Brigit herself tending the fire. Such was Gerald of Wales's story, but Clarke works in the speculation (common in scholarship of the time) that the custom was a survival of a pagan fire cult, the goddess 'templed by the flame'. As in Clarke's prose romances, we end with a visionary slippage between dream and reality:

> We wakened with the early blackbird
> Before the oaks had drawn
> An old sun-circle on the grass:

131 Clarke, *Collected Poems*, 177.

The sightly house was gone.
Yet we gave praise to that sky-woman
For wayfare and a vision shown
At night to harmless men who have
No parish of their own.

Brigit's monastery and her temple—the monastery's phantasmagoric double—have both vanished, pointing to their identity. Both Sharp and Clarke give us theophanic visions of Brigit; but in 'Wandering Men' she maintains a resonant silence, whereas Sharp's contemporary apparition has rather a lot to say.

Brigit is a potent figure with whom to end. At the time of writing, she has probably become the most popular of all Irish goddesses among Pagans—perhaps ironically, since she is also the most idiosyncratic. It is clear that in the second half of the twentieth century she came to perform the role Aengus had fulfilled in the first, that of a flexible icon of spiritual rootedness and cultural renewal. Significantly, in recent years she has been taken up in Ireland itself, where the development of Pagan spirituality has remained fairly muted in comparison to Britain and the United States.[132] This reflects her value as a simultaneously ancient and postmodern symbol of natively Irish spirituality, including its perceived pre-Christian dimension. Embodying integrity and independence, Brigit had come to provide a focus for grappling with issues around gender, authority, and justice, especially in the context of seismic changes in the position of the Church in Irish life—not least the widespread disgust with the Catholic hierarchy which climaxed with the publication of the Cloyne Report in 2011. When the consequences of recent turmoil are clearer, a full-length study of Brigit in contemporary Ireland, preferably from a scholar in religious studies, would be highly desirable. I have seen her invoked in relation to the financial crisis, revelations about child abuse, abortion, and—because of the medieval tradition of Brigit's episcopacy—in debates about women's ordination. Brigidine imagery

---

132 This is emphatically not to say that these religious trends are unknown, and the conclusion of the first scholar to make a survey of the scene is that they seem to be growing, albeit more slowly than in the UK and US; see J. Butler, 'Druidry in Contemporary Ireland', in M. Strmiska (ed.), *Modern Paganism in World Cultures: Comparative Perspectives* (Oxford, 2005), 87–125, and 'Irish Neo-Paganism: Worldview and Identity', in O. Cosgrove, et al. (eds.), *Ireland's New Religious Movements* (2011), 111–130.

can appear in unexpected places: the cover of Sinéad O'Connor's 2000 album *Faith and Courage* depicted the singer against a flame-coloured background, a triple tongue of fire descending upon her head.

It is clear that in this process the Christian Brigit has become increasingly inflected by the pre-Christian one, so that when in 1993, the leader of the Brigidine Sisters in Kildare relit the sacred flame, it was a powerful gesture to many people, all historical dubiety aside. (Ironically, it was precisely such doubts which led to reports that the Vatican had struck Brigit from the roster of saints in 1969; this was in fact untrue, but it would have had the ironic effect that she began the twentieth century as a saint and former goddess, and ended it as a goddess and former saint.) And at Imbolc 2006 a specially commissioned pillar sculpture, the St Brigid's Flame Monument, was unveiled in Kildare's Market Square by the then President of Ireland, Mary McAleese. The design of the monument showed a conscious mixing of pagan and Christian imagery in that its chief symbols are the acorn and oak leaf, both for *Cill Dara*, the 'Church of the Oak', and as an enduring symbol for Druidry. A cynic might put this gesture down to Kildare County Council acknowledging that the goddess-saint was a unique local selling point, especially to spiritual seekers from the United States. But Austin Clarke would have been pleased by Brigit's popularity, for the new monument precisely embodied the theme of his 'Wandering Men'; it would have gratified William Sharp too, no doubt, because with it one of the prophecies of 'Fiona' had—almost unbelievably—actually come to pass.

12

ARTGODS

Gods make their own importance.

—PATRICK KAVANAGH, 'EPIC'

ONE NIGHT IN EARLY 2015, persons unknown climbed Binevenagh Mountain, outside Limavady, Co. Derry, where a splendid lifesize statue of Manannán mac Lir had recently been erected as a piece of public art.[1] This is the landscape of 'The Voyage of Bran', for the statue looked down over the eastern edge of Lough Foyle—now the site of a British prison— whence Bran and his mariners had set sail for the Land of the Women. It was a striking work, showing the sea-god in his boat, arms raised to command the sea (Fig. 12.1). But whoever visited it that night was not intrigued but enraged: after sawing the figure off at the feet and throwing it down a cliff, they erected a wooden cross inscribed YOU SHALL HAVE NO OTHER GODS BEFORE ME, followed by the alpha and omega of Christ.

Only in Ulster, some might sigh, although it should be pointed out that attacks on monuments perceived to be 'pagan' still occasionally occur throughout post-Christian Europe, though they are increasingly more likely to be perpetrated by the disturbed than the devout.[2] But what was astonishing was the global publicity this act of vandalism generated: it soon became clear that the sculpture had touched many people around the world, who petitioned for its replacement in strikingly personal terms.[3] The ironies were heavy. Destroying the statue had ren-

1 Created by Darren John Sutton, a sculptor from Dungannon, Co. Tyrone.

2 See Hutton, *PB*, 452, fn.27, for the 2004 destruction of a 'sheela-na-gig' at the church in Buncton, West Sussex, ascribed to 'an act of Christian vandalism'; in the same year yellow gloss paint was spattered across an entire stone circle, the 3,500 year old Rollright Stones in Oxfordshire.

3 See for example http://www.derryjournal.com/news/facebook-campaign-to-bring -back-stolen-sea-god-statue-1-6538279, accessed 2nd April 2015.

dered it iconic, and presumably the zealots who found the image idolatrous were unaware of 'The Voyage of Bran', whose learned clerical
author had chosen to depict Manannán as a typological substitute for
the Christian god thirteen hundred years before. Whatever their denom-
inational background—it seems unfair to speculate—the vandals clearly
felt threatened by Manannán in a way that our unknown monastic *literatus*, writing only a century or so after the final decline of Irish paganism, conspicuously had not. The crime itself, plus the disgust of locals at
the vandalism of an artwork which was a symbol of their heritage as
well as a popular tourist attraction, shows that one native god at least
retained the ability to stir strong feelings among the people who lived in
the landscape with which he had long been associated, and in the world
at large. Happily, in March 2015 it was announced that the sculpture
would be replaced.

These events occurred as I finished this book, and they bring me to
some final observations. I made it clear at the beginning of this study
that it could not be exhaustive, and works that have been neglected (not
least the *Táin*) press upon my conscience. But I began not with aspirations to complete coverage but with a series of questions, of which three
were fundamental: who and what the gods of Irish myth are, why they
are so exceptional, and what has been the nature of the imaginative investment made in them. A fourth—the question of how they have been
reconstituted as a pantheon in modernity—has been answered in the
body of the text, but the others require some threads to be pulled together in response.

Answers to the question of who and what are various. The Irish divinities prefer cameo appearances: they haunt the medieval literature,
but outside the relatively restricted Mythological Cycle they are rarely
its central players. Even when they are, the question of their identity is
problematic and, significantly, continued to be so for modern writers
bent on the gods' retrieval. So constant is the harping upon the nature of
their nature that it becomes a primary leitmotif. *It is in a great síd that we
live, therefore we are called the people of the síd*, punned the nameless
woman in 'The Adventure of Connlae'. *I am of the race of Adam*, intoned
Lug in 'The Phantom's Frenzy.' The author of 'The Wasting Sickness of
Cú Chulainn' dismissed the gods as *demons from before the Faith*, prone
to beguiling mortals with delusory phantasmagorias. Adventurous
thinkers pondered whether they might belong to some exotic order of
being—perhaps 'half-fallen' angels or unfallen human beings—while the
pseudohistorians identified them as the long-dead descendants of Noah,

FIG. 12.1. *Manannán Commands the Sea* (2013, now destroyed), fibreglass and stainless steel, by John Darren Sutton. Permission and photo courtesy of the artist.

schooled in pagan lore. Later in the Middle Ages we find them depicted as quarantined, contaminated beings, and—simultaneously—as humanity's idealized twin race. Such beings might know the unearthly bliss of the *síd*, but none of them (or very few) were destined for the eternal bliss of heaven. As fairies, demons, magicians, allegories and moral *exempla*—and later as hermetic forces, relics of Indo-Europe, and Yeatsian 'immortal moods'—Ireland's native supernaturals seem to hover in a state of permanent ontological suspension.

Nonetheless, views came in two broad kinds that might be termed the 'numinous' and the 'semi-euhemeristic'. The 'numinous' position entailed the direct acknowledgement that the native supernaturals were pagan gods, which had undoubtedly once been the case for a few. This was inevitably a problematic position in the Middle Ages because it flirted with the existence of spiritual entities whose position within Christian cosmology was dubious, to say the least. It was one thing to memorialize a native deity in a glossary of vernacular terms, but quite another to breathe literary life into such a being. Sometimes, nonetheless, medieval authors did just that—earning our gratitude for the splendour of their achievement—but persistent notes of distaste are detectable. Centuries later, romantic nationalism reanimated the idea that Ireland's literary supernaturals had once been pre-Christian deities, in the process turning the medieval valuation of such beings decisively on its head: newly enthused by romantic paganism, writers now looked askance at the medieval Christian culture which had preserved the gods.

Such was the first position. The 'semi-euhemeristic' view was more authoritative for much of the Middle Ages, and beyond: it consisted of variations on the idea that the native supernaturals should be regarded as humans of some especially gifted or augmented sort. There was debate about their moral stature, as on the question of whether they had died long ago or had merely passed into another sphere of existence. The invention of demonic deities such as Crom Crúach, the 'Bloody Crookback', is telling in this regard: they suggest that there came a stage when medieval Irish writers knew that their ancestors had worshipped pagan gods, but that the human-like people of the *síd* no longer struck them as belonging to the same cognitive category. This viewpoint has dwindled in modernity: George Russell tried, but in the end even he abandoned his idea that the gods were men and women self-divinized by esoteric knowledge.

It is important to remember that both these views were standard intellectual positions in medieval Europe and, far from being unique to Ireland, they were applied to the classical and Norse gods as well. The first position was plain to see in those parts of the Old Testament which implied that gods other than the God of Israel existed; in seeking to explain such passages Augustine of Hippo affirmed that pagan divinities had been real, albeit demonic, spiritual beings. The Icelandic mythographer Snorri Sturluson, on the other hand, exemplified the second position by identifying the high god Odin as a descendant of King Priam of Troy. Like the Norse pantheon, the Irish gods were local figures, often associated with particular features in the landscape; they never occupied the lofty cosmological and allegorical roles which medieval philosophy assigned to the gods of Mediterranean antiquity. Medieval men of learning made occasional thoughtful analogies between classical and Irish deities, but symbolic readings of the pantheon only really flourished from the late nineteenth century, when classical models were so thoroughly internalized as to be inescapable.

In short, the distinctiveness of the Irish setup lies in its restless refusal to resolve. This could be richly exploited; writers could and did fine-tune the ontology of these supernatural figures to suit their literary purposes, sometimes cleverly crosshatching different takes on their nature within a single text, as in 'The Wooing of Étaín'. This was key to the gods' appeal, because it enabled literary deliberation upon *human* nature—its pleasures, potentials, and pitfalls, its limits and excellences, and its ultimate fate. In medieval Irish literature elusiveness and ambiguity occupy a position of high aesthetic value, and the hazy status of the native supernaturals was ideally suited to the creation of such effects.

One upshot of the tradition's unrelenting rumination upon ontology is that the material could have been approached in other ways, even by the present author. This book ends with writers of international fame, but I have tried to avoid implying that this represents a climax—the medieval literature is far too compelling on its own terms for that—but inevitably the narrative has emphasized how the indigenous supernaturals re-emerged in modernity as a pantheon of distinctive divinities. A certain grand respiratory rhythm has therefore been implied: the pre-Christian Irish probably had a multitude of local deities, but most of these were jettisoned during the conversion and only a small core were retained as literary figures. During the Middle Ages that core multiplied into a host of supernatural *síd*-folk. This indefinite plurality then in turn underwent another phase of thinning down, to leave us—for the second time—with a small clutch of 'ancient' gods.

The same material might have held a very different shape for a folklorist, who could with full justification have laid stress upon the concept of fairies, rather than gods. In doing so he or she might have examined the relationship between the *áes síde* of the medieval literature and those of the folklore collected since the nineteenth century. I have dealt here with the question of literary, not literal, belief, but the Irish material could be set by a folklore specialist in the context of fairy traditions across north-western Europe; the late-Victorian occult nationalism which I have placed centre stage would then be of marginal concern. Equally, features of the tradition that I have sidelined—such as the persistent connection between the fairies and the dead—would loom large. Such a study would be a valuable complement to the views expressed here, allowing a more rounded picture to emerge.

Lastly, what kind of imaginative investment in the gods does the literature imply? Three connected observations emerge. First, I suggest that the truth value of the gods is in some measure keyed to the truth value ascribed to fictive representation itself. Over recent decades an influential school of thought about medieval Irish literature has stressed its role as propaganda: writers represented events in the semi-legendary past in such a way as to bolster the political interests of specific patrons. The gods, especially various forms of the so-called sovereignty goddess, were certainly pressed into service in literary exercises of this kind. But such beings—given their ontological elusiveness and often their sheer *strangeness*—seem to me to have played a role in carving out a space in the culture for flashes of 'pure' imaginative literature, independent of propagandistic priorities. Heather O'Donoghue reminds us that 'mythology tends to be the most surreal manifestation of any culture', and the Irish supernaturals—with their ability to change shape, baffle perception, or project visions—are tied up with the very processes of representation, making that which begins in the imagination concrete.[4]

This reflects the long-lasting link between the native gods and human skill. We recall the role in the pantheon of the 'Three Gods of Skill'—mysterious, suggestive figures—and the way that many of the divinities are imagined as the exemplars of those elevated by their talent: poets, physicians, craftsmen of all sorts. As literary figures, the Irish gods are thus both the patrons and the products of shaping art, associated with in-groups that possess esoteric or specialized knowledge. It is significant that this is one area in which medieval tradition and modern reception coincide. I noted that the deities Brigit and Aengus Óg held such importance for modern Irish writers—not least Yeats—partly because they

4 *FATV*, 128.

could personify different dimensions of the poet's art, the rigours of technique and the inrush of inspiration. In spirit, if not detail, a *fili* from the tenth century might find something familiar here.

It is striking therefore that the twentieth and twenty-first centuries have come to associate these 'gods of culture' ever more closely with the natural world, especially as the most immediately impressive areas of Ireland often owe their distinctive beauty to a bitter colonial history of deforestation and depopulation. Environmentalists have often looked to them: when, in 2008, the Irish government finally went ahead with the building of a motorway through the Tara/Skryne valley, permanently scarring the nation's most precious archaeological landscape, one pro-tester, Lisa Feeney, dug herself into a tunnel on the site, strangely literal-izing of the idea of the *síd*. She occupied her tunnel for three days, read-ing Lady Gregory by candlelight.[5] But however much one may salute her courage, it is difficult not to remark on the irony that ploughing a causeway through the landscape was one of the god Midir's specialities in 'The Wooing of Étaín', while the Dagda erased forests and re-routed rivers. And 'The Book of Invasions', after all, represented the Túatha Dé Danann not as powers of wild nature, but as the sophisticated denizens of four cities.

A second observation has been repeatedly emphasized throughout this book, and this is that there is nowhere in which the divinities may be uncovered in any pristine form, for their entire history in Irish (and Scottish) culture consists of afterlife. Like Lug in 'The Phantom's Frenzy', they are their own ghosts. This is bound up with the 'shaped' quality identified above, because without the ballast provided by testimonia to pagan cult-practice—contrast Greece and Rome—the Irish pantheon was constantly open to imaginative reshaping. New gods (Lir, Danu, Dalua, Orchil) bud forth unpredictably, while others (Bres, Brigit, perhaps Finn) undergo radical reshaping. This explains why creative mythography has always burgeoned in Ireland at precisely those traumatic moments when the gods seem on the verge of evanescence—post-conversion, in the af-termath of the Viking wars, and as the Irish language and Irish folk tradition retreated under extreme pressure. At all these points, re-trieval—revealed here as an imaginative rather than a forensic process—took off, resulting in a lack of purchase in the attempt to sort the authen-tic from the ersatz in the mythology. In weighing up the achievement of 'Fiona Macleod' I used the term *neomyth*, but in a sense even a famous

5 http://www.anphoblacht.com/contents/18386, accessed 3rd April 2015.

medieval tale such as 'The Tragic Deaths of the Children of Lir' is a neo-myth. It is a religious parable in which the roles happen to be filled by native supernatural figures; that it was written in Irish does not in itself make it more authentically 'mythological' than (say) the writings of William Sharp, crowded though they are with *mochrees*, Immortal Desires, and white wandering sea-waves. And yet if the pantheon's whole history is reception, the overall impression imparted is not one of insecure artifice, but of continual, metamorphic creativity.

Thirdly, the gods are perennially handled with an odd but characteristic combination of self-consciousness and the lack thereof. Much of the story I have traced recounts efforts at conscious synthesis made by groups of intellectuals, whom we observe again and again trying to bring myth and history—and the past and the present—into an orderly relationship. The classic example is the medieval synthetic history, the most elaborate imaginative edifice ever placed around the native gods. Similarly self-conscious were the efforts of Celtic Revivalists to reconfigure the native gods as living images—easier said than done—despite the irrationalism of the enterprise. Yeats and Russell approached the national unconscious with the same self-conscious ordering impulse that the medieval pseudohistorians had brought to bear upon the obscurities of the national past. Always the focus of attention centres not upon the gods, but rather passes through them to Ireland and Irishness itself. This at least was the pattern that prevailed until the emergence of contemporary Celtic Paganism, the only sphere in which this fundamental rule has been reversed; to modern devotees, Manannán, Lug, and Brigit may be invoked in Clare, Colchester, or California alike.

INVOKING IRELAND

If the Irish gods are still with us in popular and counter-cultural incarnations, they seem, however, to have abandoned high culture. What the future holds in this regard remains to be seen. The upheavals that have transformed Ireland over the past three decades are scarcely less dramatic than those that galvanized previous revivals of mythic writing, and Ciaran Carson's sinewy rendering of the *Táin* suggests that the time may be ripe for a new wave of literary translations.[6]

6 C. Carson, *The Táin: translated from the Old Irish epic Táin Bó Cúailnge* (London, 2007).

I want to finish, however, with an extraordinary figure whose work hints that cultural mileage may yet be left in the pantheon itself. This is the Kerry-born John Moriarty (1938–2007), whom the *Dictionary of Irish Biography* arrestingly lists as a 'philosopher and shaman'. Through a number of books—written in a disarmingly spiralling and elliptical style—Moriarty advocated an enlarged Christianity that would enfold and be enriched by pre-Christian myth:

> In Christ we see it. It isn't only that we are anthropically success-ful… Christian good news has it that we are deinanthropically successful. That we didn't hear, climbing between her breasts, from Danu. That we didn't hear from Manannán singing his Song of God to us at sea. That we didn't hear from headless Cú Roí. But that is no reason why we should forget or ignore these great pagan divinities… What is so terrible about polytheistic credence so long as we know that behind the gods and the world that ema-nate from it is the eternal divine One who is One only without a second? Danu showing her breasts, Manannán singing at sea, and Cú Roí walking headlessly yet unerringly south through Ire-land are immense theophanies, are immense revelations, per-suading us surely to go not for a break but for a continuity with our pagan past.[7]

Myth for Moriarty held profound spiritual, moral, and ecological signifi-cance. It amounts to humanity's interior wilderness, bound up with and mirroring the world of wild nature 'out there'. Irish mythology in par-ticular furnished his work with an inventory of metaphor and image. He diagnosed contemporary psychic fragmentation as a 'wasting sickness' or *serglige*, like that of Cú Chulainn, and identified the eye of the Fomo-rian king Balor with the 'modern economic eye', meaning the rapacious trammelling of the earth by human intention and purpose. Moriarty is far from the only Irish writer to have sounded a warning about the pace of change during the ill-fated boom years; the year after Moriarty's death, Seamus Heaney summed the situation up with the vivid image of

---

7 J. Moriarty, *Invoking Ireland: Ailiu Iath n-hErend* (Dublin, 2005), 216–7. Represen-tative works of Moriarty's include *Dreamtime* (Dublin, 1994, revised and expanded 1999), *Turtle Was Gone a Long Time: Crossing the Kedron* (Dublin, 1996)—the first part of a tril-ogy—and a two-volume autobiography, comprising *Nostos* (Dublin, 2001) and *What The Curlew Said: Nostos Continued* (Dublin, 2007).

the 'tiger now lashing its tail and smashing its way through the harp', ancient symbol of Ireland.[8]

Moriarty used native tradition to fashion something like an Irish version of Blake's prophetic books, and indeed his penultimate work, *Invoking Ireland*, was subtitled *Ireland, A Prophecy*, in imitation of the English poet. An odd, urgent work, it marked him out as a visionary in the mode of George Russell.[9] And as in Russell's work, and that of James Cousins and James Stephens, Indian influences abound. Caíntigern—mother of Mongán and Manannán's unwitting lover in 'The Voyage of Bran'—is redefined as the sea-god's 'most passionate gopi, his most passionate bhakti, his Irish Radha'—thus delineating Manannán himself as the Irish Krishna. Moriarty's project—which he termed not philosophical but 'philomythical'—is nothing less than the psychic introjection of the gods in the face of ecological and cultural crisis, to the end of national self-reconstitution:

> In Ireland from the beginning it is philomythically that we have been philosophical. In Ireland Manannán is our Socrates, Lugh is our Descartes and Cú Roí is our Kant.[10]

Without resort to the striking of atavistic poses, Moriarty proposes a corrective to contemporary problems rooted in the country's medieval tradition and mythic history. The gods offer a counterbalancing inheritance that can restore imaginative vitality. Moriarty writes:

> Much as Oisín has a long way to go in his Paganism so has St Patrick a long way to go in his Christianity. Here in Ireland, deepest Paganism and deepest Christianity can enrich each other to unity of vision, unity of voice. ... How can we be happy that our national eye is a Balar's eye? How come that Manannán's Gita-at-Sea isn't out national anthem? How come that the silver branch isn't blazon to our national flag, silver on purple?[11]

---

8 In a radio interview for BBC Ulster, http://news.bbc.co.uk/1/hi/northern_ireland/7272705.stm, accessed 3rd April 2012.

9 In filmed interviews there is something uncanny—orphic, in fact—about Moriarty, arising from the combination of the rhapsodic voice, shaggy white hair, and the gentle, androgynous cast of his features.

10 *Invoking Ireland*, 158. Note that to Moriarty these trios are not equivalents, but *opposites*: the three philosophers named—as representatives of anti-instinctual empiricism and conceptual logic—are not being flattered but found wanting by the comparison with the native gods.

11 *Invoking Ireland*, 221, 223.

This is a visionary phenomenology of the spirit, defining the pivotal event in the national narrative, not the Anglo-Norman invasion or the Easter Rising, but as the 'dreamtime' rebellion of the Túatha Dé Danann against the Fomorians.

Inevitably a position such as this was liable to provoke befuddlement and cynicism in some quarters, and Moriarty's voice has found no immediate echo.[12] Nonetheless, it represented the first Irish response to the national gods (outside academia) since the days of the Literary Revival. And, crucially, it was also a *total* response, for his writings double back over the entire tradition—modernist, revivalist, early modern, medieval, and pre-Christian—in an attempt to render it transparent to a spiritual and depth-psychological view. Here Jung was a clear influence, and Moriarty—who described himself as attempting to 'take up where Yeats and Lady Gregory left off'—can be seen as reviving the Celtic Mysteries project of activating the archetypes of the national unconscious, but now with a conscious emphasis on the ecological as well as the spiritual and aesthetic.[13]

Often Moriarty's takes on the native gods are completely original— sometimes a startling experience for the reader. For example, he reimagined Ériu, Banba, and Fódla—the three goddesses who give their names to Ireland in 'The Book of Invasions'—as superimposed dimensions of the country's eternal being, with Fódla in particular as wild landscape, untouched by human beings and 'dreaming itself'. The same originality is visible in the handling of Manannán mac Lir—the first pagan deity to appear in surviving medieval writing—who was clearly the most important divinity for Moriarty, embodying the transfigured mode of seeing he termed 'silver-branch perception'. (He would have been delighted by the affection for the Limavady statue.) Moriarty saw the mysterious double vision of the sea-god in 'The Voyage of Bran' as the result of shifting the attention outward and away from the ego,

12 In a 2012 memorial film named *Dreamtime, Revisited*, directed by Julius Ziz and Dónal Ó Céilleachair, Moriarty's words were blended with Terence Malick-style footage of waterfowl in flight and wind stirring through grasses. I was rapt, but Donald Clarke in the *Irish Times* thought it 'a priceless parody of Celtic windbaggery' [http://www.irish times.com/culture/film/dreamtime-revisited-1.551540, accessed 30th September 2015].

13 Depth psychology has so far made little use of Irish myth, in contrast to its saturation with classical stories; but note especially P. O'Connor, *Beyond the Mist: What Irish Mythology Can Teach Us About Ourselves* (London, 2000), and Jungian analyst Jim Fitzgerald's beautiful essay 'Story and the Interface with the Sacred in Irish Myth', in *Irish Culture and Depth Psychology* [= *Spring: A Journal of Archetype and Culture* 79] (Spring, 2008), 15–30.

granting the ability to perceive mythic and spiritual currents: it amounts to a mode of simultaneous poetic dwelling and poetic seeing. The phrase 'silver-branch perception' sounds vague and New Age, but with the concept Moriarty—trained as an academic philosopher—was drawing on major strands in continental thought, particularly the work of Martin Heidegger.[14]

Always Moriarty's work articulates the intimacy between pantheon and landscape. His account of the second battle of Moytura expresses this via a neomyth, elaborating on a minor incident not discussed before, in which the Dagda's magical harp—plus its player—are stolen by the Fomorians; Ogma, Lug, and the Dagda himself have to mount a commando raid to get it back. In the ninth-century saga relating the course of the battle, the theft of the harp is merely an outrageous act of provocation on the part of the gods' enemies. But Moriarty compellingly renames the harp 'Harmonizes Us to All Things', and transmutes it into a potent symbol of humanity as a part of, rather than apart from, creation.[15] With its loss the gods lose their closeness to nature, and 'Túatha Dé Danann' and 'Fomorian' are revealed not as ethnic identities, but as spiritual states:

> That very day, their tongues the colour and shape of cormorant's tongue, the Tuatha Dé were the new Fomorians.
> Only Ogma, being who he was, didn't capitulate to the countrywide epidemic of forgetfulness and brutishness.[16]

The allegory allows Moriarty—clearly self-identified with Ogma—to make his view of industrial modernity plain.

The link between the Túatha Dé Danann and landscape also leads Moriarty into a fascinating negative reading of the coming of the sons of Míl (the Gaels), whose arrival is depicted as a fall from grace rather than a triumph. In 'The Book of Invasions', the Milesian poet Amairgen sings

14 Heidegger's (difficult) thinking on 'being-in-the-world' has intrigued other eco-critics and eco-philosophers: Jonathan Bate has made extensive use of it in *The Song of the Earth* (London, 2000), 252ff.

15 This resembles neither of the names for the harp given in 'The Second Battle of Moytura': 'Oak of Two Meadows' (*Daur Dá Bláo*) and, more mundanely, *Cóir Cethairchuir*, which might be rendered—following Elizabeth Gray (*CMT*, 113)—the 'Fittingly Four-sided One'. (Or, taking *cor/cur*, 'putting, throwing, casting', in its specialized sense 'tune', possibly the 'Seemly One of Four Melodies'?)

16 *Invoking Ireland*, 27.

a famous and much-anthologized poem identifying with all aspects of the land which his people are about to wrest from the Túatha Dé:

I am a wind in the sea
I am a sea-wave upon the land...[17]

Older Celtic scholarship detected similarities between this poem and statements made by the god Krishna in the *Bhagavad Gita*, and when Moriarty places the two side by side, the informed reader expected to find yet another iteration of that hoary theme, the archaic affinity of Celt and Hindu.[18] But no: 'Listening to Krishna we are sure the "I" of his many "I ams" is the innermost Self, is atman Brahman, the Divine Ground of all being. Listening to Amhairghin we cannot be sure that the "I" of his "I ams" isn't ego, and if it is then we are dealing with the serious insanity of ego-inflation.'[19] Amairgen's song—long taken by Celtic enthusiasts as a vision of the unity of humanity and the creation—is seen darkly here as an act of 'Fomorian' hubris and presumption.

Moriarty commends an ecological and psychic sensitivity so acute that being and seeing are fused. And indeed *what the gods are* and *how to envision them* have been the signature questions of this study, even if it has emerged that it is in the nature of deities to disappear in the course of efforts to describe them. But perhaps now, amid economic upheaval, environmental degradation, and the painful unearthing of several venal and tragic dimensions to Irish life, that elusiveness can be imagined neither as divine caprice nor enforced exile, but as ecstatic self-effacement—Moriarty's own profound re-imagining of the Túatha Dé Danann's departure into the earth. 'In truth they were a race of gods, but... it was their particular delight to be of one mind with the wind and rain', he writes. 'In the end you could walk through the land and not know they were in it.'[20]

---

17 Thus Moriarty: there is no 'on the land' in the original, given in *LGE*, ed. & trans. R. A. S. Macalister (London, 1938–56), v., 110, 111.

18 Classic statement in Rees & Rees, *Celtic Heritage*, 99–100.

19 *Invoking Ireland*, 36.

20 *Invoking Ireland*, 25–6.

ACKNOWLEDGEMENTS

IN THE COURSE of their history the Irish gods have long been imagined as fairies, and—as Angela Carter once observed—'the realm of faery has always attracted nutters, regressives and the unbalanced'. I therefore must thank all the more those who tolerated me during the four years I spent preparing this book. It was begun while I was a Research Fellow at Peterhouse, Cambridge; my gratitude is due to the Master and Fellows of that college for their stimulating company, and especially to Chris Tilmouth and Mari Jones. It was completed during my time as a Fellow of Lincoln College, Oxford, and to the Rector and Fellows of that humane institution I owe a great debt, especially to my colleagues in English, Peter McCullough and Tim Michael, and to Susan Brigden, in History. I am especially grateful to the Michael Zilkha Trust at Lincoln College, which contributed generously to the costs of obtaining permissions and reproductions for the illustrations.

I have been constantly grateful for the enthusiasm of Ben Tate, editor extraordinaire at Princeton University Press, and of his colleague Hannah Paul. My gratitude is owed also to the staff of the University and English Faculty Libraries, Cambridge, and of the Bodleian and Taylorian Libraries, Oxford; special thanks must go to Owen McKnight of the Meyricke Library in Jesus College, for his unfailing helpfulness and patience.

This project was originally conceived as I finished my doctorate at Jesus College, Oxford, where Thomas Charles-Edwards—*mo aite forcitail*—was typically supportive as I roughed out its scope. Former colleagues in Cambridge's Department of Anglo-Saxon, Norse, and Celtic commented on this book as a work in progress; I am grateful for the advice of both Máire Ní Mhaonaigh and Paul Russell. John Carey's investigations into *Lebor Gabála* and the Mythological Cycle have proved a continual encouragement. Every third footnote in this book seems to cite his work, and my gratitude for his advice runs deep. An example: after I had finished chapter 5 but a year before this book went to press, he published a typically erudite piece on *Acallam na Senórach* which independently covered the same ground. It was his suggestion that I refer to his piece in the notes without substantially altering what I had already written—a much-appreciated act of graciousness. Heartfelt thanks are also owed to the Press's two anonymous reviewers, whose feedback prompted rewrites, sharpened up my thinking, and rescued me from a hefty clutch of omissions and errors. One of the two took me to task—with seraphic patience—for judging William Sharp ('Fiona Macleod') more harshly than either fairness or scholarship demanded, and so prompted an examination of conscience.

Heather O'Donoghue's research on the afterlife of Norse myth inspired the project, and I was grateful for her encouragement. Ronald Hutton fielded flustered emails when I heard (wrongly, as it turned out) that he was engaged upon a similar project. With characteristic kindness he went on to encourage my work, and it will be apparent to informed readers just how much I owe him. Roy Foster responded to the material on the gods' modern reception with galvanizing enthusiasm, helping to tie down some crucial arguments when I was wandering—like Yeats's Aengus—in territory not my own. Lizzie Boyle, Ralph O'Connor, Alderik Blom, and Mark Zumbuhl gave expert advice and encouragement. Geraldine Parsons was typically open-handed with her expertise on the Finn Cycle. Sinéad Garrigan-Mattar generously shared her own research on Yeats. Abigail Burnyeat organized an enjoyable conference on the Celtic Revival in Scotland. Ben Morgan was a heroic and consistently encouraging friend and housemate; he gave feedback on every aspect of the book and shepherded me through the final stages. The indefatigable Maggie Ross kept me anchored in the Deep Mind, while also advising on the parts of the book that touch on Christian theology. Melanie Marshall—who like the god Lug is *samildánach*, 'equally skilled in all the arts'—took my garbled initial thoughts and turned them into persuasive sentences. Kenneth Clarke, dear friend and formidable maven, took the time to read portions of the book when busy with his own work, as did Daniel Taylor, *dyfrgi annwyl*, who made me express myself more clearly. The splendid Bill Davies gave advice on music.

Justine Robinson, Greg Hill, Pauline Kennedy Allan, Bliss Vincent, Rhian Thomas, Sally Bayley, Ian Chamberlain, Dan Hedley, Jonathan Woolley, Janet Taylor, Elen Hawke, Carmella Elan-Gaston, and my former students Dan Sperrin and Natalie Cargill all read through some or all of the book in draft, or talked to me about the project, and their comments were greatly appreciated. Zoe Parsons gave me a wonderful place to live. Joe Hyames offered wisdom and insight. My brother Nick and my parents Hugh and Yvonne were a constant support. Carmen Reynal pumped out the psychic engine room with wisdom during a difficult but transformative few years. Ana Adnan embodied Blake's dictum that Energy is Eternal Delight, while Tony Kerridge offered much-needed relaxation. Last but not least, the great, the *trismegista* Christina Harrington of Treadwells Bookshop in London provided me with invaluable opportunities to inflict my ideas on a captive audience. I am also grateful that she found a home for a section cut from chapter eleven, which has appeared as 'Ella Young and Ross Nichols: Sourcing the Irish Gods', in *Abraxas* 6 (2014), 72–82.

I owe thanks to the following individuals and institutions for permission to reproduce images, and in many cases for the images themselves: The Design and Artists Copyright Society (DACS), acting on behalf of the estate of John Duncan; The Rutland Boughton Music Trust; the Dean and Chapter of St Patrick's Cathedral (Church of Ireland), Armagh; the National Monuments Service of the Department of Arts, Heritage and the Gaeltacht; the National Museum of Ireland; Frank Prendergast; Nikki Hamilton; Dundee City Council (Dundee's Art Galleries and Museums); National Galleries Ireland; The National Gallery of Scotland; Armagh County Museum; Inverclyde Council; Brigid Campbell; John Darren Sutton; Gerard Lovett; Amanda Panitch at Lippincott Massie McQuilkin; and to the Robert Gore Rifkind Collection, Beverly Hills. The drawing of William Sharp is © National Portrait Gallery, London. To the Bodleian Libraries, University of Oxford, I owe figures 9.6 and 11.4; the first is from D. A. Mackenzie's *Wondertales from Scottish Myth and Legend* (shelfmark 930 e. 529, pl. between pages 24 and 25), while the second is from Violet Russell's *Heroes of the Dawn* (shelfmark 930 e. 488, pl. between pages 4 and 5).

My thanks also go to the University of Chicago Press and Justine Hopkins for permission to quote from Michael Ayrton's novel *The Maze Maker*; to Faber & Faber, for quotations from Heaney, Pound, and Eliot; and to John Sinclair-Stevenson for the quotation from John Cooper Powys. The excerpt from 'Bogland' from *Opened Ground: Selected Poems 1966–1996*, © 1998 by Seamus Heaney, is reprinted by permission of Farrar, Straus and Giroux, LLC. The quotation from Patrick Kavanagh's 'Epic' is reprinted from his *Collected Poems*, edited by Antoinette Quinn (Allen Lane, 2004), by kind permission of the Trustees of the Estate of the late Katherine B. Kavanagh, through the Jonathan Williams Literary Agency. The epigraph to chapter eleven is by Ezra Pound, from *Guide to*

Kulchur, copyright ©1970 by Ezra Pound, reprinted by permission of New Directions Publishing Corp. The excerpt from 'East Coker' is from *Four Quartets* by T. S. Eliot. Copyright 1940 by T. S. Eliot. Copyright (c) renewed 1968 by Esme Valerie Eliot. Reprinted by permission of Houghton Mifflin Harcourt Publishing Company. All rights reserved.

A special demon lies in wait for those who attempt to cover millennial timespans in a single book. It will have ensured that errors—all mine—remain.

GLOSSARY OF
TECHNICAL TERMS

THE FOLLOWING DEFINITIONS are not comprehensive and are merely designed to make this book more useable to non-specialist readers. I have defined all these terms more fully in the course of the text when they first appear, but a crib may be needed at points.

Cú Chulainn   the great hero among the Ulstermen, and leading warrior in the epic *Táin Bó Cúailnge*

dindshenchas   literally the 'lore of notable places', meaning prose and verse traditions about how particular places came to get the names they have, often featuring mythological beings

druid   one of the magico-religious specialists of at least some Celtic-speaking peoples in the ancient world; in Ireland, normally a class of pagan magician and prophet

fénnid   in the earliest legal and narrative sources, a young aristocratic warrior between maturity and inheritance, who belongs to a *fian*-band and engages in a period of licensed living outside the law; in later literature often a mercenary or king's man

fían, pl. *fíana*   originally (and historically) a band of warrior-hunters living on the edges of society, often consisting of noble young men who have not yet inherited and become settled members of the community; in later literature a band of warriors or mercenaries, often in the service of a king

fili, pl. *filid*   literally 'seer', but referring to the secular class of learned poet-storytellers in the early Gaelic world

Finn mac Cumaill   legendary warrior-hunter and poet; leader of the literature's most celebrated *fian*-band

Fomorians   the enemies of the *Túatha Dé Danann* and other peoples attempting to settle Ireland; a supernatural race, sometimes associated with piracy and the sea, increasingly visualized as hideously deformed or demonic as the tradition developed

geis, pl. **gessi** a prohibited act, often emanating in some manner from the powers of the otherworld

gloss a comment written into a manuscript text, often between the lines or in the margin, usually explaining the sense or significance of the main text

glossary an early form of dictionary, usually designed to analyse the meanings of vernacular terms, in ways which often seem fanciful to us but were characteristic of medieval learned discourse

Lebor Gabála Érenn 'The Book of the Taking of Ireland': a complex, artificial, and highly influential prehistory of Ireland, compiled *c*.1075 but based on older traditions

neomyth my term for a myth made up in modernity, either using the characters of the medieval mythology, or introducing newly-invented ones, or both

ogam an alphabet specifically created for the Irish language, probably in the fourth century AD. It consists of strokes and notches, and was used originally for inscriptions along the edge of a stone, perhaps also on wood; these are almost always of the form '[the memorial] of X, son/descendant of Y...' and appear to have been grave and/or boundary markers

over-king a king with authority over other, less powerful kings, in Irish *ard-rí*

polytheology a coinage borrowed from contemporary Religious Studies, meaning propositions about the nature of multiple deities, and about their relationships to one another, to humans, and to creation

pseudohistory a body of narrative and genealogical data that we know to be artificial, but in which medieval (and later) people often placed considerable faith

saga a vernacular medieval narrative in prose or a mixture of prose and verse, set in past (often the legendary or semi-legendary past) and dramatizing a specific sequence of events

senchas 'lore', 'tradition': the body of geographical, genealogical, historical, and aetiological data and narrative which it was the medieval Irish learned poet's business to command

síd, pl. **síde** a mound or hill, sometimes natural but often a prehistoric tumulus, believed to be supernaturally inhabited; by extension, an otherworldly parallel dimension contiguous to our own

'(woman of) sovereignty' a personification of the land as a supernatural feminine figure depicted as the wife or sexual partner of a king. She is often beautiful when a king rules justly, and aged or ugly when his rule becomes unjust, and probably owes something to both Irish paganism and the personifications found in Christian scripture; *also* 'sovereignty goddess', 'woman of sovereignty'

synthetic history the elaborate artificial backstory for Ireland's past developed by Irish men of learning in the early Middle Ages, which reached its climax in *Lebor Gabála Érenn* (see above); *see also* pseudohistory

Tara the archaeologically rich Hill of Tara in Co. Meath, symbolic seat of Irish over-kingship

theomachy an Indo-European mythological theme, the war of the gods against supernatural enemies, or antigods

Túatha Dé Danann the 'Peoples of the goddess Danann' (or, in a slightly dubious philological reconstruction, 'of the goddess Danu'): name for the main Irish supernatural race, some of whom are reflexes of former deities. The name was developed *c.*1000, replacing earlier *Túath Dé* (among other terms)

Túath Dé the semi-divine 'god-people', earlier name for the *Túatha Dé Danann*, the people who (according to the synthetic history) lived in Ireland before the arrival of the Gaels, the ethnic Irish

CONSPECTUS OF MEDIEVAL SOURCES

THE FOLLOWING ARE the major medieval sources examined in Part One of this book and frequently referenced in Part Two. These texts may be unfamiliar to the general reader and this conspectus is provided in order to give non-specialists a basic *aide-memoire*. The translated title is given first, followed by the Irish name for the text and a likely date of composition. Something is then said about the manuscripts in which it is found, and a brief summary is given. It must be stressed how rare it is for a medieval Irish text to survive in a contemporary manuscript—very often there are several centuries between a text's supposed date of composition and our earliest copy. Also the dates and date ranges suggested must not be taken as conclusive; some texts can be more securely dated than others. A plus sign (+) following a date indicates that a text was subject to continuing and sometimes radical revision after the date of initial composition.

The *Acallam*: see 'The Colloquy of the Elders' below.

'The Adventure of Connlae' (*Echtrae Chonnlai*)   *c*.688–750?

Probably composed between the late seventh and mid-eighth centuries in a monastery on the border between Ulster and the midlands, this mixed prose-and-verse text survives in seven manuscripts, the earliest of which dates to the early twelfth century. It describes (largely through dialogue) how Connlae, son of king Conn of the Hundred Battles, is lured away to the otherworld by a mysterious woman. It is very short and may well be the earliest vernacular narrative composed in Irish—it is almost certainly the earliest to survive—and it is often taken to be a Christian allegory.

'The Battle of Ventry' (*Cath Finntrága*)   *c*.1450

A late tale which was composed in the form in which we have it in the fifteenth century, though there is evidence that a version of the story was in circulation as early as the twelfth. It survives in two manuscripts, both from the fifteenth century. It gives an account of a great battle lasting a year and a day between Finn mac Cumaill and his *fíana* on the one hand and the hosts of Dáire Donn, 'King of the Great World', on the other. At one point the Túatha Dé Danann are persuaded to intervene to help Finn and his men because of the extensive history of intermarriage between them and the *fíana*.

'The Book of Invasions' (*Lebor Gabála Érenn*)   *c*.1075 +

Probably the single most complex text to have come down to us from medieval Ireland, this is an elaborate and influential protohistory of the island in a mixture of prose and verse. Originally composed in the final quarter of the eleventh century, it was rapidly added to and repeatedly recast, resulting in four recensions, three medieval and one Early Modern. These recensions survive in a large number of manuscripts the correlation of which with one another is exceptionally tricky. The text tells the story of Ireland and its various waves of settlers and invaders from the time of Noah's Flood down to the era of the Gaels or 'Milesians', meaning the ethnic Irish themselves. The gods or Túatha Dé Danann are imagined to have been a race of pagan enchanters who held power over the island for several hundred years immediately before the arrival of the Gaels. This text is therefore a prime example of the 'euhemerizing' approach to the native gods—the strategy of explaining them away as powerful or exceptional human beings.

'The Colloquy of the Elders' (*Acallam na Senórach*)   *c*.1220

A composition of the early thirteenth century, probably in the west of Ireland, this is a tonally varied compendium of stories centring on the adventures of the hero Finn mac Cumaill and his band of warriors, which are narrated to St Patrick. Many stories within the text involve the blessings or malice of otherworld beings. Roughly the length of an average modern novel, it has a complex narrative structure of interlocking timeframes and tales nested within tales, and is missing its ending in all of the four manuscripts which have come down to us. Three of these are fifteenth century, while one is sixteenth century.

'The Conception of Cú Chulainn' (*Compert Con Culainn*)   *c.*725?

A fairly short early narrative recounting how the hero Cú Chulainn was fathered by the god Lug, albeit in a rather nebulous way and after two false starts. It forms part of the Ulster Cycle, one of the four great cycles of medieval Irish vernacular literature. The date is uncertain; while the earliest version (of two) survives in the twelfth-century manuscript known as *Lebor na hUidhre*, we know that the tale was included in a long-lost manuscript named the *Cín Dromma Snechtai*, which may have been written during the first half of the eighth century, though this is the subject of controversy. The tale *may*, therefore, be among the oldest surviving Irish sagas. There is also a later, Middle Irish version.

'Cormac's Glossary' (*Sanas Cormaic*)   *c.*900 +

A kind of early dictionary, the first version of this text was compiled around the turn of the tenth century and is associated with the king-bishop of Cashel, Cormac mac Cuilennáin (d. 908). It is one of a number of medieval Irish glossaries, the purpose of which was to set out and curate learned discourse by commenting on the meanings of individual words, some common, some obscure. 'Cormac's Glossary' survives in eight manuscripts, though in some cases only as a fragment. There are two basic versions, an earlier, shorter one (with seven hundred or so entries) and a later, longer one (with roughly thirteen hundred). But the text was also continually revised and added to up to the time of each manuscript's writing, so that the text—and individual entries within that text—grew with time, potentially drawing on other sources now lost to us. A significant number of entries seem concerned with the lore and learning of the *filid*, the professional poets. It often gives us information about native mythological figures, and while it cannot be relied upon it is nonetheless one of our most important sources of data about the native gods.

'The Fosterage of the House of Two Vessels' (*Altrom tigi dá medar*)   *c.*1400

A late saga of high quality, composed in the fourteenth or perhaps fifteenth century, which survives only in the fifteenth-century Book of Fermoy. It tells the story of how Eithne, a woman of the Túatha Dé Danann, undergoes a mysterious alteration in her nature and so becomes a saintly convert to Christianity, eventually encountering St Patrick and being baptized. As such it is a blend of mythological figures with the conventions of hagiography; it was much loved by the twentieth-century Irish poet Austin Clarke, who drew upon it in a number of works.

'The Lore of Ireland's Notable Places' (*Dindshenchus Érenn*)

*c.*1050 +

Both a set of specific texts and a recurrent strand in Irish medieval literature, *dindshenchus* refers to a body of lore about the features of Ireland's landscape, usually explaining how they got their names with reference to legendary events and persons; such explanations are usually wildly fanciful and clearly artificial from the modern point of view. The corpus consists of nearly two hundred poems plus associated prose commentaries (the 'Metrical *Dindshenchus*'), as well as a number of independent prose anecdotes (the 'Prose *Dindshenchus*'). The earliest *dindshenchus* poetry we have dates to the eleventh century; the earliest copy of the 'Metrical *Dindshenchus*' to survive is found (complete) in the twelfth-century Book of Leinster.

'The Phantom's Frenzy' (*Baile in Scáil*)   c.800–900 +

The core of this saga was written in the ninth century but then revised in the early eleventh. It survives in two manuscripts, one from the fifteenth and one from the sixteenth century. The god Lug—the 'phantom' of the title—lures King Conn of the Hundred Battles into a otherworldly feasting-hall and, in the form of a tall, handsome, enthroned man, he enumerates to Conn the names and regnal periods of the future kings of Tara. Also present with Lug is a young woman identified as the 'Sovereignty' of Ireland—the first appearance of a figure with a very long history in Irish literature and culture.

'The Scholars' Primer' (*Auraicept na n-Éces*)   c.650 +

One of the most interesting and difficult texts to have come down to us, the *Auraicept* is a handbook of vernacular grammatical and linguistic learning which provides our prime evidence for how medieval Irish *literati* conceptualized and analysed their own language. The core of the text may be seventh century, but it was extensively added to and revised over the centuries between the composition of this core and our first manuscript, the twelfth-century Book of Leinster.

'The Second Battle of Moytura' (*Cath Maige Tuired*)　　　*c.*875

The centrepiece of the so-called Mythological Cycle, this saga was probably composed in the ninth century, though a preamble was tacked onto the beginning in the eleventh. Alarmingly for such a crucial text, it survives only in one sixteenth-century manuscript written in a peculiar orthography; some of the verse included in it in particular is difficult to translate. It tells how the 'god-peoples' come to be oppressively ruled by Bres, a bad king whose mother belongs to the god-peoples but whose father belongs to their enemies, the Fomorians. Eventually the gods, with the help of the heroic Lug of the Long Arm, throw off Fomorian rule and are triumphant—for a time. There is also an Early Modern Irish version of the story.

'The Tragic Deaths of the Children of Lir' (*Oidheadh Chloinne Lir*)　　　*c.*1450

The best known of Irish mythological tales, this late story is really a religious fable which uses native supernatural beings to exalt the Christian virtue of fortitude. It tells how Lir's four young children are persecuted by their wicked stepmother, who changes them into swans. They endure in that manner for centuries until released by a saint, whereupon they are baptized and go to heaven. It was probably originally composed in the Franciscan monastery of Multyfarnam sometime in the fifteenth century; it was obviously very popular as it survives in whole or in part in approximately seventy manuscripts, the earliest of which dates from *c.*1600.

'The Tragic Deaths of the Children of Tuireann' (*Oidheadh Chloinne Tuireann*)　　　*c.*1500

A late tale, probably dating from the fifteenth or even early sixteenth century in the form in which we have it, though because a summarized earlier version is found in 'The Book of Invasions' we know the tale goes back to the eleventh century. It survives in at least three manuscripts of the eighteenth century and one from the very early nineteenth. It tells of murder and revenge within two great families among the Túatha Dé Danann, recounting how the three sons of Tuireann murder Cían, father of Lug. Lug then sets them a series of difficult tasks to complete in expiation, but in the end he coldly allows all three brothers to die, even though he could easily have healed them. The entire plot of the saga slots into the wider narrative arc recounted in 'The Second Battle of Moytura', though it is not mentioned in that text.

'The Voyage of Bran' (*Immram Brain*)   c.690–750

A relatively brief, mysterious, and early saga, composed in a mixture of prose and verse probably in the late seventh or early eighth century, and surviving in nine manuscripts, of which the earliest is the twelfth-century *Lebor na hUidhre*. It seems to remember and revise 'The Adventure of Connlae', with which it may be more or less contemporary. It tells the story of how Bran son of Febal journeys over the sea to 'the Land of the Women', encountering the sea-god Manannán mac Lir along the way. In a hallucinatory poem the god explains to him that what he, Bran, sees as ocean, Manannán experiences as a flowery plain. He then tells Bran that he is off to father the hero Mongán mac Fíachna—a historical person who died in 625—upon a mortal woman, in a way which is paralleled with the Incarnation of Christ.

'The Wooing of Étaín' (*Tochmarc Étaíne*)   c.800–1000

A ninth- or tenth-century saga (or set of three interlinked sagas), surviving in five manuscripts, the earliest of which dates to the twelfth century; the textual history of the saga is rather complex and scholars were only in a position to produce a full edition in 1930. This is a splendid and elaborate tale of magic and reincarnation, the narrative of which spans over a millennium. It starts in the period in which the 'god-peoples' rule Ireland, deep in the past, and moves, through three narrative phases or sub-tales, all the way down to the period around the lifetime of Christ, roughly speaking. It centres on the fate of the woman Étaín, sometime wife of the god Midir. It was much beloved by Anglo-Irish romantics, who lacked a full text and so tended to reconstruct the plot in idiosyncratic and (we now know) inaccurate ways.

WORKS CITED

PRIMARY SOURCES IN CELTIC
AND CLASSICAL LANGUAGES

Acallam na Senórach, ed. & partial trans. by W. Stokes, 'Acallamh na senórach', in W. Stokes & E. Windisch (eds.), *Irische Texte* (4 vols., Leipzig, 1880–1909), iv.

Airne Fingéin, ed. J. Vendryes (Dublin, 1953).

Altrom tigi dá medar, ed. & trans. M. C. Dobbs, 'Altromh tighi da medar', *ZCP* 18 (1930), 189–230.

——, ed. & trans. L. Duncan, 'Altram Tige Dá Medar', *Ériu* 11 (1932), 184–225.

The Annals of Inisfallen (MS. Rawlinson B. 503), ed. & trans. S. Mac Airt (Dublin, 1951).

The Annals of Tigernach, ed. & partial trans. W. Stokes, *RC* 16 (1895) 374–419; *RC* 17 (1896) 6–33, 116–263, 337–420; *RC* 18 (1897) 9–59, 150–303 [repr. 2 vols., Felinfach, 1993].

Aquinas, Thomas, *Summa Theologiae*, (61 vols., New York, 1964–73, reprnt. Cambridge, 2006).

Augustine, *De Civitate Dei*, trans. G. E. McCracken and W. Green, *The City of God against the Pagans* (7 vols., London, 1957–72).

Auraicept na n-Éces, ed. & trans. A. Ahlqvist, *The Early Irish Linguist: An Edition of the Canonical Part of the Auraicept na nÉces* (Helsinki, 1983).

Baile in Scáil: The Phantom's Frenzy, ed. & trans. K. Murray [ITS 58] (Dublin, 2004).

Bechbretha: an Old Irish Law-Tract on Bee-Keeping, ed. & trans. T. Charles-Edwards & F. Kelly (Dublin, 1983).

Bethu Phátraic: The Tripartite Life of Patrick, ed. K. Mulchrone (Dublin, 1939).

Bó Bithblich meic Lonán, ed. & trans. D. Clifford, 'Bó Bithblicht meic Lonán: eagrán de scéal faoi Fhlann mac Lonán', *Celtica* 25 (2007), 9–39.

——, ed. O. Bergin, 'A story of Flann mac Lonáin', in O. Bergin, *et al.* (eds.) *Anecdota from Irish manuscripts* (5 vols., Halle, 1907–13), i., 45–50.

The Book of Leinster, formerly Lebar na Núachongbála, ed. O. Bergin & R. I. Best, *et al.* (5 vols., Dublin, 1954–83).

'Bretha Déin Chécht', ed. O. Bergin, *Ériu* 20 (1966), 1–66.

Caesar, *Commentarii de Bello Gallico*, ed. & trans. H. J. Edwards, *The Gallic War* (Cambridge, MA, 1917).

Carmina Gadelica, ortha nan Gaidheal: hymns and incantations with illustrative notes on words, rites, and customs, dying and obsolete, ed. & trans. A. Carmichael, *et al.*, (6 vols., Edinburgh, 1928–71).

Cath Finntrága, ed. & trans. K. Meyer, *Cath Finntrága* (Oxford, 1885).

——, ed. & trans. C. O'Rahilly, *Cath Finntrágha* (Dublin, 1962).

Cath Maige Tuired, ed. & trans. W. Stokes, 'The Second Battle of Moytura', *RC* 12 (1891), 52–130, 306–8.

——, ed. & trans. E. A. Gray, *Cath Maige Tuired: The Second Battle of Mag Tuired* [ITS 52] (London, 1982).

Cath Maige Tuired Cunga, ed. & trans. J. Fraser, 'Cath Maige Tuired Cunga', *Ériu* 8 (1915), 1–63.

Cath Muighe Tuireadh, ed. B. Ó Cuív, *Cath Muighe Tuireadh: The Second Battle of Magh Tuireadh* (Dublin, 1945).

'The Cauldron of Poesy' ed. & trans. L. Breatnach, *Ériu* 32 (1981), 45–93.

Clement of Alexandria, *Stromata*, ed. J.-P. Migne, *Patrologia Graeca* (161 vols., Paris, 1857–86), ix.

'Cinaed ua hArtacain's poem on Brugh na Boinne', ed. & trans. L. Gwynn, *Ériu* 7 (1914), 210–38.

Cóir Anman: A Late Middle Irish Treatise on Personal Names, i., ed. & trans. S. Arbuthnot [ITS 59] (Dublin, 2005).

Compert Con Culainn and other stories, ed. A. G. Van Hamel (Dublin, 1933 [reprinted 1978]).

Compert Mongáin and Three Other Early Mongán Tales, ed. & trans. N. White (Maynooth, 2006).

Córus Béscnai, ed. D. A. Binchy, *Corpus Iuris Hibernici* (6 vols., Dublin, 1978).

Dá ernail déc na filidheachta, ed. R. Thurneysen, in W. Stokes and E. Windisch, *Irische Texte* (4 vols. in 5, Leipzig, 1880–1909), iii, 1, §2.

Dánta Grádha: an anthology of Irish love poetry (A.D. 1350–1750), ed. T. F. O'Rahilly (Dublin, 1926).

De Gabáil in tSíde, ed. & trans. V. Hull, '*De Gabáil in t-Sída*', *ZCP* 19 (1933), 53–58.

Duanaire Fhinn: The Book of the Lays of Fionn, ed. E. MacNeill & G. Murphy (3 vols., London, 1953).

Eachtra Airt meic Cuind ocus Tochmarc Delbchaime ingine Morgain, ed. & trans. R. I. Best, 'The Adventures of Art son of Conn, and the Courtship of Delbchæm', *Ériu* 3 (1907), 149-73.

Eachtra Thaidhg meic Chéin, ed. & trans. S. H. O'Grady, *Silva Gadelica: A Collection of Tales in Irish* (2 vols., London, 1892), i, 342–59, ii, 385–401.

Early Irish Lyrics: eighth to twelfth century, ed. & trans. G. Murphy (Oxford, 1956 [new edn. Dublin, 1998]).

Echtrae Chonnlai, ed. & trans K. McCone, *Echtrae Chonnlai and the Beginnings of Vernacular Narrative Writing in Ireland* (Maynooth, 2000).

'An Edition of the Pseudo-Historical prologue to the *Senchas Már*', ed. & trans. J. Carey, *Ériu* 45 (1994), 1–32.

Fled Dúin na nGéd, ed. & trans. J. O'Donovan, *The Banquet of Dun na n-Geadh and the battle of Magh Rath, An Historical Tale* (Dublin, 1842).

'The Four Jewels of the Tuatha Dé Danann', ed. & trans. V. Hull, *ZCP* 18 (1930), 73–89.

'Das Gedicht der Vierzig Fragen von Eochaid ua Cerin', ed. & German trans. R. Thurneysen, *ZCP* 13 (1921) 130–6.

Geoffrey of Monmouth, *Vita Merlini*, ed. & trans. B. Clarke, *Life of Merlin* (Cardiff, 1973).

Gerald of Wales, *Topographia Hibernie*, ed. J. J. O'Meara, *PRIA* 52 (C) (1948–50), 113–78, & trans. as *The History and Topography of Ireland* (London, 1951, revised 1982).

Gofraidh Fionn Ó Dálaigh, 'A Poem by Gofraidh Fionn Ó Dálaigh', ed. & trans. O. Bergin, in E. C. Quiggin (ed.), *Essays and Studies presented to William Ridgeway* (Cambridge, 1913), 323–33.

Gregory of Nazianzus, *Epistles*, in J. P. Migne, *Patrologia Graeca* (161 vols., Paris, 1857–86), xxxvii.

Historia Brittonum, ed. Th. Mommsen, *Chronica Minora Saec. IV. V. VI. VII.* [Monumenta Germaniae Historica AA 13] (Berlin, 1898).

——, ed. & trans. J. Morris, in *Nennius, British History, and the Welsh Annals* (London, 1980).

'How the Dagda Got his Magic Staff', ed. & trans. O Bergin, in R. S. Loomis (ed.), *Medieval Studies in Memory of Gertrude Schoepperle Loomis* (Paris, 1927), 399–406.

——, ed. & trans. S. Mac Mathúna, *Immram Brain: Bran's Journey to the Land of the Women* (Tübingen, 1985).

Immacaldam Choluim Chille 7 int Óclaig, ed. & trans. J. Carey, 'The Lough Foyle Colloquy Texts', *Ériu* 52 (2002), 53–87.

Immacallam in Dá Thuarad, ed. W. Stokes, *RC* 26 (1905), 4–64.

Immram Brain, ed. & trans. A. Nutt & K. Meyer, *The Voyage of Bran son of Febal to the Land of the Living* (2 vols., London, 1895–7 [partial reprt. Felinfach, 1994]).

The Irish Penitentials, ed. L. Bieler (Dublin, 1963).

Isidore of Seville, *Etymologiae*, ed. W. M. Lindsay, *Isidori Hispalensis Episcopi etymologiarum sive originum libri xx* (2 vols., Oxford, 1911).

Keating, Geoffrey (Seathrún Céitinn), *Foras feasa ar Érinn*, ed. & trans. D. Comyn & P. S. Dinneen, *Foras feasa ar Érinn: the history of Ireland* (4 vols., London, 1902–14).

'*Lebar Gabála, Recension I*', ed. & trans. J. Carey [unpublished PhD dissertation, Harvard University, 1983]).

Lebor Bretnach, ed. A. G. van Hamel, *Lebor Bretnach: the Irish version of the Historia Britonum ascribed to Nennius* (Dublin, 1932).

——, ed. & trans J. H. Todd, with intro. & notes by A. Herbert, *Leabhar breathnach annso sis: the Irish version of the Historia Britonum* (Dublin, 1848).

Lebor Gabála Érenn, ed. & trans. R. A. S. Macalister [ITS 34, 35, 39, 41, 44] (5 vols., London, 1938–56 [repr. London, 1993]).

Mesca Ulad, ed. J. C. Watson (Dublin, 1941).

The Metrical Dindshenchas, ed. & trans. E. J. Gwynn (5 vols., Dublin, 1903–35).

Muirchú, *Vita Patricii*, ed. and trans. L. Bieler, *The Patrician Texts in the Book of Armagh* (Dublin, 1979).

Navigatio sancti Brendani, ed. & trans. C. Selmer, *Navigatio sancti Brendani abbatis from Early Latin Manuscripts* (Notre Dame, IN, 1959)

——, ed. G. Orlandi & R. Guglielmetti, *Navigatio sancti Brendani: alla scoperta dei segreti meravigliosi del mondo* (Florence, 2014).

Noínden Ulad: The Debility of the Ulidians, ed. & trans. V. Hull, *Celtica* 8 (1968), 1–42.

Oidheadh Chloinne hUisneach: The Violent Death of the Children of Uisneach, ed. & trans. C. Mac Giolla Léith (London, 1993).

Oidheadh Chloinne Lir, ed. & trans. E. O'Curry, 'The Tri Thruaighe na Scéalaigheachta (i.e. the "Three Most Sorrowful tales") of Erinn, ii., The fate of the Children of Lir', *Atlantis* 4 (1863), 113–57;

——, ed. & trans. R. O'Duffy, *Oidhe Chloinne Lir; The fate of the children of Lir* (Dublin, 1883, 1897).

Oidhe Chloinne Tuireann: The Fate of the Children of Tuireann, ed. & trans. R. J. O'Duffy (Dublin, 1901).

——, 'Oidheadh Chloinne Tuireann: A Sixteenth Century Latin Fragment', ed. & trans. R. B. Bhreathnach, *Éigse* 1 (1939/40), 249–57.

'An Old Irish Tract on the Privileges and Responsibilities of Poets', ed. E. J. Gwynn, *Ériu* 13 (1940–2), 1–60, 220–36.

The Patrician Texts in the Book of Armagh, ed. L. Bieler with F. Kelly (Dublin, 1979).

Patrick, *Libri Epistolorum*, ed. L. Bieler, *Libri Epistolorum Sancti Patricii Episcopi* (2 vols., Dublin, 1952 [reprt. Dublin, 1993]).

——, ed. & trans. D. Howlett, *The Book of Letters of Saint Patrick the Bishop* (Blackrock, 1994).

'The Prose Tales in the Rennes *Dindshenchas*', ed. & trans. W. Stokes, *RC* 15 (1894) 272–336, 418–84.

Sanas Cormaic, ed. K. Meyer, *Sanas Cormaic: an Old Irish glossary compiled by Cormac úa Cuilennáin king-bishop of Cashel in the tenth century*, in O. Bergin, *et al.* (eds.), *Anecdota from Irish Manuscripts* (5 vols., Dublin & Halle 1913), iv.; useful single-volume reprnt. Llanerch, 1994; trans. in W. Stokes & J. O'Donovan (ed. & tr.), *'Sanas Chormaic': Cormac's Glossary* (Calcutta, 1868).

Senchas na relec, ed. & trans. K. Kilpatrick, 'The historical interpretation of early medieval insular place-names' [unpublished D.Phil thesis, University of Oxford, 2012], 393–404.

——, ed. & trans. J. O'Donovan, 'Senchas na relec in so', in G. Petrie, *An Essay on the Origin and Uses of Round Towers of Ireland* (1846), 97–101.

Serglige Con Chulainn, ed. M. Dillon (Dublin, 1953).

Táin Bó Cúailnge: Recension I, ed. & trans. C. O'Rahilly (Dublin, 1976).

Tecosca Chormaic, ed. & trans. K. Meyer, *The Instructions of King Cormac mac Airt* [RIA Todd Lecture Series 15] (Dublin, 1909).

Tírechán, '*Collectanea*', ed. and trans. L. Bieler, *The Patrician Texts in the Book of Armagh* (Dublin, 1979).

Tochmarc Étaíne, ed. & trans. O. Bergin & R.I. Best, *Ériu* 12 (1938), 137–96.

Tochomlad mac Miledh a hEspain i nErind, ed. & trans. M.E. Dobbs, 'Tochomlad mac Miledh a hEspain i nErind: no Cath Tailten?', *ÉC* 2 (1937), 50–91.

Togail Bruidne Da Derga, ed. E. Knott (Dublin, 1936).

Tóruigheacht Dhiarmada agus Ghráinne, ed. & trans. N. Ní Shéaghdha [ITS 48] (Dublin, 1967).

Trioedd Ynys Prydein: The Welsh Triads, ed. & trans. R. Bromwich [4th edn.] (Cardiff, 2014).

Uraicecht na Ríar, ed. & trans. L. Breatnach, *Uraicecht na Ríar: the poetic grades in early Irish law* (Dublin, 1987).

Vita Prima S. Brigitae, ed. J. Colgan, *Triadis Thaumaturgae... Acta* (Louvain, 1647), 527–42.

Virgil, *Aeneid*, ed. R. A. B. Mynors, *P. Vergili Maronis Opera* (Oxford, 1969).

PRIMARY SOURCES IN ENGLISH
AND SECONDARY WORKS

Ackroyd, P., *Blake* (London, 1995).

Aitchison, B., 'Kingship, society and sacrality: rank, power, and ideology in early medieval Ireland', *Traditio* 49 (1994), 45–75.

Alaya, F., *William Sharp—"Fiona Macleod"* (Cambridge, MA, 1970).

(Aldhouse-)Green, M., *The Gods of the Celts* (Gloucester, 1986).

——, *A Dictionary of Celtic Myth and Legend* (London, 1992).

——, *Celtic Goddesses* (London, 1995).

——, 'Gallo-British Deities and their Shrines', in M. Todd (ed.), *A Companion to Roman Britain* (Oxford, 2004).

——, *Caesar's Druids: An Ancient Priesthood* (London & New Haven, 2010).

Allen, N., *George Russell (Æ) and the New Ireland, 1905–1930* (Dublin, 2003).

Amaladass, A., 'Jesuits and Sanskrit Studies', *Journal of Indo-European Studies* 30 (1992), 209–31.

d'Arbois de Jubainville, M.-H., *Le Cycle mythologique irlandais et la mythologie celtique* (Paris, 1884), trans. R. I. Best, *The Irish mythological cycle and Celtic mythology* [Dublin & London, 1903]).

Bate, J., *The Song of the Earth* (London, 2000).

Beale, D., 'Landscapes and faery', *Apollo* (December, 2004), 70–75.

Beard, M., North, J., & Price, S., *The Religions of Rome: A History* (2 vols., Cambridge, 1999).

Belier, W. W., *Decayed Gods: Origin and Development of Georges Dumézil's Idéologie Tripartite* (Leiden, 1991).

Bennett, G., 'Geologists and Folklorists: Cultural Evolution and the Science of Folklore', *Folklore* 105 (1994), 25–37.

de Bernardo Stempel, P., 'A Welsh Cognate for Gaul. ανδοουννάβο?', *BBCS* 36 (1989), 102–5.

Bernhardt-House, P. A., *Werewolves, Magical Hounds, and Dog-headed Men in Celtic Literature: A Typological Study of Shape-Shifting* (Lewiston, 2010).

Beveridge, J., *Children into Swans: Fairy Tales and the Pagan Imagination* (Montreal & Kingston, 2014).

Bhreathnach, E., (ed.), *The Kingship and Landscape of Tara* (Dublin, 2005).

——, *Ireland and the Medieval World, AD 400–1000* (Dublin, 2014).

Bieler, L., 'Two Observations Concerning the *Navigatio Brendani*', *Celtica* 11 (1976), 15–7, reprt. in J. M. Wooding (ed.), *The Otherworld Voyage in Early Irish Literature: An Anthology of Criticism* (Dublin, 2000), 91–3.

Binchy, D. A., 'The Fair of Tailtiu and the Feast of Tara', *Ériu* 18 (1958), 113–38.

Black, R., 'I Thought He Made It All Up: Context and Controversy', in D. U. Stiùbhart (ed.), *The Life and Legacy of Alexander Carmichael* (2008), 57–61.

Blair Gibson, D., *From Chiefdom to State in Early Ireland* (Cambridge, 2012).

Blamires, S., *The Little Book of the Great Enchantment* (Arcata, CA, 2008).

Bonwick, J., *Irish Druids and Old Irish Religions* (London, 1894).

Borsje, J., 'Demonising the enemy: a study of Congal Cáech', in J. E. Rekdal, *et al.* (eds.), *Proceedings of the Eighth Symposium of Societas Celtologica Nordica* (Uppsala, 2007), 21–38.

——, 'Human sacrifice in medieval Irish literature', in J. Bremmer (ed.), *The Strange World of Human Sacrifice* (Leuven & Dudley, MA, 2007), 31–54.

——, 'Druids, deer, and "words of power": coming to terms with evil in medieval Ireland', in K. Ritari, *et al.* (eds.), *Approaches to Religion and Mythology in Celtic Studies* (Newcastle, 2008), 122–49.

——, 'Monotheistic to a Certain Extent: The "Good Neighbours" of God in Ireland', in A.-M. Korte & M. de Haardt (eds.), *The Boundaries of Monotheism: Interdisciplinary Explorations into the Foundations of Western Monotheism* (Leiden & Boston, 2009), 53–82.

——, 'Bodb', in J. T. Koch, *et al.* (eds.), *The Celts: History, Life, and Culture* (Santa Barbara, CA, 2012), i., 100–1.

Bourke, A., *The Burning of Bridget Cleary* (London, 1993).

——, 'Irish Stories of Weather, Time, and Gender: Saint Brigit', in M. Cohen & N. J. Curtin, (eds.), *Reclaiming Gender: Transgressive Identities in Modern Ireland* (London, 1999), 13–32.

Bown, N., *Fairies in Nineteenth-Century Art and Literature* (Cambridge, 2001).

Boyd, M. (ed.), *Coire Sois, The Cauldron of Knowledge: A Companion to Early Irish Saga* (Notre Dame, IN, 2014) [= reprints and revisions of articles by T. Ó Cathsaigh, cited under Ó Cathsaigh below].

Boyle, E., 'Allegory, the *áes dána* and the Liberal Arts in Medieval Irish Literature', in *Grammatica and the Celtic Vernaculars in the Medieval World*, ed. D. Hayden & P. Russell [forthcoming, 2016].

——, review of E. Bhreathnach, *Ireland in the Medieval World, AD 400–1000*, in *The Historical Review* [forthcoming, (?)2016].

Bramsbäck, B., *James Stephens: A Literary and Biographical study* (Uppsala, 1959).

Breatnach, C., 'The Historical Context of *Cath Fionntrágha*', *Éigse* 28 (1994–95), 138–55.

——, 'Cath Fionntrágha', *Léachtaí Cholm Cille* 25 (1995), 128–41.

——, *Patronage, Politics and Prose* (Maynooth, 1996).

——, 'The Religious Significance of *Oidheadh Chloinne Lir*', *Ériu* 50 (1999), 1–40.

——, '*Oidheadh Chloinne Tuireann* agus *Cath Maige Tuired*: dhá shampla de mhiotas eiseamláireach', *Éigse* 32 (2000), 35–46.

Breatnach, L., 'Poets and Poetry', in K. McCone & K. Simms (eds.), *Progress in Medieval Irish Studies* (Maynooth, 1996), 65–78.

——, *A Companion to the Corpus iuris hibernici* (Dublin, 2005).

——, 'Satire, Praise, and the Early Irish Poet', *Ériu* 56 (2006), 63–84.

Brown, C., *The Death of Christian Britain: Understanding Secularisation 1800–2000* (London, 2009 [2nd edn.]).

Brown, T., *Northern Voices: Poets from Ulster* (Dublin, 1975).

——, *Ireland: A Social and Cultural History 1922–79* (London, 1981).

——, & Hayley, B., (eds.), *Samuel Ferguson: A Centenary Tribute* (Dublin, 1987).

Bruford, A., *Gaelic Folk-tales and Medieval Romances: A Study of the Early Modern Irish 'Romantic Tales' and their Oral Derivatives* (Dublin, 1969).

Bryant, S., *Celtic Ireland* (1889).

Burl, A., *Rites of the Gods* (London, 1981).

Burns, M., *Perilous Realms: Celtic and Norse in Tolkien's Middle-Earth* (Toronto, 2005).

Butler, A., *Victorian Occultism and the Making of Modern Magic: Invoking Tradition* (Basingstoke, 2011).

Butler, J., 'Druidry in Contemporary Ireland', in M. Strmiska (ed.), *Modern Paganism in World Cultures: Comparative Perspectives* (Oxford, 2005), 87–125.

——, 'Irish Neo-Paganism: Worldview and Identity', in O. Cosgrove, *et al.* (eds.), *Ireland's New Religious Movements* (2011), 111–130.

Bynum, C. W., *Holy Feast and Holy Fast: the Religious Significance of Food to Medieval Women* (Berkeley, Los Angeles, & London, 1987).

——, *Metamorphosis and Identity* (New York, 2001).

Byrne, F. J., *Irish Kings and High-Kings* (Dublin, 1973).

——, 'The Viking Age', in D. Ó Cróinín, (ed.), *A New History of Ireland I: Prehistoric and Early Ireland* (Oxford, 2005), 609–34.

——, 'Ireland and her neighbours c.1014–1072', in D. Ó Cróinín, (ed.), *A New History of Ireland I: Prehistoric and Early Ireland* (Oxford, 2005), 862–98.

——, 'The Trembling Sod: Ireland in 1169', in A. Cosgrove (ed.), *A New History of Ireland II: Medieval Ireland (1169–1534)* (Oxford, 2008), 1–42.

Caball, M., & Hollo, K., 'The literature of later medieval Ireland, 1200–1600: from the Normans to the Tudors', in M. Kelleher & P. O'Leary (eds.), *The Cambridge History of Irish Literature* (2 vols., Cambridge, 2006), i., 74–139.

Caball, M., 'Lost in translation: reading Keating's *Foras feasa ar Éireann*, 1635–1847', in M. Caball & A. Carpenter (eds.), *Oral and printed cultures in Ireland, 1600–1900* (Dublin, 2010), 47–68.

——, & Hazard, B., 'Dynamism and declicine: translating Keating's *Foras Feasa ar Éirinn* in the seventeenth century', *Studia Hibernica* 39 (2013), 49–69.

Campbell, J. G., *Superstitions of the Highlands and the Islands of Scotland* (1900) and *Witchcraft and Second Sight in the Highlands and Islands* (1902), republished as *The Gaelic Otherworld*, ed. R. Black (Edinburgh, 2005).

Carey, J., 'The Name "Tuatha Dé Danann"', *Éigse* 18 (1981), 291–4

——, 'The Location of the Otherworld in Irish Tradition', *Éigse* 19 (1982), 36–43.

——, 'Early Irish Literature: The State of Research', in G. Mac Eoin, *et al.* (eds.), *Proceedings of the Sixth International Congress of Celtic Studies* (Dublin, 1983), 113–30.

——, 'Notes on the Irish war-goddess', *Éigse* 19 (1983), 263–75.

——, '*Scél Tuáin meic Chairill*', *Ériu* 35 (1984), 93–111.

——, 'Nodons in Britain and Ireland', *ZCP* 40 (1984), 1–22.

——, 'The Irish Vision of the Chinese', *Ériu* 38 (1987), 73–80.

——, 'The Origin and Development of the Cessair Legend', *Éigse* 22 (1987), 37–48.

——, 'Time, Space, and the Otherworld', *PHCC* 7 (1987), 1–27.

——, 'Myth and Mythography in *Cath Maige Tuired*', *Studia Celtica* 24–5 (1989–90), 33–69.

——, 'The Ancestry of Fénius Farsaid', *Celtica* 21 (1990), 104–12.

——, Time, Memory, and the Boyne Necropolis', *PHCC* 10 (1990), 24–36.

——, 'The Two Laws in Dubthach's Judgment', *CMCS* 19 (1990), 1–18.

———, 'A *Tuatha Dé* Miscellany', ed. & trans. J. Carey, *BBCS* 39 (1992), 24–45.

———, *A new introduction to Lebor Gabála Érenn, the Book of the Taking of Ireland*, edited and translated by R. A. Stewart Macalister (Dublin, 1993).

———, *The Irish National Origin-Legend: Synthetic Pseudohistory* [Quiggin Pamphlets on the Sources of Mediaeval Gaelic History 1, 1994].

———, 'The Uses of Tradition in *Serglige Con Chulainn*', in J. P. Mallory & G. Stockman (eds.), *Ulidia: Proceedings of the First International Conference on the Ulster Cycle of Tales* (Belfast, 1994), 85–90.

———, 'On the interrelationships of some Cín Dromma Snechtai texts', *Ériu* 46 (1995) 71–92.

———, 'Native elements in Irish pseudohistory', in D. Edel, *Cultural Identity and Cultural Integration: Ireland and Europe in the Early Middle Ages* (Dublin, 1995), 45–60.

———, 'The Rhetoric of *Echtrae Chonlai*', *CMCS* 30 (1995), 41–65.

———, 'Obscure styles in medieval Ireland', *Mediaevalia* 19 (1996), 23–39.

———, 'Saint Patrick, the Druids, and the End of the World', *History of Religions* 36:1 (1996), 42–53.

———, 'The Three Things Required of a Poet', *Ériu* 48 (1997), 41–58.

———, *King of Mysteries: Early Irish Religious Writing* (Dublin, 1998).

———, *A Single Ray of the Sun: Religious Speculation in Early Ireland* (Andover, MA, & Aberystwyth, 1999).

———, 'Transmutations of Immortality in "The Lament of the Old Woman of Beare"' *Celtica* 23 (1999), 30–7.

———, 'Nodons, Lugus, Windos', in C.-M. Ternes, *et al.* (eds.), *Dieux des Celtes/Goetter der Kelten/Gods of the Celts* (Luxembourg, 2002), 99–126.

———, *Lebor Gabála* and the legendary history of Ireland', in H. Fulton (ed.), *Medieval Celtic Literature and Society* (Dublin, 2005), 32–48.

———, 'Tara and the Supernatural', in E. Bhreathnach (ed.), *The Kingship and Landscape of Tara* (Dublin, 2005), 32–48.

———, 'Tuath Dé', in J. T. Koch (ed.), *Celtic Culture: A Historical Encyclopedia* (5 vols., Oxford and Santa Barbara, 2006), v., 1693–6.

———, *Ireland and the Grail* (Aberystwyth, 2007).

———, 'From David to Labraid: sacral kingship and the emergence of monotheism in Israel and Ireland', in K. Ritari, *et al.* (eds.), *Approaches to Religion and Mythology in Celtic Studies* (Newcastle, 2008), 2–27.

———, 'Celtic **lugus* 'lynx': A phantom Big Cat?', in F. Josephson (ed.), *Celtic Language, Law and Letters: Proceedings of the Tenth Symposium of Societas Celtologica Nordica* (Gothenburg, 2008), 151–68.

——, '*Dee* "Pagan Deity" ', *Ériu* 62 (2012) 33–42.

——, '*Acallam na senórach*: a conversation between worlds', in A. Doyle & K. Murray, *In Dialogue with the Agallamh: Essays in Honour of Seán Ó Coileáin* (Dublin, 2014), 76–89.

——, 'In search of Mael Muru Othna', in E. Purcell & P. MacCotter, *et al.* (eds.) *Clerics, Kings and Vikings: Essays on Medieval Ireland in Honour of Donnchadh Ó Corráin* (Dublin, 2015), 429–39.

Carney, J., *Studies in Irish Literature and History* (Dublin, 1955).

——, 'The Deeper Level of Early Irish Literature', *Capuchin Annual '69* (1969), 160–71.

——, 'Language and Literature to 1169', in D. Ó Cróinín, (ed.), *A New History of Ireland I: Prehistoric and Early Ireland* (Oxford, 2005), 451–510.

Carr-Gomm, P., *The Druid Way* (Shaftesbury, 1993).

Carson, C., *The Táin: translated from the Old Irish epic Táin Bó Cúailnge* (London, 2007).

Charles-Edwards, T. M. O., 'The Social Background to Irish *Perigrinatio*', *Celtica* 11 (1976), 43–59.

——, *Early Irish and Welsh Kinship* (Oxford, 1993).

——, '*Mi a dynghaf dynghed* and related problems' in J. F. Eska, *et al.* (eds.), *Hispano-Gallo-Brittonica: Essays in honour of Professor D. Ellis Evans on the occasion of his sitxty-fifth birthday* (Cardiff, 1995), 1–15.

——, 'The Context and Uses of Literacy in Early Christian Ireland', in H. Pryce (ed.), *Literacy in Medieval Celtic Societies* (Cambridge, 1998), 62–82.

——, *The early mediaeval Gaelic lawyer* [Quiggin Pamphlets on the Sources of Mediaeval Gaelic History 4] (Department of Anglo-Saxon, Norse, and Celtic, University of Cambridge, 1999).

——, *Early Christian Ireland* (Cambridge, 2000).

——, '*Tochmarc Étaíne*: A Literal Interpretation', in J.-M. Picard & M. Richter (eds.), *Ogma: Essays in Celtic Studies in Honour of Próinséas Ní Chatháin* (Dublin, 2002), 165–181.

——, (ed.), *After Rome* (Oxford, 2003).

——, 'Introduction: Prehistoric and Early Ireland', in D. Ó Cróinín, (ed.), *A New History of Ireland I: Prehistoric and Early Ireland* (Oxford, 2005), lvii–lxxxii.

——, 'Early Irish Law', in D. Ó Cróinín, (ed.), *A New History of Ireland I: Prehistoric and Early Ireland* (Oxford, 2005), 353–4.

——, *Wales and the Britons, 350–1064* (Oxford, 2013).

Chaucer, G., *The Riverside Chaucer*, ed. L. D. Benson, *et al.*, (3rd edn., Oxford, 2008).

Chesnutt, M., 'Cath Maige Tuired—A parable of the Battle of Clontarf', in S. Ó Catháin (ed.), *Northern Lights: Following Folklore in North-Western Europe* (Dublin, 2001), 22–33.

Christensen, M. J., & Wittung, J., (eds.), *Partakers of the Divine Nature: the History of Development of Deification in the Christian Traditions* (Madison, 2007).

Clancy, T. O., 'Women poets in early medieval Ireland: stating the case' in C. Meek & K. Simms (eds.), *The Fragility of her Sex? Medieval Irishwomen in their European Context* (Dublin, 1996), 43–72.

——, 'Scotland, the "Nennian" Recension of the *Historia Brittonum*, and the *Lebor Bretnach*', in S. Taylor (ed.), *Kings, Clerics and Chronicles in Scotland, 500–1297* (Dublin, 2000), 87–107.

Clarke, A., *The Sword of the West* (Dublin, 1921).

——, *The Singing-Men at Cashel* (London, 1936).

——, *The Sun Dances at Easter: a romance* (London, 1952).

——, *Collected Poems of Austin Clarke*, ed. L. Miller (Dublin, 1974).

Clarke, M., 'The lore of the monstrous races in the developing text of the Irish *Sex aetates mundi*', *CMCS* 63 (Summer, 2012), 15–50.

——, 'Linguistic Education and Literary Creativity in Medieval Ireland', in P. Ronan (ed.), *Cahiers de l' Institut de Linguistique et des Sciences des Langues* 38 (Lausanne, 2013), 39–71.

——, 'Demonology, Allegory and Translation: the Furies and the Morrígan', in R. O'Connor (ed.), *Classical Literature and Learning in Medieval Irish Narrative* (Cambridge, 2014), 101–22.

Cleary, J. (ed.), *The Cambridge Companion to Irish Modernism* (Cambridge, 2014).

Clifton, C., *Her Hidden Children: The Rise of Wicca and Paganism in America* (Lanham, MD, 2006).

Comerford, T., *History of Ireland from the Earliest Accounts of Time to the Invasion of the English under King Henry II* (London, 1751).

Cooney, G., *Landscapes of Neolithic Ireland* (Abingdon, 2000).

Cosgrove, A., (ed.), *A New History of Ireland II: Medieval Ireland (1169–1534)* (Oxford, 2008) [= vol. 2 of F. J. Byrne, *et al.*, (eds.), *A New History of Ireland* (9 vols., Oxford, 1982–2011)].

Costello, P., *The heart grown brutal: the Irish revolution in literature from Parnell to the death of Yeats* (Dublin, 1977).

Cousins, J., *The Quest* (Dublin, 1906).

——, *Etain the Beautiful* (Dublin, 1912).

——, *The Wisdom of the West: An Introduction to the Interpretative Study of Irish Mythology* (London, 1912).

——, *The Cultural Unity of Asia* (Adyar, Madras, 1922).

——, *Collected Poems (1894–1940)* (Madras, 1940).

——, & M. Cousins, *We Two Together: A Duo-Autobiography* (Madras, 1950).

Cowell, H., *Piano Music: Volume Two* (Associated Music Publishers, New York, 1982).

Cross, J. W., *George Eliot's Life as related in her Letters and Journals* (3 vols., Edinburgh & London, 1885).

Cross, T. P., & Slover, C. H. (trans.), *Ancient Irish Tales* (1st edn. 1936, repnt. New York, 1996).

Crowe, M. J., *The Extraterrestrial Life Debate, 1750–1900: the idea of a plurality of worlds from Kant to Lowell* (Cambridge, 1986).

Cunningham, B., *The world of Geoffrey Keating: history, myth and religion in seventeenth-century Ireland* (Dublin, 2000).

Dagger, C., 'Eithne ban-dia agus ban-naomh', *Léachtaí Cholm Cille* 15 (1985), 61–78.

——, 'Eithne: the sources' *ZCP* 43 (1989), 84–124.

Dalton, J. P., 'Cromm Cruaich of Magh Sleacht', *PRIA* 36 (C) (1921–4), 23–67.

Dante Alighieri, *La Commedia secondo l'antica vulgata*, ed. by G. Petrocchi (4 vols., Florence, 1994).

Deane, J. F., *All Dressed Up: Modern Irish Historical Pageantry* (Syracuse, NY, 2014).

Deane, M., 'From sacred marriage to clientship: a mythical account of the establishment of kingship as an institution', in R. Schot, *et al.* (eds.), *Landscapes of Cult and Kingship* (Dublin, 2011), 1–21.

Deane, S., 'Literary myths of the Revival: a case for their abandonment', in J. Ronsley (ed.), *Myth and Reality in Irish Literature* (Waterloo, Ontario, 1977), 317–29.

——, *Strange Country: modernity and nationhood in Irish writing since 1790* (Oxford, 1996).

De Barra, S., 'Into the Twilight: Arnold Bax and Ireland', *The Journal of Music in Ireland* 4/3 (March–April 2004), 25–9.

Dentith, S., *Epic and Empire in Nineteenth-century Britain* (Cambridge, 2006).

Dillon, M., *Early Irish Literature* (Chicago, 1948).

Di Martino, V., *Roman Ireland* (Cork, 2003).

Doherty, C., 'Kingship in Early Ireland', in E. Bhreathnach (ed.), *The Kingship and Landscape of Tara* (Dublin, 2005), 3–31.

Doniger, W., *The Hindus: An Alternative History* (Oxford, 2010).

Dooley, A., & Roe, H., *Tales of the Elders of Ireland* (Oxford, 1999).

Dooley, A., 'Early Irish literature and contemporary scholarly disciplines', in R. Wall (ed.), *Medieval and Modern Ireland* (New Jersey, 1988), 68–71.

——, 'The Date and Purpose of *Acallam na Senórach*', *Éigse* 34 (2004), 97–126.

——, *Playing the Hero: Reading the Irish Saga* Táin Bó Cúailnge (Toronto, 2006).

——, 'Pagan Beliefs and Christian Redress in *Acallam na Senórach*', in J. Borsje *et al.* (eds.), *Celtic Cosmology: Perspectives from Ireland and Scotland* (Toronto, 2014), 249–67.

Doty, W. G., *Mythography: The Study of Myths and Rituals* (Tuscaloosa, 2000 [2nd edn.]).

Doyle, A., & Murray, K., (eds.), *In Dialogue with the Agallamh: essays in honour of Seán Ó Coileáin* (Dublin, 2014).

Doyle, A., *A History of the Irish Language from the Norman Invasion to Independence* (Oxford, 2015).

Duffy, P., Edwards, D., & FitzPatrick, E., (eds.), *Gaelic Ireland, c.1250-c.1650: land, lordship and settlement* (Dublin, 2001).

Dumbleton, W. A., *James Cousins* (Boston, MA, 1980).

Dumézil, G., *Jupiter, Mars, Quirinus* (Paris, 1941).

——, *Mythe et épopée* (Paris, 1961).

Dumville, D., 'Two Approaches to the Dating of *Navigatio Sancti Brendani*', *Studi Medievale* 29 ser. 3.1 (1988), 87–102.

——, & Abrams, L., (eds.), *Saint Patrick, A.D. 493–1993* (Woodbridge, 1999).

——, *The Early Medieval Insular Churches and Preservation of Roman Literature* (2nd edn., Department of Anglo-Saxon, Norse, and Celtic, University of Cambridge, 2004).

Dunham, S. B., 'Caesar's perception of Gallic social structures', in B. Arnold & D. Blair Gibson (eds.), *Celtic Chiefdom, Celtic State* (Cambridge, 1995), 110–5.

Duval, P.-M., *Les dieux de la Gaule* (Paris, 1993).

Earl, J. W., 'Typology and Iconographic Style in Early Medieval Hagiography', *Studies in the Literary Imagination* 8 (1975), 15–46.

Edel, D., ' "Bodily Matters" in Early Irish Narrative Literature', *ZCP* 55 (2006), 69–107.

Edwards, N., 'The Archaeology of early medieval Ireland, c.400–1169: Settlement and Economy', in D. Ó Cróinín, (ed.), *A New History of Ireland I: Prehistoric and Early Ireland* (Oxford, 2005), 235–300.

Ellis Evans, E., *Gaulish Personal Names* (Oxford, 1967).

Etchingham, C., *Church organisation in Ireland, A.D. 650 to 1000* (Maynooth, 1999).

Ettlinger, E., 'Contributions to an interpretation of several stone images in the British Isles', *Ogam* 13 (1961), 286–304.

Evans-Wentz, W. Y., *The Fairy-Faith in Celtic Countries* (Oxford, 1911).

Ewans, M., *Opera from the Greek: Studies in the Poetics of Appropriation* (Aldershot, 2007).

Feeney, D. C., *The Gods in Epic: Poets and Critics of the Classical Tradition* (Oxford, 1991).

Ferguson, S., *Congal: a poem, in five books* (Dublin & London, 1872).

Ferriter, D., *The Transformations of Ireland, 1900–2000* (London, 2004).

Fimi, D., ' "Mad" Elves and "elusive beauty": some Celtic strands of Tolkien's mythology', *Folklore* 117.2 (2006), 156–70.

——, *Tolkien, Race and Cultural History: From Fairies to Hobbits* (Basingstoke, 2008).

Fitzgerald, D., 'Early Celtic History and Mythology', *RC* 6 (1883–5), 193–259.

Fitzgerald, J., 'Story and the Interface with the Sacred in Irish Myth', in *Irish Culture and Depth Psychology* [= *Spring: A Journal of Archetype and Culture* 79] (Spring, 2008), 15–30.

Flanagan, M. T., *Irish Society, Anglo-Norman Settlers, Angevin Kingship: Interactions in Ireland in the Late Twelfth Century* (Oxford, 1989).

——, *The Transformation of the Irish Church in the Twelfth Century* (Woodbridge, 2010).

Flannery, M. C., *Yeats and Magic: The Earlier Works* (Gerrards Cross, 1977).

Flechner, R., 'Patrick's Reasons for Leaving Britain', in P. Russell & F. L. Edmonds (eds.), *Tome: Studies in Medieval History and Law* (Woodbridge, 2011), 125–34.

——, & M. Ní Mhaonaigh (eds.), *Converting the Isles* (Turnhout, 2016).

Fletcher, R., *The Conversion of Europe: From Paganism to Christianity, 371–1386 AD* (London, 1997).

Flint, K. C. [= Casey Flynn], *The Riders of the Sidhe* (New York, 1984).

——, *Champions of the Sidhe* (New York, 1985).

——, *Master of the Sidhe* (New York, 1985).

——, *Most Ancient Song* (New York, 1991).

——, *The Enchanted Isles* (New York, 1991).

Flower, R., *Catalogue of Irish manuscripts in the British Museum* (London, 1926).

Foley, T., & O'Connor, M., (eds.), *Ireland and India: Colonies, Culture and Empire* (Dublin, 2006).

Fomin, M., et al. (eds.), *Sacred Topology in Early Ireland and Ancient India: Religious Paradigm Shift* (Washington, DC, 2010).

Ford, P. K., 'The blind, the dumb, and the ugly: aspects of poets and their craft in early Ireland and Wales', *CMCS* 19 (1990), 27–40.

——, 'The *which* on the wall; obscenity exposed in early Ireland', in J. M. Ziolkowski, *Obscenity: Social Control and Artistic Creation in the European Middle Ages* (Leiden, 1998), 176–90.

Foreman, L., *Bax: a Composer and his Times* (Aldershot, 1983, 1987; 3rd edn, Woodbridge, 2007).

Foster, J. W., 'The Revival of Saga and Heroic Romance during the Irish Renaissance: The Ideology of Cultural Nationalism', in H. Kosok (ed.), *Studies in Anglo-Irish Literature* (Bonn, 1982), 126–36.

——, *Fictions of the Irish Literary Revival: A Changeling Art* (Syracuse, NY, 1987).

Foster, R., *Modern Ireland, 1600–1972* (London, 1989).

——, *Paddy and Mr Punch: Connections in Irish and English History* (London, 1993).

——, *W. B. Yeats, A Life: I. The Apprentice Mage, 1865–1914* (Oxford, 1998).

——, *The Irish Story: Telling Tales and Making It Up in Ireland* (London, 2001).

——, *W. B. Yeats, A Life: II. The Arch-Poet, 1915–1939* (Oxford, 2003).

——, *Words Alone: Yeats and his Inheritances* (Oxford, 2011), 39.

Gantz, J., *Early Irish Myths and Sagas* (London, 1981).

Garner, A., *The Weirdstone of Brisingamen: a Tale of Alderley* (London, 1960).

Garrigan-Mattar, S., 'Reviewing the Celt: The Revue Celtique and Irish Celticism', *Bullán: an Irish Studies Journal* V.2 (Winter/Spring 2001), 55–74.

——, *Primitivism, Science, and the Irish Revival* (Oxford, 2004).

——, 'Yeats, Fairies, and the New Animism', *New Literary History* 43.1 (Winter 2012), 137–57.

Gibson, M., Trower, S., et al. (eds.), *Mysticism, Myth and Celtic Identity* (New York & Abingdon, 2013).

Goss, G., 'Women, Gender, and Sexuality in Late Medieval Irish *Románsaíochtai*', in S. Sheehan & A. Dooley (eds.), *Constructing Gender in Medieval Ireland* (New York, 2013), 153–170.

Gould, W., ' "The Music of Heaven": Dorothea Hunter', *YA* 9 [= *Yeats and Women*] (2nd edn., Basingstoke, 1997), 73–134.

Graf, S. J., 'Heterodox Religions in Ireland: Theosophy, the Hermetic Society, and the Castle of Heroes', *Irish Studies Review* 11.1 (2003), 51–9.

——, *Talking to the Gods: Occultism in the Work of W. B. Yeats, Arthur Machen, Algernon Blackwood, and Dion Fortune* (Albany, NY, 2015).

Grafton, A., et al. (eds.), *The Classical Tradition* (Cambridge, MA & London, 2010).

Graham, C., *Ideologies of Epic: Nation, Empire, and Victorian Epic Poetry* (Manchester & New York, 1998).

Gray, B., 'Reading *Aislinge Óenguso* as a Christian-Platonist Parable', *PHCC* 24 (2004), 16–39.

Gray, E. A., '*Cath Maige Tuired*: Myth and Structure', *Éigse* 18 (1980–1), 183–209, and Éigse 19 (1982–3), 1–35, 230–62.

——, 'Lug and Cú Chulainn: King and Warrior, God and Man', *SC* 24/5 (1989/90), 38–52.

Graziosi, B., *The Gods of Olympus: A History* (London, 2013).

Green, P., *Classical Bearings: Interpreting Ancient History and Culture* (London, 1989).

Gregory, A., *Cuchulainn of Muirthemne* (London, 1902).

——, *Gods and Fighting Men: The Story of the Tuatha De Danaan and of the Fianna of Ireland* (London, 1904).

Gregory, T., *From Many Gods to One* (Chicago, 2006).

Gruffudd, W. J., 'Donwy', *BBCS* 7.1 (1933), 1–4

Guinness, S., 'Visions and Beliefs in the West of Ireland: Irish Folklore and British Anthropology, 1898–1920', *Irish Studies Review* 6:1 (1998), 37–46.

Guyonvarc'h, C.-J., *The Making of a Druid: Hidden Teachings from 'The Colloquy of Two Sages'* (Rochester, VT, 2002, original French edn. 1999).

Hagan, E. A., *'High Nonsensical Words': A Study of the Works of Standish James O'Grady* (Troy, NY, 1986).

Hall, A., *Elves in Anglo-Saxon England: Matters of Belief, Health, Gender, and Identity* (Woodbridge, 2007).

Hambro, C., 'Waiting for Christian Fish and Milk from India: A Textual and Contextual Analysis of *Altram Tige Dá Medar* ("The Nourishment of the House of Two Milk Vessels")' [unpublished Ph.D dissertation, University of Oslo, 2011].

Hamp, E. P., 'Varia I: 4. *Banba* again', *Ériu* 24 (1973), 169–71.

——, 'Old Irish *Credne, cerd*, Welsh *cerdd*', in J. T Koch, J. Carey, & P.-Y. Lambert (eds.), *Ildánach, Ildírech: A Festschrift for Proinsias Mac Cana* (Andover, 1999), 49–51.

——, 'The Dag(h)d(h)ae and his relatives', in L. Sawicki & D. Shalev (eds.), *Donum grammaticum: Studies in Latin and Celtic Linguistics in Honour of Hannah Rosén* (Leuven, 2002), 163–169.

Harmon, M., 'The Sword of the West (1921, 1936, 1974)', Études Irlandaises 10 (December, 1985), 93–104.

——, Austin Clarke 1896–1974: A Critical Introduction (Dublin, 1989).

——, The colloquy of the old men (Acallam na senórach) (Dublin, 2001).

——, 'The Colloquy of the Old Men; Shape and Substance', in P. A. Lynch, et al. (eds.), Back to the Present, Forward to the Past: Irish Writing and History since 1798 (2 vols., New York, 2006), ii., 123–34.

Harper, G. M., Yeats's Golden Dawn (London, 1974).

——, (ed.), Yeats and the Occult (London, 1976).

Harrington, C., Women in a Celtic Church, Ireland 450–1150 (Oxford, 2002).

Harvey, A., 'Early Literacy in Ireland', CMCS 14 (Winter, 1987), 1–15.

Heaney, M., Over Nine Waves: A Book of Irish Legends (London, 1994).

Hellmuth, P. S., 'The Dindshenchas and Irish literary tradition', in J. Carey et al. (eds.), Cín Chille Chúile, Texts, Saints and Places: Essays in Honour of Pádraig Ó Riain (Aberystwyth 2004), 116–26.

Herbert, M., 'Crossing Historical and Literary Boundaries: Irish Written Culture Around the Year 1000', in P. Sims-Williams and G. A. Williams (eds.), Crossing Boundaries/Croesi Ffiniau (Aberystwyth, 2007) [= CMCS 53/4 (2007)], 87–101.

Herren, M. W., 'Classical and Secular Learning among the Irish before the Carolingian Renaissance', Florilegium 3 (1981), 118–57.

Herron, T., Spenser's Irish Work: Poetry, Plantation and Colonial Reformation (Aldershot, 2007).

Hicks, M., Henry Cowell, Bohemian (Urbana, IL, 2002).

Hicks, R., 'Cosmography in Tochmarc Étaíne', The Journal of Indo-European Studies 37:1–2 (Spring/Summer, 2009), 115–29.

Hill, J., Lady Gregory: an Irish Life (Stroud, 2005).

Hofman, R., 'Some New Facts Concerning the Knowledge of Vergil in Early Medieval Ireland', ÉC 25 (1988), 189–212.

Hogan, E., Onomasticon Goedelicum: locorum et tribuum Hiberniae et Scotiae (Dublin, 1910).

Holdsworth, C., 'Yeats and Ireland' [review of P. A. Smith, The Tribes of Danu], English Literature in Transition, 1880–1920 32.1 (1989), 108–10.

Hollo, K., 'Allegoresis and Literary Creativity in Eighth-Century Ireland: The Case of Echtrae Chonnlai', in J. Eska (ed.), Narrative in Celtic Tradition: Essays in Honor of Edgar M. Slotkin [CSANA Yearbook 8–9] (Hamilton, NY, 2011), 117–28.

——, 'Later medieval Ireland, 1200–1600: Part II: Prose literature', in M. Kelleher & P. O'Leary (eds.), The Cambridge History of Irish Literature (2 vols., Cambridge, 2006), i., 110–36.

Hough, G., *The Mystery Religion of W. B. Yeats* (Brighton, 1984).

Hoyne, M., 'The Political Context of *Cath Muige Tuireadh*, the Early Modern Irish Version of the Second Battle of *Magh Tuireadh*', *Ériu* 63 (2013), 91–116.

Hughes, K., *The Church in Irish Society* (London, 1967).

Hull, E., *The Cuchullin saga in Irish literature* (London, 1898).

——, 'Legends and traditions of the Cailleach Beare', *Folklore* 38.3 (1927), 225–54.

Hurd, M., *Immortal Hour—the Life and Period of Rutland Boughton* (London, 1962).

Hutchinson, J., *The Dynamics of Cultural Nationalism: the Gaelic Revival and the Creation of the Irish Nation State* (London, 1987).

Hutton, R., *The Pagan Religions of the Ancient British Isles: Their Nature and Legacy* (Oxford, 1991).

——, *The Stations of the Sun: A History of the Ritual Year in Britain* (Oxford, 1996).

——, *The Triumph of the Moon* (Oxford, 1999).

——, *Witches, Druids, and King Arthur* (London, 2002).

——, *Blood and Mistletoe: The History of the Druids in Britain* (London & New Haven, 2009).

——, *Pagan Britain* (London & New Haven, 2013).

Hyde, D., 'Amadán na bruidhne', *Gadelica: A Journal of Modern-Irish Studies* 1 (1913), 271.

Imhoff, H., 'The Themes and Structure of *Aided Echach maic Maireda*', *Ériu* 58 (2008), 107–131.

Isaac, G., *Place-names in Ptolemy's Geography: an electronic data base with etymological analysis of the Celtic name-elements* [CD-ROM] (Aberystwyth, 2004).

——, 'A note on the name of Ireland in Irish and Welsh', *Ériu* 59 (2009), 49–55.

Jaski, B., *Early Irish Kingship and Succession* (Dublin, 2000).

Jeffrey, D. L., (ed.), *A Dictionary of Biblical Tradition in English Literature* (Grand Rapids, MI, 1992).

Jenkyns, R., *The Victorians and Ancient Greece* (Cambridge, MA, 1980).

Johnston, E., *Literacy and Identity in Early Medieval Ireland* (Woodbridge, 2013).

Joshi, S., *A Subtler Magick: The Writings and Philosophy of H. P. Lovecraft* (Gilette, NJ, 1982).

Joyce, J., *Finnegans Wake* ([1939] Oxford, 2012).

Jufer, N., & Luginbühl, T., *Les dieux gaulois: répertoire des noms de divinités celtiques connus par l'épigraphie, les textes antiques et la toponymie* (Paris, 2001).

Kalogera, L. S., 'Yeats's Celtic Mysteries' [unpublished PhD dissertation, Florida State University, 1977].

Kelleher, M., & O'Leary, P., (eds.), *The Cambridge History of Irish Literature* (2 vols., Cambridge, 2006).

Kelly, F., *A Guide to Early Irish Law* (Dublin, 1988).

——, *Early Irish Farming* (Dublin, 2000).

Kelly, J. F., 'Hiberno-Latin Theology' in H. Löwe (ed.), *Die Iren und Europa im früheren Mittelalter* (2 vols., Stuttgart, 1982).

Kemplay, J., *The Paintings of John Duncan: A Scottish Symbolist* (Warwick & Petaluma, CA, 2009).

Kiberd, D., *Inventing Ireland: the literature of the modern nation* (London, 1995).

King, G. G., 'Fiona Macleod', *Modern Language Notes* 33 (1918), 352–6.

Klein, A., 'Celtic Legends in Irish Opera, 1900–1930', *PHCC* 24/25 (2004/5), 40–53.

——, 'Stage-Irish, or The National in Irish Opera 1780–1925', *Opera Quarterly* 21.1 (2005), 27–67.

Koch, J. T., 'Some Suggestions and Etymologies Reflecting upon the Mythology of the Four Branches', *PHCC* 9 (1989), 1–10.

——, 'Further to *tongu do dia toinges mo thuath* etc.', *ÉC* 29 (1992), 249–61.

——, 'A Swallowed Onomastic Tale in *Cath Maige Mucrama*?', in J. Carey, et al. (eds.), *Ildánach, Ildírech: A Festschrift for Proinsias Mac Cana* (Llandysul, 1999), 69–71.

——, (ed.), *Celtic Culture: A Historical Encyclopedia* (5 vols., Oxford and Santa Barbara, 2006).

——, & J. Carey (ed. & trans.), *The Celtic Heroic Age: Literary Sources for Ancient Celtic Europe & Early Ireland & Wales* (4th edn., Aberystwyth, 2003).

Kohlfeldt, M. L., *Lady Gregory: the Woman behind the Irish Literary Renaissance* (London, 1985).

Kondratiev, A., *The Apple Branch: A Path to Celtic Ritual* (San Francisco, CA, 1998).

Kuch, P., *Yeats and A.E.: the antagonism that unites dear friends* (Gerrards Cross, 1986).

Lacey, B., *Lug's forgotten Donegal kingdom: the archaeology, history, and folklore of the Síl Lugdach of Cloghaneely* (Dublin, 2012).

Lahey-Dolega, C., 'Some Brief Observations on the Life and Work of William Sharp (Fiona Macleod)', *Ball State University Forum* 21:4 (Autumn, 1980), 18–26.

Laing, L., 'The romanization of Ireland in the fifth century', *Peritia* 4 (1985), 261–78.

Lambert, P.-Y., 'Gaulois ANΔOOYNNABO', *ÉC* 27 (1990), 197–99.

——, *La Langue Gauloise: description linguistique, commentaire d'inscriptions choisies* (Paris, 1994).

Lanters, J., *Unauthorized Versions: Irish Menippean Satire, 1919–1952* (Washington, DC, 2000).

——, 'Carnivalizing Irish Catholicism: Austin Clarke's *The Sun Dances at Easter*', in P. I. Barta et al. (eds.), *Carnivalizing Difference: Bakhtin and the Other* (London & New York, 2001), 191–208.

Larminie, W., *Fand and other poems* (Dublin, 1892).

Lawhead, S., *The Paradise War* (Oxford, 1991).

Leahy, A. H., *Heroic Irish Romances* (2 vols., London, 1905–6).

Leerssen, J., *Mere Irish and Fíor-ghael: Studies in the Idea of Irish Nationality* (Amsterdam, 1986).

——, 'Celticism', in T. Brown (ed.), *Celticism* (Amsterdam, 1996), 1–20.

——, *Remembrance and Imagination: patterns in the historical and literary representation of Ireland in the nineteenth century* (Cork, 1996).

Lennon, J., *Irish Orientalism: a Literary and Intellectual History* (Syracuse, NY, 2004).

Le Roux, F., 'Les Isles au Nord du Monde', *Hommages à Albert Grenier* (3 vols., Brussels, 1962), ii., 1051–62.

——, 'Le dieu-roi NODONS/NUADA', *Celticum* 6 (1963), 425–54.

Lindeman, F. O., 'Varia III.2: Gaulish ανδοουνναβο', *Ériu* 42 (1991), 146.

——, 'Varia VI', *Ériu* 50 (1999), 183–4.

Lopez, D. S., *The Tibetan Book of the Dead: A Biography* (Princeton, NJ, 2011).

Mac Airt, S., '*Filidecht* and *coimgne*', *Ériu* 18 (1958), 139–52.

McAteer, M., *Standish O'Grady, Æ and Yeats: History, Politics, Culture* (Dublin, 2002).

MacBain, A., *Celtic Mythology and Religion* (Inverness, 1885 [Stirling, 1917]).

——, 'Incantations and magic rhymes', *Highland Monthly* 3 (1891–2), 117–25.

McCall Smith, A., *Dream Angus: The Celtic God of Dreams* (London, 2006).

Mac Cana, P., 'The Influence of the Vikings on Celtic Literature', in B. Ó Cuív (ed.), *Proceedings of the International Congress of Celtic Studies held in Dublin 6–10 July, 1959* (Dublin, 1962), 78–118.

———, *Celtic Mythology* (London, 1970).

———, 'Mongán mac Fiachna and *Immram Brain*', *Ériu* 23 (1972), 102–42.

———, 'The Sinless Otherworld of *Immram Brain*', *Ériu* 27 (1976), 95–115.

———, *The Learned Tales of Medieval Ireland* (Dublin, 1980).

———, '*Fianaigecht* in the pre-Norman period', in B. Almqvist, et al. (eds.), *The Heroic Process: Essays on the Fenian Tradition of Ireland and Scotland* (Dublin, 1987), 75–99.

———, 'Place-names and mythology in Irish tradition', in G. W. MacLennan (ed.), *Proceedings of the first North-American Congress of Celtic Studies* (Ottawa 1988), 319–341.

———, 'Mythology and the Oral Tradition: Ireland', in M. J. Green (ed.), *The Celtic World* (London, 1995), 779–84.

McCone, K., 'Notes on the Text and Authorship of the Early Irish Bee-Laws', *CMCS* 8 (Winter, 1984), 45–50.

———, 'Werewolves, cyclopes, *díberga*, and *fíanna*: juvenile delinquency in early Ireland', *CMCS* 12 (1986), 1–22.

———, 'A Tale of Two Ditties', in L. Breatnach, K. McCone, & D. Ó Corráin (eds.), *Sages, saints and storytellers: Celtic studies in honour of Professor James Carney* (Maynooth, 1989), 122–43.

———, *Pagan Past and Christian Present in Early Irish Literature* (Maynooth, 1990).

———, 'Prehistoric, Old, and Middle Irish', in K. McCone & K. Simms (eds.), *Progress in Medieval Irish Studies* (Maynooth, 1996), 7–54.

———, 'The Celtic and Indo-European origins of the *fían*', in G. Parsons & S. Arbuthnot (eds.), *The Gaelic Finn Tradition* (Dublin, 2012), 14–30.

Macdonald, M., 'The Visual Dimension of *Carmina Gadelica*', in D. U. Stiùbhart (ed.), *The Life and Legacy of Alexander Carmichael* (Port of Ness, 2008), 135–45.

McDowell, D., *Ella Young and Her World: Celtic Mythology, the Irish Revival and the Californian Avant-Garde* (Bethesda, 2014).

McFate, P., *The Writings of James Stephens: Variations on a Theme of Love* (London, 1979).

McKenna, C., 'Apotheosis and evanescence: the fortunes of Saint Brigit in the nineteenth and twentieth centuries', in J. F. Nagy, (ed.), *The Individual in Celtic Literatures* [CSANA Yearbook 1] (Dublin, 2001), 74–108.

Mackenzie, D. A., *Wonder Tales from Scottish Myth and Legend* (London, 1917).

MacLeod, N., 'The Not-So-Exotic Law of Dian Cécht', in G. Evans, et al.

(eds.), *Origins and Revivals: Proceedings of the First Australian Conference of Celtic Studies* (Sydney, 2000), 381–400.

——, 'Irish Law and the Wars of the Túatha Dé Danann', in L. Breatnach et al. (eds.), *Proceedings of the XIV International Congress of Celtic Studies, held in Maynooth University, 1–5 August 2011* (Dublin, 2015), 75–94.

MacLeod, S. P., 'Mater Deorum Hibernensium: Identity and Cross-Correlation in Early Irish Mythology', *PHCC* 18/19 (1998/1999), 340–84.

McLeod, W., *Divided Gaels: Gaelic Cultural Identities in Scotland and Ireland, c.1200–c.1650* (Oxford, 2004).

McManus, D., *A Guide to Ogam* (Maynooth, 1991).

Mac Mathúna, S., 'The Relationship of the Chthonic World in Early Ireland to Chaos and Cosmos', in J. Borsje, et al. (eds.), *Celtic Cosmology: Perspectives from Ireland and Scotland* (Toronto, 2014), 53–76.

McNamara, M., 'Tradition and Creativity in Irish Psalter Study', in P. Ní Chatháin, et al. (eds.), *Irland und Europa: Die Kirche im Frühmittelalter* (Stuttgart, 1984).

——, *The Psalms in the Early Irish Church* (Sheffield, 2000).

Mac Neill, M., 'The Legend of the False God's Daughter', *JRSAI* 79 (1949), 100–9.

——, *The Festival of Lughnasa: A Study of the Survival of the Celtic Feast of the Beginning of Harvest* (London, 1962).

MacQuarrie, C. W., *The Biography of the Irish god of the Sea from Immram Brain (c. 700) to Finnegans Wake (1939): the Waves of Manannán* (Lewiston, NY, 2004).

McQuillan, P., 'Finn, Fothad and *fian*: some early associations', *PHCC* 8 (1990), 1–10.

Mac Shamhráin, A., & Byrne, P., 'Prosopography I: Kings named in *Baile Chuinn Chétchathaig* and The Airgíalla Charter Poem', in E. Bhreathnach (ed.), *The Kingship and Landscape of Tara* (Dublin, 2005), 159–224.

Magee, E., *Richard Wagner and the Nibelungs* (Oxford, 1990).

Maier, B., 'Is Lug to be identified with Mercury (*Bell. Gall.* vi 17, 1)? New Suggestions on an Old Problem', *Ériu* 47 (1996), 127–135.

——, 'Comparative philology and mythology: the letters of Whitley Stokes to Adalbert Kuhn', in P. Russell & E. Boyle (eds.), *The Tripartite Life of Whitley Stokes, 1830–1909* (Dublin, 2011), 119–33.

Mallory, J. P., *The Origins of the Irish* (London & New York, 2013).

Marillier, J., *Daughter of the Forest* (London, 2000).

Martin, A., *James Stephens: A Critical Study* (Dublin, 1977).

Martin, H. C., *W. B. Yeats: Metaphysician as Dramatist* (Gerrards Cross, 1986).

Martin, M., *A Description of the Western Islands of Scotland* [1703] (Edinburgh, 1999).

Matasović, R., *Etymological Dictionary of Proto-Celtic* (Leiden & Boston, 2009).

Matthews, C., *The Elements of the Celtic Tradition* (Shaftesbury, 1989).

——, & Matthews, J., *The Encyclopedia of Celtic Wisdom* (Shaftesbury, 1994).

Matthews, J., *The Celtic Shaman* (Shaftesbury, 1991).

——, (ed.), *From the Isles of Dream: Visionary Stories and Poems of the Celtic Renaissance* (Melksham, 1993).

——, *Within the Hollow Hills: an Anthology of new Celtic Writing* (Guildford, 1994);

——, & D. Sallee (eds.), *At the Gates of Dawn: A Collection of Writings by Ella Young* (Cheltenham, 2011).

Menotti, F., *Wetland Archaeology and Beyond: Theory and Practice* (Oxford, 2012).

Merivale, P., *Pan the Goat-God: His Myth in Modern Times* (Cambridge, MA, 1969).

Meyer, K., *Fianaigecht: being a collection of hitherto inedited Irish poems and tales relating to Finn and his fiana* [Todd Lecture Series 16] (Dublin, 1910).

Meyers, T. L., *The Sexual Tensions of William Sharp: A Study of the Birth of Fiona Macleod* (New York, 1996).

Miles, B., *Heroic Saga and Classical Epic in Medieval Ireland* (Cambridge, 2011).

Milligan, A., *Hero Lays* (Dublin, 1908).

Monteith, K., *Yeats and Theosophy* (London, 2008).

Moran, P., 'Their harmless calling: Stokes and the Irish linguistic tradition', in E. Boyle & P. Russell, (eds.), *The Tripartite Life of Whitley Stokes, 1830–1909* (Dublin, 2011), 175–84.

Morford, M., Lenardon, R. J., & Sham, M., (eds.), *Classical Mythology* (Oxford, 2013 [tenth edn]).

Moriarty, J., *Dreamtime* (Dublin, 1994 [revised and expanded edn. 1999]).

——, *Turtle Was Gone a Long Time: Crossing the Kedron* (Dublin, 1996).

——, *Nostos* (Dublin, 2001).

——, *Invoking Ireland: Ailiu Iath n-hErend* (Dublin, 2005).

——, *What The Curlew Said: Nostos Continued* (Dublin, 2007).

Munro, R., 'Some Survivals of Paganism in Scotland', *Good Words* 30 (1889), 333–7.

Murphy, G., 'Notes on Cath Maige Tuired', *Éigse* 7 (1953–5), 191–198, 204.

——, *Early Irish Metrics* (Dublin, 1961).

Murphy, R., *Ella Young: Irish Mystic and Rebel* (Dublin, 2008).

Murray, K., 'Interpreting the evidence: problems with dating the early *fíanaigecht* corpus', in G. Parsons & S. Arbuthnot (eds.), *The Gaelic Finn Tradition*, 31–49.

Nagy, G., *The Ancient Greek Hero in 24 Hours* (Cambridge, MA, 2013).

Nagy, J. F., *The Wisdom of the Outlaw: the Boyhood Deeds of Finn in Gaelic Narrative Tradition* (Berkeley, 1985).

——, 'In Defence of *Rómánsaíocht*', *Ériu* 38 (1987), 9–26.

——, 'Compositional Concerns in the *Acallam na Senórach*', in D. Ó Corráin et al. (eds.), *Sages, Saints and Storytellers: Celtic Studies in Honour of Professor James Carney* (Maynooth, 1989), 149–58.

——, *Conversing with Angels and Ancients: Literary Myths of Medieval Ireland* (Ithaca, NY, 1999).

——, 'Myth and Legendum in Medieval and Modern Ireland', in G. Schrempp & W. Hansen (eds.), *Myth: A New Symposium* (Bloomington, IN, 2002), 124–38.

——, review of C. Harrington, *Women in a Celtic Church: Ireland 450–1150*, in *Speculum* 79.4 (2004), 1085–88.

——, 'Orality in Medieval Irish Narrative: An Overview', *Oral Tradition* 1/2 (1986), 272–301.

——, 'Mercantile Myth in Medieval Celtic Traditions' [H. M. Chadwick Memorial Lecture 20] (Department of Anglo-Saxon, Norse, and Celtic: University of Cambridge, 2011).

——, 'Oral Tradition and Performance in Medieval Ireland', in K. Reichl (ed.), *Medieval Oral Literature* (Boston & Berlin, 2011), 279–93.

——, 'Keeping the *Acallam* together', in G. Parsons & S. Arbuthnot (eds.), *The Gaelic Finn Tradition* (Dublin, 2012), 111–21.

——, 'Some strands and strains in *Acallam na Senórach*', in A. Doyle & K. Murray (eds.), *In Dialogue with the Agallamh* (Dublin, 2014), 90–108.

Newall, V. J., 'The Adaptation of Folklore and Tradition (*Folklorismus*)', *Folklore* 98:2 (1987), 131–51.

Newman, B., *God and the Goddesses: Vision, Poetry and Belief in the Middle Ages* (Philadelphia, PA, 2002).

Ní Bhrolcháin, M., *An Introduction to Early Irish Literature* (Dublin, 2009).

Nic Cárthaigh, E., 'Surviving the Flood: Revenants and Antediluvian Lore in Medieval Irish Texts', in K. Cawsey & J. Harris, *Transmission and Transformation in the Middle Ages: Texts and Contexts* (Dublin, 2007), 40–64.

Nicholls, K. W., *Gaelic and Gaelicised Ireland in the Middle Ages* (Dublin, 1972).

Ní Dhonnchadha, M., 'The semantics of *banscál*', *Éigse* 31 (1999), 31–35.

——, 'The *Prull* narrative in *Sanas Cormaic*', in J. Carey, et al. (eds.), *Cín Chille Cúile: Texts, Saints and Places: Essays in Honour of Pádraig Ó Riain* (Aberystwyth, 2004), 163–177.

——, 'Seeing things: revelation in Gaelic literature', *CMCS* 53–4 [= *Croesi ffiniau: Trafodion y 12fed Gyngres Astudiaethau Celtaidd Ryngwladol 24–30 Awst 2003, Prifysgol Cymru, Aberystwyth / Crossing boundaries: Proceedings of the 12th International Congress of Celtic Studies, 24–30 August 2003, University of Wales, Aberystwyth*] (2007), 103–12.

Ní Mhaonaigh, M., 'The literature of medieval Ireland, 800–1200: from the Vikings to the Normans', in M. Kelleher & P. O'Leary (eds.), *The Cambridge History of Irish Literature* (2 vols., Cambridge, 2006), i., 32–73.

——, 'Literary Lochlann', in W. McLeod, et al. (eds.), *Cànan & Cultar/ Language & Culture: Rannsachadh na Gàidhlig* 3 (2006), 25–37.

——, 'Pagans and holy men: literary manifestations of twelfth-century reform', in D. Bracken & D. Ó Riain-Raedel (eds.), *Ireland and Europe in the Twelfth Century: Reform and Renewal* (Dublin, 2006), 143–161.

Nolan, J., 'The Awakening of the Fires: A Survey of AE's Mystical Writings 1897–1933', *ABEI Journal: The Brazilian Journal of Irish Studies* (2001), 89–99.

——, 'The Hindu Celticism of James Cousins (1873–1956)', *ABEI Journal: The Brazilian Journal of Irish Studies* (2005), 219–32.

Nulty, O., *George Russell–Æ.... at The Oriel's 21st Anniversary* (Dublin, ?1989).

Ó Briain, M., 'Some material on Oisín in the Land of Youth', in D. Ó Corráin et al. (eds.), *Sages, Saints and Storytellers: Celtic Studies in Honour of Professor James Carney* (Maynooth, 1989), 181–99.

O'Brien, E., 'Pagan and Christian burial in Ireland in the first millennium', in N. Edwards (ed.), *The Early Church in Wales and the West* (Oxford, 1992), 130–7.

O'Brien, S., 'Indo-European Eschatology: A Model', *Journal of Indo-European Studies* 4 (1976), 295–320.

Ó Cadhla, S., 'Gods and Heroes: Approaching the *Acallam* as Ethnography', in A. Doyle & K. Murray (eds.), *In Dialogue with the Agallamh*, 125–43.

Ó Catháin, S., *The Festival of Brigit* (Dublin, 1995).

Ó Cathasaigh, T., 'The Semantics of *síd*', *Éigse* 17 (1977–9), 137–55 [reprt. in Boyd (ed.), *Coire Sois*, 19–34].

'*Cath Maige Tuired* as Exemplary Myth', in P. de Brún, et al. (eds.), *Folia Gadelica: Essays presented by former students to R. A. Breatnach* (Cork, 1983), 1–19 [reprt. in Boyd (ed.), *Coire Sois*, 135–54].

——, 'Pagan Survivals: the Evidence of Early Irish Narrative', in P. Ní Chatháin & M. Richter (eds.), *Ireland and Europe: The Early Church/Irland und Europa: die Kirche im Frühmittelalter* (Stuttgart, 1984), 291–307 [reprt. in Boyd (ed.), *Coire Sois*, 35–50].

——, 'The Eponym of Cnogba', *Éigse* 23 (1989), 27–38 [reprt. in Boyd (ed.), *Coire Sois*, 155–64].

——, 'Mythology in *Táin Bó Cúailnge*' in H. L. Tristram (ed.), *Studien zur Táin Bó Cúailnge* (Tübingen, 1993), 114–3 [reprt. in Boyd (ed.), *Coire Sois*, 201–18].

——, '*Tóraíacht Dhiarmada agus Ghráinne*', *Léachtaí Cholm Cille* 25 (1995) 30–46 [reprt. in Boyd (ed.), *Coire Sois*, 449–65; English trans. in the same volume, 466–83].

——, 'Early Irish Narrative Literature', in K. McCone & K. Simms (eds.), *Progress in Medieval Irish Studies* (Maynooth, 1996), 55–64.

——, 'Knowledge and Power in *Aislinge Óenguso*', in A. Alqvist & V. Čapková (eds.), *Dán do oide: Essays in Memeory of Conn R. Ó Cléirigh* (Dublin, 1997), 431–38 [reprt. in Boyd (ed.), *Coire Sois*, 165–72].

——, 'Aspects of Memory and Identity in early Ireland', in J. E. Eska (ed.), *Narrative in Celtic tradition: essays in honor of Edgar M. Slotkin* [*CSANA Yearbook* 8–9] (Hamilton, NY, 2011), 201–16.

——, '*Tochmarc Étaíne* II: A Tale of Three Wooings', in P. O'Neill (ed.), *Land Beneath the Sea: Essays in Honour of Anders Alqvist's Contribution to Celtic Studies in Australia* (Sydney, 2013), 129–142.

Ó Concheanainn, T., 'The three forms of *Dinnshenchas Érenn*', *Journal of Celtic Studies* 3 (1981) 88–131.

——, 'The Textual Tradition of *Compert Con Culainn*', *Celtica* 21 (1990), 441–55.

O'Connor, D., *Keating's General History of Ireland, Translated from the original Irish, with many curious Amendments* (Dublin, 1841 [translated in 1723]).

O'Connor, L., *Haunted English: the Celtic Fringe, the British Empire, and De-Anglicization* (Baltimore, MD, 2006).

O'Connor, P., *Beyond the Mist: What Irish Mythology Can Teach Us About Ourselves* (London, 2000).

O'Connor, R., *The Destruction of Da Derga's Hostel: Kingship and Narrative Artistry in a Mediaeval Saga* (Oxford, 2013).

——, (ed.), *Classical Literature and Learning in Mediaeval Irish Narrative* (Cambridge, 2014).

Ó Corráin, D., Breatnach, L., & Breen, A., 'The Laws of the Irish', *Peritia* 3 (1984), 382–438.

Ó Corráin, D., 'Irish Origin Legends and Genealogy: Recurrent Aetiologies', in T. Nyberg, et al. (eds.), *History and Heroic Tale: A Symposium* (Odense, 1985), 51–96.

——, 'Historical Need and Literary Narrative', in D. Ellis Evans, et al. (eds.), *Proceedings of the Seventh International Congress of Celtic Studies* (Oxford, 1986), 141–58.

——, 'Legend as Critic', in T. Dunne & C. Doherty (eds.), *The Writer as Witness: Literature as Historical Evidence* (Cork, 1987), 23–38.

——, 'Creating the Past: The Early Irish Genealogical Tradition', *Peritia* 12 (1998), 177–208.

Ó Cróinín, D., *Early Medieval Ireland, 400–1200* (London & New York, 1995).

——, (ed.), *A New History of Ireland I: Prehistoric and Early Ireland* (Oxford, 2005) [= vol. 1 of F. J. Byrne, et al., (eds.), *A New History of Ireland* (9 vols., Oxford, 1982–2011)].

Ó Crualaoich, G., *The Book of the Cailleach: Stories of the Wise-Woman Healer* (Cork, 2003).

Ó Cuív, B., 'Medieval Irish Scholars and Classical Latin Literature', *PRIA* 81 (C) (1981), 239–48.

O'Curry, E., *Lectures on the Manuscript Materials of ancient Irish History* (Dublin, 1861).

——, *On the Manners and Customs of the Ancient Irish: a series of lectures* (Dublin, 1973)

O'Duffy, E., *King Goshawk and the Birds* (New York, 1926).

——, *The Spacious Adventures of the Man in the Street* (London, 1928).

——, *Asses in Clover* (London, 1933).

O'Donoghue, H., *From Asgard to Valhalla: The Remarkable History of the Norse Myths* (London, 2007).

Ó Fiannachta, P., 'Eoghan Ó Comhraí, file traidisiúnta', in D. Ó Corráin, L. Breatnach, & K. McCone (eds.), *Sages, saints and storytellers: Celtic studies in honour of Professor James Carney* (1989), 280–307.

O'Flaherty, L., *The Ecstasy of Angus* (London, 1931).

O'Flaherty, R., *Ogygia: seu, Rerum Hibernicarum chronologia […]* (London, 1685) [trans. J. Hely, *Ogygia or, A chronological account of Irish events [...]* (Dublin, 1793).

——, *Roderick O'Flaherty's Letters To William Molyneux, Edward Lhwyd, and Samuel Molyneux, 1696–1709*, ed. R. Sharpe (Dublin, 2013).

O'Grady, S. H., *Silva Gadelica* (2 vols., London, 1892).

O'Grady, S. J., *History of Ireland* (2 vols., London, 1878–80).

——, *History of Ireland: critical and philosophical* (London & Dublin, 1881).

——, *The Coming of Cuculain: a Romance of the Heroic Age* (London, 1894).

O'Halloran, C., *Golden Ages and Barbarous Nations: antiquarian debate and cultural politics in Ireland, c. 1750–1800* (Cork, 2004).

O'Halloran, S., *A General History of Ireland* (London, 1775).

O Hehir, B., 'The Passing of the Shee: After Reading a Book about Yeats and the Tribes of Danu' [review of P. A. Smith, *The Tribes of Danu*], *Yeats: An Annual of Critical and Textual Studies* 6 (1988), 245–65.

——, 'Yeats's Sources for the Matter of Ireland, I. Edain and Aengus', *Yeats: An Annual of Critical and Textual Studies* 6 (1989), 76–89.

——, 'Yeats's Sources for the Matter of Ireland: II. Edain and Midhir', *Yeats: An Annual of Critical and Textual Studies* 9 (1991), 95–106.

Ó hÓgáin, D., *Myth, Legend, and Romance: An Encyclopedia of the Irish Folk Tradition* (London, 1990).

Ó hUiginn, R., '*Tongu Do Dia Toinges Mo Thuath* and Related Expressions', in D. Ó Corráin, et al. (eds.), *Sages, Saints and Storytellers: Celtic Studies in Honour of Professor James Carney* (Maynooth, 1989), 332–41.

O'Kelly, C., *Illustrated Guide to Newgrange and the other Boyne monuments* (3rd edn., Ardnalee, 1978).

O'Kelly, M. J., Lynch, F. M., & O'Kelly, C., 'Three passage-graves at Newgrange, Co. Meath' *PRIA* 78 (C) (1978), 249–352.

O'Kelly, M. J., *Newgrange: Archaeology, Art and Legend* (London, 1982).

O'Leary, P., 'A Foreseeing Driver of an Old Chariot: Regal Moderation in Early Irish Literature', *CMCS* 11 (Summer, 1986), 1–16.

Olney, J., *The Rhizome and the Flower: The Perennial Philosophy: Yeats and Jung* (Berkeley, CA, 1980).

O'Loughlin, T., 'Reading Muirchú's Tara-event within its background as a biblical "trial of divinities" ', in J. Cartwright (ed.), *Celtic Hagiography and Saints' Cults* (Cardiff, 2003), 123–135.

Ó Mainnín, M., 'Eochaid Ua Flainn agus Eochaid Ua Flannucáin: Súil Úr ar an bhFianaise', *Léann* 2 (2009) 75–105.

O'Malley, K., *Ireland, India and Empire: Indo-Irish Radical Connections, 1919–64* (Manchester, 2009).

O'Meara, T. F., 'Christian Theology and Extraterrestrial Intelligent Life', *Theological Studies* 60 (1999), 3–30.

Oosten, J., *The War of the Gods: the Social Code in Indo-European Mythology* (London, 1985).

Oppenheim, J., *The Other World: Spiritualism and Psychical Research in England, 1850–1914* (Cambridge, 1985).

O'Rahilly, T. F., *Early Irish History and Mythology* (Dublin, 1946).

Ó Riain, P., 'Traces of Lug in early Irish hagiographical tradition', *ZCP* 36 (1977), 138–156.

——, 'Pagan Example and Christian Practice: A Reconsideration', in D. Edel (ed.), *Cultural Identity and Cultural Integration: Ireland and Europe in the Early Middle Ages* (Dublin, 1995), 144–56,

——, *Geoffrey Keating's Foras Feasa Ar Eirinn: Reassessments* [ITS Subsidiary Series 19] (London, 2008).

O'Shea, P., *The Hounds of the Mórrígan* (Oxford, 1985).

O'Sullivan, A., 'Exploring past people's interactions with wetland environments in Ireland', *PRIA* (C) 107 (2007), 147–203.

Otis, B., *Virgil: A Study in Civilized Poetry* (Oxford, 1966).

Ó Tuama, S., 'Brian Merriman and his Court', *Repossessions: Selected Essays on the Irish Poetic Heritage* (Cork, 1995), 63–77.

Owen, A., *The Place of Enchantment: British Occultism and the Culture of the Modern* (Chicago, 2007).

Parker, R., *On Greek Religion* (Ithaca & London, 2011).

Parsons, D. N., & Sims-Williams, P., (eds.), *Ptolemy: Towards a linguistic atlas of the earliest Celtic place-names of Europe* (Aberystwyth, 2000).

Parsons, G., & Arbuthnot, S., (eds.), *The Gaelic Finn Tradition* (Dublin, 2012).

Parsons, G., 'A Reading of *Acallam na Senórach* as a Literary Text' [unpublished Ph.D thesis, University of Cambridge, 2007].

——, 'The structure of *Acallam na Senórach*', *CMCS* 55 (Summer 2008), 11–39.

Patton, L. L., 'Space and time in the *Immacallam in dá Thuarad*', *Folklore* 103.1 (1992), 92–102.

Pettit, E., 'Míach's Healing of Núadu in *Cath Maige Tuired*', *Celtica* 27 (2013), 167–71.

Phelpstead, C., *Tolkien and Wales: Language, Literature and Identity* (Cardiff, 2011).

Phillip, G., *Firebrand* (Glasgow, 2010).

Phillips, N., *A Fine Anger: a Critical Introduction to the Work of Alan Garner* (London, 1981).

Pittock, M., *Scottish and Irish Romanticism* (Oxford, 2008).

Platt, L., *Joyce and the Anglo-Irish: A Study of Joyce and the Literary Revival* (Amsterdam, 1998).

Poppe, E., '*Grammatica, grammatic*, Augustine, and the *Táin*', in J. T Koch, J. Carey, & P.-Y. Lambert (eds.), *Ildánach, Ildírech: A Festschrift for Proinsias Mac Cana* (Andover, 1999), 203–10.

——, '*Imtheachta Aeniasa*: Virgil's *Aeneid* in Medieval Ireland', *Classics Ireland* 11 (2004), 74–94.

——, *Of Cycles and Other Critical Matters: Some Issues in Medieval Irish Literature and Criticism* (Department of Anglo-Saxon, Norse, and Celtic, University of Cambridge, 2008).

Puhvel, J., *Comparative Mythology* (Baltimore, 1987).

Purser, J., *Scotland's Music: a History of the Traditional and Classical Music of Scotland from Earliest Times to the Present Day* (Edinburgh, 1992).

Putzel, S., *Reconstructing Yeats: The Secret Rose and The Wind Among the Reeds* (Dublin, 1986).

Pyle, H., *James Stephens, his Work and an Account of his Life* (London, 1965).

——, 'The Hamwood ladies: Letitia and Eva Hamilton', *Irish Arts Review Yearbook* 13 (1997), 123–34.

——, & Beale, M., &. Beale, D., (eds.), *The Paintings of George W. Russell (AE)* (Sligo, 2006).

Quin, E. C., review of *Cath Maige Tuired*, ed. & trans. E. A. Gray, *CMCS* 9 (1985), 99–101.

Radner, J., '"Men Will Die": Poets, Harpers, and Women in Early Irish Literature', in *Celtic Language, Celtic Culture: A Festschrift for Eric P. Hamp* (Van Nuys, CA, 1990), 172–86.

——, 'The Combat of Lug and Balor', *Oral Tradition* 7.1 (1992), 143–9.

Raftery, B., *Pagan Celtic Ireland: The Enigma of the Irish Iron Age* (London, 1994).

——, 'Iron-age Ireland', in D. Ó Cróinín, (ed.), *A New History of Ireland I: Prehistoric and Early Ireland* (Oxford, 2005), 134–81.

Rees, A., & Rees, B., *Celtic Heritage: Ancient Tradition in Ireland and Wales* (London, 1978).

Robins, R. H., *A Short History of Linguistics* (New York, 1997).

Rodway, S., 'Mermaids, Leprachauns, and Fomorians: A Middle Irish Account of the Descendants of Cain', *CMCS* 59 (2010), 1–17.

Roe, H., 'The *Acallam*: the Church's eventual acceptance of the cultural inheritance of pagan Ireland', in S. Sheehan, et al. (eds.), *Gablánach* in *Scélaigecht: Celtic Studies in honor of Ann Dooley* (Dublin, 2013), 103–15.

Ross, A., *The Pagan Celts* (London, 1986 [revised edn.])

Ruskin, J., *Praeterita*, ed. F. O'Gorman (Oxford, 2012 [1885]).

Russell, G. W., 'A Dream of Angus Oge', *Imaginations and Reveries* (Dublin, 1915), 195–201.

——, *The Candle of Vision* (London, 1918).

——, *The Descent of the Gods: The Mystical Writings of George Russell-A.E.*, ed. R. & N. Iyer (Gerrards Cross, 1988).

Russell, P., 'The Sounds of a Silence: The Growth of Cormac's Glossary', *CMCS* 15 (Summer, 1988), 1–30.

——, '"What was best of every language": the early history of the Irish language', in D. Ó Cróinín, (ed.), *A New History of Ireland I: Prehistoric and Early Ireland* (Oxford, 2005), 405–50.

——, '*Moth, toth, traeth*: sex, gender and the early Irish grammarian', in D. Cram, et al. (eds.), *History of Linguistics 1996: selected papers from the Seventh International Congress on the History of the Language Sciences, Oxford, 12–17 September 1996* (Amsterdam, 1996), 203–16.

——, 'Poets, Power and Possessions in Medieval Ireland: Some Stories from *Sanas Cormaic*', in J. Eska (ed.), *Law, Literature and Society* [*CSANA Yearbook* 7] (Dublin, 2008), 9–45.

Russell, V., *Heroes of the Dawn* (Dublin & London, 1913).

Rynne, E., 'Celtic Stone Idols in Ireland', in C. Thomas (ed.), *The Iron Age in the Irish Sea Province* [Council for British Archaeology Research Report 9] (London, 1972), 79–98.

Sands, L., 'Survivals of Paganism in Foula' [*Glasgow Herald* 17th November 1884].

Saunders, C., *Magic and the Supernatural in Medieval English Romance* (Cambridge, 2010).

Sayers, W., 'Bargaining for the Life of Bres in *Cath Maige Tuired*', *BBCS* 34 (1987), 26–40.

——, '*Airdrech, sirite*, and other early Irish battlefield spirits', *Éigse* 25 (1991), 45–55.

——, 'Fusion and Fission in the Love and Lexis of Early Ireland', in A. Classen (ed.), *Words of Love and Love of Words in the Middle Ages and Renaissance* (Tempe, AZ, 2008), 95–109.

——, 'Netherworld and Otherworld in early Irish Literature', *ZCP* 59 (2012), 201–30.

Schirmer, G. A., *The Poetry of Austin* Clarke (Dublin, 1983).

Schlüter, D., ' "For the entertainment of lords and commons of later times": past and remembrance in *Acallam na Senórach*', *Celtica* 26 (2010), 146–60.

——, *History or Fable: The Book of Leinster as a document of cultural memory in twelfth-century Ireland* (Münster, 2010).

Schot, R., et al. (eds.), *Landscapes of Cult and Kingship* (Dublin, 2011).

Schrijver, P., *Studies in British Celtic historical phonology* (Rodopi, 1995).

——, 'On Henbane and Early European Narcotics', *ZCP* 51 (1999), 17–45.

Schumacher, S., 'Old Irish **Tucaid*, *Tocad* and Middle Welsh *Tynghaf Tynghet* Re-Examined', *Ériu* 46 (1995) 49–57.

Scott, T., 'The Fantasy of the Celtic Revival: Lord Dunsany, Fiona Macleod, and W. B. Yeats', in C. Younger (ed.), *Border Crossings: Narration, Nation and Imagination in Scots and Irish Literature and Culture* (Newcastle, 2013), 127–141.

Scowcroft, R. M., '*Leabhar Gabhála*, Part I: The Growth of the Text', *Ériu* 38 (1987), 81–142.

——, '*Leabhar Gabhála*, Part II: The Growth of the Tradition', *Ériu* 39 (1988), 1–66.

——, 'Abstract narrative in Ireland', *Ériu* 46 (1995), 121–58.

——, 'Mediaeval Recensions of the *Lebor Gabála*', in J. Carey (ed.), *Lebor Gabála Érenn: textual History and Pseudohistory* (London, 2009), 1–20.

Seaman, A. T., 'Celtic Myth as Perceived in Eighteenth- and Nineteenth-Century Literature in English', in C. J. Byrne, et al. (eds.), *Celtic Languages and Celtic Peoples: Proceedings of the Second North American Congress of Celtic Studies held in Halifax August 16–19* (Halifax, 1992), 443–60.

Semple, S., 'A Fear of the Past: the Place of the Prehistoric Burial Mound in the Ideology of Middle and Later Anglo-Saxon England', *World Archaeology* 30 (1998), 109–26.

Shakespeare, W., *King Lear*, ed. R. A. Foakes (London, 1997).

Sharp, W. [= 'Fiona Macleod'], *Pharais: A Romance of the Isles* (Derby, 1894).

——, 'Mary of the Gael', in P. Geddes (ed.), *The Evergreen, A Northern Seasonal: The Book of Autumn* (Edinburgh, 1895), 123–48.

——, *The Washer of the Ford and other legendary moralities* (Edinburgh, 1896).

——, 'The Snow-Sleep of Angus Ogue', *The Evergreen, A Northern Seasonal: The Book of Winter* (1896–7), 118–23.

——, *The Dominion of Dreams* (London, 1899).

——, 'Sea-Magic and Running Water', *Contemporary Review* 82 (1902), 568–80.

——, *The Silence of Amor: prose rhythms* (Portland, Maine, 1902).

——, *The Winged Destiny: studies in the spiritual history of the Gael* (London, 1904).

——, 'St. Bridget of the Shores', in F. Macleod, *Where the Forest Murmurs: Nature Essays* (London, 1906), 76–86.

——, *The Immortal Hour: A Drama in two Acts* (Edinburgh & London, 1908).

——, *The Works of 'Fiona Macleod'*, arr. E. Sharp (7 vols., London, 1913).

Sharpe, R., 'Hiberno-Latin *laicus*, Irish *láech* and the devil's men', *Ériu* 30 (1979), 75–92.

Shaw, M., 'William Sharp's Neo-paganism: Queer Identity and the National Family', in D. Dau & S. Preston (eds.), *Queer Victorian Families: Curious Relations in Literature* (Abingdon, 2015), 77–96.

Sheehy, J., *The Rediscovery of Ireland's Past: the Celtic Revival 1830–1930* (London, 1980).

Sheldon, A. J., *Notes on Rutland Boughton's* The Immortal Hour (Birmingham, 1922).

Silver, C., *Strange and Secret Peoples: Fairies and Victorian Consciousness* (Oxford, 1999).

Simms, K., 'Bards and Barons: The Anglo-Irish Aristocracy and the Native Culture', in R. Bartlett & A. MacKay (eds.), *Medieval Frontier Societies* (Oxford, 1989), 177–97.

Sims-Williams, P., 'The visionary Celt: the construction of an "ethnic preconception"', *CMCS* 11 (1986), 71–96.

——, review of K. McCone, *Pagan Past and Christian Present in Early Irish Literature*, *Éigse* 29 (1996), 181–96.

——, 'Celtomania and Celtoscepticism' *CMCS* 36 (1998), 1–36.

——, & Poppe, E., 'Medieval Irish literary theory and criticism', in A. Minnis & I. Johnson, (eds.) *The Cambridge History of Literary Criticism II: The Middle Ages* (Cambridge, 2005), 291–309.

——, *Ancient Celtic Placenames in Europe and Asia Minor* (Oxford, 2006).

——, *Irish Influence on Medieval Welsh Literature* (Oxford, 2011).

Sjoestedt, M.-L., *Gods and Heroes of the Celts* (London, 1949).

Slotkin, E. M., 'Medieval Irish Scribes and Fixed Texts', *Éigse* 17 (1977–9), 437–50.

——, 'What Allows Fixed Texts to Enter Gaelic Oral Tradition?', in H. C. Tristram (ed.), *(Re)Oralisierung* [*ScriptOralia* 84] (Tübingen, 1996), 55–65.

Smith, P. A., *The Tribes of Danu: Three Views of Ireland's Fairies* (Gerrards Cross, 1987).

Smith, P. J., 'Early Irish Historical Verse, the Evolution of a Genre', in P. Ní Chatháin & M. Richter (eds.), *Ireland and Europe in the Early Middle Ages: Texts and Transmission/Irland und Europa im früheren Mittelalter: Texte und Überlieferung* (Dublin, 2002), 326–41.

——, *Three Historical Poems ascribed to Gilla-Cóemáin: a Critical Edition of the Work of an Eleventh Century Irish Scholar* [Studien und Texte zur Keltologie 8] (Münster, 2007).

Smyth, M., *Understanding the Universe in Seventh-Century Ireland* (Woodbridge, 1996).

Spaan, D., 'The Place of Manannan Mac Lir in Irish Mythology', *Folklore* 76 (1965), 176–95.

Spence, L., *The Mysteries of Britain: Secret Rites and Traditions of Ancient Britain Restored* (London, 1905).

Spenser, E., *The Faerie Queene*, ed. A. C. Hamilton (London, 1980).

Squire, C., *Celtic Myth and Legend* (London, 1905).

Stacey, R. C., *Dark Speech: The Performance of Law in Early Ireland* (Philadelphia, 2007).

Stafford, F. J., & Gaskill, H., (eds.), *From Gaelic to Romantic: Ossianic Translations* (Amsterdam, 1998).

Stafford, F. J., *The Sublime Savage: a study of James Macpherson and the poems of Ossian* (Edinburgh, 1988).

Stancliffe, C., 'Red, White and Blue Martyrdom', in D. Whitelock, et al. (eds.), *Ireland in Early Mediaeval Europe: Studies in Memory of Kathleen Hughes* (Cambridge, 1982), 21–46.

Stanley, M., 'Anthropomorphic wooden figures: recent Irish discoveries', in J. Barber, et al. (eds.), *Archaeology from the Wetlands: Recent Perspectives* [Proceedings of the eleventh WARP conference] (Edinburgh, 2007), 17–30.

Stephens, J., *The Crock of Gold* (London, 1912).

——, 'The Wisdom of the West' [review of J. Cousins, The Wisdom of the West], *The Irish Review* 2:14 (April, 1912), 100–2.

——, *In the Land of Youth* (London, 1924).

——, *The Letters of James Stephens*, ed. R. J. Finneran (London, 1974).

——, *The Poems of James Stephens*, ed. S. S. Mulligan (Gerrards Cross, 2006).

Sterckx, C., 'Quand Lugh devient-il roi?', *Ollodagos* 18/2 (2004), 301–5.

Stevenson, J., 'The Beginnings of Literacy in Ireland', *PRIA* (C) 89 (1989), 137–65.

Steward, J. C., (ed.), *When Time Began to Rant and Rage: Figurative Painting from Twentieth-Century Ireland* (London, 1998).

Stewart, R. J., *Celtic Gods, Celtic Goddesses* (London, 1990).

——, *Power within the Land: the Roots of Celtic and Underworld Traditions* (Shaftsbury, 1992).

——, *The Living World of Faery* (Glastonbury, 1995).

Stiùbhart, D. U., ' "Some heathenish and superstitious rites": a letter from Lewis, 1700', *Scottish Studies* 34 (2000–6), 205–26.

——, 'Alexander Carmichael and *Carmina Gadelica*', in D. U. Stiùbhart (ed.), *The Life and Legacy of Alexander Carmichael* (Port of Ness, 2008), 1–39.

——, 'The Making of a Charm Collector: Alexander Carmichael in the Outer Hebrides, 1864 to 1882', in J. Kapaló, É. Pocs, & W. Ryan (eds.), *The Power of Words: Studies on Charms and Charming in Europe* (Budapest, 2013) 25–66.

Stocking, G. W., *Victorian Anthropology* (London & New York, 1987).

Stokes, W., 'Remarks on Mr Fitzgerald's "Early Celtic History and Mythology" ', 358–70.

Stout, G., *Newgrange and the Bend of the Boyne* (2002).

Summerfield, H., *That Myriad-Minded Man: a Biography of George William Russell, 'A.E.', 1867–1955* (Gerrards Cross, 1975).

Sweetser, E., 'Cognate Formulas for a Welsh and Irish Topos of Otherworldly Ambiguity', in G. Henley & P. Russell (eds.), *Rhetoric and Reality in Medieval Celtic Literature: Studies in Honor of Daniel F. Melia* [*CSANA Yearbook* 11–12] (Hamilton, NY, 2014), 191–4.

Swift, C., 'Pagan monuments and Christian legal centres in early Meath', *Ríocht na Midhe* 9.2 (1996), 1–26.

——, *Ogam Stones and the Earliest Irish Christians* (Maynooth, 1997).

——, '*Óenach Tailten*, the Blackwater valley, and the Uí Néill kings of Tara', in A. P. Smith, (ed.), *Seanchas: Studies in Early and Medieval Irish Archaeology, History, and Literature in Honour of Francis J. Byrne* (Dublin, 2000), 109–20.

——, 'The Gods of Newgrange in Irish Literature and Romano-Celtic Tradition', in G. Burenhult & S. Westergaard (eds.), *Stones and Bones* (Oxford, 2003), 53–63.

Swinburne, A. C., *Poems and Ballads & Atalanta in Calydon*, ed. K. Haynes (London, 2000).

Tapping, G. C., *Austin Clarke: A Study of his Writings* (Dublin, 1981).

Thanisch, E., 'Flann Mainistrech's Götterdämmerung as a Junction within *Lebor Gabála Érenn*', *Quaestio Insularis: Selected Proceedings of the Cambridge Colloquium in Anglo-Saxon, Norse, and Celtic* 13 (2013), 69–93.

Thompson, E. A., *Who Was Saint Patrick?* (Woodbridge, 1985).

Thomson, D., *The Gaelic Sources of Macpherson's Ossian* (Edinburgh, 1952).

Thuente, M. H., *W. B. Yeats and Irish Folklore* (Dublin, 1980).

Thurneysen, R., *Die irische Helden- und Königsage bis zum 17. Jahrhundert* (Halle/Saale, 1912 [repnt. Hildersheim, 1980]).

——, 'Tuirill Bicren und seine Kinder', *ZCP* 12 (1918), 239–50.

——, 'Aus Dem Irischen Recht v.', *ZCP* 18 (1930), 353–408.

Tolkien, J. R. R., *The Lord of the Rings* (London, 2007 [1st edn. 1954]).

——, *The Letters of J.R.R. Tolkien: a selection*, ed. H. Carpenter (London, 1990).

Toner, G., '*Messe ocus Pangur Bán*: structure and cosmology', *CMCS* 57 (2009), 1–22.

——, 'Landscape and Cosmology in the *Dindshenchas*', in J. Borsje, A. Dooley, et al. (eds.), *Celtic Cosmology: Perspectives from Ireland and Scotland* (Toronto, 2014), 268–83.

Toomey, D., 'Labyrinths: Yeats and Maud Gonne', *YA* 9 (1992), 95–131.

Tovar, A., 'The God Lugus in Spain', *BBCS* 29.4 (1982), 591–9.

Tuchman, G., & Fortin, N., *Edging Women Out: Victorian Novelists, Publishers and Social Change* (London, 1989).

Tucker, H. F., *Epic: Britain's Heroic Muse 1790–1910* (Oxford, 2008).

Tymoczko, M., *Translation in a postcolonial context: early Irish literature in English translation* (Manchester, 1999).

Uhlich, J., 'Einige britannische Lehnnamen im Irischen: *Brénainn* (*Brenden*), *Cathaír/Catháer* und *Midir*', *ZCP* 49/50 (1997), 893–5.

Vendler, H., *Our Secret Discipline: Yeats and Lyric Form* (Oxford, 2007).

Vendryes, J., 'Manannan mac Lir', *ÉC* 7 (1952–4), 239–54.

——, *Lexique etymologique de l'Irlandais ancien* (Dublin & Paris, 1959).

de Vries, R., 'The Names of Lí Ban', in J. F. Nagy (ed.) *Myth in Celtic Literatures* [*CSANA Yearbook* 6] (Dublin, 2007), 39–54.

Waddell, J., *Archaeology and Celtic Myth: An Exploration* (Dublin, 2014).

Wadden, P., 'Some views of the Normans in eleventh- and twelfth-century Ireland', in S. Duffy & S. Foran (eds.), *English Isles: cultural transmission and political conflict in Britain and Ireland, 1100–1500* (Dublin, 2013), 13–36.

Wagner, H., 'Studies in the Origins of Early Celtic Traditions', *Ériu* 26 (1975), 1–26.

——, 'Origins of pagan Irish religion', *ZCP* 38 (1981), 1–28.

Wallace, P. F., & Ó Floinn, R., (eds.), *Treasures of the National Museum of Ireland: Irish Antiquities* (Dublin, 2002).

Watkins, C., *How to Kill a Dragon: Aspects of Indo-European Poetics* (Oxford, 1995).

West, M. L., *Indo-European Poetry and Myth* (Oxford, 2007).

Wilde, J., *Ancient Cures, Charms, and Usages of Ireland* (London, 1890).

Wiley, D. M., 'Baptizing the Fairies: The Christian-Conversion Typescene as a Rite de Passage', *PHCC* 15 (1995), 139–146.

Williams, A. N., *The Ground of Union: Deification in Aquinas and Palamas* (Oxford, 1999).

Williams, M., *Fiery Shapes: Celestial Portents and Astrology in Ireland and Wales, 700–1700* (Oxford, 2010).

——, ' "Lady Vengeance": A Reading of Sín in *Aided Muirchertach meic Erca*', *CMCS* 62 (Winter, 2011), 1–32.

——, 'Ella Young and Ross Nichols: Sourcing the Irish Gods', *Abraxas: the International Journal of Esoteric Studies* 6 (2014), 72–82.

Wooding, J. M., 'Reapproaching the Pagan Celtic Past—Anti-Nativism, Asterisk Reality and the Late-Antiquity Paradigm', *Studia Celtica Fennica* 6 (2009), 51–74.

Wright, C. D., 'From Monks' Jokes to Sages' Wisdom: The Joca Monachorum Tradition and the Irish *Immacallam in dá Thúarad*', in M. Garrison, A. P. Orbán, & M. Mostert (eds.), *Spoken and Written Language: Relations between Latin and the Vernacular Languages in the Earlier Middle Ages* (Turnhout, 2013), 199–225.

Yeats, W. B. (ed.) *Fairy and Folktales of the Irish Peasantry* (London, 1888).

——, *The Wind Among the Reeds* (London, 1899).

——, *Ideas of Good and Evil* (London, 1903).

——, *Autobiographies* (London, 1955).

——, *The Variorum Edition of the Poems of W. B. Yeats*, ed. P. Allt & R. K. Alspach (2nd edn., New York, 1966).

——, *Druid Craft: The Writing of 'The Shadowy Waters'* [Manuscripts of W. B. Yeats I], transcribed & ed. M. J. Sidnell, D. R. Clark, et al. (Amherst, 1971).

——, *The Collected Letters of W. B. Yeats*, ed. J. S. Kelly, W. Gould, D. Toomey, et al., (4 vols., Oxford, 1986–).

——, *The Collected Works of W. B. Yeats* Volume VI: *Prefaces and Introductions*, ed. William H. O'Donnell (London, 1988).

——, *The Secret Rose, Stories by W. B. Yeats: A Variorum Edition*, ed. W. Gould, P. L. Marcus & M. J. Sidnell ([2nd edn., revised and enlarged] London, 1992).

——, *Writings on Irish Folklore, Legend, and Myth*, ed. R. Welch (London, 1993).

——, *The Collected Poems of W. B. Yeats*, ed. R. J. Finneran (New York, NY, 1996).

——, *The Collected Works of W. B. Yeats* Volume IX: *Early Articles and Reviews*, ed. J. P. Frayne & M. Marchaterre (New York, 2004), 439–441.

——, *Mythologies*, ed. W. Gould & D. Toomey (Basingstoke, 2005).

Yorke, B., *The Conversion of Britain: Religion, Politics and Society in Britain, 600–800* (Harlow, 2006).

Young, R., *Electric Eden: Unearthing Britain's Visionary Music* (London, 2010).

Ziegler, S., *Die Sprache der altirischen Ogam-Inschriften* (Göttingen, 1994).

Zimmer, S., 'The making of myth: Old Irish *Airgatlám*, Welsh *Llaw ereint*, Caledonian Ἀργεντοκόξος', in M. Richter & J.-M. Picard (eds.), *OGMA: Essays in Celtic Studies in honour of Próinséas Ní Chatháin* (Dublin, 2002), 295–7.

ONLINE RESOURCES

Dictionary of Irish Biography, ed. J. McGuire, *et al.* (2009) www.dib.org

eDIL (Electronic Dictionary of the Irish Language), ed. G. Toner, *et al.*, http://www.dil.ie/

Imbas, www.imbas.org

Tairis, http://www.tairis.co.uk/introduction/celtic-reconstructionism

The William Sharp Archive, ed. W. F. Halloran http://www.ies.sas.ac.uk /research/current-projects/william-sharp-fiona-macleod-archive /william-sharp-fiona-macleod-archive

INDEX

Page numbers in italics refer to figures and tables

CPSIA information can be obtained
at www.ICGtesting.com
Printed in the USA
LVHW091123211020
669379LV00003B/24